Security Fundamentals

A Wiley Canada Custom Publication for

British Columbia Institute of Technology

FMGT 4620

Marketing Manager: Anita Osborne
Custom Project Editor: Sara Tinteri
Production Coordinator: Lynda Jess

Printed and bound in the United States of America

WILEY

John Wiley & Sons Canada, Ltd
6045 Freemont Blvd.
Mississauga, Ontario
L5R 4J3
Visit our website at: www.wiley.ca

UNDERSTANDING INVESTMENTS

Chapter 1 provides the foundation for the study of investments by analyzing what investing is all about. The critically important trade-off between expected return and risk is explained, and the major issues that every investor must deal with in making investment decisions are analyzed. An organizational structure for the entire text is provided.

Learning Objectives

After reading this chapter, you should be able to

1. Define investment and discuss what it means to study investments.
2. Explain why risk and return are the two critical components of all investing decisions.
3. Outline the two-step investment decision process.
4. Discuss key factors that affect the investment decision process.

CHAPTER PREVIEW

This chapter lays the foundation for the study of investments. You will learn what an investment is and why it is important to study the investment process. We introduce the concept of a trade-off between expected return and risk—the basis for all investment decisions—and outline the two-step investment decision process of security analysis and portfolio management. Finally, we discuss some of the key factors that affect the investment decision process such as global markets and institutional investors.

THE PURPOSE OF THIS TEXTBOOK

The objective of this text is to help you understand the investments field as it is currently understood, discussed, and practised so that you can make sound investment decisions that will enhance your economic welfare. Key concepts are presented to provide an appreciation of the theory and practice of investments. After reading this text, you will be able to intelligently answer questions such as the following:

- The S&P/TSX Composite Index, which is the major Canadian stock index measuring stock performance on the Toronto Stock Exchange (TSX), fell 604.99 points (or 4.75 percent) on January 21, 2008, which combined with previous losses that week to produce an 11.4 percent decline for the TSX for that week's trading. The next day (January 22, 2008), the Index increased 509 points (or 4.2 percent). What causes this type of extreme volatility? With volatility such as this, should investors avoid common stocks altogether, particularly for retirement plans?

- The average return on Canadian equity mutual funds was 15.0 percent for the five-year period ending December 31, 2007.[1] This is below the 18.4 percent return achieved over this period by the S&P/TSX Total Return Index. Why is this?

- In 2007, the average returns earned on Canadian Emerging Market and Global Equity mutual funds were 18.9 percent and −3.2 percent respectively, while the average return for Canadian equity funds was 5.5 percent. Should Canadian investors be participating in developed and/or emerging global equity markets? If so, what investment options are available to them and how much wealth should they allocate to such investments?

- Is it possible to have earned 30 percent or more investing in low-risk Treasury bills in a single year?

- In January of 2008, the French bank Société Générale announced losses of €4.9 billion, or $7.14 billion (US), resulting from the fraudulent actions of a single futures trader who implemented a series of unauthorized trades that spiraled out of control. Given that such potential losses can be caused by futures trading, how is it that investors use these instruments to actually reduce or control risk?

- What is the historical average annual rate of return on common stocks and what can an investor reasonably expect to earn from stocks in the future?

Both descriptive and quantitative materials on investing are readily available in a variety of forms. Some of this material is very enlightening, much of it is entertaining but debatable because of the many controversies in investments, and some of it is simply worthless. This text seeks to cover what is particularly useful and relevant for today's investment climate. It offers some ideas about what you can reasonably expect to accomplish by using what you learn and therefore what you can realistically expect to achieve as an investor in today's investment world. Many investors have unrealistic expectations, which ultimately lead to disappointment or worse.

Learning to avoid the many pitfalls awaiting you as an investor by clearly understanding what you can reasonably expect from investing your money may be the single most important benefit to

---

[1] www.globefund.com, May 12, 2008.

be derived from this text. For example, would you entrust your money to someone offering 36 percent annual return on riskless US government Treasury securities? Some 600 investors did and lost approximately $10 million to a former Sunday school teacher. Intelligent investors learn to say no and to avoid many of the mistakes that can thus be prevented.

THE NATURE OF INVESTMENTS

Some Definitions

The term investing can cover a wide range of activities. It often refers to putting money in GICs, bonds, common stocks, or mutual funds. More knowledgeable investors would include other paper assets, such as income trusts, warrants, puts and calls, futures contracts, and convertible securities, as well as tangible assets, such as gold, real estate, and collectibles. Investing can range from very conservative to aggressive speculation. Whether you are a university graduate starting out in the workplace or a senior citizen concerned with how to get by in retirement, investing decisions will be very important to you.

An **investment** can be defined as the commitment of funds to one or more assets that will be held over some future time period. The field of **investments**, therefore, involves the study of the investment process. The study of investments is concerned with the management of an investor's wealth, which is the sum of current income and the present value of all future income. (This is why present value and compound interest concepts have an important role in the investment process.) Although the field of investments encompasses many aspects, it can be thought of in terms of two primary functions: analysis and management.

In this text, the term investments refers in general to **financial assets** and in particular to marketable securities. Financial assets are paper (or electronic) claims on some issuer such as the federal or provincial government or a corporation; on the other hand, **real assets** are tangible physical assets such as precious metals (gold, silver), gems (diamonds), art, and real estate. **Marketable securities** are financial assets that are easily and cheaply traded in organized markets. Technically, investments include both financial and real assets, and both marketable and non-marketable assets. Because of the vast scope of investment opportunities available to investors, our primary emphasis is on marketable securities; however, the basic principles and techniques discussed in this text are applicable to real assets as well.

Even when we limit our discussion primarily to financial assets, it is difficult to keep up with the proliferation of new products. One such product that was relatively unimportant a few years ago is exchange-traded funds (ETFs) (discussed in Chapter 3). Real-World Returns 1-1 refers to the recent growth of ETFs.

Investing as Part of Personal Financial Planning

The investment of funds in various assets is only part of the overall financial decision making and planning that most individuals must do. Before investing, each individual should develop a financial plan that should include the decision on whether to purchase a house, a major investment for most individuals. In addition, decisions must be made about insurance of various types—life, health, disability, and protection of business and property. Finally, the plan should provide for emergency reserve funds.[2]

This text assumes that investors have established their overall financial plan and are now interested in managing and enhancing their wealth by investing in an optimal combination of financial assets. The idea of an "optimal combination" is important because our wealth, which we hold in the form of various assets, should be evaluated and managed as a unified whole. Wealth should be evaluated and managed within the context of a **portfolio**, which is made up of the asset holdings of an investor.

Investment
The commitment of funds to one or more assets that will be held over some future time period.

Investments
The study of the investment process.

Financial Assets
Paper or electronic claims on some issuer such as the federal or provincial government or a corporation.

Real Assets
Physical assets, such as gold or real estate.

Marketable Securities
Financial assets that are easily and cheaply traded in organized markets.

Portfolio
The securities held by an investor taken as a unit.

---

[2]Personal finance decisions of this type are discussed in personal finance texts.

REAL-WORLD RETURNS 1-1

When It Comes to Paying Fund Fees, the Price Is Right with ETFs

One of the first things I ever read about exchange-traded funds was a *Wall Street Journal* piece that described them as being 2007's "It" investment. Now that's a characterization you've got to love—the investing equivalent of fashion "must-haves" like Louboutin heels or spring's bright florals and trench coats.

The problem, though, is that no one really expects to be wearing those flirty florals or bright orange trench coats in five years' time. You want more from your investments than fads: You want the equivalent of a classic tailored suit or winter coat, something that will be in your wardrobe for decades. Like Louboutins, though, once in a while a fad becomes a trend with staying power.

Last weekend, I had a chance to poll more than 10 of my friends and not one of them knew what exchange-traded funds, or ETFs, are. For the uninitiated, ETFs are like mutual funds that trade like a stock. But they are different from mutual funds in that they are baskets of stocks or bonds put together to mirror indexes, such like, say, the S&P/TSX composite index. There is no portfolio manager actively buying and selling the stocks. In theory, if the S&P/TSX composite rises 10 percent in a year, so should your TSX ETF.

In the last few years, the number of ETFs in Canada and particularly the US has skyrocketed to about 700. They have moved from covering the large indexes to zeroing in on the smallest of niches. It's fun to see how small a niche can be: For example, in the US, you can buy ETFs that track the health care sector, but you can also narrow that down further to funds that focus on just cardiology or dermatology. But that explosion in the number of ETFs, particularly in niche funds, concerns Heather Pelant, the head of business development for Barclays Global Investors in Canada. Her company runs many of the most widely traded ETFs in Canada. She worries that the investor who is looking at ETFs for the first time may be put off by all the "noise and confusion."

Ms. Pelant admits that the average investor still doesn't know much about ETFs, but predicts that will change over the next five years, probably at the expense of mutual funds. "Our belief is that this is just a better investment tool."

There is a lot to like about ETFs, the major selling point being lower fees. While the typical mutual fund has a management-expense ratio of 2.6 percent and the average money market fund, more than 1 percent, ETFs have ratios generally below one-half of 1 percent. Just how much can fees cost you? Take this example published in this paper last month: A $1,000 investment in mutual funds with an annual return of 8 percent over 20 years would produce a profit of $3,661 without fees—but only $1,807 after a typical 2.6-percent management-expense ratio.

ETFs have lower fees because management of their funds is passive, although it certainly isn't without risk. Take, for instance, a fund that aims to replicate the S&P/TSX composite. The basket wouldn't contain the exact same stocks, but a mixture of stocks or futures contracts that when put together try to achieve the same results as the index.

According to a study by Morgan Stanley reported this week in the *Wall Street Journal*, which looked at 330 ETFs south of the border, funds that tracked broad US stock market indexes last year on average delivered returns that were 0.32 of a percentage point less than those of the indexes after fees.

But, especially in niche funds, there were some whopping misfires—Vanguard Telecommunication Services ETF returned 5.5 percent, compared with the benchmark's 10.5 percent, a difference of five percentage points.

Which means, like all stock market-related investments, there's no such thing as a sure thing. The other thing to consider about ETFs is that even when they do replicate indexes, most people want their funds to do better. Everybody wants to beat the market, but maybe that's a fool's game.

To that point, Barclays' Ms. Pelant cites the Standard & Poor's Indices Versus Active Funds Scorecard, which was released last week. It found that in the five-year period ending in 2007, only 8.4 percent of actively managed Canadian equity mutual funds have outperformed the S&P/TSX composite index. In other words, just meeting the index was doing better than 90 percent of equity funds over the five-year period.

A disadvantage of ETFs is that because they are bought and sold on exchanges, you have to pay brokerage commissions. That makes it hard for the many people who set aside small amounts each month—say $200 a month—for their mutual funds. It just wouldn't make sense to buy ETFs in such small quantities.

For now, Ms. Pelant says that ETFs are only 2 percent of the total fund market, but growing at twice the pace of mutual funds. My feeling is that the numbers will continue to climb. It may be because RRSP season has just recently passed, but I've been hearing a lot of grumbling lately from friends who worry about low returns and high fees with their mutual funds.

I can't help but think that when they come to know ETFs, the low fees will be a huge lure. Whether they'll be excited by a dermatology fund is a whole other issue.

Source: Rasbach, Noreen, "When it comes to paying fund fees, the price is right with ETFs," *The Globe and Mail*, March 8, 2008, CTVglobemedia Publishing, Inc. All Rights Reserved.

Why Do We Invest?

Although everyone would agree that we invest to make money, we need to be more precise. We invest to improve our welfare, which for our purposes can be defined as monetary wealth, both current and future. Funds to be invested come from assets already owned, such as savings or inheritances, borrowed money, or "foregone consumption." By foregoing consumption today and investing the savings, investors expect to enhance their future consumption possibilities by increasing their wealth.

Investors also seek to manage their wealth effectively, obtaining the most from it while protecting it from inflation, taxes, and other factors. There are three primary investment objectives:

1. Safety

2. Income

3. Growth of capital.

These objectives are mutually exclusive to some extent in the sense that a single security cannot maximize two or more of these primary objectives. In other words, trade-offs exist, so if you wish to maximize safety, you have to be willing to make some sacrifices with respect to income and growth potential.

Secondary investment objectives include liquidity or marketability and tax minimization. They are considered secondary in the sense that investors should not allow them to dominate primary investment considerations. For example, it would be imprudent to alter an investment portfolio designed to maximize safety, simply to avoid taxes. On the other hand, it makes good sense to devise and follow tax avoidance strategies within the context of any investment plan. The point is that they should not be the overriding factor determining investment decisions.

Investors face several constraints that will affect the objectives of their investment policy and determine how effectively these objectives can be attained. The most obvious factors are the level and stability of income and the level of financial obligations faced by an investor, both now and in the future. The individual's level of investment knowledge and general tolerance for risk should also play an important role in the design of an investment policy. Some investors will be constrained by legal, moral, and ethical considerations. In addition, miscellaneous factors such as illness or a pending divorce may become an overriding factor in the investment decision. These issues are discussed in detail in Chapter 21.

CHECK YOUR UNDERSTANDING

1-1. All financial assets are real assets, but only some marketable securities are real assets. Do you agree, or disagree? Explain.

1-2. What term is used to refer to all the securities held by an investor? Why is it important to think of asset holdings taken as a unit rather than individually?

1-3. Is tax minimization one of the three primary investment objectives? If not, should this factor ever be considered when making investment decisions?

THE IMPORTANCE OF STUDYING INVESTMENTS

The Personal Aspects

It is important to remember that all individuals have wealth of some kind; if nothing else, they have the value of their services in the marketplace. Most individuals must make investment decisions sometime in their lives. These include day-to-day decisions such as how to improve the return from savings accounts by investing funds in alternative financial instruments. In fact, the decision to enroll at a postsecondary educational institution represents a significant investment decision, since it requires a large sacrifice of your time and money. The future benefits are uncertain, although they include an increase in earnings potential; intangible benefits include the sense of accomplishment individuals feel as they learn and/or achieve academic success.

A good example of the critical importance of making good investment decisions is deciding how much to contribute to a Registered Retirement Savings Plan (RRSP) (discussed in Chapter 3), and what types of assets these should include. Working taxpayers can make tax-deductible contributions up to specified limits per year (depending on their income and their contributions to other registered plans). The earnings on the contributions are not taxed until they are withdrawn, as long as the assets are RRSP-eligible.

RRSP funds can be invested in a wide range of assets, from the very safe to the very speculative. Since these funds may be invested for long periods of time, good investment decisions are critical. Over many years, the differences in the investment returns earned can be staggering. Table 1-1 demonstrates how $4,000 invested every year for 40 years will grow to over $7 million if the funds earn 15 percent per year; they will grow to $1.78 million at 10 percent and $483,200 at 5 percent—quite a large variation in final wealth.

Table 1-1 also demonstrates the importance of investing early. This is obvious from the great difference in ending wealth values that accrue after 20 years, which are dramatically smaller than the corresponding 40-year values listed in the bottom row of that table.

With so much individual investor money flowing into mutual funds, and with individual investors owning a large percentage of all stocks outstanding, the study of investments is more important than ever. After being net sellers of stocks from 1968 through 1990, individual investors have swarmed into the financial markets. Individual investor interest in the stock market since 1990 is best expressed by the power of mutual funds (explained in Chapter 3), their favourite investment vehicle. Mutual funds, pension funds, and other institutional investors are now the driving forces in the marketplace, and over half of all trades on the TSX and on the NYSE are block trades by institutional investors. In fact, the total

Table 1-1

Possible Payoffs from Long-Term Investing

Amount Invested per Year	Number of Years	Final Wealth if Funds Are Invested at		
		5%	10%	15%
$4,000	20	$132,264	$229,100	$409,760
$4,000	30	$265,756	$657,960	$1,739,000
$4,000	40	$483,200	$1,770,360	$7,116,400

assets in mutual funds in Canada grew from $24.9 billion at the end of 1990, to $697.3 billion by December 31, 2007.[3]

In the final analysis, we study investments in the hope of earning better returns in relation to the risk we assume when we invest. A careful study of investment analysis and portfolio management principles can provide a sound framework for both managing and increasing wealth. Furthermore, this knowledge will allow you to sift through and properly evaluate the many articles on investing that appear daily in newspapers and magazines, which in turn will increase your chances of reaching your financial goals.

Many of the issues discussed regularly in the financial media and by average investors are covered in the text, and learning about them will make you a much smarter investor, including the following list of topics:

1. Financial assets available to investors

2. Total rate of return versus yield

3. Compounding effects and terminal wealth

4. Realized returns versus expected returns

5. Index funds and mutual fund expenses

6. How diversification works to reduce risk

7. The asset allocation decision

8. The significance of market efficiency to investors

Investments as a Profession

In addition to the above reasons for studying investments, the world of investments offers several rewarding careers, both professionally and financially. At the end of 2005 there were 201 firms in the securities industry in Canada employing more than 39,000 individuals.[4] This number is significant but it pales in comparison to the numbers employed by the big Canadian banks. For example, the **Royal Bank of Canada** alone employed over 60,000 people in 2005. A study of investments is an essential part of becoming a professional in these fields.

Investment professionals who arrange the sale of new securities and assist in mergers and acquisitions enjoyed phenomenal financial rewards in the booming 1980s and in the latter part of the 1990s. The total value of mergers in Canada reached an all-time high of $257 billion in 2006. Experienced merger and acquisition specialists can earn over a million dollars a year, and even someone with just a few years' experience can earn $200,000 to $400,000 in this area.

Top security traders and registered representatives (investment advisors) commonly earn six-figure salaries, which escalate during periods of strong market activity, such as that displayed during the mid-1990s until early 2001, and over the 2003 to mid-2007 period. Bond traders can also

---

[3]The Investment Funds Institute of Canada (IFIC) website: www.ific.ca.

[4]Investment Industry Regulatory Organization of Canada (IIROC) website: www.iiroc.com, formerly Investment Dealers Association of Canada (IDA).

commonly earn in the six-figure range, with the salaries increasing with experience. A relatively inexperienced bond salesperson selling to institutional investors can earn $200,000 or more and, if experienced, the figure rises to the $600,000 to $700,000 range.

Although less glamorous and less profitable for the firms involved, there are good paying jobs on Bay Street and Wall Street in research. Analysts with a few years of experience can earn well over $100,000, while those with 10 years or more of experience can earn up to $500,000. A range of financial institutions—including securities firms, banks, investment companies, and insurance companies—need the services of investment analysts. Securities firms need them to support their registered representatives who in turn serve the public, for example, by preparing the research reports provided to customers. They also need analysts to assist in the sale of new securities and in the valuation of firms as possible merger or acquisition candidates. Banks, insurance companies, and investment companies need analysts to evaluate securities for possible purchase or sale from their investment portfolios.

The firms mentioned above all need portfolio managers to manage the portfolios of securities handled by these organizations. Portfolio managers are responsible for making the actual portfolio buy and sell decisions—what to buy and sell, when to buy and sell, and so forth. Portfolio performance is calculated for these managers, and their jobs typically depend on their performance relative to other managed portfolios and to market averages.

Finally, the number of financial planners continues to grow. While most provinces do not regulate the term "financial planner," many planners pursue professional designations, including the Certified Financial Planner (CFP). The CFP designation has been sanctioned by the Financial Planners Standards Council (FPSC), which was formed in 1995 to develop a set of minimum standards for financial planners in terms of education, experience, and ethical and moral conduct. The FPSC establishes and enforces uniform professional standards for financial planners who choose to recognize the internationally recognized CFP™ designation. Today, there are nearly 17,000 CFP professionals in Canada and almost 100,000 in 19 countries around the world. CFP professionals work in every segment of the financial services industry. In addition, the FPSC strives to continue to develop and regulate standards that are relevant to the current financial planning needs of Canadians.

Individuals interested in careers in the investments field, rather than financial planning, should consider studying to become a **Chartered Financial Analyst** (CFA). This is a professional designation for people in the investments area, not unlike the CA, CMA, or CGA designations for accountants. The CFA designation is widely recognized in the investments industry. It serves as an indication that areas of knowledge relevant to investing have been studied and that high ethical and professional standards have been recognized and accepted. Details of the CFA program are included in Appendix 1A. Throughout this text we will use relevant parts of the CFA curriculum, procedures, and philosophy because it directly relates to a study of investments.

UNDERSTANDING THE INVESTMENT DECISION PROCESS

learning objective 2
Explain why risk and return are the two critical components of all investing decisions.

An organized view of the investment process involves analyzing the basic nature of investment decisions and organizing the activities in the decision process.

Common stocks have produced, on average, significantly larger returns over the years than savings accounts or bonds, but these higher returns mean larger risks. Underlying all investment decisions is the trade-off between expected return and risk. Therefore, we first consider these two basic parameters that are of critical importance to all investors and the trade-off that exists between expected return and risk.

Given the foundation for making investment decisions—the trade-off between expected return and risk—we next consider the decision process in investments as it is practised today. Although numerous separate decisions must be made, for organizational purposes this decision process has traditionally been divided into a two-step process: security analysis and portfolio management. Security analysis involves the valuation of securities, whereas portfolio management involves the management of an investor's investment selections as a portfolio (package of assets), with its own unique characteristics.

The Basis of Investment Decisions

Return

Stated in simplest terms, investors wish to earn a return on their money. Cash has an opportunity cost. By holding cash, you forego the opportunity to earn a return on that cash. Furthermore, in an inflationary environment, the purchasing power of cash diminishes, with high rates of inflation (such as that in 1980) bringing a rapid decline in purchasing power.

In investments it is critical to distinguish between an **expected return** (the anticipated return for some future period) and a **realized return** (the actual return over some past period). Investors invest for the future—for the returns they expect to earn—but when the investing period is over, they are left with their realized returns. What investors actually earn from their holdings may turn out to be more or less than what they expected when they first made the investment. This point is the essence of the investments process: investors must always consider the risk involved in investing.

Risk

Investors would like their returns to be as large as possible; however, this objective is subject to constraints, primarily risk. The Toronto Stock Exchange had a reasonably good year in 2007, with total returns for the S&P/TSX Composite Index of 9.8 percent. During the same period, the returns earned by professionally managed Canadian equity mutual funds varied from as low as –27.0 percent to as high as 35.1 percent.[5] This demonstrates the riskiness associated with marketable securities that offer variable rates of return. The investment decision, therefore, must always be considered in terms of both risk and return. The two are inseparable.

There are different types, and therefore different definitions, of risk. We define **risk** as the chance that the actual return on an investment will be different from its expected return.[6] Using the term risk in this manner, the nominal (current dollar) return on a long-term Government of Canada bond can be considered free of default risk, since it is virtually assured that the government will redeem these obligations as they mature. On the other hand, there is some risk, however small, that the Royal Bank or BCE will be unable to redeem an issue of long-term bonds when they mature. And there is a very substantial risk of not realizing the expected return on any particular common stock over some future holding period.

Do investors dislike risk? In economics in general, and investments in particular, the standard assumption is that investors are rational and prefer certainty to uncertainty. It is easy to say that investors dislike risk, but more precisely, we should say that investors are risk averse. A **risk-averse investor** is one who will not assume risk simply for its own sake and will not incur any given level of risk unless there is an expectation of adequate compensation for having done so. Note carefully that it is not irrational to assume risk, even very large risk, as long as we expect to be compensated for it. In fact, investors cannot reasonably expect to earn larger returns without assuming larger risks.

Investors deal with risk by choosing (implicitly or explicitly) the amount of risk they are willing to incur. Some investors choose high levels of risk with the expectation of high levels of return. Other investors are unwilling to assume much risk at all, and they should not expect to earn large returns.

We have said that investors would like to maximize their returns. Can we also say that investors, in general, will choose to minimize their risks? No! The reason is that there are costs to minimizing the risk—specifically a lower expected return. Taken to its logical conclusion, the minimization of risk would result in everyone holding risk-free assets such as savings accounts, CSBs,

Expected Return
The anticipated return by investors for some future period.

Realized Return
Actual return on an investment for some previous period of time.

Risk
The chance that the actual return on an investment will be different from the expected return.

Risk-Averse Investor
An investor who will not assume a given level of risk unless there is an expectation of adequate compensation for having done so.

---

[5]www.globefund.com, March 12, 2008.
[6]As we shall see in Chapter 7, expected return is a precise statistical term, not simply the return the investor expects. As indicated in our definition, risk involves chances or probabilities, which will also be discussed in Chapter 7 along with measures of the dispersion in the expected return.

and Treasury bills. Thus, we need to think in terms of the expected risk–return trade-off that results from the direct relationship between the risk and the expected return of an investment.

The Expected Return–Risk Trade-Off

Within the realm of financial assets, investors can achieve virtually any position on an expected risk–return spectrum such as that depicted in Figure 1-1. The line RF to B is the assumed trade-off between expected return and risk that exists for all investors interested in financial assets. This trade-off always slopes upward, because the vertical axis is expected return, and rational investors will not assume more risk unless they expect to be compensated for doing so. The expected return must be large enough to compensate for taking the additional risk.

Figure 1-1
The Expected Return–Risk Trade-Off Available to Investors

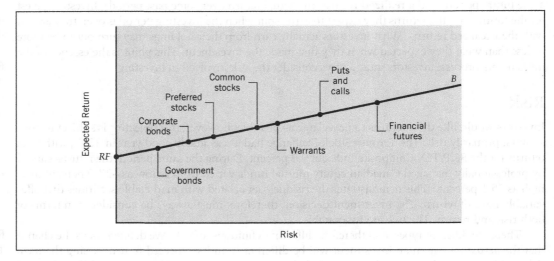

RF in Figure 1-1 is the return on a riskless asset such as Government of Canada T-bills. Since these assets have no risk, the expected return will equal (approximately) the realized return, which equals the current rate of return offered by these assets. This **risk-free rate of return**, which is available to all investors, will be designated as RF throughout the text. Using this as a starting point, we can say the following relationship will hold for expected returns on risky assets:

$$\text{Expected return} = \text{Risk-free rate (RF)} + \text{Expected risk premium}$$

This figure shows the relative positions for some of the financial assets that will be discussed in Chapter 2. As we move from riskless securities to more risky corporate bonds, equities, and so forth, we assume more risk in the expectation of earning a larger return. Common stocks are quite risky in relation to bonds, but they are not as risky as uncovered positions in options or futures contracts. (All of these terms are defined in Chapter 2.)

Obviously, we are using broad categories here. Within a particular category, such as common stocks, a wide range of expected return and risk opportunities exists at any time. The important point is that it is the trade-off between expected return and risk that should prevail in a rational environment. Investors unwilling to assume risk must be satisfied with the risk-free rate of return, RF. If they wish to try to earn a larger rate of return, they must be willing to assume a larger risk as represented by moving up the expected risk–return trade-off into the wide range of financial assets available to investors. Although all rational investors like returns and dislike risk, they are satisfied by quite different levels of expected return and risk. Put differently, investors have different limits on the amount of risk they are willing to assume and, therefore, the amount of return that can realistically be

Risk-Free Rate of Return
The return on a riskless asset, often proxied by the rate of return on Treasury securities.

expected. In economic terms, the explanation for these differences in preferences is that rational investors strive to maximize their utility, the perception of which varies among investors.[7]

It is important to remember that the risk–return trade-off depicted in Figure 1-1 is *ex ante*, meaning "before the fact." That is, before the investment is actually made, the investor expects higher returns from assets that have a higher risk, and the expected risk premium is positive. This is the only sensible expectation for risk-averse investors, who are assumed to constitute the majority of all investors. *Ex post* (meaning "after the fact" or when it is known what has occurred), for a given period of time, such as a month or a year or even longer, the trade-off may turn out to be flat or even negative. For example, the 2002 return on Canadian stocks as measured by the S&P/TSX Composite Index was –12.4 percent, while the return on long-term Government of Canada bonds that year was 10.1 percent. This implies that the actual (*ex post*) returns on the riskier common stocks were well below the realized returns on the relatively safer bonds. Such is the nature of risky investments!

Structuring the Decision Process

Investors can choose from a wide range of securities in their attempt to maximize the expected returns from these opportunities. They face constraints, the most pervasive of which is risk. Traditionally, investors have analyzed and managed securities using a broad two-step process: security analysis and portfolio management.

learning objective 3
Outline the two-step investment decision process.

Security Analysis

The first part of the investment decision process involves the valuation and analysis of individual securities, which is referred to as **security analysis**. Institutional investors usually employ professional security analysts. Of course, there are also millions of amateur security analysts in the form of individual investors.

The valuation of securities is a time-consuming and difficult job. First of all, it is necessary to understand the characteristics of the various securities and the factors that affect them. Second, a valuation model must be applied to these securities to estimate their price or value. Value is a combination of the expected future returns on a security and the risk attached. Both of these parameters must be estimated and then brought together in a model.

For bonds, the valuation process is relatively straightforward because the returns are known and the risk can be approximated from currently available data. This does not mean, however, that all the problems of bond analysis are easily resolved. Interest rates are the primary factor affecting bond prices, and no one can consistently forecast changes in these rates.

The valuation process is much more difficult for common stocks than for bonds. The investor must take into account the overall economy, the industry, and the individual company. With common stocks, estimating the expected return and the risk is not easy, but despite the difficulties, investors serious about their portfolios must perform some type of analysis. Unless this is done, one has to rely on personal hunches, suggestions from friends, and recommendations from brokers—all of which may be dangerous to one's financial health.

Security Analysis
The first part of the investment decision process, involving the valuation and analysis of individual securities.

Portfolio Management

The second major component of the decision process is **portfolio management**. After securities have been evaluated, portfolio composition must be determined. The concepts associated with building a portfolio are well known and are discussed at some length in Chapters 7 to 10, and in Chapter 21.

Portfolio Management
The second step in the investment decision process, involving the management of a group of assets (i.e., a portfolio) as a unit.

---

[7]Utility theory is a complex subject; however, for our purposes we can equate maximization of utility with maximization of welfare. Because welfare is a function of present and future wealth, and wealth in turn is a function of current and future income discounted (reduced) for the amount of risk involved, in effect, investors maximize their welfare by optimizing the expected risk–return trade-off. In the final analysis, expected return and risk constitute the foundation of all investment decisions.

Having built a portfolio, the astute investor must consider how and when to revise it. This raises a number of important questions. Portfolios must be managed, regardless of whether an investor is active or passive. If the investor pursues an active strategy, the issue of market efficiency must be considered. If prices reflect information quickly and fully, investors should consider how this would affect their buy and sell decisions. Even if investors follow a passive strategy (which involves designing or purchasing a portfolio that mirrors the performance of some market benchmark), questions to be considered include taxes, transaction costs, maintenance of the desired risk level, and so on.

Finally, all investors are interested in how well their portfolio performs. This is the bottom line of the investment process, but measuring portfolio performance is an inexact procedure and needs to be carefully considered.

CHECK YOUR UNDERSTANDING

1-4. Historically, stocks have outperformed other asset classes such as bonds, on average. Should all intelligent investors own stocks?

1-5. Rational investors always attempt to minimize their risks. Do you agree or disagree?

1-6. Investors should always seek to maximize their returns from investing. Do you agree or disagree?

1-7. The valuation and analysis of individual securities is a difficult and time-consuming task. Does this activity represent the full scope of the investment decision process?

IMPORTANT CONSIDERATIONS IN THE INVESTMENT DECISION PROCESS

learning objective 4
Discuss key factors that affect the investment decision process.

Intelligent investors should recognize that the investment decision process described above can be lengthy and involved. Regardless of individual actions, certain factors in the investment environment affect everyone. Investors should be aware of these factors as they work through the investment decision process.

The Great Unknown

"You have to understand that being wrong is part of the process." This statement by Peter Bernstein, one of the world's most prominent investment experts, illustrates the paramount factor that all investors must come to grips with—uncertainty. Investors buy various financial assets, expecting to earn certain returns over some future holding period. These returns are only what can be expected; they may never be realized. The simple fact that dominates investing is that the realized return on a risky asset is likely to be different from what was expected—sometimes, quite different.

At best, estimates are imprecise; at worst, they are completely wrong. Some investors try to handle uncertainty by building elaborate quantitative models, and others simply keep it in the back of their mind. All investors, however, are affected by it, and the best they can do is make the most informed return and risk estimates they can, act on them, and be prepared for changing circumstances. Regardless of how careful and informed investors are, the future is uncertain, and mistakes will be made. This will always be true for everyone involved with financial markets and, in fact, for anyone at all, since life itself is uncertain. For example, many experts predicted the Canadian dollar would remain stable or increase slightly during 2007, yet by the end of that year the value of the dollar had increased dramatically by 17.6 percent from $0.8581 US to $1.0088 US.

Investors often use historical data to make their estimates and modify this to incorporate what they believe is most likely to happen. It is important to remember that basing investment decisions solely on the past may lead to serious errors. Just because stocks had a 10 percent average return over the last 10 years is no guarantee of the same return next year, or 10 years from now.

Anyone can tell you what you should have bought or sold in the past—it's a matter of record. For example, the **Altamira** Canadian Equity mutual fund produced a 20-year compound average return of 12.8 percent for the period ending December 31, 2007, well above the 10.0 percent average return for the **S&P/TSX Total Return Index** over the same period. That fund outperformed the TSX in 2007 (10.82 percent versus 9.8 percent), yet underperformed in both 2006 (15.6 percent versus 17.3 percent) and in 2005 (22.5 percent versus 24.1 percent). The point is that while the past provides important information, no one can guarantee you a successful portfolio for next year or any other specified period of time. Unanticipated events will affect financial markets. No one can consistently forecast what will happen with interest rates or in financial markets, including the professionals who are paid to make recommendations.

Although uncertainty is always present, all is not lost. It is often possible to make reasonable and informed judgments about the outcomes of many investment opportunities. Investment decisions are both an art and a science. To succeed, we must think in terms of what we expect to happen. We know what has happened, but the past may or may not repeat itself. Although the future is uncertain, investors can attempt to manage it intelligently by developing a thorough understanding of the basic principles of investing. In addition, new tools and techniques are constantly being developed that may help investors to make better decisions.

The Global Investments Arena

Now more than ever, investors must think of investments in a global context. Although foreign investments have been possible for a number of years, many investors have not bought and sold on an international basis. However, astute investors can no longer afford to limit themselves to domestic investment only.

An international perspective is becoming increasingly important to all investors as we find ourselves operating in a global marketplace of round-the-clock investing. Since the Canadian stock and bond markets comprise only about 2 percent of their respective world markets, Canadian investors who ignore these markets will be cutting themselves off from a large number of investment alternatives.

Foreign markets have grown rapidly, and several are now large by any measure. The Japanese market is well known, having reached very high levels followed by very low levels. Western European markets are well developed and offer investors numerous alternatives in what some observers feel will be the premier economic power of the future.

A hot investment concept in recent years is the potential rewards of investing in **emerging markets**.[8] Indeed, much of the strength in Canadian markets can be attributed to strong commodity prices, which have been driven to a large extent by the tremendous economic growth in China and India. During 2007, the returns for the Chinese stock market were 63.1 percent, those in India were 71.2 percent, while returns in Peru were 86.0 percent. Consistent with the volatile nature of emerging markets, from January 1 to March 11, 2008, the Chinese and Indian markets had declined 21.3 and 24.5 percent respectively, while the returns in Peru were positive 11.5 percent.

Emerging Markets
Markets of less developed countries characterized by high risks but potentially large returns.

The impact of the US economy for Canadian investors is apparent on a daily basis, as we routinely observe large swings in Canadian bond and stock price levels in response to announcements by the US Federal Reserve Board, or the release of other US economic statistics. Given that the United States accounts for well over 70 percent of Canadian exports and imports, it is not surprising that the returns on Canadian stock markets are tightly tied to those on US markets. Real-World Returns 1-2 demonstrates this relationship clearly, as fears of a US recession in January of 2008 triggered a stock market selloff in global stock markets, including Canada. Indeed, the turmoil in Canadian markets that began in the summer of 2007 and has persisted throughout much of 2008 can be mainly attributed to the subprime debt market crisis in the US, and the economic fallout resulting from this crisis.

---

[8]The World Bank classifies a stock market as "emerging" if its country's economy had less than $7,910 in US dollars per capita gross domestic product (GDP) in 1991.

REAL-WORLD RETURNS 1-2

US Recession Fears Spark Global Sell Off

The looming threat of a US recession that could infect the rest of the world dealt Canadian stocks their biggest one-day blow since 9/11 yesterday as share prices plunged from London to Frankfurt to Tokyo.

In Canada, markets that had been skidding for several days fell off a cliff, with the S&P/TSX composite index tumbling 605 points or 4.75 percent. In the past week, the index has shrunk by more than 1,500 points, or 11.4 percent. Energy and mining stocks, buoyed in recent months by high commodity prices, fell the furthest yesterday.

"The market is finally starting to wake up to some realities out there," said Murray Leith, director of research at investment adviser Odlum Brown Ltd. in Vancouver. "The rest of the world is not going to decouple from the United States," which is likely headed for recession, he said.

"To think that the United States and the developed world can have a slowdown and it will not have any impact on emerging markets is really ridiculous," he said. "A big part of this correction is the world waking up to that reality."

Many analysts suggested that one reason for the worldwide decline is a feeling that the US stimulus package unveiled by President George W. Bush and Federal Reserve chief Ben Bernanke last week is insufficient.

But more action is coming. The Bank of Canada is almost certain to lower interest rates today to bolster the economy.

And the Federal Reserve Board in the United States is expected to lower its key interest rate when it makes its next setting on Jan. 30. It's now under pressure to make the move even earlier.

All this happened while US markets were closed for the Martin Luther King Day holiday. This morning, all eyes will be on Wall Street to see how the biggest and most important market reacts to what took place outside the US borders.

Trading in stock futures, which change hands when the market is closed, suggests the US markets could see losses today that will be larger than yesterday's, and the global rout was continuing last night when markets opened sharply down in Asia.

Among the hardest hit Canadian stocks was BCE Inc. It has come under increasing pressure since rumours emerged that the takeover by a group led by the Ontario Teachers' Pension Plan could get scuttled. At yesterday's close of $34.42, BCE stock is 19 percent below the takeover price of $42.75 a share.

Source: Excerpted from Blackwell, Richard, "The market is finally starting to wake up to some realities," *The Globe and Mail*, January 22, 2008, page A1.

In addition to the US, the performance of Canadian investment assets is also greatly affected by global economic activity outside North America, as alluded to above with respect to the growth in the economies in China and India, and the resulting impact on world commodity prices. In addition, we routinely observe large volatility in domestic markets being caused by international events such as concerns over the ability of Russia to meet its external debt payments in 1998 or the war in Iraq that began in 2003.

There are several reasons why global events have such a significant impact on Canadian investors. One is the very nature of Canada's economy, which consists of a relatively large proportion of commodity-based industries such as oil, mining, and forestry. Since the price of these commodities is determined in the global marketplace, our economy is greatly influenced by global supply and demand. In addition, many Canadian firms (even those that are not commodity-based) derive a large proportion of their revenues from abroad. As a result, adverse movements in foreign exchange rates can have unhappy consequences for Canadian multinational companies whose foreign currency profits are translated into fewer Canadian dollars. On the other hand, many Canadian companies benefit from a decline in the value of the dollar because their products become relatively less expensive in foreign markets, which increases demand for their products abroad.

Another important reason for Canadian investors to think in a global context is that the rates of return available in foreign securities are often higher than those available from Canadian markets. Finally, the addition of foreign securities allows investors to achieve beneficial risk reduction, since many foreign markets move differently from Canada's. For example, when Canadian stocks are doing poorly, some foreign stocks may be doing well, which would help offset the poor domestic performance. This risk reduction is a result of diversification. The simple point is that if domestic diversification in a portfolio reduces risk (as discussed in Chapter 7), which it clearly does, foreign diversification should provide even greater risk reduction—and it does! Given the increased attention paid to international investing, it is not surprising that many studies of international equity have found that global portfolio diversification does not contribute to performance as much as it did in the past; however, it still offers substantial benefits.

Thus, we should consider foreign markets as well as the domestic financial environment. We will do so throughout this text as an integral part of the discussion rather than in a separate chapter, because although the details may vary, the principles of investing are applicable to financial assets and markets wherever they exist.

The New Economy Versus the Old Economy

Investors must now cope with a changed investing environment. In the past there was one large market of securities, ranging from the tiny company to the giant company, from very shaky companies to the very successful companies, from the purely domestic company to the multinational firms. These days, investors talk about Old Economy stocks and New Economy stocks, and the same rules and analysis procedures may not apply to both.

Old Economy stocks refer to the traditional "smokestack" companies and the traditional service, consumer, and financial companies. Examples include Molson, Magna International Inc., Procter & Gamble, Imperial Oil Limited, and McDonald's Corporation. They produce and sell goods and services, show a profit, and reward their stockholders fairly consistently. These companies may be successful and have a lengthy history, but they are not considered exciting. The New Economy stocks such as Research In Motion (RIM), Nortel Networks, 724 Solutions, Cisco Systems Inc., and AOL have a heavy focus on technology. The New Economy includes many stocks that had meteoric rises and very dramatic declines, resulting in the Internet bubble of the late 1990s and subsequent burst in the early 2000s. We use the graph of the stock price of Nortel to summarize this phenomenon, as shown in Figure 1-2.

Nortel used to be a simple, telecommunications manufacturer controlled by BCE Inc. However, in the Internet mania of the late 1990s, investor interest shifted to companies making the equipment for the backbone of the Internet. Two Canadian companies, Nortel and JDS Uniphase, attracted a huge amount of interest. As can be seen from the graph that follows, Nortel's stock price jumped from the $20 to $40 range to peak at over $170, before collapsing to the penny stock range. The prices of JDS and other IT companies followed similar patterns over this time frame. At one point, Nortel and JDS combined to make up over one-third of the market value of the S&P/TSX Composite Index, and they dragged it up along with them when they soared, and dragged it back down again when they crashed.

What does this mean to investors? It illustrates that the world in general and the investing world in particular is changing faster than ever today. Investors often have to change their views and sometimes their procedures. Many of the new e-commerce companies have no earnings or cash flows, and

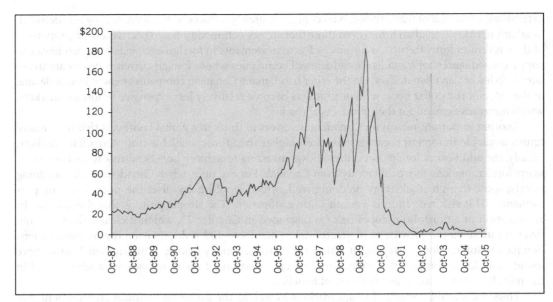

Figure 1-2
Nortel Stock Price
(1987–2005)

therefore traditional valuation approaches do not work very well, if at all. At one point, investors paid $500 per share for Amazon, a company with no profits, while eBay has sold for a P/E ratio in the thousands. This is a brave new world and one that investors must consider. After all, if they simply ignore the new technologies and trends, they will miss opportunities to acquire stocks in companies such as RIM, Cisco Systems Inc., Dell Inc., Microsoft Corporation, and Intel Corporation—all of which have rewarded their shareholders tremendously in the past.

As discussed above, during the 2001–2002 period, technology stocks in general suffered dramatic declines in value and the markets were significantly off from their previous highs. However, many technology stocks made solid recoveries during 2003. This illustrates that learning about rational investment principles that have held up over long periods of time is important. Ultimately, investors return to basic valuation principles, such as those discussed in this text.

The Role of the Internet

Any discussion of the investment decision process must focus on the role of the Internet, which has significantly changed the investments environment. Investors can access a wealth of information about investing, trade cheaply and quickly in their brokerage accounts, obtain real-time quotes throughout the day, and monitor their portfolios.

This is a true revolution. The Internet has democratized the flow of investment information. Any investor—whether at home, at work, or on vacation—can download an incredible amount of information, communicate with other investors, do security analysis, manage portfolios, check company filings with government agencies, and carry out numerous other activities not thought possible for a small investor only a few years ago. Although some of these information sources and/or services carry a fee, most are free.

Institutional Investors
Pension funds, investment companies, bank trust departments, life insurance companies, and so forth that manage huge portfolios of securities.

Institutional Investors

There are two broad categories of investors: individual and **institutional investors**. The latter group, consisting of banks, pension funds, investment companies, insurance companies, and so forth, includes professional money managers who are frequently publicized in the popular press. The amount of money managed by these institutions is staggering. For example, by October of 2007, **IGM Financial** (Investors, MacKenzie Financial) managed total net assets of $111 billion, while

RBC Asset Management Inc., a subsidiary of the Royal Bank Financial Group, managed total net assets exceeding $81 billion. At this time, IGM offered investors over 380 funds to choose from, while RBC offered over 80 funds.

The amount of assets managed by institutional investors has continued to escalate in both Canada and the United States. In addition to the rapid growth in mutual fund assets in Canada in recent years (to $697 billion by December 31, 2007), banks, pension funds, and life insurance companies are important participants in Canadian (and international) financial markets. These institutional investors do not constitute a monolithic bloc of investors, but are composed of thousands of different organizations, most of which have multiple money managers.

The first issue to note about institutional investors is that their relative importance has changed. Mutual funds became the primary buying force in North American stock markets in the 1990s, due to the large growth in popularity of these investment vehicles. The role of pension funds has also changed significantly in both Canada and the United States in recent years. Canadian pension funds have historically invested very conservatively, primarily in fixed income securities such as bonds and money market instruments. However, in recent years, they have become more aggressive and have become more important players in Canadian and foreign equity and derivative security markets. Real-World Returns 1-3 alludes to the changes in Canadian pension plan activity, and the Canada Pension Plan (CPP) in particular, over the last two decades.

REAL-WORLD RETURNS 1-3

The Changing Face of Pension Plans

What do Canadians have in common with New Zealand air travelers? More than one might expect, as a result of this week's $1.3 billion (Canadian) offer by the Canada Pension Plan Investment Board (CPPIB) to purchase New Zealand's largest airport (Auckland).

Should we be concerned about such an announcement? After all, isn't this a risky place to invest our hard earned dollars that we have contributed to the CPP?

Indeed, such an announcement would have been unheard of 20 years ago when Canadian pension fund assets were comprised almost entirely of high quality fixed income securities (mainly government bonds). In fact, the CPP's assets in particular, were entirely comprised of said fixed income securities as recently as 1999. However, in today's investing environment, announcements such as the one above are far from extraordinary.

So what has changed? It turns out that it all has to do with a change in the regulations guiding pension fund management. In particular, fund managers are bound to a duty of care to the plan beneficiaries, which was historically guided by something referred to as the *prudent man rule*. This rule required that they determine whether a prospective investment would be considered prudent based on its own individual merits, in isolation from the existing investments held by the fund.

This rule effectively prohibited pension funds from holding common stock, real estate, etc. As a result, pension fund assets were entirely invested in low-risk, low-return investments, thus restricting their return potential. In response to this important shortcoming, the current version of the *prudent investor rule* has been adopted in various provincial jurisdictions since 1990, and was officially incorporated into the Uniform Trustee Investment Act of 1997.

The new rule is based upon the basic tenets of modern portfolio theory (MPT), which asserts that that the risk of a well diversified portfolio is determined by the interaction of individual assets in that portfolio, and is therefore distinct from the risk of any one particular investment. Therefore many investments that might be viewed as high risk in isolation may in fact be suitable for inclusion in a given portfolio. Indeed, the rule specifically stipulates that it

(continued)

REAL-WORLD RETURNS 1-3 *continued*

is the duty of fund managers to adequately *diversify* the fund's assets. These ideas are not new by any stretch of the imagination, having originated in the 1950s. Why it took so long to put them into practice is anybody's guess...

So what have been the results of these changes? As of June 2007, the $120.5 billion in CPP assets were comprised of approximately 58 percent public equities, 7 percent private equities, 10 percent in inflation sensitive assets (such as real estate and commodities), and only 25 percent in bonds—quite a change indeed. In fact, the CPP was one of the last Canadian pension plans that was able to adapt to changing rules. Others including the Ontario Teachers Pension Plan ($106 billion in assets as of December 31, 2006) and La Caisse de Depot in Quebec ($143.5 billion in assets as of December 31, 2006) have been well diversified across the various asset classes and have been major "players" in domestic and global equity markets since the early 1990s.

How has this worked out so far? Over the four year-period ending March 31, 2007, the CPP provided an average annual return of 13.6 percent, and the plan assets more than doubled from $55.6 billion to $116.6 billion. Over $37 billion of this growth can be attributed to investment returns, with the rest being attributed to contributions. By comparison, long-term Canada bonds provided an average annual return of approximately 9.1 pecent over this period, which would have caused the plan assets to grow by about $23 billion. So we can say that over this brief period of time, the change in policy contributed an additional $14 billion (approximately) or more to the fund.

The new asset mix may not always perform better than holding all bonds, especially over short or even intermediate horizons. However, in the long run, there is no doubt that adding equities and other potential investments to a portfolio will enhance the expected returns. For example, since 1938, bonds have provided an average annual return of approximately 6 percent, versus 11 percent on equities.

While there have been several other factors at work, there is no doubt that the manner in which the plan's assets are now being managed is an important reason why the general consensus today is that Canadians can count on CPP payments when they retire. We may take this for granted, but as little as 10 or 15 years ago many financial planners were advising their clients to plan for retirement based on the premise that they would not receive any CPP payments. And perhaps we should not judge each investment decision until we know the whole picture.

Source: Cleary, Sean, CFA and MacKinnon, Greg, CFA, "The changing face of pension plans," *Halifax Daily News*, November 10, 2007.

The second issue to note about institutional investors is their dual relationship to individual investors. On the one hand, individuals are the indirect beneficiaries of institutional investor actions, because they own or benefit from these institutions' portfolios. On a daily basis, however, they are competing with these institutions in the sense that both are managing portfolios of securities and attempting to do well financially. Both groups are trying to make intelligent trading decisions about securities. Can individual investors hope to compete fairly with institutions, and how do these large portfolios affect the individual investor's decision process?

Institutional investors are indeed the professional investors, with vast resources at their command. They generally pay lower commission fees on security transactions than those paid by retail investors. In addition, there is evidence to suggest that some companies disclose important information selectively to some institutional investors. According to a survey by the National Investor Relations Institute (an association for investor-relations professionals), perhaps one-third of public companies disclose sensitive information concerning their stock that may put individual investors at a disadvantage.

Another advantage that institutional investors have is that they can trade in the "aftermarket" (negotiated trades conducted electronically among institutions) following exchange closings. (The

TSX closes at 4 p.m. Eastern Time.) By the time a stock opens the next morning, the price may have adjusted significantly.

Does the average investor, then, have a reasonable chance in the market? Yes, in the sense that he or she can generally expect to earn a fair return for the risk taken. On average, the individual investor may do just as well as the big institutional investors, because markets are usually quite efficient and securities fairly priced.

Some individual investors do even better than professionals due to superior skill, insight, or luck. Furthermore, some opportunities can more easily be exploited by individual investors, who have greater flexibility in adjusting their portfolio composition, than by institutional investors.

The question of how well individual investors do relative to institutional investors raises the issue of market efficiency, which we consider next. All intelligent investors who seek to do well when investing must ultimately come to grips with the issue of market efficiency.

The Issue of Market Efficiency

One of the most profound ideas affecting the investment decision process, and indeed all of finance, is the idea that the securities markets, particularly the equity markets, are efficient. In an efficient market, the prices of securities do not depart for any length of time from the justified economic values that investors calculate for them. Economic values for securities are determined by investor expectations about earnings, risks, and so on, as investors grapple with the uncertain future. If the market price of a security does differ from its estimated economic value, investors act to bring the two values together. Thus, as new information arrives in an efficient marketplace, causing a revision in the estimated economic value of a security, its price adjusts to this information quickly and, on balance, correctly. In other words, securities are efficiently priced on a continuous basis. We discuss the full implications of this statement in Chapter 10.

Obviously, the possibility that the stock market is efficient has significant implications for investors. In fact, one's knowledge of and belief in this idea, known as the **Efficient Market Hypothesis (EMH)**, will directly affect how one views the investment process and makes investment decisions. Those who are strong believers in the EMH may adopt, to varying degrees, a passive investment strategy, because of the likelihood that they will not be able to find underpriced securities. These investors will seek to minimize transaction costs and taxes, as well as the time and resources devoted to analyzing securities, which, if the EMH is correct, should be correctly priced to begin with.

Investors who do not accept the EMH, or have serious doubts, pursue active investment strategies, believing they can identify mispriced securities and/or lags that exist in the market's adjustment of securities' prices to new information. These investors generate more search costs (both in time and money) and more transaction costs but believe the marginal benefits outweigh the marginal costs incurred.

Efficient Market Hypothesis (EMH) The proposition that securities markets are efficient, with the prices of securities reflecting their economic value.

Corporate Governance

The issue of corporate governance has garnered a tremendous amount of attention in recent years in light of such financial debacles as Enron and WorldCom, and more recently Nortel in Canada. Some of the main issues that have been brought to "centre stage" as a result of these and similar abuses of the financial system include:

- The accountability of the Board of Directors and Management

- A re-examination of accounting and auditing practices

- Management compensation arrangements such as executive stock option plans, which are designed to align the interests of management and shareholders

INVESTING *tip*

An efficient market does not have to be perfectly efficient to have a profound impact on investors. All that is required is that the market be economically efficient. That is, after acting on information to trade securities and subtracting all costs (transaction costs and taxes, to name two), the investor would have been as well off with a simple buy-and-hold strategy. If the market is economically efficient, securities could depart somewhat from their true economic values, but it would not pay investors to take advantage of these small discrepancies.

- Disclosure requirements
- The effectiveness of existing regulatory bodies

Many changes have already been put in place on a number of these fronts including many regulatory changes, the imposition of stricter auditing standards, and increased accountability for top executives and company directors. More changes are still in the works. Real-World Returns 1-4 discusses the Sarbanes-Oxley (SOX) Act of 2002 that was implemented in the US in response to a complete collapse in public confidence as a result of the Enron and WorldCom fallout.

As the key provisions of SOX indicate, the main targets are the company and its auditors. There was significant belief that Enron's auditor, Arthur Andersen, was too tight with Enron, as many former Andersen people worked with Enron and the local auditors overruled head office in several key areas. In the future, the company's auditor has to be rotated every five years to ensure their objectivity. Further,

REAL-WORLD RETURNS 1-4

Sarbanes-Oxley Act of 2002

The Sarbanes-Oxley Act is a piece of legislation that combines Bills written by Senators **Paul Sarbanes** (D-MD) and **Michael G. Oxley** (R-OH) that addressed corporate auditing accountability and reporting practices. Simply put, it comprises regulations intended to control financial abuses at large public companies. The law now requires that companies boost their accounting oversight and adopt strict internal controls.

The full text of the **Sarbanes-Oxley Act** is lengthy. A few quick focal points are:

- Section 101 – Establishment of the Public Accounting Oversight Board (PCAOB) and Board Membership
- Section 102(a) – Public Accounting Firm Mandatory Registration
- Section 107 – SEC has authority over the PCAOB
- Section 201 – Services Outside The Scope Of Practice Of Auditors; Prohibited Activities
- Section 301 – "Whistleblower" procedure
- Section 402(a) – Prohibition on Personal Loans to Executives
- Section 404 – Internal controls
- Section 409 – Real-time disclosure
- Section 807 – Criminal penalties for defrauding shareholders of publicly traded companies
- Section 1350 – Failure of corporate officers to certify financial reports

Sarbanes-Oxley has passed into the vernacular as Sarbox or SOX, and has come to the forefront of many CEO and CFO task lists. Besides the beneficial, protective effects of SOX, the Act's certification requirements have also had other less-predicted effects. For example, CFOs may be reluctant to join a company and be prepared to certify its past financial statements, being criminally liable for any inaccuracies. Some smaller companies have considered returning the business to private operations to avoid the cost of SOX compliance. Adhering to SOX rules can be time-consuming and expensive, many times without a clear return on investment. The Act itself does not include best practices for complying with its rules. Internal guidelines must be set by the company.

Source: www.fiercesarbox.com/topics/sarbanesoxleyact, March 12, 2008.

the non-auditing functions of the major accounting firms were separated from their audit functions, since many felt the accounting firms were in a severe conflict of interest. This was because many felt the accounting firms were treating auditing as a "loss leader" to get consulting contracts. Consequently, they were not sufficiently objective in their audit responsibilities. This judgment is confirmed by the fact that the US government set up an oversight body to regulate audit firms and take direct control of many accounting areas.

For US companies, the major change is the requirement of stronger internal controls. One of the failures at Enron was apparently a weak audit committee that did not exercise proper oversight of the company's financial statements. In the future, the audit committee has to be composed of independent and unrelated members of the board of directors (BOD) with the power to engage external consultants and to have the external auditors report to them. Further, management has to report on and the auditor comment on the firm's internal controls with the CEO and CFO certifying the statements as fair.

SOX has had a major impact in the US in improving the public confidence in the objectivity of the financial statements of US companies. It also affects a significant number of Canadian companies (especially the large ones) that issue securities in the US and have to comply with US securities laws. Indeed, while accounting scandals in Canada have been fewer in number, and of a smaller scale than those in the US, concerns over such misrepresentations and their impact on our business environment have dictated that Canadian regulatory authorities maintain strict controls over the auditing process, similar to those employed in the US.

CHECK YOUR UNDERSTANDING

1-8. Individual investors make investing decisions under conditions of uncertainty, while professional investors make such decisions under conditions of controlled risk taking, thereby eliminating the uncertainty. Do you agree or disagree? Explain your reasoning.

1-9. Canadian investors should hold foreign securities primarily because they offer higher expected returns than domestic securities. Do you agree with this statement?

SUMMARY

This summary relates to the learning objectives for this chapter.

1. **Define investment and discuss what it means to study investments.**

   An investment is the commitment of funds to one or more assets that will be held over some future time period. The field of investments involves the study of the investment process and is concerned with the management of an investor's wealth. We study investments for both personal and professional reasons.

2. **Explain why risk and return are the two critical components of all investing decisions.**

   Risk is defined as the chance that what you expect to gain from an investment will differ from its actual return. The basis of all investment decisions is the trade-off between expected return and risk. Expected return and risk are directly related; the greater the risk, the greater the expected return, and the smaller the risk the smaller the expected return. Rational investors are risk averse, meaning they are unwilling to assume risk unless they expect to be adequately compensated.

3. **Outline the two-step investment decision process.**

   The investment decision process is generally divided into two categories: securities analysis and portfolio management. Security analysis involves the valuation and analysis of individual securities. Portfolio management involves building a portfolio of individual securities after they have been evaluated and maintaining that portfolio.

4. Discuss key factors that affect the investment decision process.

Major factors affecting the investment decision process include uncertainty, the global nature of investing, the role played by institutional investors, and the efficiency of markets. Investors should consider these factors carefully as they evaluate information and claims and make decisions.

KEY TERMS

Canadian Securities Course™ (CSC) (Appendix 1B), p.23
Chartered Financial Analyst® (CFA) (Appendix 1A), p.24
Efficient Market Hypothesis (EMH), p.19
Emerging markets, p.13

Expected return, p.9
Financial assets, p.3
Institutional investors, p.16
Investment, p.3
Investments, p.3
Marketable securities, p.3
Portfolio, p.3

Portfolio management, p.11
Real assets, p.3
Realized return, p.9
Risk, p.9
Risk-averse investor, p.9
Risk-free rate of return, p.10
Security analysis, p.11

REVIEW QUESTIONS

1-1. Define the term investments. Why study investments?

1-2. Distinguish between a financial asset and a real asset. Give two examples of each.

1-3. List three primary investing objectives and two secondary investing objectives.

1-4. Briefly describe three constraints that have an impact on the design of an investment policy.

1-5. With respect to Figure 1-1, when would an investor expect to earn the risk-free rate of return?

1-6. Distinguish between expected return and realized return.

1-7. Why should the required rate of return be different for a corporate bond and a Government of Canada bond?

1-8. A marketable security is said to be liquid if it can be easily and cheaply traded. Why is the liquidity of a marketable security an important thing for investors to consider?

1-9. Differentiate between an active investment strategy and a passive investment strategy.

1-10. List at least four categories of institutional investors. Give examples of Canadian corporations that fit in each category.

1-11. Describe the broad two-step process involved in making investment decisions.

1-12. Why is the study of investments important to most individuals?

1-13. Carefully describe the risk–return trade-off faced by all investors.

1-14. "A risk-averse investor will not assume risk." Do you agree or disagree with this statement? Why?

1-15. Summarize the basic nature of the investment decision in one sentence.

1-16. Are all rational investors risk averse? Do they all have the same degree of risk aversion?

1-17. What are institutional investors? How are individual investors likely to be affected by institutional investors?

1-18. What is meant by the expression efficient markets?

1-19. Of what significance is an efficient market to investors?

1-20. Discuss at least three reasons why Canadian investors should be concerned with global investing. Do you think the exchange rate value of the Canadian dollar will have any effect on the decision to invest globally?

1-21. Although a Treasury bill is said to be "risk free," there actually is some risk associated with investing in one. What do you think the risk (or risks) would be?

1-22. Define risk. How many specific types can you think of?

1-23. What other constraints besides risk do investors face?

1-24. What are four external factors that affect the decision process? Which do you think is the most important, and why?

1-25. What is meant by the terms *ex ante* and *ex post*?

1-26. Explain why risk and return are the two critical components of all investing decisions.

1-27. How has Internet technology influenced the nature of investing?

1-28. Construct a chart to show how the following typical investments compare in terms of expected return and expected risk: Coins and stamps, common shares, commercial real estate, residential real estate, corporate bonds, government bonds, options/futures, treasury bills, preferred shares, art objects.

1-29. What is meant by an investor's risk tolerance? What role does this concept play in investor decision making?

APPENDIX 1A

THE CHARTERED FINANCIAL ANALYST® PROGRAM

Individuals interested in careers in the investment analysis field should consider seeking the **Chartered Financial Analyst® (CFA®)** designation, which is, for people in the investment area, not unlike the CA, CGA, or CMA for accountants. The CFA charter, granted exclusively by CFA Institute, is widely recognized in the investments industry today.

Chartered Financial Analyst®(CFA®)
A professional designation for people in the investment field.

Candidates enrolled in the CFA program must show that they have mastered important material in economics, quantitative analysis, ethical and professional standards, financial accounting, fixed income securities, equity securities analysis, and portfolio management. Candidates must successfully complete three examinations, referred to as Level I, Level II, and Level III, and meet certain work experience and membership requirements, in order to be awarded the CFA designation.

The basis of the CFA study and examination program is a candidate body of knowledge (CBOK). The CBOK is organized along functional and topical lines and is structured around the investment decision-making process. The CBOK functional areas are ethics and professional standards, investment tools, asset valuation, and portfolio management.

For each level of the exam, the curriculum is organized around a functional area:

Level I study program—emphasizes tools and inputs

Level II study program—emphasizes asset valuation

Level III study program—emphasizes portfolio management

Ethical and professional standards are considered an integral part of all three functional areas and are included in all levels of the curriculum.

Six-hour examinations are given throughout Canada, the United States, and around the world once a year, around June 1, and must be completed in sequence. Level I exams are also offered in December. As a result, completion of the CFA program requires a minimum of two and a half years.

By 2008 over 81,000 investment professionals from 126 countries and territories had earned the CFA charter since it was first awarded in 1963. The most common occupations of CFA charter holders include the following:

- CEO/Principal
- Chief Investment Officer
- Equity Analyst
- Fixed Income Analyst
- Investment Banker
- Investment Counselor
- Investment Firm Manager
- Portfolio Manager
- Portfolio Strategist
- Sales/Marketing Professional

What does it mean to be awarded the CFA charter? Increasingly, employers are recognizing the value of this designation and the potential benefits that an employee with it can offer a company. The CFA charter represents a combination of academic achievement and professional experience along with a commitment to a stringent code of professional and ethical standards. CFA charter holders must renew their pledge to abide by the code every year and violations can carry severe sanctions.

The investments profession, like many others, involves lifelong learning. After receiving the CFA designation, investment professionals can participate in the CFA Professional Development program in order to remain current on investment issues. This program allows them to earn continuing education credits a number of ways including workshops, seminars, and reading on their own.

For more information about the CFA program, call its toll-free number at 1-800-247-8132 or 1-434-951-5499, or visit the CFA Institute website at www.cfainstitute.org.

APPENDIX 1B

THE CANADIAN SECURITIES INSTITUTE (CSI)

The Canadian Securities Institute (CSI) has been providing education for financial professionals and the general public since 1970, and has trained over 700,000 global professionals. CSI serves the broad financial services industry with an emphasis on securities. CSI courses, seminars, and specialized programs are recognized by regulators as the proficiency benchmarks for all levels of industry professionals.

Canadian Securities Course™ (CSC)

This course is offered by the Canadian Securities Institute (CSI) and is a mandatory requirement for individuals who wish to become licensed to sell financial securities in Canada and to register to sell mutual funds.

The **Canadian Securities Course™ (CSC)**[9] is a prerequisite for many other CSI courses and is a starting point for earning sought-after professional designations. Completion of certain CSI courses is mandatory to meet the requirements for various registration categories. Individuals who wish to become licensed to sell securities must pass the CSC as well as the Conduct and Practices Handbook (CPH). Completion of the CSC also allows individuals to become registered to sell mutual funds.

CSI's approach to professional investment education is based on extensive research and consultation with the financial services industry, regulators, and end-users. Rather than single-course offerings, CSI programs focus on career streams that lead students to specialized designations. For more information about CSI and its programs, call 1-866-866-2601 or visit its website at www.csi.ca.

---

[9]The Canadian Securities Course™ (CSC) and other courses discussed here are trademarks of the Canadian Securities Institute.

INVESTMENT ALTERNATIVES

Chapter 2 explains the most important investment alternatives available to investors, ranging from money market securities to capital market securities—bonds and stocks—to derivative securities. It organizes the types of financial assets available in the money and capital markets, and it provides the reader with a good understanding of the securities that are of primary interest to most investors, particularly bonds and stocks. The emphasis is on the basic features of these securities, providing the reader with the knowledge needed to understand the investment opportunities of interest to most investors. Recent trends such as securitization are considered, as is international investing.

Although our discussion is as up to date as possible, changes in the securities field occur so rapidly that investors are regularly confronted with new developments. Investors in the twenty-first century have a wide variety of investment alternatives available, and it is reasonable to expect that this variety will only increase. However, if investors understand the basic characteristics of the major existing securities, they will likely be able to understand new securities as they appear.

Learning Objectives

After reading this chapter, you should be able to

1. Describe the major types of financial assets and how they are organized.
2. Explain what non-marketable financial assets are.
3. Describe the important features of money market securities.
4. Describe the important features of capital market securities.
5. Distinguish among preferred stock, income trusts, and common stock.
6. Understand the basics of options and futures.

CHAPTER PREVIEW

Changes in the securities field occur so rapidly that investors are regularly confronted with new developments. However, if investors understand the basic characteristics of the major existing securities, they will likely be able to understand new securities as they appear. This chapter explains the most important investment alternatives available to investors, ranging from non-marketable financial assets to marketable investments in money market, capital market, and derivative securities. You will learn the basic features of securities that are of primary interest to most investors, particularly bonds and stocks. We also discuss recent trends such as "securitization" and international investing.

ORGANIZING FINANCIAL ASSETS

learning objective 1
Describe the major types of financial assets and how they are organized.

The emphasis in this chapter (and in the text in general) is on financial assets, which, as explained in Chapter 1, are financial claims on the issuers of securities. We focus in particular on marketable securities, which are claims that are negotiable, or saleable, in various marketplaces, as discussed in Chapter 4.

This chapter concentrates on investment alternatives available through direct investing, which involves securities that investors buy and sell themselves, primarily capital market securities and derivative securities. The taxation of income earned from these financial assets in Canada is discussed in Appendix 2A at the end of the chapter. In Chapter 3, we examine **indirect investing**. Rather than invest directly in securities, investors can invest in a portfolio of securities by purchasing the units of a financial intermediary that invests in various types of securities on behalf of its shareowners. Perhaps the most common method of indirect investing involves mutual funds. Indirect investing is a very important alternative for all investors to consider and has become tremendously popular in the last few years with individual investors.

Indirect Investing
The buying and selling of the shares of investment companies that themselves hold portfolios of securities.

People who invest directly in financial markets have a wide variety of assets from which to choose. Non-marketable investment opportunities, such as savings accounts at financial institutions, are discussed briefly at the beginning of the chapter since investors often own these assets and are familiar with them. Henceforth, we will consider only marketable securities, which may be classified into one of three categories:

1. The money market
2. The capital market
3. The derivatives market

Investors should understand money market securities, particularly Treasury bills, but they typically will not own these securities directly, choosing instead to own them through the money market funds explained in Chapter 3. Within the capital market, securities can be classified as either fixed-income or equity. Finally, investors may choose to use derivative securities in their portfolios. The market value of these securities is derived from underlying securities such as common stock.

Figure 2-1 organizes the types of financial assets to be analyzed in this chapter (under the heading of direct investing) using the above classifications. It also indicates various indirect investment alternatives, which will be discussed in more depth in Chapter 3. Although we cover direct investing and indirect investing in separate chapters, it is important to understand that investors can, and often do, both. Many individuals invest directly through the use of a brokerage account and indirectly in one or more investment companies. Furthermore, brokerage accounts that accommodate the ownership of investment company shares are becoming increasingly popular, thereby combining direct and indirect investing into one account.

	DIRECT INVESTING
Non-marketable	• Savings deposits
	• GICs
	• Canada Savings Bonds (CSBs)
Money market	• Treasury bills
	• Commercial paper
	• Eurodollars
	• Repurchase agreements
	• Bankers' acceptances (B/As)
Capital market	• Fixed-income
	Government bonds
	Government agency bonds (e.g., Ontario Hydro)
	Corporate bonds
	• Mortgage-backed securities (MBS)/
	Asset-backed securities (ABS)
	• Income trusts
	• Equities
	Preferred stock
	Common stock
Derivatives market	• Options
	• Futures contracts
	INDIRECT INVESTING
Investment funds	• Open end
	Money market mutual fund
	Stock, bond, and income funds
	• Closed end

Figure 2-1
Major Types of Financial Assets

An International Perspective

As noted in Chapter 1, investors should adopt an international perspective in making their investment decisions. The investment alternatives analyzed in this chapter, in particular some money market assets, bonds, and stocks, are available to Canadian investors from many foreign markets. Thus, the characteristics of these basic securities are relevant if we invest in domestic or foreign financial assets, or both. Canadian investors usually invest internationally indirectly through investment companies, many of which offer a wide variety of global asset funds.

CHECK YOUR UNDERSTANDING

2-1. What is the main difference between direct and indirect investing?

2-2. List the two main classifications of capital market securities, and one example of each.

NON-MARKETABLE FINANCIAL ASSETS

We begin our discussion of investment alternatives by mentioning those that are non-marketable because most individuals will own one or more of these assets regardless of what else they do in the investing arena. Furthermore, these assets represent useful contrasts to the marketable securities we will concentrate on throughout the text.

learning objective 2
Explain what non-marketable financial assets are.

A distinguishing characteristic of these assets is that they represent personal transactions between the owner and the issuer. That is, as the owner of a savings account at a bank, you must open the account personally and deal with the bank in maintaining the account or in closing it. In contrast, marketable securities trade in impersonal markets where the buyer and seller do not know one another and do not care.

Most non-marketable instruments are safe investments available from insured financial institutions or issued by the Canadian government. Most of these assets offer the ultimate in **liquidity**, which can be defined as the ease with which an asset can be converted to cash. An asset is liquid if it can be disposed of quickly with no more than small price changes, assuming no new information in the marketplace. Thus, we know we can get all of our money back from a savings account or a Canada Savings Bond very quickly.

The most familiar form of non-marketable assets is savings accounts (or demand deposits) with financial institutions such as chartered banks, trust and mortgage companies, and credit unions or caisses populaires. The funds invested here are available on demand, which guarantees the liquidity of these investments. The safety of these deposits is further enhanced through the existence of deposit insurance, as discussed in Real-World Returns 2-1.

Liquidity

The ease with which an asset can be converted to cash. An asset is liquid if it can be bought or sold quickly with relatively small price changes.

REAL-WORLD RETURNS 2-1
Protecting Canadian Investors

Most chartered banks and trust companies are members of the Canada Deposit Insurance Corporation (CDIC), an agency of the federal government. The CDIC insures qualifying deposits with member institutions, up to a maximum of $100,000 of total deposits with one financial institution. Individuals wishing to have more than $100,000 in insured deposits must maintain deposits with several institutions and ensure the total deposits with any particular institution do not exceed $100,000.

Insurance companies, credit unions and caisses populaires, and investment dealers are not eligible for CDIC membership, but generally provide other forms of protection for their clients. Credit unions generally offer protection through provincial deposit insurance or guarantee programs. For example, deposits with credit unions in British Columbia are protected through the Credit Union Deposit Insurance Corporation of BC. This corporation guarantees the total savings, chequing, and term deposits by an individual with one credit union up to a maximum of $100,000. The $100,000 maximum per individual per credit union also applies to both RRSP and RRIF plans, in addition to the $100,000 limit for savings accounts.

The maximum deposit protection and the qualifying criteria for investment protection varies across the provinces. The maximum protection per individual per institution is $60,000 of the total of savings, chequing, and term deposits in New Brunswick and Prince Edward Island. The caisses populaires in Quebec offer $60,000 coverage per investor. Coverage is limited to $100,000 in Ontario and to $250,000 in Nova Scotia. Alberta, Manitoba, and Saskatchewan all offer unlimited protection.

The Canadian Life and Health Compensation Corporation (CompCorp) came into existence in 1990 to provide protection for customers of companies that sell life and/or health insurance to the Canadian public, and became Assuris in 2005. The Property and Casualty Insurance Compensation Corporation (PACICC) performs a similar function for customers of property and casualty insurance companies. Finally, customers of investment dealers are afforded protection by the Canadian Investor Protection Fund (CIPF), which is discussed in greater detail in Chapter 5.

Guaranteed Investment Certificates (GICs) are non-transferable time deposits with chartered banks and trust companies that offer investors higher returns than those available on savings accounts. These differ from demand deposits because they are locked in for a fixed period of time, and early withdrawals are not permitted, or else are often accompanied by penalties and/or the loss of accrued interest.

Another widely used non-marketable financial asset is the Canada Savings Bond (CSB), with over $45 billion in these bonds having been sold since their introduction in 1946. Unlike other bonds, CSBs can be cashed out by the owner at full par value plus eligible accrued interest at any bank in Canada at any time. They are not transferable, and their prices do not change over time. They are only available for six months of the year (between early October through April 1st each year) and require a minimum $100 investment. They are sold in registered form to provide protection against loss, theft, or destruction. In recent years, only individuals, estates of deceased persons, and trusts governed by certain types of deferred savings and income plans have been allowed to acquire CSBs.

The published rate of return on CSBs is not always fixed. This is done to avoid having holders cash out in times of rising interest rates. However, the government often guarantees minimum rates for the future. An effective program for selling CSBs is administered through the payroll savings plans of over 12,000 organizations. The various options available to investors, as well as some of the features of these instruments, are described in Real-World Returns 2-2.

REAL-WORLD RETURNS 2-2

Bonds

Canada Savings Bonds are a safe and secure way to reach your savings and investment goals, and are also ideal for gift giving. They are issued by the Government of Canada and can be purchased with an RRSP or RRIF option from the Bank of Canada. You can choose either the Canada Savings Bond (CSB), which is cashable at any time, or the Canada Premium Bond (CPB), which is cashable once a year. Both the CSB and the CPB offer a variety of features:

The Canada Premium Bond
The CPB is fully backed by the Government of Canada and offers a higher rate of interest at the time of issue than the Canada Savings Bond on sale at the same time. The CPB can be redeemed once a year on the anniversary of the issue date and during the 30 days following.

The Canada Savings Bond
The CSB is a safe, secure investment enjoyed by millions of Canadians for over 60 years. It provides both maximum flexibility and security. It is backed by the Government of Canada and offers a minimum guaranteed rate that will be increased should market conditions warrant. It can also be purchased through payroll deduction where available at sponsoring employers.

The Canada RSP
The Canada Retirement Savings Plan is a no-fee RRSP created to allow Canadians to hold compound interest Canada Savings Bonds as RRSP investments without the need for a self-directed plan. The Canada RSP option is available where you bank or invest, through direct telephone and online purchase and via the Payroll Savings Program.

The Canada RIF
The Canada Retirement Income Fund is a no-fee RRIF, designed to hold compound interest Canada Savings Bonds as retirement income investments without the need for a self-directed plan. The Canada RIF option is available where you bank or invest.

(continued)

REAL-WORLD RETURNS 2-2 *continued*

Other Retail Products

Treasury Bills, Marketable Bonds, and Real Return Bonds have a guaranteed return if held to maturity but can be bought or sold prior to maturity at market prices, which vary from day to day. These products are available only through investment dealers.

How to Buy

The Canada Premium Bond and the Canada Savings Bond can be purchased online for ease and convenience. The site is encrypted for security, and provides a fast and easy way to become a bondholder. The CPB and the CSB can also be bought wherever you bank or invest, or by contacting us. The CSB can also be purchased through payroll deduction where available at sponsoring employers.

How to Redeem

Bonds with certificates may be redeemed at most financial institutions in Canada. CSBs purchased through the Payroll Savings Program may be redeemed online or by calling Customer Service. Bonds held within The Canada RSP and The Canada RIF may be redeemed by writing to the Trustee.

Source: www.csb.gc.ca/eng/bonds.asp, March 12, 2008.

CHECK YOUR UNDERSTANDING

2-3. Marketable securities may be referred to as impersonal assets, whereas non-marketable financial assets are not. Why is this?

2-4. Do individuals who make deposits at most chartered banks and trust companies in Canada have any risk of losing their funds?

MONEY MARKET SECURITIES

learning objective 3
Describe the important features of money market securities.

Money Market
The market for short-term, highly liquid, low-risk debt instruments sold by governments, financial institutions, and corporations. Canadian government Treasury bills are an example.

Money markets include short-term, highly liquid, relatively low-risk debt instruments sold by governments, financial institutions, and corporations to investors with temporary excess funds to invest. The returns on these instruments exceed those offered by savings accounts; however, the size of transactions is generally large ($100,000 or more). On the other hand, several financial institutions purchase large blocks of these instruments and break them up into smaller denominations (as low as $1,000) in order to make them available for their retail customers. The rates on these smaller denominations will be lower than those available on the larger blocks, which is how the intermediaries make their profits.

The money market is dominated by financial institutions (particularly banks) and governments. The maturities of money market instruments range from one day to one year, and are often less than 90 days. Some of these instruments are negotiable and actively traded, and others are not. Most of them are sold on a discount basis. For example, 91-day Treasury bills with a face (or maturity) value of $100,000 may be sold to investors for $98,500. The investor receives $100,000 at maturity, which means they have earned $1,500 in interest on their original investment of $98,500. Investors may invest directly in some of these securities, but more often they do so indirectly through money market mutual funds offered by investment companies.

Another reason that knowledge of these securities is important is the use of government **Treasury bills (T-bills)** as a benchmark asset. Although in some pure sense there is no such thing as a risk-free financial asset, on a practical basis Government of Canada Treasury bills are risk-free since there is virtually no chance of default by the federal government, and the length of the investment period is very short. The T-bill rate, denoted RF, is used throughout the text as a proxy for the nominal risk-free rate of return available to investors (e.g., the RF shown and discussed in Figure 1-1 in Chapter 1).

In summary, money market instruments are characterized as short-term, highly marketable investments, with an extremely low probability of default. Because the minimum investment is generally large, money market securities are normally owned by individual investors indirectly in the form of investment funds known as money market mutual funds, or, as they are usually called, money market funds.

Money market rates tend to move together and most rates are very close to each other for the same maturity, as can be seen in the Real-World Returns 2-3. Notice that T-bill rates are lower than those for other money market securities because of their risk-free nature.

Treasury Bill (T-bill)
A short-term money market instrument sold at discount by Canadian governments.

REAL-WORLD RETURNS 2-3

Money Markets

MONEY MARKET	24/01/08	25/01/08	+/-
Overnight rate	4.0019%	4.0137%	+ 0.0118
Target for the overnight rate	4.00%	4.00%	0.00
Overnight repo rate (CORRA)	4.0054%	4.0264%	+ 0.0210
Corporate paper, 1 month	4.05%	4.04%	- 0.01
Treasury bill, 1 month	3.48%	3.46%	- 0.02
Bankers' Acceptances, 1 month	4.05%	4.06%	+ 0.01

Source: www.globeinvestorgold.com, January 28, 2008.

The following are the major money market securities of most interest to individual investors.

1. *Treasury bills.* The premier money market instrument, a fully guaranteed, very liquid IOU from the Government of Canada or provincial governments. Government of Canada Treasury bills are sold by auction every two weeks at a discount from face value in denominations ranging from $1,000 to $1 million. The greater the discount at the time of purchase the higher the return earned by investors. Standard maturities are 91, 182, and 364 days, although shorter maturities are also offered. New bills can be purchased by investors on a competitive or non-competitive bid basis. Outstanding (i.e., already issued) bills can be purchased and sold in the secondary market, an extremely efficient market where government securities dealers stand ready to buy and sell these securities.

2. *Commercial paper.* A short-term, unsecured promissory note issued by large, well-known, and financially strong corporations (including finance companies). Denominations start at $100,000 with maturities of 30 to 365 days. Commercial paper (CP) is usually sold at a discount either directly by the issuer or indirectly through a dealer, with rates slightly above T-bills. There is an important distinction between bank-backed CP, which as the name suggests consists of CP that is guaranteed or backed by a bank (or banks), and non-bank-backed CP. This distinction came to the forefront of investor attention in the summer of 2007, as the trading in non-bank based asset backed commercial paper (ABCP) ceased entirely, and as of March 2008, trading had not resumed. This issue

Bond Characteristics

Par Value (Face Value)

The redemption value of a bond paid at maturity, generally $1,000.

The **par value (face value)** of most bonds is $1,000, and we will use this number as the amount to be repaid at maturity.[1] The bond generally matures (terminates) on a specified date and is technically known as a term bond.[2] Most bonds are coupon bonds, where coupon refers to the periodic interest that the issuer pays to the holder of the bonds.[3] Interest on bonds is generally paid semi-annually.

EXAMPLE 2-1: GOVERNMENT OF CANADA COUPON BOND

A three-year, 9.00 percent Government of Canada coupon bond was listed in the bond listings at www.financialpost.com/markets/market_data/bonds-canadian.html on March 17, 2008. Assuming the bond has a par value of $1,000, it has a dollar coupon of $90.00 (9.0 percent of $1,000); therefore, knowing the percentage coupon rate is the same as knowing the coupon payment in dollars.[4] If the interest on the bond is paid semi-annually, this bond would pay interest (the coupons) of $45.00 on a specified date every six months. The $1,000 principal would be repaid three years hence at the maturity date (hence we say the term-to-maturity is three years).

Zero Coupon Bond

A bond sold with no coupons at a discount and redeemed for face value at maturity. Also known as a strip bond.

An important innovation in the format of traditional bonds is the **zero coupon bond** (or strip bond), which does not pay any coupons, or interest, during its life. The purchaser pays less than par value for "zeroes" and receives par value at maturity. The difference in these two amounts generates an effective interest rate or rate of return. Similar to Treasury bills, the lower the price paid for the coupon bond, the higher the effective return.

Zeroes are usually created when financial intermediaries purchase traditional bonds, strip the cash flows from them, and sell the cash flows separately. These bonds first appeared in Canada in 1982. In the United States, the US Treasury created STRIPS, or Separate Trading of Registered Interest and Principal of Securities, in 1985. Under this program, all new **treasury bonds** (i.e., bonds issued by the US government) and notes with maturities greater than 10 years are eligible to be stripped to create zero coupon Treasury securities that are direct obligations of the US Treasury Department.

Treasury Bond

Long-term bonds sold by the US government.

By convention, bond prices are quoted as a proportion of par value using 100 as par rather than 1,000. Therefore, a price of 90 represents $900, and a price of 55 represents $550, using the normal assumption of a par value of $1,000. The easiest way to convert quoted bond prices to actual prices is to remember that they are quoted in percentages, with the common assumption of a $1,000 par value.

EXAMPLE 2-2: PRICE OF A GOVERNMENT OF CANADA COUPON BOND

The bid price of the three-year 9.00 percent Government of Canada coupon bond was 117.70 on March 14, 2008. This quoted price represents 117.70 percent of $1,000, or $1,177.00.

The above example suggests that an investor could purchase the bond for $1,177.00 on that day. Actually, bonds trade on an accrued interest basis. That is, the bond buyer must pay the bond seller the price of the bond as well as the interest that has been earned (accrued) on the bond since the last interest payment. This allows an investor to sell a bond any time without losing the interest that has accrued. Bond buyers should remember this additional cost when buying a bond because prices are quoted in the paper without the accrued interest.[5]

---

[1]The par value is almost never less than $1,000, although it easily can be more.
[2]The phrase term-to-maturity is used to denote how much longer the bond will be in existence. In contrast, a serial bond has a series of maturity dates. Thus, one issue of serial bonds may mature in specified amounts year after year, and each specified amount could carry a different coupon.
[3]The terms interest income and coupon income are interchangeable.
[4]The coupon rate on a traditional, standard bond is fixed at the bond's issuance and cannot vary.
[5]The invoice or cash price is the price the bond buyer must pay and will include the accrued interest.

The price of the bond in the above example is above 100 (i.e., $1,000) because market yields on bonds of this type were below the stated coupon rate of 9.00 percent on this bond (in fact, the yield associated with this price for this bond is 2.72 percent). The coupon on this particular bond became more than competitive with the going market interest rate for comparable newly issued bonds, and the price increased to reflect this fact. At any point in time some bonds are selling at premiums (above par value), reflecting a decline in market rates after that particular bond was sold. Others are selling at discounts (below par value), because the stated coupons are less than the prevailing interest rate on a comparable new issue.

The **call provision** gives the issuer the right to "call in" the bonds, thereby depriving investors of that particular fixed-income security. Exercising the call provision becomes attractive to the issuer when market interest rates drop sufficiently below the coupon rate on the outstanding bonds for the issuer to save money. Costs are incurred to call the bonds, such as a "call premium" and administrative expenses. However, issuers expect to sell new bonds at a lower interest cost, thereby replacing existing higher interest-cost bonds with new, lower interest-cost bonds.

Callable bonds give the issuer the option to call or repurchase outstanding bonds at predetermined "call prices" (generally at a premium over par) at specified times. This feature is detrimental to the bondholders who are willing to pay less for them (i.e., they demand a higher return) than for similar non-callable bonds. Generally, the issuer agrees to give 30 or more days' notice that the issue will be redeemed. Most callables have a time period (referred to as call protection) prior to the first call date during which they cannot be called. The redemption price often declines on a graduated scale, reflecting the fact that the hardship to the investor of having an issue called is reduced as the time to maturity declines. Most Government of Canada and US Treasury bonds are non-callable.[6] Provincial bonds are usually callable at 100 plus accrued interest. Usually corporate issues have a mandatory call feature for sinking fund purposes.

Retractable bonds allow the bondholder to sell the bonds back to the issuer at predetermined prices at specified times, while **extendible bonds** allow the bondholder to extend the maturity date of the bond. Both of these bonds offer investors an additional privilege, which implies they will pay more for these bonds (i.e., accept a lower return). They both tend to trade similar to short-term bonds during periods of rising interest rates, as it is likely that they will be redeemed (or not extended). Similarly, they tend to behave like long-term bonds during periods of decreasing interest rates. The holders generally must state their intentions to extend or redeem during the election period (which occurs six to 12 months prior to the extendible or retractable dates).

A sinking fund provision provides for the orderly retirement of the bond issue during its life. The provisions of a sinking fund vary widely. For example, it can be stated as a fixed or variable amount and as a percentage of the particular issue outstanding or the total debt of the issuer outstanding. All or part of the bond issue may be retired through the sinking fund by the maturity date. One procedure for carrying out the sinking fund requirement is simply to buy the required amount of bonds on the open market each year. A second alternative is to call the bonds randomly. Again, investors should be aware of such provisions for their protection.

Convertible bonds may be converted into common shares at predetermined conversion prices. This privilege is afforded to the investor in order to make the issue more saleable and to reduce the interest rate that must be offered to purchasers. The conversion price is often graduated upward through time to encourage early conversion. Most convertibles are callable. Certain convertibles include a forced conversion clause, which forces conversion by affording the issuer the right to redeem the issue once the common share price goes above pre-specified levels. Convertibles typically trade

---

Call Provision

Gives the issuer the right to call in a security and retire it by paying off the obligation.

INVESTING *tip*

The call feature is a risk to investors who must give up the higher yielding bonds. Consistent with our discussion of risk and return in Chapter 1, we generally observe that callable bonds offer investors a higher yield than similar non-callable bonds as compensation for this risk. The wise bond investor will note the bond issue's provisions concerning the call, carefully determining the earliest date at which the bond can be called, and the bond's yield if it is called at the earliest date possible. This calculation is shown in Chapter 11.

Retractable Bonds

Bonds that allow the bondholder to sell the bonds back to the issuer at predetermined prices at specified times.

Extendible Bonds

Bonds that allow investors to extend the maturity date of the bond.

Convertible Bonds

Bonds that are convertible, at the holder's option, into shares of common stock of the same corporation at predetermined prices.

---

[6]US Treasury bonds issued after February 1985 cannot be called.

similar to straight debentures when the conversion price is well below the market price of the common shares. A "premium" appears as market price approaches conversion price, and it is said to "sell off the stock" once market price exceeds the conversion price.

Floating rate bonds (or floaters) are an alternative to traditional fixed coupon bonds. They have adjustable coupons that are generally tied to T-bill rates or some other short-term interest rate. They are attractive for the protection offered in times of volatile interest rates (and/or during inflationary periods) and behave like money market securities in an investment portfolio. An example of a floating-rate bond that provides protection against increases in inflation (which is generally accompanied by an increase in interest rates) is Government of Canada Real Return Bonds. These were introduced in 1991 to provide investors with a real yield of about 4.25 percent. The variants now exist with longer terms to maturity that provide real yields of 4.0 percent and 3.0 percent respectively. The real yields are achieved by pegging the face value to the Consumer Price Index (CPI) and having the coupon rate of 4.25 (4.0 or 3.0) percent apply to the inflation-adjusted face value.

Types of Bonds

Bond certificates may be in either bearer or registered forms. Bearer bonds are presumed to be owned by the party holding them. Coupons are numbered and dated and may be clipped and redeemed for cash. Registered bonds have the name of the owner on their face and interest is paid to the registered owner by the issuer. If lost or stolen, it is difficult for anyone other than the owner to cash them. Most bonds are traded through dealers in the over-the-counter market, which is described in Chapter 4.

Bonds may be classified as domestic, foreign, or Eurobonds. Domestic bonds are issued in the currency and country of the issuer, while foreign bonds are issued primarily in a currency and country other than the issuer's. Eurobonds are issued in any number of currencies in the Euromarket or the international bond market (if issued in Canadian dollars they would be called EuroCanadian bonds, and if issued in US dollars they would be called Eurodollar bonds).

While government bonds constitute the majority of the bond market in Canada, corporate bonds are growing in importance. For example, at the end of 1995, there was $452 billion US in Canadian government bonds outstanding versus $50 billion US outstanding in Canadian corporate bonds (approximately 10 percent of the Canadian total). However, by June 2007, the corporate bond market grew in size to $418.1 billion US (or 38.4 percent of the total Canadian bond market), while the amount of Canadian government bonds outstanding stood at $670.4 billion.

Government Bonds

The Government of Canada is the largest single issuer of bonds in Canada. Like Treasury bills, they are sold at competitive auctions, but unlike bills, they are sold at approximately face value with investors submitting bids on yields (for example, 4.3 percent). Interest payments (coupons) are usually paid semi-annually. Face value denominations are $1,000, $5,000, $10,000, $100,000, $500,000, and $1 million. These bonds are considered an extremely safe credit risk because the government's ability to print money and increase taxes implies the risk of default is minimal for these securities. An investor purchases them with the expectation of earning a steady stream of interest payments and with full assurance of receiving the par value of the bonds when they mature.

Provincial governments also participate in Canadian and global bond markets through direct bond issues as well as by guaranteeing bond issues of provincially appointed authorities and commissions (e.g., Hydro Québec may have outstanding bonds that are guaranteed by the Province of Quebec). Finally, municipal governments also raise debt capital through bond markets. In recent years, municipalities have relied primarily on instalment debentures or serial bonds (described in footnote 2) to raise debt capital from the markets.

US government agencies are the second-largest issuers/guarantors of bonds in the world, with over $6.35 trillion US in outstanding debt securities by June 2007, and lagging only the Japanese government ($6.58 trillion). The US federal government issues numerous notes and bonds with maturities greater than one year through the Treasury Department (hence the name Treasury notes or Treasury bonds).[7] Various US credit agencies also compete for funds in the marketplace by selling government agency securities. Securities issued by federal agencies that are legally part of the federal government are fully guaranteed by the Treasury. The most important agency for investors is the Government National Mortgage Association (often nicknamed "Ginnie Mae"). In addition to these federal agencies, there exist several other federally sponsored credit agencies in the United States that are privately owned institutions that sell their own securities in the marketplace. They have the right to draw on Treasury funds up to some approved amount; however, their securities are not guaranteed by the government. Some of the more important federally sponsored credit agencies include the Federal Home Loan Mortgage Corporation ("Freddie Mac"), the Federal Home Loan Bank, the Farm Credit System, and the Student Loan Marketing Association. Perhaps the best known of these federally sponsored agencies is the Federal National Mortgage Association (FNMA, referred to as "Fannie Mae"), which is designed to help the mortgage markets.[8]

Corporate Bonds

Several of the larger corporations issue **corporate bonds** to help finance their operations. An investor can find a wide range of maturities, coupons, and special features available from corporate bonds. The average corporate bond pays semi-annual interest, is callable, carries a sinking fund provision, and is sold originally at a price close to par value, which is usually $1,000.[9]

Corporate bonds are **senior securities**. That is, they are senior to any preferred stock and to the common stock of a corporation in terms of priority of payment and in case of bankruptcy and liquidation. However, within the bond category itself there are various degrees of security. Mortgage bonds are secured by real assets, which means that holders have legal claim to specific assets of the issuer. **Debentures** are generally unsecured and are backed only by the issuer's overall financial soundness. In addition, debentures can be "subordinated," resulting in a claim on income that stands below (subordinate to) the claim of the other debentures.[10]

Corporate bonds carry a greater risk of default by the issuer than government bonds, and as a result, their indentures (or contracts) often include protective covenants, which are clauses that restrict the actions of the issuer. Negative covenants prohibit certain actions (e.g., restrict dividend payments or prevent pledging of any assets to lenders). Positive covenants specify actions that the firm agrees to undertake (e.g., furnish quarterly financial statements or maintain certain working capital levels).

Rating services perform detailed analysis of bond issuers to determine their ability to maintain uninterrupted payments of interest and repayment of principal. The Dominion Bond Rating Service (DBRS) and the Canadian Bond Rating Service (CBRS) are the two major Canadian **bond rating** services. Standard & Poor's (S&P) Corporation and Moody's Investors Service Inc. are two major US rating agencies that rate bond issuers (both government and corporate) across the world.

Corporate Bonds
Long-term debt securities of various types sold by corporations.

Senior Securities
Those securities that are senior, because they are ahead of common and preferred stock in terms of payment in case of liquidation or bankruptcy.

Debenture
An unsecured bond backed by the general financial worthiness of the firm.

Bond Rating
Letters assigned to bonds by rating agencies to express the relative probability of default.

---

[7]US Treasury securities with maturities greater than one year and less than 10 years technically are referred to as Treasury notes, while those with maturities greater than 10 years are referred to as Treasury bonds.
[8]At the time of writing, Fannie Mae and Freddie Mac held approximately $5 trillion in secured and unsecured mortgages in default, and were being bailed out by the US government.
[9]There are various exceptions to this generalization, of course, including bonds with warrants attached, mortgage-backed bonds, collateral trust bonds (which are backed by financial assets), and zero coupon bonds.
[10]Other types of corporate bonds exist, including collateral trust bonds, which are backed by other securities. For example, a parent firm may pledge the securities of one of its subsidiaries as collateral. Equipment obligations (or equipment trust certificates) are backed by specific real assets such as railway engines or airplanes. A trustee is used to hold the assets involved with both collateral trust bonds and equipment obligations.

The following are the debt ratings categories for CBRS and DBRS:

CBRS		DBRS	
A++	highest quality	AAA	highest credit quality
A+	very good quality	AA	superior credit quality
A	good quality	A	upper medium grade credit quality
B++	medium quality	BBB	medium grade credit quality
B+	lower medium quality	BB	lower medium grade credit quality
B	poor quality	B	speculative credit quality
C	speculative quality	CCC	highly speculative credit quality
D	default	CC	in default
Suspended	rating suspended	C	second tier of debt of an entity in default

Ratings may also be modified by high or low to indicate the relative ranking or the trend within the category, such as high A+ or low A+. Investment grade bonds are defined as those with bond ratings of BBB (DBRS and S&P), B++ (CBRS), or Baa (Moody's), or higher. Generally, institutional investors such as insurance companies must confine themselves to investment grade bonds. Other things being equal, bond ratings and bond coupon rates are inversely related. Junk (or high-yield or low-grade) bonds have bond ratings below these. These bonds are regarded as speculative securities in terms of the issuer's ability to meet its contractual obligations.

Despite their widespread acceptance, bond ratings have their limitations, and debt rating agencies have come under extreme criticism in light of their inability to predict many of the problems that arose as a result of the US sub-prime crisis that began in 2007. Real-World Returns 2-5 elaborates.

REAL-WORLD RETURNS 2-5

DBRS to Roll Out a New Road Map on Risk

Canadian bond-rating firm **DBRS Ltd.** is planning new disclosure demands designed to help investors better understand the risks of complex securities, a response to a blowup in credit markets that led to heavy criticism of rating companies for not giving enough warning.

The idea is to give investors a simple, easy-to-follow outline of the risks and the setup of so-called "structured" securities that are based on large pools of underlying assets such as mortgages. Toronto-based DBRS has been consulting with regulators, investors, issuers and banks since March and may unveil the disclosure proposal as soon as next month, said Huston Loke, head of global structured finance at DBRS.

"In the credit crunch it became clear that a number of investors weren't aware of all the risks they were entering into in acquiring their investments, and the disclosure frameworks demanded by the regulators and what the issuers were willing to put out were not always sufficient," Mr. Loke said.

Rating agencies around the world are revamping their ratings and policies to address criticism and demands from regulators after the collapse in the US subprime loan market created a domino effect that led to hundreds of downgrades of securities based on the loans.

Many investors were blindsided when securities that were triple-A-rated had their ratings slashed as defaults on mortgages piled up. DBRS itself has come under fire for giving top ratings to some of the asset-backed commercial paper that ended up frozen last August when the credit crunch hit.

"What we want to see is investors having a shot at getting the right information, where they can look at it, do some of their own analytics, get an appreciation for the risk and then decide, yes, I will invest in this."

(continued)

REAL-WORLD RETURNS 2-5 *continued*

DBRS rival **Standard & Poor's Corp.** yesterday announced a 27-step plan to increase investor confidence in ratings. Another big US player in bond ratings, **Moody's Investors Service Inc.**, is considering switching ratings of complex debt securities from letter grades that are also used for standard corporate bonds and government debt to numerical grades, driving home to investors that the debt is different.

S&P's proposals encompass enhanced disclosure, including a "flag" to help investors differentiate between traditional corporate or government bonds and structured securities. The firm also introduced broader reforms focused on governance, such as creating an ombudsman to watch for conflicts of interest and rotating analysts periodically so they do not become too close to bond issuers.

A key plank in S&P's plan is to educate investors about credit ratings, both how they work and what they mean.

"Part of the misunderstanding in the market is that when you assign a triple-A, people believe it's never going to change," said Vickie Tillman, an executive vice-president at S&P.

"Ratings do change. They change with circumstances, and they change with economic changes."

S&P consulted with regulators and central banks around the world, Ms. Tillman said, before settling on the package of reforms. Indeed, Canada's central bank has been vocal in calls for more clarity in ratings of structure products.

"Whatever helps to improve transparency and give investors confidence, that's just good for the market," said Mr. Loke of DBRS.

However, DBRS isn't planning a wholesale revamp of its governance structure like S&P. Mr. Loke said ratings agencies are better off focusing on ensuring that securities are structured robustly enough to withstand market turmoil, rather than on "pretty complicated governance frameworks. Because ultimately these transactions were unable to withstand the stress of the slump in the US housing market because they didn't have adequate amounts of credit enhancements to protect them against the unknown."

S&P'S PLANS

- Create an ombudsman to watch for potential conflicts of interest and analysis problems.
- Rotate analysts periodically to keep them from getting too close to issuers.
- Focus on training.
- Simplify ratings criteria.
- Add "What if" scenarios that help investors judge risks.
- Publish a manual to explain what ratings are for and how they should be used.
- Launch "market outreach" to promote understanding of complex securities.

Source: Erman, Boyd, www.globeinvestorgold.com, March 17, 2008.

We conclude by noting that while the Canadian market for corporate bonds has grown in importance in recent years, it is still smaller than the Canadian government bond market, as discussed above. In addition, the $418 billion US in Canadian corporate bonds outstanding in June 2007 is very small relative to corporate bond markets in other countries. For example, the United States, Japan, France, Italy, and Germany had $17.0 trillion, $1.6 trillion, $1.1 trillion, $1.1 trillion, and $1.01 trillion US of corporate debt outstanding at that time. In fact, the Canadian figure accounts for only approximately 1.5 percent of the world corporate debt market.

Asset-Backed Securities

Asset-Backed Securities (ABS)

Securities issued against some type of asset-linked debts bundled together, such as credit card receivables or mortgages.

The money and capital markets are constantly adapting to meet new requirements and conditions. This has given rise to new types of securities that were not previously available. "Securitization" refers to the transformation of illiquid, risky individual loans into more liquid, less risky securities referred to as **asset-backed securities (ABS)**. The best example of this process is mortgage-backed securities (MBS). These are created when a financial institution purchases (or originates) a number of mortgage loans that are then repackaged and sold to investors as mortgage pools. Investors in MBSs are, in effect, purchasing a piece of a mortgage pool. MBS investors assume little default risk because most mortgages are guaranteed by a federal government agency, as described below.

The Canada Mortgage and Housing Corporation (CMHC) introduced MBSs in Canada in 1987. Similar to the GNMA in the United States (which fully supports Ginnie Mae issues), the CMHC issues fully guaranteed securities in support of the mortgage market. These securities have attracted considerable attention in recent years because the principal and interest payments on the underlying mortgages used as collateral are "passed through" to the bondholder monthly as the mortgages are repaid. However, these securities are not completely riskless because they can receive varying amounts of monthly payments depending on how quickly homeowners pay off their mortgages. Although the stated maturity can be as long as 40 years, the average life of these securities has actually been much shorter.

ABSs are created when an underwriter, such as a bank, bundles some type of asset-linked debt (usually consumer oriented) and sells investors the right to receive payments made on that debt. As a result of the trend to securitization, other asset-backed securities have proliferated as financial institutions have rushed to securitize various types of loans.

Marketable securities have been backed by car loans, credit-card receivables, railway car leases, small-business loans, leases for photocopiers or aircraft, and so forth. The assets that can be securitized seem to be limited only by the imagination of the packagers, as evidenced by the fact that new asset types include items such as royalty streams from films, student loans, mutual fund fees, tax liens, monthly hydro bills, and delinquent child support payments!

The original use of securitization was to enhance the liquidity of the residential mortgage market, and MBSs grew from about 15 percent of mortgages in 1980 to more than 63 percent in 2003. In fact, the market value of global MBSs exceeded $8 trillion in 2006, which begs the question: Why do investors like these securities? The attractions are relatively high yields and relatively short maturities (often five years) combined with investment-grade credit ratings, typically the highest two ratings available. Investors are often protected by a bond insurer. Institutional investors, such as pension funds and life insurance companies, have become increasingly attracted to these securities because of the higher yields; the same is true of foreign investors.

As for risk, securitization works best when packaged loans are homogeneous, so that income streams and risks are more predictable. This is clearly the case for home mortgages, for example, which must adhere to strict guidelines, but for some of the newer loans being considered for packaging—such as loans for boats and motorcycles—the smaller amount of information results in a larger risk from unanticipated factors.

However, as we have seen in 2007 and 2008, investors underestimated the risks associated with many of these investments. Indeed, the market value of MBSs had fallen to $6.5 trillion by February of 2008, as a result of the massive market write-downs emanating from the sub-prime crisis fallout. This decline in value occurred despite the fact that the actual number of low grade (i.e., sub-prime) mortgages comprising MBSs was "supposed to be" relatively small. Indeed, many investors (mainly institutional investors—the so-called "experts") holding various MBSs and ABSs experienced severe losses as the market values of these instruments declined substantially. Investors in the Canadian non-bank backed ABCP market are still waiting to see how large will be their losses, when (and if) trading begins again in this market. As alluded to in Real-World Returns 2-5, the utter collapse of these markets has caused massive damage to the reputations of the debt rating agencies, since they failed to identify the inherent risks in these types of investments, and many market participants relied heavily (too heavily) on these ratings.

Rates on Fixed-Income Securities

Interest rates on fixed-income securities have fluctuated widely over the years as inflationary expectations as well as supply and demand conditions for long-term funds change. As one would expect on the basis of the return–risk trade-off explained in Chapter 1, corporate rates generally exceed government rates because of the higher risk, and lower-rated corporate securities yield more than do higher-rated ones.

Equity Securities

Unlike their fixed-income counterparts, equity securities represent an ownership interest in a corporation. These securities provide a residual claim—after payment of all fixed-income obligations—on the income and assets of a corporation. There are three forms of equities: preferred stock, income trusts, and common stock. Investors have traditionally been more interested in common stocks; however, income trusts have attracted a lot of attention from investors in recent years.

learning objective 5
Distinguish among preferred stock, income trusts, and common stock.

Preferred Stock

Most preferred shares in Canada are traded on the TSX and in the United States on the NYSE. They generally offer fixed monthly or quarterly dividends and are rated as to credit risk (similar to bonds and commercial paper). Although technically an equity security, **preferred stock** is often referred to as a hybrid, because it resembles both equity and fixed-income instruments.

As an equity security, preferred stock has an infinite life and pays dividends. It resembles fixed-income securities in that the amount of the dividend is fixed and known in advance, providing a stream of income very similar to that of a bond. The difference is that the stream continues forever, unless the issue is called or otherwise retired. Similar to bonds, the prices of preferreds are very sensitive to interest rates, but their price fluctuations often exceed those in bonds due to their long-term nature.

Preferred shareholders rank below creditors but above common shareholders in terms of priority of payment of income and in case the corporation is liquidated. While payment of preferred dividends is not obligatory like interest payments, payment to common shareholders has to wait until preferred shareholders receive full payment of the dividends to which they are entitled. Most preferred shares are non-voting; however, once a stated number of dividend payments have been omitted, it is common practice to assign voting privileges to the preferred. In addition, failure to pay anticipated preferred dividends weakens investor confidence in the issuer, which has an impact on its general credit and borrowing power. Finally, preferred shares usually have a "cumulative" feature associated with their dividends. This requires the firm to pay all preferred dividends (both current and arrears) before paying any dividends to common shareholders, and that makes the preferred less risky than common shares from the investor's point of view.

Preferred dividends are paid from after-tax earnings, and, unlike interest payments, they do not provide the issuer with a tax-deductible expense. However, individual investors receive relief in the form of a dividend tax credit, which implies they will pay lower taxes on a dollar of dividend income than on interest income. In addition, dividends received by one Canadian corporation from another Canadian corporation are not taxable. As a result of this tax incentive many Canadian financial institutions (banks and insurance companies, in particular) used to be large participants in the market for preferred shares. However, tax laws were changed in 1987, which required specified financial institutions (including banks and insurance companies) to treat preferred dividend payments as the equivalent to interest (which is fully taxable). The result of this change in tax laws is that fewer new issues of preferred shares have occurred since then.

Companies issue preferred shares as a compromise between the demands created by debt, and the dilution of common equity caused by the issuance of additional common shares, or when market conditions are unfavourable for new common share issues. Investors may be attracted to them if they want dividend income, which offers tax advantages over interest income. In addition, some issues have

Preferred Stock
A hybrid security that is part equity and part fixed-income because it increases in value but also pays a fixed dividend.

special features that make them attractive to investors. For example, some preferred issues are convertible into common stock at the owner's option. Similar to convertible debt, most convertible preferred shares are callable at a premium over par value.

Other types of preferred shares include

1. Retractable preferreds, which can be tendered by the holder to the issuer for redemption;

2. Variable-rate or floating-rate preferreds, which have the dividend rate tied to current market interest rates;

3. Participating preferreds, which have certain pre-specified rights to a share in company earnings over and above their specified rate.

In addition, some preferreds require the company to purchase a specified amount in the open market if they are available at or below the stipulated price. This provides built-in market support for these shares. Sinking fund provisions are less common for preferred share issues. They have the potential disadvantage to investors that the required purchases may be called in by lot at the sinking fund price plus accrued and unpaid dividends if the fund's open market operations are unsuccessful.

Income Trusts

Income Trusts

Investment instruments that pay out a substantial portion of cash flows generated from the underlying revenue-generating assets.

While **income trusts** have been around for a long time, they have grown in importance dramatically over the last few years, as discussed in Chapter 1. They are usually structured so that the trust itself invests in the shares and debt obligations of an underlying operating company. Since it is a trust, all the income is passed through to trust unitholders without any tax consequences to the trust. Further, since the trust owns both the debt and equity of the company, the use of debt can be maximized to reduce (or eliminate) any corporate income tax, provided the trust pays out most (or all) of its income to unitholders. Obviously this structure provides the businesses with the ultimate incentive to pay out most of their earnings in order to avoid paying taxes. This feature, in turn, made trusts very popular among investors.

The tax efficient structure of trusts, along with their popularity among investors, led to dramatic growth in this market. As of March 31, 2006, there were 238 income trusts listed on the Toronto Stock Exchange (TSX), up from 73 in 2001, and only a handful in the mid 1990s. In fact, the total market capitalization of these instruments grew from $1.4 billion in 1994 to $192 billion by March of 2006, representing approximately 10 percent of the quoted market value of the TSX.[11] Income trusts became the major source of equity initial public offerings (IPOs) in Canada during the 2000s, often accounting for over half of all new equity IPOs. Some of these trust IPOs provided financing for new businesses, while others were associated with existing companies "converting" to the trust structure. As a result of this growth, the TSX fully incorporated income trusts into the S&P/TSX Composite Index as of March 2006.

On October 31, 2006, Finance Minister Jim Flaherty announced unexpectedly, and in contradiction of a key election promise, that the distributions made by newly created trusts would be taxed at prevailing corporate tax rates, and that this new tax would apply to existing trusts beginning in 2011. This announcement was made just as Canadian telecommunications giants TELUS Corp. and BCE Inc. were in the midst of preparing to convert from the traditional corporate structure to the income trust structure, which would have added another $50 billion or so in market cap to the income trust market.

Not surprisingly, both BCE Inc. and TELUS Corp. subsequently cancelled their plans to convert to the trust structure, and many other planned income trust IPOs were also cancelled. Indeed, the October 31 announcement brought a dramatic end to the growth of income trusts, and severely damaged the Canadian equity IPO market, as can be seen in Real-World Returns 2-6.

---

[11]TSX website: www.tsx.com.

REAL-WORLD RETURNS 2-6

Income Trust Tax Slowed Canada's IPO Pace in 2007

The value of Canadian initial public offerings was down substantially last year despite a fourth-quarter surge, PricewaterhouseCoopers said in a report Monday.

It said there were 90 IPOs last year on the Toronto Stock Exchange and the TSX Venture, worth a total of $3.4 billion in 2007. That was down from 109 new offerings in 2006, worth $5.6 billion.

"A host of different factors conspired against the IPO market last year," Ross Sinclair, national leader of PricewaterhouseCoopers' IPO and income-trust services, said in a statement, noting the impact of the federal government announcing in October 2006 it would start taxing new income trusts as corporations in the new year.

"The environment in 2007 was anything but predictable and stable," he added. "The impact of the loss of income trusts in the market was felt most of the year, as potential issuers tried to chart a course for the future."

In the fourth quarter of 2007, PricewaterhouseCoopers counted 19 IPOs, worth $2.1 billion. That compared with five launches in the same quarter a year earlier for $987 million.

One particular IPO that made the difference last in the year was the one for Franco-Nevada Corp. for $1.1 billion. PricewaterhouseCoopers said without that deal, the annual total for IPOs would have been $2.3 billion. That's close to the $2.1 billion worth of IPOs in 2001, which was the lowest level in a decade.

Common Stock

Common stock represents the ownership interest of corporations or the equity of the shareholders, and we can use the term equity securities interchangeably. If a firm's shares are owned by only a few individuals, the firm is said to be closely held. Many companies choose to go public, or they sell common stock to the general public, primarily to let them raise additional capital more easily. If a corporation meets certain requirements, it may choose to be listed on one or more exchanges such as the TSX. Otherwise, it will be listed in the over-the-counter market (this process is discussed in Chapter 4).

As the residual claimants of the corporation, shareholders are entitled to income remaining after the fixed-income claimants such as the preferred shareholders have been paid; also, in case of liquidation of the corporation, they are entitled to the remaining assets after all other claims (including preferred stock) are satisfied.

As owners, the holders of common stock are entitled to elect the directors of the corporation and vote on major issues.[12] Each shareholder is allowed to cast votes equal to the number of shares owned when such votes take place at the annual meeting of the corporation, which each shareholder is allowed to attend.[13] Most stockholders vote by proxy, meaning that they authorize someone else

Common Stock
An equity security representing the ownership interest in a corporation.

---

[12]The voting rights of the shareholders give them legal control of the corporation. In theory, the board of directors controls the management of the corporation, but in many cases the effective result is the opposite. Shareholders can regain control if they are sufficiently dissatisfied.

[13]Most shareholders do not attend, often allowing management to vote their proxy. Therefore, although technically more than 50 percent of the outstanding shares are needed for control of a firm, effective control can often be exercised with considerably less because not all of the shares are voted.

(most often management) to vote their shares. Sometimes proxy battles occur, whereby one or more groups unhappy with corporate policies seek to bring about changes.

The amount of protection afforded shareholders by this right to vote is a matter of debate. The value of this privilege is in fact a function of several elements of corporate governance, including the effectiveness of the board of directors in serving in the best interests of shareholders.

There often exists a clause in a corporation's charter that grants existing shareholders the first or pre-emptive right to purchase any new common stock sold by the corporation. The right is a piece of paper giving each stockholder the option to buy a specified number of new shares, usually at a discount, during a specified short period of time. These rights are valuable and can be sold in the market.

Finally, shareholders also have limited liability, meaning they cannot be held responsible for the debts of the company or lose more than their original investment. In the event of financial difficulties, creditors have recourse only to the assets of the corporation, leaving the stockholders protected. This is perhaps the greatest advantage of the corporation and the reason why it has been so successful.

Characteristics of Common Stocks

The par value for a common stock, unlike that of a bond or preferred stock, is generally not a significant economic variable. Corporations can make the par value any number they choose and an often-used par value is $1. New stock is usually sold for more than par value, with the difference recorded on the balance sheet as "capital in excess of par value" or "additional paid-in capital." Canadian corporations incorporated under the Canada Business Corporations Act (CBCA) and under most provincial acts can no longer issue shares with par value.

Book Value

The accounting value of common equity as shown on the balance sheet.

The **book value** of a corporation is the accounting value of the common equity as shown on the books (i.e., balance sheet). It is the total value of common equity for a corporation, represented by the sum of common stock outstanding, capital in excess of par value and/or contributed surplus, and retained earnings. Dividing this sum—total book value—by the number of common shares outstanding, produces the book value per share. In effect, book value is the accounting value of the stockholders' equity. Although book value per share plays a role in making investment decisions, market value per share is the critical item of interest to investors.

EXAMPLE 2-3: BOOK VALUE FOR MAGNA INTERNATIONAL INC.

Magna International Inc. reported $7.157 billion in common shareholders' equity for fiscal year end 2006. This is the book value of common equity. Based on the year-end common shares outstanding of 109.880 million for that year (a figure obtained from the company's annual report), the book value per share was $65.13.

The market value or price of the equity is the variable of concern to investors. The aggregate market value for a corporation is calculated by multiplying the market price per share of the stock by the number of shares outstanding. This represents the total value of the firm as determined in the marketplace. The market value of one share of stock, of course, is simply the "observed" current market price. At the time the observation for Magna's book value was recorded, the market price was in the $93.87 range. This implies that Magna's market-to-book ratio (discussed in Chapter 13) was $93.87/$65.13 = 1.44.

Dividends

Cash payments declared and paid by corporations to stockholders.

Dividends are the only cash payments regularly made by corporations to their stockholders. They are decided upon and declared by the board of directors quarterly and can range from zero to virtually any amount the corporation can afford to pay (up to 100 percent of present and past net earnings). Roughly half of the companies listed on the TSX (and three-fourths of the companies listed on the NYSE) pay dividends. However, the common stockholder has no specific promises to receive any cash from the corporation since the stock never matures and dividends do not have to be paid. Therefore, common stocks involve substantial risk because the dividend is at the company's discretion and stock prices can fluctuate sharply, which means that the value of investors' claims may rise and fall rapidly over relatively short periods of time.

The two dividend terms dividend yield and payout ratio are important considerations for investors.

The **dividend yield** is the income component of a stock's return stated on a percentage basis. It is one of the two components of total return, which is discussed in Chapter 6. Dividend yield is commonly calculated as the most recent annual dividend amount divided by the current market price.

The **payout ratio** is the ratio of dividends to earnings. It indicates the percentage of a firm's earnings paid out in cash to its stockholders. The complement of the payout ratio is the retention ratio, and it indicates the percentage of a firm's current earnings retained by it for reinvestment purposes.

Dividend Yield
The income component of a stock's return, generally calculated by dividing the current annual dividend by the prevailing market price.

Payout Ratio
The percentage of a firm's earnings paid out in cash to its stockholders, calculated by dividing dividends by earnings.

EXAMPLE 2-4: PAYOUT RATIO FOR MAGNA INTERNATIONAL INC.

Magna's 2006 earnings were $4.86 per share, and it paid an annual dividend on its common shares of $1.52 per share. Assuming a price for Magna of $93.87, the dividend yield would be $1.52/$93.87, or 1.62 percent. The payout ratio was $1.52/$4.86, or 31.28 percent, and the retention ratio was 68.72 percent (i.e., 100 percent − 31.28 percent).

Dividends are commonly declared and paid quarterly, but to receive a declared dividend, an investor must be a holder of record on the specified date that a company closes its stock transfer books and compiles the list of stockholders to be paid (which is generally done two to four weeks before the payment date). The ex dividend date is set at the second business day before the record date, and shares trade without the right to the associated dividend on and after this date. Since stock trades settle on the third business day after a trade, a purchaser of the share two days before the record date would not settle until the day after the record date, and would thus not be entitled to receive the dividend. Shares are said to trade cum dividend up to the ex dividend date, and trade ex dividend thereafter. This will be reflected in the share price, which typically falls by an amount close to the dividend amount on the ex rights date.

EXAMPLE 2-5: ANNOUNCING DIVIDENDS FOR MAGNA INTERNATIONAL INC.

Assume that the board of directors of Magna meets on April 24 and declares a quarterly dividend, payable on June 30. April 24 is called the declaration date. The board will declare a holder-of-record date, say, June 9. The books close on this date, but Magna goes ex-dividend on June 7 (assuming June 7 and June 8 are regular business days). To receive this dividend, an investor must purchase the stock by June 6. The dividend will be mailed to the stockholders of record on the payment date, June 30.

Stock dividends and stock splits attract considerable investor attention. A **stock dividend** is a payment by a corporation in shares of stock instead of cash.[14] A **stock split** involves the division of a corporation's stock by issuing a specified number of new shares while simultaneously lowering the face value of outstanding shares. With a stock split, the book value and par value of the equity are changed; for example, each would be cut in half with a 2-for-1 split. However, on a practical basis, there is little difference between a stock dividend and a stock split since the net result of both actions is an increase in the number of shares outstanding.

Stock Dividend
A payment by a corporation of a dividend in shares of stock rather than cash.

Stock Split
The division of a corporation's stock by issuing a specified number of new shares while simultaneously lowering the face value of outstanding shares.

---

[14]The amount of the stock dividend received by an investor equals the number of shares he or she receives, times the prevailing market price per share. The amount is taxable in the same manner as a cash dividend for this dollar amount.

EXAMPLE 2-6: SPLITTING STOCK 2-FOR-1

A 5 percent stock dividend would entitle an owner of 100 shares of a particular stock to an additional five shares. A 2-for-1 stock split would double the number of shares of the stock outstanding, double an individual owner's number of shares (e.g., from 100 shares to 200 shares), and cut the price in half at the time of the split.

Stock data, as reported to investors in most investment information sources and in the company's reports to stockholders, are adjusted for all stock dividends and stock splits. These adjustments must be made when splits or dividends occur in order for legitimate comparisons to be made for the data.

The important question to investors is the value of the distribution, whether a dividend or a split. It is clear that the recipient has more shares (i.e., more pieces of paper), but has anything of real value been received? Other things being equal, these additional shares do not represent additional value because proportional ownership has not changed. Quite simply, the pieces of paper—stock certificates—have been repackaged. For example, if you own 1,000 shares of a corporation that has 100,000 shares of stock outstanding, your proportional ownership is 1 percent; with a 2-for-1 stock split, you now own 2,000 shares out of a total of 200,000 shares outstanding, but your proportional ownership is still 1 percent.

Regardless of the above, some evidence does suggest that the stock price receives a boost following a split. A recent study by a university professor, David Ikenberry, finds that such stocks tend to outperform the market in the first year following a split by an average eight percentage points and that the effect continues for some three years following the split. According to S&P data, split shares tend to outperform the market for some 18 months following the split. Typically, the dividend is raised at the time of the split, which would have a positive effect by itself. If the above findings are correct, it suggests that management signals with splits and dividends that they are confident about future prospects, which in turn should boost investor confidence.

P/E Ratio

The ratio of stock price to earnings, using historical, current, or estimated data. Also known as earnings multiplier. (*See also* E/P Ratio.)

The **P/E ratio**, also referred to as the earnings multiplier, is generally calculated as the ratio of the current market price to the firm's most recent earnings, although it can also be based on expected future earnings. It is an indication of how much the market as a whole is willing to pay per dollar of earnings. It is standard investing practice to refer to stocks as selling at, say, 10 or 15 times earnings. Investors have traditionally used such a classification to categorize stocks. Growth stocks, for example, generally sell at high multiples, compared with the average stock, because of their expected higher earnings growth.

The P/E ratio is a widely reported variable, appearing in daily newspapers and websites carrying stock information, in brokerage reports covering particular stocks, in magazine articles recommending various companies, and so forth. It is usually reported in the media as the current price divided by the latest 12-month earnings. For example, the P/E ratio for Magna International Inc. based on the information above would be \$93.87/\$4.86 = 19.31. However, variations of this ratio are often used in the valuation of common stocks. In fact, the P/E ratio in its various forms is one of the best-known and most often cited variables in security analysis and is familiar to almost all investors.[15] The P/E ratio is discussed in great detail in Chapters 13 through 17, which deal with common stock valuation.

Investing Internationally in Equities

Canadians can invest internationally in a variety of ways. First, they may purchase shares of foreign companies that list directly on Canadian exchanges or in the Canadian over-the-counter market. Alternatively, they may purchase shares of foreign companies in the country of origin or purchase options or

[15]In calculating P/E ratios on the basis of either the latest reported earnings or the expected earnings, problems can arise when comparing P/E ratios among companies if some of them are experiencing, or are expected to experience, abnormally high or low earnings. To avoid this problem, some market participants calculate a normalized earnings estimate. Normalized earnings are intended to reflect the "normal" level of a company's earnings; that is, transitory effects are presumably excluded, thus providing the user with a more accurate estimate of "true" earnings.

futures contracts on foreign stock indexes. Finally, they can purchase foreign securities indirectly by purchasing units (or shares) of investment companies (mutual funds, closed-end funds, or exchange traded funds) specializing in foreign securities, as discussed in Chapter 3. The latter method is the approach used by the vast majority of Canadians wishing to invest globally.

CHECK YOUR UNDERSTANDING

2-7. Consider two corporate bonds: one rated AAA, the other rated BBB. Could you say with confidence that the first bond will not default while for the second bond there is some reasonable probability of default?

2-8. Should risk-averse investors avoid junk bonds?

2-9. Why might investors opt to hold preferred stocks rather than bonds in their portfolios?

2-10. Is it fair to say that income trusts became popular investment vehicles primarily because of the tax efficiency of the payments they make to investors?

2-11. Suppose you own common stock in a company that has just declared bankruptcy because it cannot pay the amounts owing to its bondholders. Can the bond investors expect you to pay off the debt? Why or why not?

DERIVATIVE SECURITIES

learning objective 6
Understand the basics of options and futures.

We focus our attention here on the two types of derivative securities that are of interest to most investors. Options and futures contracts are **derivative securities**, so named because their value is derived from their connected underlying security. Numerous types of options and futures are traded in world markets. Furthermore, there are different types of options other than the puts and calls discussed here. For example, a **warrant** is a corporate-created, long-term option on the underlying common stock of the company. It gives the holder the right to buy the stock from the company at a stated price within a stated period of time, often several years. They are often issued as "sweeteners" attached to a debt, preferred share, or common share issue to make the issue more attractive to investors.

Options and futures contracts share some common characteristics. Both have standardized features that allow them to be traded quickly and cheaply on organized exchanges. In addition to facilitating the trading of these securities, the exchange guarantees the performance of these contracts and its clearing house allows an investor to reverse his or her original position before maturity. For example, a seller of a futures contract can buy the contract and cancel the obligation that the contract carries. The exchanges and associated clearing houses for both options and futures contracts have worked extremely well.

Options and futures contracts are important to investors because they provide a way for them to manage portfolio risk. For example, investors may incur the risk of adverse currency fluctuations if they invest in foreign securities, or they may incur the risk that interest rates will adversely affect their fixed-income securities. Options and futures contracts can be used to limit some, or all, of these risks, thereby providing risk-control possibilities.

Options and futures contracts have important differences in their trading, the assets they can affect, their risk factor, and so forth. Perhaps the biggest difference to note now is that a futures contract is an obligation to buy or sell, but an options contract is only the right as opposed to an obligation to do so. The buyer of an option has limited liability, but the buyer of a futures contract does not.

Options

In today's investing world, the word **options** refers to **puts** and **calls**. Options are created not by corporations but by investors seeking to trade in claims on a particular common stock, stock index, or futures contract. A standard equity call (put) option gives the holder (buyer) the right to purchase

Derivative Securities
Securities that derive their value in whole or in part by having a claim on some underlying security.

Warrant
An option created by a corporation to purchase a stated number of common shares at a specified price within a specified time (often several years).

Options
Rights to buy or sell a stated number of shares of stock within a specified period at a specified price.

Puts
Options to sell a specified number of shares of stock at a stated price within a specified period.

Calls
Options to buy a specified number of shares of stock at a stated price within a specified period.

LEAPs

Options to buy (calls) or
sell (puts) securities with
longer maturity dates of up
to several years, also known
as long-term options.

(sell) 100 shares of a particular stock at a specified price (called the exercise price) within a specified time.[16] The maturities on most new puts and calls are available up to several months away, although **LEAPs** have maturity dates of several years. Many exercise prices are created for each underlying common stock, giving investors a choice in both the maturity and the price they will pay or receive.

Holders (buyers) of calls receive the right to purchase a specified number of shares at a specified price. These investors are betting that the price of the underlying common stock will rise, making the call option more valuable. Put buyers receive the right to sell a specified number of shares at a specified price. They are betting that the price of the underlying common stock will decline, making the put option more valuable. Both put and call options are written (created) by other investors who are betting the opposite of their respective purchasers. The sellers (writers) receive an option premium for selling each new contract while the buyer pays this option premium.

Once the option is created and the writer (seller) receives the premium from the buyer, it can be traded repeatedly in the secondary market. The premium is simply the market price of the contract as determined by investors. The price will fluctuate constantly, just as the price of the underlying common stock changes. This makes sense, because the option is affected directly by the price of the stock that gives it value. In addition, the option's value is affected by the time remaining to maturity, current interest rates, the volatility of the stock, and the price at which the option can be exercised.

Puts and calls allow both buyers and sellers (writers) to speculate on the short-term movements of certain common stocks. Buyers obtain an option on the common stock for a small, known premium, which is the maximum that the buyer can lose. If the buyer is correct about the price movements on the underlying assets, gains are magnified in relation to having bought (or sold short) the assets because a smaller investment is required. However, the buyer has only a short time in which to be correct. Writers (sellers) earn the premium as income, based on their beliefs about a stock. They win or lose, depending on whether their beliefs are correct or incorrect.

Options can be used in a variety of strategies, giving investors opportunities to manage their portfolios in ways that would be unavailable in the absence of such instruments. For example, since the most a buyer of a put or call can lose is the cost of the option, the buyer is able to truncate the distribution of potential returns. That is, after a certain point, no matter how much the underlying stock price changes, the buyer's position does not change. Some basic options strategies are discussed in Chapter 19.

Forward and Futures Contracts

Forward Contracts

Commitments today to
transact in the future.

Forward contracts are commitments today to transact in the future. Two parties agree to exchange an underlying asset, such as gold, in the future at a price that is determined today. Both parties have agreed to a deferred delivery at a sales price that is currently determined. These contracts are sold through the over-the-counter market, with no funds being exchanged initially.

Forward contracts are centuries old, while organized futures markets, on the other hand, only go back to the mid-nineteenth century in Chicago. Futures markets are, in effect, organized and standardized forward markets. An organized futures exchange standardizes the non-standard forward contracts, establishing such features as contract size, delivery dates, and condition of the items that can be delivered. Only the price and number of contracts are left for futures traders to negotiate. Individuals can trade without personal contact with each other because of the centralized marketplace. Performance is guaranteed by a clearing house, relieving one party to the transaction from worry that the other party will fail to honour its commitment.

Futures contracts have been available on commodities such as corn and wheat for a long time. Today, they are also readily available on several financial instruments, including stock market indexes, currencies, Treasury bills, bankers' acceptances, and government bonds.

---

[16]Option expiry dates are expressed in terms of the month in which they expire. Option contracts expire on the Saturday following the third Friday of the month, so the third Friday is the last trading day for these instruments.

A **futures contract** is an agreement that provides for the future exchange of a particular asset between a buyer and a seller. The seller contracts to deliver the asset at a specified delivery date in exchange for a specified amount of cash from the buyer. Although the cash is not required until the delivery date, a "good faith deposit," called the margin, is required to reduce the chance of default by either party. The margin is small compared with the value of the contract.

Futures Contracts
Agreements providing for the future exchange of a particular asset between a buyer and seller at a specified date for a specified amount.

Most futures contracts are not exercised. Instead, they are "offset" by taking a position opposite to the one initially undertaken. For example, a purchaser of a May Government of Canada bond futures contract can close out the position by selling an identical May contract before the delivery date, while a seller can close out the same position by purchasing that contract.

Most participants in futures are either hedgers or speculators. Hedgers seek to reduce price uncertainty over some future period. For example, by purchasing a futures contract, a hedger can lock in a specific price for the asset and be protected from adverse price movements. Similarly, sellers can protect themselves from downward price movements. Speculators, on the other hand, seek to profit from the uncertainty that will occur in the future. If prices are expected to rise, contracts will be purchased, and if prices are expected to fall, contracts will be sold. Correct anticipations can result in very large profits because only a small margin is required. Futures are discussed at length in Chapter 20.

In addition to traditional options and futures contracts, there also exist options on futures. Calls on futures give the buyer the right, but not the obligation, to assume the futures position.

CHECK YOUR UNDERSTANDING

2-12. What is the most significant conceptual difference between a futures contract and an options contract?

2-13. Suppose you believed that the price of a particular common stock would soon fall dramatically. Which type of derivative contract would be best suited to allowing you to profit from the situation?

SUMMARY

This summary relates to the objectives for this chapter.

1. **Describe the major types of financial assets and how they are organized.**
   Investors may invest either directly in non-marketable assets, money market instruments, capital market securities (divided into fixed-income and equity securities), and derivative securities, or indirectly in the form of investment company shares (e.g., mutual funds).

2. **Explain what non-marketable financial assets are.**
   Non-marketable financial assets are highly liquid, safe investments available from insured financial institutions or issued by the Canadian government. In contrast to marketable securities, these assets represent personal transactions between the owner and the issuer. Non-marketable financial assets are widely owned by investors and include savings deposits, GICs, and Canada Savings Bonds.

3. **Describe the important features of money market securities.**
   Money market investments are characterized as short-term, highly liquid, very safe investments. These include (but are not limited to) Treasury bills, commercial paper, Eurodollars, repurchase agreements, and banker's acceptances.

4. **Describe the important features of capital market securities.**
   Capital market securities have maturities in excess of one year and are of two types: fixed-income securities and equity securities. Fixed-income securities have a specified payment and/or

repayment schedule and are issued by governments and corporations. Equity securities represent an ownership interest in a corporation or trust and are of three forms: preferred stock, common stock, and income trusts.

5. **Distinguish among preferred stock, income trusts, and common stock.**

   Preferred stock, while technically an equity security, is often regarded by investors as a fixed-income type of security because of its stated (and fixed) dividend. Preferred stock has no maturity date but may be retired by calls or other means. Common stock (equity) represents the ownership of the corporation. The stockholder is the residual claimant in terms of both income and assets.

6. **Understand the basics of options and futures.**

   Options allow both buyers and sellers (writers) to speculate on and/or hedge the price movements of stocks for which these claims are available. Calls are multiple-month rights to purchase a common stock at a specified price, while puts are the same rights to sell. Futures contracts provide for the future exchange of a particular asset between a buyer and a seller. A recent innovation is options on futures.

KEY TERMS

Asset-backed securities (ABS), p.40	Dividends, p.44	Payout ratio, p.45
Bonds, p.33	Dividend yield, p. 45	P/E ratio, p.46
Bond rating, p.37	Extendible bonds, p.35	Preferred stock, p.41
Book value, p.44	Fixed-income securities, p.33	Puts, p.47
Calls, p.47	Forward contracts, p.48	Retractable bonds, p.35
Call provision, p.35	Futures contract, p.49	Senior securities, p.37
Capital markets, p.33	Income trusts, p.42	Stock dividend, p.45
Common stock, p.43	Indirect investing, p.26	Stock split, p.45
Convertible bonds, p.35	LEAPs, p.48	Treasury bill (T-bill), p.31
Corporate bonds, p.37	Liquidity, p.28	Treasury bond, p.34
Debenture, p.37	Money market, p.30	Warrant, p.47
Derivative securities, p.47	Options, p.47	Zero coupon bond, p.34
	Par value (Face value), p.34	

REVIEW QUESTIONS

2-1. Outline the classification scheme for marketable securities used in the chapter. Explain each of the terms involved.

2-2. What is the difference between a savings deposit and a GIC?

2-3. What does it mean for Treasury bills to be sold at a discount?

2-4. Why is the common stockholder referred to as a "residual claimant"?

2-5. Do all common stocks pay dividends? Who decides?

2-6. Distinguish between a serial bond and a term bond.

2-7. What is meant by "indirect" investing?

2-8. Why should we expect that the six-month Treasury bill rate will be less than the six-month commercial paper rate?

2-9. What types of securities are traded on the money markets? What types are traded on the capital markets? Give examples of each type obtained from a daily business newspaper.

2-10. From the investor's perspective, what is the difference between a warrant and a call option?

2-11. What are the advantages and disadvantages of investing in Government of Canada bonds versus corporate bonds?

2-12. What are the differences between a Canada Savings Bond and a Government of Canada long-term bond?

2-13. Why is preferred stock referred to as a "hybrid" security?

2-14. What is meant by the term derivative security? What is the major determinant of the price of a derivative security?

2-15. What is meant by the term securitization? Give at least two examples of asset-backed securities.

2-16. Why are convertible and retractable features generally advantageous for bondholders? How do they pay for these privileges?

2-17. What is the value to investors of stock dividends and splits?

2-18. What are the advantages and disadvantages of being a holder of the common stock of Bombardier Inc. as opposed to owning a Bombardier bond?

2-19. Assume that a company whose stock you are interested in will pay regular quarterly dividends soon. Looking at the stock listings on-line, you observe a dividend figure of $3.20 listed for this stock. The board of directors has declared the dividend payable on September 1, with a holder-of-record date of August 15. When must you buy the stock to receive the dividend, and how much will you receive if you buy 150 shares?

2-20. List three types of derivative securities. Explain the difference between each type.

2-21. Under what conditions might a bondholder utilize the convertible feature of a bond?

2-22. Under what conditions might a bondholder utilize the retractable feature of a bond?

2-23. How is it possible that an investor who buys shares in a company may make a profit even if the share price drops?

2-24. Do you think that a stock with a high dividend yield will be more or less risky than a stock that does not pay any dividend? Why?

2-25. Is the call provision on a bond an advantage to the investor or an advantage to the issuing corporation? Given your knowledge of risk and return, what effect should the call feature have on the pricing of a bond; in other words, will the bond offer a higher or lower rate of interest? Why?

2-26. From the corporation's perspective, what are the differences between a warrant and a call option? If the call option is exercised, what will happen to the share price of the underlying company? If the warrant is exercised, what might happen to the share price of the underlying company?

2-27. What do you think some of the contributing factors might be when a company's management determines what the dividend payout ratio will be?

2-28. Name and briefly describe four types of money market securities.

2-29. Give at least two examples of asset-backed securities.

2-30. What kind of investment would be attractive to an individual who is in a high tax bracket?

2-31. Why might an individual be interested in investing in a strip bond?

2-32. What kind of issuers would you expect to offer the lowest yield for their long-term bonds?

2-33. Why do junk bonds offer high yields?

2-34. What are bearer bonds? What are the advantages and disadvantages of holding this type of bond?

2-35. What are Eurobonds? Why might these be attractive to an investor?

2-36. Name the four issuers of bonds discussed in this chapter. Which do you think would be most risky as a general proposition?

2-37. Why is the call provision on a bond generally a disadvantage to the bondholder?

2-38. With regard to bond ratings, which of the following statements is incorrect?

    a. The first four categories represent investment-grade securities.

    b. Ratings reflect the absolute probability of default.

    c. Both corporates and municipals are rated.

    d. Ratings are current opinions on the relative quality of bonds.

2-39. Choose the statement that best completes the sentence: Preferred stocks and common stocks are similar in that

    a. Both are equity securities.

    b. Both pay a stated and fixed dividend.

    c. The expected return for each can be estimated with precision for the next period.

    d. Both have an equal claim on the income stream of the company.

PROBLEMS

2-1. Suppose a resident of Ontario will earn an extra $100 of investment income in 2008. For the various levels of taxable income shown below, determine how much of the $100 the investor will keep (the after-tax income) if it is earned as: (a) dividends from a large Canadian company; (b) interest from a Government bond; and (c) profit from selling some stock (a capital gain).

    The federal and provincial tax rates are provided in Appendix 2A. Note that in addition to the federal dividend tax credit, there is also an Ontario dividend tax credit of 6.75 percent of the taxable amount of the dividend (145 percent of the dividend received). You may want to lay out your spreadsheet as follows:

Taxable Income	Marginal Tax Rate		Dividends		After-Tax Income		
	Federal	Ontario	Tax	Tax Credit	Dividends	Interest	Capital Gain
12,500							
37,500							
50,000							
75,000							
87,500							
112,500							
125,000							

APPENDIX 2A

TAXATION OF INVESTMENT INCOME IN CANADA

General Information

The basic federal tax rates (as of 2008) are:

1. 15 percent for taxable income up to $37,885

2. 22 percent on the next $37,884 up to $76,769

3. 26 percent on the next $47,415 up to $123,184

4. 29 percent on any amount above $123,184

In addition, each province operates a separate provincial tax system. It used to be that provincial taxes were a simple multiple of federal taxes, so that Ontario for example would add on 52 percent (at its peak) of the federal taxes. However, things have changed over the last 10 years and each province except Quebec has developed a parallel tax system that works similar to the federal system. The 2008 provincial/territorial tax rates[17] are provided in Table 2A-1.

Table 2A-1

Provincial and Territorial Tax Rates

Province/Territories:	Rates
Newfoundland and Labrador	8.2% on the first $30,215 of taxable income, + 13.3% on the next $30,214, + 16% on the amount over $60,429
Prince Edward Island	9.8% on the first $31,984 of taxable income, + 13.8% on the next $31,985, + 16.7% on the amount over $63,969
Nova Scotia	8.79% on the first $29,590 of taxable income, + 14.95% on the next $29,590, + 16.67% on the next $33,820 + 17.5% on the amount over $93,000
New Brunswick	10.12% on the first $34,836 of taxable income, + 15.48% on the next $34,837, + 16.8% on the next $43,600, + 17.95% on the amount over $113,273
Ontario	6.05% on the first $36,020 of taxable income, + 9.15% on the next $36,021, + 11.16% on the amount over $72,041
Manitoba	10.9% on the first $30,544 of taxable income, + 12.75% on the next $35,456, + 17.4% on the amount over $66,000
Saskatchewan	11% on the first $39,135 of taxable income, + 13% on the next $72,679, + 15% on the amount over $111,814
Alberta	10% of taxable income
British Columbia	5.24% on the first $35,016 of taxable income, + 7.98% on the next $35,017, + 10.5% on the next $10,373, + 12.29% on the next $17,230, + 14.7% on the amount over $97,636
Yukon	7.04% on the first $37,885 of taxable income, + 9.68% on the next $37,884, + 11.44% on the next $47,415, + 12.76% on the amount over $123,184
Northwest Territories	5.9% on the first $35,986 of taxable income, + 8.6% on the next $35,987, + 12.2% on the next $45,038, + 14.05% on the amount over $117,011
Nunavut	4% on the first $37,885 of taxable income, + 7% on the next $37,885, + 9% on the next $47,414, + 11.5% on the amount over $123,184

Source: Reproduced with permission of the Canada Revenue Agency and the Minister of Public Works and Government Services Canada, 2008.

Interest, Dividend, and Capital Gains Income

Interest income from debt securities (including bonds and money market securities) is taxable at the full marginal rate; however, dividends and capital gains afford investors a tax break. Dividends (whether they are cash, stock, or reinvested dividends) received from Canadian corporations are taxable in the following manner for all provinces except Quebec. First, the amount of the dividend is "grossed-up" by 45 percent (as of the May 2006 budget) to obtain the taxable amount of dividend that is used in determining net income. The taxpayer is then able to claim a federal tax credit of 18.97 percent of the taxable amount of the dividend. The investor then claims a provincial tax credit that varies with the province or territory of residence. This is done to reduce the amount of "double taxation," which refers to the fact that dividends are paid by companies out of after-tax earnings (i.e., these earnings have been taxed), and then investors pay taxes on the dividends they receive from the businesses.

---

[17]www.cra-arc.gc.ca/tx/ndvdls/fq/txrts-eng.html#provincial, March 18, 2008.

The marginal tax rates on dividends are lower than on interest and are lower on capital gains for investors in lower marginal tax brackets, with the cut-off points varying by province. This lower effective tax rate enhances the investor's after-tax return.

In response to the 2008 federal budget, which will reduce corporate taxes from 19.5 percent in 2008 to 15 percent in 2012, the amount of the federal dividend gross-up will be reduced from 45 percent to 38 percent, and the credit will be reduced to 15 percent from 19 percent by 2012. This will effectively increase the marginal rate on dividends from 14.55 percent to 19.29, assuming no further changes.

Foreign dividends are usually taxed by the source country and there is an allowable credit, which is essentially the lower of the foreign tax paid and the Canadian tax payable on foreign income subject to certain adjustments.

A capital gain arises from the disposition of capital assets for proceeds in excess of their cost. Only 50 percent of the capital gain is taxable, provided the transaction involved a taxpayer whose ordinary business does not involve the trading of securities, or that Canada Revenue Agency did not determine the trading to be speculative in nature. The general rule is that capital gains equal the proceeds from distribution minus the adjusted cost base (which includes commission costs, etc.) plus any costs of disposing of assets.

The adjusted cost base is complicated when shares were purchased at different prices and is based on the average cost method. For example, if 200 shares were purchased for $5 (including commission) and an additional 300 shares were purchased for $6 (including commission), then the average adjusted cost per share would be ($1,000 + $1,800) ÷ 500 = $5.60 per share. Taxes on disposition of debt securities are applied as above; however, the accrued interest portion of a bond purchase price is not included as part of the adjusted cost base and is treated as taxable income in the hands of the bond seller.

Capital losses cannot be claimed by the security holder unless ownership is transferred in writing to another person. One exception to this rule is where the security becomes worthless due to bankruptcy of the underlying company. Superficial losses are those that result from the sale and purchase of the same security within a given time frame and are not tax deductible. However, the taxpayer eventually receives the tax benefit since the amount of the superficial loss is added to the cost base of the repurchased shares, which lowers the ultimate capital gain. A superficial loss occurs when securities are sold at a loss but are repurchased and still held 30 days after the sale. They do not apply to losses resulting from leaving Canada, death of a taxpayer, expiry of an option, or a deemed disposition of securities by a trust or to a controlled corporation.

Certain items related to investment income are tax deductible including carrying charges such as interest on borrowed funds, investment counselling fees, fees paid for administration or safe custody of investments, safety deposit box charges, and accounting fees paid for recording investment income. Interest on borrowed funds is deductible only if the investor had a legal obligation to pay the interest, the purpose of the borrowing was to earn income, and the income earned from the investment is not tax exempt. (Note: it does not need to be an arm's-length transaction.) In addition, the interest charge:

1. Cannot exceed the amount of interest earned on debt securities unless they are convertible

2. Is disallowed as a deduction if it exceeds the grossed-up amount of preferred dividends

3. Is for the most part deductible if it is for the purchase of common shares

Table 2A-2 breaks down the various marginal provincial and territorial tax rates on ordinary income (i.e., interest income), dividends, and capital gains for a taxable income of $75,000 as of 2008.

Table 2A-2

Personal Tax Calculator

Province/ Territory	Tax Payable	After-Tax Income	Average Tax Rate	Marginal Tax Rate	Marginal Rate on Capital Gains	Marginal Rate on Eligible Dividends*	Marginal Rate on Ineligible Dividends
B.C.	$17,077	$57,923	22.77%	32.50%	16.25%	4.40%	17.58%
Alberta	$18,291	$56,709	24.39%	32.00%	16.00%	5.85%	17.71%
Sask.	$20,391	$54,609	27.19%	35.00%	17.50%	7.30%	19.58%
Manitoba	$20,948	$54,052	27.93%	39.40%	19.70%	13.68%	28.65%
Ontario	$17,923	$57,077	23.90%	39.41%	19.71%	13.81%	22.59%
Quebec	$21,818	$53,182	29.09%	38.37%	19.19%	15.42%	24.05%
N.B.	$21,370	$53,630	28.49%	38.80%	19.40%	11.36%	25.21%
N.S.	$21,590	$53,410	28.79%	38.67%	19.34%	15.74%	22.04%
P.E.I.	$21,043	$53,957	28.06%	38.70%	19.35%	13.39%	23.58%
Nfld.	$20,615	$54,385	27.49%	38.00%	19.00%	17.96%	24.58%
N.W.T.	$17,266	$57,734	23.02%	34.20%	17.10%	5.42%	18.58%
Yukon	$17,992	$57,008	23.99%	31.68%	15.84%	4.40%	17.37%
Nunavut	$16,067	$58,933	21.42%	29.00%	14.50%	5.50%	14.58%

Source: Ernst & Young, www.ey.com/GLOBAL/content.nsf/Canada/Tax_-_Calculators_-_2008_Personal_Tax, June 19, 2008.

Derivative Securities

When convertible features are exercised, it is not deemed to be a disposition of property, so no capital gain or loss is recorded. Instead, the adjusted cost base of the new shares will be that of the original securities. For example, if 100 preferred shares are purchased for a total cost of $5,000 and each share is convertible into 10 common shares, the adjusted cost base of one common share (after conversion), will be $5,000/100/10 or $50/10 = $5 per share.

Warrants and rights may be acquired through direct purchase, by owning shares, or by purchasing units with rights or warrants attached. When they are purchased they are treated the same as convertibles; however, if they are the result of owning underlying shares, the adjusted cost base of the original shares is altered. When warrants or rights are not exercised, a capital gain or loss may result, unless they were acquired at zero cost.

There are two basic types of options—calls and puts. At the time of the sale of either option, the seller receives consideration for the option and has disposed of a right. This sale of a right generates a capital gain calculated as the cost of the option, which is nil or zero subtracted from the consideration received. As with all capital gains, only one-half of it is included in income. The buyer or purchaser of either option has acquired a right with a cost equal to the amount of consideration paid.

There are no further tax consequences to the buyer until the option is either exercised or allowed to expire.

If either option expires, then the buyer has disposed of it for no consideration. Since the disposition has occurred, the selling price is zero and the buyer has a capital loss equal to the amount paid to acquire the option subtracted from the selling price, which is zero.

If a call option is exercised, then the price paid to acquire the option is added to the price paid to acquire the underlying asset. The option holder now owns the underlying asset with a cost calculated as the price paid for the underlying asset plus the price paid for the option to acquire the asset. The seller of the underlying asset through the call option contract (the call seller) must add the price received for the option to the selling price of the asset that was sold. This increased selling price becomes the proceeds of disposition of the asset and a capital gain (or loss) is calculated by subtracting the original cost of the asset from these increased proceeds of disposition. When the original option was sold, the seller included a capital gain in their income as described by the above paragraph. This seller must now file an amended tax return if the option was sold in a year previous to the year the actual underlying asset was sold.

If a put option is exercised, the tax consequences are similar to the above. The purchaser of the asset (the put seller) has received consideration for the put option. Therefore the purchaser of the underlying asset deducts the amount received for the option and the cost of the underlying asset is calculated as the actual consideration paid to acquire the asset minus the amount received for the option to sell. Since the buyer of the asset through the put option (the put seller) has already reported a capital gain on the sale of the put option, an amended tax return must be filed to remove this income from the previous year. The seller of the underlying asset (the put buyer) has paid an amount for the put option and has received consideration for the actual sale of the asset. The selling price of the asset is reduced by the amount paid for the option. The seller calculates a capital gain (or loss) equal to the selling price of the asset minus the amount paid for the option minus the purchase price of the asset through exercise of the put option.

Profits or losses on hedging futures contracts, which is normally part of risk management for businesses, are considered normal business income or loss and are included, or deductible, in the annual financial statements.

For the general investor, speculating in futures contracts can generate either capital gains or losses or normal income. The choice of which approach to take is left open to the speculator. The only requirement is that once a choice has been made, that selection must be adhered to in the future. One of the main considerations in this selection is that if the investor is using borrowed funds for the purpose of speculating in futures contracts, the interest on the borrowed funds is deductible against the income that is being generated. Therefore, the normal investor must select income treatment for speculation purposes. If capital gains treatment was selected, and the investor was using borrowed funds, the interest on these funds is not deductible.

CHAPTER 3

INVESTMENT FUNDS

Chapter 2 was primarily concerned with direct investing, meaning investors make decisions to buy various securities, typically in a brokerage account, and eventually sell them. The investor makes the decisions and controls the actions involving the investments. Chapter 3, in contrast, discusses the very important alternative of indirect investing used by many investors—buying and selling mutual funds, closed-end funds, unit investment trusts, and exchange-traded funds.

All four types of funds are analyzed in this chapter, with primary emphasis on mutual funds and on the increasingly popular exchange-traded funds. The key point about indirect investing is that the investor turns his or her money over to one of these types of funds, thereby relinquishing direct control of the securities in the portfolio. In contrast, an investor with a portfolio of 10 stocks in his or her brokerage account can decide exactly how long to hold each one before selling, when to realize capital losses for tax purposes, or what to do with any dividends generated by the portfolio, as examples.

Learning Objectives

After reading this chapter, you should be able to

1. Distinguish between direct and indirect investing.
2. Define open-end and closed-end investment funds.
3. State the major types of mutual funds and give their features.
4. Explain the transactions behind indirect investments.
5. Define exchange-traded funds (ETFs).
6. Understand how the performance of investment funds is measured.
7. Discuss the opportunities for investing indirectly internationally.

CHAPTER PREVIEW

Investors may choose to invest either directly or indirectly in the instruments that we described in Chapter 2. In this chapter, we focus on investing indirectly through investment funds, chiefly through the buying and selling of mutual funds. You will learn about the two major types of investment funds (open-end and closed-end), the transactions behind them, and how we measure the performance of these funds. Finally, we turn to opportunities for investing indirectly internationally and discuss hedge funds.

INVESTING INDIRECTLY

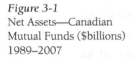
Distinguish between direct and indirect investing.

Basically, households have three choices with regard to savings:

1. Hold the liabilities of traditional intermediaries, such as banks, trust companies, and insurance companies. These include savings accounts, GICs, and so forth.

2. Hold securities directly by purchasing stocks and bonds through brokers and other intermediaries.

3. Hold securities indirectly through investment companies and pension funds.

There has been a pronounced shift toward indirect investing in North America in recent years. Individuals have increasingly turned away from the direct holding of securities and the liabilities of traditional intermediaries and toward indirect holdings of assets through pension funds and mutual funds.

A substantial proportion of Canadian families own investment funds of some type. Mutual fund assets reached an all-time high of $697.3 billion by the end of 2007. In fact, mutual fund assets in Canada have increased approximately 30 times over the 19-year period ending December 31, 2007—from $23.5 billion in 1989. In the United States, mutual funds grew tenfold during the 1980s to $1 trillion, and by 2005 the amount approximated $8.9 trillion. The dramatic growth in mutual fund assets in Canada is clearly demonstrated in Figure 3-1. This may well be the most important trend in recent years affecting the average household with regard to its investing activities and programs.

Figure 3-1
Net Assets—Canadian Mutual Funds ($billions) 1989–2007

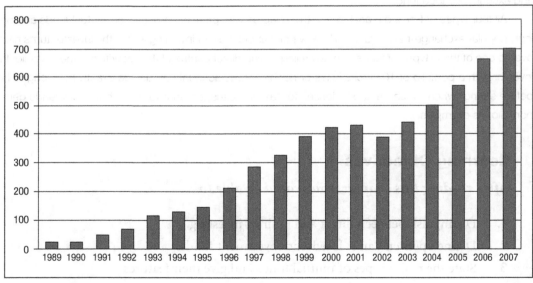

Source: The Investment Funds Institute of Canada (IFIC)

The rising ownership of pension fund assets and mutual fund shares, an alternative to the direct investing methods discussed in Chapter 2, is very important to every investor in accomplishing his or her investing goals. Investors now rely heavily on indirect investing. A significant contributor to the growth in investment fund assets in Canada has been the steady increase in contributions to

Registered Retirement Savings Plans (RRSPs) by Canadian investors throughout the 1990s and through the early 2000s. The nature of RRSPs is discussed in detail in the following Investing Tip.

In 1997, Canadians contributed $27.4 billion to RRSPs, representing a 71 percent increase over 1991. However, by 2004, RRSP contributions were only $25.2 billion, with the average contribution being $6,402 per person. In fact, despite a record 6.2 million contributors during 2007, they only used about 7 percent of their total contribution room, as discussed in Real-World Returns 3-1.

INVESTING *tip*

Registered Retirement Savings Plans (RRSPs)

Registered Retirement Savings Plans (RRSPs) are important tax deferral investment alternatives that allow Canadian taxpayers to make annual tax-deductible contributions up to predetermined limits. The income earned on the plan is tax-free as long as it remains in the plan, and provided the plans are registered with Canada Revenue Agency.

Most individuals contribute to their RRSPs by purchasing one or more pooled or mutual funds that are managed by fund managers. However, some investors choose to contribute through self-directed RRSPs. Under these arrangements, the investor funds or contributes certain acceptable securities into a registered plan that is administered for a fee; however, the investment transactions are directed by the investor.

RRSPs are trust accounts for the investor's benefit upon retirement and access to funds cannot be gained immediately without paying a withholding tax. In addition, RRSPs cannot be used as collateral for loan purposes. RRSP contributions must be made within 60 days of year end. Contributions are limited to the lesser of 18 percent of the previous year's earnings or the dollar limit (presently $20,000, and scheduled to increase to $21,000 in 2009 and to $22,000 in 2010) less the previous year's Pension Adjustment and Past Service Pension Adjustment plus the unused RRSP deduction room.

A penalty tax of 1 percent per month is levied on "overcontributions" of $2,000 or more. When a planholder contributes securities already owned to an RRSP (referred to as a "contribution in kind"), the taxpayer pays taxes on any capital gains but is unable to claim any capital losses that result.

A married taxpayer may contribute to an RRSP with the spouse named as the beneficiary, to the extent it does not use the maximum contribution to the contributor's plan. The contribution does not affect the contribution limits of the spouse. For example, if a wife contributes $9,000 of her $12,000 available contribution room to her own plan, she may also contribute $3,000 to her husband's plan without affecting his contribution limits. The proceeds from de-registering a spousal plan are taxable income for the spouse (not the contributor), except for contributions made in the year of de-registration and the two calendar years before the plan is de-registered.

An RRSP holder may de-register the plan at any time, but mandatory de-registration is required at the age of 71 (which was increased from 69 in 2007). There are several available options for de-registering RRSPs upon retirement. The least desirable from a tax perspective is to withdraw the full lump sum amount, which is then fully taxable. To spread out the taxes paid on withdrawn funds, the proceeds from the plan may be used to purchase a life annuity with a guaranteed term or a fixed term annuity that provides annual benefits to age 90. Similarly, the funds may be used to purchase a Registered Retirement Income Fund (RRIF) that provides annual income to age 90 or life.

Subsequent to retirement, if a plan owner dies, remaining benefits on an annuity or RRIF can be transferred to a spouse or child, or else the value is included in the deceased's income in the year of death and is fully taxable. RRIF holders must withdraw and pay income tax on a set fraction of the total assets in the fund (the annual minimum amount). The annual fraction is determined by a formula designed to provide benefits for a desired term; however, the payout may be accelerated if the owner elects. A taxpayer may own more than one RRIF and these may be self-directed if desired.

There are several advantages associated with RRSPs, some of which are discussed in Real-World Returns 3-1. First, they allow taxpayers to reduce taxable income during high taxation years. Second, they allow investors to shelter certain types of income from taxation by transferring them into an RRSP. Third, RRSPs are tax-efficient mechanisms for accumulation of retirement funds, with the funds earning income on a tax-free basis, thus allowing deferment of some taxes. Finally, RRSPs provide investors with an opportunity to split retirement income (through spousal RRSPs), which may result in lower total tax payments.

REAL-WORLD RETURNS 3-1

RRSP Contribution Tips for Your Clients

For some clients, contributing to their RRSP is harder to do than visiting the dentist. Last year Canadians used just 7 percent of the total room available to eligible tax filers, despite a record 6.2 million Canucks contributing.

Why aren't people saving more? Because Canadians like their stuff. "It doesn't come as second nature to go put money in an RRSP when you can buy something with those funds," says Gena Katz, executive director at Ernst & Young. "But it makes good sense. The earlier your clients start, the better off they are. It's something advisors should always encourage clients to do."

To help advisors convince their clients that making an RRSP contribution is beneficial, the company put out its list of "Eight Tips to Tackle RRSP Crunch Time."

One of the suggestions on the list deals with a problem that's likely common to many of your clients: they don't have enough cash to contribute this year.

Katz says borrowing money to put into an RRSP is a good option for those Canadians lacking funds. "The borrowing often comes up because people go on their merry way all year and don't put money in an RRSP."

However, she adds that using borrowed money is not for everyone. The benefits depend on a number of things, including age. If a client is 60, contributing with loaned money doesn't make much sense, as the investment will not likely grow significantly before he or she retires. It's a different story for someone who's 30 and will see his or her investment grow substantially over 40 years.

Borrowing also makes sense if the client can pay off the loan in a reasonable amount of time. "If the funds are going to be there for quite a number of years, and the client can repay the loan in a reasonable amount of time, like one to four years, then borrowing does make sense," Katz says.

Clients can also make contributions with non-registered investments, but there will be an accrued gain if that contribution is in the form of stocks. "The client will be paying tax up front right now, and later on they'll be taxed on the full amount coming out," says Katz.

But with equity markets in turmoil, dumping your lower-priced stocks into an RRSP might be a wise move, as your gains could be less than they would be in an up market.

Another tip that Ernst & Young offers is contributing to a spousal RRSP. Katz says a lot of people think pension splitting, which was introduced in 2007, replaces spousal RRSPs, but that is not the case.

"Spousal RRSPs still make sense because there's no limitation," she says. "Income splitting is only half of eligible pension income. For spousal RRSPs, individuals can potentially put all contributions in the plan and they can get more income in their spouse's hand. And they're not limited by eligible pension income."

Ernst & Young lists several other ways to maximize your clients' RRSP contributions, like suggesting they pay the $2,000 penalty-free excess contribution so they can contribute less down the road or, if they're making a large "catch-up" contribution, spread the deduction over a couple of years to increase the related tax benefit.

But more important than any of these strategies is to make sure your client contributes sooner rather than later.

"The final suggestion is 'now that you know that your RRSPs are so wonderful, instead of just doing 2007 now, how about contributing for 2008 too?'" says Katz.

Source: Borzykowski, Bryan, Advisor.ca. Retrieved from www.advisor.ca, January 29, 2008.

INVESTING INDIRECTLY THROUGH INVESTMENT FUNDS

An investment fund such as a mutual fund is a clear alternative for an investor seeking to own stocks and bonds. Rather than purchase securities and manage a portfolio, investors can, in effect, indirectly invest by putting their money into an investment fund, and allowing their investment advisor to do all the work and make all the decisions (for a fee, of course). Investment funds are ideal for investors

- with small capital bases who cannot properly diversify on their own

- who do not have adequate time to manage their own investments

- who do not wish to manage their own portfolio

Indirect investing in this discussion refers to the buying and selling of the units of investment funds that consist of portfolios of securities. Investors who purchase units of a particular fund managed by an investment company are buying an ownership interest in the fund portfolio and are entitled to a portion of the dividends, interest, and capital gains generated. Shareholders must also pay a share of the fund expenses and its management fee, which will be deducted from the portfolio's earnings as it flows back to the shareholders.

The contrast between direct and indirect investing is illustrated in Figure 3-2, which shows that indirect investing essentially accomplishes the same thing as direct investing. The difference is that the investment companies that manage and sell the fund units stand between investors and the portfolio of securities. Although technical qualifications exist, the point about indirect investing is that investors gain and lose through the investment fund's activities in the same manner that they would gain and lose from holding a portfolio directly. The differences are the costs (any sales charges plus the management fee) and the additional services gained from the investment fund, such as record-keeping and cheque-writing privileges.

The choice between direct or indirect investing is very important to all investors. Since each has advantages and disadvantages, the choice may not be straightforward. Investors can be classified as active (those who are interested in participating in managing their portfolios), or passive (those who do not get involved in managing their portfolios). Moreover, it is possible to have both classes of investors invest directly or indirectly.

The line between direct and indirect investing is becoming blurred. For example, investors can invest in investment funds directly through their brokerage accounts, generally at no additional expense. In addition, brokerage firms offer alternatives to mutual funds in several forms, which will be discussed in Chapter 5.

Figure 3-2
Direct Versus Indirect
Investing

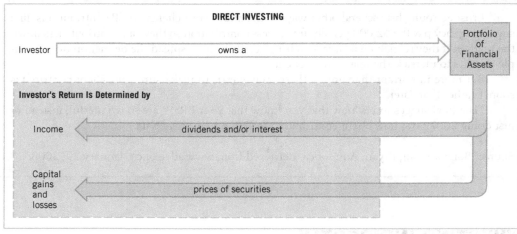

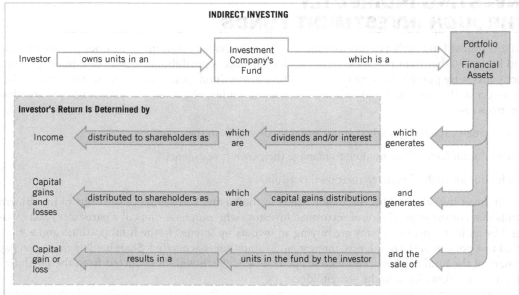

CHECK YOUR UNDERSTANDING

3-1. What trend is felt to be a significant factor in the growth of investment fund assets in Canada?

3-2. Why do many investors choose the indirect investing route when there are significant costs (fees to an advisor or investment company) to doing so?

3-3. Although there is not always a clear distinction, who would you expect to be more likely to invest indirectly through an investment company: active or passive investors?

Investment Fund

A financial company or trust fund that sells shares in itself or units of the trust fund to the public and uses the funds to invest in a portfolio of securities such as money market instruments, stocks, and bonds.

WHAT IS AN INVESTMENT FUND?

An **investment fund** sells shares or units in a trust fund to the public and invests these funds in a portfolio of securities such as money market instruments, stocks, and bonds. By pooling the funds of thousands of investors, a widely diversified portfolio of financial assets can be purchased. Investment companies usually manage several funds simultaneously and offer their customers a variety of services.

EXAMPLE 3-1: RBC ASSET MANAGEMENT INC.

RBC Asset Management Inc. had the largest dollar amount of mutual fund assets under its management in Canada in September 2008 at $101.8 billion. Real-World Returns 3-2 includes excerpts from its June 27, 2008 "Simplified Prospectus" for RBC Funds, which refers to the basic characteristics of mutual funds and the general risks associated with investing in mutual funds.

REAL-WORLD RETURNS 3-2

What Is a Mutual Fund and What Are the Risks of Investing in a Mutual Fund?

A mutual fund is a pool of investments made on behalf of people with a similar investment objective. When you invest in a mutual fund, your money is working together with that of many other investors. A professional investment manager invests this money on behalf of the whole group.

Investors share a mutual fund's income, expenses, gains and losses in proportion to their interest in the mutual fund. Mutual funds can give individuals the advantages of a simpler, more accessible, less expensive and less time-consuming method of investing in a portfolio of securities.

Mutual funds own different kinds of investments, depending on their objectives. These include equities like stocks, fixed income securities like bonds and cash or cash equivalents like treasury bills. The value of these investments will change from day to day, reflecting changes in interest rates, economic conditions, financial markets and company news.

When you invest in a mutual fund trust, you are buying a portion of the fund called a unit. Mutual funds keep track of all the individual investments by recording how many units each investor owns. The more money you put into a mutual fund, the more units you get. The price of a unit changes every day, depending on how the investments are performing. When the investments rise in value, the price of a unit goes up. When the investments drop in value, the price of the unit goes down.

Some mutual funds offer units in more than one series. A multi-series structure recognizes that different investors may seek the same investment objective, yet require different investment advice and/or service. Each series represents an investment in the same investment portfolio of each fund. However, each series may charge a different management fee and and incur its own specific expenses. As a result, a separate net asset value per unit is calculated for each series on a daily basis.

Your investment in any mutual fund is not guaranteed. Unlike bank accounts or guaranteed investment certificates (GICs), mutual fund units are not covered by the Canada Deposit Insurance Corporation or any other government deposit insurer.

Under exceptional circumstances, you may not be able to redeem your units.

Risk and Return

As an investor, there is always a risk you could lose money. Mutual funds are no exception, but the degree of risk varies considerably from one mutual fund to the next. As a general rule, investments with the greatest risk also have the greatest potential return. The key is to recognize the risk involved with your investment, understand it, and decide whether it is a risk you are comfortable accepting.

Although the value of your investments may drop in the short term, a longer investment horizon will help to lessen the effects of short-term market volatility. A shorter investment horizon may result in you having to sell your investments in adverse conditions. Ideally, investors in equity funds have a five- to 10-year investment horizon, which generally provides enough time for their investments to overcome any short-term volatility and grow.

(continued)

REAL-WORLD RETURNS 3-2 *continued*

The following chart shows the relationship between risk and potential return. As you can see, money market funds are the least volatile and generally have the lowest returns. At the other end of the scale, equity funds are usually the most risky, but also tend to have the highest potential return.

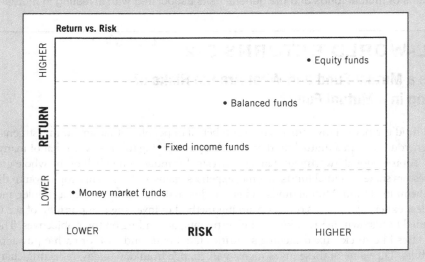

Source: RBC Asset Management Inc., 2008 Simplified Prospectus (June 27, 2008), pp. 3-4.

An investment fund acts as a conduit, flowing dividends, interest, and realized capital gains through to its unitholders, who pay taxes on this income at their own marginal tax rates. In effect, fund owners are treated as if they held the securities in the fund's portfolio. During the year, funds make capital gains and losses when they sell securities. These gains are taxable in the hands of the investor. Therefore, investors should determine if a capital gains distribution is pending before purchasing a fund, since this will result in a decline in the fund's value corresponding to the amount of the tax liability incurred.

In addition to taxes on income earned by the investment fund, when a fund owner redeems the shares or units in a fund, the transaction is considered a disposition for tax purposes and is subject to capital gains or losses. A complication arises due to the reinvestment of interest and dividends, which implies that investors (or their investment advisors) must keep track of the actual purchase prices of all units in a fund.

Most Canadian investment funds fall under the jurisdiction of the securities acts of the provinces in which they operate. While management of mutual funds is regulated by the securities commissions, distribution of funds is regulated by the Mutual Fund Dealers Association (MFDA), which is the mutual fund industry's self-regulatory organization (SRO). Since most funds continually issue new shares, they are in a continuous state of primary distribution, and must annually file a prospectus or simplified prospectus. Usually, funds file simplified prospectuses similar to the one provided by RBC Asset Management Inc. referred to in Real-World Returns 3-2. The prospectus must contain all material information and must be amended when material changes occur. Fund buyers must receive copies of this document no later than two business days after an agreement of purchase has been made.

Investment fund managers, distributors, and their sales personnel must be registered with the securities commissions in which they do business, and must adhere to industry code of practice guidelines. Salespeople must have successfully completed the CSC or the education program offered by the Investment Funds Institute of Canada (IFIC).

TYPES OF INVESTMENT FUNDS

All investment funds begin by selling shares or units in the associated trust fund to the public. Most are managed by investment companies that offer professional supervision of the portfolio as one of the benefits.

Unit Investment Trusts

An alternative form of investment company that deviates from the normal managed type is the **unit investment trust**, which typically is an unmanaged, fixed-income security portfolio put together by a sponsor and handled by an independent trustee. Redeemable trust certificates representing claims against the assets of the trust are sold to investors at net asset value plus a small commission. All interest (or dividends) and principal repayments are distributed to the holders of the certificates. Most unit investment trusts hold tax-exempt securities. The assets are almost always kept unchanged and the trust ceases to exist when the bonds mature, although it is possible to redeem units of the trust.

In general, unit investment trusts are passive investments. They are designed to be bought and held, with capital preservation as a major objective. They enable investors to gain diversification, provide professional management that takes care of all the details, permit the purchase of securities by the trust at a cheaper price than if purchased individually, and ensure minimum operating costs. If conditions change, however, investors lose the ability to make rapid, inexpensive, or costless changes in their positions. Assets of unit investment trusts currently represent a very small part of total investment company assets.

Closed-End Investment Funds

A **closed-end investment fund** usually sells no additional shares after the initial public offering (IPO). Therefore, the fund capitalization is fixed unless a new public offering is made. The shares of a closed-end fund trade in the secondary markets—that is, on the exchanges—exactly like any other stock. To buy and sell, investors use their brokers, paying the current price at which the shares are selling plus brokerage commissions, or receiving that price less the commissions.

Because shares of closed-end funds trade on stock exchanges, their prices are determined by the forces of supply and demand. Interestingly, however, the market price is seldom equal to the actual per-share value of the closed-end shares. We examine the issue of closed-end discounts and premiums later in the chapter.

Closed-end funds have been around for a long time; in fact, they were a popular investment before the great crash of 1929. After that, they lost favour and were relatively unimportant until they started to attract significant investor interest again following the crash of 1987. By 2005, for example, the amount of fund assets in closed-end funds in the United States had grown to approximately $275 billion. There were approximately 240 closed-end funds in Canada by March of 2008.

Open-End Investment Funds (Mutual Funds)

Open-end investment funds (or **mutual funds**) account for a large majority of aggregate funds invested in Canada. As stated earlier, the growth in mutual funds and their assets has been one of the important developments in recent years. The number of mutual funds has grown rapidly as well. At the beginning of 1988, there were 294 Canadian mutual funds, with assets totalling $20.4 billion, and by the end of 2007 there were 2,038 funds, with total assets of $697.3 billion. Growth in the United States was even more spectacular, where the number of mutual funds increased from 564 in 1980 to more than 7,000, with total assets exceeding $8.9 trillion by 2005.

As mentioned, mutual funds are formed either by creating a mutual fund company and selling shares in it, or by creating a mutual fund trust and selling "units" in the mutual fund trust. Mutual funds continue to sell their treasury shares or units to investors after the initial sale that starts the fund. The capitalization of an open-end investment fund is frequently changing as it continually

Unit Investment Trust
An unmanaged form of investment company, typically holding fixed-income securities, offering investors diversification and minimum operating costs.

learning objective 2
Define open-end and closed-end investment funds.

Closed-End Investment Fund
An investment fund with a fixed capitalization whose shares trade on exchanges and over-the-counter (OTC) markets.

Open-End Investment Fund
An investment fund whose capitalization constantly changes as new shares or trust units are sold and outstanding units are redeemed. Popularly known as mutual funds.

Mutual Funds
The popular name for open-end investment funds whose capitalization constantly changes as new shares are sold and outstanding shares are redeemed.

issues and redeems shares or units on demand. This right of redemption is the hallmark of open-end funds. In fact, that is what makes it open-ended, as new investors buy additional shares or units and owners cash in by selling their shares or units back to the company.

Mutual funds are purchased in two ways:

1. Directly from a fund company by mail, telephone, or at office locations;

2. Indirectly from a sales agent, including securities firms, banks, life insurance companies, and financial planners.

Mutual funds may be affiliated with an underwriter, who usually has an exclusive right to distribute shares to investors. Most underwriters distribute shares through broker/dealer firms.

Most mutual funds are corporations or trusts formed by an investment advisory firm that selects the board of trustees (directors) for the company. In turn, the trustees hire a separate management company, normally the investment advisory firm, to manage the fund. The management company is contracted by the investment company to perform necessary research and to manage the portfolio, as well as to handle the administrative chores. For that it receives a fee.

There are economies of scale in managing portfolios—expenses rise as assets under management increase, but not at the same rate as revenues. Because investment managers can oversee various amounts of money with few additional costs, management companies seek to increase the size of the fund(s) being managed. Most investment companies operate several different funds simultaneously. Investors can choose from a large number of mutual fund complexes. A fund complex is a group or family of funds managed by the same fund management company.

EXAMPLE 3-2: IGM FINANCIAL AND RBC ASSET MANAGEMENT INC.

As of October 2007, IGM Financial (**Investors Group, MacKenzie**) was the largest mutual fund company in Canada with total net assets exceeding $111.0 billion, while **RBC Asset Management Inc.**, a subsidiary of the Royal Bank of Canada, was the second largest, with assets of $81.8 billion. As of March 2008, IGM offered investors a choice of 387 funds (many through subsidiaries), while RBC offered 81. These included a variety of the categories of funds described in the subsequent sections of this chapter.

Mutual funds are the most popular form of investment funds for the average investor. One reason is the small minimum investment requirements. Most funds require a minimum initial investment of $1,000 to get started, although some larger funds only need as little as $200. In addition, most funds that are RRSP-eligible have a lower required initial investment for RRSP contributions. After the initial investment, minimum contributions are typically much lower.

EXAMPLE 3-3: RBC CANADIAN EQUITY FUND

RBC Asset Management Inc.'s **Canadian Equity Fund** requires a minimum initial investment of $1,000, but only $500 if the fund is purchased for an RRSP. Subsequent contributions must be in amounts of $25 or more (whether for an RRSP or not). Most funds will accept less than $500 if a monthly commitment is made (e.g., commit to contribute $50 per month).

Net Asset Value (NAV)
The total market value of the securities in an investment company's portfolio divided by the number of investment fund units currently outstanding.

Owners of fund units can sell them back to the company any time they choose; the mutual fund is legally obligated to redeem them. Investors purchase new units and redeem their existing ones at the **net asset value (NAV)** plus (less) commission fees. The NAV for any investment fund unit is computed by calculating the total market value of the securities in the portfolio, subtracting any accounts payable, and dividing by the number of fund shares or units currently outstanding.[1]

---

[1] Total market value of the portfolio is equal to the sum of the product of each security's current market price multiplied by the number of shares of that security owned by the fund.

EXAMPLE 3-4: RBC CANADIAN EQUITY FUND

Using the numbers from RBC Asset Management Inc.'s June 2007 semi-annual report for the RBC Canadian Equity Fund, the year-end NAV is calculated as follows (all numbers are in 000's except for the per unit NAV figures):

Total assets	$5,015,725
Total liabilities	69,770
Net assets	$4,945,955
Net Assets (series A)	$4,933,523
Units outstanding series A	169,261
NAV series A	$29.15
	(i.e., $4,933,523/169,261)

As this example shows, the net asset value is the per unit value of the portfolio of securities held by the investment fund. Over the course of the year, this will change as the value of the securities held changes and as income from the securities is received.

CHECK YOUR UNDERSTANDING

3-4. Which regulatory agency guarantees the money entrusted to investment funds?

3-5. Why do you think mutual funds are by far the most popular type of investment with investors?

3-6. Why is the number of outstanding shares (or units) of a mutual fund continually changing?

MAJOR TYPES OF MUTUAL FUNDS

learning objective 3
State the major types of mutual funds and give their features.

There are two major types of mutual funds:

1. Money market mutual funds (short-term funds)

2. Equity and bond & income funds (long-term funds)

These two types of funds parallel our discussion in Chapter 2 of money markets and capital markets. Money market funds concentrate on short-term investing by holding portfolios of money market assets, whereas equity and bond & income funds concentrate on longer term investing by holding mostly capital market assets. We will discuss each of these types of mutual funds in turn.

Money Market Funds

A major innovation in the investment company industry has been the creation, and subsequent phenomenal growth, of **money market funds (MMFs)**, which are open-end investment funds whose portfolios consist of money market instruments. Created in 1974, when interest rates were at record-high levels, MMFs grew tremendously in 1981–82 when short-term interest rates were again at record levels. Investors seeking to earn these high short-term rates found they generally could not do so directly because money market securities were only available in large denominations, and so they turned to MMFs. By October 2007, the total assets of Canadian MMFs was $50 billion, accounting for 7.0 percent of the total assets of all Canadian mutual fund assets ($710 billion at that time).

The objective of MMFs is to achieve a high level of income and liquidity through investment in short-term money market instruments such as Treasury bills, commercial paper, and short-term government bonds. These funds are attractive to investors seeking low risk and high liquidity. The average maturity of money market portfolios ranges from one to three months.

Investors in money market funds earn and are credited with interest daily. The shares can be redeemed at any time by phone or wire. Money market funds (MMFs) provide investors with a chance to

Money Market Funds (MMFs)
Open-end investment (mutual) funds that invest in short-term money market instruments such as Treasury bills, commercial paper, and short-term government bonds.

earn the going rates in the money market while enjoying broad diversification and great liquidity. The rates have varied as market conditions changed. The important point is that their yields correspond to current market conditions. Although investors may assume little risk because of the diversification and quality of these instruments, money market funds are not insured. Banks and other financial institutions have emphasized this point in competing with money market funds for the savings of investors.

Equity and Bond and Income Funds

The board of directors (or trustees) of an investment fund must specify the objective that the fund will pursue in its investment policy. The companies try to follow a consistent investment policy, according to their specified objective(s), which may have a great deal of influence on the typical investor's purchase decision.

EXAMPLE 3-5: RBC CANADIAN DIVIDEND FUND

The objective of the RBC Canadian Dividend Fund is "To achieve long-term total returns consisting of regular dividend income and modest long-term capital growth by investing primarily in common and preferred shares of major Canadian companies with above average dividend yields."

Given these objectives, it is not surprising to see the fund's holdings as of November 30, 2007, were heavily weighted in sectors that traditionally pay substantial amounts of dividends (e.g., 44 percent in financial services). At that time, the fund had 7.8 percent of its holdings in cash and 3.8 percent in bonds at that time.

EXAMPLE 3-6: RBC BALANCED FUND

The investment objective for RBC's Balanced Fund is stated below:[2]

"This "one-decision" Fund seeks potential for moderate interest income, dividends and capital appreciation. The Fund invests primarily in Canadian equities, bonds and short-term debt securities and may also invest up to 20 percent of its assets in foreign equities. The proportion of the Fund invested in each asset type is periodically changed to respond to changes in the market outlook for that asset."

The holdings of this fund as of November 30, 2007, reflected this objective of balancing growth and income. At that time, the portfolio was composed of 55.1 percent equities, 30.1 percent bonds, and 14.7 percent cash and short-term securities.

The following list identifies and describes several of the major categories of investment objectives, most of which relate to equity and bond and income funds. Investors in these funds have a wide range of investment objectives from which to choose. Traditionally, investors have favoured growth funds, which strive for capital appreciation, or balanced funds, which seek both income and capital appreciation. Today's investors can choose from global funds (either bonds or stocks), precious metal funds, mortgage funds, bond funds, and so forth.

- **Money Market Funds:** Objective is to achieve a high level of income and liquidity through investment in short-term money market instruments such as T-bills, commercial paper, and short-term government bonds. These funds will be attractive to investors seeking low risk and high liquidity.

- **Mortgage Funds:** Riskier than money market funds since terms of investments may be five years or greater, so there is more interest rate risk (although it is less than most bond funds, which have longer maturities).

---

[2]www.globefund.com, March 19, 2008.

- **Bond Funds:** Primary goals are income and safety. However, they are still subject to capital gains and losses due to inherent interest rate risk.

- **Dividend Funds:** Objective is to benefit from the tax advantage afforded by dividends. Therefore, they are not that appropriate for RRSPs or RRIFs where the credit cannot be applied. Price changes tend to be driven by changes in interest rates and general market trends.

- **Balanced Funds:** Main objective is to provide a mixture of safety, income, and capital appreciation. Usually, the prospectus stipulates minimum and maximum weighting in each asset class.

- **Asset Allocation Funds:** Similar objectives to balanced funds, but they are usually not restricted to holding specified minimum percentages in any class of investment.

- **Equity or Common Stock Funds:** Primary objective is capital gains. The bulk of assets are in common shares, although they maintain limited amounts of other assets for liquidity, income, and diversification purposes. Equity funds may vary greatly in degree of risk and growth objectives.

- **Index Funds:** Their objective is to mirror the performance of a market index such as the S&P/TSX Composite Index, or the ScotiaMcLeod Bond Index. The management fees are generally much lower than for actively managed funds. An alternative to these are exchange-traded funds (ETFs), which are discussed later in this chapter.

- **Specialty Funds:** These funds seek capital gains and are willing to forego broad diversification benefits in the hopes of achieving them. They typically concentrate on companies in one industry, one segment of the capital market, or in one geographical location.

- **International or Global Funds:** These can be considered subsets of the specialty funds, and invest in markets that offer the best prospects, regardless of location. They carry the additional risk of foreign exposure.

- **Real Estate Funds:** Invest in income-producing property in order to achieve long-term growth through capital appreciation and the reinvestment of income. The valuation of real estate funds is done infrequently (monthly or quarterly) and is based on appraisals of properties in the portfolio. They are less liquid than other funds and may require investors to give advance notice of redemption.

- **Hedge Funds:** Professionally managed portfolios that are traditionally sold to "sophisticated," wealthy investors. Minimum investments are usually between $90,000 and $150,000. Hedge fund managers often pursue strategies not available to traditional mutual fund managers, which may involve additional risks. These funds may try to hedge against a variety of factors such as market risks (domestic or foreign), foreign exchange risk, commodity price risk, or inflation. Some of the more aggressive funds may use leverage to magnify gains or losses, further contributing to their risk.

- **Ethical Funds:** These funds are guided by moral criteria that may prevent the funds from investing in companies that produce tobacco, for example.

Figure 3-3 shows that Canadian and foreign equity funds constituted close to half of the assets of Canadian mutual funds in October 2007. The nature of these equity funds can vary significantly and it is common to categorize equity funds based on investment objectives such as "growth" and "growth and income." These categorizations may change in the future as many observers believe it is more important to describe a fund's investment style and actual portfolio holdings rather than state that the fund is seeking "growth of capital," which could be accomplished in several different ways. As part of this new trend, Morningstar Inc., a well-known Chicago mutual fund research firm, uses nine categories for equity funds. These categories, such as large cap, mid cap, small cap, value, blend, and growth, are intended to describe investment styles, as shown in Figure 3-4, where Morningstar categorizes the Altamira Growth Portfolio as a Large Cap, Growth style equity fund.[3]

---

[3]"Cap" refers to capitalization, or market value for a company, calculated as the price of the stock times the total number of shares outstanding. A mutual fund that invests in stocks with large market capitalizations would be a large cap fund, while a small cap fund is one that invests in companies with small market capitalizations.

Figure 3-3
Mutual Fund Assets
(October 2007)

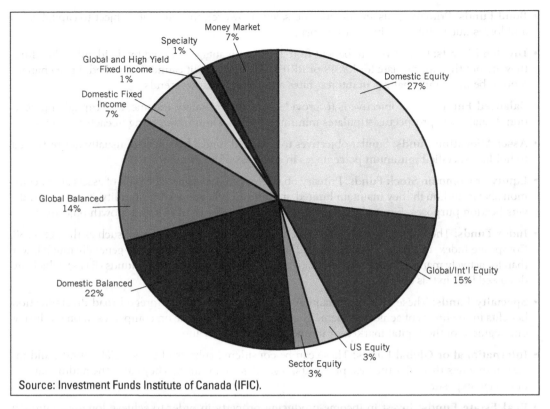

Source: Investment Funds Institute of Canada (IFIC).

Figure 3-4
Morningstar Classification
of Altamira Growth
Portfolio

	Value	Blend	Growth
Large			X
Mid			
Small			

Source: Retrieved from www.morningstar.ca, March 18, 2008.

Most stock funds can be divided into two categories based on their approach to selecting stocks—value funds and growth funds. A value fund generally looks for stocks that are cheap on the basis of standard fundamental analysis yardsticks, such as earnings, book value, and dividend yield. Growth funds, on the other hand, seek companies that are expected to show rapid future growth in earnings, even if current earnings are poor or even non-existent.

Value funds and growth funds tend to perform well at different times. Therefore, fund investors should distinguish between the two types, which is not always easy to do. A more risk-averse investor worrying about a market decline may wish to emphasize value funds, while more aggressive investors seeking good performance in an expected market rise might favour growth funds. Given the evidence on efficient markets, the best strategy could be to buy both types of funds. However, there is some evidence to suggest that value stocks outperform growth stocks over the long run. These and other issues relating to market efficiency are considered in Chapter 10.

While Figures 3-3 and 3-4 and the discussion above provide some useful guidelines for investors regarding what particular types of funds are all about, one must be wary of reading too much into the classification of a fund into a particular category. For example, it may be surprising to some readers to observe that close to 12 percent of the holdings of the RBC Canadian Dividend Fund referred to in the example above consisted of cash and short-term securities and bonds (which pay interest and not dividends). This is not uncommon among funds and it is typical to see funds composed of securities that do not appear to be obvious choices for inclusion in that portfolio based upon the fund name or objectives. This illustrates two important points regarding mutual funds and other professionally managed portfolios:

1. The name of the fund does not always provide a sufficient description of the nature of the securities that are found within the portfolio.

2. There is a great deal of variation in the composition of the portfolio holdings across funds, even when they are classified within the same fund category.

CHECK YOUR UNDERSTANDING

3-7. Why are money market funds the safest type of mutual fund an investor can hold?

3-8. Why might investors prefer a balanced fund to either a stock fund or a bond fund?

INDIRECT INVESTMENT TRANSACTIONS

learning objective 4
Explain the transactions behind indirect investments.

Investors transact indirectly via investment companies by buying, holding, and selling shares of closed-end funds, mutual funds, exchange-traded funds (ETFs), segregated funds, and Labour Sponsored Venture Capital Corporations (LSVCCs). In this section, we analyze some of the details involved in these transactions.

Closed-End Funds

Historically, the market prices of closed-end funds have varied widely from their net asset values (NAVs). A discount refers to the situation in which the closed-end fund is selling for less than its NAV. If the market price of the fund exceeds the NAV the fund is said to be selling at a premium. That is,

If NAV > market price, the fund is selling at a discount.
If NAV < market price, the fund is selling at a premium.

Although several studies have addressed the question of why these funds sell at discounts and premiums, no totally satisfactory explanation has been widely accepted by all market observers. On average, closed-end funds tend to sell at a discount from their NAV. For example, on March 18, 2008, the average discount on the 241 closed-end funds in Canada was 6.8 percent from their NAV per share, with only 24 (or 10 percent) of these funds not trading at a discount.

Some explanations that have been cited to explain discounts in various closed-end funds include illiquidity (either for the fund's holdings or in the fund's shares themselves) high expenses, poor performance, and unrealized capital gains. Another of these explanations—anti-takeover provisions— would prevent investors from taking over the fund and liquidating it in order to realize the full NAV.[4]

By purchasing a fund at a discount, an investor is actually buying shares in a portfolio of securities at a price below their market value. Therefore, even if the value of the portfolio remains unchanged, an investor can gain or lose if the discount narrows or widens over time. That is, a difference exists between the portfolio's return, based on net asset values, and the shareholder's return, based on closing prices.

While most of these funds trade at a discount, some also trade at premiums, and the amount of the discounts or premiums vary through time. For example, as of March 18, 2008, SL Split Corp shares sold at a 32 percent premium to their NAV of $45.64, while the shares in Global Diversified Inv Grade Inc Tr I traded at a 66.5 percent discount from their NAV of $7.77.

Mutual Funds

Some mutual funds use a sales force to reach investors, with shares or units available from brokers and financial planners. In an alternative form of distribution called direct marketing, the company uses advertising and direct mailing to appeal to investors.

---

[4]As for premiums such as those enjoyed by several closed-end funds that hold foreign securities, it is hard to short these funds because of the difficulty in borrowing the shares to do so. Thus, they end up selling at premiums.

INVESTING *tip*

Initial public offerings (IPOs) of closed-end funds typically involve brokerage commissions of 6 or 7 percent. Brokers often support the price in the after-market temporarily, but then the price drops to NAV or below. Many small investors would do well not to purchase the IPOs of closed-end funds.

Most mutual funds permit purchase of fractional shares or units. Purchase methods include lump sum cash purchases, accumulation purchase plans, and buying by reinvesting dividends. Lump sum purchases generally involve initial and subsequent minimum purchase amounts as discussed previously. Accumulation purchase plans may be voluntary or contractual arrangements, although the latter have declined in popularity due to their restrictive nature. In addition, many funds automatically reinvest dividends and interest to acquire new shares or units, unless instructed otherwise.

Mutual funds can be subdivided into load funds (those that charge a sales fee) and no-load funds (those that do not). Load funds charge investors a sales fee for the costs involved in selling the fund. Investors either pay the fee initially when the fund units are purchased (front-end sales charges), or in the future when the shares are redeemed by the investors (back-end or redemption charges). When an investor purchases units in a fund that charges an upfront sales charge, the offering or purchase price relates the sales charge to the net asset value (NAV) in the following manner:

Offering or purchase price = (NAV) ÷ (100 percent less the sales charge)

EXAMPLE 3-7: CALCULATING OFFERING PRICE

For example, the offering price for a fund that has a NAV of $10 and a 5 percent upfront sales charge is

Offering price = $10 ÷ (1.0 − 0.05) = $10.53

Notice that $0.53 is 5.3 percent of the NAV (or net amount invested). Regulators require that firms report sales charges in prospectuses as both the percentage of amount paid by investor (i.e., 5 percent), and the percentage of net amount invested (i.e., 5.3 percent).

The load or sales charge goes to the marketing organization selling the shares, which could be the investment company itself or brokers. The fee is split between the salesperson and the company employing that person. The load fee percentage usually declines with the size of the purchase. The old adage in the investment company business is that "mutual fund shares are sold, not bought," meaning that the sales force aggressively sells the shares to investors. The current norm for front-end loads is 5 percent of the offering price or less, as a result of increased competitiveness.

Figure 3-4 shows that 71 percent of Canadian mutual funds charged loads in 2008, with 8 percent having front-end sales charges, 19 percent back-end (redemption) charges, and 44 percent giving the investor the option of front- or back-end loads. The other 29 percent of funds were no-loads, which did not charge direct selling charges. However, no-load funds typically levy modest administration fees and charge other management fees that may add up. Investors should read the prospectus carefully to determine the net cost of these services. In addition, some funds are subject to an early redemption fee (often 2 percent) if the funds are redeemed within 90 days of purchase. Finally, some funds charge a distribution charge to pay commissioned salespeople, while trailer fees (or service fees) are those paid by a manager to the selling organization.

The level of management fees paid to compensate mutual fund managers in Canada varies widely depending on the fund, from 1 percent for some money market and index funds to 3 percent for some equity funds. It is normally expressed as a percentage of fund assets. Other fund expenses such as brokerage fees, audit, legal, safekeeping and custodial, and informational fees are also included in the management expense ratio (MER) calculation. These expenses decrease the returns to fund holders, and both management fees and expense ratios for the past five years must be included in the fund prospectus. Generally, sales charges are higher for mutual funds than for a bond or stock, but they offer much more in the package.

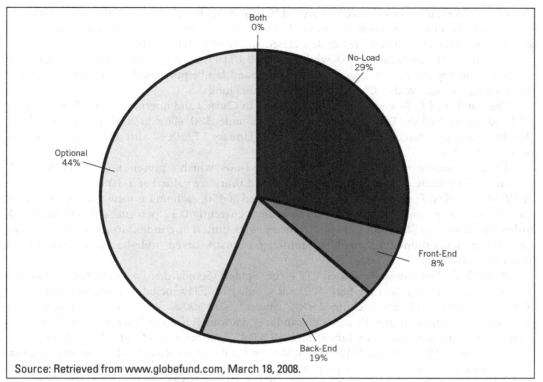

Figure 3-4
Load Versus No-Load
Funds (March 18, 2008)

Source: Retrieved from www.globefund.com, March 18, 2008.

Mutual funds redeem their shares or units on written request at a price that is either equal or close to the fund's net asset value per share (NAVPS). All funds must compute the NAVPS at least once a month (once a week for equity funds and once a year for real estate funds), and most of the larger ones do so on a daily basis (quarterly for real estate funds). Payment must be made for redeemed shares within five business days from the determination of NAVPS, although most funds reserve the right to suspend redemptions under certain highly unusual or emergency conditions—for example, if trading is suspended on securities comprising more than 50 percent of portfolio value.

There is normally no charge to redeem funds unless they are back-end loads, in which case the charge is usually a stated percentage of market value at the time of redemption (although some funds charge a percentage of the original amount invested). Systematic withdrawal plans may be arranged to meet investors' cash flow requirements. There are four general types of withdrawal plans:

1. Ratio withdrawal plan—a specified percentage of fund shares are redeemed at fixed intervals (amounts will vary according to prevailing market values).

2. Fixed dollar withdrawal plan—a specified dollar amount is withdrawn at regular intervals.

3. Fixed period withdrawal plan—a specified amount is withdrawn over a predetermined period of time with the intent that all capital will be exhausted when the plan ends.

4. Life expectancy adjusted withdrawal plan—a variation of number 3 designed to provide as high an income as possible during the holder's expected life; the amounts withdrawn vary in relation to the amount of capital remaining in the plan and the plan holder's revised life expectancy.

Exchange-Traded Funds (ETFs)

A new investing trend of increasing importance is the emergence of **exchange-traded funds (ETFs)**. An ETF is an index fund holding a diversified portfolio of securities, priced and traded on public exchanges. Most ETFs are passively managed funds owning a basket of stocks (or bonds) designed to mimic the performance of a market index such as the S&P/TSX 60 Index, the S&P 500, or the DJIA.

learning objective 5
Define exchange-traded funds (ETFs).

Exchange-Traded Funds (ETFs)
An index fund holding a diversified portfolio of securities, priced and traded on public exchanges.

However, unlike mutual funds, investors are not buying shares from an investment company directly, but rather from another investor. Therefore, ETFs involve regular brokerage transactions and brokerage fees. This makes the ETF resemble a closed-end fund in many respects.

Canadian ETFs trade on the TSX while US-based ETFs trade on US exchanges. Most ETFs are priced continually during the day, can be sold short, and can be purchased on margin (margin and short selling are explained in Chapter 5), unlike mutual funds.

The number of ETFs continues to grow rapidly in Canada and internationally. There was over US $450 billion in Global ETF assets in 2005, up from under $80 billion in 2000. In Canada, IShares (Barclays Canada) offered 24 ETFs in Canada as of January 17, 2008, with total NAV of approximately $15 billion.[5]

The most widely traded Canadian ETFs are the **I-60s**, which represent units in the S&P/TSX 60 Index. They trade on the TSX (ticker: XIU) and units are valued at 1/10th the value of the S&P/TSX 60 Index. For example, if the index is valued at 450, each unit is valued at approximately $45. Dividends are paid every quarter. The MER is currently 0.17 percent. The **TD S&P/TSX Index Fund** has the S&P/TSX Composite Index as its underlying index. In addition, there is a large and growing number of small-cap, mid-cap, industry-based, style-based, and bond ETFs available on the TSX.

Probably the best-known US-based ETF is the "Spider" (Standard & Poor's Depositary Receipt), introduced in 1993 to reflect the S&P 500 Index. Other US ETFs include "Diamonds" (the DJIA), "Cubes" (Nasdaq-100 Index Tracking Stock), "iShares" (S&P 500 as well as other S&P indexes for small-cap, mid-cap, and growth and value indexes, various Russell indexes, various Dow Jones Sector funds, and various country funds), and "HOLDRS" (various sector funds). Most of the global-focused iShares MSCI (formerly WEBS) track Morgan Stanley International indexes of various countries, providing investors with an opportunity to hold well-diversified country portfolios.

What happens when an investor wishes to sell his or her ETF? The shares are simply sold to another investor, thereby having no direct effect on the fund. As a result, it is important to ensure there is adequate liquidity in the form of trading volume (at least a few thousand shares traded daily). This is a direct result of the unique feature of ETFs involving discounts. Recall that many closed-end funds sell at discounts, meaning the price of the shares is less than the NAV of the fund. ETFs, in turn, have devised an unusual process to ensure that the shares always sell for the approximate value of the portfolio holdings. This is accomplished by granting special trading rights to institutional investors interacting with the ETF company. ETF companies include the Bank of New York, Barclays Global Investors, State Street, and Vanguard. If the ETF share price is less than the actual value of the underlying assets, an institutional investor can buy the ETF shares and turn them in to the sponsoring company for an equivalent amount of the underlying stocks, which the institution then sells for an immediate profit. If the ETF share price is greater than the underlying assets, the process is reversed. This unique process essentially ensures that the price of the ETF shares will approximate very closely the value of the underlying assets.

The "in-kind" feature described earlier, involving special trading rights for institutions, also leads to some tax efficiency. The ETF manager does not have to sell shares to pay for redemptions; therefore, redemptions do not create capital gains that must be distributed to the shareholders. Redemptions do not involve the fund at all, but rather one investor selling to another. Therefore, even though both index funds offered by an investment company and ETFs avoid capital gains as a result of no active trading, the ETF also avoids redemptions and the capital gains that could result from this activity. Note, however, that ETFs may still distribute capital gains as well as income as a part of holding a particular set of stocks.

We know that index funds have much lower operating expenses than do actively managed funds because they are passively managed. ETFs have even lower expenses. Although the average domestic stock index fund charges about 0.50 percent a year, the average ETF charges about 0.34 percent, and some (such as the I-60s) charge even less. This is because even though the investment company is responsible for the index fund and for sending investors statements, a brokerage firm does that in the

---

[5]www.ishares.ca.

case of ETFs, leaving the fund itself with very low expenses. ETFs are not for all investors. Regular purchases will incur ongoing brokerage fees, while trading ETFs on a short-term basis leads to taxable capital gains.

Distinguishing Among ETFs, Closed-End Funds, and Mutual Funds

Due to the rise of ETFs, it is sometimes difficult to distinguish them from the typical investment company products such as closed-end funds and mutual funds. It is worthwhile to remember the following:

1. Both closed-end funds and ETFs trade all day on exchanges, can be bought on margin, and can be shorted. Mutual funds, on the other hand, are bought and sold at the end of the trading day when the NAV is calculated. Thus, an investor urgently wanting to buy or sell such assets during the day would be out of luck with the typical mutual fund.

2. Closed-end funds and most mutual funds (exceptions are index funds) are actively managed, for better or for worse. ETFs, in contrast, are currently passive in nature, following an index.

3. Mutual funds trade at NAV (although buyers of load funds pay a sales charge).Closed-end funds typically trade at discounts and premiums, with discounts predominating in many years. ETFs can trade at discounts or premiums, but their mechanics are such that they are very likely to trade close to their NAV.

4. ETFs offer an important advantage over funds with regard to flexibility on taxes. Mutual fund managers may have to sell shares to pay those who want to leave the fund, thereby generating capital gains. Market makers in ETFs, in contrast, are paid for ETFs with a swap of the underlying shares. In these transactions, no capital gains occur. However, ETFs can generate taxable distributions.

Segregated Funds

Segregated funds are offered by insurance companies as alternatives to conventional mutual funds. They are legally considered to be insurance products and the funds must be separated from other assets of the insurance company. They have the unique feature of guaranteeing that, regardless of how poorly the fund performs, investors are entitled to at least a minimum percentage of their total contributions to the fund after a certain period of time. The minimum required by law is 75 percent after 10 years, although most funds guarantee 100 percent. They may also be structured so that the assets within the fund cannot be seized by creditors if the investor declares bankruptcy.

These funds have grown in popularity in recent years, with assets growing from $20 billion in 1991 to $89 billion in 2002, to over $310 billion by 2007. Much of this growth has been fuelled by investor concerns about growing volatility in financial markets. As a result of this demand, investment companies and banks have begun to offer similar products referred to as guaranteed funds or protected funds. While these funds represent attractive alternatives to the risk-averse investor who wishes to participate in increasing stock market prices without exposing themselves to an undue amount of risk, there are a couple of things investors should keep in mind. The first point to recognize is that the guarantee is only good after a certain period of time, and if investors sell their fund units before this date, they could end up receiving less than the guaranteed percentage of their investment. The second important point is that segregated funds (as well as the similar funds offered by investment companies and banks) tend to have higher load fees and some firms insist they be purchased through a contractual purchase plan.

Labour Sponsored Venture Capital Corporations (LSVCCs)

Labour Sponsored Venture Capital Corporations (LSVCCs) offer investors a tax credit and are usually provincially based. They must be sponsored by labour organizations and their specific mandate is to invest in small to medium-size businesses. Their main purposes are to create and protect jobs, promote economic growth and diversification, increase the supply of venture capital, and encourage greater participation in share ownership and business development. They presently account for approximately 40 percent of all venture capital raised in Canada. Eligible investments for LSVCCs include shares, ownership interests, or certain debt securities of eligible corporations or partnerships. Eligibility is restricted to taxable Canadian businesses that are active in Canada and meet specific criteria. These investments may be considered hybrid securities since they are speculative investments that also provide tax benefits.

LSVCC investors are eligible to receive a federal tax credit of 15 percent and provincial credits that are usually in the 15–20 percent range. While there is no maximum amount an investor may invest in an LSVCC, the total tax credit cannot exceed $1,500 in any year; therefore the maximum investment eligible for tax credits is $5,000 (since $1,500 is 30 percent of $5,000). These tax credits are subject to recapture by tax authorities if they are redeemed before they have been held for a certain period of time.

Aside from the available tax credits and foreign content advantages, LSVCCs provide other advantages to investors. In particular, most LSVCCs are RRSP and RRIF eligible, which implies the potential for a double tax advantage. For example, an investor in the 50 percent tax bracket who purchases $5,000 worth of LSVCCs for RRSP purposes can deduct $2,500 (50 percent of $5,000) from their taxable income, in addition to receiving the $1,500 in federal and provincial tax credits (as described above). Hence, an investor could potentially invest $5,000 in LSVCCs, at a net after-tax cost of $1,000.

The potential for higher after-tax returns offered by these investments does not come without the assumption of additional risk. Investors must be aware of the highly speculative and illiquid nature of these investments, which make them suitable only for investors with a high risk tolerance. The portfolios are generally not well diversified geographically and/or across industries and are composed of venture capital investments in small to medium-size companies that often lack an established track record. The companies are typically private companies that may not have been analyzed by a large number of outsiders, and they are not subject to the disclosure requirements of public companies. In fact, their financial statements may not even be audited. The nature of these investments implies that not only are they speculative in nature, but since the companies likely do not trade publicly, there is a great deal of illiquidity associated with the investments. Indeed, Real-World Returns 3-3 discusses the poor performance of these funds over the last decade.

REAL-WORLD RETURNS 3-3
Labour-Sponsored Funds

What Are We Looking For?
Top-performing, labour-sponsored investment funds over the long haul. These investments—now called retail venture funds—were marketed on their long-term potential and juicy tax credits.

Today's Search
We looked at their performance over the decade to the end of 2007—specifically, average annual returns over one, three, five and 10 years.

So What Did We Turn Up?
Ugly returns. Dead funds. Funds reinventing themselves. Many took a hit after the technology bubble burst. And high management fees have taken a big bite from returns.

GrowthWorks Canadian, formerly Working Ventures Canadian Fund, posted an average annual loss of 3 percent over the decade.

Canadian Medical Discoveries (series I), formed from the merger of the first two original series, fared even worse. It suffered an average annual loss of 6.6 percent. And VenGrowth Investment Fund Class A (series E) declined an average of 1.1 percent a year.

(continued)

REAL-WORLD RETURNS 3-3 *continued*

Some funds managed to stay in the black. At the lower end was BEST Discoveries, up 1 percent annually. Dynamic Venture Opportunity (series I) posted a 6.8 percent average annual return—the best in the group. Still, they underperformed the 9.8 percent average for Canadian small-to-mid-capitalization equity funds.

While Crocus Investment Fund is listed as active, it's on life support. The scandal-ridden fund has been mired in legal woes, and its assets are still being liquidated.

Sportfund merged with Retrocom Growth Fund, which filed for bankruptcy protection in 2006 and proceedings are continuing. And Covington Fund I was wound down last year. Out of 20 funds, 13 are listed as non-active. Some of them are under new managers, or have merged with other funds.

Triax Growth I merged with the Covington Venture Fund Inc. (series I). York Labour Fund, formerly Centerfire Growth, has become Lawrence Enterprise V Fund.

Impax Venture Income Fund, formerly DGC Entertainment Ventures, merged with Impax Venture Fund to become Horizons Advantaged Equity Fund (series I).

Capital Alliance Ventures, Canadian Science & Technology Growth and First Ontario (which took over Trillium Growth Capital and FESA Enterprise Venture Capital) merged with Growth-Works Canadian to start a new series. ENSIS Growth will soon amalgamate with GrowthWorks Canadian too. Workers Investment Fund has merged with GrowthWorks Atlantic Venture Fund.

When funds start a new life, the performance clock often starts all over again. So much for long-term potential.

Labour-Sponsored Funds Existing in 1998

Fund Name*	Inception date	Net assets (millions) as of Dec. '07	% return as of Dec. 2007					Active/Not active fund as of today	MER effective date	Last reported MER
			1-year	3-year	5-year	10-year	Since inception			
GrowthWorks Canadian	2/8/1990	227.4	−0.19%	2.87%	3.76%	−2.96%	0.12%	Active	2/28/2005	4.9
Working Opportunity Balncd Ser 1	4/1/1992	154.9	−2.84%	−2.48%	−1.90%	1.62%	2.66%	Active	9/30/2005	2.63
Crocus Investment Fund	3/1/1993								1/30/2004	4.04
Dynamic Venture Opport Series 1	2/28/1994	61.9	−6.52%	5.78%	5.22%	6.79%	1.78%	Active	6/29/2007	3.99
Impax Venture Income Fund Inc.	3/1/1994							Not Active		
Canadian Medical Discoveries	10/7/1994	156.4	−19.84%	−13.93%	−9.93%	−6.60%	−4.32%	Active	5/31/2005	3.71
Trillium Growth Capital Inc.	10/25/1994							Not Active		
First Ontario LSIF Ltd.	1/31/1995							Not Active		
Covington Fund 1	2/28/1995							Not Active		
Capital Alliance Ventures	2/28/1995							Not Active		
Sportfund	2/28/1995							Not Active		
FESA Enterprise Venture Capital	3/1/1995							Not Active		
VenGrowth Invst Fund Inc.	3/1/1995	95.7	−9.57%	−2.70%	−4.35%	−1.12%	0.58%	Active	8/31/2007	4.17
Retrocom Growth	4/13/1995							Not Active		
Triax Growth-I	1/10/1996							Not Active		
Canadian Science & Tech Growth	12/2/1996							Not Active		
B.E.S.T. Discoveries I	12/31/1996	56.9	20.32%	6.59%	1.38%	0.97%	0.70%	Active	9/28/2007	5.72
Workers Investment Fund Inc.	1/10/1997							Not Active		
York Labour Fund Inc.	3/1/1997							Not Active		
ENSIS Growth Fund Inc.	1/5/1998	96.0	2.15%	−3.13%	−2.13%		−2.10%	Active	10/29/2004	4.95
Avg Return - Canadian Small-Mid Cap Equity Fund			7.23%	12.46%	16.95%	9.78%				
Median Return - Canadian Small -Mid Cap Equity Fund			8.02%	11.61%	16.24%	10.47%				
BMO Nesbitt Burns Cdn Small Cap Index			2.01%	12.51%	18.33%	9.68%				

*Note: The list does not include the Quebec Solidarity Fund because it is valued semi-annually and data is incomplete. Source: Globefund.

Source: Won, Shirley. "The ugly truth about labour-sponsored funds," *The Globe and Mail*, February 16, 2008, p. B15.

Disclosure requirements for LSVCCs are similar to those for mutual funds, through a prospectus offering, since shares are continually being issued. Registered salespeople must have passed the CSC exam and follow the IFIC Code of Conduct guidelines. However, LSVCCs differ from mutual funds in several ways. Unlike mutual funds, LSVCCs

1. Are not restricted to 10 percent ownership in given companies (in fact, they may exceed 20 percent)

2. Have restrictions on transferability and redemption

3. May not be valued based exclusively on the market, but rather, may require valuation by independent qualified persons that are to be updated by management

In short, LSVCCs are only suitable as long-term investments due to their speculative and illiquid nature, as well as to restrictions regarding the provision of tax credit benefits.

CHECK YOUR UNDERSTANDING

3-9. ETFs and closed-end funds both trade on exchanges. Why, then, have ETFs become so popular while closed-end funds, as a group, have languished?

3-10. Given the wide availability of no-load funds, why do many investors choose to buy load funds and pay sales charges?

3-11. The tax credits available on LSVCCs are a very appealing feature. Why do you suppose these funds have not surpassed other investment funds in popularity?

INVESTMENT FUNDS PERFORMANCE

learning objective 6
Understand how the performance of investment funds is measured.

Few topics in investments are as well reported on a regular basis as the performance of investment funds, and in particular mutual funds. *The Globe and Mail, National Post, Business Week, Forbes,* and *Money,* among other popular publications, regularly cover the performance of mutual funds, emphasizing their returns and risks. Real-World Returns 3-4 provides an example of fund performance reports available at www.globefund.com.

We will discuss the calculation of investment returns in much more detail in Chapter 6, but the primary focus in that chapter is on individual securities and indexes of securities and the actual mechanics involved. Furthermore, we discuss the evaluation of portfolio performance in detail in Chapter 22 and therefore do not consider the evaluation of mutual fund performance in depth now. Nevertheless, it is instructive at this point to consider some of the basic points about mutual fund returns.

Throughout this text we will use total return (explained in detail in Chapter 6) to measure the return from any financial asset, including a mutual fund. Total return for a mutual fund includes reinvested dividends, interest payments and/or capital gains, and therefore includes all of the ways investors make money from financial assets. It is stated as a percentage and can cover any time period—one day, one month, one year, or several years.

Standard practice in the mutual fund industry is to calculate and present the average annual return, a hypothetical rate of return that, if achieved annually, would have produced the same cumulative total return if performance had been constant over the entire period. The average annual return is a geometric mean (discussed in Chapter 6) and reflects the compound rate of growth at which money grew over time.

Average annual total returns allow investors to make direct comparisons among funds as to their performance, assuming they do so legitimately, as explained in Chapter 22 when we discuss the evaluation of performance. In particular, the risk of the funds being compared should be equivalent, and the funds should have the same general objectives. In addition to various average return figures, Real-World Returns 3-4 includes two measures of risk (3-year risk, which is actually the standard deviation; and beta) that will be discussed in subsequent chapters. For example, we expect equity funds to outperform bond funds and money market funds on average. Another complexity arising in the comparison of fund performance is that, as discussed above, funds with the same stated objectives often have significant variation in the nature of the assets included in their portfolios.

REAL-WORLD RETURNS 3-4

Average Total Returns RBC Asset Management Inc.'s Canadian Equity Fund

Returns as at February 29, 2008

	Fund	Index*
1 Month	3.62%	3.45%
3 Months	-1.31%	-0.12%
6 Months	-0.41%	0.70%
1 Year	4.92%	6.75%
2 Year Avg	9.74%	10.52%
3 Year Avg	13.77%	14.58%
5 Year Avg	16.56%	18.11%
10 Year Avg	8.95%	8.67%
15 Year Avg	11.21%	11.72%
20 Year Avg	9.26%	10.05%
Since Inception	10.19%	-
2007	9.37%	9.83%
2006	17.54%	17.26%
2005	22.99%	24.13%
3 year risk	11.02	10.99
3 year beta	0.99	1.00

*S&P/TSX Total Return

Source: Retrieved from www.globefund.com, February 29, 2008.

Benchmarks

Investors need to relate the performance of a mutual fund to some benchmark in order to judge relative performance with (hopefully) a comparable investment alternative. RBC Asset Management Inc.'s Canadian Equity Fund, presented above, was compared to the S&P/TSX Total Return Index. Other funds are compared to different benchmarks based on their objectives and asset allocation parameters. For example, small-cap funds are compared to small-cap indexes, and bond funds are compared to bond indexes.

How Important Are Expenses?

An important issue for all fund investors is that of expenses. Should they be overly concerned about the load charges, given the large number of no-load funds? What about annual operating expenses, as reflected in MERs? There is considerable evidence that funds with lower MERs provide better returns for investors in the long run, which makes sense to the extent that this expense is passed on to investors (i.e., it reduces their returns). While this will not always be the case, it certainly makes sense to be aware of the level of MER when purchasing funds.

Mutual Fund Ratings

Many agencies provide ratings for mutual funds. One of the best known rating systems is provided by Morningstar. Globefund is a major provider of information and ratings of Canadian mutual funds. Real-World Returns 3-5 shows Globefund's reports for selected RBC funds. Real-World Returns 3-6 describes Globefund's five-star rating system and lists some of the 547 funds that had a five-star rating as of March 18, 2008.

Mutual fund ratings such as those provided by Morningstar and Globefund are widely used by investors as a screening device when searching for a fund to buy. However, it is important to note the measures reflect historical performance, which is no guarantee of "future" performance, as discussed in the next section.

REAL-WORLD RETURNS 3-5

Global Fund Reports

Selected RBC Funds

Fund Report – Standard

Fund name	Price $	1 day $ Chg	30 day %	3 mo %	6 mo %	1 yr %	3 yr %	Incep (mm/yy)
RBC $U.S. Income (US$)	10.275	-0.011	0.83	-0.34	1.75	2.93		3.87 (05/05)
RBC Advisor Canadian Bond	11.215	0.028	2.62	2.41	5.25	4.03	4.28	5.97 (11/99)
RBC Asian Equity	8.631	-0.138	-10.59	-13.44	-12.08	-12.62	4.73	3.91 (07/02)
RBC Balanced	11.785	-0.171	-2.37	-3.29	-1.94	-0.30	7.46	7.87 (01/88)
RBC Balanced - T	12.681	-0.184	-2.37	-3.28	-1.92			-3.49 (07/07)
RBC Balanced Growth	12.038	-0.112	-2.83	-4.79	-3.70	-2.95	6.68	5.27 (04/98)
RBC Balanced Growth - T	12.598	-0.117	-2.83	-4.78	-3.67			-5.37 (07/07)
RBC Bond	6.023	0.026	2.09	1.75	4.11	1.55	3.33	8.32 (11/72)
RBC Canadian Bond Index	11.419	0.024	2.74	2.75	6.15	5.66	4.59	5.81 (06/00)
RBC Canadian Dividend	43.209	-0.846	-5.33	-4.65	-4.80	-0.20	10.51	13.35 (01/93)
RBC Canadian Dividend - T	12.192	-0.239	-5.33	-4.64	-4.79			-6.35 (07/07)
RBC Canadian Index	23.473	-0.784	-5.30	-0.24	0.50	6.31	13.97	11.49 (10/98)
RBC Canadian Money Market	10.000	0.000	0.30	1.00	2.03	3.81	3.01	4.98 (12/86)
RBC Canadian Short-Term Income	10.827	0.001	1.36	2.46	4.20	4.37	2.79	5.20 (01/92)
RBC Canadian T-Bill	10.000	0.000	0.25	0.83	1.72	3.45	2.83	3.81 (01/91)
RBC Cash Flow Portfolio	9.689	-0.036	-0.61	-0.12	1.61	2.06	4.06	4.82 (08/04)
RBC Cdn Diversified Income Trust	16.671	-0.401	-2.77	4.80	4.92	8.39		5.45 (08/06)
RBC Cdn Equity	24.891	-0.811	-4.73	-1.31	-0.41	4.92	13.77	10.19 (04/67)
RBC DS Aggressive All Eq Global Prt	11.002	-0.208	-4.36	-8.08	-6.66	-4.82		5.50 (09/05)

Fund — As of March 19, 2008

Fund Report – Key Facts

Fund name	Asset Class	Assets ($M)	MER %	Load Type	Minimum Investment	RSP
RBC $U.S. Income (US$)	Global Fixed Income Balanced	53.0	1.85	NL	1000	Yes
RBC Advisor Canadian Bond	Canadian Fixed Income	157.6	0.88	FE	10000	Yes
RBC Asian Equity	Asia Pacific Equity	592.4	2.69	NL	1000	Yes
RBC Balanced	Canadian Neutral Balanced	8886.5	2.28	NL	1000	Yes

Fund Report – Key Facts (continued)

Fund name	Asset Class	Assets ($M)	MER %	Load Type	Minimum Investment	RSP
RBC Balanced Growth	Canadian Neutral Balanced	1135.0	2.36	NL	1000	Yes
RBC Bond	Canadian Fixed Income	3869.2	1.46	NL	1000	Yes
RBC Canadian Bond Index	Canadian Fixed Income	189.4	0.70	NL	1000	Yes
RBC Canadian Dividend	Canadian Dividend and Income Equity	9268.3	1.73	NL	1000	Yes
RBC Canadian Index	Canadian Equity	485.3	0.71	NL	1000	Yes
RBC Canadian Money Market	Canadian Money Market	4913.2	0.98	NL	500	Yes
RBC Canadian Short-Term Income	Canadian Short Term Fixed Income	1849.2	1.45	NL	1000	Yes
RBC Canadian T-Bill	Canadian Money Market	1425.8	0.97	NL	500	Yes
RBC Cash Flow Portfolio	Canadian Fixed Income Balanced	706.2	1.54	NL	5000	Yes
RBC Cdn Diversified Income Trust	Canadian Equity	13.1	2.14	OPT	1000	Yes
RBC Cdn Equity	Canadian Equity	4919.2	1.99	NL	1000	Yes
RBC DS Aggressive All Eq Global Prt	Global Equity	69.3	2.44	NL	1500	Yes

Source: Retrieved from www.globefund.com, March 18, 2008.

REAL-WORLD RETURNS 3-6

Globefund 5-Star Ratings

Globefund.com in conjunction with Algorithmics Inc. is pleased to introduce the Globefund 5-Star Ratings service, a simple rating for most mutual funds in Canada. Globefund 5-Star Ratings will help you understand how well each fund has been doing relative to similar funds. The ratings are available on the new 5-Star Rating Fund Report, on the Annual and Long-Term Fund Reports and on the Fund Profile. You can also use the Fund Filter to screen funds based on their Globefund 5-Star Rating.

Funds are ranked from one to five stars, with the top ranked funds getting five stars and the lowest ranked funds getting one star. While past performance does not guarantee future performance, our historical testing of this rating system has shown that on average, top-rated funds have tended to outperform their peers over a six-month to two-year horizon.

Our rating system provides a useful gauge of the funds we follow. However, we do not suggest you use it as the single decision point for the suitability of a fund for your needs. Be sure to study all of the information you can gather on any fund before you invest.

(continued)

REAL-WORLD RETURNS 3-6 *continued*

Globefund 5-Star Funds
as of March 19, 2008

Fund Name	Globefund 5-Star Rating	1 Yr Return%	2 Yr Return%	3 Yr Return%	Asset Class
AGF American Growth Class (US$)	★★★★★	5.30	6.31	9.29	International Growth
AGF Canada Class (US$)	★★★★★	22.73	18.36	20.18	Growth
AGF Canadian Balanced	★★★★★	1.11	7.33	8.87	Growth and Income
AGF Canadian Balanced D	★★★★★	1.61	7.88	9.43	Growth and Income
AGF Canadian Conservative Income	★★★★★	1.70	2.58	2.06	Growth and Income
AGF China Focus Class (US$)	★★★★★	45.82	40.89	33.11	Aggressive Growth
AGF Emerging Markets Value (US$)	★★★★★	26.61	24.82	31.79	Aggressive Growth
AGF Glo Government Bond (US$)	★★★★★	14.83	8.46	4.87	Income
AGF Global Equity Class (US$)	★★★★★	5.42	9.32	11.85	International Growth
AGF Global High Yield Bond (US$)	★★★★★	11.26	9.60	10.81	Income
AGF Global Resources Class	★★★★★	24.41	24.14	26.22	Aggressive Growth
AGF Global Resources Class (US$)	★★★★★	47.80	33.48	36.04	Aggressive Growth
AGF Precious Metal	★★★★★	12.21	29.27	31.30	Aggressive Growth
AGF Short Term Income (US$)	★★★★★	22.44	10.81	10.56	Income
AGF World Companies (US$)	★★★★★	5.13	9.64	12.73	International Growth
AGF World Opportunities (US$)	★★★★★	3.85	7.03	10.85	International Growth
AIC Global Focused (US$)	★★★★★	9.37	10.98		International Growth
AIC Global Focused Corp Cl (US$)	★★★★★	9.56	11.63		International Growth
AIC PPC Global Fixed Inc Pool (US$)	★★★★★	10.50	7.11		Income
AIC World Equity (US$)	★★★★★	1.21	8.59	8.01	International Growth
AIC World Equity Corporate Cl (US$)	★★★★★	0.87	8.33	7.64	International Growth
AIM European Growth (US$)	★★★★★	1.26	13.38	14.34	International Growth
AIM European Growth Class (US$)	★★★★★	1.57	13.08	14.18	International Growth
AIM International Growth Class(US$)	★★★★★	4.28	13.08	15.40	International Growth
AIM Short-Term Income 'A' (US$)	★★★★★	22.11	10.27	9.99	Capital Preservation
AIM Short-Term Income 'B' (US$)	★★★★★	21.80	9.96	9.63	Capital Preservation
APEX Balanced (AGF)	★★★★★	2.84	6.62	7.30	Growth and Income
APEX Canadian Value (Dynamic)	★★★★★	2.15	13.95	16.31	Growth
Acuity Pooled Fixed Income	★★★★★	4.27	3.52		

How It Works

We have divided mutual funds into six broad fund categories that closely match the asset allocation categories used by financial planners, as follows:

- Growth (primarily mid-size and large cap Canadian equity funds)
- Growth and Income (primarily balanced, dividend, and asset allocation funds)
- International Growth (foreign equity funds)
- Aggressive Growth (primarily small cap, geographic, and specialty funds)
- Income (fixed income and mortgage funds)
- Capital Preservation (Canadian and foreign money market funds)

The only qualification for including a fund in the rating system is that it must have at least two years of history. Currently, that means we compute a rating for approximately 80 percent of the 6,000 Canadian mutual funds that we track.

Once classified into one of these broad categories, all the funds within that category compete with each other in terms of the best score, and hence the best rating. A fund's score is a combination of return and regret and is determined as follows. On a monthly basis, for each fund, we compute month-by-month returns and subtract from these the return of the 90-day Canadian T-Bill to get what is known as the risk-free return for each month. If this result is positive for any one month, it contributes to the fund's return. If it is negative, it contributes to the fund's regret. We then use an averaging method across each of these returns and regrets (with increasing weight on the most recent data) to derive a final measure for return and for regret for each fund. The final score for a fund is then computed as the return score minus an adjusted regret score, where the adjustment factor for the regret component is unique for each broad asset category. Using the final scores for each of the funds in a category, we rank them and then allocate a star rating for each. The top 10 percent of funds receive a five-star rating, the next 22.5 percent a four-star rating, the middle 35 percent a three-star rating, the next 22.5 percent a two-star rating and the bottom 10 percent of funds a one-star rating.

The Globefund 5-Star Ratings use many of the elements of the Mark-to-Future methodology pioneered by Algorithmics: www.mark-to-future.com. Algorithmics, www.algorithmics.com, was founded in 1989 in response to the complex issues surrounding financial risk management for the enterprise. Today, as the leading provider with the largest and most experienced team in the industry, Algorithmics continues to focus its efforts on creating and implementing enterprise risk management software that meets the evolving needs of its customers. Continuing its tradition of leading the way in risk measurement and management tools and processes, Algorithmics recently introduced Mark-To-Future™ (MtF), an open and comprehensive framework for measuring risk and reward. Headquartered in Toronto, with 14 offices around the world, Algorithmics serves more than 90 global financial institutions with 140 installations worldwide.

Source: Retrieved from www.globefund.com, March 19, 2008. Globefund 5-Star ratings provided by *The Globe and Mail*. Methodology provided by Algorithmics Inc.

Consistency of Performance

Can the returns numbers above, widely available for mutual funds, help investors choose this year's, or next year's, winner? The consistency of performance of mutual funds has long been a controversy, and this continues to be true. Early studies tended to find no consistency in fund performance, but some recent studies did find some. For example, in the 1990s, Grinblatt and Titman found persistence in differences between funds over time. More recently Elton, Gruber, and Blake also found evidence of performance differences.[6]

Princeton University professor Burton Malkiel has also found evidence of such differences, although he found that the historical period had an effect, with differences persisting in the 1970s but not in the 1980s.[7] Malkiel, famous for many years as a strong believer in market efficiency, would have a difficult time saying past performance matters in selecting a fund. However, in a recent interview, Malkiel suggests that investors may gain when selecting funds by relying on recent good performance; however, there are no guarantees when investing, but a possible advantage is to be appreciated.

---

[6]Mark Grinblatt and Sheridan Titman, "The Persistence of Mutual Fund Performance," *The Journal of Finance* 47 (December 1992), pp. 1977–1984; Edwin Elton, Martin J. Gruber, and Christopher Blake, "The Persistence of Risk-Adjusted Mutual Fund Performance," *Journal of Business* 69 (April 1996), pp. 133–157; and Martin J. Gruber, "Another Puzzle: The Growth in Actively Managed Mutual Funds," *The Journal of Finance* 51 (July 1996), pp. 783–810.
[7]Burton G. Malkiel, "Returns from Investing in Equity Mutual Funds: 1971 to 1991," *The Journal of Finance* 50 (June 1995), pp. 549–572.

A study by MPL Communications Inc. of Toronto also documents a lack of persistence in Canadian mutual fund performance. They find that none of the 76 Canadian equity funds that were in existence for the 10-year period ended September 30, 1997, were able to surpass the category average for all 10 years. Further, only one fund was able to beat the average nine times, only three beat the average eight times, while only four could beat the average seven times. In fact, less than half (34) of the funds were able to beat the average in five or more years.[8]

Evidence compiled from www.globefund.com confirms this lack of persistence in Canadian equity fund performance over the 1993–2007 period, as shown in Table 3-1. The table is based on the number of Canadian equity funds that existed throughout the 10- and 15-year periods ending in 2007.

Referring to column two of Table 3-1, we can see that no funds were able to beat the group average for 12, 13, 14, or 15 years, while only two funds were able to outperform for 10 years or 11 years. Closer examination shows that only 16 of the 46 funds (or 34.8 percent) were able to outperform more than half the time (i.e., 8 years or more). Similar results are evident if we look at column three, where we can see that none of the funds were able to outperform in 9 or 10 years, and only 27 of the 82 funds (or 32.9 percent) were able to outperform more than half the time.

In conclusion, although past fund performance provides useful information to investors, strong past performance is no guarantee of strong future performance.

Table 3-1

Canadian Equity Funds Performance

Number of Times Fund Performed Above Average	Number of Funds (1993–2007; 15-year period)	Number of Funds (1998–2007; 10-year period)
0	0	0
1	0	2
2	1	10
3	2	10
4	1	15
5	6	18
6	11	15
7	9	8
8	7	4
9	5	0
10	2	0
11	2	n/a
12	0	n/a
13	0	n/a
14	0	n/a
15	0	n/a
Total number of firms during period	46	82

Source: www.globefund.com, March 19, 2008.

INVESTING INTERNATIONALLY THROUGH INVESTMENT FUNDS

learning objective 7
Discuss the opportunities for investing indirectly internationally.

The mutual fund industry has become a global industry. Open-end funds around the world have grown rapidly, including those in emerging market economies. Worldwide assets were approximately $14.4 trillion US by mid-2004.

---

[8]Peter Brewster, "Better than average: Not very often," *The Globe and Mail/Report on Mutual Funds*, November 6, 1997, p. C1.

Canadian investors can invest internationally by buying and selling investment funds that specialize in international securities. These funds have become both numerous and well-known in recent years. By March 2008, Canadians could choose from a large number of foreign funds, including 649 US equity funds; 94 small- and mid-cap US equity funds; 125 European equity funds; 1,001 global equity funds; 324 international equity funds; 78 North American equity funds; 37 Japanese equity funds; 38 Asia Pacific (excluding Japan) equity funds; 67 emerging market equity funds; 980 global balanced funds; 90 global fixed income funds; and 32 US money market funds.

So-called international funds tend to concentrate primarily on international stocks, while global funds tend to keep a minimum percentage of their total in domestic assets. Another alternative in indirect investing, the single-country funds, concentrate on the securities of a single country. International closed-end funds usually sell at either a discount or a premium to their net asset value as do their domestic counterparts. Some developing countries restrict access to foreign equity ownership, with the result that a single-country fund may be an investor's only readily available alternative for investing in that particular country.

Another alternative for international fund investing is through country funds, which concentrate on each of several different countries. The typical single-country fund is closed-end, and is usually passively managed—geared to match a major stock index of a particular country. Each of these offerings will typically be almost fully invested, have little turnover, and offer significantly reduced expenses to shareholders. For example, Morgan Stanley offers iShares (formerly WEBS), which tracks a pre-designated index (one of Morgan Stanley's international capital indices) for many countries.

THE FUTURE OF INDIRECT INVESTING

One of the hottest new movements concerning indirect investing is the fund "supermarket" in which investors can buy the funds of various mutual fund families through one source, such as a brokerage firm. Supermarket refers to the fact that an investor has hundreds of choices available through one source and does not have to go to other sources to obtain his or her choices. The funds participating in the supermarket pay the firms offering the funds distribution fees (0.25 percent to 0.40 percent of assets per year). Investors often use the Internet to access these supermarkets, with Schwab and Fidelity reporting that about 60 percent of mutual fund trades are done online.

Hedge Funds

We close our discussion of investment companies by considering an offshoot, an unregulated investment company. The Investment Company Act of 1940 gave primacy to the open-end investment company (or mutual fund) as the way to protect investors from the excesses of the unregulated companies of the 1920s. The key was that such companies would be heavily regulated as to investor protections. However, the Act also left open the possibility of a money manager handling funds for a small group of sophisticated investors in an unregulated format. In 1949, a fund was started to "hedge" market risk by both buying and selling short, thus initiating the hedge fund industry.

Hedge funds are unregulated companies that seek to exploit various market opportunities and thereby earn larger returns than are ordinarily available. For example, they may use leverage or derivative securities, or they may invest in illiquid assets, strategies not generally available to the typical mutual fund. They require a substantial initial investment from investors, and may have restrictions on how quickly investors can withdraw their funds. Unlike mutual funds, they traditionally do not disclose information to their investors about their investing activities. Hedge funds charge substantial fees and take a percentage of the profits earned, typically at least 20 percent.

Over time, the average performance of hedge funds has been good, with larger returns and less risk than the typical mutual fund. However, there have been some well-known failures, such as Bayou in 2005 whereby the principals are alleged to have drained investor monies for their own purposes. The most spectacular failure was Long Term Capital in 1998, which got in trouble as a result of Russia defaulting on its debt. In this case, the Federal Reserve had to step in to calm the waters.

In Canada, by 2006, it was estimated there were over 250 funds and $30 billion in assets. Globally, by 2005 there were more than 8,000 hedge funds, with an estimated $1 trillion under management. A legitimate issue to consider is whether there are enough talented managers to run this many funds. Furthermore, are more and more funds competing for the same opportunities in the market? If so, does this not diminish the returns to be expected from hedge funds?

THOSE WHO LIVE IN GLASS HOUSES

In late 2003, Edward D. Jones & Co., a large retail brokerage firm with offices in the US, Canada, and UK, took out ads criticizing the "anything goes" approach that led to abuses in the US mutual fund industry. In late 2004, the US Securities and Exchange Commission finalized a US$75-million settlement agreement with the company. The company was charged with accepting tens of millions of dollars secretly from seven preferred mutual fund groups, which could lead its brokers to favour those funds with their clients even if it were not in the best interest of the clients. Brokers received bonuses and other incentives to sell these particular funds.

It was also found that the brokerage firm did not have in place the proper systems to prevent late trading of mutual funds from taking place. Late trading occurs when fund buyers are able to execute mutual fund orders after 4 p.m. using the 4 p.m. closing price. Thus, favourable market-moving developments after 4 p.m. could cause a fund's value to go up the next day, and buying the shares at the same-day 4 p.m. price can allow favoured clients to earn profits at the expense of long-term fund shareholders.

DISCUSSION QUESTIONS

1. Should Edward Jones have told clients that its brokers were given incentives to sell particular funds, or should it have stopped the practice altogether?

2. Financial advisors not connected with brokerage firms often receive commissions for selling mutual funds. Is that unethical?

3. If customers were to profit from buying mutual funds their broker was receiving incentives for selling, would that make it less unethical?

CHECK YOUR UNDERSTANDING

3-12. If a mutual fund were purchased and held for exactly one year, would the change in unit price represent the total return on the investment?

3-13. Can you be confident that mutual funds with a 5-star Globefund rating will perform well in the future? Would you recommend that investors only invest in these highly rated funds?

3-14. Would an International fund or a Global fund likely be the better choice for an investor seeking a single investment fund to provide broad geographic diversification including both domestic stocks and those from around the world?

3-15. Why are most investors restricted from investing in hedge funds, despite their strong performance records?

SUMMARY

This summary relates to the learning objectives for this chapter.

1. **Distinguish between direct and indirect investing.**

   As an alternative to purchasing financial assets themselves, all investors can invest indirectly, which involves the purchase of shares (or trust units) of an investment fund.

2. **Define open-end and closed-end investment funds.**

   Investment funds are composed of portfolios of securities that are held on behalf of their shareholders. Investment funds are classified as either open-end or closed-end, depending on whether their own capitalization (number of shares or units outstanding) is constantly changing or relatively fixed.

3. **State the major types of mutual funds and give their features.**

   Open-end funds, or mutual funds, can be divided into two categories: money market funds and stock and bond & income funds. Money market mutual funds concentrate on portfolios of money market securities, providing investors with a way to own these high face value securities indirectly. Stock, bond, and income funds own portfolios of stocks and/or bonds, allowing investors to participate in these markets without having to purchase these securities directly.

4. **Explain the transactions behind indirect investments.**

   Investors transacting indirectly in closed-end funds encounter discounts and premiums, meaning that the price of these funds is unequal to their net asset values. Mutual funds can be load or no-load funds, depending on whether they have a sales charge (load) or not. All investment companies charge a management fee.

5. **Define exchange-traded funds (ETFs).**

   An exchange-traded fund is an index fund holding a diversified portfolio of securities designed to mimic the performance of a market index such as the S&P/TSX 60 Index. They are priced and traded on public exchanges.

6. **Understand how the performance of investment funds is measured.**

   Total return for a mutual fund includes reinvested dividends, interest payments, and/or capital gains. A cumulative total return measures the actual performance over a stated period of time, such as the past three, five, or 10 years. The average annual return is a hypothetical rate of return that, if achieved annually, would have produced the same cumulative total return if performance had been constant over the entire period.

7. **Discuss the opportunities for investing indirectly internationally.**

   International funds concentrate primarily on international stocks, while global funds keep a minimum percentage of their total in domestic assets. Single-country funds concentrate on the securities in a single country.

KEY TERMS

Closed-end investment fund, p.65	Investment fund, p.62	Net asset value (NAV), p.66
Exchange-traded funds (ETFs), p.73	Money market funds (MMFs), p.67	Open-end investment fund, p.65
	Mutual funds, p.65	Unit investment trust, p.65

REVIEW QUESTIONS

3-1. What is meant by indirect investing?

3-2. What is a money market fund? Why would it appeal to investors?

3-3. Distinguish between a value fund and a growth fund.

3-4. Distinguish between the direct and indirect methods by which mutual fund units are typically purchased.

3-5. What are passively managed country funds?

3-6. What is the difference between the management fee and the management expense ratio for a mutual fund?

3-7. What is an investment fund? Distinguish between an open-end and a closed-end fund.

3-8. It has been said that many closed-end funds are worth more dead than alive. What is meant by this expression?

3-9. What is meant by an investment fund's objective? What are some of the objectives pursued by an equity, bond, and income fund?

3-10. What is the difference between the average annual return for a fund and the cumulative total return?

3-11. How would the owner of some units of RBC Asset Management Inc.'s Canadian Equity Fund "cash out" when he or she was ready to sell the shares?

3-12. Who owns a mutual fund? Who determines investment policies and objectives?

3-13. What does it mean when someone says "Mutual funds involve investment risk"?

3-14. What is the difference between a load fund and a no-load fund?

3-15. Distinguish between segregated funds and mutual funds.

3-16. Identify three ways in which LSVCCs differ from other mutual funds.

3-17. How does the NAVPS affect the price of an open-end investment fund (mutual fund) as compared to the price of a closed-end fund? Explain.

3-18. As a small investor, what are the major benefits of indirect investing (in a mutual fund, for example) as compared to investing directly in stocks or bonds? What are the drawbacks?

3-19. The Crabtree Canadian Equity Fund has 500,000 units issued to investors. The fund currently has liabilities of $100,000. If the fund's portfolio is composed of the three securities listed below, calculate the fund's NAVPS.

Security	# of Shares	Price / Share
Evergreen Inc.	100,000	$10
Atlantic Fisheries Ltd.	500,000	8
Great Northern Gas Inc.	1,000,000	1.10

3-20. How is the net asset value for a mutual fund calculated?

3-21. Identify the risks associated with investments in LSVCCs.

3-22. Does a closed-end fund normally trade at a discount or a premium from its NAVPS?

3-23. List at least four reasons why it is believed that the situation in Question 22 occurs. How does this phenomenon impact on the concept of market efficiency?

3-24. Although most closed-end funds trade at a discount to their NAVPS, this is not always the case. Why do you think that some closed-end funds trade at a premium (sometimes a substantial premium) to their NAVPS?

3-25. List the benefits of a money market fund for investors. List the disadvantages.

3-26. List some reasons an investor might prefer a closed-end fund to an open-end fund.

3-27. Distinguish between a global fund and an international fund.

3-28. How have investors' preferences with regard to mutual fund investing changed over time?

3-29. What is meant by a "family of funds"?

3-30. List and briefly describe three differences between ETFs and mutual funds.

3-31. What does the term open-end mean with regard to an investment company?

3-32. What is the value to investors of Morningstar and Globefund ratings? What is the weakness of these ratings?

3-33. What does it mean to say an index fund is related to passive investing?

3-34. How does a hedge fund differ from a mutual fund?

3-35. What is a fund supermarket?

PROBLEMS

3-1. The years 2001 to 2008 witnessed some big increases and some significant declines in the Canadian stock market. The data below show the percentage annual returns for two mutual funds in the Mackenzie Financial family of funds: the Focus Canada Fund and the Maxxum Canadian Equity Growth Fund. Note that the figures for 2008 reflect performance for the first eight months of the year, but we will assume they are full-year figures.

	Focus	Maxxum
2001	-6.64	-6.79
2002	-12.00	-8.60
2003	13.38	15.48
2004	14.48	7.78
2005	6.18	25.98
2006	16.61	14.46
2007	7.73	2.01
2008	-7.46	1.34

a. Calculate the average performance for each fund for the eight-year period. Use the spreadsheet function { = average(B4:B11)} where B4:B11 represents the cells holding the annual returns for the fund.

b. Now calculate how much $1,000 invested in each fund at the beginning of 2001 would have grown to by the end of 2004, when the market was entering a growth phase. To do this calculation, construct two new columns, one for each fund, showing the decimal equivalent of the fund's return added to 1.0 (call this the *return relative*—to find it, divide each return by 100 and add 1.0). For example, for Focus, the first entry would be 0.9336. Then for each fund multiply $1,000 by each of the first four return relatives in turn. How much money would an investor in each fund have at the end of 2004? Which fund performed better up to that point?

c. Using the answer determined in (b), calculate the amount of money an investor would have in each fund at the end of 2008. Do this in a manner similar to compounding the result you found at the end of 2005 by each of the four remaining return relatives.

d. What is the difference in ending wealth between the two funds, having started with $1,000 in each fund?

e. Now calculate the average annual total return (geometric mean) for each fund using the spreadsheet function {= geomean (D4:D11)} assuming, for example, that the return relatives for one fund are in the cells D4:D11.

f. How does the difference in the average annual total returns for each fund compare to the arithmetic averages for each over the eight-year period?

PREPARING FOR YOUR PROFESSIONAL EXAMS

CFA PRACTICE QUESTIONS

3-1. An open-ended fund holds three stocks at the end of the business day: 500,000 shares of A valued at $20 each; 100,000 shares of B valued at $10 each; and 200,000 shares of C valued at $15 each plus $1 million in cash. The fund currently has one million shares outstanding. What is the NAV per share?

   a. $10
   b. $13
   c. $14
   d. $15

3-2. Which of the following statements about load funds is true?

   a. Trade their shares on the registered exchanges.
   b. Offer shares at the fund's net asset value plus a sales charge.
   c. Guarantee returns consistent with the fund's systematic risk.
   d. Deduct up to 1.25 percent of average assets per year to cover marketing expenses.

CHAPTER 4

SECURITIES MARKETS

Chapter 4 outlines the structure of the markets where investors buy and sell securities. Although primary markets, including the role of investment bankers, are considered here, the emphasis is on secondary markets where most investors are active. Equity markets are covered in detail because most investors are primarily interested in stocks; bond markets and derivative markets are also discussed. Changes in the securities markets are considered, including globalization. The structure and operating mechanisms of the securities markets in the United States have changed drastically in the last 20 years. Accordingly, this chapter concludes with a look at some of these changes and what the future may hold.

Learning Objectives

After reading this chapter, you should be able to

1. Distinguish between primary and secondary markets.
2. Describe how the equity markets are organized and how they operate.
3. State the major stock market indicators.
4. Describe, briefly, the bond and derivatives markets.
5. Discuss some of the factors behind rapid change in the securities markets.

CHAPTER PREVIEW

Whether you choose to invest directly or indirectly through investment funds, you need to understand the structure of the markets where securities are bought and sold. Financial markets are of two main types: primary markets (new securities are issued, often through investment dealers) and secondary markets (existing securities are traded among investors). In this chapter, we focus on secondary markets in Canada and the United States, as Canadian investors are active mostly in these markets. Secondary markets include the equity, bond, and derivatives markets. We concentrate on equities, because these are the securities that investors most often buy and sell. Bond and derivatives markets are discussed in greater detail in later chapters. We close this chapter with a look at how the structure and operating mechanisms of the securities markets have changed drastically in the past 20 years. Notably, we consider the dramatic changes that have occurred to the structure of Canadian stock markets.

THE IMPORTANCE OF FINANCIAL MARKETS

In order to finance their operations as well as expand, business firms must invest capital in amounts that are beyond their capacity to save in any reasonable period of time. Similarly, governments must borrow large amounts of money to provide the goods and services that people demand of them. Financial markets permit both business and government to raise the needed funds by selling securities. Simultaneously, investors with excess funds are able to invest and earn a return, enhancing their welfare.

Financial markets are absolutely vital for the proper functioning of capitalistic economies, since they serve to channel funds from savers to borrowers. Furthermore, they provide an important allocative function by channelling the funds to those who can make the best use of them—presumably, the most productive users of these funds. In fact, the chief function of a capital market is to allocate resources optimally.[1]

The existence of well-functioning secondary markets, where investors come together to trade existing securities, assures the purchasers that they can quickly sell their securities if the need arises. Of course, such sales may involve a loss, because there are no guarantees in the financial markets. A loss, however, may be much preferred to having no cash at all if the securities cannot be sold readily.

In summary, secondary markets are indispensable to the proper functioning of the primary markets, which are, in turn, indispensable to the proper functioning of the economy.

learning objective 1
Distinguish between primary and secondary markets.

THE PRIMARY MARKETS

Primary Market
The market for new issues of securities such as government Treasury bills or a corporation's stocks or bonds often involving investment dealers. The issuers of the securities receive cash from the buyers who in turn receive financial claims on the issuing organization.

A **primary market** is one in which a borrower issues new securities in exchange for cash from an investor (buyer or lender). New sales of, for example, T-bills, Bank of Montreal common stock, or Hydro-Québec bonds all take place in the primary markets. The issuers of these securities—the Canadian government, the Bank of Montreal, and Hydro-Québec—receive cash from the buyers of these new securities, who, in turn, receive financial claims that previously did not exist. Note that in all three examples, each of these organizations already had outstanding securities before the latest new sales occurred. In other words, these were offerings of *new* securities but they were *not* initial public offerings (IPOs).

Corporate bonds are issued through public offerings or private placements, which are described in the following section. Federal government debt securities are issued in the primary market by the minister of finance through the Bank of Canada using the competitive tender system, which is described below.

The auction or competitive tender system is used for most issues (i.e., Treasury bills and coupon bonds) by the federal government. Primary distributors that are eligible to tender include the chartered banks, investment dealers, and active foreign dealers. Competitive bids may consist of one or

---

[1] A securities market with this characteristic is said to be allocationally efficient. An operationally efficient market, on the other hand, is one with the lowest possible prices for transactions services.

more bids in multiples of $1,000 (minimum $100,000 per individual bid). The bid must state the yield to maturity to three decimal places. A primary distributor may also submit one non-competitive tender in multiples of $1,000, which is subject to a $1,000 minimum and a $3 million maximum. This bid will be executed at the average price of the accepted competitive tenders.

If a new maturity of bond is being offered, the coupon rate is set to within 25 basis points of the average yield of the accepted competitive tenders, which produces an average issue price at or below par (100). In addition to bidding for its own requirements, the Bank of Canada stands ready to absorb the entire tender if required, which implies that the Bank theoretically could set the yield at each tender.

On the day of tender, the Bank releases complete information about the tender so that bidders can determine their net position. No commissions are paid to dealers who purchase the bonds, and there are no selling price restrictions for the successful buyers.

New issues of provincial direct and guaranteed bonds are usually sold at a negotiated price through a fiscal agent (i.e., an underwriting syndicate). Direct bonds are issued directly by the government (e.g., Province of Manitoba bonds), while guaranteed bonds are issued in the name of a Crown corporation, but are guaranteed by the provincial government (e.g., Hydro-Québec).

Municipal bond and debenture issues are more likely to be placed in institutional portfolios and pension accounts. Non-market sources of investment capital that purchase municipal securities include: (i) the Canada Pension Plan (CPP) and Quebec Pension Plan (QPP), which commit a pro-rata portion of each province's obligation to the purchase of municipal securities; (ii) provincial and municipal pension funds, which directly invest in municipal securities; and (iii) the federal government, which often loans funds to municipalities for specific projects.

Sales of common stock of a publicly traded company are called "seasoned" new issues. If the issuer is selling securities for the first time, this is referred to as an **initial public offering (IPO)**. Once the original purchasers sell the securities, they trade in secondary markets. New securities may trade repeatedly in the secondary market, but the original issuers will be unaffected in the sense that they receive no additional cash from these transactions.

Initial Public Offering (IPO)
Common stock shares of a company being sold for the first time.

It is generally argued that firms would want to issue securities when they have good uses for the funds and when market prices are high. The latter observation is consistent with the observed record levels of IPOs on the TSX in 2000, in response to high stock market price levels at the beginning of that year, which carried over from the high levels of 1999. Table 4-1 shows the Canadian IPO levels over the 2000 to 2007 period. During 2000, the TSX set a record of $5.3 billion raised by initial public offerings (IPOs). On the other hand, IPO activity declined to $2.1 billion in 2001 before recovering to $5.8 billion in 2002 and reaching a high of $6.8 billion in 2005 in response to favourable market conditions during those years. As discussed in Real-World Returns 2-6, IPO activity was hampered by the government's October 31, 2006, decision to alter the tax structure that applies to income trusts. As a result, many planned income trust IPOs were cancelled, with a corresponding impact on IPO activity during the last quarter of 2006 and throughout 2007, when IPOs declined to $3.4 billion.

Table 4-1

Canadian IPO Activity

Year	Amount ($ billions)
2000	5.3
2001	2.1
2002	5.8
2003	4.6
2004	6.2
2005	6.8
2006	5.4
2007	3.4

Sources: Stewart, Sinclair, "IPO activity set to tumble in the wake of trust crackdown," *The Globe and Mail*, January 5, 2007, p. B5. "Income trust tax slowed Canada's IPO pace in 2007," *Financial Post*, January 7, 2008. Retrieved from ww.financialpost.com.

Pricing of initial offerings is an extremely important and complex decision. Firms do not want to set their offering price too low, since the higher the price obtained by the firm per share, the fewer shares have to be issued to raise the same amount of money. However, they do not want to overprice the issue and have it "undersubscribed," thus not raising the required funds. The following well-known example of IPO underpricing illustrates the difficulties associated with determining a fair issue price for companies with no previous trading history.

EXAMPLE 4-1: 724 SOLUTIONS INC.

During January 2000, 724 Solutions Inc. went public at $37 a share. The shares closed their first day of trading at three times the issue price, and then skyrocketed to $345 before falling back to the $55 range by October 2000.

This example indicates the complexity and high degree of uncertainty involved in the pricing of some IPOs, particularly for companies with new products or those operating in rapidly changing industries. Other IPOs for well-known companies in well-defined industries are easier to price with relative accuracy.

There is substantial Canadian, US, and global evidence that, on average, IPOs are underpriced. Underpricing is generally measured as the difference between the first trading day closing price minus the issue price, divided by the issue price. For the 724 Solutions Inc. example, this implies underpricing of $(111 - 37) / 37 = 200.0\%$. Loughran, Ritter, and Rydqvist provide summary evidence for international IPOs and find that average underpricing ranged from a low of 4.2 percent in France to highs of 78.5 percent in Brazil and 166.6 percent in Malaysia (during the 1970s and 1980s).[2] Loughran et al. also show that average underpricing in Germany (1978–92), the United Kingdom (1959–90), the US (1960–92), and Japan (1970–91) was 11.1 percent, 12.0 percent, 15.3 percent, and 32.5 percent respectively.

Jog and Riding provide Canadian evidence for 100 IPOs over the 1971–83 period and find average underpricing of 11.0 percent. However, the degree of underpricing varied significantly and approximately 40 percent of the new issues were actually overpriced.[3] Jog and Srivastava extend Canadian evidence to the 1984–92 period and find that average underpricing falls to 5.67 percent during this period, with only 47.4 percent of the issues being underpriced.[4] It is important to note that not all IPOs are underpriced—some are overpriced. There is also substantial Canadian and US evidence that the subsequent performance of IPOs is below average, which implies that investors could lose any short-term gains in the long run.

Investment Dealers

Investment Dealer

An organization specializing in the sale of new securities, usually by purchasing the issue and reselling it to the public. Known as investment bankers in the US.

In the course of selling new securities, issuers often rely on an **investment dealer** (or an investment banker in the US) for the necessary expertise as well as the ability to reach widely dispersed suppliers of capital. Along with performing activities such as helping corporations in mergers and acquisitions, investment dealers specialize in the design and sale of securities in the primary market while operating simultaneously in the secondary markets. For example, **BMO Nesbitt Burns** offers investment services while operating a large retail brokerage operation throughout the country.

Investment dealers act as intermediaries between issuers and investors. For firms seeking to raise long-term funds, the investment dealer can provide important advice to their clients during the planning stage preceding the issuance of new securities. This advice includes providing information about the type of security to be sold, the features to be offered with the security, the price, and the timing of the sale.

[2]Loughran, T., J. Ritter, and K. Rydqvist, "Initial Public Offerings: International Insights," *Pacific-Basin Finance Journal* 2 (May 1994), pp. 165–200.
[3]Jog, V., and A. Riding, "Underpricing in Canadian IPOs," *Financial Analysts Journal* 43 (Nov–Dec 1987), pp. 48–55.
[4]Jog, V., and A. Srivastava, "Underpricing in Canadian IPOs 1971–1992 — An Update," 3 *FINECO* (November 1995).

Investment dealers participate in primary markets as principals when they take on the task of **underwriting** new issues by purchasing the securities (once the details of the issue have been negotiated) and assuming the risk of reselling them to investors. Investment dealers provide a valuable service to the issuers at this stage. The issuer receives its cheque and can spend the proceeds for the purposes for which the funds are being raised. The investment dealers own the securities until they are resold. Although many issues are sold out quickly—sometimes on the first day they are offered to the public—others may not be sold for days or even weeks. Investment dealers are compensated by a spread, which is the difference between what they pay the issuer for the securities and what they sell them for to the public. The securities are purchased from the issuer at a discount.

In addition to having expertise in these matters and closely scrutinizing any potential issue of securities, investment dealers often protect themselves by forming an underwriting syndicate or group of investment dealers. This allows them to diversify their risk and enhance the marketability of the issue. One investment dealer serves as the lead underwriter overseeing the underwriting syndicate. This syndicate becomes part of a larger group that sells the securities. A primary offering of securities through this process is referred to as a syndicated offering.

Investment dealers may also assume the role of agents in primary markets when they market newly issued securities on a "best efforts" basis. Under these arrangements, they receive compensation in the form of a commission, and it is the issuer that assumes the risk of the issue not selling. This arrangement is more common for issues of smaller or more speculative companies, or for "private placements" (discussed below) for large companies with good credit ratings where the risk of the issue not selling is negligible.

All public offerings are regulated by the Canada Business Corporations Act (CBCA) and provincial securities regulations. They require that a **prospectus** be prepared that includes "full, true, and plain disclosure of all material facts relating to the securities offered." A material fact is one that significantly affects, or would reasonably be expected to have a significant effect on, the securities' market price.

Prospectuses are lengthy, legal documents that contain relevant financial statements, proposed use of funds from the issue, future growth plans, and the relevant information regarding the share issue. Normally, before a final prospectus may be issued, it is necessary to prepare and distribute copies of a "preliminary prospectus" to the securities commission and prospective investors. This contains most of the information to be included in the final prospectus except the price to the dealers and public, and sometimes the auditor's report. Because the prospectus is for information only and does not solicit the selling of securities, it is often referred to as a "red herring." A statement, in red, must be displayed on the front page to the effect that it is not final and is subject to completion or amendment before shares can be issued. The dealer may also prepare a "greensheet," which is an information circular, for in-house use only. It includes salient features of the issue, both pro and con, and would be used by the sales department to solicit interest in the new issue.

During the waiting period (between the issuance of red herrings and the receipt of final prospectuses), dealers are prohibited from activities considered to be furthering the issuance of securities (such as entering into purchase and sale agreements), other than solicitation of expressions of interest. However, the dealer will proceed along other lines, attempting to formalize the details of items such as the trust deed or indenture (for debt issues); the underwriting or agency agreement between issuer and distributor; the banking group agreement; the selling group agreement; and final price to the public and to the dealer.

Once the prospectus has been prepared, it will be filed with the relevant securities commissions, and approval generally takes three weeks. Any changes must be agreed upon with the issuers before final approval. The issue is then "blue skied" and may be distributed to the public. It must be accompanied by the consent of all experts whose opinions are referred to in the prospectus. This process prevents investors from investing in companies with few or no assets—that is, from purchasing "the blue sky." The prospectus must be mailed or delivered to all purchasers of the securities, not later than midnight on the second business day after the trade.

Underwriting
The process by which investment dealers purchase an issue of securities from a firm and resell it to the public.

Prospectus
Legal documents that contain relevant financial statements about the proposed use of the funds raised by the stock issue, future growth plans and other relevant information regarding the share issue. Provides information about a public offering of securities to potential buyers.

The Underwriting Process

A typical example of the underwriting process is depicted in Figure 4-1. The first step in the process has the issuing company selling the securities to the financing group (also known as managing underwriters or syndicate managers), which consists of one or two firms. The financing group accepts the liability of the issue on behalf of the banking group members, which includes themselves, as well as other dealers who have agreed to participate based on certain terms.

Figure 4-1
A Primary Offering of
Securities

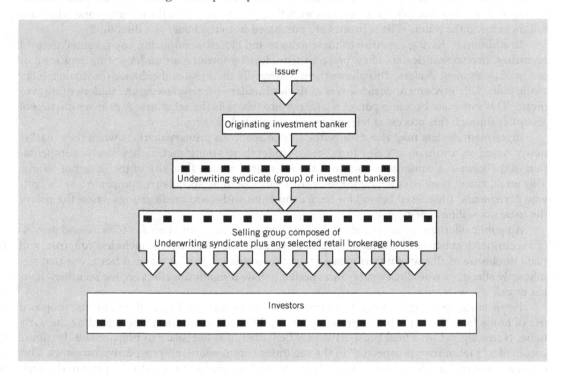

Second, the financing group sells the securities to the marketing group at a "draw down" price, which provides a differential that enables the financing group to recover expenditures undertaken on behalf of the entire banking group.

Third, the securities are distributed for sale to the public, with a certain proportion being allocated to

1. The banking group (the largest proportion)

2. The exempt list, which usually includes only large professional buyers, mostly financial institutions, who are exempt from prospectus requirements

3. The selling group, which consists of other dealers who are not part of the banking group

4. Casual dealers, who are not members of the banking or selling groups, and may be brokers, broker dealers, foreign dealers, banks, etc.

5. Special groups, which may include the issuer's banker or dealer, etc.

Prompt Offering Qualification (POP) System

Allows qualifying senior reporting issuers to put out short form prospectuses in lieu of full ones.

The Prompt Offering Qualification (POP) System

The **Prompt Offering Qualification (POP) System** allows senior reporting issuers, who have made public distributions and who are subject to continuous disclosure requirements, to issue "short form" prospectuses. The rationale is that there is already a great deal of information available on the company that would normally be included in a prospectus. These short form prospectuses save issuers a great deal of time and money, and generally focus on details of the securities being issued such as price, distribution spread, use of proceeds, and security attributes.

Issuers under the POP System

1. Have been filing annual and interim statements for 12 months prior to the issue
2. Have filed or will file an annual information form (AIF) with the appropriate administrator
3. Are not in default of any requirements under the relevant securities legislation
4. Have a large public float (equity shares listed on an exchange and held by non-insiders with a market value of at least $75 million)

Issuers satisfying the first three conditions may also use the POP System for issues of high quality non-convertible debt and/or preferred shares.

Short form prospectuses are commonly used for "bought deals" and have contributed to the growth of these arrangements. Bought deals are the most popular form of underwriting in Canada. The issuer sells the entire issue to one investment dealer or to a group that attempts to resell it and accepts all of the price risk. Generally, the dealer has pre-marketed the issue to a few large institutional investors. Issuers are usually large, well-known firms that qualify for the use of POP. Therefore, bought deals are usually executed very swiftly.

An additional option available to Canadian companies since 1991 is to register securities in advance of issuance, which is referred to as "shelf registration." This alternative, which has been available in the United States since 1982, permits companies to "place on the shelf" securities to be sold. The issuing company can sell the new securities over time by auctioning pieces of the issue, which provides flexibility and savings.

The Listing Process

New share issues are usually initially traded over-the-counter (OTC) and are considered for listing on an exchange only after proof of satisfactory distribution is available. Often, the underwriting agreement will require the underwriters to provide some market support for the new security issue for a specified time period. Sometimes a market develops for new issues prior to their actual listing, and trading is handled by dealers in what is known as the "grey market." This is an unofficial OTC market composed of dealers wishing to execute customers' orders and support an issue until official listing occurs.

Global Security Issues

The global perspective now in place allows companies in various countries to raise new capital in amounts that would have been impossible only a few years earlier because these companies were often limited to selling new securities in their own domestic markets. The global equity offering has changed all that. An important new development for investment dealers is the emphasis on managing the global offerings of securities. A lead investment dealer can act as a "global coordinator," linking separate underwriting syndicates throughout the world in selling equity issues. Many Canadian companies issue bonds in the United States or in the Euromarket.

A number of Canadian companies are "interlisted" on more than one stock market, primarily markets in the United States, such as Nasdaq or the New York Stock Exchange (NYSE). The motivation for Canadian firms to interlist on US markets is to increase the stock's potential market and enhance its visibility. However, empirical evidence is inconclusive regarding share price benefits obtained from interlisting in the United States.

Private Placements

An increasing number of corporations have executed private placements, whereby new securities issues are sold directly to financial institutions, such as life insurance companies and pension funds, bypassing the open market. While private placements have been very common for debt issues for quite some time, they have been used more frequently for equity issuances. For example, in the first quarter of 2004, $2.898 billion (56 percent) of total equity issues were raised through private placements. One advantage is that the firm does not have to prepare a full prospectus, only a specific contract (or offering memorandum).[5] Investment dealer fees are also reduced because the dealer usually acts as an agent for the issuer for a finders fee, which is well below normal underwriting spreads. The disadvantages of private placements include a higher interest cost, because the financial institutions usually require a higher return than would be required from a public subscription, and possible restrictive provisions on the borrower's activities.[6]

CHECK YOUR UNDERSTANDING

4-1. In a typical underwriting, the procedure is referred to as a firm commitment. What do you think this means?

4-2. It is said that IPOs are often underpriced relative to the price at which they could be marketed. What are some possible reasons for this?

4-3. If a company with publicly traded stock issues more shares through a seasoned offering, would the sale of these securities occur in the primary or secondary market?

Secondary Markets
Markets where existing securities are traded among investors; the TSX is the largest stock market in Canada.

learning objective 2
Describe how the equity markets are organized and how they operate.

Auction Market
A securities market with a physical location, such as the Toronto Stock Exchange, where the prices of securities are determined by the bidding (auction) actions of buyers and sellers.

Brokers
Intermediaries who represent both buyers and sellers and attempt to obtain the best price possible for either party in securities transactions; they receive a commission for this service.

THE SECONDARY MARKETS

Once new securities have been sold in the primary market, an efficient mechanism must exist for their resale if investors are to view securities as attractive opportunities. **Secondary markets** give investors the means to trade existing securities.[7]

Secondary markets exist for the trading of common and preferred stock, rights, warrants, bonds, and puts and calls. Figure 4-2 diagrams the structure of Canadian secondary markets in 2008, which is discussed below in the following order: equities, bonds, and derivative securities.

Equity Securities—Auction Markets

Common stocks, preferred stocks, income trusts, and warrants are traded in the equity markets. Some secondary equity markets are **auction markets**, involving an auction (bidding) process in a specific physical location. Investors are represented by **brokers**, intermediaries who represent both buyers and sellers and attempt to obtain the best price possible for either party in a transaction. Brokers collect commissions for their efforts and generally have no vested interest in whether a customer places a buy order or a sell order, or, in most cases, in what is bought or sold (holding constant the value of the transaction).

---

[5]The savings in time can sometimes be important, for market conditions can change rapidly between the time an issue is registered and sold.

[6]In addition, a lack of marketability exists because the issue is unregistered. Therefore, the buyer may demand additional compensation from the issuer in the form of a higher yield.

[7]Again, this does not directly affect the issuer, who sells new securities in the primary market in order to raise funds.

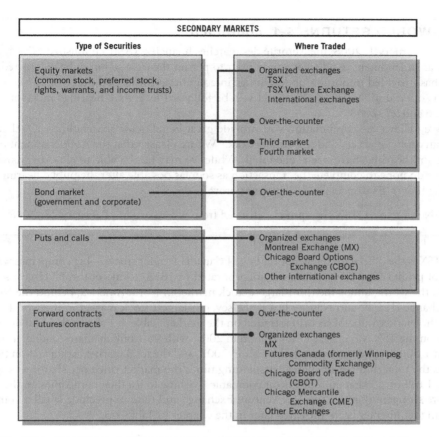

Figure 4-2
The Structure of
Secondary Markets

Canadian Exchanges

Canadian stock exchanges have undergone significant changes. At the start of 1999, there were five stock exchanges in Canada: the **Toronto Stock Exchange (TSX)**, the Montreal Exchange (MX), the Vancouver Stock Exchange (VSE), the Winnipeg Stock Exchange (WSE), and the Alberta Stock Exchange (ASE). A complete overhaul of that structure occurred during 1999 and 2000, and as a result of this restructuring, there are two remaining stock exchanges in Canada: the TSX and the TSX Venture Exchange. In addition, by March 2000 the Montreal Exchange (MX) assumed its role as the Canadian national derivatives market, and it now carries on all trading in financial futures and options that previously occurred on the TSX, the MX, and the now-defunct Toronto Futures Exchange. On May 1, 2008, the TSX Group and the MX merged to create the TMX Group Inc. The February announcement, which describes the process leading up to May 1, is described in Real-World Returns 4-1. This merger is a Canadian example of a broader global trend toward exchange mergers, several of which are discussed in the next sections.

Toronto Stock Exchange (TSX)

Canada's national stock market for senior companies.

REAL-WORLD RETURNS 4-1

Key Milestone Achieved in TSX Group Inc. and MX Combination

Shareholders of Montréal Exchange Inc. today voted 99.6 percent in favour of the combination with TSX Group Inc. to form TMX Group Inc., as announced December 10, 2007.

"This is a significant step towards completing the transaction," said Michael Ptasznik, Interim Co-CEO, TSX Group. "Our efforts are now focused on obtaining the necessary regulatory approvals needed to finalize the combination."

(continued)

> **REAL-WORLD RETURNS 4-1 continued**
>
> On February 1, 2008, the Autorité des marchés financiers (AMF) published MX's application for an amendment to its recognition order to permit the transaction to be completed. TSX Group has provided important undertakings in conjunction with that process. The comment period is open until March 3, 2008 and will be followed by public hearings in Montreal on March 26 and 27, 2008.
>
> "We believe the combination will provide great benefits for shareholders, Quebec and Canadian capital markets", added Mr. Ptasznik. "We are pleased that the AMF comment period is open and hearings have been scheduled. While we may not be able to close by March 31, 2008, we do hope to complete the transaction as soon as possible after the public hearings and receiving the AMF's decision and all other approvals."
>
> Source: News release, TSX Group Inc. Retrieved from www.tsx.com, February 13, 2008.

The TSX is the official exchange for trading of Canadian senior stocks—big companies with solid histories of profits. The TSX, which was incorporated in 1878, is one of the 10 largest stock exchanges in the world, and is the third-largest stock market in North America, behind the New York Stock Exchange (NYSE) and Nasdaq.It was the seventh-largest stock market in the world in 2006, based on the market value of securities traded on the market. Table 4-2 shows the total dollar value of trading on the TSX was close to $1.7 trillion in 2007, with 96.1 billion shares traded. There were more than 1,600 listed companies on the TSX in 2007, and the total market capitalization (which is defined as the total number of shares outstanding times the market price per share) was approximately $2.1 trillion.[8] The requirements for companies wishing to list their companies on the TSX are much more stringent than for the TSX Venture Exchange and tend to preclude smaller companies. These listing requirements are provided later in the chapter in Table 4-3.

Table 4-2

TSX and TSX Venture Exchange Trading Statistics (2006–2007)

	2006	2007
TSX		
Trading volume (millions)	82,050	96,109
Trading value ($ billions)	1,416	1,697
Market capitalization ($ billions)	2,061	2,093
Number of listed companies	1,598	1,613
TSX Venture Exchange		
Trading volume (millions)	37,364	53,147
Trading value ($ billions)	33.3	45.0
Market capitalization ($ billions)	55.3	58.5
Number of listed companies	2,244	2,338

Source: Retrieved from www.tsx.com, March 23, 2008.

---

[8]Retrieved from www.tsx.com, March 23, 2008.

The TSX Venture Exchange is Canada's public venture capital marketplace, and like the TSX, it is part of the TSX Group. It provides emerging companies with access to capital while offering investors a well-regulated market for making venture investments. By the end of 2007, the TSX Venture Exchange had 2,338 companies listed and the total market capitalization of this market had reached $58.5 billion. TSX Venture Exchange-listed companies are active primarily in the mining, oil and gas, manufacturing, technology, and financial services sectors. It provides the Canadian economy with a capital-raising infrastructure for the small and medium-size businesses that are driving economic growth in Canada. With offices in Vancouver, Calgary, Winnipeg, Toronto, and Montreal, the TSX Venture Exchange provides corporate finance and business development expertise in key markets across the country.

Trading operations for both the TSX and the TSX Venture Exchange are conducted by TSX Markets, also a member of the TSX Group. The TSX closed its trading floor on April 23, 1997, and trading is now completely computerized. Trading occurs through continuous electronic auction markets, with all trades being settled through the Canadian Depository for Securities Limited (CDS). Stock exchange memberships (in the form of stock exchange "seats") are sold to individuals, which permits them to trade on the exchange. These seats are valuable assets that may be sold, subject to certain exchange conditions.

Exchange member firms must be publicly owned, maintain adequate capital requirements, and key personnel must complete required courses of study. Exchanges are governed by bodies that consist of at least one permanent exchange official (e.g., the president), plus governors selected from member firms, as well as two to six highly qualified public governors appointed or elected from outside the brokerage community. Exchanges qualify as non-profit associations and are not subject to corporate income tax.

Exchanges have the power to suspend the trading or listing privileges of an individual security temporarily or permanently. Temporary withdrawals of trading and/or listing privileges include

1. Delayed opening (which may arise if there exist a large number of buy and/or sell orders)

2. Halt in trading (to allow significant news such as merger activity to be reported)

3. Suspension of trading, which may occur for more than one session until an identified problem is rectified by the company to the exchange's satisfaction (if the company fails to meet requirements for continued trading or does not comply with listing requirements)

   A listed security can be cancelled or delisted for a variety of reasons:

1. It no longer exists (e.g., a preferred share issue that has been redeemed)

2. The company has no assets or is bankrupt

3. Public distribution of the security is no longer sufficient

4. The company has failed to comply with the terms of its listing agreement

US Exchanges

The US auction markets include two national exchanges and several regional ones. The national exchanges include the **New York Stock Exchange (NYSE)** and the American Stock Exchange (Amex). The NYSE was founded in 1792 and is the oldest and most prominent secondary market in the United States. It is generally regarded as the best regulated exchange in the world and has proven its ability to function in crisis. On Black Monday in October 1987, for example, this exchange handled some 600 million shares when other exchanges were experiencing significant problems.

The NYSE has historically been a not-for-profit corporation and members could transfer seats, by sale or lease, subject to the approval of the exchange. The number of seats remained constant at 1,366 for over 50 years; however, their price varied sharply in response to market conditions. The value of a seat was less than $100,000 in the mid-1970s but had increased to $2 million by February 1998, before eventually falling to $1,225,000 by the end of that year. On December 1, 2005, $4 million was paid for a seat, which was the all-time maximum.

New York Stock Exchange (NYSE)
The largest secondary market for the trading of equity securities in the world.

On December 30, 2005, member seat sales officially ended and were replaced by the sale of annual trading licences, in anticipation of the NYSE's transformation into a publicly held company. This transformation occurred on March 7, 2006, as the NYSE Group Inc. was formed out of the merger of the New York Stock Exchange and Archipelago Exchange. The merger was the largest-ever among securities exchanges up to this time. Shares in the NYSE Group Inc. began trading under the symbol NYX on March 8, 2006.

The changes did not stop there, as the NYSE Group Inc. combined with Euronext N.V. to create NYSE Euronext (a holding company) on April 4, 2007, thereby creating "...the world's largest and most liquid exchange group.... NYSE Euronext, which brings together six cash equities exchanges in five countries and six derivatives exchanges, is a world leader for listings, trading in cash equities, equity and interest rate derivatives, bonds and the distribution of market data."[9]

Specialists

Members of an organized exchange who are charged with maintaining an orderly market in one or more stocks by buying or selling for their own accounts.

Professionals with trading licences for the exchange can combine with others to operate as a member organization and do business with the public. Market **specialists** play an important role on the NYSE and are assigned to trading posts on the floor of the NYSE, where they handle one or more of the stocks traded at that post. Specialists are responsible for maintaining an orderly market in one or more stocks by buying or selling shares for his or her own account. Some specialists firms are part of well-known brokerage operations, while many others are virtually unknown to the public. (Specialists are discussed in more detail in Chapter 5.)

As mentioned previously, a number of Canadian companies are interlisted on the NYSE. Table 4-3 shows that the qualifying criteria for TSX-listed companies pale in comparison to those that must be satisfied by NYSE-listed companies.[10] As a result, only the largest Canadian companies are able to list their shares on this exchange.

Table 4-3

TSX versus NYSE Initial Listing Requirements*

Criteria	TSX (Cdn $)	NYSE (US $)
Net Tangible Assets	> = $2M	> = $40M
Pre-Tax Income	> = $200,000 in most recent year	> = $10M in the aggregate the last three years and > = $2m in the two most recent fiscal years (positive amounts in all three years) OR
Pre-Tax Cash Flow	> = $500,000 previous year	(1) > = $50M in global market capitalization (2) > = $100M in revenues during the most recent year (3) > = $25M aggregate cash flows for the last three fiscal years with positive amounts in all three years
Market Value of Publicly Held Shares	> = $4M	> = $60M (companies that list either at the time of their IPOs or as a result of spin-offs or under the Affiliated company standard)
	> = $10M (technology companies)	> = $100M for other companies
Number of Outstanding Shares	1M	1.1M
Number of shareholders of "board" (Can.) or "round" (US) lots (generally 100 shares)	300	400, OR 2,200 total shareholders, AND 100,000 in monthly trading volume; OR,

[9]Retrieved from www.nyse.com, March 23, 2008.
[10]Continuing listing requirements must also be met, or a firm could be delisted from the exchange.

Criteria	TSX (Cdn $)	NYSE (US $)
		500 total shareholders, AND 1,000,000 in monthly trading volume.
Working Capital (W/C) Requirements	Adequate W/C and capitalization to carry on the business	N/A

*The TSX requirements are for "profitable" Canadian industrial companies. Requirements vary for Industrials that are: (i) forecasting profitability; (ii) technology companies; or, (iii) research and development companies. They are also different for mining, oil and gas, and non-Canadian companies, as well as for junior companies.

Sources: Toronto Stock Exchange, www.tsx.com and New York Stock Exchange, www.nyse.com.

The NYSE is the dominant capital market in the world based on trading volume and on the market capitalization of its firms (which is defined as the total number of shares outstanding multiplied by the market price per share). During 2007, the NYSE had 2,805 listed companies and trading volume was $21.9 trillion US (about $87.1 billion US per trading day). The market value of NYSE-listed companies was $17.5 trillion US as of December 2007.[11]

A trend of potential significance that is often discussed in the popular press is **program trading**, which may be defined as the computer-generated trading of large blocks of securities. It is used to accomplish certain trading strategies, such as arbitrage against futures contracts and portfolio accumulation and liquidation strategies. The NYSE published its first report on program trading activities in 1988. During 2007, program trading volume accounted for over 30 percent of total NYSE volume.

Program Trading
The computer-generated trading of large blocks of securities. It is often implemented to take advantage of price discrepancies between markets (arbitrage opportunities).

The American Stock Exchange (Amex) is the only other national organized exchange in the United States. Relative to the NYSE, the Amex is much smaller and the listing requirements for stocks on the Amex are less stringent than the NYSE. Trading volume is significantly below that of the NYSE (the NYSE generally does more trading in the first hour than the Amex does during the entire day). The Amex does a large business in ETFs, offering over 380 in 2007, comprising over $250 billion in assets, as well as options and other derivative securities. NYSE Euronext is in the process of acquiring Amex, as discussed in Real-World Returns 4-2.

REAL-WORLD RETURNS 4-2

NYSE Euronext and Amex Announce Early Termination of the Hart Scott-Rodino Waiting Period for NYSE Euronext's Acquisition of Amex

NYSE Euronext (NYSE Euronext: NYX) and the American Stock Exchange® (Amex®) today announced that the two companies received notification from the Federal Trade Commission that early termination of the waiting period under the Hart-Scott-Rodino (HSR) Antitrust Improvements Act of 1976 has been granted in connection with the proposed acquisition of Amex by NYSE Euronext. The proposed acquisition remains subject to the satisfaction of other conditions including the approval of Amex seat owners and the U.S. Securities and Exchange Commission. The parties expect the transaction to close in the third quarter of this year.

Source: News release retrieved from www.amex.com, March 23, 2008.

---

[11]www.nyse.com.

The United States also has several regional exchanges, although their listing requirements are considerably more lenient. Some of the largest of these are the Chicago Exchange, the Pacific Stock Exchange, the Philadelphia Exchange, the Boston Stock Exchange, and the Cincinnati Stock Exchange. In 2001, the Pacific Exchange combined with an Electronic Communications Network (ECN) (which are discussed below) to form the Archipelago Exchange, which subsequently merged with the NYSE in 2006, as discussed above. Regional exchanges accounted for a very small percentage of both share volume and dollar volume in the United States.

Global Stock Markets

There are numerous stock markets in nations all over the world. The New York, Tokyo, Nasdaq, London, and Euronext markets are the largest, and the TSX is one of the top 10 in terms of market capitalization.

As noted, investors have become increasingly interested in equity markets around the world. Important global equity markets exist in developed countries including the United Kingdom, France, Germany, Italy, Switzerland, Japan, Hong Kong, and Australia. Investors are also interested in emerging markets such as Mexico, Brazil, and Indonesia.[12] Because of the large number and variety of foreign markets, we will consider only a few highlights here.

Western Europe has several mature markets that are mostly electronic. The London Stock Exchange (LSE) is an important equity market, with $3.8 trillion US in market cap as of December 2006. Euronext is Europe's leading cross-border exchange, providing an integrated trading platform for Brussels, Amsterdam, and Paris. Switzerland is home to some of the largest global companies in the world, including Nestlé (food and beverage) and Hoffman La Roche (drugs).

Europe's emerging markets include the Czech Republic, Hungary, and Poland, where potential profits are great but risks are also. Illiquidity is a common problem, corporate information is difficult to obtain, and political risk can be an important factor. Turkey is another example of an emerging market.

The Far East is the fastest growing region in the world, with growth rates twice that of Canada and the United States. North American investors have been particularly active in the Far Eastern markets. These markets also have been very volatile, with large gains and losses because of illiquidity (a scarcity of buyers at times) as well as political and currency risks.

Japan, the dominant Asian economic power, had the second-largest stock market in the world in 2006 based on market capitalization. Although Japan has eight stock exchanges, the Tokyo Stock Exchange with a 2006 market cap of $4.6 trillion US dominates that country's equity markets. Both domestic and foreign stocks are listed on the Tokyo Exchange, and among domestic issues, relatively few are traded on the floor of the exchange; the rest (as well as foreign stocks) are handled by computer.

Hong Kong is the second-largest Asian market in terms of market capitalization. Other Asian markets include India, Indonesia, Japan, South Korea, Malaysia, Pakistan, the Philippines, Singapore, Sri Lanka, Taiwan, and Thailand. Of course, some of these markets are quite small. The Four Dragons—Hong Kong, Singapore, South Korea, and Taiwan—dominate these markets when Japan is excluded.

The big unknown in Asian markets is, of course, China. An emerging economy of potentially great importance, China is booming as an economy but with great risks, for politics strongly affects investments in China. Its financial markets are still tiny by other countries' standards. Chinese companies do trade on the Hong Kong exchange as well as on exchanges in China such as Shanghai and Shenzen.

Latin America is the remaining emerging marketplace that has been of great interest to investors. The markets in Latin America include Argentina, Brazil, Chile, Colombia, Mexico, Peru, and Venezuela. Mexico's market is the largest, followed by Brazil, with the others small by comparison in terms of market capitalization. As we would expect in emerging markets, profit potentials are large, but so are risks—volatile prices, liquidity problems, and political risks such as the assassination of Mexico's leading presidential candidate in 1994. Brazil (1999) and Argentina have also suffered financial crises.

---

[12]There is no precise definition of an emerging market, but generally it involves a stable political system, fewer regulations, and less standardization in trading activity.

Equity Securities—Negotiated Markets

Unlike the exchanges, **over-the-counter (OTC) markets** or dealer markets do not have a physical location but consist of a network of dealers who trade with each other over the phone or over a computer network. It is a **negotiated market**, where only the **dealers'** bid and ask quotations are entered by those dealers acting as "market makers" in a particular security. Market makers execute trades from their inventories of securities in which they have agreed to "make a market" (discussed in Chapter 5). This market essentially handles securities that are not listed on a stock exchange, although some listed securities are now traded in this market.

The Canadian OTC Market

The volume of unlisted or OTC equity trading in Canada has traditionally been much smaller than the volume of exchange-traded equity transactions. From 1991 to 2000, Canadian OTC trading for unlisted securities occurred through the Canadian Dealing Network Inc. (CDN), a subsidiary of the TSX. The CDN consisted of a large network linking dealers across Canada, where trading went on longer than exchange hours. In 2000, OTC stocks began trading on the Canadian Venture Exchange, which has since been replaced by the TSX Venture Exchange as Canada's national junior stock market. Today, the TSX Venture Exchange handles trades in all junior stocks except for those of issuers that do not meet its ongoing listing standards. These stocks trade OTC on the NEX board, a separate board of the TSX Venture Exchange. As one would expect, this market is more speculative in nature than the exchanges and is also generally referred to as a "thin" or illiquid market, since it is characterized by low trading volume and relatively few bids or offers.

The US OTC Market

Thousands of stocks trade in the OTC market in the United States. Many of these are small, thinly traded stocks that do not generate much interest.[13] The most important part of the negotiated market is the **Nasdaq Stock Market**, or **Nasdaq**. Nasdaq represents a national and international stock market consisting of communications networks for the trading of thousands of stocks.

The Nasdaq Stock Market consists of a network of market makers or dealers linked together by communications devices who compete freely with each other through an electronic network of terminals, rather than on the floor of an exchange. These dealers conduct transactions directly with each other and with customers. Each Nasdaq company has a number of competing dealers who make a market in the stock, with a minimum of two and an average of 11 dealers. (Some large Nasdaq companies have 40 or more dealers.)

Nasdaq features an electronic trading system as the centrepiece of its operations. This system provides instantaneous transactions as Nasdaq market makers compete for investor orders. An investor who places an order with his or her broker for a Nasdaq security will have this order executed in one of two ways:

1. If the broker's firm makes a market in the security, the order will be executed internally at a price equal to, or better than, the best price quoted by all competing market makers.

2. If the broker's firm is not a market maker in this security, the firm will buy from or sell to a market maker at another firm.

The **Nasdaq National Market System (Nasdaq/NMS)** is a component of the Nasdaq market. The NMS is a combination of the competing market makers in OTC stocks and the up-to-the-minute reporting of trades. The system uses data similar to that shown for the exchanges (specifically, high, low, and closing quotations, volume, and the net change from one day to the next). The vast majority of the roughly 4,000 Nasdaq-listed securities trade as NMS securities, and on a volume basis NMS issues account for over 90 percent of all Nasdaq volume.

---

[13] Traditionally, the prices of these stocks were reported only once a day on what are called Pink Sheets. Current prices on these stocks are now available electronically.

Over-the-Counter (OTC) Market
A network of securities dealers linked together by phone and computer to make markets in securities.

Negotiated Market
A market involving dealers such as the OTC.

Dealer
An individual or firm who makes a market in a stock by buying from and selling to investors.

Nasdaq Stock Market (Nasdaq)
A national and international OTC stock market consisting of communication networks for the trading of thousands of stocks.

Nasdaq National Market System (Nasdaq/NMS)
The largest secondary market for the trading of equity securities in the world.

The other distinct segment of Nasdaq is the Nasdaq SmallCap Market, which involves trading in smaller stocks that have not yet reached a suitable size for the NMS, and those that no longer qualify for trading on the NMS. More than 800 companies trade in this market. Several thousand US OTC stocks trade via the OTC Bulletin Board or through the "Pink Sheets" market, which are markets for very thinly traded securities, many of which trade infrequently.

When we think of the Nasdaq market, we typically think of it as a network of market makers. However, today the Nasdaq network connects other trading systems such as Alternative Trading Systems (ATSs) / Electronic Communications Networks (ECNs). These systems allow investors to trade electronically with each other at preset prices and are described later in the chapter. They do not involve a market maker and are simply order-matching systems.

The Nasdaq Stock Market has become a major player in the securities markets. In 2007, there were more companies listed on Nasdaq (over 3,900) than on the NYSE (2,805), and the volume of shares traded exceeded that on the NYSE. However the market capitalization was $5.3 trillion, well below the $17.5 trillion market capitalization of NYSE firms.[14] In November of 2007, they entered into an agreement to acquire the Philadelphia Stock Exchange, and in 2008, Nasdaq combined with OMX AB to form the Nasdaq OMX Group Inc., as discussed in Real-World Returns 4-3.

REAL-WORLD RETURNS 4-3

Nasdaq Completes OMX Transaction to Become The Nasdaq OMX Group, Inc.

The Nasdaq Stock Market, Inc. (Nasdaq:NDAQ) (NASDAQ(r)) has completed its combination with OMX AB, creating the world's largest exchange company, The NASDAQ OMX Group, Inc. (NASDAQ OMX Group).

NASDAQ OMX Group has operations around the world, spanning developed and emerging markets. Its global offerings include trading across multiple asset classes, capital formation solutions, financial services and exchanges technology, market data products, and financial indexes.

"NASDAQ OMX Group is a new type of exchange company. It is unique in its ability to serve customers at multiple levels, from trading platforms supporting multiple asset classes to listings, financial services technology, and data and financial products," said Bob Greifeld, Chief Executive Officer of The NASDAQ OMX Group.

As part of the transaction, NASDAQ OMX Group also became a 33 1/3 percent shareholder in DIFX, Dubai's international financial exchange. As previously announced and approved, Borse Dubai is a 19.9 percent shareholder of NASDAQ OMX Group.

Greifeld added, "We are grateful for the support of OMX shareholders. We look forward to executing on our plan that will benefit all of our constituencies, including investors, shareholders and customers." The NASDAQ OMX Group, Inc. is the world's largest exchange company. It delivers trading, exchange technology and public company services across six continents, and with over 3,900 companies, it is number one in worldwide listings among major markets. NASDAQ OMX offers multiple capital raising solutions to companies around the globe, including its US listings market; the OMX Nordic Exchange, including First North; and the 144A PORTAL Market. The company offers trading across multiple asset classes including equities, derivatives, debt, commodities, structured products and ETFs. NASDAQ OMX technology supports the operations of over 60 exchanges, clearing organizations and central securities depositories in more than 50 countries. OMX Nordic Exchange is not a legal entity but describes the common offering from Nasdaq OMX exchanges in Helsinki, Copenhagen, Stockholm, Iceland, Tallinn, Riga, and Vilnius. For more information about NASDAQ OMX, visit www.nasdaqomx.com.

Source: The Nasdaq Stock Market, Inc. news release, February 27, 2008, PrimeNewswire via COMTEX News Network.

---

[14]World Federation of Exchanges (formerly International Federation of Stock Exchanges) website: www.world-exchanges.org.

In summary, the common stock issues traded on Nasdaq vary widely in size, price, quality, and trading activity. These stocks range from small start-up companies to huge successful companies that have chosen to remain Nasdaq companies rather than move on to the NYSE.

The Third and Fourth Markets

The **third market** is an OTC market for the trading of securities that are listed on organized exchanges. This market has traditionally been important in the United States for block trades or extremely large transactions. This was done in order to avoid minimum exchange-regulated commission fees, although with the abolition of these fees this market has become less important.

The **fourth market** refers to transactions made directly between large institutions (and wealthy individuals), bypassing brokers and dealers. Essentially, the fourth market is a communications network among investors interested in trading large blocks of stock, often referred to as Electronic Communications Networks. Several different privately owned automated systems exist to provide current information on specific securities that the participants are willing to buy or sell.

Electronic Communications Networks (ECNs) (or alternative trading systems (ATSs)) are taking business away from Nasdaq, the NYSE, and the TSX (having been permitted in Canada as of December 1, 2004). An ECN is a computerized trading network that matches buy and sell orders electronically entered by customers. If no match is currently possible, the ECN acts sort of like a broker, posting its best bid and ask offer (under its own name) on Nasdaq's trading screen. Another party who sees these prices and wants to perform transactions may enter the appropriate buy or sell order. Trading was initially limited to members only, meaning institutional investors or large traders. However, day traders can now link to them through direct-access brokers and Instinet (described below), which began to allow retail access in 2001.

ECNs offer automation, lower costs, and anonymity to buyers and sellers. There are no spreads, or conflicts of interest with a broker (as explained in Chapter 5). Costs are about one cent a share. **Instinet (Institutional Network)**, which is owned by Reuters, is the original electronic trading network. It started in 1969 long before the ECNs. It is a system offering equity transactions and research services to brokers, dealers, exchange specialists, institutional fund managers, and plan sponsors who pay commissions of about one cent a share and who also receive free proprietary terminals. Instinet is always open for trading stocks on any of the exchanges worldwide to which Instinet belongs.

Instinet offers anonymous trading, thereby allowing large traders to bypass brokers with their often attendant leaks on who is transacting. Trades are often less than 10,000 shares each, and an institution can do multiple trades to get into or out of a position in a stock without others knowing.

The prospect is for these electronic networks to grow and consolidate, as seen with the merger of Instinet and Island in 2002. Since April 1999, ECNs have been allowed to register as exchanges under Securities and Exchange Commission (SEC) rules. This led to the development of a new exchange (the Archipelago Exchange), which was formed by combining an ECN and the Pacific Exchange, before merging with the NYSE in 2006. Similar to the US experience, ATSs have grown in Canada, with the TSX offering its own ATS, called NEX, as discussed in Real-World Returns 4-4.

Third Market
An OTC market for the trading of securities that are listed on organized exchanges.

Fourth Market
Transactions made directly between large institutions or wealthy individuals bypassing brokers and dealers. It is a communications network among these large institutional investors.

Electronic Communications Networks (ECNs)
Computerized trading networks for institutions and large traders.

Instinet (Institutional Network)
An electronic trading network that has become the largest computerized brokerage. It is part of the fourth market and only open to those brokers and institutions who pay to use it.

REAL-WORLD RETURNS 4-4

TSX Group's NEX Market Shows Strong Trading Growth

Alternative marketplaces continue to launch in Canada but it is TSX Group's own NEX market that is showing the fastest trading growth of any of these marketplaces.

According to current TSX Group trading data during Q1 2008, NEX activity has recently grown to over 2.6 million shares a day. That's up from the Q4 2007 daily average of 1.3 million shares—and accounts for a growth of 100 percent. NEX is a separate board of TSX Venture Exchange. It provides an alternative trading forum for listed companies that have fallen below

(continued)

REAL-WORLD RETURNS 4-4 *continued*

TSX and TSX Venture Exchange's ongoing listing standards, which otherwise would no longer be eligible to trade on a TSX Group exchange or seek listing on a competitive Canadian exchange.

Comparatively, CNQ's average trading volume is at 1.5 million shares per day. As a percentage of overall Canadian trading, NEX's market share by volume is also greater than each of the competitive Alternative Trading Systems operating in Canada including Pure, Chi-X, CNQ, Triact, Liquidnet, and Blockbook for the month of February.

"NEX meets the needs of the investor community for those trading this segment of issuers and its trading structure was designed with customer needs in mind," said Thomas Kalafatis, Vice-President, Sales and Trading with TSX Markets. "Our most recent changes to NEX streamlined the fee structure to be in-line with a volume based trading fee model, like the TSX and TSX Venture Exchange. The lower rate per share for NEX trading fee reflects smaller market cap of issuers. This fee structure has aided in adding liquidity. We continue to believe that TSX focus on the specific needs of customers will reinforce the growth of markets and address competitive forces. We are excited at continuing to develop new products for the marketplace."

NEX companies benefit from the support and visibility provided by a listing and trading environment tailored to their needs, while the profile and reputation of TSX Venture Exchange companies will be enhanced as a result of the overall improved quality of the main TSX Venture Exchange stock list.

Source: Retrieved from www.tsx.com, March 23, 2008.

After-Hours Trading

ECNs allow investors to trade after exchange hours, which primarily means 4 to 8 p.m. ET, and sometimes early in the morning. Instinet, however, operates around the clock.

On-line brokerage firms offer their clients access to this trading using the computerized order matching systems of the ECNs. It is important to note that such trading is completely independent from the standard trading during market hours. Investors must, in effect, find someone willing to fill their orders at an acceptable price. Liquidity may be thin, although heavily traded NYSE stocks are good candidates for trading, as are most Nasdaq 100 stocks. Limitations exist on the types of orders that can be placed and the size of the orders. As of the beginning of 2001, less than half of on-line brokerage firms allowed customers this option.

In-House Trading

Along with the electronic networks, a new trend that has significant implications for the NYSE is the internal trading, or in-house trading, by fund managers without the use of a broker or an exchange. At a large institution with several funds or accounts, traders agree to buy and sell in-house, or cross-trade, perhaps at the next closing price. For example, at a large bank with several pension fund accounts, the manager of Account A might wish to buy Inco stock at the same time that the manager of Account B is selling a position in Inco.

Fidelity Investments, the largest mutual fund company, operates an in-house trading system for its own funds because of the tremendous amount of buying and selling it does every day. In addition, it has set up the Investor Liquidity Network, which is now used by other brokerage firms and institutional clients. This electronic routing system is said to handle 5 percent of the NYSE's volume, and Fidelity's in-house trading accounts for at least that much more.

Comparison of International Equity Markets

Figure 4-3 shows the market capitalization for the top 10 major world stock markets for 2005 and 2006. As we can see by this measure, New York was by far the largest market, followed by Tokyo, Nasdaq, London, Euronext, and so forth. The Toronto Stock Exchange ranked seventh in 2006 and was sixth in 2005. Based on market capitalization (and on trading volumes), the TSX is the dominant Canadian stock market, while the NYSE remains the dominant market in the United States, followed by Nasdaq.

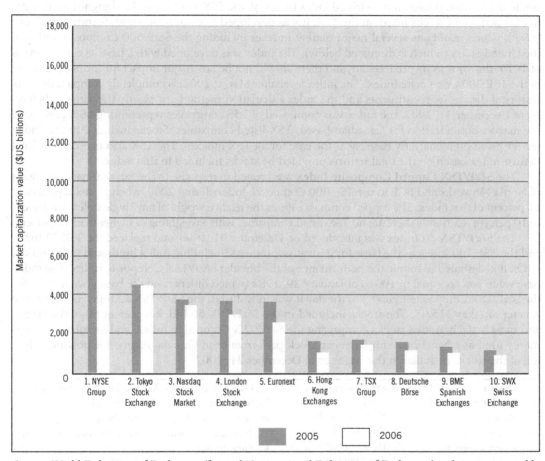

Figure 4-3
The Ten Biggest Stock Markets in the World by Market Capitalization (in Billions of US Dollars, 2005–2006)

Source: World Federation of Exchanges (formerly International Federation of Exchanges) website: www.world-exchanges.org.

Stock Market Indicators

The most popular question asked about stock markets is probably, "What did the market do today?" To answer this question, we need a composite report on market performance, which is what stock market averages and indexes are designed to provide. Because of the large number of equity markets, both domestic and foreign, there are numerous stock market indicators.

An index is a series of numbers that represent a combination of stock prices in such a manner that percentage changes in this series may be calculated over time. They are used primarily for performance comparisons and to gauge the overall direction of movements in the stock market. An average is used in the same manner as an index but differs from it because it is composed of equally weighted items. In this section, we outline only some basic information on these averages and indexes, with subsequent chapters containing more analysis and discussion as needed. The appendix at the end of this chapter provides additional details on these indicators, including composition and construction details.

Canadian Market Indexes

S&P/TSX Composite Index

The S&P/TSX Composite Index measures changes in market values of a portfolio of 300 Canadian stocks due to alterations in the total market capitalization (the number of common shares outstanding multiplied by the market price per share) of these stocks.

The TSE 300 Composite Index, which was widely considered to be the benchmark for Canadian equities, was renamed the **S&P/TSX Composite Index** effective May 1, 2002. The S&P/TSX Composite Index is a capitalization-weighted index (as are all the TSX indexes) and is designed to measure market activity of stocks listed on the TSX. It was developed in conjunction with Standard & Poor's (S&P), which maintains several major market indexes including the S&P 500 Composite Index in the United States (which is discussed below). The index was developed with a base level of 1,000 as of 1975, the same as its predecessor, and there should not be any major impact for former end users of the TSE 300 Composite Index. The index level after May 1, 2002, is completely comparable to its historical data as its constituents and the index calculation method are exactly the same as before. As of December 31, 2007, the index was composed of 258 companies representing 68.5 percent of the market capitalization for Canadian-based, TSX-listed companies. Stocks included in this index are reviewed on a quarterly basis, as is the case for all TSX indexes. The TSX also maintains a Total Return Index based on the total returns provided by stocks included in this index.

The **S&P/TSX Capped Composite Index** was created in response to the extraordinary weighting of Nortel Networks and BCE in the TSE 300 Composite Index during 2000, when Nortel represented 37 percent of that index. The capped composite limits the relative weight of any single index constituent to 10 percent. Currently there are no TSX-listed companies with a weighting of higher than 10 percent.

The **S&P/TSX 60 Index** was introduced on December 31, 1998, and replaced the TSE 35 Index and the TSE 100 Index as the basis for derivative products, including index funds and index-linked GICs. It is designed to mimic the performance of the broader S&P/TSX Composite Index. The index base value was set equal to 100 as of January 29, 1982 (which differs from the base year of 1975 for the S&P/TSX Composite Index). On the day it was introduced, the S&P/TSX 60 Index closing value was reported as 375.98. The stocks included in the S&P/TSX 60 Index represent 60 of the largest and most actively traded stocks comprising the S&P/TSX Composite Index, and as such it is commonly used as a benchmark for large-cap stock performance in Canada. Figure 4-4 provides a listing of the stocks included in this index as of December 31, 2007.

Figure 4-4
The S&P/TSX 60
(December 2007)

1. Research in Motion Ltd.	18. Manulife Financial Corp.	32. Cdn. Tire Corp. Ltd. A	48. Talisman Energy Inc.
2. Potash Corp. of Sask.	19. Shaw Comm. Inc. B	33. Nexen Inc.	49. Biovail Corp.
3. Alcan Inc.	20. Kinross Gold Corp.	34. Nova Chemicals Corp.	50. Thomson Corp.
4. EnCana Corp.	21. Husky Energy Inc.	35. TransCanada Corp.	51. Cdn. National Railway Co.
5. Suncor Energy Inc.	22. TransAlta Corp.	36. Enbridge Inc.	52. Bank of Nova Scotia
6. BCE Inc.	23. Novelis Inc.	37. Toronto-Dominion Bank	53. National Bank of Canada
7. Cdn. Natural Resources Ltd.	24. ACE Aviation Holdings Inc.	38. MDS Inc.	54. Penn West Energy Trust
8. Rogers Comm.	25. Agnico-Eagle Mines Ltd.	39. Domtar Inc.	55. Cameco Corp.
9. Barrick Gold Corp.	26. Shoppers Drug Mart Corp.	40. Celestica Inc.	56. Teck Cominco Ltd. B
10. Agrium Inc.	27. Cognos Inc.	41. Cott Corp.	57. Royal Bank of Canada
11. Sun Life Financial Inc.	28. Tim Hortons Inc.	42. George Weston Ltd.	58. Bank of Montreal
12. Imperial Oil Ltd.	29. Yellow Pages Income Fund	43. Brookfield Asset Management Inc.	59. Nortel Networks Corp.
13. Bombardier Inc.	30. Goldcorp Inc.	44. Lundin Mining Corp.	60. Cdn. Imperial Bank of Commerce
14. Cdn. Oil Sands Trust	31. Cdn. Pacific Railway Ltd.	45. TELUS Corp.	
15. Petro-Canada		46. Loblaw Companies Ltd.	
16. IPSCO Inc.		47. Magna Intl. Inc. A	
17. Fording Cdn. Coal Trust			

Source: "Market Statistics & Returns," TD Newcrest, January 2008.

In addition to the three indexes above, the TSX also maintains several other indexes such as the S&P/TSX 60 Capped Index (which is capped similar to the S&P/TSX Capped Composite Index), the S&P/TSX Mid-Cap Index, and the S&P/TSX Small-Cap Index. The Mid-Cap Index and the Small-Cap Index contain mid-cap and small-cap stocks respectively that meet specific inclusion criteria and are included in the S&P/TSX Composite Index. The TSX also maintains 13 capped industry indexes and one income trust index, as well as two income trust sub-indexes.

The S&P/TSX Venture Index is a broad market indicator for the Canadian venture capital market, which replaced the CDNX Index in December 2001. As of March 2008, it was composed of 484 companies. However, the number of companies included in the index can vary from one period to the next.

US Market Indexes

The **Dow Jones Industrial Average (DJIA)** is the most widely quoted measure of NYSE stock performance, despite the fact that it includes only 30 stocks that trade on the NYSE and Nasdaq. The DJIA is computed from 30 leading industrial stocks whose composition changes slowly over time to reflect changes in the economy. This average is said to be composed of **blue chip stocks**, meaning large, well-established, and well-known companies.

The DJIA is price-weighted and is therefore affected more by changes in higher priced stocks. It is calculated by adding the prices of the 30 stocks together and dividing by a divisor. The divisor was initially 30, but has been revised downward through the years to reflect the impact of stock splits. It is now below 1.0 and was approximately 0.135 by early 2005. The DJIA includes only blue chip stocks with a low-risk profile and it tends to underperform broader based indexes in the long term as a result of this lower risk. Other Dow Jones indexes include the Transportation Average (20 companies), a Utility Average (15 companies), and a Composite Average (65 companies), which are all price-weighted.

There are several other US indexes, of which the **Standard & Poor's 500 Composite Index (S&P 500)** is the most important. The S&P 500 Index is a broadly based market-weighted index that measures US stock performance. The S&P 500 is obviously a much broader measure than the Dow, and it should be more representative of the general market. However, it consists primarily of NYSE stocks, and it is clearly dominated by the largest corporations.[15] Nevertheless, the S&P 500 Index is typically the measure of the market preferred by institutional investors who most often compare their performance to this market index.

Other US indexes include NYSE-maintained market-valued indexes that include all listed equities for a given group: composite, industrials, transportation, finance, real estate, and utilities. The Amex Index includes all stocks that trade on the American Stock Exchange and is value-weighted. The Nasdaq Composite Index was set equal to 100 as of January 1971, and is market-valued. The Russell Indexes are well known. The Russell 1000 is closely correlated with the S&P 500 because it is largely composed of "large-cap" stocks, with the stocks in the index having an average market cap of about $4 billion. The Russell 1000 comprises 90 percent of the market cap of the Russell 3000 Index, with the remaining 10 percent being composed of 2,000 small-cap stocks, with an average market cap of $200 million. The Dow Jones Equity Market Index is capitalization-weighted and consists of 700 stocks covering about 80 percent of the US equity market. Finally, the Wilshire 5,000 Equity Index is a market-valued index that attempts to measure all stocks for which quotations are available; it is the most broadly based US index.

Foreign Stock Market Indicators

Stock market indexes are available for most foreign markets, but the composition, weighting, and computational procedures vary widely from index to index. This makes it difficult to make comparisons. To deal with these problems, some organizations have constructed their own set of indexes on

Dow Jones Industrial Average (DJIA)

A price-weighted series of 30 leading industrial stocks that trade on the US markets, used as a measure of stock market activity and of changes in the economy in general.

Blue Chip Stocks

The stocks of large, well-established, and well-known companies that have long records of earnings and dividends.

Standard & Poor's 500 Composite Index (S&P 500)

Broadly based, market-weighted index of US stock market activity covering 500 stocks. It is generally the measure of the market preferred by institutional investors.

---

[15]The S&P 500 contains some stocks traded on Nasdaq.

a consistent basis to facilitate international market performance comparisons. The largest provider of international indexes is Morgan Stanley Capital International (MSCI). They maintain several global indexes including the MSCI World Index, which is a market-valued index that includes stocks from 21 developed countries. MSCI also maintains 45 country and numerous regional indexes including the **EAFE Index** (the Europe, Australia, and Far East Index), the Emerging Markets Index, and several others.

EAFE Index

The Europe, Australia, and Far East Index is a value-weighted index of the equity performance of major foreign markets.

Similar to the MSCI World Index, the Dow Jones World Stock Index covers Canada, Mexico, and the United States, as well as the Pacific Region and Europe. It is designed to be a comprehensive measure and represents approximately 80 percent of the world's stock markets. Unlike the DJIA, the World Stock Index is a capitalization-weighted index.

The best-known measure of the Japanese stock market is the Nikkei 225 Average, an arithmetic average of prices for 225 actively traded stocks on the Tokyo Stock Exchange. Similar to the Dow Jones Average, it traditionally has been a price-weighted series. In contrast, the Financial Times Actuaries Share Indexes are market-value indexes covering stocks on the London Stock Exchange, the most widely followed being the FT London FT-SE 100 Index. These indexes, as well as those for other foreign markets, can be seen daily in the media.

Bond Markets

learning objective 4
Describe, briefly, the bond and derivatives markets.

Just as stockholders need good secondary markets to be able to trade stocks and thus preserve their flexibility, bondholders need a viable market in order to sell before maturity. Otherwise, many investors would be reluctant to tie up their funds for up to 30 years. At the very least, they would demand higher initial yields on bonds, which would hinder raising funds by those who wish to invest productively.

Investors can purchase either new bonds being issued in the primary market or existing bonds outstanding in the secondary market. Yields for the two must be in equilibrium. If, for example, **Loblaw Co. Ltd.'s** existing bonds are trading to provide a 5 percent yield over a 15-year period, comparable, new Loblaws bonds will be sold with approximately the same yield.

Although some bonds trade on the exchanges (convertible bonds only on the TSX), the secondary bond market is primarily an OTC market, with a large network of dealers making markets in the various bonds. Investors can buy and sell bonds through their brokers, who, in turn, trade with bond dealers. The volume of bond trading in the OTC market in Canada dwarfs the volume of bonds traded on all the exchanges combined. The situation is similar in the United States where OTC trading of bonds dominates, although a few thousand bonds are traded on the NYSE and a very few on the Amex.

The Canadian bond market represents a relatively small percentage of the global bond market. For example, in June 2007, there was approximately $1.09 trillion US in outstanding domestic debt or 2.1 percent of the global market. The size of the Canadian market pales in comparison to several international bond markets such as those in the United States and Japan, where there was $23.4 and $8.1 trillion US in outstanding debt in June 2007.

Government bonds comprised about 61.6 percent of the Canadian bond market at that time, with Government of Canada bonds representing the major component. These are widely purchased, held, and traded, resulting in a broad and deep market, with a large volume of transactions. The market is not as deep for provincial, municipal, or corporate bonds, despite an increase in trading in corporate issues over the past few years. By June 2007, the amount of Canadian corporate bonds outstanding was $418.1 billion US, accounting for approximately 2 percent of the world corporate market. At the same time, there was over $17 trillion US in outstanding corporate bonds in the United States.

Corporate issues are not traded as actively as government issues, which is likely attributable to the fact that over 40 percent of these bonds are held by institutional investors. Most corporate bond trades by institutions involve large amounts. As a result, liquidity is not always good for small transactions in corporate bonds, with delays occurring in the trade, and price concessions often have to be made. Investors should be careful in trading small amounts of corporate bonds and be prepared for delays and costs.

Derivatives Markets

We discuss the details of derivatives markets in their respective chapters. However, at this point we note that options can be bought or sold through an exchange facility or privately arranged (OTC options). All exchange-traded options or financial securities in Canada trade on the Montreal Exchange (Canada's national derivatives market), as shown in Figure 4-5. As discussed previously, the MX agreed to merge with the TSX Group to form the TMX Group in 2008.

Derivative Type	Underlying Asset	Symbol	Contract Specifications
Options	Equities (individual stocks)	Vary	American style 100 shares of underlying stock
Options	S&P/TSX 60 Index	SXO	European style Cash settlement based on $100 × S&P/TSX 60 Index value
Options	S&P/TSX 60 iShare Fund Units	XIU	American style 100 iShares (i.e., S&P/TSX 60 Index Fund units)
Options	Barclays iShares Sector Funds	XEG, XFN, XGD, XGI, XIT	American style 100 iShares for one of the following funds: XEG, XEX: iShares S&P/TSX Capped Energy Index Fund XFN: iShares S&P/TSX Capped Financials Index Fund XGD, XGL: iShares S&P/TSX Capped Gold Index Fund XIT: iShares S&P/TSX Capped Information Technology Index Fund
Futures	S&P/TSX 60 Index	SXF	Cash settlement C$200 times the future value
Futures	Sectoral Index	SXA, SXB, SXH, SXY	Cash settlement SXH (Information Technology): C$500 times the futures value SXY (Energy): C$200 times the futures value SXB (Financials): C$200 times the futures value SXA (Gold): C$200 times the futures value
Futures	Three-Month Canadian Bankers' Acceptance Futures	BAX	Cash settlement C$1,000,000 nominal value of Canadian Bankers' Acceptance with a three-month maturity

Figure 4-5
Montreal Exchange
Product Offerings
(March 2008)

Derivative Type	Underlying Asset	Symbol	Contract Specifications
Options	Options on Three-Month Canadian Bankers' Acceptance Futures	OBX	American style One three-month Canadian Bankers' Acceptance futures
Futures	30-day Overnight Repo Rate Futures	ONX	Cash settlement Each contract shall be for a nominal value of C$5,000,000
Futures	Two-Year Government of Canada Bond Futures	CGZ	Physical delivery C$200,000 nominal value Government of Canada bond with 4% notional coupon
Futures	Ten-year Government of Canada Bond Futures	CGB	Physical delivery C$100,000 nominal value of Government of Canada bond with 6% notional coupon
Futures	Ten-year Government of Canada Bond Futures	CGB	Physical delivery C$100,000 nominal value of Government of Canada bond with 6% notional coupon
Futures	30-year Government of Canada Bond Futures	LGB	Physical delivery C$100,000 nominal value of Government of Canada bond with 4% notional coupon
Options	One Ten-year Government of Canada Bond Futures	OGB	American style
Options	US dollars	USX™	Cash settlement American exercise style Based on $10,000 US trading units
Options	Sponsored Options	Vary	Cash settlement European exercise style

Source: *The Montreal Exchange website: www.m-x.ca.*

In 1973, the Chicago Board of Options Exchange (CBOE) was formed to begin trading in options. It is the best-known options market in the world and operates using a system of market makers. Bid and ask prices are quoted by the market maker, and floor brokers can trade with the market maker or with other floor brokers. Liquidity problems, which had plagued the OTC options markets, were overcome by

1. Standardizing option contracts
2. Introducing a clearing corporation that would guarantee the performance of the seller of an options contract (it effectively becomes the buyer and seller for each option contract)

In Canada, all equity, bond, and stock index option positions are issued and guaranteed by a single clearing corporation, the Canadian Derivatives Clearing Corporation (CDCC), which is wholly owned by the ME. In the US, all listed options are cleared through the Options Clearing Corporation (OCC).

Exercise of options is accomplished by submitting an exercise notice to the clearing corporation, which assigns it to a member firm, which then assigns it to one of its accounts.

In contrast to options, futures contracts are traded on exchanges in designated "pits," using an open-outcry process as a trading mechanism. Under this system, the pit trader offers to buy or sell contracts at an offered price and other pit traders are free to transact if they wish. This open-outcry system is unique in securities trading. There are few sights in the financial system that can rival frenzied trading activity in a futures market pit. Another unique feature of these markets is that the delivery time period can vary, from four to six weeks for commodities such as corn or wheat, to one day for an index contract.

In Canada, the only commodity exchange is the ICE Futures Canada™, which resulted from the Winnipeg Commodity Exchange being acquired by the IntercontinentalExchange Inc. in August of 2007, and was officially renamed as of January 1, 2008. Canola futures are by far the most active product on this exchange, as can be seen in Figure 4-6. The ME trades a wide variety of futures contracts on interest rate products, stock indexes, and even on individual stocks, as seen in Figure 4-5.

Options

Year		2006	2005	2004	2003	2002
Canola	Calls	14,295	6,929	10,718	16,650	16,138
	Puts	12,228	20,182	4,871	11,718	19,332
	Total	26,523	27,111	15,589	28,368	35,470
Feed Wheat	Calls	0	0	0	4	92
	Puts	0	1,460	0	0	9
	Total	0	1,460	0	4	101
Flaxseed	Calls	0	0	0	10	97
	Puts	0	0	0	0	0
	Total	0	0	0	10	97
Western Barley	Calls	484	28	411	66	1,668
	Puts	596	848	1,496	2,712	151
	Total	1,080	876	1,907	2,778	1,819
Total	Calls	14,779	6,957	11,129	16,730	17,995
	Puts	12,824	22,490	6,367	14,430	19,492
Total Options		27,603	29,947	17,496	31,160	37,487

Futures

Year	2006	2005	2004	2003	2002
Canola	2,427,697	1,661,463	1,591,039	1,422,794	1,710,345
Canola Meal*	0	0	0	0	155
Feed Wheat	65,802	81,348	84,151	56,186	84,042
Field Peas**	0	0	0	0	729
Flaxseed	0	0	70	3,358	21,206
Western Barley	193,324	133,460	196,973	190,120	203,1049
Total Futures***	2,686,823	1,876,271	1,872,233	1,672,458	2,019,581

Figure 4-6
Futures Canada (formerly Winnipeg Commodity Exchange) Options and Futures Trading (2002–2006)

* The WCE Canola Meal futures contract was listed on June 26, 2001 and de-listed September 16, 2003.
** The WCE Field Peas futures contract was listed on April 5, 1999 and de-listed October 15, 2002.
*** Totals include volume from de-listed contracts.

Source: ICE Futures Canada (formerly Winnipeg Commodity Exchange) website: www.theice.com.

The centre of commodity futures trading in North America is the Chicago Board of Trade (CBOT) and the Chicago Mercantile Exchange (CME). However, there are several other important exchanges in New York including the Commodity Exchange, the New York Mercantile Exchange, the New York Coffee, Sugar, and Cocoa Exchange, the New York Cotton Exchange, and the New York Futures Exchange.

CHECK YOUR UNDERSTANDING

4-4. The TSX and the NYSE are both secondary markets for equities. How else are they similar? How do they differ (other than country of origin)?

4-5. Distinguish between Nasdaq and the over-the-counter market.

4-6. Why might a company opt to have its shares traded on Nasdaq rather than the NYSE? What about the reverse?

4-7. Is the S&P/TSX Composite Index affected by the size of the companies in the index?

THE CHANGING SECURITIES MARKETS

learning objective 5
Discuss some of the factors behind rapid change in the securities markets.

Over the last two decades, the securities markets have been changing rapidly, with more of the same expected over the coming years. In Canada, a massive restructuring of the security exchanges has resulted in drastic changes to Canadian secondary markets. Globally, there have been numerous combinations of markets, and most markets have also been transformed into for-profit, publicly listed businesses.

Several factors explain why markets have undergone such rapid changes. First, institutional investors have different requirements and often different views from individual investors, and their emergence as the dominant force in the market has necessitated significant shifts in market structure and operation.

Blocks
Transactions involving at least 10,000 shares or $100,000 in value; block trades are usually executed by institutional investors.

Institutional investors often trade in large **blocks**. Large-block activity is an indicator of institutional participation, and the average size of trades on the TSX and NYSE has grown sharply over the years.

Another factor stimulating changes in our markets is the growth of computerized trading of securities, which has made possible the inter-market trading of securities. Inter-market trading permits brokerage houses to electronically route orders to whatever market is offering the best price to a buyer or a seller. This system should enhance market efficiency, by promoting competition and lowering bid-ask spreads, because the dealers with the most attractive prices would automatically receive the orders.

Most of the world's major stock exchanges have moved to computerized trading (including the TSX), the most notable exception being the largest exchange in the world, the NYSE. It continues to justify its nearly 200-year-old specialist system, despite criticisms that it is not attuned to the needs of the modern market. The NYSE defends the specialist system vigorously, citing such evidence as the 1987 market crash, when the specialists stayed at their posts to handle orders while many over-the-counter dealers refused to answer the phone. ECNs will likely have an even larger impact on traditional security markets as we move forward. Finally, the global nature of security markets in today's world has put extreme pressure on all markets to compete aggressively for security listings.

The Globalization of Securities Markets

The move toward around-the-clock trading—which many expected to be the wave of the future—began in the early 1990s. Through such sources as Instinet, stock prices can change quickly even though the exchanges themselves are closed. The after-hours trading is particularly important when significant news events occur, or when an institutional investor is simply anxious to trade a position. Such activity could, in a few years, lead to the 24-hour trading of stocks, just as currency trading now does.

What about bonds? In today's world, bonds increasingly are being traded at all hours around the globe, more so than stocks. The emergence of global offerings means that bonds are traded around the clock and around the world. The result of this global trading in bonds is that bond dealers and investors are having to adapt to the new demands of the marketplace, being available to react and trade at all hours of the day and night. This includes new employees in various locales, expanded hours, and computer terminals in the home.

Foreign markets are changing rapidly, with many merging or simply forming alliances. This is done to reduce costs and attract business as electronic trading costs are lower than those on an exchange. Most stock markets around the world are almost totally computerized, with the remaining ones moving in that direction.

INVESTMENT DEALER FINED FOR LACK OF CONTROLS

The Investment Industry Regulatory Organization of Canada (IIROC) regulates members of the profession to ensure they uphold strict standards when acting on behalf of clients. Violations can result in steep penalties.

In 2007, IIROC's predecessor, the Investment Dealers Association of Canada (IDA), reached a settlement with member National Bank Financial Inc., whereby the firm would pay $795,000 in fines for violating IDA regulations, bylaws, and policies. One violation involved two staff members in one branch, who began to open options accounts for their clients. But neither representative was trained in or approved to trade in options contracts.

The IDA found that a colleague who was approved to trade in options approved the opening of the accounts and entered options trades without ever communicating with the clients or verifying whether the trades matched their actual risk tolerance and investment objectives. Most clients wanted to reduce risk in their portfolio, yet some trades involved high-risk options. For nearly a year, about 100 options accounts were created, with more than 1,100 options trades performed.

The IDA said that National Bank Financial acknowledged its responsibility and took the necessary steps to remedy the situation, including paying "substantial amounts" to clients to compensate them, and stepping up supervision, controls, and approvals. The IDA determined there was little risk the violations would reoccur.

DISCUSSION QUESTIONS

1. What ethics, if any, were breached?

2. If National Bank Financial had not fully cooperated with the IDA investigation, should the penalty have been higher?

3. If the violations had concerned investments less risky than options, would the ethical situation have changed?

SUMMARY

This summary relates to the learning objectives for this chapter.

1. **Distinguish between primary and secondary markets.**
   Financial markets include primary markets, where new securities are sold, and secondary markets, where existing securities are traded. Primary markets involve investment dealers who specialize in selling new securities. They offer the issuer several functions, including advisory, underwriting, and

marketing services. Secondary markets consist of equity, bond, and derivative markets. The Toronto Stock Exchange (TSX) is the largest stock market in Canada, and trading on it has been completely computerized since April 1997. The New York Stock Exchange (NYSE) is the world's premier stock market and operates using a specialist system.

2. Describe how the equity markets are organized and how they operate.

The equity markets consist of auction markets (exchanges) and negotiated markets (over-the-counter—OTC—markets). Brokers act as intermediaries, representing both buyers and sellers; dealers make markets in securities, buying and selling for their own account. The OTC market is a network of dealers making markets in unlisted securities.

3. State the major stock market indicators.

The best-known market indicator in Canada is the S&P/TSX Composite Index, a market-weighted index. The best-known stock market indicator in the United States is the Dow Jones Industrial Average (DJIA), a price-weighted average computed from 30 leading industrial stocks. The S&P 500 Composite Index (which is value-weighted, similar to the S&P/TSX Index), is carried in the popular press, and investors often refer to it as a good measure of what the overall US stock markets are doing, at least for large NYSE stocks.

4. Describe, briefly, the bond and derivatives markets.

Although some bonds are traded on the exchanges, most bond trading occurs in the OTC market. Federal government bonds enjoy broad markets, while the markets for provincial, municipal, and corporate bonds are often less liquid. Derivatives markets involve options and futures contracts. Puts and calls are traded on option exchanges using market makers or on the OTC market, while futures contracts are traded in pits using an open-outcry system.

5. Discuss some of the factors behind rapid change in the securities markets.

The securities markets are changing rapidly, stimulated by the demands of institutional investors and by computerized and inter-market trading of securities. The markets are increasingly linked globally.

KEY TERMS

Auction market, p.98
Blocks, p.116
Blue chip stocks, p.111
Brokers, p.98
Dealer, p.105
Dow Jones Industrial Average (DJIA), p.111
EAFE Index, p.112
Electronic Communications Networks (ECNs), p.107
Fourth market, p.107
Initial public offering (IPO), p.93
Instinet (Institutional Network), p.107

Investment dealer, p.94
Nasdaq National Market System (Nasdaq/NMS), p.105
Nasdaq Stock Market (Nasdaq), p.105
Negotiated market, p.105
New York Stock Exchange (NYSE), p.101
Over-the-counter (OTC) market, p.105
Primary market, p.92
Program trading, p.103
Prompt offering qualification (POP) system, p.96
Prospectus, p.95

Secondary markets, p.98
Specialists, p.102
Standard & Poor's 500 Composite Index (S&P 500), p.111
S&P/TSX Composite Index, p.110
Third market, p.107
Toronto Stock Exchange (TSX), p.98
Underwriting, p.95

REVIEW QUESTIONS

4-1. Distinguish between the third market and the fourth market.

4-2. What are two primary factors accounting for the rapid changes in securities markets?

4-3. What is the S&P/TSX Composite Index?

4-4. What is the Dow Jones Industrial Average? How does it differ from the S&P 500 Composite Index?

4-5. What is meant by the term blue chip stocks? Cite three examples.

4-6. What is the EAFE Index?

4-7. What is meant by block activity? How important is it on the TSX and NYSE?

4-8. What is meant by the statement "The bond market is primarily an OTC market"?

4-9. What does it mean to say an IPO has been underwritten by BMO Nesbitt Burns?

4-10. Briefly describe the POP system. What kind of companies qualify to use this system?

4-11. What are "bought deals"?

4-12. What are the advantages and disadvantages of private placements?

4-13. What might cause an investment dealer to market newly issued securities on a "best efforts" basis instead of underwriting them?

4-14. What is the chief function of a capital market?

4-15. Why do some large Canadian firms want to be interlisted on US stock exchanges?

4-16. Discuss the importance of financial markets to the Canadian economy. Can primary markets exist without secondary markets?

4-17. Discuss the functions of an investment dealer. How do they serve as principals and how do they serve as agents in primary markets?

4-18. Outline the process for a primary offering of securities involving investment dealers.

4-19. Outline the structure of equity markets in Canada. Distinguish between auction markets and negotiated markets.

4-20. What is Instinet? How does it affect the over-the-counter market?

4-21. What is a prospectus?

4-22. What are some of the concerns that the issuing company takes into account when deciding on the pricing of an initial public offering (IPO)?

4-23. Comment on the global evidence of underpricing in IPOs. How is underpricing measured? Why do you think this phenomenon exists, given your understanding of efficient markets?

4-24. Explain the difference between a price-weighted index and a market-weighted index.

4-25. In what way is an investment dealer similar to a commission broker?

4-26. Describe the roles performed by specialists. How do they maintain an orderly market?

4-27. Is there any similarity between an over-the-counter dealer and a specialist on an exchange?

4-28. What is meant by "in-house trading"? Who is likely to benefit from this activity?

4-29. Explain what an ECN is.

4-30. What advantages do ECNs offer?

4-31. Assume that Pfizer and Altria, both of which are in the DJIA and in the S&P 500, have approximately equivalent market values (price multiplied by the number of shares outstanding) but very different market prices (which in fact is the case). Would a 5 percent move in each stock have about the same effect on the S&P 500 Index?

PROBLEM

4-1. Appendix 4A provides details on how the S&P/TSX Composite Index (a value index) and the Dow Jones Industrial Average (a price index) are constructed. Create both a price index and a value index for a group of 10 imaginary stocks (labelled "Stock 1" through "Stock 10"). In the base case, each stock has a price of $10 per share. Stock 1 has 100 shares outstanding; Stock 2 has 200 shares, and so on up to 1,000 shares outstanding for Stock 10. Use a divisor of 1.0 for the price index so that the starting index value is 100.00; for the value index use a multiplier (or base number) of 100 so that the index also starts at 100.00.

Determine the value of each of the two indices for the following three scenarios. Observe how the different indexing methods are impacted by different types of changes in the stocks.

Case A: The price of Stocks 1 to 5 increases by 10% (to $11 each) but the price of Stocks 6 to 10 fall by 10% (to $9 per share).

Case B: Stock 1 splits its shares 2 for 1 (so there are now 200 outstanding); its price therefore is cut in half. No other stock changes at all from the base case. For the price index, your divisor should now change to 0.95 to account for the stock split.

Case C: The changes from Cases A and B both occur. Note that the price of Stock 1 will now be $5.50 per share with 200 shares outstanding.

PREPARING FOR YOUR PROFESSIONAL EXAMS

CFA PRACTICE QUESTIONS

Use the table below to answer the following three questions.

Company	Price A	B	C	Shares A	B	C
Day 1	10	25	50	500	350	250
Day 2	10	20	55	500*	350	250
Day 3	9	25	51	1,000	350	250**
Day 4	8	25	17	1,000	350	750

* 2:1 Split on Stock A after Close of Day 2
**3:1 Split on Stock C after Close of Day 3

4-1. The price-weighted index for Day 1, 2, 3, and 4 respectively, is closest to:

   a. 28.34   13.34   30.10   16.67
   b. 28.33   28.33   30.10   29.51
   c. 88.34   13.43   28.66   29.51
   d. 88.34   28.33   2.82   16.67

4-2. Assuming that the initial index value is 100, a value-weighted index for Day 1 would be closest to:

   a. 1
   b. 100
   c. 98.10
   d. 112.38

4-3. Assuming that the initial index value is 100, a value-weighted index for Day 4 would be closest to:

   a. 1
   b. 100
   c. 98.10
   d. 112.38

4-4. Which of the following statements is false?

   a. The Nikkei 225 is a price-weighted index.
   b. The Standard & Poor's indexes are equal-weighted indexes.
   c. A market-weighted index automatically adjusts for stock splits.
   d. Because of stock splits the denominator of a price-weighted index will decrease over time.

CFA CURRICULUM AND SAMPLE EXAM QUESTIONS (©CFA INSTITUTE)

4-1. The divisor for the Dow Jones Industrial Average (DJIA) is *most likely* to decrease if a stock in the DJIA:

   a. has a stock split.
   b. has a reverse split.
   c. pays a cash dividend.
   d. is removed and replaced.

APPENDIX 4A
STOCK MARKET INDEXES

Several issues must be dealt with in the construction of a stock market index or average. The most important involve its composition, the weighting procedure used, and the method of calculation.

What is the composition of the market measure? Is it a sample of one exchange to be used or a sample from the major exchanges? Should a sample from the over-the-counter (OTC) market be included? Alternatively, should every stock on an exchange(s) be used, and if so, how should OTC stocks be handled? (Do you include every active OTC stock or just those for which daily quotes are available?)

If investors need a broad measure of stock performance, several markets (TSX, TSX Venture Exchange, and OTC) need to be included. If investors want to know the performance of the largest stocks, a measure of TSX performance may be sufficient. Some market measures use sub-samples of one or more markets, whereas others use every stock on one or more markets. It is important to be aware of compositional differences among the various market measures.

A second issue involves the weighting procedure used in constructing the index or average. Does each stock receive equal weight or is each weighted by its market value (i.e., market price multiplied by shares outstanding)? Alternatively, the measure could be price-weighted, resulting in higher priced stocks carrying more weight than lower priced ones.

The third issue is the calculation procedures used. The primary question here is whether an index or an average is being used. A market average is an arithmetic mean of the prices for the sample of securities being used, showing the arithmetic average of the prices at a given time.

A market index measures the current price behaviour of the sample in relation to a base period established for a previous time. Indexes, therefore, are expressed in relative numbers, whereas averages are simply arithmetic means (weighted or unweighted). The use of an index allows for more meaningful comparisons over long periods of time because current values can be related to established base period values.

The Dow Jones Averages are arithmetic averages, but virtually all the other market measures are indexes.

The S&P/TSX Composite Index

To determine the index, the market value of all firms is calculated (current market price multiplied by number of shares), and this total value is divided by the market value of all the securities for the base period. This relative value is multiplied by 1,000, representing the base period value.[16] In equation form, the S&P/TSX Composite Index is calculated as:

(4-1)
$$\text{S\&P/TSX Index} = \frac{\Sigma P_{it} Q_{it}}{\Sigma P_{ib} Q_{ib}}(k)$$

P_{it} = the price of a stock i at time t
Q_{it} = number of shares of stock i at time t
P_{ib} = the price of a stock i at the base period time b
Q_{ib} = number of shares of stock i at the base period time b
b = the base period
k = the base number

A current value of 13,000 for the S&P/TSX Index indicates that the average price of the stocks in the index has increased by a factor of 13 in relation to the base period. If the Royal Bank of Canada was included in the index and had a market value that was seven times as great as that of the National Bank of Canada, a 1 percent change in Royal's price would have more than seven times the impact of a 1 percent change in National's price.

The Dow Jones Industrial Average

In principle, calculation of the DJIA involves adding up the prices of the 30 stocks and dividing by 30 to obtain the average, but it is not that simple because of stock splits and dividends. Instead, the number is adjusted to reflect the stock splits and dividends that have occurred and today is much less than 1.0. As a result, a one-point change in the DJIA does not represent a change of $1 in the value of an average share; rather, the change amounts to only a few cents. You should keep this in mind the next time someone gets excited about a 10- or 20-point rise in one day in the DJIA.

The DJIA is calculated as:
$$\text{DJIA}_t = \Sigma P_{it}/n^*$$

where P is the price of a stock i at time t and n^* indicates an adjusted divisor.

---

[16]Before multiplying by 1,000, the S&P/TSX Index at any point can be thought of as the price, in relation to the beginning price of $1, of all stocks in the index weighted by their proportionate total market values.

HOW SECURITIES ARE TRADED

In Chapter 4 we considered how securities markets are organized. In this chapter we learn the mechanics of trading securities, which investors must know in order to operate successfully in the marketplace. Chapter 5 discusses various details involved in trading securities, critical information for every investor. Brokerage firms and their activities are analyzed, as are the types of orders to buy and sell securities, and the handling of these orders. The regulation of the securities markets is discussed. Finally, the various aspects of trading securities that investors often encounter are considered. Although the details of trading, like the organization of securities markets, continue to evolve, the basic procedures remain the same.

Learning Objectives

After reading this chapter, you should be able to

1. Explain the role of brokerage firms and stockbrokers.
2. Describe how brokerage firms operate.
3. Outline how orders to buy and sell securities are executed.
4. Discuss the regulation of the Canadian securities industry.
5. Explain the importance of margin trading and short selling to investors.

CHAPTER PREVIEW

Now that we have explained the basic types of securities and the markets where they are traded, we turn to the mechanics of trading—that is, what actually happens when a trade takes place. Similar to the organization of securities markets, the details of trading continue to evolve, but the basic procedures remain the same. In this chapter, you will learn about brokerage firms and stockbrokers and how they operate. We introduce the three major types of orders—market orders, limit orders, and stop orders—and explain how they are executed on the exchanges and in the over-the-counter market. (Appendix 5A features the specialist system used by the NYSE.) We discuss the regulation of the Canadian securities industry and its role in protecting investors (Appendix 5B considers regulation in the United States). Finally, you will learn about the importance of margin trading and short selling to investors.

BROKERAGE TRANSACTIONS

Brokerage Firms

learning objective 1
Explain the role of brokerage firms and stockbrokers.

In general, it is quite easy for any responsible person to open a brokerage account. An investor selects a broker or brokerage house by personal contact, referral, reputation, and so forth. Licensed traders of the exchanges are supposed to learn certain basic facts about potential customers, but only minimal information is normally required. Actually, personal contact between broker and customer seldom occurs, with transactions carried out by telephone, in writing, or increasingly, by computer.

Full-Service Brokers
Brokerage firms offering a full range of services, including information and advice.

Customers can choose the type of broker they wish to use and brokers can be classified according to the services offered and fees charged. **Full-service brokers** offer a variety of services to investors, particularly information and advice. Thus, investors can obtain a wide variety of information about the economy, particular industries, individual companies, and the bond market, for example. Full-service brokers in Canada are primarily owned by the large banks. Familiar names include RBC Dominion Securities, Scotia Capital Markets, CIBC World Markets (formerly CIBC Wood Gundy), and BMO Nesbitt Burns.

Discount Brokers
Brokerage firms offering execution services for buying and selling securities at prices significantly less than full-service brokerage firms. They provide little, if any, investing information and give no advice.

In contrast to the full-service brokers, **discount brokers** concentrate on executing orders and are able to charge lower fees. Most offer services frequently used by investors in a manner similar to the full-service brokers, but they provide little, if any, investing information and give no advice. Thus, investors pay less and receive less. Most of the full-service brokerage firms also maintain discount brokerage operations. Familiar names include Bank of Montreal Investor Line, ScotiaBank Discount Brokerage, Royal Bank Action Direct Discount Brokerage, TD Waterhouse (formerly TD Greenline), and CIBC Investor's Edge Discount Brokerage.

Today, there are numerous on-line discount brokerage firms—including E*TRADE Canada and most of the traditional discount brokerage firms—that allow reduced commissions for trading of securities using the Internet. This provides many investors with an attractive option for investing.

Stockbrokers or Financial Consultants?

Traditionally, investors dealt with stockbrokers at large retail brokerage firms who executed their customers' orders, provided advice, and sent them publications about individual stocks, industries, bonds, and so forth. These brokers earned most of their income from their share of the commissions generated by their customers. The key to being a successful broker was to build a client base and to service the accounts, making money as customers traded.

As noted above, investors can now choose to use a discount broker who will provide virtually all of the same services except advice and publications and will charge less for the execution of trades. Smart investors choose the alternative that is best for them in terms of their own needs. Some investors need and want personal attention and research publications and are willing to pay higher brokerage commissions. Others, however, prefer to do their own research and to pay only for order execution.

What about today's full-service stockbrokers? In the first place, they go by different titles, such as financial consultants or investment advisors (or simply registered representatives). This change in title reflects the significant changes that have occurred in the industry. Brokerage firms now derive a smaller percentage of their revenues from commissions paid by individual investors than in the past. And the typical full-service stockbroker, whatever he or she is called, now derives less of their income from customer commissions.

How do brokers earn the rest of their income? One alternative is to sell mutual funds owned by their own firms. These funds carry a load or sales charge, and the broker selling shares in these funds earns part of this sales charge. Although a large brokerage firm may sell dozens or hundreds of different funds, there is evidence that brokers are pressured to put their customers into the in-house funds.

Another alternative involves "principal transactions," or brokerage firms trading for their own accounts. When these firms want to sell some shares from their own account, brokers are often encouraged to sell these securities to their customers, with some additional financial incentives provided. Smart investors, when given a recommendation to buy a security by their broker, ask if the firm has issued a public buy recommendation or if the broker is being compensated to sell this security. This activity now accounts for an increasingly important source of income for brokerage firms.

Yet another source of income is the sale of new issues of securities (IPOs), discussed in Chapter 4. Underwriting new issues is a profitable activity for brokerage firms, and brokers may have an incentive to steer their customers into the new issues.

Other sources of revenue today that were non-existent or much smaller in the past include administrative fees resulting from imposing charges on customer accounts. For example, fees for inactive accounts, transfers, and maintenance may be imposed on customers. Obviously, commissions on products sold by brokers will vary depending on the product. Government bonds or T-bills may carry commissions of less than 1 percent, whereas limited partnerships, which are more complicated instruments, may carry commissions of 8 percent or more.

Types of Brokerage Accounts

The most basic type of account is the **cash account**, whereby the customer pays the brokerage house the full price for any securities purchased. Many customers open a **margin account**, which allows the customer to borrow from the brokerage firm to purchase securities. (Margin is explained in some detail later in this chapter.) An alternative to these accounts is for clients of investment dealers to maintain discretionary or managed accounts. Managed accounts are client portfolios that are managed on a continuing basis by the dealer, usually for a management fee. Discretionary accounts are similar but are generally opened as a convenience to clients who are unwilling or unable to attend to their own accounts (for example, if they are seriously ill or are out of the country). Managed accounts may be solicited, whereas discretionary accounts may not. Both accounts require written consent of the client, and the authorization must include investment objectives. These accounts generally require minimum account balances of $100,000 or $200,000 and charge management fees in the 2 percent range.

In an important development in brokerage accounts, brokers now act as middlemen, matching clients with independent money managers. Brokerage houses offer **wrap accounts** to investors with a minimum of $100,000 to commit. Using the broker as a consultant, the client chooses one or more outside money managers from a list provided by the broker. Under this wrap account, all costs—the cost of the broker-consultant and money manager, transactions costs, custody fees, and the cost of detailed performance reports—are wrapped in one fee. For stocks, fees are typically in the 2 to 3 percent range of the assets managed, dropping as the size of the account gets larger.[1]

learning objective 2
Describe how brokerage firms operate.

Cash Account
The most common type of brokerage account in which the customer pays the brokerage house the full price of any securities purchased.

Margin Account
A brokerage account that allows the customer to borrow from the brokerage firm to purchase securities.

Wrap Account
A type of brokerage account where all costs are wrapped in one fee.

---

[1]Fees are generally lower for bond portfolios or combinations of stocks and bonds.

Commissions

For most of their long history, North American exchanges have required their members to charge fixed (and minimum) commissions (although on transactions involving more than $500,000, they were negotiable in Canada). In the United States, the requirement of fixed commissions applied to all trades and fuelled the growth of the third market for block trading, as discussed in Chapter 4. The United States eliminated fixed commissions requirements in 1975, and Canada followed suit in 1983. The result of these changes is that in today's environment, fees are supposed to be negotiated, with each firm free to act independently.

These changes have lead to lower commission fees, as well as the growth of discount brokerage firms. Today's investors can attempt to negotiate with their brokers, and different brokers charge different commissions. In practice, the larger full-service brokerage houses have specified commission rates for the small investor. However, the overall competition in the industry has an effect on the rates that are set. Customers are free to shop around, and smart ones do so because differences in commissions among major firms can be substantial in some cases.

In contrast, negotiated rates are the norm for institutional customers, who deal in large blocks of stock. The rates charged institutional investors have declined drastically, from an average of 25 cents a share in 1975 to only a few cents a share for exchange-listed stocks. Institutional investors also receive a better deal when trading in OTC stocks.

Electronic Trading and the Internet

Obviously, we are now in the age of electronic trading. In addition to contacting brokerage firms the traditional way by phone, many investors now trade with dedicated software using their personal computer. In 1992, E*TRADE (and **E*TRADE Canada**) became the first brokerage service to offer on-line trading, and by December 2003, Canadian investors could make equity trades for as low as $6.99. As one would expect, other firms rushed to offer their services on the Internet, and investors now have a wide variety of brokerage firms to choose from. Real-World Returns 5-1 provides a report card for 14 on-line brokerages surveyed by *The Globe and Mail* in October 2007.

While discount brokerages offer on-line trading, full-service firms do not. Such firms do not want to give up their higher commissions, nor break the direct link between broker and client that currently exists. Full-service brokers claim that regardless of the information investors can obtain on the Internet, "Technology can't replace advice."

Individual investors now have three choices when executing trades:

1. Full-service brokers: example, BMO Nesbitt Burns

2. Large discount brokers: example, TD Waterhouse (formerly TD Greenline)

3. Internet discount brokers: example, E*TRADE Canada.

Brokerage costs have changed rapidly because of competition and the rise of the Internet. The following example is only one illustration, and fees are continually changing. Investors need to check out various brokers themselves for brokerage and other costs and the services provided.

REAL-WORLD RETURNS 5-1

Rating Canada's On-line Brokerages

Investors have the on-line brokerage business right where they want it.

To start with, stock-trading commissions are plunging. After years of being stuck in the $24-to-$29 range, more and more brokers are charging just under $10 as long as your accounts have at least $50,000 to $100,000 in total assets. At the same time, these firms are giving clients more for their money with better tools for finding investments and managing their accounts.

(continued)

REAL-WORLD RETURNS 5-1 *continued*

Pay less, get more. The brokers that best followed this line are the front-runners in the 2007–08 version of *The Globe and Mail's* annual ranking of on-line brokers. Qtrade Investor takes top honours for the second year in a row after chopping commissions and revamping its research offerings. E*Trade Canada, TD Waterhouse, BMO InvestorLine and Credential Direct filled out the other top spots.

A total of 14 brokers were included in this year's ranking, including a pair of newcomers called Questrade and TradeFreedom. As always in this ranking, the focus is strictly on on-line services and the target audience is the mainstream investor who has a registered retirement account and is interested in more than stocks.

Costs and fees are a key criterion in this year's ranking because investors rate it as their top concern when choosing a broker. That bit of intelligence comes from an on-line survey we ran on *Globe and Mail* websites last month in which participants were asked to choose what issue matters most to them in choosing an on-line broker. The other rating criteria are the following.

Customer satisfaction: Based on three questions in our on-line survey about customer perceptions of their broker.

Tools and research: An evaluation of resources for choosing securities and also for broader financial planning matters.

Website utility: Does a broker's website help you save time and effort in managing your money?

Website security: A guarantee that clients won't lose money if a hacker accesses their account gets a broker an easy five points in this survey.

Trading: Focuses mainly on how efficient a broker's stock-trading platform is; bonds and funds are also considered.

Trading scores were tweaked slightly to address one of the most contentious issues for on-line brokerage customers today: the treatment of US cash in registered retirement accounts. The background here is that on-line brokers don't yet have computer systems capable of allowing clients to hold US cash in registered accounts. Net result: investors can be dinged on foreign exchange fees.

To help alleviate this problem, a few brokers allow US cash to be channelled in and out of US-dollar money market funds without any currency conversion.

The 14 players in the 2007/2008 *Globe and Mail* ranking of on-line brokers were rated in seven different categories. Here's how they did.

How They Rank

Rank	Broker	Fees & Commisions (/25)	Trading (/25)	Tools & research (/20)	Customer satisfaction (/10)	Website/ account info (/10)	Investment selection (/5)	Security (/5)	Total (/100)
1	Qtrade Investor	19	19	16	10	8.5	4	5	81.5
2	E*Trade Canada	23.5	20	14.5	6.4	6.5	3	5	78.9
3	TD Waterhouse	17.5	17	17	7.2	4.8	4	5	72.5
4	BMO InvestorLine	17.5	17.5	14	4.8	9.8	3.5	5	72.1
5	Credential Direct	16	14	15	8.8	8.8	2.5	5	70.1
6	RBC Direct Investing	17.5	14.5	17	2.8	5.3	3	5	65.1
7	ScotiaMcLeod Direct Investing	11	18.5	15	3.6	4.8	1.5	5	59.4
8	Questrade	23.5	13	8	10	2.8	1	0	58.3
9	TradeFreedom	22	15	6	6.4	5	1.5	0	55.9
10	Disnat	11	16	11.5	6	6	3	0	53.5
11	CIBC Investor's Edge	14.5	13.5	13	5.2	4.3	3	0	53.5
12	National Bank Direct Investing	10.5	13	13	2.4	4.3	3	5	51.2
13	HSBC InvestDirect	11.5	16	13	2.8	4	2.5	0	49.8
14	eNorthern	11.5	12	3	8	3	1	0	38.5

(continued)

REAL-WORLD RETURNS 5-1 *continued*

1. Qtrade Investor
qtrade.ca
Ownership: Privately held

Comments

Qtrade is what you might end up with if you built an on-line brokerage by adopting the best features and practices of all the competitors in the sector. The net result is a low-cost broker that does things right on matters big and small. Qtrade has lots of stock research, it's much better than most at showing you how your portfolio is doing, it removes any worries about hackers getting into your account with a security guarantee and it allows clients trading US stocks to stash their cash in US-dollar money market funds. Last word: Qtrade's customers seem to love the service.

2. E*Trade Canada
canada.etrade.com
Ownership: E*Trade Financial Corp.

Comments

E*Trade used to fancy itself a service for aggressive traders, and it still puts a lot of importance in this market. But in many ways, E*Trade is the friend of the mainstream investor who only trades occasionally, and even beginners. You can trade for $9.99 flat if you have $50,000 in assets with the firm or make at least 30 trades per quarter; otherwise, the minimum charge is a reasonable $19.99. There are no fees of any kind for registered accounts and all funds are commission-free. Looking for a high-interest savings account to park some cash? E*Trade's Cash Optimizer Investment Account now pays an impressive 4.15 percent.

3. TD Waterhouse
tdwaterhouse.ca
Ownership: Toronto-Dominion Bank

Comments

After years of clinging to its $29 minimum commission, TD became a cost-cutting leader among bank-owned firms last month by introducing stock trades for a flat $9.99 if you have $100,000 in any number of accounts with the firm (with less you pay $29). Couple this price cut with TD's solid trading platform and you have a strong package. What would make it better is more attention to small things like showing clients how their portfolios are doing. Note: TD's in the minority of brokers that let clients direct cash from US stock trades into US-dollar money market funds without conversion fees.

4. BMO InvestorLine
bmoinvestorline.com
Ownership: Bank of Montreal

Comments

BMO has been among the top-ranked brokers since this survey began in 1999 and the reason is that it has a unique vision of helping clients invest successfully, even while not providing any advice. Just recently, a feature called MyLink has been introduced to send reminders to clients about developments they need to attend to in their portfolios. BMO is also a leader in account performance reporting and in helping clients build portfolios of mutual funds and exchange-traded funds to suit their needs. BMO is improving on costs now that it has announced it will emulate TD's commission cut starting Nov. 1.

(continued)

REAL-WORLD RETURNS 5-1 *continued*

5. Credential Direct

credentialdirect.com

Ownership: The credit union movement

Comments

The credit union bloodline is evident in Credential through its user-friendly website, reasonable fees and well-satisfied clients. It's also apparent in the sometimes bland look of Credential's website and its lack of resources and tools that would get sophisticated investors excited. So big deal. This is a broker that offers an unflashy but well-rounded service ideal for the masses. Much like credit unions.

6. RBC Direct Investing

rbcdirectinvesting.com

Owner: Royal Bank of Canada

Comments

A broker on the rise, even if it's still in the middle of the pack. RBC is building a premier stock research centre, and it has introduced a new low-fee class of mutual fund in the RBC family for do-it-yourself investors. Some day, all brokers will sell funds this way. RBC's weak spot is corner-cutting in areas such as helping clients track their personal returns. On the other hand, RBC is addressing its high-cost status by matching TD's commission deal as of Dec. 22.

7. ScotiaMcLeod Direct Investing

Scotiamcleoddirect.com

Owner: Bank of Nova Scotia

Comments

SMDI is out of step on stock-trading commissions, it still doesn't offer on-line bond trading (it says its clients aren't interested) and its website, long a sore spot in this ranking, remains as navigationally impaired as ever. The reason why you shouldn't write off SMDI is that it does as good a job as anyone at feeding clients a bracing diet of analyst research on stocks, bonds and funds. If you're looking for guidance in selecting investments, SMDI delivers.

8. Disnat

disnat.com

Owner: Groupe Desjardins

Comments

Canada's oldest discount broker—Disnat dates back to 1982, long before the Internet let brokers go on-line—may well be the most improved as well. Disnat used to be dismal—so neglected was this broker that using its website was like an archeological expedition back to the Internet's prehistoric days. Today, Disnat is revitalized with improved stock research tools, on-line bond trading and a much crisper website. Still missing are competitive stock-trading commissions and proper tools for monitoring your account. A security guarantee would be nice, too.

9. CIBC Investor's Edge

investorsedge.cibc.com

Owner: Canadian Imperial Bank of Commerce

Comments

There's one flash of originality at this otherwise middling broker. Through a deal called Edge Advantage, clients can pay a flat $395 a year for 50 on-line trades of any type, which works out to $7.90 a crack. After that, you pay $6.95 for any additional trades. The question is whether an investor who trades enough to be interested in this deal would be happy with

(continued)

REAL-WORLD RETURNS 5-1 *continued*

Investor's Edge. The answer is yes, if you plan to take advantage of CIBC's offering of on-line bonds and guaranteed investment certificates and its reservoir of stock research from CIBC World Markets.

10. National Bank Direct Brokerage

nbdb.ca

Owner: National Bank of Canada

Comments

The quintessential "nothing special but still adequate" on-line broker. The rudiments are here—including plenty of stock market and mutual fund research, some good portfolio planning and monitoring tools and an on-line bond trading platform that differs from most other bank-owned firms in offering high-yield, speculative bonds. What would really help are lower commissions. Active traders get attractive rates, but regular clients pay a minimum of $28.95.

11. HSBC InvestDirect

investdirect.hsbc.ca

Owner: HSBC Group

Comments

E*Trade's US parent introduced on-line trading on six global stock markets. Given HSBC's status as one of the most global banks, this is exactly the kind of service that HSBC InvestDirect should be offering, but isn't. There's an attempt to play up the global angle, but there's on-line access only to the Hong Kong Stock Exchange and telephone trades are required for other global markets. Blah is the word to describe InvestDirect's service for investors focusing on Canada and the US market, although it is one of the better ones for helping clients avoid currency costs.

12. enorthern

enorthern.com

Owner: Northern Securities

Comments

A skeletal service where the main attraction is a minimum stock-trading commission of $24. That used to be cheap.

13. Questrade

Questrade.com

Owner: Privately held

Comments

A service for active traders that is reaching out to mainstream investors with commissions as low as $4.95, no matter how often you trade or how big your account is. The website is as basic as they come, but a planned redesign should help.

14. TradeFreedom

Tradefreedom.com

Owner: Bank of Nova Scotia

Comments

Another service for active traders, this one offering mainstream investors a deal where they can trade for $9.95 on orders of up to 1,000 shares. Low commissions are the main story here, and they undercut Scotiabank's SMDI by a big margin. How long will that last?

Source: *The Globe and Mail*'s On-Line Broker Survey, retrieved from http://gold.globeinvestor.com, March 25, 2008. © *The Globe and Mail.*

Investing without a Broker

Hundreds of North American companies now offer **dividend reinvestment plans (DRIPs)**. There are over 60 in Canada. For investors, the company uses the dividends paid on shares owned by investors enrolled in these plans to purchase more of the company's shares, and there is usually no brokerage or administrative fees. One of the advantages of such plans is dollar cost averaging, whereby more shares are purchased when the stock price is low than when it is high. In addition, some of the plans (approximately 30 percent of the Canadian plans) offer a 3 to 5 percent discount for share purchases.[2]

In order to be in a company's dividend reinvestment plan, investors buy the stock through their brokers, although some companies do sell directly to individuals. On becoming shareholders, investors can join the dividend reinvestment program and invest additional cash at specified intervals. DRIPs are starting to resemble brokerage accounts. Investors can purchase additional shares by having money withdrawn from bank accounts periodically, and shares can even be redeemed by phone at many companies.

It is possible to invest in the market without a stockbroker or a brokerage account in the traditional sense. As an outgrowth of their dividend reinvestment plans, a number of companies now offer no-load stock purchase programs to first-time investors. By early 2008, close to half of all Canadian companies offering DRIPs also offered direct stock purchase programs.

Dividend Reinvestment Plans (DRIPs)
Plans offered by a company that allow shareholders to reinvest dividends to purchase additional shares of stock at no additional cost.

EXAMPLE 5-1: NATIONAL BANK

National Bank permits investors to buy, each quarter, up to $5,000 worth of their common or preferred stock from the company itself by reinvesting their cash dividend, with no brokerage commissions or administrative charges. Some other well-known Canadian companies offering similar plans in 2008 included Aliant, CIBC, Magna, and Imperial Oil Company.

Investors make their initial purchase of stock directly from the company for purchase fees ranging from zero to about 7 cents a share. The price paid is normally based on the closing price of the stock on designated dates, and no limit orders are allowed. The companies selling stock by this method view it as a way to raise capital without underwriting fees and as a way to build goodwill with investors.

CHECK YOUR UNDERSTANDING

5-1. On-line trading has made investing easier and cheaper, as it has been accompanied by reduced commissions. A more significant reduction in commission fees actually occurred well before the advent of the Internet, however. What prompted this fee reduction?

5-2. State two reasons why an investor establishing a brokerage account might prefer a wrap account to the more traditional asset management account.

HOW ORDERS WORK

Orders on the Organized Exchanges

learning objective 3
Outline how orders to buy and sell securities are executed.

The TSX introduced the world's first computer-assisted trading system (CATS) in 1977, and most exchanges in the world have followed in its footsteps. On April 23, 1997, the TSX closed all floor trading, and all TSX and TSX Venture Exchange trades are now handled electronically. The trading system consists of a central computer terminal that links traders from licensed traders with the TSX. The central terminal processes, records, and monitors all trades.

---

[2]Stingy Investor website: www.ndir.com.

An order from an investor for 100 shares of **Bombardier** might be handled as follows: The investor phones his or her broker and asks how Bombardier is doing. The broker has immediate access to information regarding the last trade for Bombardier, as well as other information such as the high and low for the day and the number of shares traded.

Assuming that the investor is willing to pay the last trade price or a price close to that, the broker can be instructed to buy 100 shares of Bombardier "at the market." For example, if the last trade price was $5.55 and the investor placed a market order for 100 shares of Bombardier, the order will be transmitted to the firm's registered trader who is responsible for trading in that stock (both for customers and on the member firm's behalf). The purchase order will then be executed immediately, at the best available ask price, which could be $5.55, but might be higher, at $5.60. Confirmation of the transaction details will be sent immediately to the brokerage firm, which will then convey the information to the client.

Had the investor indicated a specific price (the bid price) that he or she was willing to pay for the 100 shares of Bombardier, the order would be considered a limit order (discussed below). Under these circumstances, the limit order would be executed immediately if the bid price was at or above existing ask prices for Bombardier. However, if the bid price is below the existing ask prices, it would be included in the limit order book, and would only be executed when potential sellers were willing to accept that price. Limit orders are executed in order of price. For example, a limit purchase order with a bid of $35 is filled before one with a bid of $34.50, while a limit sell order with an ask price of $36 is filled before one with an ask price of $36.50.

As mentioned in Chapter 4, the NYSE has resisted the move to complete trading automation. The NYSE continues to carry on trading activity on the floor of the exchange using its specialist system, which is described in Appendix 5A. It is often called an agency auction market because agents represent the public at an auction where the interactions of buyers and sellers determine the price of stocks traded on the NYSE.

Orders in the Over-the-Counter Market

Traditionally, market makers (dealers) in the OTC market arrive at the prices of securities by both negotiating with customers specifically and making competitive bids. They match the forces of supply and demand, with each market maker making a market in certain securities. They do this by standing ready to buy a particular security from a seller or to sell it to a buyer. Dealers quote bid and ask prices for each security; the **bid price** is the highest price offered by the dealer, and the **ask price** is the lowest price at which the dealer is willing to sell. The dealer profits from the spread between these two prices. Market makers are required to provide continuous bid and ask quotations throughout the trading day, and there may be more than one market maker for any particular stock.

Types of Orders

Investors can buy or sell stocks in "board lots" ("round lots" in the United States) or "odd lots," or a combination of both. Canadian exchanges define board lots as orders in multiples of 100 shares in most cases. A trade for less than 100 shares is considered to be an odd lot. Thus, an order for 356 shares would be for three board lots and one odd lot of 56 shares.

Investors use three basic types of orders: market orders, limit orders, and stop orders.

1. **Market orders**, the most common type of order, instruct the broker to buy or sell the securities immediately at the best price available. As a representative of the buyer or seller, it is incumbent upon the broker to obtain the best price possible. A market order ensures that the transaction will be carried out, but the exact price at which it will occur is not known until its execution and subsequent confirmation to the customer.

2. **Limit orders** specify a particular price to be met or bettered. They may result in the customer obtaining a better price than with a market order or in no purchase or sale occurring because the market price never reaches the specified limit. The purchase or sale will occur only if the broker obtains

Bid Price

The price at which the specialist or dealer offers to buy shares.

Ask Price

The price at which the specialist or dealer offers to sell shares.

Market Order

An order to buy or sell at the best price when the order reaches the trading floor.

Limit Order

An order that is executed only if the buyer (seller) obtains the stated bid (ask) price.

that price or betters it (lower for a purchase, higher for a sale). Limit orders can be tried immediately or left with the broker for a specific time or indefinitely. In turn, the broker leaves the order with the specialist, who enters it in the limit book.

EXAMPLE: Assume the current market price of a stock is $50. An investor might enter a buy limit order at $47; if the stock declines in price to $47, this limit order, which is on the specialist's book, will then be executed. Similarly, another investor might enter a sell limit order for this stock at $55; if the price of this stock rises to $55, this investor's shares will be sold.

3. **Stop orders** specify a certain price at which a market order takes effect. For example, a stop order to sell at $50 becomes a market order to sell as soon as the market price reaches (or declines to) $50. However, the order may not be filled exactly at $50 because the closest price at which the stock trades may be $49⅞. The exact price specified in the stop order is therefore not guaranteed and may not be realized.

Stop Order
An order specifying a certain price at which a market order takes effect.

EXAMPLE 1: A sell stop order can be used to protect a profit in the case of a price decline. Assume, for example, that a stock bought at $32 currently trades at $50. The investor does not want to limit additional gains, but may wish to protect against a price decline. To lock in most of the profit, a sell stop order could be placed at $47.

EXAMPLE 2: A buy order could be used to protect a profit from a short sale. Assume an investor sold short at $50, and the current market price of the stock is $32. A buy stop order placed at, say, $36 would protect most of the profit from the short sale.

Because market orders specify the buying or selling of a certain number of shares at the best price available, investors are often advised to enter limit orders that name a particular price whenever possible in order to avoid the range of prices that may result from a market order. Investors can enter limit orders as day orders, which are effective for only one day.[3] Alternatively, they may enter good-until-cancelled (GTC) orders or open orders, which remain in effect unless cancelled or renewed.[4] "Good through" orders are good for a specified number of days and then are automatically cancelled if unfilled. There is no guarantee that all orders will be filled at a particular price limit when that price is reached because orders are filled in a sequence determined by the rules of the various exchanges.

Limit orders can be filled in whole or in part until completed (involving more than one trading day) in several ways. All or none (AON) orders are only executed if the total number of shares specified in the order can be obtained or sold, and are often referred to as "fill or kill" orders. An order may be given under this heading that states the minimum number of shares that is acceptable to the client. The advantage of this type of order is that it prevents accumulation of odd lots, which can be more expensive to trade and/or less marketable since most investors prefer to purchase shares in board lots. Any part orders are the opposite of AON orders, and may be more costly to execute since they may entail the purchase of all stock in odd, broken, or board lots.

Stop orders are used to buy and sell after a stock reaches a certain price level. A buy stop order is placed above the current market price, while a sell stop order is placed below the current price. Stop loss orders are orders to sell (as market orders) if the price drops below a certain level. They are used to limit losses on long positions. Stop buy orders are the opposite of stop loss orders. A market buy order is generated if the price rises above a certain level to limit losses on short positions.

Clearing Procedures

Clients who do not wish to or are unable to obtain credit from the securities firm open cash accounts and are expected to make full payment for purchases by the settlement date. The settlement date is the same day for government T-bills; two business days after for other Government of Canada direct liabilities and guarantees up to three years; and three business days after for all other securities

---

[3]A market order remains in effect only for the day.
[4]Many firms limit GTC orders for a specified time period such as 30, 60, or 90 days.

(including long-term government bonds and common shares). On the settlement date, the customer becomes the legal owner of any securities bought (or gives them up if sold) and must settle with the brokerage firm by that time.[5]

Street Name

When customers' securities are held by a brokerage firm in its own name.

Most customers allow their brokerage firm to keep their securities in a **street name**—that is, the name of the brokerage firm. If the certificate is in registered form, the seller must properly endorse and deliver it. Customers receive monthly statements showing the position of their accounts in cash, securities held, any funds borrowed from the broker, and so on.

Brokerage houses must settle all transactions with the other party to the transaction, who may be another brokerage house, a market specialist, or market maker. A clearing house facilitates this process by taking the records of all transactions made by its members during a day, verifying both sides of the trades, and netting out the securities and money due or to be paid each member. Members of clearing houses include brokerage houses, banks, and others involved with securities. Once the transaction is completed on the floor (or electronically), the details of the trade are reported to the exchange, and the buying and selling firms are provided with specific details of the trade such as price, time, and the identity of the other party. The firms phone their clients to confirm the transaction and then mail written confirmation to them.

Today, in Canada, most stock and bond certificates are cleared through the Canadian Depository for Securities (CDS). The CDS is a clearing corporation that electronically settles all transactions between members on a daily basis without physically moving the certificates. When an investment dealer trades from its own account, the trade occurs at current market value as determined by the exchange. There are detailed regulations that licensed traders must observe to avoid potential conflicts of interest. In the United States, the National Securities Clearing Corporation operates a central clearing house for trades on the New York and American stock exchanges and in the OTC markets.

Use of stock certificates as part of the settlement process is dying out in both Canada and the United States, since computers handle most transactions. Members (brokers and dealers) who own certificates (in street name) deposit them in an account and can then deliver securities to each other in the form of a bookkeeping entry. This book-entry system, as opposed to the actual physical possession of securities in either registered or "bearer" form, is essential to minimize the tremendous amount of paperwork that would otherwise occur with stock certificates. Such a system also reduces the potential for securities to be lost or stolen.

CHECK YOUR UNDERSTANDING

5-3. Suppose you purchased some shares in a company for $40 each. The stock has now increased in price to $60. While you think the price may go higher (hence you are unwilling to sell the shares right now), you want to protect most of your gain if the price were to fall. What type of order could you place to accomplish this?

5-4. How do market makers or dealers in the OTC market earn a profit, regardless of what happens to the price of the stock they are trading?

INVESTOR PROTECTION IN THE SECURITIES MARKETS

learning objective 4
Discuss the regulation of the Canadian securities industry.

Investors should be concerned that securities markets are properly regulated for their protection. Our financial system depends heavily on confidence in that system. In the late nineteenth and early twentieth centuries, significant abuses in securities trading did occur; at the same time there was a lack of information disclosure, and trading procedures were not always sound. The market crash in

---

[5]The purchaser of securities usually will not be able to take physical delivery of the securities on the settlement date because they will not be available by then.

1929 and the Great Depression served as catalysts for reforms that effectively began in the 1930s. As mentioned in Chapters 1 and 2, debacles such as the Enron and WorldCom scandals have led to a preoccupation with investor protection, and many regulatory changes have occurred.

Investor protection can be divided into government regulation, at the federal and provincial level, and self-regulation by the industry. Real-World Returns 5-2 discusses a new organization that has been organized to help protect small investors.

REAL-WORLD RETURNS 5-2

Protection for Small Investors

There's almost no job more mystifying and intimidating than going after an investment professional who lost your money through bad or unscrupulous advice.

Lawyers can help, but they're expensive and it's not easy to find one conversant in securities law. Solution: Join the Small Investor Protection Association (SIPA) and take advantage of the free lawyer referral service it set up last month for aggrieved members.

For close to a decade, SIPA has quietly worked to organize individual investors and help them pursue complaints against the financial industry. A few years ago, the non-profit group set up an information-sharing database that helps link up members with complaints against the same adviser.

The lawyer referral service originates in SIPA founder Stan Buell's belief that investors should get legal advice before going after an adviser to recover losses. "The idea is for our members to go in and sit down with a lawyer, or talk to him on the telephone, and get some advice on what their options are," Mr. Buell said.

The options in most cases are these:

Try and get the firm to fix the problem: This may work in egregious cases of investor abuse, but you're just as likely to get the runaround.

Try an ombudsman: Clients of bank-owned investment firms should try the bank's own ombudsman office; for other firms, and if the bank ombudsman doesn't see things your way, there's the Ombudsman for Banking Services and Investments (OBSI).

Try regulators: The Investment Dealers Association of Canada, Mutual Fund Dealers Association of Canada and provincial securities commissions will look into whether an adviser has broken the rules, but they won't try to get your money back.

Try arbitration: The IDA offers an arbitration plan for claims of less than $100,000 and member firms must participate if a client initiates action.

Try legal action: A growing number of lawyers are specializing in representing investors trying to recover losses.

Mr. Buell believes legal action is the best way, although the heavy costs make it prohibitively expensive for some people. Even if you don't end up suing, it's still worth consulting a lawyer before trying to get redress for a serious loss.

"You need to know what you're going to be up against and what the process is," Mr. Buell said. "If you go to see your adviser with a complaint, he'll say, 'Oh, yeah, we'll get that sorted out' and suddenly you're being led down the garden path. Suddenly, you discover you've gone a year and you're no further ahead."

One of the most important matters a lawyer will discuss has to do with a limitation period in Ontario and some other provinces that blocks you from suing if two years or more have gone by since you suffered the loss prompting your legal action. The relevance of these limitation periods is that pursuing a complaint against a broker through regular channels can easily take more than two years, Mr. Buell said.

(continued)

REAL-WORLD RETURNS 5-2 *continued*

There are five lawyers with experience in securities litigation on the SIPA referral roster and they all have agreed to work on a pro bono basis, which means they're donating the time. Mr. Buell said it's possible that the lawyers will pick up business if SIPA members choose them to pursue a legal case. All the lawyers are located in Toronto or Southern Ontario, but Mr. Buell said members across the country can easily deal with them by phone.

To see one of the lawyers, SIPA members have to submit a short summary of their case along with some supporting documents. If the case is legitimate, the information is then forwarded to the lawyer.

SIPA membership costs $20 a year, which is a very small investment to make if you've run into trouble with an adviser. In addition to the information-sharing and lawyer-referral services, SIPA maintains a list of 25 or so lawyers across the country who handle investor cases. These lawyers are not SIPA-endorsed, but they have been recommended by the group's members.

Mr. Buell set up SIPA after a costly run-in with a rogue broker in the 1980s and has been fighting ever since to advance the cause of investor protection. Lately, he's become a touch more optimistic that regulators are starting to take investor concerns seriously. Specifically, he mentioned the IDA's proposals that would give member firms five business days to acknowledge a client complaint and 90 days to issue a final decision.

Long delays are but one of the obstacles to getting your money back when you've been victimized by a bad adviser. For a full list of these complications, and some ideas for surmounting them, consult one of SIPA's lawyers.

The goods on SIPA
Full Name: Small Investor Protection Association
Mission: Advocate for better investor protection and act as a voice for small investors
Founded: 1998
Home Base: Markham, Ont.
Membership cost: $20 a year
Members: 600, up from 22 at the beginning
Services: Assists individuals trying to recoup money lost due to bad investment advice
Website: sipa.ca

Source: Carrick, Rob, "Protection for small investors just got a bit stronger," Globeinvestor.com. Retrieved from www.globeinvestor.com, March 25, 2008.

The Canadian Regulatory Environment

The Office of the Superintendent of Financial Institutions was established in 1987 by legislation that amalgamated the Department of Insurance and the Office of the Inspector General of Banks. It regulates and supervises banks, insurance, trust, loan and investment companies, and cooperative credit associations that are chartered federally. It also supervises over 900 federally regulated pension plans. However, it does not regulate the Canadian securities industry.

The 1987 legislation also established the Financial Supervisory Committee, which is composed of the superintendent (the committee chair), the governor of the Bank of Canada, the deputy minister of finance, and the chairman of the Canada Deposit Insurance Corporation (CDIC). Its purpose is to simplify the confidential exchange of information among its members on all matters relating to supervising financial institutions.

Figure 5-1 provides an overview of the regulatory environment in the Canadian securities industry, discussed below.

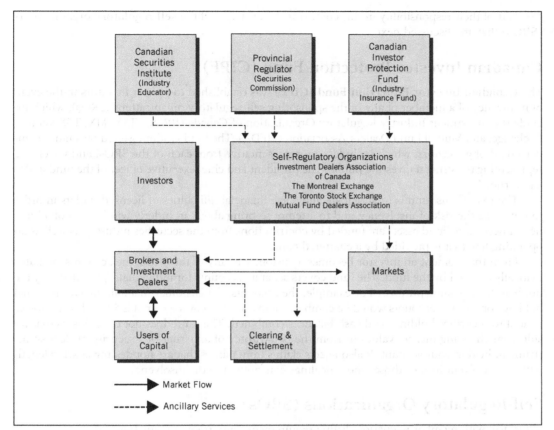

Figure 5-1
Securities Industry
Flowchart

Source: *Canadian Securities Course Textbook* (Toronto: Canadian Securities Institute, Fall 2001); pp. 1–2.
© Fall 2001 Canadian Securities Institute. Modified version. Reprinted with permission.

The Provincial Regulators

Canada has no central federal regulatory agency for the securities industry, unlike the Securities and Exchange Commission (SEC) in the United States. (US regulators are discussed in Appendix 5B.) This is because regulation of the securities business is a provincial responsibility that is delegated to securities commissions in most provinces and is handled by appointed securities administrators in others. The provincial regulators work closely with the Canadian Investor Protection Fund and self-regulatory organizations to maintain high standards.

The Canadian Securities Administrators (CSA), a group representing the 13 provincial and territorial securities regulators, has proposed the adoption of a common "platform" of rules for the investment industry to follow. Many involved parties, including the Minister of Finance, as well as spokespeople for the TSX Group and for the CFA Institute's Canadian Advocacy Committee, recommend the adoption of a "national" securities regulator. Only time will tell how this plays out.

Due to the dominance of the TSX for Canadian stock trading activity, the Ontario Securities Commission (OSC) is one provincial regulatory body of particular importance. The OSC's mandate is to

• protect investors from unfair, improper, or fraudulent practices

• foster fair and efficient capital markets

• maintain public and investor confidence in the integrity of those markets

Self-Regulatory Organizations (SROs)

Organizations in the Canadian securities industry that regulate their own activities. They include the Investment Industry Regulatory Organization of Canada (IIROC), TSX, MX, and the MFDA.

Canadian Investor Protection Fund (CIPF)

A fund established by the Canadian stock exchanges and other organizations to protect investors in the event of the insolvency of any of its members.

Investment Industry Regulatory Organization of Canada (IIROC)

The Canadian investment industry's national self-regulatory organization, which oversees all investment dealers and trading activity on debt and equity marketplaces in Canada.

Part of their responsibility in this context is the oversight of the **self-regulatory organizations** (**SROs**) that are discussed next.[6]

Canadian Investor Protection Fund (CIPF)

The **Canadian Investor Protection Fund (CIPF)** was established to protect investors in the event of insolvency of a member of any of the sponsoring self-regulatory organizations (SROs), which include the Investment Industry Regulatory Organization of Canada (IIROC) TSX, MX, TSX Venture Exchange, and Mutual Fund Dealers' Association (MFDA). The fund is administered by a nine-member board of governors, which includes one representative from each of the SROs, and governors representing the general investing public. The president and chief executive officer of the fund is also a governor.

The role of this fund is to anticipate and solve financial difficulties of licensed traders in order to minimize the risk of insolvency, and to attempt to bring about an orderly wind-down of a business if necessary. Fund assets are funded by contributions from the securities industry, as well as an operating line that is provided by a chartered bank.

From the moment an investor becomes a customer of any of the SROs, the accounts are automatically covered by the fund. The fund covers separate accounts for individuals, provided they are not held for the same purpose. For example, the accounts of a customer maintaining two personal holding corporation accounts would be combined into one. The coverage limit is $1 million for losses related to securities holdings and cash balances combined. The fund does not cover losses that result from changing market values or from the bankruptcy of an issuer of a security or deposit instrument held in your account. It also rejects claims from parties that are not dealing at arm's length with the insolvent firm or those whose dealings contributed to the insolvency.

Self-Regulatory Organizations (SROs)

SROs deal with member regulation, listing requirements, and trading regulation.

The **Investment Industry Regulatory Organization of Canada (IIROC) (formed through the merger of the Investment Dealers' Association of Canada and Market Regulation Services Inc.)** is the Canadian investment industry's national self-regulatory organization. Its mission is to "set high quality regulatory and investment industry standards, protect investors and strengthen market integrity while maintaining efficient and competitive capital markets." These dual roles as both industry regulator and trade association are complementary.

The responsibilities of the IIROC include monitoring licensed traders for capital adequacy and business conduct, as well as regulating the qualifying and registration process of these firms. As Canada's only national SRO, it has the additional responsibility of ensuring that national policies and rules reflect the various perspectives of people in all parts of the country. In its efforts to foster more efficient capital markets, the IIROC serves as a market regulator by

1. Playing a key role in formulating policies and standards for primary debt and equity markets

2. Monitoring activities of licensed traders, and developing trading and sales practices

The IIROC also serves as an international representative and as a public policy advocate by striving to provide accurate information and practical advice to government agencies on matters related to the securities industry.

The IIROC strives to ensure the integrity of the marketplace and protection of investors. This requires that licensed traders maintain financial standards and conduct their business within appropriate guidelines. The IIROC conducts financial compliance reviews as well as business conduct compliance reviews.

---

[6]OSC website: www.osc.gov.on.ca.

The Canadian Securities Institute (CSI)

The **Canadian Securities Institute (CSI)** was created in 1970 as the national educator of the Canadian securities industry. Completion of CSI courses is mandatory to meet the requirements for various registration categories.

Canadian Securities Institute (CSI)
The national educational body of the Canadian securities industry.

CHECK YOUR UNDERSTANDING

5-5. If an investor purchases shares of a company that subsequently goes bankrupt (resulting in a total loss of the investment), the Canadian Investor Protection Fund (CIPF) will cover the loss, up to $1 million. Do you agree or disagree?

5-6. What reasons might be used to support the adoption of a national securities regulator in Canada? Why do some parties oppose such a move?

MARGIN

learning objective 5
Explain the importance of margin trading and short selling to investors.

As previously noted, accounts at brokerage houses can be either cash accounts or margin accounts. Opening a margin account requires some deposit of cash or securities such as T-bills, bonds, or other equity securities. With a margin account, the customer can pay part of the total amount due and borrow the remainder from the broker, who charges the customer the "margin interest rate." The rate charged to the customer is usually based on the prime lending rate plus a percentage added on by the brokerage firm.[7] Investment firms are allowed the use of customers' free credit balances but must give them written notice to this effect.

A margin account can be used to purchase additional securities by leveraging the value of the eligible shares to buy more. They also permit investors to borrow money from a brokerage account for personal purposes, at the margin interest rate, which is comparable to a bank's prime rate.

The **margin** is that part of the total value of a security transaction that a customer must pay to initiate the transaction; that is, the part that cannot be borrowed from the broker. Cash has 100 percent loan value, which means that $100,000 in cash deposits constitutes a $100,000 margin. Other assets such as stock securities may have 50 percent (or lower) loan value because of potential fluctuations in their market value. This means you would have to deposit $200,000 (market value) of common stocks to satisfy a $100,000 margin requirement.

Margin
The part of the total value of a sale of securities that a customer must pay to initiate the transaction with the other part being borrowed from the broker.

Margin requirements for stocks traded in Canada with exchange and licensed traders range from 30 percent to 100 percent, depending on the price at which the stock is selling.[8] The margin requirements increase as the stock price decreases, reflecting the additional risk associated with lower-priced stocks. The word margin refers to the amount of funds the investor must personally provide in a margin account, with the balance being provided by the investment dealer in the form of a loan. Maximum loan values by exchange and IIROC members for long positions in securities other than bonds and debentures, expressed as maximum percentages of market value, are provided in Table 5-1.

Initial margin requirements for stocks trading in the US have historically ranged between 40 and 100 percent, with a current level of 50 percent since 1974.[9]

---

[7]The prime lending rate is the rate at which banks will lend short-term funds to their best customers. It is usually set at a rate slightly above the bank rate, which is the rate the Bank of Canada lends short-term funds to the chartered banks.
[8]Securities firms can demand more initial margin than required by the SROs if they wish.
[9]In addition, US margin purchases require investors to sustain a "maintenance margin," below which the actual margin cannot go. Maintenance margin requirements for NYSE firms require an investor to maintain equity of 25 percent of the market value of any securities held (and in practice brokers usually require 30 percent or more) on long positions.

Table 5-1

Canadian Margin Requirements

On listed securities selling:	Maximum Loan Values
Securities eligible for reduced margin	70% of market value
At $2.00 and over	50% of market value
At $1.75 to $1.99	40% of market value
At $1.50 to $1.74	20% of market value
Under $1.50	No loan value

Figure 5-2 describes the eligibility criteria to be considered "eligible for special margin."

Figure 5-2
List of Securities Eligible
for Reduced Margin

Eligibility Criteria

For the selection of securities eligible for a reduced margin rate, the securities must meet the following criteria.

General Inclusion Requirements

Price volatility measures
- Calculated price volatility margin interval <= 25%
- Market value per share >=$2.00 per share

Liquidity measures
- Dollar value of public float greater than $50 million
- Average daily trade volume for each month in the quarter >= 10,000 shares per day for at least two out of the three months in the quarter

  OR

- An equivalent average daily traded value amount for each month in the quarter ended >= $500,000 per day [to accommodate high price securities]

Listing requirements
- Listed on a Canadian exchange for six months

  OR

- Listed on a Canadian exchange less than six months, with:
  - Market value per share >= $5.00 per share
  - Dollar value of public float greater than $500 million and
  - In the discretion of IDA staff, the issuer company is in an industry sector known for low price volatility

Other Inclusion Requirements
- A new security listing resulting from an issuer reorganization that:
  - is substantially the same as a previous security listing,
  - has a combined calculated price volatility margin interval for the old and the new listings of <=25%, and
  - meets all the other General Inclusion Requirements for ongoing listings.

For the purposes of this requirement, the term "substantially the same" means a new security listing that represents between 80% and 120% of the public float of a previous security listing.

- A Canada/United States inter-listed security against which options issued by The Options Clearing Corporation are traded
- A security that is senior to or convertible into a security that meets the General Inclusion Requirements or Other Inclusion Requirements above

Source: "List of Securities Eligible for Special Margin," The Investment Dealers Association of Canada December 2003. Retrieved from www.iiroc.ca.

EXAMPLE 5-2: MEETING MARGIN REQUIREMENT

If the margin requirement is 30 percent on a $10,000 transaction (100 shares at $100 per share), the customer must put up $3,000, borrowing $7,000 from the broker.[10] The customer could satisfy their margin requirement by putting up $3,000 in cash or by depositing $6,000 in marginable securities that qualify for 50 percent loan value.

As the stock price changes, so does the investor's equity. This is calculated as the market value of the collateral stock minus the amount borrowed. The market value of the stock is equal to the current market price multiplied by the number of shares. Securities firms calculate the actual margin in their customers' accounts daily to determine whether a "margin call" is required. This is known as having the brokerage accounts "marked to market." If the investor's equity exceeds the required margin, the excess margin can be withdrawn from the account or used to purchase more stock. Conversely, if the investor's equity declines below the required margin, an investor may receive a margin call (described below).[11]

A **margin call** (or maintenance call) occurs when the market value of the margined securities less the debit balance (amount owed) of the margin account declines below the required margin. This type of call is payable on demand, and the brokerage house may reserve the right to take action without notice if market conditions are deteriorating badly enough. In other words, the firm may sell enough shares from the margin account to satisfy the margin requirements.

Margin Call
A demand from the broker for additional cash or securities as a result of the actual margin declining below the margin requirement.

EXAMPLE 5-3: CALCULATING MARGIN

Assume that the required margin is 30 percent, and that the price of the 100 shares of stock (from the previous example) declines from $100 to $95 per share. The following equation is used to calculate actual margin:

$$\text{Actual Margin} = \frac{\text{Market value of securities} - \text{Amount borrowed}}{\text{Market value of securities}}$$

$$26.32\% = (\$9,500 - \$7,000) \div \$9,500$$

Notice that the investor's equity position is now $2,500 (down from $3,000), while the dealer's loan is still for $7,000. The actual margin is now below the required 30 percent and the customer will receive a margin call to restore the investor's equity to the required margin. Thus, the investor should have an equity position of 30 percent of $9,500 (or $2,850), and the broker's maximum loan value is only 70 percent of $9,500 (or $6,650). In order to restore the margin, the investor can contribute $350, which will reduce the loan from $7,000 to the required $6,650, and increase the equity position from $2,500 to the required $2,850.

---

[10]If the margin requirement was 50 percent, the customer would have to initially put up $5,000.
[11]In the United States, investors would only be able to withdraw funds if the actual margin exceeded the initial margin requirement—not just the maintenance margin. On the other hand, they would only receive a margin call when the actual margin fell below the maintenance margin—not the initial margin.

EXAMPLE 5-4: MARGIN REQUIREMENTS

An investor purchases common shares of two companies on margin. The first share (A) is eligible for special margin and is presently trading for $10, while the second share (B) is trading at $2.

a. What is the total margin requirement if the investor purchases 1,000 shares of A and 1,000 shares of B?

b. If the price of A immediately increases to $11 and the price of B falls rapidly to $1.50, how much (if any) will be the required deposit in your margin account?

Solution:

a.
Total cost A = $10 × 1,000	= $10,000	Total cost B = $2 × 1,000	=	$2,000
Less: Maximum loan (@70%)	= $ 7,000	Less: Maximum loan (@50%)	=	$1,000
Equals: Margin requirement (A)	= $ 3,000	Equals: Margin requirement (B)	=	$1,000

Total margin requirement (A + B) = $ 3,000 + $1,000 = $4,000

b.
Original cost A	= $10,000	Original cost B	= $2,000
Less: Revised maximum loan A (@70%)		Less: Revised maximum loan B (@ 20%)	
= 0.70 × $11 × 1,000	= $ 7,700	= 0.20 × $1.50 × 1,000 =	$300
Gross Margin Requirement	= $ 2,300		$1,700
Margin deficit (surplus)	surplus ($700)		deficit $700

Therefore, the net required deposit is zero, since your margin surplus in one account ($700) offsets your deficit in the other.

While margin requirements for common stocks may be as low as 30 percent, the margin option does not have to be fully employed. That is, investors could limit their borrowing to less than 70 percent to reduce the volatility of the investment returns, as well as reducing the probability of ever encountering a margin call.

The traditional appeal of margin trading to investors is that it magnifies any gains on a transaction by the reciprocal of the margin requirement (i.e., 1/margin percentage). Unfortunately, the use of margin also magnifies any losses. This magnification is generally referred to as creating "leverage."

We refer to the example "Meeting Margin Requirement" above to demonstrate this relationship. Commission fees and interest costs on margin loans are ignored for the sake of simplicity. In the example, the margin requirement is 30 percent (which magnifies gains or losses by a factor of 1/0.3 = 3.33). First, let's consider the profits to an investor who purchased 100 shares for $100 each, for a total investment of $10,000. If the share price increased (decreased) 10 percent to $110 ($90), that investor would have gained (lost) $1,000 ($10 per share price change multiplied by 100 shares). This gain (loss) represents 10 percent of the original investment. Consider another investor who purchased 100 shares at $100 per share on margin, at the 30 percent margin rate. This investor's initial investment was $3,000 (30 percent of the $10,000 total cost). If the share price increased (decreased) by $10 to $110 ($90), the total gain (loss) would still be $1,000. However, since the original cash outlay was only $3,000, the investor's gain (loss) is 3.33 times greater, at 33.3 percent of the original investment (or $1,000/$3,000).

Regardless of what happens, the margin trader must pay the interest costs on the margin account. An investor considering a margined stock purchase should remember that the stock price can go up, remain the same, or go down. In two of these three cases, the investor loses. Even if the stock rises, the break-even point is higher by the amount of the interest charges.

SHORT SALES

The purchase of a security technically results in the investor being "long" in the security. The security is bought and owned because the investor believes the price is likely to rise. But what if the investor thinks that the price of a security will decline? If he or she owns it, it would be wise to sell. If the security is not owned, the investor wishing to profit from the expected decline in price can sell the security short. **Short sales** are a normal part of market transactions.

How can an investor sell short, which is to say sell something he or she does not own? Not owning the security to begin with, the investor will have to borrow from a third party. The broker, on being instructed to sell short, will make these arrangements for this investor by borrowing the security from those held in street-name margin accounts and, in effect, lending it to the short seller.[12]

The short seller's broker sells the borrowed security in the open market, exactly like any other sale, to some investor who wishes to own it. The short seller expects the price of the security to decline. Assume that it does. The short seller instructs the broker to repurchase the security at the currently lower price and cancel the short position (by replacing the borrowed security). The investor profits by the difference between the price at which the borrowed stock was sold and the price at which it was repurchased.

Short Sales

The sale of a stock not owned by the investor but borrowed from a third party in order to take advantage of an expected decline in the price of the stock.

EXAMPLE 5-5: SELLING SHORT ON POWER FINANCIAL CORP.

An investor named Helen believes that the price of **Power's** shares will decline over the next few months and wants to profit from her conviction. She calls her broker with instructions to sell 100 shares of Power short (she does not own Power) at its current market price of $36 per share. The broker borrows 100 shares of Power from another client, Kellie, who has a brokerage account with the firm and currently owns Power ("long"). The broker sells the 100 shares at $36 per share, crediting the $3,600 proceeds (less commissions, which we will ignore for this example) to Helen's account.[13]

Six months later, the price of Power has declined, as Helen predicted, and is now $30 per share. Satisfied with this drop in the price of Power, she instructs the broker to purchase 100 shares of Power and close out the short position. Her profit is $3,600 minus $3,000, or $600 (again, ignoring commissions). The broker replaces Kellie's missing stock with the just-purchased 100 shares, and the transaction is complete.[14]

Several technicalities are involved in a short sale, which are outlined in Table 5-2. Keep in mind that to sell short, an investor must be approved for a margin account because short positions involve the potential for margin calls. The margins are expressed in terms of the liability arising from the "borrowing" of the securities from another investor, as outlined in the example, "Margin Requirement for Selling Short on Power Financial Corp.," on the following page. Short selling is defined as

---

[12]The securities could be borrowed from another broker. If the lending firm calls back the stock loan, the broker may be forced to close the short position. Also, individuals sometimes agree to lend securities to short sellers in exchange for interest-free loans equal to the collateral value of the securities sold short. Collateral value equals the amount of funds borrowed in a margin transaction.

[13]Note that Kellie knows nothing about this transaction, nor is she really affected. Kellie receives a monthly statement from the broker showing ownership of 100 shares of Power. Should Kellie wish to sell the Power stock while Helen is short, the broker will simply borrow 100 shares from Elizabeth, a third investor who deals with this firm and owns Power stock, to cover the sale. It is important to note that all of these transactions are book entries and do not involve the actual stock certificates.

[14]Notice that two trades are required to complete a transaction or "round trip." Investors who purchase securities plan to sell them eventually. Investors who sell short plan to buy back eventually; they have simply reversed the normal buy-sell procedure by selling and then buying.

the sale of securities that the seller does not own. The investor is said to be in a short position since he or she must repay it in the future (hopefully it can be repurchased after prices have fallen). The investor must leave the proceeds of the short sale with the dealer (who then has free use of these funds), and deposit a certain portion of the market value in addition to the proceeds.

Required margin amounts for trades with dealers and exchange members in Canada, expressed as percentages of market value, are provided in Table 5-3.

Table 5-2

The Details of Short Selling

1. Dividends declared on any stock sold short must be covered by the short seller. After all, the person from whom the shares were borrowed still owns the stock and expects all dividends paid on it.

2. Short sellers must have a margin account to sell short and must put up margin as if they had gone long. The margin can consist of cash or any restricted securities held long.

3. The net proceeds from a short sale, plus the required margin, are held by the broker; thus, no funds are immediately received by the short seller. The lender must be fully protected. To do this, the account is marked-to-the-market (as mentioned earlier in connection with margin accounts.) If the price of the stock declines as expected by the short seller, he or she can draw out the difference between the sale price and the current market price. If the price of the stock rises, however, the short seller will have to put up more funds.

4. There is no time limit on a short sale. Short sellers can remain short indefinitely. The only protection arises when the lender of the securities wants them back. In most cases the broker can borrow elsewhere, but in some situations, such as a thinly capitalized stock, this may not be possible.

5. Short sales are permitted only on rising prices or an uptick. A short seller can sell short at the last trade price only if that price exceeded the last different price before it. Otherwise, they must wait for an uptick. Although the order to the broker can be placed at any time, it will not be executed until an uptick occurs.

Table 5-3

Canadian Short Sale Margin Requirements

On listed securities selling:	Maximum margin required
Securities eligible for reduced margin	130% of market value
At $2.00 and over	150% of market value
At $1.50 to $1.99	$3.00 per share
At $0.25 to $1.49	200% of market value
Under $0.25	100% of market + $0.25 per share

EXAMPLE 5-6: MARGIN REQUIREMENT FOR SELLING SHORT ON POWER FINANCIAL CORP.

Suppose Power Financial Corp. is eligible for special margin and requires a margin of 130 percent. When Helen short sells the 100 shares of Power for $36 each, the sale proceeds of $3,600 (which represent 100 percent of Helen's liability at that time) will remain in an account with her securities firm. In addition, she will be required to deposit 30 percent of her liability (or $1,080) with the firm in order to bring the margin account up to 130 percent (with a total of $4,680).

Should the price of Power rise to $42, Helen's liability increases to $4,200 ($42/share $\times$ 100 shares), and she would be required to have 130 percent of $4,200, or $5,460, in the account. Since there was only $4,680 in the account, Helen would be required to deposit an additional $780 ($5,460 − $4,680) to restore the margin. Alternatively, if the price of Power fell to $30, her liability would be $3,000, and her required margin would be $3,900 (1.30 $\times$ $3,000). Hence, Helen would find herself in an excess margin position and be able to withdraw $780.

There is no time limit on the maintenance of a short position. However, the client must buy the necessary shares to cover the position if the broker is unable to borrow sufficient shares to do so. Because of this potential problem, many experienced traders confine short sales activities to stocks that are actively traded. Members are required to disclose which trades are short sales, and the TSX compiles and publicly reports total short positions regularly.

Difficulties and hazards of short selling include problems in borrowing a sufficient number of shares; responsibility of maintaining an adequate margin; liability for any dividends paid; threat of being required to purchase shares at undesirable prices if the margin is not maintained and/or if originally borrowed stock is called by its owners and cannot be replaced; difficulty in obtaining up-to-date information on total short sales; possibility of volatile prices should a rush to cover occur; and unlimited potential loss.

EXAMPLE 5-7: SHORT SALE MARGIN REQUIREMENTS

a. What amount must an investor put in a margin account, if he or she short sells 1,000 shares of an option-eligible security trading for $10?

b. What will happen if the price of the shares, which were sold short immediately, increases to $12?

Solution:

a.
Minimum account balance (@130%)	=	1.30 $\times$ $10 $\times$ 1,000	= $13,000
Less: Proceeds from short sale	=	$10 $\times$ 1,000	= $10,000
Equals: Minimum margin requirement			= $ 3,000

b.
Minimum account balance (@130%)	=	1.30 $\times$ $12 $\times$ 1,000	= $15,600
Less: Proceeds from short sale	=	$10 $\times$ 1,000	= $10,000
Equals: Minimum margin requirement			= $ 5,600

Required deposit = margin deficit = $5,600 − $3,000 = $ 2,600

CHECK YOUR UNDERSTANDING

5-7. As an investor you should be concerned with the rate of return you earn on the amount of money you actually invest (your equity). Write out an equation that allows you to calculate your return on invested capital, taking into account the following five items: the amount of your equity at purchase, the value of the stock at time of purchase, the value of the stock at time of sale, the total income received while holding the stock, and the total margin interest paid on the transaction.

5-8. What benefits do brokerage firms derive from offering margin accounts?

5-9. What does it mean to say the losses from short selling are infinite while the gains are finite?

DO YOU HAVE AN OBLIGATION FOR GOOD ADVICE UNSOLICITED?

Investors have a choice of brokers, ranging from those providing advice and recommendations (and typically charging more), and those offering little or no advice (and typically charging less). While we generally think of an investor seeking out a broker, brokers often seek out customers. Assume you as an investor have a brokerage account of your own choosing where you transact your investing decisions. Out of the blue one day a broker you have never met, employed at a brokerage firm you are not familiar with, calls you. (For obvious reasons, this is referred to in the business as "cold-calling.") He offers to send you free some investing ideas. You accept the offer. You later decide to invest in one of the stocks he has recommended because after thinking about it and checking further, you decide this stock has merit. You execute the transaction in your regular brokerage account rather than through a new account with the broker who called. Is this ethical behaviour on your part?

Most observers would agree that in this situation you are under no obligation to transact with the broker who sought you out as a potential customer. Had you solicited the recommendation, you would have an obligation, but in this case you do not. Of course, you may not receive any more recommendations from this broker.

DISCUSSION QUESTIONS

1. If you were a broker, would you make cold calls to potential clients? What if some attractive commissions were offered?

2. If you had to make cold calls and you found out that someone took your advice but made a transaction with another broker, how would you react?

3. Is there such a thing as objective financial advice?

SUMMARY

This summary relates to the learning objectives for this chapter.

1. **Explain the role of brokerage firms and stockbrokers.**

    Brokerage firms consist of full-service brokers, discount brokers, and/or Internet brokers who execute stock trades for clients. Full-service stockbrokers earn their incomes from a variety of sources including individuals' trades, in-house mutual fund sales, principal transactions, new issues, and fees.

2. **Describe how brokerage firms operate.**

    With a cash brokerage account, the customer pays in full on the settlement date, whereas with a margin account money can be borrowed from the broker to finance purchases. Wrap accounts, where all costs are wrapped in one fee, are becoming increasingly popular. Brokerage commissions are negotiable. Full-line brokerage houses charge more than discount brokers but offer advice and recommendations, while Internet brokers tend to charge the least. Investors can also invest without out a broker through dividend reinvestment plans (DRIPs), whereby companies sell shares directly to investors through share purchase plans.

3. **Outline how orders to buy and sell securities are executed.**

    The TSX was the first stock exchange in the world to go electronic and now handles all trades electronically. Most exchanges are now highly automated, although the NYSE still handles orders using its specialist system. Specialists on the NYSE are charged with maintaining a continuous, orderly market in their assigned stocks. Market orders are executed at the best price available, whereas limit orders specify a particular price to be met or bettered. Stop orders specify a certain price at which a market order is to take over.

4. **Discuss the regulation of the Canadian securities industry.**

Investor protection includes government regulation, primarily at the provincial level, and self-regulation by the industry. Self-regulatory organizations (SROs) deal with member regulation, listing requirements, and trading regulation. SROs include the Investment Industry Regulatory Organization of Canada (IIROC), TSX, TSX Venture Exchange, MX, and the MFDA. The IIROC is the Canadian investment industry's national self-regulatory organization.

5. **Explain the importance of margin trading and short selling to investors.**

Margin is the equity an investor has in a transaction. Required margins are set by the appropriate SROs. The appeal of margin to investors is that it can magnify any gains on a transaction, but it can also magnify losses. An investor sells short if a security's price is expected to decline. The investor borrows the securities sold short from the broker, hoping to replace them through a later purchase at a lower price.

KEY TERMS

Ask price, p.132

Bid price, p.132

Canadian Investor Protection Fund (CIPF), p.138

Canadian Securities Institute (CSI), p.139

Cash account, p.125

Discount brokers, p.124

Dividend reinvestment plans (DRIPs), p.131

Full-service brokers, p.124

Investment Industry Regulatory Organization of Canada (IIROC), p.138

Limit order, p.132

Margin, p.139

Margin account, p.125

Margin call, p.139

Market order, p.132

Self-regulatory organizations (SROs), p.138

Short sales, p.143

Stop order, p.133

Street name, p.134

Wrap account, p.125

REVIEW QUESTIONS

5-1. What is the normal settlement date for common stocks? For long-term government bonds? For T-bills?

5-2. What are the maximum loan values applicable to IIROC and exchange licensed traders in establishing margin accounts for clients who wish to purchase common shares at various price levels?

5-3. What conditions result in a margin call?

5-4. How can an investor sell a security that is not currently owned?

5-5. What is a wrap account? How does it involve a change in the traditional role of the broker?

5-6. Distinguish between a full-service broker and a discount broker.

5-7. How can investors invest without a broker?

5-8. What is the difference between a day order and an open order?

5-9. Why are investors interested in having margin accounts? What risk do such accounts involve?

5-10. Given the lower brokerage costs charged by discount brokers and Internet brokers, why might an investor choose to use a full-service broker?

5-11. Explain the role of the specialists on the NYSE, describing the two roles they perform. How do they act to maintain an orderly market?

5-12. Is there any similarity between an over-the-counter dealer and a specialist on an exchange?

5-13. Discuss the advantages and disadvantages of a limit order versus a market order.

5-14. How does a stop order differ from a limit order?

5-15. What is the role of SROs in the regulation of securities markets?

5-16. What are the risks associated with short selling?

5-17. What role is performed by the Canadian Investor Protection Fund (CIPF)? What losses does it cover, and what losses does it not cover?

5-18. What conditions must be met for an investor to sell short?

5-19. Explain the difference, relative to the current market price of a stock, between the following types of orders: sell limit, buy limit, buy stop, and sell stop.

5-20. How has technology influenced how securities are traded?

5-21. What is an all or none order and what are the advantages of this type of order?

5-22. What is meant by having margin accounts "marked to the market" daily?

5-23. Is there any link between margin accounts and short selling?

PROBLEMS

5-1.   a. Consider an investor who purchased a stock at $100 per share. The current market price is $125. At what price would a limit order be placed to ensure a profit of $30 per share?

     b. What type of stop order would be placed to ensure a profit of at least $20 per share?

5-2. Assume an investor sells short 200 shares of stock at $75 per share. At what price must the investor cover the short sale in order to realize a gross profit of $5,000? Of $1,000?

5-3. Assume that an investor buys 100 shares of stock at $50 per share and the stock rises to $60 per share. What is the gross profit, assuming a margin requirement of 30 percent? Of 50 percent? Of 60 percent?

5-4. An investor buys 100 shares of an option eligible stock on margin at $60 per share. The price of the stock subsequently drops to $50.

     a. What is the actual margin at $50? Is there a margin call?

     b. If the price declines to $45, what is the amount of the margin call? At $35?

     c. If the price increased to $70, how much, if any, funds would the investor have available to them from this account?

5-5. An investor short sells 200 shares of a stock trading at $3. How much must he or she deposit in order to complete the transaction? Suppose the price subsequently falls to $2. How much money can the investor withdraw? If the price rises to $4.50, how much must the investor deposit?

5-6.   a. What is your required margin deposit if you short sell 200 shares of a common stock for $20 per share, and the required margin is 130 percent?

     b. If the price of the common stock above rises to $25 per share, how much cash will you be required to deposit in order to restore your margin position?

     c. What is the leverage factor associated with the margin purchase of 100 shares of a $5 stock if the initial margin requirement is 40 percent?

     d. What will be your annualized return (expressed as a percentage) if you purchase 1,000 shares of a stock for $12 per share on margin and hold them for two months before eventually reselling them for $15 per share? Assume the required margin is 50 percent, and that your broker charges you interest at an annual rate of 8 percent, and you do not receive any margin calls during the two-month period. Ignore transaction costs.

5-7. You open a margin account at Chas. Pigeon, a discount broker. You subsequently short Exciting.com at $286, believing it to be overpriced. This transaction is done on margin, which has an annual interest rate cost of 9 percent. Exactly one year later Exciting has declined to $54 a share, at which point you cover your short position. You pay brokerage costs of $20 on each transaction you make.

    a. The margin requirement is 50 percent. Calculate your dollar gain or loss on this position, taking into account both the margin interest and the transaction costs.

    b. Calculate the percentage return on your investment (the amount of money you put up initially, counting the brokerage costs to buy).

5-8. Using your same brokerage account as in Problem 5-7 (same margin rate and transaction costs), assume that you buy IBM at $156 a share, on 60 percent margin. During the year IBM pays a dividend of $1.30 per share. One year later you sell the position at $233.

    a. Calculate the dollar gain or loss on this position.

    b. Calculate the percentage return on your investment.

5-9. An investor buys 100 shares of Altria at $82 per share on margin. The initial margin requirement is 50 percent, and the maintenance margin is 30 percent.

    a. The price of Altria drops to $61 per share. What is the actual margin now?

    b. The price of Altria declines further to $59.50. Show why a margin call is generated, or is not warranted.

    c. The price declines yet again to $55.25. Show by calculations why a margin call is generated.

    d. Using the information in (c), how much cash must be added to the account to bring it into compliance with the margin requirements?

5-10. You have been watching six stocks (call them "Stock 1" through "Stock 6") and now believe that three of them are poised to move upward, while the other three are likely to fall in price. Therefore, you intend to take a long position (buy 100 shares each) in Stocks 1, 2 and 3 and a short position (sell 100 shares each) in Stock 4, 5, and 6. Each stock is currently trading at $10 per share; you may ignore trading commissions.

    First determine the amount of cash you will have to deposit to your brokerage account (margin) to make the six investments. Now assume you have made this minimum cash deposit and taken the desired positions (made the investments). For the following two scenarios, determine whether your cash balance is now in surplus or deficit as compared to the updated minimum margin amount. Also calculate the total value of the account assuming you do not make any further deposits or withdrawals. Note: margin requirement is 50 percent.

    Scenario 1 ("Good" price changes): Stocks 1 and 2 increase by 10 percent, as expected; Stocks 3 and 4 do not change in price; Stocks 5 and 6 fall by 10 percent.

    Scenario 2 ("Bad" price changes): Stocks 1 and 2 decrease by 10 percent (to $9 per share); Stocks 3 and 4 do not change; Stocks 5 and 6 increase in price by 10 percent.

PREPARING FOR YOUR PROFESSIONAL EXAMS

CFA PRACTICE QUESTIONS

5-1. An investor sold a stock short and is worried about rising prices. To protect against rising prices, the investor would place a

    a. Stop order to sell

    b. Stop order to buy

    c. Limit order to sell

    d. Limit order to buy

5-2. A stock is purchased on margin at $20 per share (assume 50 percent margin requirement). At what price would you receive a margin call if the maintenance margin is 25 percent?

    a. $13.33

    b. $15.00

    c. $18.67

    d. $24.00

5-3. Which of the following rules does not apply to short sale transactions?

    a. They are only permitted on an uptick.

    b. The short position must be closed out within 60 days.

    c. Any dividends declared must be covered by the short seller.

    d. The margin account is "marked-to-the-market"

5-4. You purchase 100 shares of a stock for $30 per share and immediately initiate a stop-loss order at a price of $25 per share. Ignoring transaction costs, your maximum loss:

    a. is $500.

    b. is $600.

    c. is $400.

    d. cannot be determined exactly.

5-5. What difficulties and hazards are associated with short selling a stock?

    i. There can be difficulties borrowing the required quantity of the security sold short to cover the short sale.

    ii. The short seller is not liable for any dividends paid during the period the account is short.

    iii. There are difficulties in obtaining up-to-date information on total short sales on a security.

    iv. The short seller is responsible for maintaining adequate margin in the short account.

        a. i, ii, iii, iv

        b. i, ii, iv

        c. ii, iii

        d. i, iii, iv

APPENDIX 5A
TRADING ON THE NYSE

NYSE Trading and the Specialist System

Assume an investor places an order to buy or sell shares of a NYSE-listed company and that the brokerage firm transmits the order to the NYSE trading floor. The Common Message Switch/SuperDot system used by the NYSE will transmit the order to either a broker's booth or directly to the specialist assigned to that stock. Having received the order, the firm's floor broker would take the order to the trading post, compete for the best price, and make the trade. The specialist will expose the order and make the trade, and will seek the best price for the customer. Upon completion of the trade, a report is sent back to the originating brokerage firm and to the Consolidated Tape Displays worldwide. The brokerage firm processes the transaction electronically, settling the investor's account.

NYSE trades appear on the NYSE consolidated tape, which prints transactions for all NYSE-listed securities on participating markets. This involves several stock exchanges (in addition to the NYSE), the over-the-counter market, and Instinet. Daily papers such as *The Wall Street Journal* report the high and low prices for each stock wherever they occur.

The role of the specialist is critical on the NYSE. Also referred to as NYSE-assigned dealers by the NYSE and discussed in Chapter 4 in connection with the NYSE, specialists are expected to maintain a fair and orderly market in those stocks assigned to them. They act as both brokers and dealers:

• As brokers, specialists maintain the limit book, which records all limit orders, or orders that investors have placed to buy or sell a security at a specific price (or better) and that will not be executed until that price is reached. The commission brokers leave the limit orders with the specialist to be filled when possible; therefore, the specialist receives part of the broker's fee.

• As dealers, specialists buy and sell shares of their assigned stock(s) to maintain an orderly market. The stock exchanges function essentially as a continuous market, assuring investors that they can almost always buy and sell a particular security at some price. Assuming that public orders do not arrive at the same time, so that they can be matched, the specialist will buy from commission brokers with orders to sell and will sell to those with orders to buy, hoping to profit by a favourable spread between the two sides.

Since specialists are charged by the NYSE with maintaining a continuous, orderly market in their assigned stocks, they often must go "against the market," which requires adequate capital. The NYSE demands that specialists be able to assume a position of 5,000 shares in their assigned stocks.[15] However, the NYSE does not require specialists to fund all the liquidity for the market at a particular time, and these stabilization trades are only a small part of total trading.

Most of the NYSE volume results from public orders interacting directly with other public orders. Using NYSE data, in 2005, specialist participation—measured as the total shares bought and sold by specialists divided by twice total volume—accounted for about 15 percent of the share volume traded. This implies that 85 percent of share volume resulted from public and licensed trader orders meeting directly in the NYSE market. It is important to note that specialists are not on both sides of any trade.

How well does the system work? According to NYSE figures, in one year, some 98.2 percent of all transactions occurred with no change in price or within the minimum change permissible on the NYSE. The quotation spread between bid and asked prices was one-fourth of a point or less in 93 percent of NYSE quotes. As an indication of market depth, for volume of 3,000 shares or more, the average stock price showed no change, or one-eighth point change, 91 percent of the time.

Automation of the NYSE

Given the volume of shares handled by the NYSE, trading must be highly automated. About 99 percent of orders and almost half of the volume is handled electronically. An electronic system matches buy and sell orders entered before the market opens, setting the opening price of a stock. SuperDot is the electronic order routing system for NYSE-listed securities. Licensed traders send orders directly to the specialist post where the securities are traded, and confirmation of trading is returned directly to the member firm over the same system. The system's peak capacity has been increased to an order processing capability of 2 billion shares per day.

As part of SuperDot, the Opening Automated Report Service (OARS) automatically and continuously scans the licensed traders' preopening buy and sell orders, pairing buy and sell orders and presenting the imbalance to the specialist up to the opening of a stock. This helps the specialist determine the opening price. OARS handles preopening market orders up to 30,099 shares.

SuperDot also includes a postopening market order system designed to accept postopening market orders of up to 3 million shares. These market orders are executed and reported back to the member firm, sending the order within 17 seconds, on average.

The specialist's volume-handling and volume-processing capabilities have been enhanced electronically by creating the Specialist's Electronic Book, which is yet another part of the SuperDot system. This database system assists in recording and reporting limit and market orders. Not only does it help eliminate paperwork and processing errors, but it now also handles about 98 percent of all SuperDot orders.

The NYSE now allows large institutional investors to avoid trading on the floor of the exchange under certain conditions. The "clean-cross" rule now permits brokers to arrange trades of 25,000 shares or more between customers without considering orders at the same price from other investors

---

[15]Specialists must be approved by the Board of Governors of the NYSE and must have experience, ability as dealers, and specified minimum capital.

on the NYSE floor. However, orders at a better price would have to be accepted.

Financial markets are changing as new techniques and processes are developed. ECNs are an obvious example. Long-standing institutions such as the NYSE must also change, and it is doing so.

APPENDIX 5B

SECURITIES REGULATION IN THE UNITED STATES

Since many Canadian institutional and individual investors transact in securities that are traded in US markets, and since many Canadian companies list their securities in US markets, it is important for Canadians to be familiar with US regulatory practice. The Securities and Exchange Commission (SEC) was created by the US Congress in 1934. It is an independent, quasi-judicial agency of the US government. Its mission is to administer laws in the securities field and to protect investors and the public in securities transactions. The commission consists of five members appointed by the SEC president for five-year terms. Its staff consists of lawyers, accountants, security analysts, and others divided into divisions and offices (including nine regional offices). The SEC has approximately 200 examiners.

The SEC is required to investigate complaints or indications of violations in securities transactions. In general, the SEC administers all securities laws. Thus, under the Securities Act of 1933, the SEC ensures that new securities being offered for public sale are registered with the commission, and under the 1934 Act it does the same for securities trading on national exchanges. The registration of securities in no way ensures that investors purchasing them will not lose money. Registration means only that the issuer has made adequate disclosure. In fact, the SEC has no power to disapprove securities for lack of merit.

Investment advisors and companies must also register with the SEC and disclose certain information. The SEC ensures that these two groups will meet the requirements of the laws affecting them.

Similar to Canada, self-regulation is a defining characteristic of the US securities industry. Stock exchanges regulate and monitor trading for the benefit of investors and the protection of the financial system. The NYSE in particular has a stringent set of self-regulations and declares that it "provides the most meaningful market regulation in the world." The NYSE regulates itself as part of a combined effort involving the SEC, itself, and licensed traders, and NYSE rules and regulations are self-imposed and approved by the SEC. Together, this triad enforces federal legislation and self-regulation for the benefit of the investing public.

In 2007, the National Association of Securities Dealers (NASD) and the member regulation committee of the New York Stock Exchange (NYSE) merged to form the Financial Industry Regulatory Authority (FINRA), the largest non-governmental regulator for securities firms in the US. FINRA, which oversees nearly 5,000 brokerage firms, about 174,000 branch offices and approximately 677,500 registered securities representatives, is "dedicated to investor protection and market integrity through effective and efficient regulation and complementary compliance and technology-based services."[16]

FINRA is involved in almost every area of the securities business including registering and educating industry professionals; examining securities firms; writing rules; enforcing those rules and US federal securities laws; promoting investor protection by educating the investing public; and administering a dispute resolution forum for investors and registered firms. FINRA also performs market regulation under contract for The NASDAQ Stock Market and the American Stock Exchange.

Similar to the CIPF in Canada, the Securities Investor Protection Corporation (SIPC), a quasi-government agency, insures each customer account of member brokers against brokerage firm failure.[17]

---

[16]www.finra.org/AboutFINRA

[17]In addition, many brokerage firms carry additional insurance, often for several million dollars, to provide even more protection for customers.

CHAPTER 11

BOND YIELDS AND PRICES

You have recently inherited $1 million, so you begin studying stocks for potential investment. Following your study of stocks, you realize you also need to understand the basics about bonds. After all, portfolio theory stresses the virtues of diversification, and that includes asset classes. A little math quickly tells you that $1 million invested in bonds returning 6 percent produces an income stream of $60,000 a year, which seems like a nice annual annuity. By now, however, you have learned that when it comes to investing, things are not always what they seem. Maybe bond returns are not as straightforward as they appear. Furthermore, you have heard people say that when interest rates rise, bond prices decline, and you wonder why. It becomes apparent to you that knowing something about bond prices and yields could be useful to you as you manage your inheritance.

Learning Objectives

After reading this chapter, you should be able to

1. Calculate the price of a bond.
2. Explain the bond valuation process.
3. Calculate major bond yield measures, including yield to maturity, yield to call, and horizon return.
4. Account for changes in bond prices.
5. Explain and apply the concept of duration.

CHAPTER PREVIEW

This chapter builds on the background developed in Part I. Having introduced the characteristics of bonds in Chapter 2, we can now examine bond yields and prices. In addition to calculating bond price, in this chapter we lay out the basic principles of valuation, which we will use again when considering other investing alternatives, particularly common stocks (Chapter 13). As part of valuation, you will learn to calculate major bond yield measures such as yield to maturity, yield to call, and horizon return. You will also learn about the factors that affect bond price changes, notably changes in interest rates. Finally, we discuss duration, a concept used by investors to deal with the effect of yield changes.

BOND PRICES

learning objective 1
Calculate the price of a bond.

In addition to the total return concept considered in Chapter 6 (which is applicable to any security), bond investors must also understand specific measures of bond yields. It is traditional in the bond markets to use various yield measures and to quote potential returns to investors on the basis of these measures. However, these gauges can mislead unwary investors who fail to understand the basis on which they are constructed. Investors must understand that bond yields reported daily in various media sources do not necessarily represent the true yield an investor will achieve when he or she buys bonds in the marketplace and holds them to maturity.

The Valuation Principle

What determines the price of a security? The answer is that a security's estimated value determines the price that investors place on it in the open market.

Intrinsic Value

The estimated or true value of a security as determined by an investor after examining a firm's underlying variables.

A security's **intrinsic value**, or estimated value, is the present value of the expected cash flows from that asset. Any security purchased is expected to provide one or more cash flows some time in the future. These could be periodic, such as interest or dividends, or simply a final price or redemption value, or a combination of these. Since these cash flows occur in the future, they must be discounted at an appropriate rate to determine their present value. The sum of these discounted cash flows is the estimated intrinsic value of the asset. Calculating that value, therefore, requires the use of present value techniques. Equation 11-1 expresses the concept:

(11-1)

$$\text{Value}_{t=0} = \sum_{t=1}^{n} \frac{\text{Cash flow (at time } t)}{(1 + k)^t}$$

where
Value $_{t=0}$ = the value of the asset now (time period 0)
Cash flow (at time t) = the future cash flow (at time t) that results from ownership of the asset
k = the appropriate discount rate or rate of return required by an investor for an investment of this type
n = number of periods over which the cash flows are expected

To solve Equation 11-1 and derive the intrinsic value of a security, it is necessary to determine the following:

1. The *expected cash flows* from the security. This includes the size and type of cash flows, such as dividends, interest, face value expected to be received at maturity, or the expected price of the security at some point in the future.

2. The *timing* of the expected cash flows. Since the returns to be generated from a security occur at various times in the future, they must be properly documented for discounting back to time period 0

(today). Money has a time value, and the timing of future cash flows significantly affects the value of the asset today.

3. The *discount rate* or required rate of return demanded by investors will reflect the time value of money and the risk of the security. It is an opportunity cost, representing the rate foregone by an investor in the next best alternative investment with comparable risk.

Bond Valuation

The intrinsic value of any asset is calculated from the present value of its expected cash flows. This is true for short-term instruments such as T-bills, as well as for long-term ones such as bonds or common stocks. Appendix 11A at the end of this chapter discusses the valuation of T-bills, and we focus here on the valuation of traditional bonds.

learning objective 2
Explain the bond valuation process.

The interest payments (coupons) and the principal repayment for bonds are known in advance—coupons are paid at regular intervals (either annually or semi-annually) and the principal repayment occurs at the maturity date. The coupons are all for the same amount, which is determined by multiplying the coupon rate (which is stated on an annual basis) by the face value of the bond (F). For example, a bond with a coupon rate of 10 percent and a face value of $1,000 would pay annual coupons of $100 ($50 if paid semi-annually). Hence, the fundamental value of a bond is determined by discounting these future payments from the issuer at an appropriate required yield, r, for the issue. Equation 11-2 is used to solve for the value of a coupon bond.[1]

$$P = \sum_{t=1}^{n} \frac{C_t}{(1 + r)^t} + \frac{F}{(1 + r)^n}$$

(11-2)

where
P = the price of the bond today (time period 0)
C = the regular coupons or interest payments (paid annually or semi-annually)
F = the face value (or par value) of the bond
n = the number of periods to maturity of the bond (the periods may be for a full year or for six months, depending on payment interval)
r = the appropriate period discount rate or market yield (which may be an annual or semi-annual rate depending on how frequently coupons are paid)

Finance students should immediately realize that the stream of interest income to be received in the form of coupons represents an annuity. This is because it represents a series of cash flows that provide the same payment at the same interval (every year or six months), and we are determining the present value of these cash flows using the same discount rate. Recalling some introductory mathematics of finance concepts, we can use the present value annuity (PVA) factor to determine the present value of any cash stream that represents an annuity. Combining this result with the fact that $\frac{1}{(1 + r)^n}$ is generally referred to as the discount or present value factor for a discount rate of r for n periods ($PV_{r,n}$), we can rewrite Equation 11-2 as:

$$P = C \times (PVA_{r,n}) + F \times (PV_{r,n})$$

(11-3)

where
$PVA_{r,n}$ = the present value annuity factor for an n period annuity using a discount rate of r
$PV_{r,n}$ = the present value or discount factor for discounting an amount to be received at time n, using a discount rate of r

---

[1]This formulation is nothing new; John Burr Williams stated it in a book in 1938. *See* J. B. Williams, *The Theory of Investment Value* (Cambridge, MA: Harvard University Press, 1938).

Bond prices can be calculated by referring to the PV and PVA tables at the end of the textbook, or simply using Equation 11-2 and a calculator, or using a computer program such as Excel. Throughout this chapter we will also present solutions calculated using the Texas Instruments BA II Plus financial calculator (which is one of two calculators that CFA candidates are permitted to use in writing the CFA examinations). Although there may be minor variations in the required input procedures, most calculators can be used in a similar fashion to obtain these results (so check your calculator user guide). The present value process for a typical coupon-bearing bond involves three steps, given the dollar coupon on the bond, the face value, and the current market yield applicable to a particular bond:

1. Using the present value of an annuity (PVA) factor (defined in Table A4, which is available in the appendix on the textbook's companion website), determine the present value of the coupons (interest payments).

2. Using the present value (PV) table (Table A-2 in the appendix on the textbook's companion website), determine the present value of the face (par) value of the bond; for our purposes, the face value will usually be $1,000.

3. Add the present values determined in steps 1 and 2 together.

EXAMPLE 11-1: CALCULATING BOND PRICES—ANNUAL COUPONS

To determine the price of a three-year bond with a face value of $1,000 that paid annual coupons at a rate of 10 percent when the appropriate discount rate was 12 percent, we would input the following information into Equation 11-3: C = $100; F = $1,000; n = 3; and r = 12 percent.

$$P = C \times (PVA_{r,n}) + F \times (PV_{r,n}) = \$100 \times (PVA_{12\%,3}) + \$1,000 \times (PV_{12\%,3})$$

$$= \$100 \times (2.40183) + \$1,000 \times (.71178) = \$240.18 + \$711.78 = \$951.96$$

Solution by Financial Calculator (Texas Instruments BA II Plus)

Inputs:
PMT = $100 (i.e., the coupon payment); n = 3 (i.e., the number of payments); FV = 1,000 (i.e., the face value); i = 12 (i.e., the current market rate in percentage terms).

Then compute (CPT) PV, which will give an answer of –$951.96 (ignore the negative sign). This is the present value of the future cash flows (both coupons and face value); therefore, the price is $951.96.

Notice that these bonds sell below their face value (at a discount from par), which is always the case when the discount rate exceeds the stated coupon rate. We will talk about this result in greater detail later in this chapter.

Generally bonds pay interest semi-annually rather than annually, so the discount rate is calculated by dividing the annual discount rate by two, while the number of semi-annual periods to maturity is determined by multiplying the number of years to maturity by two.

EXAMPLE 11-2: CALCULATING BOND PRICES—SEMI-ANNUAL COUPONS

Assume the three-year bond in the Example 11-1 paid semi-annual coupons instead of annual ones and that all the other information above remained the same. To determine its value we would input the following information into Equation 11-3: C = $50; n = 6; and r = 6 percent.

$$P = \$50 \times (PVA_{6\%,6}) + \$1,000 \times (PV_{6\%,6})$$

$$= \$50 \times (4.91732) + \$1,000 \times (0.70496) = \$245.87 + \$704.96 = \$950.83$$

Solution by Financial Calculator (Texas Instruments BA II Plus)

Inputs:

PMT = $50; n = 6; FV = 1,000; i = 6; CPT then PV = −$950.83
So, the price = $950.83.

Thus, while we can see the processes are similar for the annual-pay bonds in Example 11-1 and the semi-annual pay bonds here, they do differ slightly, and it is essential to use the correct equation to obtain the correct answer.

While the PV and PVA factors for various discount rates and periods are found in Appendices A2 and A4 on the textbook's companion website, it is often necessary to use the equations provided at the top of these appendices, which are given below:

$$PV = \frac{1}{(1 + r)^n} \quad \text{and,}$$

$$PVA_{r,n} = \frac{1 - \dfrac{1}{(1 + r)^n}}{r}$$

EXAMPLE 11-3: CALCULATING BOND PRICES

A bond with 10 years to maturity has an 8 percent coupon rate, with coupons being paid semi-annually. If its face value is $1,000 and the appropriate discount rate is 6.52 percent, we can determine its value as follows:

$$P = \$40 \times (PVA_{3.26\%,20}) + \$1,000 \times (PV_{3.26\%,20}) = \$40 \times \left[\frac{1 - \dfrac{1}{(1.0326)^{20}}}{.0326}\right] + \frac{\$1,000}{(1 + .0326)^{20}}$$

$$= \$40 \times (14.52606) + \$1,000 \times (0.52645) = \$581.04 + \$526.45 = \$1,107.49$$

Solution by Financial Calculator (Texas Instruments BA II Plus)

Inputs:
PMT = $40; n = 20; FV = 1,000; i = 3.26; CPT then PV = −$1,107.49
So, the price = $1,107.49.

Notice that these bonds sell above their face value (at a premium over par), which is always the case when the discount rate is less than the stated coupon rate. As with Example 11-1 in which we calculated the price for a three-year bond that paid annual coupons, we defer our discussion of this result until later.

Notice that for zero-coupon bonds, the first term of Equation 11-2 is zero, so we are left with the following equation that can be used to determine the price of these bonds:

$$P = \frac{F}{(1 + r)^n}$$

(11-4)

In the examples above, the bonds are valued, as are any other assets, on the basis of their future stream of expected benefits (cash flows), using an appropriate market yield. Since the numerator is always specified for coupon-bearing bonds at the time of issue, the only problem in valuing a typical bond is to determine the denominator or discount rate. The appropriate discount rate is the bond's required yield.

The required yield, r, in Equations 11-3 and 11-4 is specific for each particular bond. It is the current market rate being earned by investors on comparable bonds with the same maturity and the same credit quality. (In other words, it is an opportunity cost.) Thus, market interest rates are incorporated directly into the discount rate used to establish the fundamental value of a bond.

Since market interest rates fluctuate constantly, required yields do also. When calculating a bond price it is customary to use the yield to maturity (YTM), which is discussed in the next section, as the appropriate discount rate. If the YTM is used, we can restate Equation 11-3 as

(11-5)
$$P = C \times (PVA_{YTM,n}) + F \times (PV_{YTM,n})$$

Real-World Returns 11-1 contains a list of bond quotations reported on www.financialpost.com. The closing bid prices and corresponding yields are for April 21, 2008, therefore the Newfoundland government bonds that mature on April 17, 2028 have a term to maturity of almost exactly 20 years. These bonds have a 6.15 percent coupon rate, and the reported yield is 4.87 percent (which refers to the yield to maturity). These bonds are selling at a premium over their face value since the coupon rate exceeds the yield. If we assume coupons are paid semi-annually, use Equation 11-3 and the yield of 4.87 percent for this bond, and assume a face (or par) value of $100 (since bond prices are usually reported per $100 of face value), we can determine that the price will equal

$$P = \$3.075 \times \left[\frac{1 - \frac{1}{(1.02435)^{40}}}{.02435} \right] + \frac{\$100}{(1.02435)^{40}} = \$3.075 \times (25.3798) + \$100 \times (0.3820) = \$116.24$$

Solution by Financial Calculator (Texas Instruments BA II Plus)

Inputs:
PMT = $3.075; n = 40; FV = 100; i = 2.435; CPT then PV = −$116.24
So, the price = $116.24

This is exactly the price reported for this bond, because the reported yields are determined based on the day's closing bid prices, which are the reported prices in this case. In other words, once we are given the yields (and the coupon rate and term to maturity), we can determine the corresponding price and vice versa. We deal with the issue of estimating the implied yield from a given price in the next section.

Calculating the price of a bond is an easy procedure in today's financial world using either a financial calculator or personal computer. For example, by using a basic financial calculator, price can be determined after entering the cash flows and required yield.

Before proceeding to the next topic, we would point out that the prices discussed in this section are typically referred to as "quoted" prices. These differ from the actual prices investors pay for bonds whenever bonds are sold at a date other than the one of a coupon. The reason is that interest will accrue to bondholders in between such payment dates, although they will have not actually received the portion of the next coupon to which they are rightfully entitled. As a result, bond purchasers must pay the bond seller the quoted price plus the accrued interest on the bond. This amount is referred to as the cash price of the bond.

Real-World Returns 11-1
Bond Quotes

Canadian Bonds on April 21, 2008

FEDERAL

Issuer	Coupon	Maturity Date	Bid $	Yield %
Canada	5.500	Jun 01/09	102.84	2.87
Canada	3.750	Jun 01/09	100.95	2.87
Canada	11.000	Jun 01/09	108.78	2.87
Canada	4.250	Sep 01/09	101.82	2.87
Canada	10.750	Oct 01/09	111.04	2.87
Canada	4.250	Dec 01/09	102.15	2.87
Canada	5.500	Jun 01/10	105.40	2.84
Canada	3.750	Jun 01/10	101.85	2.84
Canada	9.500	Jun 01/10	113.52	2.84
Canada	4.000	Sep 01/10	102.54	2.88
Canada	9.000	Mar 01/11	116.19	3.04
Canada	8.500	Jun 01/11	116.04	3.04
Canada	6.000	Jun 01/11	108.68	3.05
Canada	3.750	Sep 01/11	102.06	3.10
Canada	3.750	Jun 01/12	102.24	3.16
Canada	5.250	Jun 01/12	107.97	3.16
Canada	5.250	Jun 01/13	109.39	3.24
Canada	3.500	Jun 01/13	101.22	3.24
Canada	10.250	Mar 15/14	136.82	3.32
Canada	5.000	Jun 01/14	109.19	3.32
Canada	11.250	Jun 01/15	149.10	3.41
Canada	4.500	Jun 01/15	106.77	3.42
Canada	4.000	Jun 01/16	103.18	3.55
Canada	4.000	Jun 01/17	102.57	3.67
Canada	4.250	Jun 01/18	103.85	3.79
Canada	10.500	Mar 15/21	165.87	3.94
Canada	9.750	Jun 01/21	158.94	3.95
Canada	9.250	Jun 01/22	156.66	3.97
Canada	8.000	Jun 01/23	144.93	4.01
Canada	9.000	Jun 01/25	160.25	4.07
Canada	8.000	Jun 01/27	150.81	4.13
Canada	5.750	Jun 01/29	122.46	4.14
Canada	5.750	Jun 01/33	125.03	4.14
Canada	5.000	Jun 01/37	114.77	4.12
CHT	4.650	Sep 15/09	102.08	3.11
CHT	3.750	Mar 15/10	100.97	3.22
CHT	3.550	Sep 15/10	100.48	3.34
CMHC	5.500	Jun 01/12	107.05	3.63
EDC	5.000	Feb 09/09	101.70	2.82
EDC	5.100	Jun 02/14	106.75	3.85

PROVINCIAL

Issuer	Coupon	Maturity Date	Bid $	Yield %
B C	6.000	Jun 09/08	100.38	2.87
B C	6.375	Aug 23/10	106.64	3.39
B C	5.750	Jan 09/12	107.18	3.66
B C	8.500	Aug 23/13	122.10	3.87
B C	6.150	Nov 19/27	117.46	4.77
B C	5.700	Jun 18/29	112.06	4.79

Issuer	Coupon	Maturity Date	Bid $	Yield %
B C	4.700	Jun 18/37	98.59	4.79
B C MF	5.900	Jun 01/11	106.31	3.73
HydQue	6.500	Feb 15/11	107.88	3.53
HydQue	10.250	Jul 16/12	124.82	3.83
HydQue	11.000	Aug 15/20	158.30	4.71
HydQue	6.000	Aug 15/31	113.78	4.99
HydQue	6.500	Feb 15/35	122.34	4.98
HydQue	6.000	Feb 15/40	116.18	4.98
HydQue	5.000	Feb 15/45	100.35	4.98
Manit	5.750	Jun 02/08	100.29	2.87
Manit	7.750	Dec 22/25	134.76	4.81
NewBr	5.700	Jun 02/08	100.29	2.88
NewBr	6.000	Dec 27/17	112.25	4.43
Newfld	6.150	Apr 17/28	116.24	4.87
NovaSc	6.600	Jun 01/27	121.88	4.83
Ontario	4.000	May 19/09	100.94	3.09
Ontario	6.200	Nov 19/09	104.52	3.22
Ontario	4.000	May 19/10	101.35	3.32
Ontario	6.100	Nov 19/10	106.46	3.45
Ontario	6.100	Dec 02/11	108.17	3.66
Ontario	4.400	Dec 02/11	102.48	3.66
Ontario	5.375	Dec 02/12	106.56	3.81
Ontario	4.500	Dec 02/12	102.89	3.81
Ontario	4.750	Jun 02/13	104.14	3.85
Ontario	5.000	Mar 08/14	105.49	3.94
Ontario	4.500	Mar 08/15	102.70	4.05
Ontario	4.400	Mar 08/16	101.64	4.15
Ontario	4.300	Mar 08/17	100.17	4.28
Ontario	8.100	Sep 08/23	137.37	4.67
Ontario	7.600	Jun 02/27	134.87	4.79
Ontario	6.500	Mar 08/29	122.15	4.81
Ontario	6.200	Jun 02/31	119.07	4.82
Ontario	5.850	Mar 08/33	114.56	4.84
Ontario	4.700	Jun 02/37	98.18	4.82
OntHyd	5.600	Jun 02/08	100.28	2.87
Quebec	5.500	Jun 01/09	102.52	3.15
Quebec	6.250	Dec 01/10	106.84	3.48
Quebec	6.000	Oct 01/12	108.72	3.84
Quebec	5.250	Oct 01/13	106.26	3.96
Quebec	5.500	Dec 01/14	107.95	4.11
Quebec	5.000	Dec 01/15	105.00	4.22
Quebec	4.500	Dec 01/16	100.96	4.37
Quebec	4.500	Dec 01/17	100.07	4.49
Quebec	4.500	Dec 01/18	99.15	4.60
Quebec	9.375	Jan 16/23	147.89	4.80
Quebec	8.500	Apr 01/26	141.87	4.95
Quebec	6.000	Oct 01/29	113.59	4.96
Quebec	6.250	Jun 01/32	117.54	4.99
Quebec	5.750	Dec 01/36	111.78	4.97
Quebec	5.000	Dec 01/38	100.41	4.97
Saskat	5.500	Jun 02/08	100.27	2.87
Saskat	8.750	May 30/25	145.92	4.79
Toronto	6.100	Dec 12/17	110.96	4.67

CORPORATE

Issuer	Coupon	Maturity Date	Bid $	Yield %
AGT Lt	8.800	Sep 22/25	120.73	6.76
Bell	6.550	May 01/29	74.17	9.39

(continued)

REAL-WORLD RETURNS 11-1 *continued*

Issuer	Coupon	Maturity Date	Bid $	Yield %	Issuer	Coupon	Maturity Date	Bid $	Yield %
BMO	6.903	Jun 30/10	103.17	5.34	HydOne	7.350	Jun 03/30	122.21	5.59
BMO	6.647	Dec 31/10	103.00	5.43	HydOne	6.930	Jun 01/32	117.65	5.59
BMO	6.685	Dec 31/11	102.90	5.80	IntrAm	4.400	Jan 26/26	94.27	4.89
BMO	5.200	Jun 21/12	99.58	5.31	IPL	8.200	Feb 15/24	128.19	5.51
BMO	5.040	Sep 04/12	99.90	5.06	Loblaw	6.650	Nov 08/27	83.86	8.34
BNS	3.930	Feb 18/10	99.15	4.42	MLI	6.240	Feb 16/11	105.01	4.33
BNS	7.310	Dec 31/10	105.88	4.94	MLI	6.700	Jun 30/12	103.99	5.61
BNS	4.580	Feb 15/11	100.08	4.55	Nexen	6.300	Jun 02/08	100.23	4.04
BNS	5.250	Nov 01/12	100.23	5.19	RoyBnk	7.288	Jun 30/10	104.38	5.14
BNS	4.990	Mar 27/13	98.91	5.24	RoyBnk	5.130	Sep 27/10	101.37	4.53
BNS	4.560	Oct 30/13	97.72	5.04	RoyBnk	7.183	Jun 30/11	104.86	5.50
CIBC	3.750	Sep 09/10	97.39	4.93	RoyBnk	4.580	Apr 30/12	97.91	5.16
CIBC	4.400	Mar 07/11	99.13	4.73	RoyBnk	5.200	Aug 15/12	101.21	4.88
CIBC	4.550	Mar 28/11	98.85	4.98	RoyBnk	4.840	Mar 11/13	98.41	5.21
CIBC	4.350	Nov 01/11	98.24	4.90	SNCLav	7.700	Sep 20/10	107.50	4.38
CIBC	5.000	Sep 10/12	99.56	5.11	SunLife	6.865	Dec 31/11	105.51	5.20
Domtar	10.000	Apr 15/11	118.07	3.55	TD Bnk	7.600	Dec 31/09	104.60	4.72
GE CAP	5.730	Oct 22/37	92.56	6.29	TD Bnk	5.382	Nov 01/12	100.67	5.21
GrTAA	6.450	Dec 03/27	107.82	5.78	TD Bnk	5.141	Nov 19/12	100.92	4.91
GWLife	6.750	Aug 10/10	105.23	4.33	TD Bnk	4.779	Dec 14/16	89.39	6.40
GWLife	5.995	Dec 31/12	101.96	5.51	TD Bnk	5.763	Dec 18/17	94.32	6.57
GWLife	5.691	Jun 21/17	93.39	6.67	TorHyd	6.110	May 07/13	107.24	4.49
GWLife	6.140	Mar 21/18	105.50	5.42	UniGas	8.650	Nov 10/25	130.73	5.83
GWLife	6.740	Nov 24/31	108.77	6.04	WelFarg	4.450	Feb 28/11	100.06	4.43
GWLife	6.670	Mar 21/33	108.09	6.04	WelFarg	4.380	Jun 30/15	95.03	5.22
HSBC	7.780	Dec 31/10	106.53	5.14	Wstcoa	6.750	Dec 15/27	108.12	6.04
HydOne	7.150	Jun 03/10	106.75	3.79					
HydOne	6.400	Dec 01/11	107.81	4.05					
HydOne	5.770	Nov 15/12	106.39	4.21					

Source: www.financialpost.com, April 21, 2008.

EXAMPLE 11-4: CASH VERSUS QUOTED PRICES

Consider a bond with a $1,000 face value and an 8 percent coupon rate that is sold on July 15 at a quoted price of $980. If interest payments on this bond are made annually on July 1, the purchaser would have to pay the seller the cash price, equal to $980 plus 15 days of accrued interest at the coupon rate of 8 percent, or

Cash price = Quoted price + Accrued interest

Cash price = $980 + [($1,000) × (0.08) × (15/365)] = $980 + $3.29 = $983.29

CHECK YOUR UNDERSTANDING

11-1. Name the two cash flow components that must be discounted to determine the current price of a traditional bond. When would a bond investor receive these cash flows?

11-2. Why does the quoted price on a bond almost always differ from the "cash price" that an investor actually pays (or receives)?

BOND YIELDS

Bond yields and interest rates refer to the same concept. Therefore, we begin our discussion of the former with a brief consideration of the latter. Interest rates measure the price paid by a borrower to a lender for the use of resources over some time period—that is, interest rates are the price for the funds loaned. The price differs from case to case, based on the supply and demand for these funds, resulting in a wide variety of interest rates. The spread between the lowest and highest rates at any time could be as much as 10 to 15 percentage points. In bond parlance, this would be equivalent to 1,000 to 1,500 basis points, since one percentage point equals 100 **basis points**.

It is convenient to focus on the one interest rate that provides the foundation for other rates. This rate is referred to as the short-term riskless rate (designated RF in this text) and is typically proxied by the rate on short-term government Treasury bills. All other rates differ from RF because of two factors: maturity differentials and risk premiums.

Basis Points

100 basis points is equal to one percentage point.

The Basic Components of Interest Rates

Explaining interest rates is a complex task that involves substantial economics reasoning and study, and it is not feasible in this text. In this chapter, we analyze the basic determinants of nominal (current) interest rates with an eye toward recognizing the factors that affect such rates and cause them to fluctuate. The bond investor who understands the foundations of market rates can then rely on expert help for more details and be in a better position to interpret and evaluate such help.

The basic foundation of market interest rates is the opportunity cost of foregoing consumption, representing the rate that must be offered to individuals to persuade them to save rather than consume. This rate is sometimes called the **real risk-free rate of interest**, because it is not affected by price changes or risk factors.[2] We will refer to it simply as the *real rate* and designate it RR in this discussion.

Nominal interest rates on T-bills consist of the RR plus an adjustment for inflation. A lender who lends $100 for a year at 10 percent will be repaid $110. But if inflation is 12 percent a year, that $110 that the lender receives upon repayment of the loan is worth only $98.21(1/1.12)($110) in today's dollars. Lenders therefore expect to be compensated for the expected rate of price change in order to leave the real purchasing power of wealth unchanged or improved. As a result, interest rates display a strong relationship with inflation as discussed in Real-World Returns 11-2.

Real Risk-Free Rate of Interest

The opportunity cost of foregoing consumption, given no inflation.

Real-World Returns 11-2

Interest Rates and Inflation

Consensus has the Bank of Canada lowering its target overnight bank rate by half a percentage point when it meets tomorrow. But not all economists and market watchers are convinced of the merits of such an aggressive reduction at this time.

What to Keep an Eye On

A 50-basis point lowering would drop the overnight lending rate to 3 percent and bring the decline since the central bank started shaving the rate late last year to 1.5 percentage points. (A basis point is 1/100th of a percentage point.)

The case for a substantial rate cut was boosted last week when it was reported that the March consumer price index dropped to a 14-month low of 1.4 percent annualized, down from 1.8 percent in February, a noteworthy achievement when most other economies are facing

(continued)

---

[2]The real rate of interest cannot be measured directly. It is often estimated by dividing $(1.0 + \text{MIR})$ by $(1.0 + \text{EI})$, where MIR is the market interest rate and EI is expected inflation. This result can be approximated by subtracting estimates of inflation from nominal (market) interest rates (on either a realized or expected basis).

REAL-WORLD RETURNS 11-2 *continued*

rising prices. The CPI is well below the central bank's target of 2 percent. The core inflation rate, which excludes the volatile food and energy prices, was even lower—at 1.3 percent.

The Bank of Canada's spring business outlook survey, which indicated that Canadian business has become more pessimistic, also raised the odds of a 50-point cut.

Added to that are the worrying sounds coming from south of the border. Last week's Federal Reserve Board's Beige Book, which details US economic conditions, showed that nine of the 12 Fed districts are seeing conditions deteriorate.

That is not good news for Canada, given the trade ties between the two countries.

Avery Shenfeld, an economist at CIBC World Markets Inc., works from the assumption that if a 25-basis point reduction would be helpful, 50 basis points "would be even better," considering that the spread between the central bank's target rate and relevant three-month private sector rates remains wide, inflation is well contained and economic growth is sluggish. He anticipates that not only will the central bank lower rates by half a percentage point, it will, in the accompanying statement, also not rule out further cuts.

Douglas Porter, deputy chief economist at BMO Nesbitt Burns, doesn't share Mr. Shenfeld's view. He looks at the situation and wonders whether an aggressive cut is warranted at this time, given that "domestic demand remains incredibly healthy." In his latest commentary, he points to the fact that in the first quarter, "auto sales look to have posted their strongest quarter on record, housing starts had their second-best quarter in 20 years and more than 100,000 net new jobs were added."

Furthermore, he suggested that the good news on inflation could be a result of the strong Canadian dollar and trends could reverse as wage pressures increase and if global commodity prices continue to rise.

While the Bank of Canada rate will be the big event this week on the Canadian economic scene, it won't be the only one. Retail sales data for February are scheduled to be released on Wednesday.

South of the border, the key numbers will be existing home sales tomorrow and durable goods orders on Thursday, the same day as the new-home sales figures come out.

Source: Barnes, Angela, "Low inflation bolsters case for interest rate cut to 3%," *The Globe and Mail*, April 21, 2008, p. B8.

As an approximation for discussion purposes, this inflation adjustment can be added to the real risk-free rate of interest. Unlike RR, which is often assumed by market participants to be reasonably stable over time, adjustments for expected inflation vary widely. Thus, for short-term, risk-free securities, such as T-bills, the nominal interest rate is a function of the real rate of interest and the expected inflationary premium. This is expressed as Equation 11-6, which is an approximation.[3]

(11-6)
$$RF \approx RR + EI$$

where
RF = short-term T-bill rate
RR = the real risk-free rate of interest
EI = the expected rate of inflation over the term of the instrument

Equation 11-6 is known as the Fisher hypothesis (named after economist Irving Fisher). It implies that the nominal rate on short-term risk-free securities rises point-for-point with anticipated

---

[3]The precisely correct procedure is to multiply (1 + the real rate) by (1 + the expected rate of inflation), and subtract 1.0. For purposes of our discussion, the additive relationship is satisfactory, provided that levels of inflation are relatively low.

inflation, with the real rate of interest remaining unaffected.[4] Turning Equation 11-6 around, estimates of the real risk-free rate of interest can be approximated by subtracting the expected inflation rate from the observed nominal interest rate.[5] The expected rate of inflation can be determined by reference to various economic projections from the government, banks, and securities firms.

All market interest rates are affected by a time factor that leads to maturity differentials. That is, although long-term government bonds are virtually free from default risk in the same manner as government T-bills, they generally yield more than medium-term bonds, which, in turn, yield more than T-bills. This typical relationship between bond maturity and yield applies to all types of bonds, whether they are corporate, or federal, provincial, municipal, or government debt securities. The term structure of interest rates, discussed in Chapter 12, accounts for the relationship between time and yield—that is, the maturity differentials.

Market interest rates, other than those for riskless government securities, are also affected by a third factor, a risk premium, which lenders require as compensation for the risk involved. This risk premium is associated with the issuer's own particular situation or with a particular market factor. The risk premium is often referred to as the yield spread or yield differential.

Measuring Bond Yields

learning objective 3
Calculate major bond yield measures, including yield to maturity, yield to call, and horizon return.

Several measures of the yield on a bond are used by investors. It is very important for bond investors to understand which yield measure is being discussed and what the underlying assumptions of any particular measure are.

Current Yield

Current yield is defined as the ratio of the coupon interest to the current market price. The current yield is clearly superior to simply citing the coupon rate on a bond because it uses the current market price as opposed to the face amount of a bond (almost always, $1,000). However, current yield is not a true measure of the return to a bond purchaser because it does not account for the difference between the bond's purchase price and its eventual redemption at par value. In effect, it is a one-period rate of return that measures the interest payment return relative to the initial investment.

Current Yield
A bond's annual coupon divided by the current market price.

EXAMPLE 11-5: CALCULATING CURRENT YIELD

Consider one of the bonds listed in Real-World Returns 11-1—the Mar 08/16 Ontario bonds with the 4.4 percent coupon rate, approximately eight years remaining to maturity, and paying coupons semi-annually. The bond is selling at a small premium over par with a current market price of $1,016.40. Because of the inverse relation between bond prices and market yields, it is clear that yields have fallen since the bond was originally issued, because the price is greater than $1,000.

The current yield (CY) on this bond = $44/$1,016.40 = 4.33%

Notice that this CY is less than the coupon rate of 4.4 percent for the bond, which will always be the case for bonds selling at a premium.

Yield to Maturity

The rate of return on bonds most often quoted for investors is the **yield to maturity (YTM)**, which is defined as the *promised* compounded rate of return an investor will receive from a bond purchased at

Yield to Maturity (YTM)
The promised compounded rate of return on a bond purchased at the current market price and held to maturity.

---

[4]Fisher believed that inflation expectations were based on past observations as well as information about the future and that inflation expectations were slow to develop and slow to disappear.

[5]While estimates of the real rate associated with government funds can be made by subtracting actual inflation for the same quarter because government funds are of very short duration, estimates of real rates on instruments with longer maturities require measures of expected inflation over the term of the instrument.

the current market price and held to maturity. This is the yield that was referred to in Real-World Returns 11-1 in the previous section. It captures the coupon income to be received on the bond as well as any capital gains and losses realized by purchasing the bond for a price different from face value and holding to maturity. Similar to the internal rate of return (IRR) in financial management, the yield to maturity is the periodic interest rate that equates the present value of the expected future cash flows (both coupons and face value) to be received on the bond to the initial investment in the bond, which is its current price.

To calculate the yield to maturity for a bond, we use Equation 11-5, where the market price, the coupon, the number of years to maturity, and the face value of the bond are known, and the discount rate or yield to maturity is the variable to be determined.

$$P = C \times (PVA_{YTM,n}) + F \times (PV_{YTM,n})$$

Since both the left-hand side of Equation 11-5 and the numerator values (cash flows) on the right side are known, the equation can be solved for YTM. When the bond pays semi-annual coupons, all terms are expressed in terms of six-month periods. (The resulting semi-annual rate must be doubled to obtain the annual YTM.)

To estimate the YTM requires a trial-and-error process to find the discount rate that equates the inflows from the bond (coupons plus face value) with its current price (cost). Different rates are tried until the left-hand and right-hand sides are equal. It is relatively easy today to find financial calculators or computer programs to solve YTM problems. We illustrate a simple example of the trial-and-error process involved in a yield-to-maturity calculation by referring to the present value tables at the end of the text. The purpose is simply to demonstrate conceptually how to calculate the YTM. Investors will normally use a calculator, computer, or the approximation formula described below to do computations such as these.

EXAMPLE 11-6: CALCULATING YIELD TO MATURITY

Consider the eight-year, 4.4 percent bond in Example 11-5 that was selling for $1,016.40. Because of the inverse relation between bond prices and market yields, it is clear that yields have fallen somewhat since the bond was originally issued, because the price is greater than $1,000. Using Equation 11-5 to determine yield to maturity,

$1,016.40 = $22.00 \times (PVA_{YTM,16}) + $1,000 \times (PV_{YTM,16})$

Trying a semi-annual rate of 2.08 percent for YTM, we get

$1,016.40 = $22.00 \times (PVA_{2.08\%,16}) + $1,000 \times (PV_{2.08\%,16})$

$1,016.40 = $22.00 (13.49206) + $1,000 (0.67362)$

$1,016.40 \approx $1,016.19$ (difference due to rounding error)

In this example, the solution is approximately 2.08 percent on a semi-annual basis, which by convention is doubled to obtain the annual YTM of 4.16 percent. However, since the price calculated using 4.16 percent is too low, we know the true YTM is "slightly" below 4.16 percent (and in fact the reported value is 4.15%).

The example above was simplistic because we were able to approximate a discount rate that equated the present value of the future cash flows almost exactly with its price. In practice, the trial-and-error process will be much more complicated and time consuming.[6]

In practice, every basis point counts and we need to be able to estimate the YTM more precisely. This is where it pays to know how to use your financial calculator! The following example shows how you can use a financial calculator to estimate the YTM of a bond, using the previous example.

---

[6]One commonly used approach for estimating the appropriate rate involves the use of an estimation technique referred to as linear interpolation, which students may have come across in other quantitative courses.

EXAMPLE 11-7: CALCULATING YIELD TO MATURITY BY FINANCIAL CALCULATOR

Consider again the eight-year, 4.4 percent bond in the previous example that is selling at $1,016.40. We can calculate its YTM using a financial calculator as follows:

Inputs:
PMT = 22.00; n = 16; FV = 1000; PV = –1016.40 (be sure to make the PV negative or make both FV and PMT negative for this calculator; for other calculators it may not be necessary).

Then we compute (CPT) i, which gives i = 2.078 (which is a semi-annual rate).

Annualizing this rate, we get YTM = 2.078% × 2 = 4.156%.

Current Yield, Yield to Maturity, and Coupon Rates

Notice that the YTM of 4.16 percent for the bond in Example 11-7 is below its current yield of 4.33 percent (as calculated for this bond in Example 11-5), which is in turn below the bond's coupon rate of 4.4 percent. This will always be the case for bonds selling at a premium (i.e., coupon rate > current yield > YTM). The relationship will be reversed for bonds selling at a discount, while all three rates will be equal only when bonds are selling at par. These relationships are expressed in the box below:

If: Coupon Rate > Current Yield > YTM	⟶ Bond is selling at a **Premium**
If: Coupon Rate = Current Yield = YTM	⟶ Bond is at **Par**
If: Coupon Rate < Current Yield < YTM	⟶ Bond is selling at a **Discount**

The YTM calculation for a zero-coupon bond is based on the same process shown in Equation 11-5—equating the current price to the future cash flows. Because there are no coupons, the process reduces to Equation 11-7, with all terms as previously defined, and n is generally expressed in semi-annual periods, producing an estimate for the semi-annual YTM:

$$YTM = [F/P]^{1/n} - 1$$

(11-7)

EXAMPLE 11-8 CALCULATING YTM FOR ZERO-COUPON BONDS

A zero-coupon bond has 12 years to maturity and is sold for $300. Given the 24 semi-annual periods to maturity, the power to be used in raising the ratio of $1,000/$300, or 3.333, is 0.04167 (calculated as 1/24). Using a calculator with a power function produces a value of 1.0514. Subtracting the 1.0 and multiplying by 100 leaves a semi-annual yield of 5.145 percent. Because YTM numbers are usually stated on an annual basis, this figure is doubled, which produces an annual yield of 10.29 percent.

It is important to understand that YTM is a promised yield, because investors earn the indicated yield only if the bond is held to maturity and the coupons are reinvested at the calculated YTM. Obviously, no trading can be done for a particular bond if the YTM is to be earned. The investor simply buys and holds. What is not so obvious to many investors, however, is the reinvestment implications of the YTM measure. Because of the importance of the reinvestment rate, we consider it in more detail by analyzing the reinvestment risk.

Yield to Call

Most corporate, as well as some government, bonds are callable by the issuers after some deferred call period. For bonds likely to be called, the yield-to-maturity calculation is an inappropriate measure of

Yield to Call

The promised return on a bond from the present to the date that the bond is first eligible to be called.

its expected return. A better measure in such situations is the promised **yield to call**. The end of the period when a bond can first be called is often used for the yield-to-call calculation. This yield is particularly appropriate for bonds selling at a premium (i.e., high-coupon bonds with market prices above par value) since they are highly likely to be called by the issuer at the first available call date.[7]

To calculate the yield to first call, the YTM formula (Equation 11-5) is used, but with the number of periods until the first call date substituted for the number of periods until maturity and the call price substituted for face value. These changes are shown in Equation 11-8.

(11-8)

$$P = C \times (PVA_{YTC,c}) + CP \times (PV_{YTC,c})$$

where
c = the number of periods until the first call date
YTC = the yield to first call
CP   = the call price to be paid if the bond is called

Bond prices are calculated on the basis of the lowest yield measure. Therefore, for premium bonds selling above a certain level, yield to call replaces yield to maturity, because it produces the lowest (and most appropriate) measure of yield.[8]

EXAMPLE 11-9: CALCULATING YIELD TO CALL

Consider the eight-year, 4.4 percent bond used in the previous examples that is selling for $1,016.40. Assuming this bond is callable after four years at a call price of $1,050, we can estimate its first yield to call (YTC) using a financial calculator as follows:

> Inputs:
> PMT = 22.00; n = 8 (i.e., number of periods to first call date or c); FV = 1050 (i.e., the call price or CP); PV = –1016.40
> Then CPT i gives us i = 2.542 (which is a semi-annual rate).
> Annualizing this rate, we get YTC = 2.542% × 2 = 5.084%.

Notice that for this example, the bond would be priced using the YTM of 4.16 percent, since it is lower than the YTC. This is because the call price is above the current market price, and thus the bond is not likely to be called unless interest rates decline before the call date.

Reinvestment Risk

Interest on Interest

The process by which bond coupons are reinvested to earn interest.

The YTM calculation assumes that the investor reinvests all coupons received from a bond at a rate equal to the computed YTM on that bond, thereby earning **interest on interest** over the life of the bond at the computed YTM rate. In effect, this calculation assumes that the reinvestment rate is the yield to maturity.

If the investor spends the coupons, or reinvests them at a rate different from the assumed reinvestment rate, the realized yield that will actually be earned at the end of the investment in the bond will differ from the promised YTM. And, in fact, coupons almost always will be reinvested at rates higher or lower than the computed YTM, resulting in a realized yield that differs from the promised yield. This gives rise to **reinvestment rate risk**.

Reinvestment Rate Risk

That part of interest rate risk resulting from uncertainty about the rate at which future interest coupons can be reinvested.

---

[7]That is, bonds with high coupons (and high yields) are prime candidates to be called.
[8]The technical name for the point at which yield to call comes into play is the "crossover point," which is a price and is approximately the sum of par value and one year's interest. For a discussion of this point, see S. Homer and M. Leibowitz, *Inside the Yield Book* (Englewood Cliffs, NJ: Prentice Hall, 1972), Chapter 4.

This interest-on-interest concept significantly affects the potential total dollar return. The exact impact is a function of coupon and time to maturity, with reinvestment becoming more important as either coupon or time to maturity, or both, rises. Holding everything else constant

- the longer the maturity of a bond, the greater the reinvestment risk; and
- the higher the coupon rate, the greater the dependence of the total dollar return from the bond on the reinvestment of the coupon payments.

To illustrate the importance of interest on interest in YTM calculations, Table 11-1 shows the realized yields under different assumed reinvestment rates for a 10 percent non-callable 20-year bond purchased at face value of $1,000. If the reinvestment rate exactly equals the YTM of 10 percent, the investor would realize a 10 percent compound return when the bond is held to maturity, with $4,040 of the total dollar return from the bond attributable to interest on interest. At a 12 percent reinvestment rate, the investor would realize an 11.14 percent compound return, with almost 75 percent of the total return coming from interest on interest ($5,738/$7,738). With no reinvestment of coupons (spending them as received), the investor would achieve only a 5.57 percent return. In all cases, the bond is held to maturity.

Clearly, the reinvestment portion of the YTM concept is critical. In fact, for long-term bonds the interest-on-interest component of the total realized yield may account for more than three-quarters of the bond's total dollar return.

INVESTING tip

Consider what happens when investors purchase bonds at high YTMs, such as when interest rates reached exceptionally high levels in the summer of 1982. Unless they reinvested the coupons at the promised YTMs, investors did not actually realize these high promised yields. For that to happen, coupons had to be reinvested at the record rates existing at that time, an unlikely situation especially for a high-YTM bond with a long maturity. The subsequent decline in interest rates during the fall of 1982 illustrates the fallacy of believing that one has "locked up" record yields during a relatively brief period of very high interest rates. On the other hand, if the investor chose to sell the bond before maturity, it would sell at a premium as a result of falling interest rates, resulting in capital gains.

Table 11-1

Realized Yields, Using Different Reinvestment Rate Assumptions, for a 10 Percent 20-Year Bond Purchased at Face Value of $1,000

Coupon Income[a] ($)	Assumed Reinvestment Rate (%)	Amount Attributable to Reinvestment[b] ($)	Total Return[c] ($)	Realized Yields[d] (%)
2000	0	0	2000	5.57
2000	5	1370	3370	7.51
2000	8	2751	4751	8.94
2000	9	3352	5352	9.46
2000	10	4040	6040	10.00
2000	11	4830	6830	10.56
2000	12	5738	7738	11.14

[a]Coupon income = $50 coupon received *semi-annually* for 20 years = $50 × 40 periods.

[b]Amount attributable to reinvestment = total return minus coupon income. This is also known as the interest on interest.

[c]Total return = sum of an annuity for 40 periods, $50 semi-annual coupons (Example: at 10 percent reinvestment rate, $50 × [5 percent, 40 period factor of 120.80] = $6,040.)

[d]Realized yield = [Future Value per Dollar Invested]$^{1/N}$ − 1, where future value per dollar invested = (total return + the selling price of bond) / cost of the bond. The result of this calculation is the potential yield on a semi-annual basis. To put this on an annual basis, this figure must be doubled. This has been done for the yields in Table 11-1.

The realized yield (RY) shown in Table 11-1 can be calculated using the following formula: (Note that RY assumes a constant reinvestment rate.)

(11-9)

$$RY = \left[\frac{\text{Total future dollars}}{\text{Purchase price of bond}} \right]^{1/n} - 1.0$$

EXAMPLE 11-10: CALCULATING REALIZED YIELD

For the bond calculations shown in Table 11-1, consider the yield an investor would achieve at an assumed reinvestment rate of 12 percent. The total future dollars equals the total dollar return shown in Table 11-1, $7,738, plus the selling price of the bond, $1,000, or $8,738. Therefore,

$$RY = [\$8,738/1,000]^{1/40} - 1.0$$
$$= [8.738]^{.025} - 1 = 1.05569 - 1.0$$
$$= 0.05569, \text{ or } 5.569\% \text{ on a semi-annual basis}$$
$$(= 11.14\% \text{ on an annual basis}).$$

One advantage of a zero-coupon bond is the elimination of reinvestment rate risk because there are no coupons to be reinvested. At the time of purchase, investors know the YTM that will be realized when the bond is held to maturity.

Horizon Return

Horizon Return
Bond returns to be earned based on assumptions about future reinvestment rates.

Bond investors today often make specific assumptions about future reinvestment rates in order to cope with the reinvestment rate problem illustrated earlier. This is sometimes referred to as horizon analysis. Given their explicit assumption about the reinvestment rate, investors can calculate the **horizon return** to be earned if that assumption turns out to be accurate.

The investor makes an assumption about the reinvestment rate expected to prevail over the planned investment horizon. The investor may also make an assumption about the yield to maturity expected to prevail at the end of the planned investment horizon, which in turn is used to estimate the price of the bond at that time. Based on these assumptions, the total future dollars expected to be available at the end of the planned investment horizon can be determined. The horizon return is then calculated as the interest rate that equates the total future dollars to the purchase price of the bond.

CHECK YOUR UNDERSTANDING

11-3. Justify the fact that the coupon rate is greater than the current yield, which in turn is greater than the yield to maturity, whenever a bond sells at a premium.

11-4. "Investors are routinely quoted the yield to maturity on a bond, but the chances of actually earning this quoted yield at the termination of the investment is almost zero." Do you agree with this statement? Explain your reasoning.

11-5. Assume that an investor holds a bond guaranteed not to default. Can the YTM on this bond be described as the actual return the investor will receive rather than a promised return?

BOND PRICE CHANGES

learning objective 4
Account for changes in bond prices.

Bond Price Changes Over Time

We know how to calculate the price of a bond using the cash flows to be received and the YTM as the discount rate. Assume that we calculate the price of a 20-year bond issued five years ago and discover that it is $910. The bond still has 15 years to maturity. What can we say about its price over the next 15 years?

When everything else is held constant, including market interest rates, any bond price that differs from the bond's face value (assumed to be $1,000) must change over time. Why? On a bond's specified maturity date, it must be worth its par or face value. Therefore, over time, holding all other factors constant, a bond's price must converge to $1,000 on the maturity date. In other words, the bond's price is "pulled to par."

After bonds are issued, they sell at discounts from par (prices less than $1,000) and premiums over par (prices greater than $1,000) during their lifetimes. Therefore, holding all other factors constant, a bond selling at a discount will experience a rise in price over time, and a bond selling at a premium will experience a decline in price over time as the bond's remaining life approaches the maturity date.

Figure 11-1 illustrates bond price movements over time, assuming constant yields. Bond 2 depicts a 10 percent coupon, 30-year bond assuming that yields remain constant at 10 percent. The price of this bond does not change, beginning and ending at $1,000. Bond 1, on the other hand, depicts an 8 percent coupon, 30-year bond assuming that required yields start, and remain constant, at 10 percent. The price starts below $1,000 because bond 1 is selling at a discount as a result of its coupon of 8 percent being less than the required yield of 10 percent. Bond 3 illustrates a 30-year bond with a 12 percent coupon, assuming that required yields start and remain constant at 10 percent. The price of bond 3 begins above $1,000 because it is selling at a premium (12 percent is greater than the required yield of 10 percent).

If all other factors are held constant, the price of all three bonds must converge to $1,000 on the maturity date. In actuality, however, other factors do not remain constant. In particular, interest rates or yields to maturity change constantly, as do bond prices. Furthermore, the sensitivity of the price change is a function of certain variables, especially coupon and maturity. We now examine these variables.

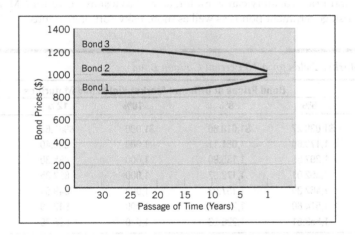

Figure 11-1
Bond Price Movements Over Time Assuming Constant Yields of 10 Percent for Three 30-Year Bonds

Bond Price Changes as a Result of Interest Rate Changes

Bond prices change with interest rates and required yields. Understanding how bond prices change in relation to interest rates is critical to successful bond management. The basics of bond price movements as a result of interest rate changes have been known for many years. For example, over 30 years ago, Burton Malkiel derived five theorems about the relationship between bond prices and yields.[9] Using the bond valuation model, he showed the changes that occur in the price of a bond (i.e., its volatility) given a change in yields, as a result of bond variables such as time to maturity and coupon. We will use Malkiel's bond theorems to illustrate how interest rate changes affect bond prices.

---

[9]B. G. Malkiel, "Expectations, Bond Prices, and the Term Structure of Interest Rates," *Quarterly Journal of Economics*, May 1962, pp. 197–218.

Bond Prices Move Inversely to Interest Rates

Investors must always keep in mind a fundamental fact about the relationship between bond prices and bond yields: Bond prices move inversely to market yields. When the level of required yields demanded by investors on new bond issues changes, the required yields on all bonds already outstanding will also change. For these yields to change, the prices of these bonds must change, since the coupon and maturity payments are fixed when the bond is originally issued. This inverse relationship, which was evident in the bond valuation examples presented earlier in the chapter, is the basis for understanding, valuing, and managing bonds.

Table 11-2 shows prices for a 10 percent coupon bond for market yields from 6 to 14 percent and for maturity dates from one to 30 years. For any given maturity, the price of the bond declines as the required yield increases and increases as the required yield declines from the 10 percent level. Figure 11-2 shows this relationship using data from Table 11-2.

An interesting corollary of the inverse relationship between bond prices and interest rates is as follows: *Holding maturity constant, a decrease in rates will raise bond prices on a percentage basis more than a corresponding increase in rates will lower bond prices.*

EXAMPLE 11-11: BOND PRICES AND INTEREST RATE CHANGES

Table 11-2 shows that for the 15-year, 10 percent coupon bond, the price would be $1,172.92 if market rates were to decline from 10 percent to 8 percent, resulting in a price appreciation of 17.29 percent. On the other hand, a rise of two percentage points in market rates from 10 percent to 12 percent results in a change in price to $862.35, a price decline of only 13.77 percent.

Obviously, bond price volatility can work for, as well as against, investors. Money can be made (and lost) in low-risk government bonds as well as more risky corporate bonds.

Table 11-2

Bond Price and Market Yields for a 10 Percent Coupon Bond

Years to Maturity	Bond Prices at Different Market Yields and Maturities				
	6%	8%	10%	12%	14%
1	$1,038.27	$1,018.86	$1,000	$981.67	$963.84
5	1,170.60	1,081.11	1,000	926.40	859.53
10	1,297.55	1,135.90	1,000	885.30	788.12
15	1,392.01	1,172.92	1,000	862.35	751.82
20	1,462.30	1,197.93	1,000	849.54	733.37
25	1,514.60	1,214.82	1,000	842.38	723.99
30	1,553.51	1,226.23	1,000	838.39	719.22

Although the inverse relationship between bond prices and interest rates is the basis of all bond analysis, a complete understanding of that relationship requires additional information. An increase in interest rates will cause bond prices to decline, but the exact amount of decline will depend on important variables unique to each bond such as time to maturity and coupon. We will examine each of these in turn.

The Effects of Maturity

The effect of a change in yields on bond prices depends on the maturity of the bond. An important principle is that for a given change in market yields, changes in bond prices are directly related to time to maturity. Therefore, as interest rates change, the prices of longer-term bonds will change more than the prices of shorter-term ones, everything else being equal.

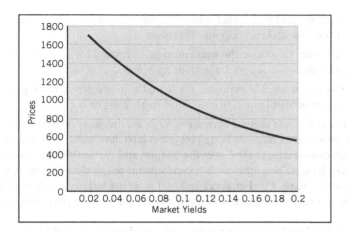

Figure 11-2
The Relationship between
Bond Prices and Market
Yields

EXAMPLE 11-12: MATURITY AND BOND PRICES

Given two 10 percent coupon bonds and a drop in market yields from 10 to 8 percent, we can see from Table 11-2 that the price of the 15-year bond will be $1,172.92, while that of the 30-year bond will be $1,226.23.

The principle illustrated here is simple but important. Other things being equal, bond price volatility is a function of maturity. Long-term bond prices fluctuate more than short-term ones. A related principle regarding maturity can be stated as follows: *The percentage price change that occurs as a result of the direct relationship between a bond's maturity and its price volatility increases at a diminishing rate as the time to maturity increases.*

EXAMPLE 11-13: MATURITY AND PRICE VOLATILITY

As we saw above, a two percentage point drop in market yields (from 10 to 8 percent) increased the price of the 15-year bond to $1,172.92, a 17.29 percent change, while the price of the 30-year bond changed to $1,226.23, a 22.62 percent change.

This example shows that the percentage of price change resulting from an increase in time to maturity increases, but at a decreasing rate. Put simply, a doubling of the time to maturity will not result in a doubling of the percentage price change resulting from a change in market yields.

The Effects of Coupon

In addition to the maturity effect, the change in the price of a bond as a result of a change in interest rates depends on the coupon rate of the bond. We can state this principle as follows (other things being equal): *Bond price fluctuations (volatility) and bond coupon rates are inversely related.* Note that we are talking about percentage price fluctuations; this relationship does not necessarily hold if we measure volatility in terms of dollar price changes rather than percentage price changes. This result is intuitive since a greater proportion of total income on higher coupon bonds is received in earlier periods; therefore the discount rate effect is lower for such bonds.

The Implications of Malkiel's Theorems for Investors

Malkiel's derivations for bond investors lead to the practical conclusion that the two bond variables of major importance in assessing the change in the price of a bond, given a change in interest rates, are its coupon and its maturity. This conclusion can be summarized as follows: A decline in interest rates will cause a rise in bond prices (and vice versa), with the most volatility in bond prices occurring in longer maturity bonds and bonds with low coupons. Therefore

1. A bond buyer, in order to receive the maximum price impact for an expected change in interest rates, should purchase low-coupon, long-maturity bonds.

2. If an increase in interest rates is expected (or feared), an investor contemplating their purchase should consider bonds with large coupons, short maturities, or both.

These relationships provide useful information for bond investors by demonstrating how the price of a bond changes with interest rates. Although investors have no control over the change and direction in market rates, they can exercise control over the coupon and maturity, both of which have significant effects on bond price changes. Nevertheless, it is cumbersome to calculate various possible price changes on the basis of these theorems. Furthermore, maturity is an inadequate measure of the sensitivity of a bond's price change to changes in yields because it ignores the coupon payments and the principal repayment.

Investors managing bond portfolios need a measure of time designed to more accurately portray a bond's "average" life, taking into account all of the bond's cash flows, including both coupons and the return of principal at maturity. Such a measure—called duration—is available and is widely used.

CHECK YOUR UNDERSTANDING

11-6. "The price of a bond is certain to change if it is selling for either a discount or a premium." Do you agree with this statement?

11-7. We know that the prices of long-term bonds are more sensitive to interest rate changes than the prices of short-term bonds. Why then, is maturity alone not sufficient to measure interest rate sensitivity?

Measuring Bond Price Volatility: Duration

learning objective 5
Explain and apply the concept of duration.

In managing a bond portfolio, perhaps the most important consideration is the effect of yield changes on the prices and rates of return for different bonds. The problem is that a given change in interest rates can result in very different percentage price changes for the various bonds that investors hold. We saw earlier that both maturity and coupon affect bond price changes for a given change in yields.

Although maturity is the traditional measure of a bond's lifetime, it is inadequate because it focuses only on the return of principal at the maturity date. Two 20-year bonds, one with an 8 percent coupon and the other with a 15 percent coupon, do not have identical economic lifetimes. An investor will recover the original purchase price much sooner with the 15 percent coupon bond. Therefore, a measure is needed that accounts for the entire pattern (both size and timing) of the cash flows over the life of the bond—the effective maturity of the bond. Such a concept, called duration, was conceived over 50 years ago by Frederick Macaulay.[10] Duration is very useful for bond management purposes because it combines the properties of maturity and coupon.

Duration Defined

Duration

A measure of a bond's economic lifetime based on the weighted present value of expected cash flows over the life of the bond.

Duration measures the weighted average maturity of a bond's cash flows on a present value basis; that is, the present values of the cash flows are used as the weights in calculating the weighted average maturity. Thus,

Duration = number of years needed to fully recover purchase price of a bond, given present values of its future cash flows

= weighted average time to recovery of all interest payments plus principal[11]

---

[10]F. R. Macaulay, *Some Theoretical Problems Suggested by the Movement of Interest Rates, Bond Yields and Stock Prices in the United States Since 1856* (New York: National Bureau of Economic Research, 1938).

[11]This discussion applies only to option-free bonds.

Figure 11-3 illustrates the concepts of both time to maturity and duration for a bond with five years to maturity, a 10 percent coupon, and selling for $1,000. As the figure indicates, the stream of cash flows generated by this bond over the term to maturity consists of $50 every six months, or $100 per year, plus the return of principal of $1,000 at the end of the five years. The last cash flow combines the interest payment of $50 with the principal repayment of $1,000 that occurs at the maturity date.

Although the term to maturity for the bond illustrated in Figure 11-3 is five years, its Macaulay duration is only 4.17 years as indicated by the arrow. This means that the weighted average maturity of the bond's cash flows is 4.17 years from the beginning date. It is important that we understand how this duration value is calculated.

Calculating Duration

To calculate Macaulay duration, it is necessary to consider a weighted time period. The time periods at which the cash flows are received are expressed in terms of years and denoted by CF_t in this discussion. When all of these cash flows (CF_ts) have been weighted and added together, the result is the duration, stated in years.

The present values of the cash flows serve as the weighting factors to apply to the time periods. Each weighting factor shows the relative importance of each cash flow to the bond's total present value, which is simply its current market price. The sum of the weighting factors will be 1.0, indicating that all cash flows have been accounted for. Putting this all together gives us the equation for duration:

$$\text{Macaulay Duration} = D = \sum_{t=1}^{n} \frac{PV(CF_t)}{\text{Market price}} \times t \qquad \textbf{(11-10)}$$

where

t	= the year at which the cash flow is expected to be received
n	= the number of years to maturity
$PV(CF_t)$	= value of the cash flow in period t discounted at the annual yield to maturity
Market price	= the bond's current price (or the present value of all the cash flows)

As Equation 11-10 shows, duration is obtained by multiplying each year's weighted cash receipt (weighted by the price of the bond) by the number of years when each is to be received, and adding. Note that duration is measured in years, and that for ease of exposition, we state the equation on an annual basis although interest on bonds is often paid semi-annually.

EXAMPLE 11-14: CALCULATING DURATION

Table 11-3 provides an example of calculating the duration for a bond, using the same bond as shown in Figure 11-3, except now for ease of exposition, the calculation is done on an annual basis. This is a 10 percent coupon bond with five years remaining to maturity. The bond is priced at $1,000 for simplicity, and the YTM is 10 percent.[12]

---

[12]A shortcut formula can be used for coupon bonds selling at face value:

$$\text{Duration} = \frac{1 + YTM}{YTM} [1 - (1/(1 + YTM)^n)]$$

Using a semi-annual rate and doubling the number of periods, we must divide the answer by 2.0 to put it on an annual basis.

Figure 11-3
Illustration of the
Cash Flow Pattern of a
10 Percent Coupon,
Five-Year Maturity Bond
Paying Interest Semi-
Annually and Returning
the Principal of $1,000
at Maturity

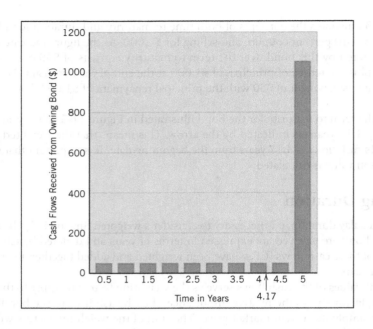

The cash flows consist of five $100 coupons plus the return of principal at the end of the fifth year. Notice that the fifth-year cash flow of $1,100 ($100 coupon plus $1,000 return of principal) accounts for 68 percent of the value of the bond and contributes 3.42 years to the duration of 4.17 years. In this example, the other cash flows combined contributed less than one year to the duration. The duration of 4.17 years is almost one year less than the term to maturity of five years. As we will see, duration will always be less than time to maturity for bonds that pay coupons.

Table 11-3

An Example of Calculating the Duration of a Bond Using a 10 Percent Coupon, Five-Year Maturity Bond Priced at $1,000 and Paying Annual Interest

(1) Years	(2) Cash Flow	(3) PV Factor	(4) $ (2) × (3)	(5) (4) / Price	(6) (1) × (5)
1	$100	.909	90.90	.0909	.0909
2	100	.826	82.60	.0826	.1652
3	100	.751	75.10	.0751	.2253
4	100	.683	68.30	.0683	.2732
5	1100	.621	683.10	.6831	3.4155
					Duration = 4.1701

Understanding Duration

How is duration related to the key bond variables previously analyzed? An examination of Equation 11-10 shows that the calculation of duration depends on three factors:

1. The maturity date of the bond
2. Coupon payments
3. Yield to maturity.

1. *The maturity date of the bond.* Holding the size of coupon payments and the yield to maturity constant, duration expands with time to maturity but at a decreasing rate, particularly beyond 15 years to maturity. Even between five and 10 years time to maturity, duration is expanding at a significantly lower rate than was the case before the five-year mark, where it expands rapidly.[13] Note that for all coupon-paying bonds, duration is always less than maturity. For a zero-coupon bond, duration is equal to time to maturity.

2. *Coupon payments.* Holding maturity and yield to maturity constant, coupon is inversely related to duration. This is logical because higher coupons lead to quicker recovery of the bond's value, resulting in a shorter duration, relative to lower coupons.

3. *Yield to maturity.* Holding coupon payments and maturity constant, yield to maturity is inversely related to duration.

Why is duration important in bond management and analysis? First, it tells us the difference between the effective lives of alternative bonds. Bonds A and B, with the same duration but different years to maturity, have more in common than bonds C and D with the same maturity but different durations. For any particular bond, as maturity increases the duration grows at a decreasing rate.[14]

EXAMPLE 11-15: DURATION AND TERM TO MATURITY

Given the 10 percent coupon bond discussed above with a yield to maturity of 10 percent and a five-year life, we saw that the duration was 4.17 years. If the maturity of this bond was 10 years, it would have an effective life (duration) of 6.76 years, and with a 20-year maturity it would have an effective life of 9.36 years—quite a different perspective. Furthermore, under these conditions, a 50-year maturity for this bond would change the effective life to only 10.91 years. The reason for the sharp differences between the term to maturity and the duration is that cash flows received in the distant future have very small present values and therefore add little to a bond's value.

Second, the duration concept is used in certain bond management strategies, particularly immunization, as explained later in the chapter.

Third, duration is a measure of bond price sensitivity to interest rate movements, a very important part of any bond analysis. Malkiel's bond price theorems are inadequate to examine all aspects of bond price sensitivity. This issue is considered in some detail below because of its potential importance to bond investors.

Estimating Price Changes Using Duration

The real value of the duration measure to bond investors is that it combines coupon and maturity, the two key variables that investors must consider in response to expected changes in interest rates. As noted earlier, duration is related positively to maturity and negatively to coupon. However, bond price changes are directly related to duration; that is, the percentage change in a bond's price, given a change in interest rates, is proportional to its duration. The reason for this relationship is that Macaulay's duration can be derived by taking the first derivative of the bond pricing equation with respect to $(1+r)$. Most students who have studied calculus will recall that the first derivative of a function (in this case the bond pricing equation) is its slope. The slope, in turn, measures the responsiveness of the function value (or the bond price) with respect to changes in the chosen variable [in this case $(1+r)$]. Therefore, duration can be used to measure interest rate exposure.

---

[13]The duration of a perpetuity is $(1 + \text{YTM})/\text{YTM}$. This indicates that maturity and duration can differ greatly since the maturity of a perpetuity is infinite, but duration is not. That is, perpetuities have an infinite maturity but a finite duration.

[14]Deep discount bonds are an exception to the general rule. Their duration first increases with time to maturity, up to some distant point, and then decreases in duration beyond this point. This is because deep discount bonds with very long maturities behave like perpetuities.

Modified Duration
Duration divided by
(1 + yield to maturity).

(11-11)

The term **modified duration** refers to Macaulay's duration in Equation 11-10 divided by $(1+r)$, or

$$\text{Modified duration} = D^* = D / (1 + r)$$

where
D^* = modified duration
r = the bond's yield to maturity

EXAMPLE 11-16: CALCULATING MODIFIED DURATION

Using the duration of 4.17 years calculated earlier and the YTM of 10 percent, the modified duration based on annual interest would be

$$D^* = 4.17 / (1 + 0.10) = 3.79$$

The modified duration can be used to calculate the percentage price change in a bond for a given change in r, using Equation 11-12, which is an approximation:[15]

(11-12)

$$\text{Percentage change in bond price} \approx \frac{-D}{(1 + r)} \times \text{Percentage point change in } r$$

or

(11-13)

$$\Delta P/P \approx -D^* \Delta r$$

where
ΔP = change in price
P = the price of the bond
$-D^*$ = modified duration with a negative sign
Δr = the instantaneous change in yield

EXAMPLE 11-17: MODIFIED DURATION AND CHANGES IN BOND

Using our same bond with a modified duration of 3.79, assume an instantaneous yield change of 20 basis points (+0.0020) in the YTM, from 10 to 10.20 percent. The approximate change in price, based on Equation 11-13, would be

$$\Delta/P = -(3.79)(+0.0020)(100) = -0.758\%$$

Given the original price of the bond of $1,000, this percentage price change would result in an estimated bond price of $992.42. This is very close to the price of $992.32 (0.768 percent decline) that we would get if we determined the bond price based on a YTM of 10.20 percent using the bond valuation equation. For very small changes in yield, Equations 11-12 or 11-13 provide good approximations. However, for larger changes, such as 100 or 200 basis points, the approximate percentage price change is less accurate. This is because the relationship is derived using the first derivative of the bond valuation equation. First derivatives measure the slope of a function (bond prices in this case) accurately over small intervals or for small changes in the variable that is being allowed to vary (interest rates in this case).

An alternative measure of duration, called *effective duration*, is equivalent to modified duration for option-free bonds. It has the additional benefit that it may also be used for measuring price volatility of bonds with options such as callable or retractable features attached. This method of estimating

---

[15]This formula provides a reasonable approximation for "option-free" bonds if the change in yield is very small, and if the yield curve undergoes a parallel shift in rates.

duration, along with a method for estimating *effective convexity*, is presented in Appendix 11B. These approaches are used extensively in the current CFA curriculum.

Convexity

Although Equation 11-12 is only an approximation for very small changes in the required yield, the approximation is quite close. However, as the changes become larger, the approximation becomes poorer. The problem is that modified duration produces symmetric percentage price change estimates using Equation 11-10 (if *r* had decreased 0.20 percent, the price change would have been +0.758 percent), when, in actuality, the price–yield relationship is not linear. This relationship is, in fact, convex, and calculations of price changes should properly account for the convexity of the price–yield relationship. **Convexity** is the term used to refer to the degree to which duration changes as the yield to maturity changes.[16]

To understand the convexity issue, Figure 11-4 repeats the analysis from Figure 11-2 that shows a 10 percent coupon bond at different market yields and prices. We can think of modified duration graphically as the slope of a line that is tangent to the convex price–yield curve of Figure 11-4 at the current price and yield of the bond, which is assumed to be $1,000 and 10 percent.[17]

In effect, we are using a tangent line to measure the slope of the curve that depicts the inverse relationship between bond price and yield. For a very small change in yield, such as a few basis points, the slope of the line—the modified duration—provides a good approximation for the rate of change in price, given a change in yield. As the change in yield increases, the error that results from using a straight line to estimate a bond's price behaviour as given by a curve increases.[18]

As we move away from the point of tangency in Figure 11-4 in either direction, we underestimate the price of the bond using modified duration; that is, the price change is always more favourable than suggested by the modified duration. Notice that the shaded area in Figure 11-4 captures the convexity areas both above and below the starting point of 10 percent and $1,000. If yields decrease, prices increase, and the duration tangent line fails to indicate the true higher price. Conversely, when yields increase, prices decrease, but the duration tangent line overstates the amount of the price decrease relative to the true convex relationship. This helps illustrate what is meant by the term positive convexity.

Convexity
A measure of the degree to which the relationship between a bond's price and yield departs from the straight line; that is, the degree to which duration changes as the yield to maturity changes.

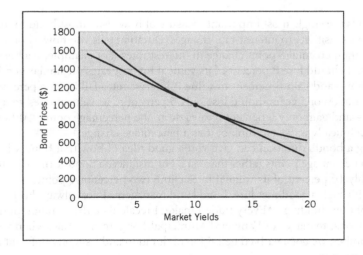

Figure 11-4
Convex Relationship between Yields and Prices and Tangent Line Representing Modified Duration for a 10 Percent, 10-Year Bond

---

[16]An in-depth discussion of convexity is beyond the scope of this text; however, we would note that it is derived by taking the second derivative of the bond valuation equation with respect to interest rates. For a more detailed discussion, see F. J. Fabozzi and T. D. Fabozzi, *The Handbook of Fixed Income Securities*, Fifth Edition (Irwin Professional Publishing, 1997).
[17]Technically, the slope of the tangent line in Figure 11-4 is equal to the negative of modified duration multiplied by the bond's current market price.
[18]As the yield changes, the tangency line and slope also change; that is, modified duration changes as yield changes.

Convexity is largest for low coupon bonds, long-maturity bonds, and low yields to maturity. If convexity is large, extensive changes in duration are implied, with corresponding inaccuracies in forecasts of price changes. Convexity calculations can be made similar to those with modified duration discussed earlier. These calculations produce an approximate percentage price change due to convexity that can be added to the one based on duration discussed earlier. This total percentage price change is still an approximation, but it is considerably improved over that using only duration.

Some Conclusions on Duration

What does this analysis of price volatility mean to bond investors? The message is simple—to have the maximum (minimum) price volatility from a bond, investors should choose bonds with the longest (shortest) duration. If an investor already owns a portfolio of bonds, he or she can act to increase the duration of the portfolio if a decline in interest rates is expected and the investor is attempting to achieve the largest price appreciation possible. Fortunately, duration is additive, which means that a bond portfolio's duration is a weighted average of each individual bond's duration.

The duration concept has become so popular in today's investment world that it is widely known and discussed in the popular press. Investors can find duration numbers in a variety of sources, particularly with regard to bond funds. As Real-World Returns 11-3 suggests, investors should basically forget maturity and think in terms of duration.

Although duration is an important measure of bond risk, it is not necessarily always the most appropriate one. Duration measures volatility, which is important but is only one aspect of the risk in bonds. If an investor considers price volatility an acceptable proxy for risk, duration is the measure of risk to use along with the correction for convexity. Duration may not be a complete measure of bond risk, but it does reflect some of the impact of changes in interest rates.

REAL-WORLD RETURNS 11-3
Using Duration to Estimate the Risk of a Bond

To predict how your bond fund will perform when the bond market gets walloped, look at its duration.

Duration is the single most important measure of how risky most bond funds are because it measures their sensitivity to interest-rate changes. Duration tells you how a bond or bond fund will react to a one-percentage-point change in interest rates. For example, if a bond has a duration of 8 years, it should lose 8 percent of its value if interest rates on similar bonds rise by one percentage point—and gain 8 percent in value if interest rates fall by one percentage point. A bond with a duration of 5 years should lose only 5 percent of its value if rates go up by one percentage point—and gain only 5 percent if rates drop one percentage point. (Although duration is expressed technically in years, think of it as a percentage change.)

Doubling a bond's duration can give you a good idea of how that bond will react if rates change by two percentage points rather than one. For instance, a bond with a duration of 8 years will lose roughly 16 percent of its value if rates climb two percentage points.

Because it's such a good measure, bond-fund managers almost always keep a tight grip on the duration of their holdings. "Every trade I make, I recalculate the duration of the portfolio," says Jerome Jacobs, manager of Vanguard Municipal Long Term. (Alas, when we called Vanguard's 800 number, we got a garbled definition of duration and a slightly different number from the one Jacobs quoted.)

Investors don't need to analyze their holds with pinpoint accuracy any more than they need to know the precise braking distance on a new car. But it's good to have at least a rough idea of the duration of the bonds and bond funds you own—as well as those that you're considering buying.

Duration is of far more value than the number that many inexperienced investors focus on: yield. "People who buy bond funds tend to do so on the basis of yield, but often the higher the yield the higher the duration," says Kurt Brouwer, a San Francisco investment adviser. A lot of investors who left the safety of certificates of deposit last fall for the higher yields of bond funds have found out the hard way that concentrating too much on yield can be costly.

While many investors don't understand duration, most are at least familiar with a less-precise measure of bond funds' interest-rate risk: maturity. Maturity is simply the number of years until a bond pays back its principal. Measure the maturities of the bonds in a fund and weight each bond according to how big a position it has in the portfolio, and you have the fund's weighted average maturity. The longer a fund's maturity, the more affected it tends to be by interest-rate swings.

But maturity is a flawed measure of interest-rate risk. "Duration is a much better guide for quantifying risk than is maturity," says Tom Poor, portfolio manager of Scudder Short-Term Bond fund. Why? Simply because duration takes into account both the amount paid on maturity and the value of the interest payments made along the way.

Consider two hypothetical 20-year bonds. One, a zero-coupon bond, doesn't pay a penny in interest until the day it matures. The other pays 7 percent interest annually. Common sense tells you that a bond that pays 7 percent annually is less volatile than one that pays nothing for 20 years.

But duration gives a more precise method of comparing the interest-rate sensitivity of the two bonds. Because the zero-coupon bond doesn't pay any interest until it matures, its duration is virtually the same as its maturity—20 years. Meanwhile, the other bond, priced at $100 and yielding 7 percent annually, has a duration of 10.7 years. Other things being equal, the higher a bond's yield, the *shorter* its duration. Take a 20-year bond also priced at $100 but with a 10 percent yield. Its duration is 8.6 years, or more than two years shorter than the duration of the 7 percent bond.

Some of the equations used in determining duration are so complex that without today's computers, duration would be an impractical tool. Fortunately, investors don't have to bother with the math. Even many portfolio managers don't know exactly how durations are figured. "If you call a bond trader and ask him how he calculates a duration, he's going to say he punches up a computer screen and looks at it," says Vanguard's Jacobs.

If you could know only one number about a bond fund, it should be its duration. But there is a second important number to use in choosing a bond fund—total return. While duration measures interest-rate risk, total return shows an investor how much a bond fund has earned, both in yield and in capital gains.

A good general rule in investing is that the more risk you take the higher your potential rewards should be. But the best funds manage to produce top returns without undue risk.

Keeping Names Straight

As good a measure as it is, duration isn't perfect. One flaw is that it changes as interest rates change. When interest rates climb, bond-fund durations shorten. When rates fall, durations lengthen. Unless rates shift dramatically, however, changes in duration should be fairly small, particularly for short- and intermediate-term bond funds. A bond fund's duration can also change when the fund trades the bonds in its portfolio. Check your fund's duration periodically to avoid unpleasant surprises.

There are a few other things to be aware of in using duration as an evaluation tool. It won't tell you anything about the credit quality of your bonds. A high-yield junk bond reacts as much to investor concerns about the stability of the economy and the issuing company as it does to interest rates. For that reason, duration is of less value in assessing junk bonds or funds. Similarly, foreign bonds change in value with currency swings, as well as with changes in interest rates. So duration isn't all that helpful in evaluating foreign bonds, either.

(continued)

REAL-WORLD RETURNS 11-3 *continued*

It also pays to keep in mind that duration is a theoretical measure of interest-rate risk. The ultimate test of a bond's worth is the marketplace. During times of extreme volatility—such as the first quarter of this year—liquidity can dry up and buyers may become scarce, regardless of what duration indicates the price should be. "In a rapidly moving market environment, bonds aren't necessarily going to behave the way bond math suggests," cautions Brad Tank, manager of Strong Short-Term Bond fund. This is particularly true of complex derivatives, used by some bond-fund managers to enhance returns.

Be aware that duration can be expressed in more than one way. The most accurate measure is *effective duration*, which takes into account the impact of bonds being called—that is, redeemed early by the issuer. In the municipal-bond market, bonds are often issued with maturities of 20 or 30 years but contain a provision that allows the issuer to pay them off earlier, typically after ten years. Effective duration also takes into account the prepayment risk in mortgage-backed bonds. If rates decline, many homeowners will refinance, lowering the duration of the bonds in mortgage-securities funds.

Although it's not as accurate, modified duration is the number that funds are most willing to make public. It does not take into account the probable effect of prepayments and calls. In municipal-bond and mortgage funds, especially, modified duration is likely to overstate slightly the interest-rate risk.

Source: Adapted and reprinted with permission from *Kiplinger's Personal Finance Magazine*, June 1994. Copyright © 1994. The Kiplinger Washington Editors, Inc.

JUNK BONDS ARE RISKY BUSINESS

In 2001, credit card company American Express sustained heavy losses because it was overly aggressive in investing in junk bonds. In the second quarter of the year, it reduced pre-tax earnings by US$826 million. After the announcement, company stock traded as low as $37.17, down from a two-year high of $62.00.

American Express CEO Kenneth I. Chenault admitted the firm "did not fully comprehend the risk" in its $3.5 billion portfolio of junk bonds.

Some of the high-yield bonds had ratings as low as single B, which had the potential for huge losses if default rates in the junk bond market increased, which they did.

DISCUSSION QUESTIONS

1. If American Express executives approved the junk bond investments in good faith, hoping to increase shareholder wealth, did that make their actions unethical?

2. What can companies do to better understand and manage investment risk?

3. Should financial advisors steer their clients away from junk bonds?

CHECK YOUR UNDERSTANDING

11-8. Holding maturity constant, a bond with a larger coupon will have a shorter duration than a bond with a smaller coupon. Agree or disagree, and explain your reasoning.

11-9. Using the duration concept, if you expect a decline in interest rates and you want to use this decline to your advantage, how should you adjust your bond portfolio?

SUMMARY

This summary relates to the learning objectives for this chapter.

1. **Calculate the price of a bond.**

   A bond's intrinsic value is its estimated value, or the present value of the expected cash flows from that asset. Bond prices are determined according to Equation 11-2.

2. **Explain the bond valuation process.**

   Bonds are valued using a present value process. The expected future cash flows for a bond—interest payments and principal repayments—are discounted at the bond's required yield. Bond prices change in response to changes in the level of market interest rates on similar instruments.

3. **Calculate major bond yield measures, including yield to maturity, yield to call, and horizon return.**

   The yield to maturity is defined as the promised compounded rate of return an investor will receive from a bond purchased at the current market price and held to maturity. The yield to call is the promised yield to the end of the period when a bond can first be called. The horizon return is the total rate of return earned on a bond over some time period given certain specified reinvestment rates of return.

4. **Account for changes in bond prices.**

   Bond prices move inversely with interest rates; prices increase as the required yield decreases and vice versa. Changes in bond prices are directly related to time to maturity and inversely related to bond coupons. Given change in interest rates the two most important bond variables in assessing the change in a price of a bond are its coupon and its maturity.

5. **Explain and apply the concept of duration.**

   Duration is the weighted average time to recovery of all interest payments plus principal repayment. Duration expands with time to maturity but at a decreasing rate, and it is inversely related to coupon and yield to maturity. The modified duration can be used to calculate the percentage price change in a bond for a given change in the bond's yield to maturity. The bond price–yield relationship is not linear but convex, and precise calculations of price changes should properly account for this convexity.

KEY TERMS

Basis points, p.327
Conversion premium
   (Appendix 11C), p.356
Conversion price
   (Appendix 11C), p.356
Conversion ratio
   (Appendix 11C), p.356
Conversion value
   (Appendix 11C), p.356

Convertible securities
   (Appendix 11C), p.356
Convexity, p.343
Current yield, p.329
Duration, p.338
Horizon return, p.334
Interest on interest, p.332
Intrinsic value, p.320
Modified duration, p.342

Real risk-free rate of interest,
   p.327
Reinvestment rate risk, p.332
Yield to call, p.332
Yield to maturity (YTM), p.329

REVIEW QUESTIONS

11-1. When a bond is issued, its coupon rate is set at approximately _____.

11-2. Why is current yield an incorrect measure of a bond's return?

11-3. What does it mean to say that YTM is a promised yield?

11-4. What is meant by interest on interest?

11-5. Distinguish between promised yield and realized yield. How does interest on interest affect realized return?

11-6. How is the intrinsic value of any asset determined? How are intrinsic value and present value related?

11-7. How is the price of a bond determined? Why is this process relatively straightforward for a bond?

11-8. What effect does the use of semi-annual discounting have on the value of a bond in relation to annual discounting?

11-9. When is a bond selling at a discount, based on coupon rate, current yield, and YTM? When is it selling at a premium?

11-10. Define YTM. How is YTM determined?

11-11. Why is YTM important?

11-12. If YTM is merely a promised yield, why do investors not use some other measure of yield?

11-13. Which bond is more affected by interest-on-interest considerations?

    a. Bond A — 12 percent coupon, 20 years to maturity
    b. Bond B — 6 percent coupon, 25 years to maturity

11-14. How can bond investors eliminate the reinvestment rate risk inherent in bonds?

11-15. How does duration differ from time to maturity? What does duration tell you?

11-16. Assume that a bond investor wishes to maximize the potential price volatility from a portfolio of bonds about to be constructed. What should this investor seek in the way of coupon, maturity, and duration?

11-17. Is duration a complete measure of bond risk? Is it the best measure? Why?

11-18. What assumptions are involved in calculating the horizon return?

11-19. Differentiate between yield to call and yield to maturity. Will the yield be the same for both? Explain.

11-20. What are the implications of Malkiel's bond price theorems to bond investors? Which two bond variables are of major importance in assessing bond price changes?

11-21. How is duration related to time to maturity? To coupon payments? To the yield to maturity? Do the same relationships hold for a zero-coupon bond?

11-22. What is convexity? Why should bond investors consider it?

11-23. With the exception of zero-coupon bonds, a bond's duration will always be less than the bond's time to maturity. Why?

11-24. Yield to maturity can be thought of as the internal rate of return on a bond investment. Do you agree or disagree? Explain your reasoning.

11-25. Given two bonds with identical risk, coupons, and maturity date, with the only difference between the two being that one is callable, which bond will sell for the higher price?

11-26. What two characteristics of a bond determine its reinvestment rate risk?

11-27. The bond price curve is said to have a convex shape. What does this mean in terms of increases in interest rates relative to changes in bond prices?

11-28. Why is the duration of a zero-coupon bond equal to its time to maturity?

PROBLEMS

11-1.   a. Consider a bond with a coupon rate of 10 percent, a face value of $1,000, and with three years to maturity, while the appropriate discount rate is 8 percent. Show that the price of the bond is $1,051.54 with annual discounting and $1,052.24 with semi-annual discounting. Use a calculator to determine the discount factors.

   b. What would be the price of this bond if both the coupon rate and the discount rate were 10 percent?

11-2. With reference to Problem 1(a), what would be the price of the bond if the coupons were paid quarterly?

11-3. Calculate the price of a 10 percent coupon bond with eight years to maturity, given an appropriate discount rate of 12 percent, using both annual and semi-annual discounting.

11-4. Calculate the price of the bond in Problem 11-3 if the maturity is 20 years rather than eight years, using semi-annual discounting. Which of Malkiel's principles are illustrated when comparing the price of this bond to the price determined in Problem 11-3?

11-5. The YTM on a 10 percent, 15-year bond is 12 percent. Calculate the price of the bond if coupons are paid semi-annually.

11-6. Consider a junk bond with a 12 percent coupon (paid annually) and 20 years to maturity. The current required rate of return for this bond is 15 percent. What is its price? What would its price be if the required yield rose to 17 percent? 20 percent?

11-7.   a. Calculate the YTM for a 10-year zero-coupon bond sold at $400. Recalculate the YTM if the bond had been priced at $300.

   b. Determine the price of a 15-year zero-coupon bond if the required rate of return is 12 percent.

11-8. Calculate the realized compound yield for a 10 percent bond paying semi-annual coupons with 20 years to maturity and an expected reinvestment rate of 8 percent.

11-9. Consider a 12 percent, 10-year bond paying annual coupons purchased at face value. Based on Table 11-1 and assuming a reinvestment rate of 10 percent, calculate

   a. The interest on interest
   b. The total return
   c. The realized return given the 10 percent reinvestment rate

11-10. Consider a 4 percent coupon bond with 15 years to maturity that pays semi-annual coupons. Determine the YTM that would be necessary to drive the price of this bond to $300.

11-11. Calculate the YTM for the following bonds that all pay coupons semi-annually.

   a. A 12 percent, 20-year bond with a current price of $975
   b. A 6 percent, 10-year bond with a current price of $836
   c. A 9 percent, eight-year bond with a current price of $714

11-12. Laurentian Bank's bonds, with a coupon rate of 6.50 percent, are selling at 104.92 and pay semi-annual coupons. Exactly two years remain to maturity. Determine the

   a. Current yield
   b. Yield to maturity

11-13. TD Bank's bonds, with a coupon rate of 6.5 percent, sell to yield 6.66 percent. Exactly 25 years remain to maturity. What is the current market price of the bonds assuming semi-annual coupons? If the YTM had been 5.5 percent, what would the price of the bonds be? Explain why this difference occurs.

11-14. A 12 percent coupon bond has 20 years to maturity and pays annual coupons. It is currently selling for 20 percent less than face value. Determine its YTM.

11-15. Given a 10 percent, three-year bond with a price of $1,052.24 that pays semi-annual coupons, if the market yield is 8 percent, calculate its duration using the format illustrated in Table 11-3.

11-16. A 12 percent coupon bond with 10 years to maturity is currently selling for $913.50. Determine the modified duration for this bond.

11-17. Calculate the yield to first call for a 10 percent, 10-year bond that pays annual coupons and is callable five years from now. The current market price is $970, and the call price is $1,050.

11-18. Using Problem 11-12, assume that 18 years remain to maturity. How would the yield to maturity change? Does the current yield change?

11-19. Using the duration from Problem 11-15, determine:

a. The modified duration
b. The percentage change in the price of the bond if r changes 0.50 percent.

11-20. Calculate the duration of a 12 percent coupon bond with 10 years remaining to maturity and selling at par.

11-21. Given the duration calculated in Problem 11-20, calculate the percentage change in bond price if the market discount rate for this bond changes by 0.75 percent.

11-22. The yield to maturity on a bond can be calculated using the IRR function. Enter the bond price as a negative number, and the coupons (on a semi-annual basis) and face value as cash flows. Use the spreadsheet formula = *IRR (A1:An) where n is the last cell with a cash flow.*

Calculate, using the spreadsheet, the YTM for a 6-year, 7 percent coupon bond currently selling for $949.75.

11-23. Using the spreadsheet, calculate the yield to call for a 6 percent, 12-year bond callable in five years at a call price of $1,040.

11-24. YTM can also be calculated directly in the spreadsheet using the function = YIELD (A1,A2,An) where n is the last cell with inputs for the problem. The user inputs settlement date, maturity date, coupon rate, current bond price, face value (par value), and number of coupons paid per year. You can set the settlement date as the current date, and the maturity date as the same month and day in the year of maturity (5 years from now, 8 years from now, etc.). Price is stated as a percentage of par (e.g., 100 = $1,000). The following format can be used to solve the YTM for the bond.

Settlement date

1/1/2007 = YEAR (year,month,day)*

Maturity date

1/1/2010 =	YEAR (year,month,day)*
0.1	Annual coupon rate
105.242	Bond price
100	Face value = par value
2	Coupon payments per year
0.08	Yield to maturity as a decimal

*Be sure under the Format settings for the spreadsheet (Format, Cells, Number) to select for Date the format m/d/year. Note: Settlement date is not important—use the current date. Maturity date should reflect the number of years to maturity and the same month and day as the settlement date.

11-25. Using the same basic format as in Problem 11-24, we can solve for bond price by entering the settlement date, the maturity date, the annual coupon rate, the YTM, the par value of the bond expressed as a percentage (100), and the number of coupons per year. Use the function = PRICE (A1, A2, A3, A4, A5, A6). Problem: solve for the price of a 6-year, 7 percent coupon bond if the YTM is 8.25 percent.

11-26. Duration can be calculated using spreadsheet formulas. Data must be entered as follows (see Problem 11-24 for DATE information):

Settlement date	Date is entered as DATE(year, month, day)
Maturity date	Date is entered as DATE(year, month, day)
Coupon as a decimal	
Required yield as a decimal	
Frequency of payments	

Use the formula = DURATION (A1, A2, A3, A4, A5) for duration and = MDURATION (A1, A2, A3, A4, A5) for modified duration. Example—Calculate the duration and modified duration for a 6 percent, 7-year bond with a required yield of 5 percent. This is done as follows (note that the dates are seven years apart; also note the format for the date):

2/16/2006	Settlement date = DATE(year,m,d)
2/16/2013	Maturity date = DATE(year,m,d)
0.06	coupon rate as decimal
0.05	required yield as decimal
2	frequency of coupons
5.86	Macaulay Duration
5.71	Modified Duration

Using this format, calculate the duration for the bond in Table 11-3.

11-27. Real World Returns 11-1 provides data for a large sample of Canadian bonds. Use the data for the first 10 corporate bonds: AGT, Bell, BMO (five bonds) and BNS (three bonds) to complete this problem. You can assume that the settlement date (when the exchange of funds would occur) is April 22, 2008; also assume that all the bonds pay coupon interest semi-annually and that the face value for each is $100.

    a. Use the given yield and the "=PRICE(...)" function to calculate the price for each bond. Do your calculated prices match the quoted prices? (As the given yields are specified to only two decimal places, you will find that several calculated prices differ from the corresponding quote by a few cents.)

    b. Use the given price to calculate the yield-to-maturity for each bond. Do your figures match the given yields?

    c. Use the "=DURATION(...)" function to determine the Macaulay duration for each bond.

    d. Use the "=MDURATION(...)" function to calculate the modified duration value for each of the bonds.

    e. Why do you think the Bell corporate bond has a shorter duration than the AGT bond, even though the latter matures sooner?

11-28. The following bonds all have a face value of $1,000 and pay annual coupons.

Bond	A	B	C	D
Maturity (years)	10	10	5	10
Coupon Rate	6%	8%	7%	7%

    a. Consider bonds A and B, which are identical other than their coupons. Calculate the price of each bond for the following range of market interest rates (yields): 4 percent, 4.5 percent, ..., 9.5 percent, 10 percent. Using the function "= -PV(...)" is the easiest approach here as the maturities are an exact number of years in the future. Next, determine the change in price (in percentage terms) that occurs as the market rate increases (from 4 percent to 4.5 percent, from 4.5 percent to 5 percent, etc.) Graph these price changes (percents) versus the market rate to verify that Bond A (the lower coupon bond) is more sensitive to yield changes.

    b. Consider bonds C and D, which are identical other than their maturities. Calculate and graph the prices and price changes for these bonds as you did above. Does your graph confirm that Bond D (the longer maturity bond) is more sensitive to yield changes?

PREPARING FOR YOUR PROFESSIONAL EXAMS

CFA PRACTICE QUESTIONS

11-1. Which bond has the longest duration?

  a. 8-year maturity, 6 percent coupon
  b. 15-year maturity, 6 percent coupon
  c. 8-year maturity, 11 percent coupon
  d. 15-year maturity, 11 percent coupon

11-2. The interest rate risk of a bond is normally:

  a. lower for higher coupons.
  b. lower for longer duration.
  c. greater for shorter maturities.
  d. all of the above.

11-3. A bond with a call feature:

  a. is attractive because the immediate receipt of principal plus premium produces a high return.
  b. would usually have a higher yield than a similar non-callable bond.
  c. is more apt to be called when interest rates are high, because the interest saving will be greater.
  d. none of the above.

11-4. What would be the market price of a 10 percent non-callable corporate bond with a face value of $1,000 and 14 years to maturity, if it pays interest semi-annually, and the required rate of return on similar bonds is presently 8.4 percent?

  a. $1,129
  b. $1,130
  c. $1,000
  d. None of the above.

11-5. How much accrued interest would have to be paid if you purchased the bond in Question 11-4 on February 8, 2002 and the bond matures on December 31, 2015?

  a. $5.34
  b. $9.56
  c. $10.44
  d. More information is needed.

11-6. In which one of the following cases is the bond selling at a discount?

  a. Coupon rate is greater than current yield, which is greater than yield to maturity
  b. Coupon rate is less than current yield, which is less than yield to maturity
  c. Coupon rate equals current yield, which equals yield to maturity
  d. Coupon rate is less than current yield, which is greater than yield to maturity

11-7. A $1,000 par value, 10 percent semi-annual, 20-year debenture bond is currently selling for $1,100. What is this bond's current yield?

  a. 10.5 percent
  b. 10.0 percent
  c. 9.1 percent
  d. 8.9 percent

11-8. What is the yield to maturity for the bond in Question 11-7?

  a. 8.9 percent
  b. 9.3 percent
  c. 9.5 percent
  d. 10.6 percent

CFA CURRICULUM AND SAMPLE EXAM QUESTIONS (©CFA INSTITUTE)

11-1. An analyst made the following statement: "We should purchase Treasury notes because they are risk-free. Default risk is essentially nonexistent." State whether this analyst's statement is correct with respect to:

	Risk free	Default risk
a.	No	No
b.	No	Yes
c.	Yes	No
d.	Yes	Yes

11-2. An analyst accurately calculates that the price of an option-free bond with a 9 percent coupon would experience a 12 percent change if market yields increase 100 basis points. If market yields decrease 100 basis points, the bond's price would most likely:

    a. increase by 12%.
    b. increase by less than 12%.
    c. decrease by less than 12%.
    d. increase by more than 12%.

11-3. The duration of an option-free bond priced t $900 is 8.5. If yields decrease by 150 basis points, the most accurate statement about the actual price of the bond after the decrease in yields is that the actual price will be:

    a. equal to $1,014.75.
    b. greater than $1,014.75.
    c. lower than $1,014.75 because of the convexity adjustment.
    d. lower than $1,014.75 because the lower level of yields increases the bond's interest rate risk.

11-4. If an investor's required return is 12 percent, the value of a 10-year maturity zero-coupon bond with a maturity value of $1,000 is closest to:

    a. $312.
    b. $688.
    c. $1,000.
    d. $1,312.

APPENDIX 11A

TREASURY BILL YIELDS AND PRICES

Treasury bills are sold in Canada on a discount basis, based on their bond equivalent yield, which is determined using the following equation:

$$r_{BEY} = \frac{Face - P}{P} \times \frac{365}{n} \times 100$$

where
r_{BEY} = the bond equivalent yield
P   = the T-bill price
Face = the T-bill face value
n = the number of days to maturity

For example, the yield on an 89-day Government of Canada Treasury bill that is presently selling at a price (P) of 99 per 100 of face value, can be determined in the following manner:

$$r_{BEY} = \frac{100 - 99}{99} \times \frac{365}{89} \times 100 = 4.1425\%$$

Rearranging this equation, we can see that T-bills are priced according to the following relationship:

$$P = \frac{Face}{(1 + r_{BEY} \times \frac{n}{365})}$$

For example, a 91-day T-bill with a $100 face value that is priced to yield 3.20 percent would be selling for $99.2085, as calculated below:

$$P = \frac{100}{[1 + (.0320 \times \frac{91}{365})]} = \frac{100}{1.007978} = 99.2085$$

Yields on US T-bills are quoted based on the bank discount yield, which is determined using a slightly different procedure than that used to calculate the bond equivalent yield in Canada. The differences arise from the use of face value instead of price in the denominator of the first term, and that 360 days, instead of 365, is used to annualize the rate. The resulting equation is given by:

$$r_{BDY} = \frac{Face - P}{Face} \times \frac{360}{n} \times 100$$

where
r_{BDY} = the bank discount yield

APPENDIX 11C

CONVERTIBLE BONDS

Convertible Securities

Bonds or preferred stock convertible into common stock.

The convertible bond is a form of equity-derivative securities (discussed in Chapter 19) that permits the owner to convert it into common stock under specified conditions. **Convertible securities** or "convertibles," which also encompass convertible preferred stock, carry a claim on the common stock of the issuer, which is exercisable at the owner's initiative. If the option is never exercised, the convertible bond remains in existence until its maturity date, whereas a convertible preferred could remain in existence forever, since preferred stock has no maturity date.[19]

Unlike puts and calls and warrants, convertible securities derive only part of their value from the option feature (i.e., the claim on the underlying common stock). These securities are valuable in their own right, as either bonds or preferred stock. Puts and calls and warrants, on the other hand, are only as valuable as the underlying common stock and have no value beyond their claim on the common stock. Convertibles have increased in popularity because they offer a unique combination of equity and bond characteristics.

Terminology for Convertible Securities

Convertible securities, whether bonds or preferred stock, have a certain terminology.

Conversion Ratio

The number of shares of common stock that the owner of a convertible security receives upon conversion.

1. The **conversion ratio** is the number of shares of common stock that a convertible holder receives on conversion, which is the process of tendering the convertible security to the corporation in exchange for common stock.[20]

2. The **conversion price** is the par value of the bond or preferred divided by the conversion ratio.[21]

Conversion Price

The par value of a convertible security divided by the conversion ratio.

(11-17) $$\text{Conversion price} = \text{Par value}/\text{Conversion ratio}$$

3. The **conversion value** is the convertible's value based on the current price of the common stock. It is defined as

(11-18) $$\text{Conversion value} = \text{Conversion ratio} \times \text{Current price of common stock}$$

Conversion Value

A convertible security's value based on the current price of the common stock.

4. The **conversion premium** is the dollar difference between the market price of the security and its conversion value.

(11-19) $$\text{Conversion premium} = \text{Market price of convertible} - \text{Conversion value}$$

Convertible securities are, by construction, hybrid securities. They have some characteristics of debt or preferred stock and some of the common stock on which they represent an option.

Therefore, to value them one must consider them in both contexts.

Conversion Premium

The dollar difference between the market price of a convertible security and its conversion value.

EXAMPLE 11A-2: ESTIMATING CONVERSION PREMIUM

Consider the convertible debentures of a company that mature in nine years and have a coupon rate of 5 percent, with coupons paid semi-annually. Its conversion ratio is $100 worth of par value for 3.49 common shares. The conversion price is $28.63, or approximately $100/3.49.[22] Its common stock is selling at $16.05 while its debentures are selling at $87.00 per $100 par value. The conversion value of these convertibles is therefore 3.49 × $16.05 = $56.01. Thus, the conversion premium is $87.00 − $56.01 = $30.99 (or 55.3 percent of the conversion value of $56.01).

---

[19]Many convertible bonds cannot be converted for an initial period of six to 24 months.
[20]Forced conversion results when the issuer initiates conversion by calling the bonds.
[21]It is obvious that the conversion privilege attached to a convertible can be expressed in either conversion ratio or conversion price terms. Both the conversion price and the conversion ratio are almost always protected against stock splits and dividends.
[22]Many convertible bonds have a conversion price that increases over time.

The Basics of Convertible Bonds

Convertible bonds are issued by corporations as part of their capital-raising activities. Similar to a warrant, a convertible feature can be attached to a bond as a sweetener to make the issue more attractive to investors. They allow the issuer to pay a lower interest rate by offering investors a chance for future gains from the common stock. Convertibles are sometimes sold as temporary financing instruments with the expectation that over a period of months (or years) the bonds will be converted into common stock. The bonds are a cheaper source of financing to the issuer than the common stock, and their gradual conversion places less price pressure on the common stock. Finally, convertibles offer a corporation the opportunity to sell common stock at a higher price than the current market price. If the issuer feels that the stock price is temporarily depressed, convertible bonds can be sold at a 15 to 20 percent premium. The result of this premium is that the price of the stock must rise by that amount before conversion is warranted.

Most bonds, whether convertible or not, are callable by the issuer. This results in additional concerns for the convertible bondholder.

Convertible bonds are typically issued as debentures. They are often subordinated to straight (non-convertible) debentures, increasing their risk. According to bond rating agencies, most convertible bonds are one class below a straight debenture issue. Nevertheless, convertible bonds enjoy good marketability. Large issues are often more actively traded than many non-convertible issues of the same quality.

Analyzing Convertible Bonds

A convertible bond offers the purchaser a stream of interest payments and a return of principal at maturity. It also offers a promise of capital gains if the price of the stock rises sufficiently. To value a convertible bond, it is necessary to account for all of these elements. The convertible bond model is illustrated graphically in Figure 11-5 to provide a framework for analysis. We shall then illustrate the components of value individually.

Graphic Analysis of Convertible Bonds

Figure 11-5 shows the components of the convertible bond model. This diagram depicts the expected relationships for a typical convertible bond. The horizontal line from PV (par value) on the left to the face value (F) on the right provides a reference point; any bond sold at par value would start out at PV, and all bonds will mature at their face value. If such a bond is callable, the call price will be above the par value in the early years because of the call premium; by maturity this price would converge to the face value.

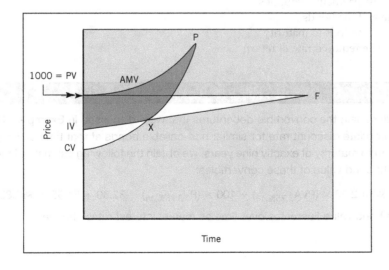

Figure 11-5
Conceptual Model for Understanding Convertible Bonds

Each convertible bond has an investment value (IV) or straight-debt value, which is the price at which a convertible would sell to equal the yield on a comparable non-convertible. In other words, the investment value is the convertible's estimated value as a straight bond. By evaluating the coupons and the face value of the convertible at the going required rate of return for a comparable straight bond, the beginning investment value can be determined. Remember that the straight (i.e., non-convertible) bond has a higher market yield because it does not offer a speculative play on the common stock. The investment value is represented in Figure 11-5 by the line from IV to F, the face value.

Each convertible has a conversion value at any time. The original conversion value (point CV) is established by multiplying together the conversion ratio and the price of the common stock at the time the convertible is issued. The conversion value curve in Figure 11-5 is then drawn on the assumption that the price of the stock will grow at a constant rate, g; that is,

$$P_1 = P_0(1 + g)$$
$$P_2 = P_1(1 + g)$$

and so forth. Obviously, this is an expected relationship and may not occur in this manner. Using this assumption, the conversion value rises above the par value as the price of the stock rises, tracing out the curve CV-P in Figure 11-5.

Finally, because the convertible often sells at a premium, it is necessary to draw an actual market value (AMV) curve, which is shown in Figure 11-5 as AMV-P. This curve eventually approaches the conversion value curve as the conversion value increases. This is primarily because the convertible may be called, forcing conversion. If this occurs, the convertible holder can receive only the conversion value. Therefore, investors are not likely to pay more than this for the convertible.

The shaded area in Figure 11-5 is the premium over conversion value, which declines as the market price of the convertible rises. This reflects the fact that the bond is callable.

Bond Value

Every convertible bond has a *straight bond value* or an investment value, which is the price at which the bond would sell with no conversion option. This price is given by the present value calculations for a bond, as explained in Chapter 11.

(11-20)
$$SBV = C \times (PVA_{r,n}) + F \times (PV_{r,n})$$

where
SBV = straight bond value (or investment value)
C   = the interest payments (coupons)
F   = face value of the bonds
n   = number of periods to maturity
r   = appropriate required rate of return

EXAMPLE 11A-3: STRAIGHT BOND VALUE

Let's consider again the convertible debentures that were discussed in Example 11A-2. Assuming an appropriate discount rate for similar non-callable bonds at that time of 7.5 percent, and assuming a term to maturity of exactly nine years, we obtain the following estimate of the investment value or straight bond value of these convertibles:

$$SBV = 2.50 \times (PVA_{3.75\%,18}) + 100 \times (PV_{3.75\%,18}) = 32.30 + 51.55 = \$83.85$$

Of course, the bond value fluctuates over time as market interest rates change.

Conversion Value

Every convertible bond has a conversion value that is the value of the common stock received upon conversion. At the time it is issued, a convertible bond has a conversion value equal to the market price of the common stock multiplied by the number of shares of stock that can be received by converting. As noted, the conversion price is usually set 15 to 20 percent above the current market price of the common, so that conversion would not be worthwhile. Over time, if the price of the common stock increases, the conversion value should also grow at the same rate.

Minimum (Floor) Value

Every convertible bond has a minimum or floor value. A convertible will always sell for no less than the greater of (1) its bond (straight) value or (2) its conversion value. In other words,

$$\text{Floor value of a convertible} = \text{Maximum (straight bond value; conversion value)} \qquad (11\text{-}21)$$

Even if the value of the conversion feature is zero, with virtually no prospect of a change in this value, a convertible bond would have a minimum price of its investment or straight bond value (i.e., its value as a non-convertible debt instrument). If the price were to decline below this value, bond investors would buy it because its yield would be greater than alternative comparable bonds. The straight bond value for the debentures in Example 11A-3 on the valuation date was $83.85, the absolute minimum price for this bond as of that time.

Actual Bond Value (Price)

Convertible bonds usually sell at prices above their minimum value, and, as we have seen, that is the higher of the bond value or the conversion value. For example, the convertible debentures in the previous example sold for $87.00, $4.15 above its bond value (and floor value), and was $30.99 above its conversion value.

Two of the reasons convertibles sell at premiums are:

1. The conversion option has a positive value because the right to convert any time during the life of the bond is valuable and investors are willing to pay for it. In effect, this is equivalent to owning a call option on the stock, and calls command positive premiums (as explained in Chapter 19).

2. A convertible bond offers investors downside protection, thereby decreasing their risk. If the price of the common stock declines sharply, resulting in a sharp decline in the conversion value, the convertible will still sell as a bond and will have a bond value determined by the present value of interest payments and principal. This dual minimum-price feature of convertibles reduces investors' risk and commands a premium in doing so.

In evaluating convertible bonds, certain details in addition to the preceding factors should be kept in mind. When a convertible bond is converted, the holder loses the accrued interest from the last interest payment date. Furthermore, if a holder converts after the ex dividend date, the common stock dividend on the newly received common shares could be lost. Since the issuer can call the bonds and force conversion, these factors can be important, and it is not unusual for issuers to choose a time favourable to themselves.

INVESTING *tip*

In a similar manner, a convertible bond cannot sell below its conversion value. If it did, arbitrageurs would buy the bond, convert it into common stock, and sell the shares, or simply establish a position in the underlying common stock at a cost lower than would otherwise be possible. Since the conversion value of $56.01 in Example 11A-2 was lower than its bond value, the bond value was its minimum, or floor value, at the time of these calculations. In Figure 11-5, the line/curve IV-X-P represents the minimum market value for the convertible bond. This minimum market value is made up of part of the investment value line (IV to X) and part of the conversion value curve (X to P). We can call this the effective market value floor.

A bond is subject to call if the market price exceeds the call price. Investors who pay a premium over the conversion value in these circumstances run a risk of having the bond called as the company forces conversion.

Should Investors Buy Convertible Bonds?

Why should investors consider convertible bonds? As for advantages, convertible bonds offer investors a unique combination of an income stream from a fixed-income security and a chance to participate in the price appreciation of the common stock. Convertibles offer downside protection in relation to owning the common stock, because regardless of what happens to the price of the common stock, the convertible bond will not decline below its value as a straight bond. They offer upside potential, because a convertible bond must always be worth at least its conversion value as the price of the common stock rises. Furthermore, the yield on a convertible bond usually exceeds the dividend yield of the underlying common stock, and interest payments have first order of priority. Compared to common stock owners, convertible bond holders enjoy a yield advantage while awaiting appreciation in the stock price.

As for disadvantages, convertible bonds yield less than do straight bonds of similar risk and maturity. Investors must give up some yield to receive the conversion feature. Convertibles are callable, and in many cases the issuer can and will force conversion. When a convertible bond is called, the holder will choose the better alternative—accept the call price or convert into common stock. If a corporation calls a bond at, say, $1,100 (face value of $1,000 plus one year's interest of $100 for a call premium), and the conversion value is, say, $1,200, the bondholders in effect are forced to convert. They give up their fixed-income security and the chance for future capital gains from the common stock.

CHAPTER 13

COMMON STOCK VALUATION

The moment you have been waiting for is almost at hand. Having prepared yourself to manage your inheritance by dealing with the numerous issues you have now reviewed, whether it be mutual funds, or selling short, or basic portfolio theory, or the CAPM, what you really want to do is what most people are itching to do—get out there and buy some stocks. After all, you know someone who bought Cisco at $20 and it went to $90, and you know for sure this person is not the brightest bulb in the chandelier. On the other hand, you have read all the horror stories about the folks who bought the technology stocks, which subsequently collapsed, if indeed they even survived—and some of these people were surely smart. So there must be more to it than is at first apparent. Once again you decide you have to bite the bullet and learn about valuation. The bad news, as you are about to learn, is that valuation is as much an art as it is a science—it requires judgement as well as skill. The good news is that learning the basic principles of valuation, though not a guarantee of success, will in fact give you an advantage over many investors.

Learning Objectives

After reading this chapter, you should be able to

1. Name two approaches to the valuation of common stocks used in fundamental security analysis.
2. Explain the present value approach.
3. Use the dividend discount model to estimate stock prices.
4. Explain the P/E ratio approach.
5. Outline other relative valuation approaches.

CHAPTER PREVIEW

In the next few chapters, we explore the approaches that investors use to value and select common stocks. In this chapter, we concentrate on two valuation methods used in fundamental security analysis, which seeks to estimate the intrinsic value of a stock: present value and P/E ratio or earnings multiplier. Under present value, we explain how to use the dividend discount model to estimate stock prices; Appendix 13B discusses another widely used present value approach, the free cash flow model. We then consider the P/E ratio, the approach most widely used by practising security analysts, as well as other valuation methods.

THE PRESENT VALUE APPROACH

learning objective 1
Name two approaches to the valuation of common stocks used in fundamental security analysis.

learning objective 2
Explain the present value approach.

The classic method of calculating intrinsic (estimated or formula) value involves the use of present value analysis, which is often referred to as the capitalization of income method. As explained in Chapter 11, a present value process involving the capitalization (discounting) of expected future cash flows can be used to estimate the value of any security. That is, the intrinsic value of a security can be estimated as the discounted (present) value of the future stream of cash flows that an investor expects to receive from the asset. Repeating from Chapter 11,

(13-1)
$$\text{Estimated value of security} = \sum_{t=1}^{n} \frac{\text{Cash Flows}}{(1 + k)^t}$$

where
k = the appropriate discount rate or required rate of return[1]

To use such a model, an investor must

1. Estimate an appropriate required rate of return.
2. Estimate the amount and timing of the future stream of cash flows.
3. Use these two components in a present value model to estimate the value of the security, which is then compared with the current market price of the security.

Figure 13-1 summarizes the present value process commonly used in fundamental analysis. It emphasizes the factors that go into valuing common stocks. The exact nature of the present value process used by investors in the marketplace depends upon assumptions made about the growth rate in the expected stream of cash flows, as explained later in this chapter.

The Required Rate of Return

An investor who is considering the purchase of a common stock must assess its risk and the associated minimum expected rate of return that will be required to induce the investor to make the purchase. This minimum expected return, or *required rate of return*, is an opportunity cost. It is the same concept as the required yield used in Chapter 11 to value bonds.

The *required rate of return, capitalization rate,* and *discount rate* are interchangeable terms in valuation analysis. Regardless of which term is used, it is challenging to determine the numerical value to use for a particular stock. While in theory we know what this variable is, in practice it is not easy to arrive at the precise number to use. Because of this complexity, we will generally assume that we know the capitalization rate and concentrate on the other issues involved in valuation, which are difficult enough. In the next chapter, we consider the required rate of return in more detail.

---

[1]The concept of required rate of return is explained in more detail in Chapter 14.

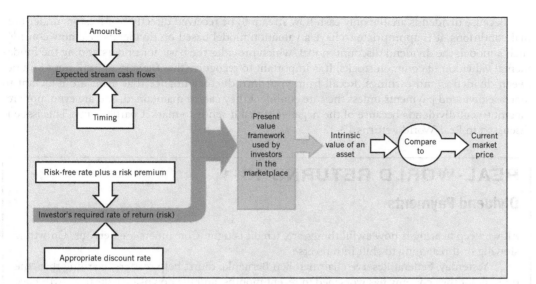

Figure 13-1
The Present Value
Approach to Valuation

The Expected Cash Flows

The other component that goes into the present value framework is the expected stream of cash flows. Just as the value of a bond is the present value of all interest payments plus the present value of the bond's face value that will be received at maturity, the value of a common stock is the present value of all the cash flows to be received from the issuer (corporation). The questions that arise are

1. What are the cash flows to use in valuing a stock?
2. What are the expected amounts of the cash flows?
3. When will the expected cash flows be received?

Shareholders may plan to sell their shares sometime in the future, resulting in a cash flow from the sales price. As we will see later, however, even if investors think of the total cash flows from common stocks as a combination of dividends and a future price at which the stock can be sold, this is equivalent to using the stream of all dividends to be received on the stock.

What about earnings? Are they important? Can they be used in valuing a stock? The answer to both questions is yes. Dividends are paid out of earnings and are clearly important. An alternative approach to fundamental analysis, which is considered later, uses the earnings and a P/E ratio to determine intrinsic value. Therefore, earnings are an important part of fundamental analysis; in fact, earnings receive more attention from investors than any other single variable.

If the corporation retains earnings, they presumably will be reinvested, thereby enhancing future earnings and, ultimately, future dividends. The present value analysis should not count the earnings reinvested currently and paid later as dividends. If properly defined and separated, these two variables produce the same results. This means that more than one present value model is possible.[2] However, it is theoretically correct to use dividends in the present value analysis, and this is what is usually done when investors use the present value approach to valuation.

INVESTING tip

To find which cash flows are appropriate in the valuation of a common stock, ask yourself the following question: If I buy a particular common stock and place it in a special trust fund for the perpetual benefit of myself and my heirs, what cash flows will be received? The answer is dividends, because this is the only cash distribution that a corporation actually makes to its shareholders. Although a firm's earnings per share in any year technically belong to the shareholders, corporations generally do not pay out all their earnings but reinvest a portion into the firm.

---

[2]In addition to dividends and earnings, the variable referred to as "free cash flow" (defined later) is often used for these models.

Because dividends are the only cash flow stream to be received directly by investors under normal conditions, it is appropriate to have a valuation model based on dividends. We now consider such a model, the dividend discount model, which provides the basis for understanding the fundamental valuation of common stocks. It is important to recognize that there is an important link between dividends and earnings. Recall from your introductory finance that firms are reluctant to increase dividend payments unless they are confident they can be maintained, and are even more reluctant to cut dividends because of the negative signal it sends to market participants. This issue is discussed in Real-World Returns 13-1.

REAL-WORLD RETURNS 13-1
Dividend Payments

All we keep hearing is how awful things are. Credit is tight. Consumers are nervous. Growth is slowing or threatening to shift into reverse.

Yesterday, Federal Reserve chairman Ben Bernanke didn't help matters, warning that "the outlook for the economy has worsened in recent months, and the downside risks to growth have increased."

But if everything is so terrible, why are so many companies raising their dividends? Do they know something we don't know?

Let's look at the evidence.

Yesterday, EnCana doubled its quarterly dividend to 40 cents (US) a share after fourth-quarter profit leaped 63 percent to $1.08-billion. Canada's biggest oil and gas company—whose dividend is now more than four times as large as it was in 2006—cited "confidence in the sustainability of its business model" for the latest hike.

That doesn't sound like a company bracing for an economic slowdown.

But, you say, energy companies are enjoying an era of high resource prices, so of course they're raising their dividends. They're the exception, right?

Wrong. Two of Canada's biggest life insurers also raised their payouts yesterday. Sun Life Financial boosted its quarterly dividend to 36 cents from 34 cents, even as profit rose less than expected and investors hammered the stock. A few hours later, Great-West Lifeco raised its dividend to 29.25 cents from 27.5 cents, after quarterly profit jumped 9 percent.

What about mutual fund companies? With stock markets in disarray and investors heading for the nearest fallout shelter, you'd think fund companies would be cutting their payouts, or at least not raising them.

Wrong again. Late last month, AGF Management hiked its dividend by a hefty 25 percent. After the close yesterday, the country's biggest mutual fund company, IGM Financial, was also expected to raise its quarterly payout, for the third time in the past 12 months.

What's going on here? Simple: Companies are expressing their confidence that, although the economy may be heading for a slowdown, their profits will keep growing—perhaps not as quickly as before, and maybe with a hiccup here or there, but growing nonetheless.

Companies do not treat dividend increases lightly. After all, when a board declares a dividend, it is not merely a promise to make this quarter's payment. It is an implicit promise to pay at least the same level of dividends in subsequent quarters, too, for there is no greater sin a company can commit than cutting its dividend. To do so means certain death for its stock, not to mention all those executive options tied to the share price.

And while it's true that several US financial institutions, including Citigroup, have cut their dividends because of the subprime debacle, Canadian banks are generally in a much stronger financial position. Bank dividend increases may be smaller this year than in years past, but they're still expected to grow. And that growth will pick up when the economy gets back on track.

(continued)

The Dividend Discount Model

learning objective 3
Use the dividend discount model to estimate stock prices.

Since dividends are the only cash payment a shareholder receives directly from a firm, they are the foundation of valuation for common stocks. In adapting Equation 13-1 specifically to value common stocks, the cash flows are the dividends expected to be paid in each future period. An investor or analyst using this approach carefully studies the future prospects for a company and estimates the likely dividends to be paid. In addition, the analyst estimates an appropriate required rate of return or discount rate based on the risk foreseen in the dividends and given the alternatives available. Finally, he or she would discount to the present, the entire stream of estimated future dividends (properly identified as to amount and timing).

The present value approach to calculating the value of a common stock is conceptually no different from the approach used in Chapter 11 to value bonds or in Appendix 13A at the end of the chapter to value preferred stock. Specifically, Equation 13-1 adapted for common stocks, where dividends are the expected future cash flows, results in Equation 13-2. This equation, known as the **dividend discount model (DDM)**, states that the value of a stock today is the discounted value of all future dividends:

Dividend Discount Model (DDM)

A model for determining the estimated price of a stock by discounting all expected future dividends by the appropriate required rate of return for the stock.

$$\hat{P}_{CS} = \frac{D_1}{(1 + k_{CS})^1} + \frac{D_2}{(1 + k_{CS})^2} + \dots + \frac{D_\infty}{(1 + k_{CS})^\infty} \qquad \textbf{(13-2)}$$

$$= \sum_{t=1}^{\infty} \frac{D_t}{(1 + k_{CS})^t}$$

= Dividend discount model (DDM)

where

$\hat{P}_{CS}$ = intrinsic or estimated value of a common stock today based on the model user's estimates of the future dividends and the required rate of return

$D_1, D_2, \dots$ = the dividends expected to be received in each future period

k_{CS} = the required rate of return for this stock, which is the discount rate applicable for an investment with this degree of riskiness (again, the opportunity cost of a comparable risk alternative)

There are two immediate problems with Equation 13-2:

1. The last term in Equation 13-2 indicates that investors are dealing with infinity. They must value a stream of dividends that may be paid forever, since common stock has no maturity date.

2. The dividend stream is uncertain:

   a. There are no specified number of dividends, if, in fact, any are paid at all. If dividends are to be paid, they must be declared periodically by the firm's board of directors. (Usually, they are declared quarterly but conventional valuation analysis uses annual dividends.)

   b. The dividends for most firms are expected to grow over time; therefore, investors usually cannot simplify Equation 13-2 to a **perpetuity** as in the case of a preferred stock.[3] Only if

Perpetuity

An annuity with no maturity date.

[3]Refer to Appendix 13A at the end of the chapter for details regarding the valuation of preferred stock.

dividends are not expected to grow can such a simplification be made. Although such a possibility exists and is covered below, it is unusual.

How are these problems resolved? The first problem, that Equation 13-2 involves an infinite number of periods and dividends, will be resolved when we deal with the second problem, specifying the expected stream of dividends. However, from a practical standpoint, this problem is not as troublesome as it first appears. At reasonably high discount rates, such as 12, 14, or 16 percent, dividends received 40 or 50 years in the future are worth very little today, so that investors need not worry about them. For example, if the discount rate is 15 percent, the present value of $1 to be received 50 years from now is $0.0009.

The conventional solution to the second problem, that the dollar amount of the dividend is expected to grow over time, is to make some assumptions about the expected growth rate of dividends. That is, the investor or analyst estimates or models the expected percentage rate of growth in the future stream of dividends. To do this, he or she classifies each stock to be valued into one of three categories based on the expected growth pattern in dividends. In summary: We operationalize the dividend discount model by estimating the expected growth rate(s) in the dividend stream.

A timeline will be used to represent the three alternative growth rate versions of the dividend discount model. All stocks that pay a dividend, or that are expected to in the future, can be modelled using this approach. It is critical to remember in using the DDM that an investor must account for all dividends from now to infinity by modelling the growth rate(s). As shown below, the mechanics of this process are such that we don't actually see all of these dividends because the formulas reduce to a simplified form, but nevertheless we are accounting for all future dividends when we use the DDM.

It is necessary in using the DDM to remember that the dividend currently being paid on a stock (or the most recent dividend paid) is designated as D_0 and is, of course, known. However, investors must estimate the future dividends to be paid, starting with D_1, the dividend expected to be paid in the next period.

The three growth rate models for dividends are

1. A dividend stream with a zero-growth rate resulting from a fixed dollar dividend equal to the current dividend, D_0, being paid every year from now to infinity. This is typically referred to as the no-growth rate or zero-growth rate model:

D_0	D_0	D_0	D_0	$+ \dots +$	D_0	Dividends
0	1	2	3	$+ \dots +$	∞	Time period

2. A dividend stream that is growing at a constant rate, g, starting with D_0. This is typically referred to as the constant or normal growth version of the dividend discount model:

D_0	$D_0(1+g)^1$	$D_0(1+g)^2$	$+ \dots +$	$D_0(1+g)^\infty$	Dividends
0	1	2	$+ \dots +$	∞	Time period

3. A dividend stream that is growing at variable rates, for example, g_1 for the first two years and g_2 thereafter, is referred to as the multiple-growth version of the dividend discount model:

D_0	$D_1 = D_0(1+g_1)$	$D_2 = D_1(1+g_1)$	$D_3 = D_2(1+g_2) + \dots + D_\infty = D_{\infty-1}(1+g_2)$	Dividends
0	1	2	3 $+ \dots +$ ∞	Time period

CHECK YOUR UNDERSTANDING

13-1. What are the two key inputs when using the present value approach to value common stock?

13-2. Why is the required rate of return for a stock critical in the valuation process?

13-3. What does it really mean to say that the estimated value of a stock today is the discounted value of all future dividends?

The Zero-Growth Model

Under the non-growth case, the dividend model reduces to a perpetual annuity or perpetuity. Assuming a constant dollar dividend, Equation 13-2 simplifies to the no-growth model shown as Equation 13-3.

$$\hat{P}_0 = \frac{D_0}{k_{CS}} = \text{Zero} - \text{growth version of the DDM} \tag{13-3}$$

where D_0 is the constant dollar dividend expected for all future time periods and k_{CS} is the opportunity cost or required rate of return for this particular common stock.

The no-growth case is equivalent to the valuation process for a preferred stock discussed at the end of this chapter because, exactly like a preferred stock, the dividend (numerator of Equation 13-3) remains unchanged. Therefore, the dividends arising from a zero-growth rate common stock represent a perpetuity that can be easily valued once k_{CS} is determined.

It is extremely important in understanding the valuation of common stocks using the DDM to recognize that in all cases an investor is discounting the future stream of dividends from now to infinity. This fact tends to be overlooked when using the perpetuity formula involving the zero-growth rate case because the discounting process is greatly simplified. Nevertheless, in this case, as in all others, we are accounting for all dividends from now to infinity. It is simply a mathematical fact that dividing a constant dollar amount by the discount rate, k, produces a result equivalent to discounting each dividend from now to infinity separately and summing all of the present values.

The Constant Growth Model

The other two versions of the DDM indicate that to establish the cash flow stream of expected dividends, which is to be subsequently discounted, it is first necessary to compound some beginning dividend into the future. Obviously, the higher the growth rate used, the greater the future amount, and the longer the time period, the greater the future amount.

A well-known scenario in valuation is the case in which dividends are expected to grow at a constant rate over time. This constant- or normal-growth model[4] is shown as Equation 13-4.

$$\hat{P}_0 = \frac{D_0(1+g)}{(1+k_{CS})^1} + \frac{D_0(1+g)^2}{(1+k_{CS})^2} + \frac{D_0(1+g)^3}{(1+k_{CS})^3} + \ldots + \frac{D_0(1+g)^\infty}{(1+k_{CS})^\infty} \tag{13-4}$$

where D_0 is the current dividend being paid and growing at the constant rate g, and k_{CS} is the appropriate discount rate.

Equation 13-4 can be simplified to the following equation:[5]

$$\hat{P}_0 = \frac{D_1}{k_{CS} - g} \tag{13-5}$$

where D_1 is the dividend expected to be received at the end of Year 1. Notice that k must be greater than g, or else the results are uninformative.

---

[4]The constant-growth model is often referred to as the Gordon model named after Myron J. Gordon, who played a large part in its development and use.

[5]Equation 13-4 represents a geometric series that is being multiplied by $(1 + g)/(1 + k)$ every period. The sum of this series is represented by Equation 13-5 as the number of periods involved approaches infinity.

Equation 13-5 is used whenever the growth rate of future dividends is estimated to be constant to infinity. It is used quite often in actual practice because of its simplicity and because in many circumstances, it is a reasonable description of the actual behaviour of a large number of companies, as well as the market as a whole.

EXAMPLE 13-1: ESTIMATING PRICE FOR SUMMA CORPORATION

Summa Corporation is currently paying $1 per share in dividends and investors expect those to grow at the rate of 7 percent a year for the foreseeable future. For investments at this risk level, investors require a return of 15 percent a year. The estimated price of Summa is

$$\hat{P}_0 = \frac{D_1}{k_{CS} - g} = \frac{\$1.00(1.07)}{0.15 - 0.07} = \$13.38$$

Note that a current dividend (D_0) must be compounded for one period because the constant growth version of the DDM specifies the numerator as the dividend expected to be received one period from now, which is (D_1). This is consistent with the model's general approach of valuing stocks based on expected future cash flows. In valuation terminology, D_0 represents the dividend currently being paid, and D_1 represents the dividend expected to be paid in the next period. If D_0 is known, D_1 can always be estimated:

$$D_0 = \text{Current dividend}$$
$$D_1 = D_0(1 + g)$$

where g is the expected growth rate of dividends.[6]

To completely understand the constant-growth model, which is widely used in valuation analysis, it is instructive to think about the process that occurs under constant growth. Table 13-1 illustrates the case of Summa's growth stock with a current dividend of $1 per share ($D_0$), an expected constant growth rate of 7 percent, and a required rate of return, k, of 15 percent.

Table 13-1

Present Value of 60 Years of Dividends
(current dividend = $1   g = 7%   k = 15%)

Period	Dollar Dividend	PV Factor	PV of Dollar Dividend
1	1.07	0.8696	0.93
2	1.14	0.7561	0.87
3	1.23	0.6576	0.81
4	1.31	0.5718	0.75
5	1.40	0.4972	0.70
6	1.50	0.4323	0.65
7	1.61	0.3759	0.60
8	1.72	0.3269	0.56
9	1.84	0.2843	0.521
10	1.97	0.2472	0.49
11	2.10	0.2149	0.45
12	2.25	0.1869	0.42
13	2.41	0.1625	0.39
14	2.58	0.1413	0.36

[6]Similarly, D_2 can be determined in the constant growth model as $D_0(1 + g)^2$ or $D_1(1 + g)$.

Period	Dollar Dividend	PV Factor	PV of Dollar Dividend
15	2.76	0.1229	0.34
16	2.95	0.1069	0.32
17	3.16	0.0929	0.29
18	3.38	0.0808	0.27
19	3.62	0.0703	0.25
20	3.87	0.0611	0.24
21	4.14	0.0531	0.22
22	4.43	0.0462	0.20
23	4.74	0.0402	0.19
24	5.07	0.0349	0.18
25	5.43	0.0304	0.16
26	5.81	0.0264	0.15
27	6.21	0.0230	0.14
28	6.65	0.0200	0.13
29	7.11	0.0174	0.12
30	7.61	0.0151	0.11
31	8.15	0.0131	0.11
32	8.72	0.0114	0.10
33	9.33	0.0099	0.09
34	9.98	0.0086	0.09
35	10.68	0.0075	0.08
36	11.42	0.0065	0.07
37	12.22	0.0057	0.07
38	13.08	0.0049	0.06
39	13.99	0.0043	0.06
40	14.97	0.0037	0.06
41	16.02	0.0032	0.05
42	17.14	0.0028	0.05
43	18.34	0.0025	0.05
44	19.63	0.0021	0.04
45	21.00	0.0019	0.04
46	22.47	0.0016	0.04
47	24.05	0.0014	0.03
48	25.73	0.0012	0.03
49	27.53	0.0011	0.03
50	29.46	0.0009	0.03
51	31.52	0.0008	0.03
52	33.73	0.0007	0.02
53	36.09	0.0006	0.02
54	38.61	0.0005	0.02
55	41.32	0.0005	0.02
56	44.21	0.0004	0.02
57	47.30	0.0003	0.02
58	50.61	0.0003	0.02
59	54.16	0.0003	0.01
60	57.95	0.0002	0.01

Sum of dividends = $870.47

Sum of first 60 years of discounted dividends = $13.20

As Table 13-1 shows, the expected dollar dividend for each period in the future grows by 7 percent. Therefore, $D_1 = \$1.07$, $D_2 = \$1.14$, $D_{10} = \$1.97$, and so forth. Only the first 60 years of growth are shown, at the end of which time the dollar dividend is $57.95. The last column of Table 13-1 shows the discounted value of each of the first 60 years of dividends. Thus, the present value of the dividend for Period 1, discounted at 15 percent, is $0.93. While the actual dollar amount of the expected dividend in Year 60 is $57.95, its present value in today's dollars is only $0.01. Obviously, dividends received far in the future, assuming normal discount rates, are worth very little today.

Figure 13-2 depicts the growth in the dollar dividend for only the first 30 years in order to provide some scale to the process. Because k is greater than g, the present value of each future dividend is declining, since the dividends are growing at a rate (g) that is below the discount rate (k) being used in the denominator of the discount procedure. For example, the present value of $D_1 = \$0.93$, the present value of $D_2 = \$0.87$, and the present value of $D_{10} = \$0.49$. Therefore, the present-value-of-dividends curve at the bottom of Figure 13-2 is declining more rapidly than the estimated-dollar-dividend-over-time curve above it is increasing.

The estimated price of Summa, as illustrated in Table 13-1 and Figure 13-2, is the sum of the present values of each of the future dividends. Adding each of these present values together from now to infinity would produce the correct estimated value of the stock. Note from Table 13-1 that adding the present values of the first 60 years of dividends together produces an estimated value of $13.20. The correct answer, as obtained from adding all years from now to infinity, was calculated as $13.38 in the example above, for a difference of only $0.18. This implies that the dividends received from Years 61 to infinity add a total value of $0.18 to the stock price (i.e., the present value of all dividends received from Year 61 to infinity is only $0.18 in year 0). The reason for this is the extremely low values for the PV factors as the number of periods increases.

Figure 13-2
The Constant Growth Model

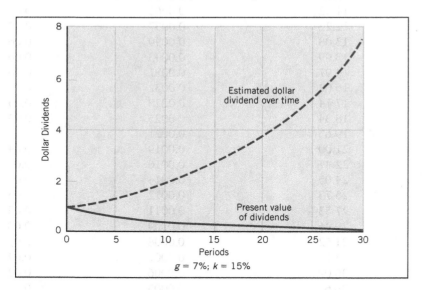

Table 13-1 illustrates the very important point about these valuation models that was explained earlier. The constant-growth version of the DDM given in Equation 13-5 takes account of all future cash flows from now to infinity, although this is not apparent from simply looking at the equation itself. Although Equation 13-5 has no summation or infinity sign, the results produced by this equation are equivalent to the sum that would be obtained by adding together the discounted value of all future dividends (as described in footnote 5). As was the case for the zero-growth model, the mathematics of the process involving a constant growth rate to infinity reduces to a very simple expression, masking the fact that all dividends from now to infinity are being accounted for.

The constant-growth DDM can also provide a useful assessment of the market's perception of growth opportunities available to a company. For example, let's assume that a firm with no profitable growth opportunities should not reinvest residual profits in the company, but rather pay out all its earnings in the form of dividends. This implies $g = 0$, and $D_1 = EPS_1$, where EPS_1 represents the expected earnings per common share in the upcoming year. Under these assumptions, the constant-growth DDM reduces to the following expression:

$$\hat{P}_0 = \frac{EPS_1}{k_{CS}}$$ (13-6)

Although we may not find many no-growth firms in practice, the result above can be applied to firms that do have growth opportunities available to them. Thus, at any given time we can view the share price of any common stock (that satisfies the assumptions of the DDM), as being composed of two components: its no-growth component and the present value of growth opportunities (PVGO). This can be expressed as

$$\hat{P}_0 = \frac{EPS_1}{k_{CS}} + PVGO$$ (13-7)

EXAMPLE 13-2: ESTIMATING PVGO FOR SUMMA CORPORATION

Assume the expected year one earnings per share (EPS_1) for Summa is $2.00. If their shares were trading at the intrinsic value of $13.38 (estimated in Example 13-1), it implies that only $0.05 for the present value of growth opportunities (PVGO) is factored by market participants into Summa's share price:

$$\widehat{PVGO} = P_0 - \frac{EPS_1}{k_{CS}} = 13.38 - \frac{2.00}{0.15} = 13.38 - 13.33 = \$0.05$$

This suggests that very little of Summa's share price is attributable to future growth opportunities.

To fully understand the constant growth rate version of the DDM, it is also important to realize that the model shows that the stock price for any one period is estimated to grow at the same rate as the dividends, which is g. This means that the expected growth rate in price, plus the expected percentage return received in the form of dividends, will equal the required rate of return (k). This is obvious if we rearrange the constant-growth DDM in the following manner, using the present market price in place of intrinsic value, to obtain an estimate of the return required by investors on a particular share:

$$k_{CS} = \frac{D_1}{P_0} + g$$ (13-8)

The first term in Equation 13-8 represents the expected dividend yield on the share, therefore, we may view the second term, g, as the expected capital gains yield, since the total return must equal the dividend yield plus capital gains yield. This provides an appropriate approximation for required return, only if the conditions of the constant-growth DDM are met (in particular the assumption regarding constant growth in dividends to infinity must be satisfied). It also assumes that markets are reasonably efficient, by assuming that the market price equals the intrinsic value.

EXAMPLE 13-3: ESTIMATING PRICE CHANGE FOR SUMMA CORPORATION

For Summa, the estimated price today is $13.38, while the estimated dividend at the end of this year (D_1) is $1.07, and the estimated long-term growth rate in dividends, g, is 7 percent. This implies an expected rate of return of 15 percent:

$$k_{CS} = \frac{D_1}{P_0} + g = \frac{1.07}{13.38} + 0.07 = 0.08 + 0.07 = 0.15$$

This suggests that the expected return on Summa is composed of a dividend yield of 8 percent and a capital gains yield of 7 percent. In other words, we expect Summa's share price to increase by 7 percent over this year. We can check this out by using Equation 13-5 to estimate the intrinsic value of Summa at the end of Period 1:

$$\hat{P}_1 = \frac{D_2}{k_{CS} - g} = \frac{\$1.07(1.07)}{0.15 - 0.07} = \$14.31$$

This estimated price at the end of Period 1 is 7 percent higher than the estimated price today of $13.38 (rounding causes slight differences):

$$Price\ change = \frac{Ending\ price\ -\ Beginning\ price}{Beginning\ price}$$

$$= (\$14.31 - \$13.38) / \$13.38 = 7\%$$

This result is intuitive, since the equation used to determine $\hat{P}_1$ is the same equation used to determine P_0, multiplied by $(1 + g)$.

EXAMPLE 13-4: ESTIMATING IMPLIED RATE OF RETURN FOR SUMMA CORPORATION

Notice that in Example 13-3, our estimate of the expected return exactly equals the required return of 15 percent that we used to determine the intrinsic value of Summa. This is because we assumed the share is trading at its intrinsic value. What if Summa was actually trading in the market at a price of $15? Under these circumstances, we estimate an expected return of 14.13 percent:

$$k_{CS} = \frac{D_1}{P_0} + g = \frac{1.07}{15.00} + 0.07 = 0.0713 + 0.07 = 0.1413$$

At a price of $15, Summa's shares are not attractive investments, since they offer a rate of return of 14.13 percent, which is below our required rate of return of 15 percent. In other words, based on our analysis, they are overpriced at $15.

Similarly, if Summa's shares were trading below $13.38, they would be undervalued according to our analysis, and we would expect to earn above our required rate of return. For example, if they were trading at $12, the expected rate of return would be 15.92 percent, well above 15 percent:

$$k_{CS} = \frac{D_1}{P_0} + g = \frac{1.07}{12.00} + 0.07 = 0.0892 + 0.07 = 0.1592$$

An examination of Equation 13-5 quickly demonstrates the factors affecting the price of a common stock, assuming the constant-growth version of the dividend discount model to be the applicable valuation approach:

1. If the market lowers the required rate of return for a stock, price will rise (other things being equal).

2. If investors decide that the expected growth in dividends will be higher as the result of some favourable development for the firm, price will also rise (other things being equal).

Of course, the converse for these two situations also holds—a rise in the discount rate or a reduction in the expected growth rate of dividends will lower price.

The present value or intrinsic value calculated from Equation 13-5 is quite sensitive to the estimates used by the investor in the equation. Relatively small variations in the inputs can change the estimated price by large percentage amounts.

EXAMPLE 13-5: EFFECT OF THE DISCOUNT RATE ON PRICE FOR SUMMA CORPORATION

For Summa, assume the discount rate used, k, is 16 percent instead of 15 percent, with other variables held constant:

$$\hat{P}_0 = \frac{\$1.00(1.07)}{0.16 - 0.07} = \$11.89$$

In this example, a one-percentage-point rise in k results in an 11.14 percent decrease in price, from \$13.38 to \$11.89.

EXAMPLE 13-6: EFFECT OF THE GROWTH RATE ON PRICE FOR SUMMA CORPORATION

Assume that for Summa the growth rate, g, is 6 instead of 7 percent, with other variables held constant:

$$\hat{P}_0 = \frac{\$1.00(1.06)}{0.15 - 0.06} = \$11.78$$

In this example, a one percentage point decline in g results in an 11.96 percent decrease in price, from \$13.38 to \$11.78.

EXAMPLE 13-7: EFFECT OF MULTIPLE VARIABLES ON PRICE FOR SUMMA CORPORATION

Assume that for Summa the discount rate rises to 16 percent, and the growth rate declines to 4 percent:

$$\hat{P}_0 = \frac{\$1.00(1.04)}{0.16 - 0.04} = \$8.67$$

In this example, the price declines from \$13.38 to \$8.67, a 35.20 percent change.

These differences demonstrate why stock prices constantly fluctuate as investors make their buy and sell decisions. Even if all investors use the constant-growth version of the dividend discount model to value a particular common stock (which in practice they don't), many different estimates of value will be obtained because of the following:

1. Each investor has his or her own required rate of return based on their estimate of the risk associated with the stock and future market conditions, resulting in a relatively wide range of values of k.

2. Each investor has his or her own estimate of the expected growth rate in dividends. Although this range may be reasonably narrow in many valuation situations, small differences in g can produce significant differences in price, everything else held constant. In addition, there are several situations under which there will be large ranges of possible estimates for k and g, which suggests why investors can hold such varied opinions about the true value of common shares.

Thus, at any time, some investors are willing to buy, whereas others wish to sell a particular stock, depending on their evaluation of its prospects. This helps to make markets active and liquid.

The Multiple-Growth Case

Many firms grow at a rapid rate (or rates) for a number of years and then slow down to an "average" growth rate. Other companies pay no dividends for a period of years, often during their early growth period. The constant-growth model discussed earlier is not formulated to deal with these situations. A model that can incorporate such a variation of the DDM is the multiple-growth model.

In addition, short-term earnings and dividend estimates should be much more reliable than those covering a longer period of time, which are often calculated using some very general estimates of future economic, industry, and company conditions. In order to use the best information available at any time, it often makes sense to estimate growth as precisely as possible in the short term before assuming some long-term rate of growth.

Multiple growth is defined as a situation in which the expected future growth in dividends must be described using two or more growth rates. Although any number of growth rates is possible, most stocks can be described using just two or three. It is important to remember that at least two different growth rates are involved; this is the distinguishing characteristic of multiple-growth situations.

A number of companies have experienced rapid growth that could not be sustained forever. During part of their lives their growth exceeded that of the average company in the economy, but later the growth rate slowed. This seems reasonable since we would expect that competitive pressures and/or business cycle influences will prevent firms from maintaining extremely high growth in earnings for long periods of time. Some well-known examples from the past include **McDonald's**, **Disney**, **Xerox**, and **IBM**.

To capture the expected growth in dividends under this scenario, it is necessary to model the dividend stream during each period of different growth. It is reasonable to assume that at some point the company's growth will slow down to some steady rate such as that of the economy as a whole. At this time, the company's growth in future dividends can be described by the constant-growth model (Equation 13-5). What remains, therefore, is to model the exact dividend stream up to the point at which dividends slow to a normal growth rate and to find the present value of all the components. This can be described in equation form as

(13-9)
$$\hat{P}_0 = \frac{D_1}{(1+k_{CS})^1} + \frac{D_2}{(1+k_{CS})^2} + \dots + \frac{D_n}{(1+k_{CS})^n} + \frac{\hat{P}_n}{(1+k_{CS})^n}$$

where
$$\hat{P}_n = \frac{D_{n+1}}{k_{CS} - g}$$

n = the time at which constant growth in dividends to infinity is assumed to begin[7]

Essentially, we estimate dividends up to the beginning of the period where it is reasonable to assume constant growth to infinity. Then we can use the constant version of the DDM to estimate the intrinsic value or market price of the stock at that point in time ($\hat{P}_n$). Finally, we discount back to the beginning of the evaluation period (time 0): (1) all of the estimated dividends up to the beginning of constant growth period; and (2) the estimated intrinsic value at that time. This provides us with today's estimate of the share's intrinsic value.

How does this approach provide us with the present value of all expected future dividends from Period 1 to infinity? Recall from the constant growth version of the DDM that the intrinsic value determined at time n ($\hat{P}_n$), represents the present value of all expected dividends (at time $t = n$), from $n+1$ to infinity. Because $\hat{P}_n$ is the expected price of the stock at the end of period n, it must be discounted back to the present. When we discount $\hat{P}_n$ back to time 0, and add it to the present value of all dividends from $t = 1$ to $t = n$, we end up with the present value (at time $t = 0$) of all expected future dividends from time $t = 1$ to infinity. This is the estimated value of the stock today, according to the DDM.

Figure 13-3 illustrates the concept of valuing a multiple-growth rate company that is expected to pay a dividend of $1.50 at the end of this year, a $2.00 dividend at the end of Year 2, and a $2.30 dividend at the end of Year 3. It is estimated dividends will grow at a constant rate of 5 percent per year thereafter. To determine the intrinsic value of this company's common shares if the required rate of

[7]The dividend at period $n + 1$ is equal to the dividend paid in period n compounded up by the growth rate expected from period n to infinity. The designation $n + 1$ refers to the first period after the years of abnormal growth.

return is 10 percent, the first step is to estimate dividends up to the start of constant growth to infinity—$D_1 = \$1.50$, $D_2 = \$2.00$, $D_3 = \$2.30$. Next, you must estimate the intrinsic value at the beginning of the constant growth to infinity period:

$$\hat{P}_3 = \frac{D_4}{k_{CS} - g} = \frac{(2.30)(1.05)}{0.10 - 0.05} = \$48.30$$

Finally, discount back the relevant cash flows to time 0 and add:

$$\hat{P}_0 = \frac{1.50}{(1.10)^1} + \frac{2.00}{(1.10)^2} + \frac{2.30}{(1.10)^3} + \frac{48.30}{(1.10)^3} = 1.364 + 1.653 + 1.728 + 36.288 = \$41.03$$

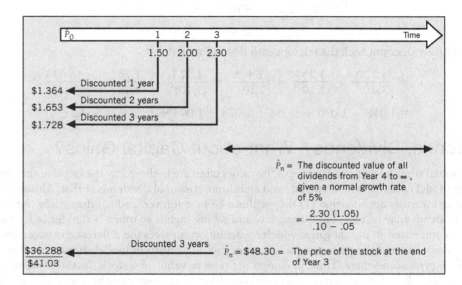

Figure 13-3
Valuing a Multiple-Growth
Rate Company

A well-known multiple-growth model is the two-stage growth rate model. This model assumes near-term growth at a rapid rate for some period (typically, 2 to 10 years) followed by a steady long-term growth rate that is sustainable (i.e., a constant-growth rate as discussed earlier).

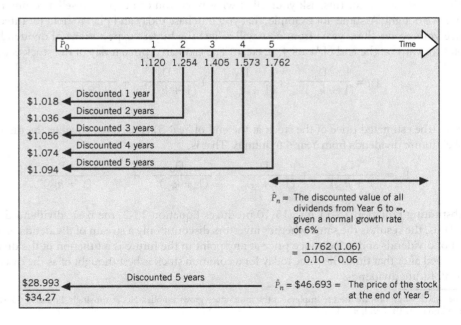

Figure 13-4
Valuing a Two-Stage
Growth Rate Company

Figure 13-4 illustrates the concept of valuing a multiple-growth rate company displaying growth in two stages. The current dividend is $1 and is expected to grow at the higher rate (g_1) of 12 percent a year for five years, at the end of which time the new growth rate (g_c) is expected to be a constant 6 percent a year. The required rate of return is 10 percent.

First estimate dividends up to the start of constant growth to infinity, done by compounding the beginning dividend, $1, at 12 percent for each of five years, producing the following: $D_0 = \$1.00$, $D_1 = \$1.00(1.12) = \$1.120$, $D_2 = \$1.00(1.12)^2 = \$1.254$, $D_3 = \$1.00(1.12)^3 = \$1.405$, $D_4 = \$1.00(1.12)^4 = \$1.573$, $D_5 = \$1.00(1.12)^5 = \$1.762$.

Then estimate the price at the beginning of the constant growth to infinity period:

$$\hat{P}_5 = \frac{D_6}{k_{CS} - g} = \frac{(1.762)(1.06)}{0.10 - 0.06} = \$46.693$$

And finally discount back the relevant cash flows to time 0:

$$\hat{P}_0 = \frac{1.120}{(1.10)^1} + \frac{1.254}{(1.10)^2} + \frac{1.405}{(1.10)^3} + \frac{1.573}{(1.10)^4} + \frac{1.762}{(1.10)^5} + \frac{46.693}{(1.10)^5}$$

$$= 1.018 + 1.036 + 1.056 + 1.074 + 1.094 + 28.993 = \$34.27$$

Dividends, Dividends—What about Capital Gains?

In their initial study of valuation concepts, investors often are bothered by the fact that the dividend discount model contains only dividends and an infinite stream of dividends at that. Although this is true, many investors are sure that (1) they will not be here forever, and (2) they really want capital gains. Dividends may be nice, but buying low and selling high is so much better! Since so many investors are interested in capital gains, which by definition involves the difference between the price paid for a security and the price at which it is later sold, a valuation model should seemingly contain a stock price somewhere. Thus, in computing present value for a stock, investors are interested in the present value of the expected price two years from now, or six months from now, or whatever the expected holding period is. How can price be incorporated into the valuation—or should it be?

According to the DDM, the only cash flows that an investor needs to be concerned with are dividends. Expected future price is built into the dividend discount model given by Equation 13-2; it is simply not visible. To see this, ask yourself at what price you can expect to sell a common stock that you have bought. Assume, for example, that you purchase today and plan to hold for three years. The price you receive three years from now will reflect the buyer's expectations of dividends from that point forward (at the end of Years 4, 5, etc.).[8] The estimated price today of the stock is equal to

(13-10)
$$\hat{P}_0 = \frac{D_1}{(1 + k_{CS})^1} + \frac{D_2}{(1 + k_{CS})^2} + \frac{D_3}{(1 + k_{CS})^3} + \frac{\hat{P}_3}{(1 + k_{CS})^3}$$

But $\hat{P}_3$ (the estimated price of the stock at the end of Year 3) is, in turn, equal to the discounted value of all future dividends from Year 4 to infinity. That is,

(13-11)
$$\hat{P}_3 = \frac{D_4}{(1 + k_{CS})^1} + \frac{D_5}{(1 + k_{CS})^2} + \frac{D_6}{(1 + k_{CS})^3} + \cdots + \frac{\hat{P}_\infty}{(1 + k_{CS})^{\infty - 3}}$$

Substituting Equation 13-11 into 13-10 produces Equation 13-2, the basic dividend discount model. Thus, the result is the same whether investors discount only a stream of dividends or a combination of dividends and price. Since price at any point in the future is a function of the dividends to be received after that time, the price today for a common stock is best thought of as the discounted value of all future dividends.

---

[8]This is the exact assumption we used to implement the multi-stage growth model. Not surprisingly, Equation 13-10 is identical to Equation 13-9 with $n = 3$.

Intrinsic Value

After making careful estimates of the expected stream of benefits and the required rate of return, the intrinsic value of the stock can be determined using present value analysis via the dividend discount model. Determining the intrinsic value is the objective of fundamental analysis. What does intrinsic value imply? Traditionally, investors and analysts specify a relationship between the estimated intrinsic value (IV) of an asset and its current market price (CMP). Specifically,

If IV > CMP, the asset is undervalued and should be purchased or held if already owned.
If IV < CMP, the asset is overvalued and should be avoided, sold if held, or possibly sold short.
If IV = CMP, this implies an equilibrium in that the asset is correctly valued.

Does the problem of varying estimates of value render valuation models useless? No, because individual investors cannot make intelligent investment decisions without having an intelligent estimate of the value of an asset. If the common shares of **Emera Inc.** are currently priced at $21.42 a share, is it a good buy for you? It may or may not be, depending on your own required rate of return (discount rate), your estimate of the future benefit stream to be derived from owning Emera, and certain other factors.[9]

EXAMPLE 13-8: INTRINSIC VALUE OF EMERA INC.

Assume that you require 9 percent return to invest in Emera; that is, your best estimate of the opportunity cost for alternative investment opportunities of similar risk is 9 percent. Also assume that the most recent dividend was $0.95 and you expect it to grow at the rate of 4 percent a year for the indefinite future. Based on these figures and using the constant-growth dividend discount model, the intrinsic value (justified price) of Emera to you would be estimated at $19.76 per share. Based on the intrinsic value principle, Emera is overvalued at $21.42 and should not be purchased, should be sold if held, or sold short if not held.

Notice that this valuation process tells you that if you pay $19.76 per share for Emera, you will earn your required rate of return of 9 percent, if the assumed dividend growth rate is correct. You can, therefore, pay less, say $19 or $16 per share, and earn more than the required rate of return.[10]

Other investors with different estimates for *k* and *g* may be at the margin valuing this security, with estimated values only slightly higher or lower than $21.42. They are potential traders if the price moves slightly or if a news event causes even slight variations in their *k* or their *g*.

The Dividend Discount Model in Practice

Many money managers and investment services firms use the DDM in various ways to estimate the intrinsic values of stocks. Regardless of who uses the model, and how it is used, estimates are always involved. Investors should always remember this in using or evaluating output from these models.

> ### INVESTING *tip*
>
> Intrinsic value is generally derived from a present value process involving estimates of uncertain (future) benefits and the use of (varying) discount rates by different investors. Therefore, the same asset may have many estimated intrinsic values, depending on who, and how many, are doing the evaluation. This is why, for a particular asset on a particular day, some investors are willing to buy and some to sell. Because future benefits and the required rate of return are uncertain and must be estimated, investors will arrive at different inputs to be used in the valuation process. In addition, it is unlikely that investors will all use the same valuation models. All of these factors result in varying estimates of the intrinsic value of an asset. The market price of an asset at any point is, in this sense, the consensus intrinsic value of that asset for the market.

---

[9]As we know from Part II, securities should be chosen on the basis of a portfolio concept—that is, how they fit together to form a unified whole.

[10]To determine the expected return for an investor who purchases the shares at $16, we can use Equation 13-8, along with an estimate for $D_1 = (\$0.95)(1.04) = \$0.988$ to obtain the following expected annual return: $k_{CS} = (0.988)/(16) + 0.04 = 0.1018$, or 10.18 percent (well above the required return of 9 percent).

INVESTING *tip*

The valuation process can establish justified prices for assets or indicate whether or not you can expect to earn your required rate of return on a prospective asset. Remember, however, that you are not assured of earning your required rate of return. Investment decisions always involve a forward-looking process. Estimates are based on the best information available, but there is always uncertainty. Even the best estimates may not be realized. As discussed in Chapter 1, uncertainty will always be the dominant feature of the environment in which investment decisions are made. Furthermore, other factors are at play, including the psychology of the market. On-line investors can interact with each other, and information—sometimes false or misleading—can spread quickly, and prices affected accordingly.

The DDM has a great deal of intuitive appeal because it links equity prices to two important fundamentals:

1. Corporate profitability (through their link with dividends)
2. The general level of interest rates (through their impact on the discount rate)

In particular, the model predicts that the intrinsic value of common shares will increase as a result of increases in expected dividends (which are closely related to profitability); increases in the growth rate of these dividends; and/or decreases in the appropriate discount rate. From previous chapters, we know that the discount rate will be an increasing function of the general level of interest rates, as well as the riskiness of the underlying security.

For these reasons, the DDM provides a great deal of insight into the factors affecting the general level of security prices in an economy. While the DDM provides great insight into the valuation process, it has its limitations. A key limitation is the large number of inputs that must be estimated regarding the uncertain future. In addition, the DDM tends to work best for large, stable companies that have positive and growing earnings and that pay a significant portion of these earnings as dividends. Examples of such companies include large utility companies, large manufacturing companies, and banks. However, the DDM does not work at all (without modification) for companies that do not pay dividends (or pay very low dividend amounts), or for those that have very volatile earnings. In other words, the DDM is not likely to work well for small companies in the early stages of growth, new technology companies that have negative or low earnings, or commodity-producing companies (such as mining and oil companies) since they have very volatile earnings, and many do not pay dividends. Real-World Returns 13-2 provides a good overview of the uses and limitations of the DDM.

A present value model that is being used more frequently is the free cash flow valuation model, which is discussed in Appendix 13B. This model overcomes some of the limitations of the DDM, specifically the discretionary nature of dividends, which are determined by a company's board of directors. Rather than focusing on dividends, this model focuses on "free" cash flows or the cash flows that are available to common shareholders after all expenses have been paid and all capital expenditures have been funded. Conceptually, this is the amount of cash that could be paid out in dividends without affecting the company's future growth plans. This model is an important part of the current CFA curriculum, as is the DDM.

REAL-WORLD RETURNS 13-2

Digging into the Dividend Discount Model

It's time to dust off one of the oldest, most conservative methods of valuing stocks—the dividend discount model (DDM). It's one of the basic applications of a financial theory that students in any introductory finance class must learn. Unfortunately, the theory is the easy part. The model requires loads of assumptions about companies' dividend payments and growth patterns, as well as future interest rates. Difficulties spring up in the search for sensible numbers to fold into the equation.

The Dividend Discount Model

Here is the basic idea: any stock is ultimately worth no more than what it will provide investors in current and future dividends. Financial theory says that the value of a stock is worth all of the future cash flows expected to be generated by the firm, discounted by an appropriate risk-adjusted rate. According to the DDM, dividends are the cash flows that are returned to the shareholder. (We're going to assume you understand the concepts of time value of money and discounting.)

To value a company using the DDM, you calculate the value of dividend payments that you think a stock will throw-off in the years ahead. The classic dividend discount model works best when valuing a mature company that pays a hefty portion of its earnings as dividends, such as a utility company.

Assumptions—The Problem of Forecasting

Proponents of the dividend discount model say that only future cash dividends can give you a reliable estimate of a company's intrinsic value. Buying a stock for any other reason—say, paying 20 times the company's earnings today because somebody will pay 30 times tomorrow—is mere speculation.

In truth, the dividend discount model requires an enormous amount of "speculation" in trying to forecast future dividends. Even when you apply it to steady, reliable, dividend-paying companies, you still need to make plenty of assumptions about their future. The model is subject to the axiom "garbage in, garbage out," meaning that a model is only as good as the assumptions it is based upon. Furthermore, the inputs that produce valuations are always changing and susceptible to error.

The first big assumption that the DDM makes is that dividends are steady, or grow at a constant rate indefinitely. But even for steady, reliable, utility-type stocks, it can be tricky to forecast exactly what the dividend payment will be next year, never mind a dozen years from now.

Multi-Stage Models

To get around the problem posed by unsteady dividends, multi-stage models take the DDM a step closer to reality by assuming that the company will experience differing growth phases. Stock analysts build complex forecast models with many phases of differing growth to better reflect real prospects. For example, a multistage DDM may predict that a company will have a dividend that grows at 5 percent for seven years, 3 percent for the following three years and then at 2 percent in perpetuity.

However, such an approach brings even more assumptions into the model—although it doesn't assume that a dividend will grow at a constant rate, it must guess when and by how much a dividend will change over time.

What Should Be "Expected"?

Another sticking point with the DDM is that no one really knows for certain the appropriate expected rate of return to use. It's not always wise simply to use the long-term interest rate because the appropriateness of this can change.

The High-Growth Problem

No fancy DDM model is able to solve the problem of high-growth stocks. If the company's dividend growth rate exceeds the expected return rate, you cannot calculate a value —because you get a negative denominator in the formula. Stocks don't have a negative value. Consider a company with a dividend growing at 20 percent while the expected return rate is only 5 percent: in the denominator $(r - g)$ you would have −15 percent $(5\% - 20\%)$!

In fact, even if the growth rate does not exceed the expected return rate, growth stocks, which don't pay dividends, are even tougher to value using this model. If you hope to value a

(continued)

REAL-WORLD RETURNS 13-2 *continued*

growth stock with the dividend discount model, your valuation will be based on nothing more than guesses about the company's future profits and dividend policy decisions. Most growth stocks don't pay out dividends. Rather, they reinvest earnings into the company with the hopes of providing shareholders with returns by means of a higher share price.

Consider Microsoft, which didn't pay a dividend for decades. Given this fact, the model might suggest the company was worthless at that time—which is completely absurd. Remember, only about a third of all public companies bother to pay dividends. Furthermore, even companies that do offer payouts are allocating less and less of their earnings to shareholders.

Conclusion

The dividend discount model is by no means the be-all and end-all for valuation. That being said, learning about the dividend discount model does encourage thinking. It forces investors to evaluate different assumptions about growth and future prospects. If nothing else, the DDM demonstrates the underlying principle that a company is worth the sum of its discounted future cash flows. (Whether or not dividends are the correct measure of cash flow is another question.) The challenge is to make the model as applicable to reality as possible, which means using the most reliable assumptions possible.

Source: Excerpted from McClure, Ben, "Digging into the Dividend Discount Model," Investopedia.com, April 14, 2004. Retrieved from www.investopedia.com. Reprinted with permission from Investopedia.com.

CHECK YOUR UNDERSTANDING

13-4. The equations for the zero-growth and constant-growth rate DDM do not include the discounting factor that we associate with finding a present value. How, then, can the DDM be said to involve a present value process?

13-5. Assume that a group of investors uses the constant-growth version of the DDM to value Power Corp., a Canadian conglomerate. Are they likely to come up with different estimates of value?

13-6. Can the intrinsic value of a stock be determined with a formula, or is it something that can only be estimated?

RELATIVE VALUATION APPROACHES

P/E Ratio (Earnings Multiplier)
The price to earnings (P/E) ratio for a stock measures the stock price relative to the earnings per share.

Relative valuation approaches determine the value of common shares by comparing the market prices of "similar" companies, relative to some common variable such as earnings, cash flow, book values, or sales. Although relatively simple to apply, using multiples based on comparable companies has the potential to build market errors into the value estimation process. This section discusses the application and appropriateness of some of these approaches, with particular emphasis on the P/E ratio, the most commonly cited one for common share valuation.

The P/E Ratio Approach

learning objective 4
Explain the P/E ratio approach.

An alternative fundamental analysis method of valuation frequently used by practising security analysts is the **P/E ratio** or **earnings multiplier** approach. The P/E ratio is the number of times investors value earnings as expressed in the stock price.

Practising security analysts probably use this method more often than dividend discount models as alluded to in Real-World Returns 13-3. Although the P/E ratio model appears easier to use than the DDM, its very simplicity causes investors to forget that estimation of the uncertain future is also involved here. This is an important point to remember. Every valuation model and approach, properly done, requires estimates of the uncertain future.

REAL-WORLD RETURNS 13-3

P/E Ratio

Here's a quotation to live by: "Why not invest your assets in the company you really like? As Mae West said, 'Too much of a good thing can be wonderful.'"

It comes from Warren Buffett, the legendary chairman and CEO of Berkshire Hathaway Inc. I love his quote because of its positive spirit —the idea that you shouldn't have to invest in companies you don't like.

On the other hand, I've learned enough to know that kind of sentiment comes with many caveats, enough, probably, to fill several columns. It's important for me to like the company, but I also have to make sure it's a good investment.

On that subject, I have heard a lot from readers, who fill my inbox every week with e-mails full of advice and reflection, of praise and mild rebuke (like the one that started with "I'm going to try to be kind.") By far, the message experienced investors want to pass on is that in picking stocks, consider price but also look at other indicators of a stock's value.

The most-cited indicator, by readers and experts, is the P/E (price-to-earnings) ratio, the ratio that gives investors an idea of how much they are paying for a company's earnings. (For those like me that are new to this calculation, it is simple: Take the stock price and divide it by the company's earnings per share. But you don't really need to figure out each ratio yourself; most services that provide stock quotes (like globeandmail.com) also offer up the P/E ratio.)

Take Apple, for example, a company I really like and have been watching very closely over the past couple of months. Its P/E ratio is about 27. That is pretty high. In fact, many of the "value investors" who wrote to me indicate that they would never buy a company's shares if the P/E ratio is above 14 or 15.

To put that in perspective, consider this analogy: It's like buying a store and paying a price equivalent to 27 years worth of profits from that store.

But P/E ratios are a little more complicated than that. It's never simple, is it? To take the analogy of the store further, a price equivalent to 27 years worth of profits would not be as crazy if you thought profits were going to soar by 20 or 30 percent a year. High-growth companies— Apple and other technology companies—tend to have higher P/E ratios because they are expected to grow faster than, say, financial institutions.

One way to see if a P/E is high or low is to compare it with similar firms. While Apple's P/E was 27 yesterday, Intel's was 18, Hewlett Packard's stood at 16, Dell at 15 and Research In Motion's was 47. Knowing those numbers helped me put Apple's ratio in context—at the higher end of technology stocks.

I know I have a huge affinity for technology stocks, so this week I also decided to broaden my horizons a little and look at some other companies I really like, although maybe not in Mae West territory. I picked blue-chip Canadian stocks that I know something about—Canadian Imperial Bank of Commerce, Thomson Corp., Imperial Oil and Manulife Financial. Two of the companies' P/E ratios were in the single digits (CIBC at 7 and Thomson at 6), while Manulife Financial's stood at 13 and Imperial Oil, 15.

(continued)

REAL-WORLD RETURNS 13-3 *continued*

After weeks of following technology stocks, with their volatility and high P/E ratios, I was momentarily lulled by these firms and their comparatively low P/E ratios. They seem so comfortable and safe.

It strikes me that I have a decision to make: What kind of investor will I be? Will I pick stocks of companies that are solid but are growing relatively slower, or will I tend to the high-growth, more volatile stocks, like Apple?

Eventually, I think I'll want a mix of both, but I can say this so far: I'm comfortable buying higher P/E stocks. I want to buy a growth stock like Apple, so I'm willing to take the risk that comes with it.

It's just a matter of when to take that risk. I read this paper's report on Warren Buffett's visit to Toronto this week, titled "Buffett sitting on his wallet." The great value investor doesn't see a lot of bargains yet on the equity markets despite the huge declines over the past few weeks.

His words made me feel concerned because the financial news keeps getting worse and experts like Mr. Buffett don't think it will end soon. This week, I noticed that analysts and experts stopped using words like "may" or "likely" or "probable" when referring to a recession in the US. In their minds, it seems to be a done deal.

So if Warren Buffett can't find a bargain, who am I to disagree? I'm sitting on my wallet with Warren.

Source: Rasbach, Noreen, "High P/E, low P/E. I'm sitting still right now… just like Warren," *The Globe and Mail*, February 9, 2008, p. B10.

The conceptual framework for the P/E model is not as solidly based on economic theory as the DDM. However, a P/E ratio model is consistent with the present value analysis because it concerns the intrinsic value of a stock or the aggregate market, exactly as before.

The P/E ratio as reported daily in the financial media is simply an identity calculated by dividing the current market price of the stock by the latest 12-month earnings. As such, it tells investors the price being paid for each $1 of the company's most recent earnings. For example, in April 2008, investors were willing to pay 15.8 times (the most recent 12-month) earnings for **Emera Inc.** but only 12.5 times earnings for **Laurentian Bank**. These P/E ratios, however, provide no basis for valuation other than showing the underlying identity on which the P/E valuation model is based: This identity is[11]

(13-12)
$$P_0 = \text{Current market price} = E_0 \times P_0/E_0$$

To implement the earnings multiplier model and estimate the value of the stock today, we must estimate the values on the right-hand side of Equation 13-12. The typical P/E formulation uses estimated earnings for the next 12 months. The basic equation then becomes

(13-13)
$$P_0 = \text{Estimated earnings} \times \text{Justified P/E ratio}$$
$$= E_1 \times P_0/E_1$$

EXAMPLE 13-9: EFFECT OF P/E RATIO ON PRICE

If investors are willing to pay 15 times expected earnings, a stock with estimated earnings of $3 per share for the next 12 months will sell for $45. This price will change as estimates of earnings or the justified P/E changes.

___

[11]E_0 here refers to the earnings used to calculate the P/E ratio as reported; usually it is the most recent 12-month earnings.

Determinants of the P/E Ratio

What determines a P/E ratio? The P/E ratio can be derived from the dividend discount model, which, as we have seen, is the foundation of valuation for common stocks. We will illustrate this process only for the case of constant growth. If a multiple-period growth model is applicable to the stock being considered, a more complicated formulation than the one presented here is required.

Start with Equation 13-5, the estimated price of a stock using the constant-growth version of the model. We use P_0 to represent estimated price from the model.

$$P_0 = \frac{D_1}{k_{CS} - g} \tag{13-14}$$

Dividing both sides of Equation 13-14 by expected earnings, E_1,

$$\frac{P_0}{E_1} = \frac{D_1/E_1}{k_{CS} - g} \tag{13-15}$$

Equation 13-15 indicates those factors that affect the estimated P/E ratio.

1. The expected dividend payout ratio (D_1/E_1)
2. The required rate of return (k_{CS})
3. The expected growth rate of dividends (g)

The following relationships should hold, other things being equal:

- The higher the expected payout ratio, the higher the P/E.
- The higher the expected growth rate, g, the higher the P/E.
- The higher the required rate of return, k, the lower the P/E.

It is important to remember the phrase "other things being equal," because usually other things are not equal and the preceding relationships do not hold by themselves. It is quite obvious, upon reflection, that if a firm could increase its estimated P/E ratio, and therefore its market price, by simply raising its payout ratio, it would be very tempted to do so. However, such an action would in all likelihood reduce future growth prospects, lowering g, and thereby defeating the increase in the payout. Similarly, trying to increase g by taking on particularly risky investment projects would cause investors to demand a higher required rate of return, thereby raising k. Again, this would work to offset the positive effects of the increasing growth rate.

Variables 2 and 3 are typically the most important factors in the preceding determination of the P/E ratio because a small change in either can have a large effect on its value.

EXAMPLE 13-10: EFFECT OF RATE OF RETURN AND GROWTH RATE ON THE P/E RATIO

Assume that the expected payout ratio is 53.5 percent (i.e., $D_1/E1 = 1.07/2.00 = 0.535$). By varying k and g, and therefore changing the difference between the two (the denominator in Equation 13-15), investors can assess the effect on the P/E ratio as follows:

Assume $k_{CS} = 0.15$ and $g = 0.07$

$$\frac{P_0}{E_1} = \frac{D_1/E_1}{k_{CS} - g} = \frac{0.535}{0.15 - 0.07} = 6.69$$

Now assume k increases to 0.16, while g falls to 0.06, the justified P/E ratio falls to 5.35.

$$\frac{P_0}{E_1} = \frac{D_1/E_1}{k_{CS} - g} = \frac{0.535}{0.16 - 0.06} = 5.35$$

This is not surprising since both of these events produce a negative impact on the justified P/E ratio.

Now assume that k falls to 14 percent, while g increases to 8 percent, which are both favourable events.

$$\frac{P_0}{E_1} = \frac{D_1/E_1}{k_{CS} - g} = \frac{0.535}{0.14 - 0.08} = 8.92$$

Think about each of these P/E ratios being used as a multiplier with expected earnings for Summa for next year of $2. The possible prices for Summa would be $13.38, $10.70, and $17.84, respectively, which is quite a range, given the small changes in k and g that were made.

Understanding the P/E Ratio

Most investors intuitively realize that the P/E ratio should be higher for companies whose earnings are expected to grow rapidly. However, it is not easy to determine how much higher. The market will assess the degree of risk involved in the expected future growth of earnings—if the higher growth rate carries a high level of risk, the P/E ratio will be affected accordingly, by the corresponding increase in the required rate of return (k_{CS}). Furthermore, the high growth rate in earnings may be attributable to several different factors, some of which are more desirable than others. For example, rapid growth in unit sales owing to strong demand for a firm's products is preferable to favourable tax situations, which may change, or liberal accounting procedures, which may cause future reversals in the firm's situation.

P/E ratios reflect investors' expectations about the growth potential of a stock and the risk involved. However, evidence provided in Chapter 10 suggests that stocks with low P/E ratios tend to outperform those with higher P/E ratios, on a risk-adjusted basis. Some analysts also make reference to the PEG ratio, which scales the P/E ratio by the company's growth rate in earnings, to adjust for the influence of growth.

Estimating the P/E Ratio

Estimates of the justified P/E ratio ultimately involve a great deal of subjectivity. While the valuation procedure itself is relatively easy, the estimation of an appropriate P/E ratio is difficult. As the discussion in the previous section suggests, determining an appropriate P/E ratio requires much analysis and judgement regarding the firm's growth opportunities, position within the industry, and the riskiness associated with the firm, its industry, and the economy as a whole.

Despite the intuitive appeal of estimating the justified P/E ratio based on Equation 13-15, it is only appropriate under certain conditions, since it is merely a reformulation of the constant-growth DDM. It will only work well for firms that exhibit stable and growing dividends, at a rate below the required return on their common shares (i.e., k_{CS} must be $> g$). An alternative approach is to find "comparable" companies, rate one company relative to the others, and estimate a target P/E ratio for the company being analyzed, based on this comparison, and based on the P/E ratios of the comparable companies. Often this approach involves scaling an industry average P/E ratio up or down, based on the analyst's opinion regarding how well the company stacks up against its peers.

A comparison of one company with its peers also involves a great deal of subjectivity regarding several company-specific characteristics including risk, potential for growth, and overall financial health of the company. Some other approaches to estimating justified P/E multiples include using historical averages for the company or the company's industry. An alternative approach is to determine the ratio based on its historic relationship to P/E multiples in the market as a whole. For example, a company or industry may historically have traded at P/E ratios that average 90 percent of the P/E ratio for the S&P/TSX Composite Index, so you could estimate an appropriate P/E multiple based on 90 percent of the S&P/TSX's current P/E ratio. The problem with any of these ways of estimating justified P/E ratios is that they may build market errors into the value estimation process. For example, we could overestimate the appropriate P/E multiple based on industry averages if the market has systematically overvalued the particular industry that the company is in. Similar results would occur if we scale the S&P/TSX Index multiple by 90 percent but find that the entire market is overvalued.

Aside from the difficulties in estimating an appropriate P/E ratio, there are several other practical concerns regarding how informative P/E ratios are. One important concern is that P/E ratios are uninformative when companies have negative (or very small) earnings. Finally, the volatile nature of earnings implies a great deal of volatility in P/E multiples. For example, the earnings of cyclical companies fluctuate much more dramatically throughout the business cycle than their stock prices. As a result, their P/E ratios tend to peak during recessionary periods (in response to low earnings) and hit low points during the peak of business cycles (in response to high earnings). In response to some of these concerns, there are a number of similar approaches described below, which are often used for valuation purposes.

Market-to-Book Ratio (M/B)

learning objective 5
Outline other relative valuation approaches.

Book value, the accounting value of the firm as reflected in its financial statements, measures the actual values recorded under accounting conventions. As such, book values have the advantages and disadvantages of accounting numbers. The book value of equity is defined as the book value of assets minus the book value of liabilities. It represents an accounting measure of the amount of unencumbered assets to which equity holders are entitled. In Canada and the United States, the book value of assets equals their original cost minus allowable depreciation, while the liability values reflect their values when incurred.

The **market-to-book ratio (M/B)** or **price-to-book value** is determined using the following equation: $M/B = P_0/BV_0$, where P_0 is the market price per common share and BV_0 is the book value per common share (determined by dividing the net book value of the firm by the number of common shares outstanding). This variable is followed closely by investors and analysts. Stocks selling below the book value of equity represent good candidates for "value" portfolios, while stocks trading at high multiples, relative to book value, are often categorized as "growth" stocks.

Market-to-Book Ratio (M/B) or Price-to-Book
The ratio of stock price to per share shareholders' equity.

Estimates of the intrinsic value of a share can be determined by multiplying the justified M/B ratio times the company's book value per share (which is easily determined from the balance sheet). We end up with the following valuation equation, similar to Equation 13-13, which was used for valuing shares based on their justified P/E ratio:

$$P_0 = \text{Book value per share} \times \text{Justified M/B ratio}$$
$$= BV_0 \times M/B$$

(13-16)

There are several reasons why valuing stocks relative to their M/B is attractive. Book value provides a relatively stable, intuitive measure of value relative to market values, which can be easily compared with those of other companies, provided accounting standards do not vary greatly across the comparison group. It eliminates the problems arising from the use of P/E multiples, since book values are rarely negative and do not exhibit the volatility associated with earnings levels. On the other hand, book values are sensitive to accounting standards and practices, which often vary from firm to firm. In addition, they may be uninformative for companies that do not have a large proportion of fixed assets (such as service firms or emerging high-technology firms).

Similar to P/E ratios, the justified M/B ratio can be estimated by comparing with industry ratios, aggregate market ratios and past trends, and by relating to the fundamentals used in the DDM. In order to relate M/B ratios to the constant-growth version of the DDM provided in Equation 13-5, we begin by noting that D_1 may be expressed as: $D_1 = EPS_1 \times \text{Payout ratio}$. Next, we note that EPS_1 can be expressed as $EPS_0 \times (1+g)$, if we assume that earnings and dividends grow at the same rate. Thus we can say that $D_1 = EPS_0 \times (1+g) \times \text{Payout ratio}$. Finally, it is an accounting identity that $EPS_0 = ROE_0 \times BV_0$, so we can say that $D_1 = ROE_0 \times BV_0 \times (1+g) \times \text{Payout ratio}$.[12]

---

[12] It is an accounting identity that $EPS_0 = ROE_0 \times BV_0$, because EPS = net income/number of common shares outstanding, ROE = net income/total common equity, while BV = total common equity/number of common shares outstanding.

When we substitute this expression for D_1 into the numerator of the constant-growth DDM equation, we obtain the following relationship:

$$P_0 = \frac{ROE_0 \times BV_0 \times \text{Payout ratio} \times (1 + g)}{k_{CS} - g}$$

Finally, dividing both sides by book value per share (BV_0), we are left with:

(13-17)

$$\frac{P_0}{BV_0} = \frac{ROE_0 \times \text{Payout ratio} \times (1 + g)}{k_{CS} - g}$$

This equation provides a method of estimating a justified M/B ratio based on underlying fundamentals. It implies that M/B is positively related to its profitability (as measured by ROE), and to its expected growth rate. Similar to the P/E ratio, it will increase as a result of decreases in the discount rate k_{CS}.

EXAMPLE 13-11: ESTIMATING MARKET-TO-BOOK RATIO FOR SUMMA CORPORATION

Suppose that in addition to the previous information, we are given that Summa's most recent return on equity (ROE_0) is 16 percent, while its current book value per share (BV_0) is \$12.40. The justified M/B ratio is 1.145.

$$M/B = \frac{P_0}{BV_0} = \frac{ROE_0 \times \text{Payout ratio} \times (1 + g)}{k_{CS} - g} = \frac{(0.16)(0.535)(1.07)}{0.15 - 0.07} = 1.145$$

Using Equation 13-16, we obtain an estimated value of \$14.20 for Summa's shares:

$$\hat{P}_0 = M/B \times BV_0 = (1.145)(12.40) = \$14.20$$

Several analysts recommend choosing stocks with low price-to-book value ratios as a stock selection rule. The M/B ratio has received support in empirical tests, several of which were discussed in Chapter 10. The most notable evidence is provided by the 1992 study by Eugene Fama and Kenneth French. They found that two basic variables, size (as measured by the market value of equity) and book-to-market value of equity (which is the reciprocal of the M/B ratio), effectively combined to capture the cross-sectional variation in average stock returns during the period 1963–90. Furthermore, the book-to-market equity ratio had a consistently stronger role in average returns.[13]

Price/Sales Ratio (P/S)

Price/Sales (P/S) Ratio
A company's total common equity market value divided by its sales.

A valuation technique that has received increased attention is the **price/sales (P/S) ratio** calculated by dividing a company's total market value (price times number of shares) by its sales. In effect, it indicates what the market is willing to pay for a dollar of the firm's revenues.

The P/S ratio has several properties that make it attractive for valuation purposes. Unlike earnings and book values, sales are relatively insensitive to accounting decisions and are never negative. Sales are not as volatile as earnings levels, hence, P/S ratios are generally less volatile than P/E multiples. In addition, sales figures provide useful information about corporate decisions such as the impact of pricing and credit policies. On the other hand, sales do not impart much information about cost control and profit margins, which are important determinants of company performance.

The expression for obtaining the share value estimate using this approach is similar to Equation 13-12 for using the P/E ratio and Equation 13-16 for using the M/B ratio:

---

[13]E. Fama and K. French, "The Cross-Section of Expected Stock Returns," *Journal of Finance* 47 (June 1992), pp. 427–465.

$$\hat{P}_0 = \text{Sales per share} \times \text{Justified price-to-sales ratio}$$
$$= \text{Sales}_0 \times \text{P/S}$$

(13-18)

Similar to P/E multiples and M/B ratios, justified P/S ratios can be estimated by reference to industry peers, market ratios, and past trends. We also alter the DDM to determine an estimate of an appropriate P/S ratio based on fundamentals. We focus on the constant-growth version of the DDM, and begin by noting as we did in the previous section, that D_1 can be expressed as $D_1 = \text{EPS}_0 \times (1+g) \times \text{Payout ratio}$. We also note that $\text{EPS}_0 = \text{Net income margin (NI\%)} \times \text{Sales per share (Sales}_0)$. By making the appropriate substitution for D_1 in the numerator of Equation 13-5, we can rewrite the constant-growth DDM as:

$$P_0 = \frac{\text{NI\%} \times \text{Sales}_0 \times \text{Payout ratio} \times (1+g)}{k_{CS} - g}$$

Finally, dividing both sides by Sales_0, we get:

$$\frac{P_0}{\text{Sales}_0} = \frac{\text{NI\%} \times \text{Payout ratio} \times (1+g)}{k_{CS} - g}$$

(13-19)

This calculation shows that the P/S ratio will increase in response to growth in profit margins and the growth rate and decreases in k_{CS}.

EXAMPLE 13-12: ESTIMATING THE PRICE/SALES RATIO FOR SUMMA CORPORATION

Suppose Summa has a net income margin (NI%) of 5 percent, and sales per share (Sales$_0$) of $40. This implies Summa's shares are worth $14.32 each.

$$\frac{P_0}{\text{Sales}_0} = \frac{\text{NI\%} \times \text{Payout ratio} \times (1+g)}{k_{CS} - g} = \frac{(0.05)(0.535)(1.07)}{0.15 - 0.07} = 0.358$$

$$\hat{P}_0 = \text{Sales}_0 \times \text{P/S} = (40)(0.358) = \$14.32$$

A well-known 1997 book, *What Works on Wall Street*, by James O'Shaugnessy,[14] gives new emphasis to the price/sales ratio. Using Compustat data back to 1951, he analyzed all of the basic investment strategies used to select common stock, such as book value, cash flow, P/E, ROE, yield, and so forth. O'Shaugnessy found that the 50 stocks with the lowest P/S ratios, based on an annual rebalancing of the portfolio, performed at an annual rate of 15.42 percent over the 40 years from 1954 through 1994, compared with 12.45 percent annually for his universe of stocks. Stocks with the highest P/S ratios earned only 4.15 percent annually. Furthermore, combining low P/S stocks (generally, a P/S of 1.0 or lower) with stocks showing momentum (the best 12-month price performance) produced results of 18.14 percent annually over the full 40-year period.

Other Relative Valuation Approaches

Another commonly used ratio is the multiple of price-to-cash flow (P/CF). Generally, cash flow (CF) is estimated as CF = net income + depreciation + deferred taxes.[15]

---

[14]James P. O'Shaugnessy, *What Works on Wall Street: A Guide to the Best-Performing Investment Strategies of All Time* (New York: McGraw-Hill, 1997).
[15]Some analysts focus on "free" cash flow available to equity holders, which is estimated as: net income + non-cash charges (such as depreciation and deferred taxes) + − capital spending − the change in net working capital − principal repayments + new external finance, as discussed in Appendix 13B.

This ratio alleviates some of the accounting concerns regarding accounting measures of earnings.

Finally, the price-to-earnings before interest and taxes (EBIT) ratio can also be used for valuation purposes. Using EBIT instead of net earnings eliminates a significant proportion of volatility caused in EPS figures by the use of debt. This is useful if we want to reduce the impact of capital structure on our valuation process.

CHECK YOUR UNDERSTANDING

13-7. What problem occurs when using comparable companies to estimate justified P/E ratios?

13-8. The definition of the P/E ratio seems straightforward. Why can it be problematic to use this relative valuation technique?

OTHER VALUATION ISSUES

There is growing interest in two value-added performance measures: economic value added and market value added. These measures are used by a number of companies to evaluate the performance of managers in enhancing firm value. These measures are also being used by security analysts as possible indicators of future equity returns.

Economic Value Added

Economic Value Added (EVA)

A technique for focusing on a firm's return on capital in order to determine if shareholders are being rewarded.

Economic value added (EVA) is a variation of the cash flow valuation approach.[16] In particular, it considers economic profit, which is similar to the net present value (NPV) approach for making capital budgeting decisions. NPV determines asset values based upon the present value of the cash flows it generates during its useful life. However, EVA advocates suggest firm managers cannot be evaluated based on the determination of firm value in this manner. The reason is that it is hard to determine the value impact of cash flows without due regard to their intended use. For example, negative cash flows in a particular period could be detracting from firm value (i.e., when it's losing money), or adding to firm value (i.e., reinvesting in profitable long-term projects). The same can be said of positive cash flows, which could be enhancing value (i.e., increasing profits) or destroying value (i.e., disposing of valuable long-term assets).

EVA addresses these concerns by considering not only profitability, but also the amount of capital resources used to generate these profits. It may be calculated using two approaches: using residual income or refined earnings. The residual income approach determines EVA in the following manner:

(13-20)
$$EVA = (ROC - WACC) \times Capital$$

where ROC is the return on total capital, WACC is the firm's weighted average cost of capital, and Capital is the average total capital (or net assets) employed by the company during the period.

Notice from Equation 13-20 that this measure penalizes decreases in capital (which proxies for growth) as well as decreases in profitability. As a result, managers who are evaluated on this measure will be less likely to enter into short-term, high-return projects if they detract from overall long-term growth in capital assets. In essence, managers are penalized to some extent if they attempt to sacrifice either profitability or growth at the expense of the other.

---

[16]The term economic value added (EVA) has been trademarked by Stern Stewart, a consulting firm that pioneered the use of this concept.

EVA is also calculated using the refined earnings approach in the following manner:

$$EVA = NOPAT - (WACC \times Capital) \tag{13-21}$$

where NOPAT is the firm's net operating profit after taxes. This approach results in a comparison of the dollar cost of capital (i.e., WACC × Capital) with the operating profits generated by the employed capital. Any negative EVA is a bad signal because it means that value is being destroyed; however, even if it is negative, the goal should be to improve upon the value in the previous period.

EXAMPLE 13-13: ESTIMATING EVA FOR SUMMA CORPORATION

Suppose that Summa's ROC is 14 percent, its WACC is 12 percent, its NOPAT is $21 million, and it employs $150 million worth of capital. Equations 13-20 and 13-21 both result in EVA of $3 million:

EVA = (ROC − WACC) × Capital = (0.14 − 0.12) × ($150m) = $3 million

EVA = NOPAT − (WACC × Capital) = $21m − (0.12 × $150m) = $3 million

Some studies have shown that stock price is more responsive to changes in EVA than to changes in earnings, the traditional variable of importance.[17] Some mutual funds are now using EVA analysis as the primary tool for selecting stocks for the fund to hold. One recommendation for investors interested in this approach is to search for companies with a return on capital in excess of 20 percent because this will, in all likelihood, exceed the cost of capital, and, therefore, the company is adding value.

Market Value Added

Unlike EVA, which evaluates internal performance, market value added (MVA) is a measure of external performance. It determines how the market has evaluated the firm's performance as reflected in the market prices of its outstanding debt and equity, relative to the capital invested in the company. MVA can be estimated for any period as follows:

$$MVA = Market\ value\ of\ the\ firm - Capital \tag{13-22}$$

Similar to EVA, it is the changes in this measure that are important. MVA relies on market perceptions and is more forward looking than EVA (which measures the performance in one period only).

EXAMPLE 13-14: ESTIMATING MVA FOR SUMMA CORPORATION

We can determine the MVA for Summa for the most recent period, if we are given a year-end market value for their total equity and debt of $172 million.

MVA = Market value − Capital = $172m − $150m = $22 million

which is a very positive result.

The use of EVA and MVA to evaluate management performance has attracted a great deal of support from the corporate world. Proponents suggest there is an important relationship between EVA and firm market values. On the other hand, detractors criticize EVA for its reliance on accounting measures and for its short-term focus. Empirical evidence regarding the relationship between EVA

---

[17]This discussion is based on Maggie Topkis, "A New Way to Find Bargains," *Fortune*, December 6, 1996, pp. 265–266.

and MVA is fairly limited at this time, and the conclusions offered by prospective researchers are mixed. For example, O'Byrne documents a strong relationship between market values and EVA, while Kramer and Pushner find evidence to the contrary.[18] The relative merit of these approaches will be evaluated in the years to come, but it seems likely they will to continue to grow in importance.

WHICH VALUATION METHOD TO USE?

We have described several valuation procedures here, including two of the most frequently used—the dividend discount model and the P/E ratio (multiplier) model. Which of these should be used?

In theory, the dividend discount model is a correct, logical, and sound position. The best estimate of the current value of a company's common stock is probably the present value of the (estimated) dividends to be paid by that company to its shareholders. However, some analysts and investors feel that this model is unrealistic. After all, they argue, no one can forecast dividends into the distant future with very much accuracy. Technically, the model calls for an estimate of all dividends from now to infinity, which is an impossible task. Finally, many investors want capital gains and not dividends, and some of these investors feel that focusing solely on dividends is not desirable. The discussion in previous sections has dealt with these objections that have been raised about the dividend discount model.

Possibly because of the objections to the dividend discount model cited here, or simply because it is easier to use, the earnings multiplier or P/E model remains the most popular approach to valuation. It is a less sophisticated and more intuitive model. In fact, understanding the P/E model can help investors comprehend the dividend discount model. Because dividends are paid out of earnings, investors must estimate the growth in earnings before they can figure out the growth in dividends or dividends themselves.

Rather than view these approaches as competing alternatives, it is better to view them as complements. Each is useful, and together they provide analysts with a better chance of valuing common stocks. There are several reasons for viewing them as complementary:

1. The P/E model can be derived from the constant growth version of the dividend discount model. They are, in fact, alternative methods of looking at value. In the dividend discount model, the future stream of benefits is discounted. In the P/E model, an estimate of expected earnings is multiplied by a P/E ratio or multiplier.

2. Dividends are paid out of earnings. To use the dividend discount model, it is necessary to estimate the future growth of earnings. The dividends used in the dividend discount model are a function of the earnings of the firm, an estimate of which is used in the earnings multiplier model.

3. Finally, investors must always keep in mind that valuation is no less an art than a science, and estimates of the future earnings and dividends are subject to error. In some cases it may be desirable to use one or the other method, and in other cases both methods can be used as a check on each other. The more procedures investors have to value common stocks, the more likely they are to obtain reasonable results.

In addition, certain techniques will be more appropriate for certain companies and industries.[19] Regardless of which method is used, it is important to remember that valuation employing fundamental analysis, or any other approach, is always subject to error. This is because we are dealing with the uncertain future. No matter who does the analysis, or how it is done, mistakes will be made.

In Chapters 15, 16, and 17, we utilize the overall logic of the fundamental valuation approach—

---

[18]S. O'Byrne, "EVA and the Shareholder," *Financial Practice and Education* 7 (Spring/Summer 1997), pp. 50–54; J. Kramer and G. Pushner, "An Empirical Analysis of Economic Value Added as a Proxy for Market Value Added," *Financial Practice and Education* 7 (Spring/Summer 1997), pp. 41–49.

[19]For an excellent review of the techniques most commonly employed for valuing firms in different industries in Canada, refer to Joe Kan, Editor, *Handbook of Canadian Security Analysis: A Guide to Evaluating the Industry Sectors of the Market, from Bay Street's Top Analysts* Volume 2 (Toronto: John Wiley & Sons Canada, 2000).

namely, that the intrinsic value of a common stock, or the aggregate market, is a function of its expected returns and accompanying risk, as proxied by the required rate of return. The dividend discount model and the P/E ratio model are both used to illustrate the fundamental valuation process.

Bursting the Bubble of New Economy Stocks— A Lesson in Valuation

At the end of the 1990s and into 2000, investors were caught up in a speculative bubble involving "New Economy" stocks, such as **eToys** and **Dr.Koop.com**. These Internet companies were thought to represent the wave of the future and to be more desirable than "Old Economy" stocks such as **Gillette** or **Procter & Gamble**. In Canada, **Nortel Networks** and **JDS Uniphase** attracted a huge amount of investor interest. Nortel's stock price jumped from the $20 to $40 range to peak at over $170, before collapsing to the penny stock range. The prices of JDS and other IT companies followed similar patterns over this time. At one point, Nortel and JDS combined to make up more than one third of the market value of the S&P/TSX Composite Index, and they pushed it up along with them when they soared, and dragged it back down again when they crashed. There seemed to be no limit on the price of these New Economy stocks as their prices were bid higher and higher. Tremendous fortunes, mostly on paper, were being made.

From early in 1998 through late March 2000, the Amex Interactive Week Internet Index rose to 689 from a starting point of about 87 (split adjusted). Therefore, in just over two years this index showed a gain of almost 700 percent. Because these companies involved revolutionary new technology, many investors argued that they should be valued using revolutionary techniques because the old methods no longer applied. As one of the leading Internet gurus at Merrill Lynch proclaimed in early 2000, "Valuation is often not a helpful tool in determining when to sell hyper-growth stocks." Other star analysts brought up "usage metrics" when discussing these stocks. Usage metrics refers to non-financial metrics such as customer loyalty, website hits, and "engaged shoppers." Many analysts and investors did not want to discuss traditional valuation methods such as EPS, cash flows, and P/E ratios. Of course, for many of these companies these variables did not exist. They had no profitability, and in many cases, little hope of profitability for the foreseeable future.

In the past, companies had to show profitability, or the likely prospect thereof, in order to go public. In 1995, for example, about two-thirds of new companies going public were profitable at the time. In contrast, in the first quarter of 2000, less than 20 percent of companies going public were profitable at the time.

As we now know, the bubble started to burst in March 2000, and continued with horrific declines in early 2001. Many of the hot New Economy stocks dropped 80 percent or more in value and hundreds of Internet companies went out of business. The aggregate dollar loss in the value of investor portfolios was staggering—roughly $4 trillion US from March 2000 to March 2001. The Internet index mentioned above declined to about 280 by the end of 2000 (a 60 percent loss) and declined even further in early 2001.

By early 2001, it became apparent that the old metrics of valuation really did apply. To survive and succeed, companies sooner or later had to generate cash flows and be profitable. Investors no longer believed statements such as that of a major brokerage firm report, which argued that cash burned by dot-com companies was "primarily an investor sentiment issue" and not a long-term risk for the sector.[20]

The bottom line is that valuation standards apply—at least in part—to New Economy stocks, and that stocks must be valued on a rational basis. Revenues and profits do matter and so do P/E ratios, especially when these new economy stocks get too far out of line. For example, at the peak of the Nasdaq market rise, which occurred on March 10, 2000, **Cisco Systems Inc.** had a P/E ratio of about 150, **Yahoo! Inc.** about 650, and **JDS Uniphase Corporation** about 640. One year later, the same companies had P/E ratios of 31, 35, and 41 respectively.

---

[20]This statement and some of the thoughts in this section are based on Gretchen Morgenson, "How Did They Value Stocks? Count the Absurd Ways," *The New York Times*, March 18, 2001.

Some Final Thoughts on Valuation

Valuing stocks is difficult under the best of circumstances. Judgements must be made and variables estimated. No one knows exactly which valuation model should be used for a particular stock. It is almost impossible to prove that an investor's calculations for a valuation model are correct or incorrect (although many calculations could be judged by most people to be "reasonable" or "not reasonable").

In the final analysis, stocks are worth what investors pay for them. Valuations may appear out of line, but market prices prevail.

TRUTH IN THE FINANCIAL MARKETS

Investors seeking to value stocks using valuation principles have a difficult enough job without having to worry about the accuracy of corporate disclosures of important financial information. There have been a number of corporate scandals involving the manipulation of corporate earnings to make them appear more favourable. Prominent cases have included Enron, WorldCom, Nortel, and ImClone.

The manipulation of numbers so that they appear more favourable has serious implications for financial markets, so many hope that these cases and the convictions of a number of top corporate executives will send the message that lying about issues that affect the valuation of a company's shares will not be tolerated. It is unrealistic, of course, to think that the prominent trials and headlines will stop all false statements that are issued by corporate executives, because the potential payoffs are often very large.

DISCUSSION QUESTIONS

1. Why is corporate ethical behaviour and investors' perception of ethical behaviour critical to the orderly functioning of the stock market?

2. Are investors who turn a blind eye to corporate misdeeds in order to earn higher profits just as unethical as the companies they invest in?

3. Will efforts to tighten corporate accountability, such as the Sarbanes-Oxley Act in the US, and a move to adopt international financial reporting standards, help eliminate unethical corporate behaviour?

CHECK YOUR UNDERSTANDING

13-9. What did the extraordinary rise in stock valuations in the late 1990s, ending in March 2000, demonstrate about the valuation of common stock?

SUMMARY

This summary relates to the learning objectives for this chapter.

1. **Name two approaches to the valuation of common stocks used in fundamental security analysis.**

   One commonly employed approach for analyzing and selecting common stocks is fundamental analysis, which should take into account efficient market considerations. Fundamental analysis seeks to estimate the intrinsic value of a stock, which is a function of its expected returns and risk. Two fundamental approaches to determining value are present value and the earnings multiplier (P/E ratio).

2. **Explain the present value approach.**

The present value approach for common stocks is similar to that used with bonds. A required (minimum) expected rate of return must be determined, based on the risk-free rate and a risk premium. As for expected returns, since dividends are the only cash flows directly paid by a corporation, they are the usual choice for expected future cash flows to be discounted in a present value model. However, in Appendix 13B, we discuss the Free Cash Flow valuation approach, which is growing in popularity.

3. **Use the dividend discount model to estimate stock prices.**

According to the dividend discount model, the value of a stock today is the discounted value of all future dividends. This model implicitly accounts for the terminal price of a stock. To account for an infinite stream of dividends, stocks to be valued are classified by their expected growth rate in dividends. If no growth is expected, the dividend discount model reduces perpetuity to a valuation problem. If two or more growth rates are expected, a multiple growth model must be used in which the future stream of dividends is identified before being discounted. The constant-growth version of the dividend discount model is used most frequently. It reduces the ratio of the dividend expected next period to the difference between the required rate of return and the expected growth rate in dividends. The dividend discount model is sensitive to the estimates of the variables used in it; therefore, investors will calculate different prices for the same stock while using an identical model.

4. **Explain the P/E ratio approach.**

The P/E ratio or multiplier approach is based on the identity that a stock's current price is the product of its actual earnings per share and the P/E ratio. It follows that the P/E ratio can be calculated by dividing the current price by the actual earnings per share. To implement the P/E ratio to estimate the value of a stock, we must estimate the earnings and the P/E ratio for the next period. The P/E ratio itself may be expressed as a function of the dividend payout ratio, the required rate of return, and the expected growth rate of dividends (under uncertain conditions). P/E ratios are also inversely related to interest rates because interest rates are directly related to required rates of return.

5. **Outline other relative valuation approaches.**

Other relative valuation approaches include the use of market-to-book ratios, price-to-sales ratios, price-to-cash flow ratios, and price-to-EBIT ratios.

KEY TERMS

Dividend discount model (DDM), p.399

Economic value added (EVA), p.422

Market-to-book ratio (M/B) or Price-to-book value, p.419

P/E ratio (Earnings multiplier), p.414

Perpetuity, p.399

Price/sales (P/S) ratio, p.420

REVIEW QUESTIONS

13-1. What is meant by intrinsic value? How is it determined?

13-2. Why can earnings not be used as readily as dividends in the present value approach?

13-3. What problems are encountered in using the dividend discount model?

13-4. Describe the three possibilities for dividend growth.

13-5. Since dividends are paid to infinity, how is this problem handled in the present value analysis?

13-6. Once an investor calculates intrinsic value for a particular stock, how does he or she decide whether or not to buy it?

13-7. Why is the required rate of return for a stock the discount rate to be used in valuation analysis?

13-8. What is the dividend discount model? Write this model in equation form.

13-9. Demonstrate how the dividend discount model is the same as a method that includes a specified number of dividends and a terminal price.

13-10. How valuable are the P/E ratios reported daily in the financial media?

13-11. What factors affect the P/E ratio? How sensitive is it to these factors?

13-12. Assume that two investors are valuing a company and have both decided to use the constant-growth version of the dividend valuation model. Both use $3 a share as the expected dividend for the coming year. Are these two investors likely to derive different prices? Why or why not?

13-13. Some investors prefer the P/E ratio model to the present value analysis on the grounds that the latter is more difficult to use. State these alleged difficulties and respond to them.

13-14. Indicate the likely direction of change in a stock's P/E ratio, and the reason(s) why, if

    a. The dividend payout decreases.
    b. The required rate of return rises.
    c. The expected growth rate of dividends rises.
    d. The riskless rate of return decreases.

13-15. Indicate the likely direction of change in a stock's M/B ratio, and the reason(s) why, if

    a. The dividend payout decreases.
    b. The required rate of return rises.
    c. The expected growth rate of dividends rises.
    d. The riskless rate of return decreases.
    e. The firm's ROE increases.

13-16. Indicate the likely direction of change in a stock's P/S ratio, and the reason(s) why, if

    a. The dividend payout decreases.
    b. The required rate of return rises.
    c. The expected growth rate of dividends rises.
    d. The riskless rate of return decreases.
    e. The firm's net income margin decreases.

13-17. Which of the following statements concerning price-to-book value is true?

    a. There is an inverse relationship between price-to-book values and market prices.
    b. It is calculated as the ratio of price to the book value of assets.
    c. There is supporting evidence that stocks with low price-to-book values significantly outperform the market.
    d. Price-to-book value ratios for many stocks range from 5.5 to 10.5.

13-18. If the dividend growth rate increases for a firm, its P/E will, other things being the same:

    a. increase.
    b. stay the same.
    c. decrease.
    d. increase or decrease but not stay the same.

13-19. Other things being equal, if the:

    a. required rate of return increases, the P/E ratio will rise.
    b. risk premium increases, the P/E ratio will rise.
    c. risk-free rate rises, the P/E ratio will fall.
    d. dividend payout increases, the P/E ratio will fall.

13-20. In general, are P/E ratios and dividend yields positively or negatively related? Briefly explain why, in either case.

13-21. Assume that you are trying to value a company using relative valuation techniques but the company has no earnings. Which techniques could you use?

13-22. List two advantages of using the price/sales ratio as a valuation technique. How is this ratio calculated without using per-share numbers?

DEMONSTRATION PROBLEMS

13-1. Puglisi Pharmaceuticals is currently paying a dividend of $2 per share, which is not expected to change. Investors require a rate of return of 20 percent to invest in a stock with the riskiness of Puglisi. Calculate the intrinsic value of the stock.

Solution:

The first step to solving a common stock valuation problem is to identify the type of growth involved in the dividend stream. The second step is to determine whether the dividend given in the problem is D_0 or D_1.

In this problem it is clear that the growth rate is zero and that we must solve a zero-growth valuation problem (Equation 13-3). The second step is not relevant here because all of the dividends are the same.

$$\hat{P}_0 = \frac{D_0}{k_{CS}} = \frac{2.00}{0.20} = \$10.00$$

13-2. Richter Construction Company is currently paying a dividend of $2 per share, which is expected to grow at a constant rate of 7 percent per year. Investors require a rate of return of 16 percent to invest in stocks with this degree of riskiness. Calculate the implied price of Richter.

Solution:

Since dividends are expected to grow at a constant rate, we use the constant-growth version of the dividend discount model (Equation 13-5). Note carefully that this equation calls for D_1 in the numerator and that the dividend given in this problem is the current dividend being paid, D_0. Therefore, we must compound this dividend up one period to obtain D_1 before solving the problem.

$$D_1 = D_0 (1 + g) = \$2.00 (1.07) = \$2.14$$

and

$$\hat{P}_0 = \frac{D_1}{k_{CS} - g} = \frac{2.14}{0.16 - 0.07} = \$23.78$$

13-3. Baddour Legal Services is currently selling for $60 per share and is expected to pay a dividend of $3. The expected growth rate in dividends is 8 percent for the foreseeable future. Calculate the required rate of return for this stock.

Solution:

To solve this problem, note first that this is a constant-growth model problem. Second, note that the dividend given in the problem is D_1 because it is stated as the dividend to be paid in the next period. To solve this problem for k, the required rate of return, we simply rearrange Equation 13-5:

$$k_{CS} = \frac{D_1}{P_0} + g = \frac{3.00}{60} + 0.08 = 0.13$$

13-4. Wrenn Restaurants has been undergoing rapid growth for the last few years. The current dividend of $2 per share is expected to continue to grow at the rapid rate of 20 percent a year for the next three years. After that time Wrenn is expected to slow down, with the dividend growing at a more normal rate of 7 percent a year for the indefinite future. Because of the risk involved in such rapid growth, the required rate of return on this stock is 22 percent. Calculate the implied price for this stock.

Solution:

We can recognize at once that this is a multiple-growth case of valuation because more than one growth rate is given. To solve for the value of this stock, it is necessary to identify the entire stream of future dividends from Year 1 to infinity, and discount the entire stream back to time period zero. After the third year a constant growth model can be used that accounts for all dividends from the beginning of Year 4 to infinity.

First, estimate dividends up to the start of constant growth to infinity by compounding the beginning dividend, $2, at 20 percent for each of three years, which produces the following:

$$D_1 = \$2.00\,(1 + 0.20) = \$2.40$$
$$D_2 = \$2.00\,(1 + 0.20)^2 = \$2.88$$
$$D_3 = \$2.00\,(1 + 0.20)^3 = \$3.456$$

Second, estimate the price at the beginning of constant growth to infinity period

$$\hat{P}_3 = \frac{D_4}{k_{CS} - g} = \frac{(3.456)(1.07)}{0.22 - 0.07} = \$24.653$$

Third, discount back the relevant cash flows to time 0 and sum

$$\hat{P}_0 = \frac{2.40}{(1.22)^1} + \frac{2.88}{(1.22)^2} + \frac{3.456}{(1.22)^3} + \frac{24.653}{(1.22)^3}$$

$$= 1.967 + 1.935 + 1.903 + 13.577 = \$19.38$$

13-5. Company BDC has an expected dividend payout ratio of 0.43 next year, and their dividends are expected to grow at an annual rate of 8 percent to infinity. The required rate of return on their shares is 11.81 percent, and the expected EPS is $3.45.

a. Using the information above, determine an appropriate P/E multiple based on company fundamentals, and estimate an appropriate share price for BDC.

b. Re-estimate the value of BDC's shares based on their five-year average P/E ratio of 8.62.

c. Repeat using the average industry P/E ratio of 8.83.

Solution:

$$P/E = \frac{D_1/E_1}{k_{CS} - g} = \frac{0.43}{0.1181 - 0.08} = 11.29$$

a. Based on this multiple, BDC's shares are worth

$$P_0 = (P/E) \times (EPS_1) = (11.29)\,(\$3.45) = \$38.95$$

b. Based on BDC's historical P/E multiple of 8.62, BDC's shares are worth

$$P_0 = (P/E) \times (EPS_1) = (8.62)\,(\$3.45) = \$29.74$$

c. Based on the industry average P/E multiple, BDC's shares are worth

$$P_0 = (P/E) \times (EPS_1) = (8.83)\,(\$3.45) = \$30.46$$

PROBLEMS

13-1. Billingsley Products is currently selling for $45 a share with an expected dividend in the coming year of $2 per share. If the growth rate in dividends expected by investors is 5 percent to infinity, what is the implied required rate of return for this stock?

13-2. Assume that Chance Industries is expected by investors to have a dividend growth rate over the foreseeable future of 6 percent a year and that the required rate of return for this stock is 13 percent. The current dividend being paid (D_0) is $2.25. What is the price of the stock?

13-3. Mittra Motors is currently selling for $50 per share and pays $3 in dividends ($D_0$). Investors require 15 percent return on this stock. What is the expected perpetual growth rate of dividends?

13-4. Howe Poultry pays $1.50 a year in dividends, which is expected to remain unchanged. Investors require a 15 percent rate of return on this stock. What is its price?

13-5. Refer to Appendix 13A for this question.

    a. Given a preferred stock with an annual dividend of $3 per share and a price of $40, what is the required rate of return?

    b. Assume now that interest rates rise, leading investors to demand a required rate of return of 9 percent. What will be the new price of this preferred stock?

13-6. The required rate of return for Peterson Industries is 15.75 percent. The stock pays a current dividend of $1.30, and the expected annual growth rate is 5.5 percent to infinity. Calculate the intrinsic value.

13-7. In Problem 13-6, assume that the expected annual growth rate is 7 percent to infinity. Calculate the intrinsic value for this stock.

13-8. Brockbank Computer Suppliers is currently paying a dividend of $1.60 per year, and this dividend is expected to grow at a constant rate of 4 percent a year forever. Investors require a 16 percent rate of return on Brockbank. What is its estimated price?

13-9. Wilson Industries is currently paying a dividend of $1 per share, which is not expected to change in the future. The current price of this stock is $12. What is the implied required rate of return on this stock?

13-10. Cascade Gas is currently selling for $40. Its current dividend is $2, and this dividend is expected to grow at a rate of 7 percent a year forever. What is the expected rate of return for this stock?

13-11. General Foods is currently selling for $50. It is expected to pay a dividend of $2 next period. If the required rate of return is 10 percent, what is the expected perpetual growth rate?

13-12. An investor purchases the common stock of a well-known house builder, DeMong Construction Company, for $25 per share. The expected dividend for the next year is $3 per share, and the investor is confident that the stock can be sold one year from now for $30. What is the implied required rate of return?

13-13.   a. The current risk-free rate (RF) is 10 percent, and the expected return on the market for the coming year is 15 percent. Calculate the required rate of return for

      i. stock A, with a beta of 1.0
      ii. stock B, with a beta of 1.7
      iii. stock C, with a beta of 0.8.

    b. How would your answers change if RF in part (a) were to increase to 12 percent, with the other variables unchanged?

    c. How would your answers change if the expected return on the market changed to 17 percent with the other variables unchanged?

13-14. Wingler Company is currently selling for $36, paying $1.80 in dividends, and investors expect dividends to grow at a constant rate of 5 percent a year forever. CEO Tony Wingler believes the stock is undervalued.

    a. If an investor requires a rate of return of 14 percent for a stock with the riskiness of Wingler Company, is it a good buy for this investor?

    b. What is the maximum an investor with a 14 percent required return should pay for Wingler Company? What is the maximum if the required return is 15 percent?

13-15. The Hall Dental Supply Company sells at $32 per share, and CEO Randy Hall estimates the latest 12-month earnings are $4 per share with a dividend payout of 50 percent.

    a. What is Hall's current P/E ratio?

    b. If an investor expects earnings to grow by 6 percent a year forever, what is the projected price for next year if the P/E ratio remains unchanged?

    c. Ray Parker, president of Hall Dental Supply, analyzes the data and estimates that the payout ratio will remain the same. Assume the expected growth rate of dividends is 6 percent per year forever, and an investor has a required rate of return of 16 percent. Would this stock be a good buy? Why or why not?

    d. If interest rates are expected to decline, what is the likely effect on Hall's P/E ratio?

13-16. McEnally Motorcycles is a rapidly growing firm. Dividends are expected to grow at the rate of 18 percent annually for the next 10 years. The growth rate after the first 10 years is expected to be 7 percent annually to infinity. The current dividend is $1.82. Investors require a rate of return of 19 percent on this stock. Calculate the intrinsic value of this stock.

13-17. BSC Ltd. is expected to earn $2 per share next year. BSC has a payout ratio of 40 percent. Earnings and dividends have been growing at a constant rate of 10 percent per year, but analysts are estimating that the growth rate will be 7 percent a year for the indefinite future. Investors require a 15 percent rate of return on BSC. What is its estimated price?

13-18. General Foundries is expected to pay a dividend of $0.60 next year, $1.10 the following year, and $1.25 each year thereafter. The required rate of return on this stock is 18 percent. How much should investors be willing to pay for this stock?

13-19. Griggs Company is not expected to pay a dividend until five years have elapsed. At the beginning of Year 6, investors expect the dividend to be $3 per share and to remain at that amount forever. If an investor has a 25 percent required rate of return for this stock, what should he or she be willing to pay for Griggs?

13-20. Poindexter Industries is expected to pay a dividend of $10 per year for 10 years and then increase the dividend to $15 per share for every year thereafter. The required rate of return on this stock is 20 percent. What is the estimated stock price for Poindexter?

13-21. Roenfeldt Components recently paid a dividend of $1 per share. This dividend is expected to grow at a rate of 25 percent a year for the next five years, after which it is expected to grow at a rate of 7 percent a year forever. The required rate of return for this stock is 18 percent. What is the estimated price of the stock?

13-22. Agrawa Corporation makes advanced computer components. It pays no dividends currently, but it expects to begin paying $1 per share four years from now. The expected dividends in subsequent years are also $1 per share. The required rate of return is 14 percent. What is the estimated price for Agrawa?

13-23. Rader Chocolate Company is currently selling for $60 and is paying a $3 dividend.

    a. If investors expect dividends to double in 12 years, what is the required rate of return for this stock?

    b. If investors had expected dividends to approximately triple in six years, what would be the required rate of return?

13-24. Avera Free Range Poultry is currently paying a dividend of $1.20. This dividend is expected to grow at the rate of 30 percent a year for the next five years, followed by a growth rate of 20 percent a year for the following five years. After 10 years the dividend is expected to grow at the rate of 6 percent a year forever. CEO Bill Avera estimates that the required rate of return for this stock is 21 percent. What is its intrinsic value?

13-25. In Problem 13-24, assume that the growth rate for the first five years is 25 percent rather than 30 percent. How would you expect the value calculated in Problem 13-24 to change? Confirm your answer by calculating the new intrinsic value.

13-26. Rocky Mountain Power and Gas is currently paying a dividend of $1.80. This dividend is expected to grow at a rate of 6 percent in the foreseeable future. Rocky Mountain Power is 10 percent less risky than the market as a whole. The market risk premium is 7 percent, and the risk-free rate is 5 percent. What is the estimated price of this stock?

13-27. Rendleman Software is expected to enjoy a very rapid growth rate in dividends of 30 percent a year for the next three years. This growth rate is then expected to slow to 20 percent a year for the next five years. After that time, the growth rate is expected to level out at 6 percent a year forever. D_0 is $2. The required rate of return is 20 percent. What is the estimated price of the stock?

13-28. Poindexter Industries is expected to pay a dividend of $10 per year for 10 years and then increase the dividend to $15 per share for every year thereafter. The required rate of return on this stock is 20 percent. What is the estimated stock price for Poindexter?

13-29. SLC Ltd. has an expected Year 1 EPS of $3.45, an expected Year 1 payout ratio of 0.456, and an expected annual growth rate in dividends to infinity of 8 percent. Shareholders require a 9.68 percent return on these shares. SLC's five-year average P/E ratio is 26.68, and the present industry average P/E ratio is 27.93. Determine three estimates of SLC's value.

13-30. Using the information for SLC Ltd. provided in Problem 13-29, and assuming the company's most recent ROE was 17.92 percent, and that its current book value per share (BV_0) is $17.86, determine the value of SLC based on the M/B ratio approach.

13-31. Using the information for SLC Ltd. provided in Problem 13-29, and assuming the company's most recent net income margin (NI%) was 3.31 percent, and that its most recent sales per share ($Sales_0$) is $85.71, determine the value of SLC based on the P/S ratio approach.

13-32. Bilco Limited has a policy of paying out 60 percent of its earnings as cash dividends to its shareholders. Bilco recently paid out a $3 per share annual dividend. The required rate of return on stocks with similar risk is 13 percent. Bilco's earnings and dividends are expected to grow at an annual rate of 8 percent forever.

    a. What is Bilco's implied P/E ratio?

    b. If Bilco changed its policy to one where it paid out 80 percent of its earnings as dividends, what would Bilco's implied P/E ratio be?

13-33. Ladslow Incorporated has a required rate of return of 14 percent, and expects that its earnings and dividends will grow at an annual rate of 6 percent forever. Its dividend payout ratio is 40 percent. Ladslow's most recent return-on-equity (ROE) was 20 percent.

    a. What is the implied market-to-book (M/B) ratio?

    b. If the company has assets of $1,000,000 (book value), has 100,000 shares outstanding, and has no debt, what should the price per share be?

13-34. Using the Price/Sales (P/S) ratio approach, what should a company's stock price be, based on the following information: required rate of return of 16 percent; perpetual annual growth rate of earnings and dividends of 6 percent; assets of $100,000,000 (book value); no debt; 20,000,000 shares outstanding; most recent annual sales of $50,000,000; most recent net income of $5,000,000; 50 percent dividend payout ratio.

13-35. The stock for Crazy Horse Corporation is trading at $75. The firm paid out $2.20 in dividends during the last year. If the payout ratio of the firm is 45 percent, what is the price-earnings ratio that will be reported to the pubic?

13-36. The current market price of the stock of Stryker Ltd. is $30 per share. The company just paid a dividend of $0.50 per share last year. If its return on assets (ROA) is 5 percent, its leverage ratio is 2, and its EPS was $2.00 last year, what is the implied rate of return assuming dividends are growing at a constant rate?

 13-37. WestTec Corporation, a technology company, has been growing rapidly. After examining the company's operations very carefully, analysts at Meril Link have estimated that dividends and earnings will grow at a rate of 22 percent a year for the next 8 years, followed by 16 percent growth for another 6 years. After 14 years, the expected growth rate is 5 percent. The risk-free rate appropriate for this analysis is 5.5 percent, and the expected return on the market is 10.5 percent. The beta for WestTec is 1.1. It currently pays a dividend of $1.10. Using the spreadsheet format below, estimate the intrinsic value of this stock today. Note the following:

a. Calculate the required rate of return for WestTec in cell H2 using the CAPM.
b. Calculate the dollar amount of each dividend for the first 14 years in cells B5 through B18, and the present value of these amounts in cells C5 through C18. Be sure to allow for the change in growth rates in year 9.
c. In cell G19, calculate the price of the stock at the beginning of year 15 using the then constant-growth rate of 5 percent.
d. In cell G20, discount the price found in (c) back to today using the proper number of periods for discounting.
e. Sum the present value of the dividends in cell C21. Add to this the present value of the price found in (d) by putting this value in C22.
f. In cell C23, add the values found in (e) in cell C24.

Curr div		Ist gr rate	2nd gr rate	normal gr	RF	Exp Mk Rt	Beta	k
	1.1	0.22	0.16	0.05	5.5	10.5	1.1	0.11
		8yrs	6yrs					
Year		Dividend	PV of Div					
1								
2								
3								
4								
5								
6								
7								
8								
9								
10								
11								
12								
13								
14								
				Price at beginning of year 15 =		0.00		
				PV of price today =		0.00		
			Sum of PV of dividends for first 14 years				0.00	
			+ PV of price at beginning of year 15				0.00	
			Sum of PV of dividends and PV of price				0.00	

13-38. Zoom Boards Inc. designs high-end skateboards. Sales have been growing rapidly, and with cash rolling in, the Board of Directors has decided to begin paying dividends to the company's shareholders. Each year, the dividend payout ratio will be 60 percent of net income. Assume that the shareholders have a required return of 12 percent on this stock.

   a. It is now October 1, 2008; Zoom has just declared its first dividend of $0.30 per share to be paid in one year. Analysts expect dividends to increase by $0.15 per year for another two years. After 2011 (when the dividend will be $0.60 per share), dividend growth is expected to settle down to a more moderate long-term rate of 5 percent. How much are the shares worth today?

   b. The management of Zoom is confident that the current level of earnings can be maintained without investing in new assets (i.e., the full amount of earnings could be paid out as dividends). What share price would this no-growth situation imply? What is the value of the growth opportunities (PVGO) built into the share price from part (a)?

   c. Suppose the long-term growth rate is projected to be only 4 percent. What is the impact on the current share price and the value PVGO? What percentage change in these values does the small change in the growth rate create? Repeat these calculations assuming a growth rate of 6 percent.

13-39. Morton's Clothing store has experienced some operating difficulties in recent years. As a result, the stock price has fallen below $20 per share, and the company is thought to be a take-over candidate. The company has 68,200 shares outstanding with a book value of $2,615,200 and no long-term debt. A Pro Forma Income Statement for the upcoming year is presented below.

   a. Use the ratios provided for Elegant Fashions Inc., a comparable firm, to determine a range of share prices that might be justified for Morton's.

   b. Use the free cash flow to the firm (FCFF) method presented in Appendix 13B to find the highest share price that you would be willing to pay for this company. You can make the following assumptions about the company's future operations.

     • In the upcoming year, the increase in net working capital will be $48,000 and capital expenditures will total $140,000.

     • Free cash flow will grow at a perpetual rate of 3.5 percent per year after next year.

     • Risk-free-rate = 4.5%; expected return on market = 10%; beta =1.10.

     • All cash flows occur at the end of the year.

Ratio	Value for Elegant
P/E (forward)	20.8
Price / Sales	0.50
Price / Book	1.25

Pro Forma Income Statement for Morton's Clothing

Revenues	$ 7,300,000
Expenses	6,955,400
EBITDA	344,600
Depreciation	194,620
EBIT	149,980
Income Taxes	37,495
Net Income	112,485

PREPARING FOR YOUR PROFESSIONAL EXAMS

CFA PRACTICE QUESTIONS

13-1. An analyst has gathered the following data about a stock:

The stock paid a $1 dividend last year.

Next year's dividend is projected to be 10 percent higher.

The stock is projected to sell for $25 at the end of the year.

The risk-free rate of interest is 8 percent and the market return is 13 percent.

The stock's beta is 1.2.

What is the value of the stock?

   a. $19.45

   b. $22.89

   c. $24.00

   d. $26.74

13-2. Use the following data to analyze a stock's P/E ratio:

The stock's beta is 1.2.

The dividend payout ratio is 60 percent.

The stock's expected growth rate is 7 percent.

The risk-free rate is 6 percent and the expected rate of return on the market is 13 percent.

Using the dividend discount model, what would you expect the stock's P/E ratio to be?

   a. 5.4

   b. 8.1

   c. 10.0

   d. 12.0

13-3. Assuming all other factors remain unchanged, which of the following would reduce a company's P/E ratio?

   a. The dividend growth rate increases.

   b. The dividend payout ratio increases.

   c. The company's beta increases.

   d. The company's return on equity is expected to increase.

13-4. A company's stock is selling for $45 per share. The firm's earnings and dividends have been growing at an annual rate of 8 percent, and this growth is expected to continue in the future. The firm's earnings per share this past year was $5, and it maintains a 40 percent dividend payout policy. Based on the dividend discount model, what rate of return are stockholders requiring?

   a. 4.5 percent

   b. 8.0 percent

   c. 12.8 percent

   d. 14.2 percent

13-5. A stock is not expected to pay dividends for the next four years. However, it is expected to pay a $0.50 dividend five years from today with dividends expected to grow at 5 percent per year thereafter. What is the price of the stock if the required rate of return is 12 percent?

   a. $7.14

   b. $4.05

   c. $4.54

   d. $4.77

CFA CURRICULUM AND SAMPLE EXAM QUESTIONS (©CFA INSTITUTE)

13-1. An analyst made the following statement: "According to empirical research, differences in both price-to-earnings ratios and price-to-book value ratios may be related to differences in long-run average common stock returns." Is the analyst's statement correct with respect to:

Price-to-earnings ratios?	Price-to-book value ratios?
a. No	No
b. No	Yes
c. Yes	No
d. Yes	Yes

13-2. An analyst gathered the following per-share data about a company for a given year:

Market value of common stock at end of year	$55
Unadjusted book value of common stock at end of year	$25
Adjusted book value of common stock at end of year	$28
Gross sales for year	$48
Net sales for year	$44
Cash flow for year	$7
Earnings for year	$3
Forecasted earnings for next year	$4

What should be the analyst's year-end estimate of the company's

Price-to-sales ratios?	Price-to-book value ratios?
a. 1.15	1.12
b. 1.15	1.96
c. 1.25	1.12
d. 1.25	1.96

13-3. An analyst made the following statement: "When using either price-to-earnings ratios or price-to-cash-flow ratios, differences among companies with respect to quality of earnings are not a major concern." Is the analyst's statement correct with respect to:

Price-to-earnings ratios?	Price-to-cash-flow ratios?
a. No	No
b. No	Yes
c. Yes	No
d. Yes	Yes

13-4. An analyst made the following statement: "Neither price-to-book value ratios nor price-to-sales ratios are useful in valuing firms whose earnings are abnormally high or low." Is the analyst's statement correct with respect to:

Price-to-book value ratios?	Price-to-sales ratios?
a. No	No
b. No	Yes
c. Yes	No
d. Yes	Yes

13-5. An analyst made the following statement: "Compared with price-to-earnings ratios, price-to-sales ratios and price-to-cash-flow ratios are generally less subject to distortion or manipulation." The analyst's statement is correct with respect to:

    a. price-to-sales ratios, but not price-to-cash-flow ratios.

    b. price-to-cash-flow ratios, but not price-to-sales ratios.

    c. both price-to-sales ratios and price-to-cash-flow ratios.

    d. neither price-to-sales ratios nor price-to-cash-flow ratios.

13-6. An analyst gathered the following information about Fallow Corporation:

Current dividend per share	$1.00
Required rate of return	15%
Expected annual growth rate for the next two years	20%
Expected annual growth rate for year three and thereafter	20%

The value of a share of Fallow's common stock is *closest* to:

    a. $10.50.

    b. $12.00.

    c. $13.55.

    d. $15.21.

APPENDIX 13A

THE ANALYSIS AND VALUATION OF PREFERRED STOCK

In Chapter 2, preferred stock was classified for investment analysis purposes as a fixed-income security, although technically it is an equity security. It is best described as a hybrid security, having some characteristics similar to fixed-income securities (i.e., bonds) and some similar to common stocks.

Analysis

Preferred stock can be described as a perpetuity, or perpetual security, since it has no maturity date, and it will pay the indicated dividend forever. Although perpetual, many preferred stock issues carry a sinking fund, which provides for early retirement of the issue, usually over a period of many years. Furthermore, many preferred stocks are callable by the issuer, which also potentially limits the life of preferreds. Finally, roughly half of all preferred stocks issued in recent years are convertible into common stock. Therefore, although preferred stock is perpetual by definition, in reality many of the issues will not remain in existence forever.

Dividends from preferred stock, unlike those from common stock, are fixed when the stock is issued and do not change. These dividends are specified as an annual dollar amount (although paid quarterly) or as a percentage of par value, which is often either $25 or $100. The issuer can forgo paying the preferred dividend if earnings are insufficient. Although this dividend is specified, failure to pay it does not result in default of the obligation, as is the case with bonds. However, most preferred issues have a cumulative feature, which requires that all unpaid preferred dividends, both current and arrears, must be paid before those for common stocks.

Investors regard preferred stock as less risky than common stock because the dividend is specified and must be paid before a common stock dividend can be paid. They regard preferreds as more risky than bonds, however, because bondholders have priority in being paid and in case of liquidation. That is why investors require higher rates of return on preferred stock than on bonds but a smaller required return than on common stocks. However, since most dividends received by individuals qualify for the dividend tax credit, they are taxed at a lower rate than interest income. As a result of this tax advantage, preferred stocks often carry slightly lower yields than bonds of comparable quality.

Valuation

The value of any perpetuity can be calculated as follows:

$$V_p = \frac{C}{(1 + k_p)^1} + \frac{C}{(1 + k_p)^2} + \cdots + \frac{C}{(1 + k_p)^\infty}$$ (13-23)

$$= \frac{C}{k_p}$$

where

V_p = the value of a perpetuity today
C = the constant annual payment to be received
k_p = the required rate of return appropriate for this perpetuity

Because the dividends provided by a straight preferred share represent a perpetuity, Equation 13-23 is applicable in its valuation. We simply substitute the preferred dividend (D) for C and the appropriate required return (k_{ps}) for k_p, resulting in Equation 13-24.[21]

$$V_{ps} = \frac{D}{k_{ps}}$$ (13-24)

A preferred stock, or any perpetuity, is easy to value because the numerator of Equation 13-24 is known and fixed forever. No complex present value calculations are needed for a perpetuity, which simplifies the valuation process considerably. If any two of the values in 13-24 are known, the third can easily be found.

As an example of the valuation analysis, consider preferred shares with a fixed annual dividend of $1.93. To value this preferred, investors need to estimate the required rate of return appropriate for its degree of riskiness. Suppose the required rate of return (k_{ps}), is 10 percent. The value of this preferred would be

$$V_{ps} = \frac{D}{k_{ps}} = \frac{1.93}{0.10} = \$19.30$$

On the other hand, a required rate of return of 11 percent would result in a value of $17.54.

If the current price for this preferred, as observed in the marketplace (P_{ps}), is substituted into Equation 13-24 for V_{ps}, the yield can be solved by using Equation 13-25.

$$k_{ps} = \frac{D}{P_{ps}}$$ (13-25)

In the case of the company above, if we observed a price of $27, this implies the yield, or required rate of return, is 7.15 percent.

$$k_{ps} = \frac{D}{P_{ps}} = \frac{1.93}{27.00} = 0.0715$$

Notice from Equation 13-24 that as the required rate of return rises, the price of the preferred stock declines; obviously, the converse is also true. Because the numerator is fixed, the value (price) of a

---

[21]Notice that this equation is identical to the no-growth version of the DDM expressed in Equation 13-3, with D= D_0 and k_{ps} = k_{CS}. This is because the dividend paid on a preferred share is a constant, or given amount.

preferred stock changes as the required rate of return changes. Clearly, investors' required rates of return fluctuate across time as interest rates and other factors change. As rates fluctuate, so do preferred stock prices. In fact, because they are fixed income securities with no maturity date, we observe that their prices will be extremely sensitive to changes in the level of interest rates, similar to long-term bonds.

CHAPTER 14

COMMON STOCKS: ANALYSIS AND STRATEGY

Given your new $1 million portfolio, you will need to manage it. You now realize that the market has a substantial impact on individual stocks and portfolios, and therefore you realize you need to better understand the impact of the overall market on individual stocks. Also, you now appreciate the role the required rate of return plays when evaluating stocks, another issue you decide warrants additional analysis. Both issues are considered here.

One of the most important decisions each investor must make is whether to take an active approach or a passive approach to investing. A passive approach will save costs and will often produce as good or better results as an active approach. Or, if you choose an active approach, you will need to give some thought to whether you want to select stocks or try to time the market. These issues will be covered here.

Learning Objectives

After reading this chapter, you should be able to

1. Discuss the impact of the overall market on common stock investors.
2. Explain the importance of the required rate of return.
3. Distinguish between passive and active investment strategies.
4. Differentiate between technical and fundamental analysis.
5. Describe the bottom-up and top-down approaches in fundamental analysis.

CHAPTER PREVIEW

This chapter covers the analysis and strategy for selecting and holding common stocks. Similar to the passive approach to bond investing, common stock investors can follow a buy-and-hold strategy, or buy index funds or exchange-traded funds that mimic some market index. Under the active approach, we analyze the primary alternatives of stock selection, sector rotation, and market timing and consider the implications of the Efficient Market Hypothesis (which was discussed in Chapter 10). We conclude by considering the two basic methods used in security analysis: technical and fundamental analysis.

TAKING A GLOBAL PERSPECTIVE

In the New Economy, investors cross borders more and more when they invest. And the investing is more sophisticated. Rather than start with a portfolio of Canadian-listed stocks and add selected foreign equities, investors today search for the truly "good" companies (e.g., industry giants, innovative leaders, those with proven track records), regardless of the country in which they are located. What matters today is being a world leader, whether that is Cisco Systems Inc. in the United States or Nokia in Finland. When it comes to important sectors such as pharmaceuticals and telecommunications, globalization is the name of the game.

Many Canadian investors have traditionally been myopic, focusing only on companies they are familiar with, such as Nortel Networks, Bombardier Inc., or The Bank of Nova Scotia. Although this has paid off some of the time, this will not always be the case. Even though Canadian equities have outperformed many foreign equity markets since 1990, they have also underperformed several others. Regardless of this historical performance, we are now in an age of globalization, and investors should therefore take a global perspective.

How much of a Canadian investor's portfolio should be allocated to foreign securities? A general consensus among market observers is that a typical investor should have 10 to 20 percent of his/her portfolio in international markets. However, many suggest that much higher proportions are reasonable. In fact, many experts suggest that it is difficult to construct a portfolio that is well-diversified across industry sectors using only Canadian companies, because of the small number of "quality" companies we have at any given time in a particular industry. Of course, all foreign markets are not the same. Emerging markets are generally much riskier than developed economies and investors should probably not have a large percentage of their portfolio in emerging markets.

SOME IMPORTANT ISSUES INVOLVING COMMON STOCKS

In Chapter 11 we analyzed bonds in terms of interest rates because of the fundamental relationship between interest rates and bond prices. In similar fashion, we now consider the impact of market risk on common stock investors. The impact of the market on every investor in common stocks is pervasive and dominant and must be fully appreciated by investors if they are to be successful.

We also consider the required rate of return in detail. This variable is important in any analysis of common stocks. As we saw in Chapter 13, the required rate of return is a very important component of the valuation process using the dividend discount model, as well as in other valuation approaches.

The Impact of the Overall Market on Individual Stocks

learning objective 1
Discuss the impact of the overall market on common stock investors.

Overall, market risk is the single most important risk affecting the price movements of common stocks. The aggregate market remains the largest single factor explaining fluctuations in both individual stock prices and portfolios of stocks. This is particularly true for a diversified portfolio of stocks, and as we know, the basic tenet of portfolio theory is to diversify into a number of properly chosen securities. For adequately diversified portfolios, market effects often account for 90 percent and more of the variability in the portfolio's return. In other words, for a well-diversified portfolio, the market is the dominant factor affecting the variability of its return. Although any given portfolio may clearly outperform the market, it will usually be significantly influenced by what happens on an overall basis.

EXAMPLE 14-1: MARKET RISK AND AIC ADVANTAGE EQUITY FUND

Consider the performance of **AIC Advantage Equity Fund** over a specific five-year period, as shown in Figure 14-1. This fund, part of the well-known AIC family of funds, invests primarily in Canadian common shares. Notice that although this fund underperformed the aggregate market (as measured by the S&P/TSX Composite Index), with an average annual return of 9.33 percent versus 18.49 percent for the S&P/TSX Total Return Index over this period, its movements roughly paralleled those of the market.

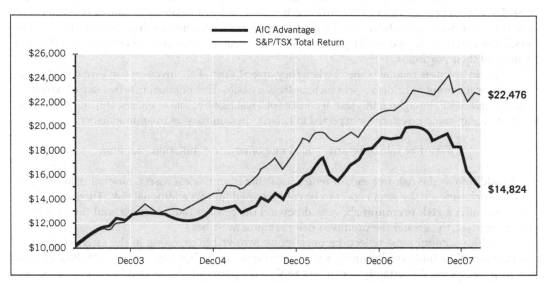

Figure 14-1
Returns for a Well-Diversified Portfolio and the S&P/TSX Composite Index

Source: Globefund website: www.globefund.com. Reprinted with permission from *The Globe and Mail*.

The International Perspective

Canadian investors buying foreign stocks face the same issues as they do at home when it comes to market risk. Some of these markets have performed very well, and some have performed poorly over specified periods of time. The investor fortunate enough to have invested in the Bolivian stock market in 2000 experienced an average gain of more than 160 percent, whereas in the South Korean market he or she would have lost about 51 percent during the same period. Many foreign markets are even more volatile than our own. For example, during 2007, the returns for the Chinese stock market were 63.1 percent and those in India were 71.2 percent; however, from January 1 to late October in 2008, the Chinese and Indian markets had declined 68 and 59 percent respectively.

Perhaps the best foreign example of the impact of the overall market on investors is Japan, clearly an economic superpower. In the 1980s, Japan seemed invincible in its economic performance, and its stock market, as measured by the Nikkei stock index, reflected Japan's success with seemingly unending rises in stock prices. By the 1990s, however, this situation had changed dramatically, with assets in Japan down sharply from the previous record levels.

> ### EXAMPLE 14-2: IMPACT OF FOREIGN MARKETS—THE NIKKEI
>
> The Nikkei stock index described in Chapter 4 peaked at the end of 1989 at a level of almost 39,000. By mid-1992, the index had declined below the 15,000 level, representing a staggering decline of some 60 percent. As one well-known magazine put it, this was the "biggest erasure of wealth in history." The Japanese stock market continued its slump, falling below 8,000 in the spring of 2003. It has recovered a significant amount since then and was just under 14,000 by April 2008.

The Required Rate of Return

learning objective 2
Explain the importance of the required rate of return.

Required Rate of Return
The minimum expected rate of return necessary to induce an investor to purchase a security.

The required rate of return was used in the previous chapter as the discount rate for valuing common stocks and in Chapter 11 to determine the price of a bond. Recall that the **required rate of return** for any security is defined as the minimum expected rate of return needed to induce an investor to purchase it. That is, given its risk, a security must offer some minimum expected return before a particular investor can be persuaded to buy it.

This discussion is directly related to the Capital Asset Pricing Model (CAPM) discussion in Chapter 9. The CAPM provides investors with a method of actually calculating a required (expected) rate of return for a stock, an industry, or the market as a whole. Our interest here is to think of the required rate of return on an overall basis as it affects the strategies that investors employ and the management of their portfolios.

What do investors require (expect) when they invest? First of all, investors can earn a riskless rate of return by investing in riskless assets such as Treasury bills. This nominal risk-free rate of return has been designated RF throughout this text. It consists of a real risk-free rate of interest and an inflation premium (to compensate investors for expected inflation).[1] In summary, as an approximation,[2]

(14-1)
$$\text{Risk-free rate of return} = \text{Real rate of return} + \text{Inflation premium}$$

In addition to the risk-free rate of return available from riskless assets, rational risk-averse investors purchasing a risky asset expect to be compensated for this additional risk. Therefore, a risky asset must offer a **risk premium** above and beyond the riskless rate of return, and the greater the risk of the asset, the greater the promised risk premium must be.

Risk Premium
That part of a security's return above the risk-free rate of return. The greater the risk of the asset, the greater the associated risk premium.

The risk premium must reflect the uncertainty involved in investing in the asset. Thinking of risk in terms of its traditional sources, such components as the business risk and the financial risk of a corporation would certainly contribute to the risk premium demanded by investors for purchasing the common stock of the corporation. After all, the risk to the investor is that the expected income (return) will not be realized because of unforeseen events.

The particular industry in which a company operates will significantly affect the risk to the investor. For example, data from the S&P/TSX Composite Index showed that information technology companies comprised the worst performing industry in 2002 with a loss of 59.0 percent, while gold companies represented the top-performing industry with a return of 42.5 percent. However, in 2003, information technology was the second-best performing industry category, with a return of +59.3 percent, while gold was the worst performing industry with a return of 13.6 percent, well below the S&P/TSX Composite Index return of 24.3 percent. Similarly, energy stocks were the top performers in 2005 with average returns of 61.3 percent, but were well below average in 2006 and were slightly

---

[1] The real risk-free rate of interest (i.e., the real time value of money) is the basic exchange rate in the economy or the price necessary to induce someone to forego consumption and save in order to consume more in the next period. It is defined within a context of no uncertainty and no inflation.

[2] The more precise calculation involves adding 1.0 to both the real rate and the inflation premium, multiplying the two together, and subtracting the 1.0 from the product. For example, assuming a real rate of 2 percent and an inflation rate of 5 percent:

$$(1 + \text{RF}) = (1 + \text{Real rate})(1 + \text{Inflation premium}) = (1 + 0.02)(1 + 0.05) = (1.071).$$

This implies RF = 0.071, or 7.1%.

below average in 2007, providing returns of 3.2 and 8.2 percent respectively, versus TSX returns of 17.3 and 9.8 percent.

In addition to business risk, the financial decisions that a firm makes (or fails to make) will also affect the riskiness of the stock.

Understanding the Required Rate of Return

The required rate of return for any investment opportunity can be expressed as Equation 14-2. One commonly used version of this equation is the CAPM, and another variation is the Fama and French three-factor model, both discussed in Chapter 9.

$$\text{Required rate of return} = \text{Risk-free rate} + \text{Risk premium}$$ **(14-2)**

It is important to note that there are many financial assets and therefore many different required rates of return. The average required rate of return on bonds is different from that on preferred stocks, and both are different from what is generally required from common stocks, warrants, or puts and calls. Furthermore, within a particular asset category such as common stocks, there are many required rates of return. Common stocks cover a relatively wide range of risk, from conservative utility stocks to small, risky high-technology stocks.

It is also important to be aware that the level of required rates of return changes over time. For example, required rates of return change with inflationary expectations, because the inflation premium is a component of the risk-free rate of return, which, in turn, is a component of the required rate of return. The level also changes as the risk premiums change. Investor pessimism will increase the risk premium and the required rate; investor optimism lowers both.

Risk and the Required Rate of Return

We know from Chapter 9 that the CAPM suggests the trade-off between the required rate of return and risk is linear and upward sloping, as shown in Figure 14-2. In other words, the required rate of return increases as the risk, measured by beta, increases. Taken as a whole, the stock market has a beta of 1.0, indicated by Point M in the diagram. The required rate of return for all stocks is therefore k_m. Stock C, with a beta lower than 1.0, has a required rate of return below k_m because its risk (beta) is less than that of the market. On the other hand, a stock with a beta greater than 1.0 has a required rate of return greater than that of the market. Stock A has a beta of 2.0 and Stock B a beta of 1.5.

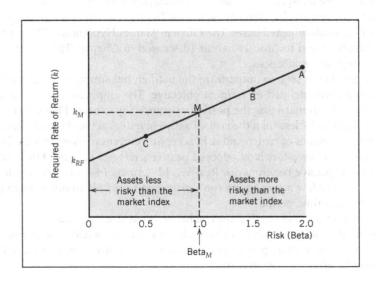

Figure 14-2
Required Rate of Return
Versus Risk for Common
Stocks

CHECK YOUR UNDERSTANDING

14-1. Suppose you knew with certainty that the next three years would be strong up years for the stock market. Assuming that you are willing to hold common stocks, would you be comfortable letting someone choose for you a broadly diversified subsample of the S&P/TSX Composite Index?

14-2. If you expect a severe gasoline shortage for a period of a few months, what would you predict will happen to the required rate of return for stocks?

BUILDING STOCK PORTFOLIOS

learning objective 3
Distinguish between passive and active investment strategies.

We now consider how investors go about selecting stocks to be held in portfolios. As noted in Chapter 8, individual investors often consider the investment decision as consisting of two steps:

1. Asset allocation

2. Security selection

We will assume that the asset allocation decision has been made so that our focus is only on common stocks. The common stock portion could constitute 100 percent of the total portfolio or some other percentage an investor chooses. For example, the **AIC Advantage Equity Fund** discussed in Example 14-1 consisted of 99.33 percent equity, 0.28 percent other assets, and 0.39 percent cash and short-term securities as of March 31, 2008.

Recall that in our discussion of bond strategies we considered the passive and active approaches. These are also applicable to investors as they select and manage common stock portfolios or select investment company managers who will oversee such portfolios on their behalf. Which of these to pursue will depend on a number of factors, including the investor's expertise, time, and temperament, and, importantly, what an investor believes about the efficiency of the market, as discussed in Chapter 10. We will consider each of these two strategies in turn.

THE PASSIVE STRATEGY

A natural outcome of a belief in efficient markets is to employ some type of passive strategy in owning and managing common stocks. If the market is totally efficient, no active strategy should be able to beat the market on a risk-adjusted basis. The Efficient Market Hypothesis (EMH) has implications for fundamental analysis and technical analysis (discussed in Chapter 18), which are both active strategies for selecting common stocks.

Passive strategies do not seek to outperform the market, but simply to do as well as the market or achieve some other well-defined investment objective. The emphasis is on minimizing transaction costs and time spent in managing the portfolio because any expected benefits from active trading or analysis are likely to be less than the costs. Passive investors act as if the market is efficient and accept the consensus estimates of return and risk, accepting current market price as the best estimate of a security's value. Many investors have adopted passive strategies in light of the inability of active fund managers to beat passive benchmarks. Real-World Returns 14-1 provides evidence in this regard, suggesting that very few active equity fund managers were able to outperform passive index-based ETFs over a recent time period.

Paralleling our discussion of passive approaches to bond management, an investor can simply follow a buy-and-hold strategy for whatever portfolio of stocks is owned. Alternatively, a very effective way to employ a passive strategy with common stocks is to invest in an indexed portfolio. We will consider each of these strategies in turn.

REAL-WORLD RETURNS 14-1

How Canadian Equities Stack Up Against an ETF

What We're Looking For

The performance of mutual funds is best measured against the appropriate benchmark stock or bond index, but let's get practical for a moment. Wouldn't it be more useful to compare mutual funds to low-fee exchange-traded funds (ETFs), which are the best way for individual investors to actually buy an index's returns? This brings us to today's screen, which pits Canadian equity funds against an ETF called the iShares CDN Composite Index Fund (ETFs trade like stocks and the symbol for this one is XIC on the Toronto Stock Exchange).

Today's Search

There are 100 or so funds in the Canadian equity category that have been around for the five years to Sept. 30. Let's compare their compound average annual returns to the composite index ETF. Just for fun, we'll toss another ETF into the mix. It's called the iShares CDN LargeCap 60 Index Fund (XIU-TSX) and it tracks big blue-chip stocks only. We'll also look at a risk measure called beta. The S&P/TSX composite has a beta of one and funds on either side of that number are said to be more or less volatile.

So What Did We Turn Up?

Nothing flattering to the mutual fund industry, that's for sure. Just five funds beat the composite index ETF over the past five years, and one of them was the LargeCap 60 ETF. You might put up with somewhat lower returns from a fund if it had a lower risk profile than an index-hugging ETF, but the beta numbers in our chart suggest that most top-performing funds are similar to the index.

Pay close attention to the effect that management expense ratios have in this comparison. ETFs have ultra-low MERs, while the funds on our list are as high as 2.85 percent. With lower fees, several funds would have put up a much stiffer challenge to ETFs.

We'd ideally use a longer-term comparison for funds and ETFs, but the current selection of Canadian ETFs haven't been around long enough to establish a 10-year track record. Meantime, keep ETFs in mind as an effective way to get some exposure to the same indexes and sectors that mutual funds match up against.

| Fund name | As of September 2007 | | | | |
	Net assets (000s)	Last reported MER date	MER %	5-yr return	5-yr beta
Acuity All Cap 30 Canadian Equity	347,766	31-Jan-07	2.85	27.96	1.385346
imaxx Canadian Equity Growth	20,179	28-Sep-07	2.76	24.54	0.986167
Altafund Investment Corp.	72,394	28-Sep-07	2.72	22.02	1.042311
TD Canadian Equity	3,091,347	28-Sep-07	2.09	21.39	1.145336
iShares CDN LargeCap 60 Index	9,992,080	28-Sep-07	0.15	21.39	0.980728
TD Canadian Equity-A		28-Sep-07	2.09	21.09	1.130500
iShares CDN Composite Index	451,582	28-Sep-07	0.25	20.94	1.002607
Desjardins Environment	120,715	31-Jan-07	2.35	20.71	0.985526
OTG Diversified		29-Sep-06	1.30	20.51	0.981718
Altamira Precision Cdn Index	199,164	28-Sep-07	0.53	20.45	0.983078
iShares CDN MidCap Index	246,361	28-Sep-07	0.55	20.45	0.983592

(continued)

REAL-WORLD RETURNS 14-1 *continued*

Hartford Canadian Stock D	21,537	28-Sep-07	1.88	20.43	0.949451
Integra Canadian Value Growth	64,937	30-Dec-05	2.24	20.04	0.906116
TD Canadian Index - e		28-Sep-07	0.31	19.93	0.987276
National Bank Canadian Index	17,445	28-Sep-07	1.14	19.84	0.983619
Leith Wheeler Canadian Equity B	169,359	28-Sep-07	1.50	19.72	0.720842
Ferique Equity	368,655	28-Sep-07	0.66	19.58	0.964336
Manulife Sector Rotation Fund	123,915	29-Dec-06	2.69	19.55	1.012749
RBC Canadian Index	500,469	28-Sep-07	0.71	19.55	0.996493
GGOF Canadian Lrg Cap Equ Mutual	168,581	29-Dec-06	2.39	19.54	0.878637
Hartford Canadian Stock B	28,404	28-Sep-07	2.60	19.53	0.952128
Acuity Social Values Canadian Equ	51,189	31-Jan-07	2.85	19.52	1.178193
Sceptre Canadian Equity - A	29,179	29-Dec-06	1.69	19.42	0.939199
TD Canadian Index	884,466	28-Sep-07	0.85	19.41	0.997669
FMOQ Canadian Equity	30,850	28-Sep-07	0.95	19.34	0.933744
CIBC Canadian Index	864,472	29-Dec-06	0.97	19.30	0.995622
Scotia Canadian Stock Index	206,428	28-Sep-07	1.03	19.20	0.997593
BMO Equity Index	478,876	28-Sep-07	1.01	19.12	0.994472
PH&N Canadian Equity-A	1,194,834	28-Sep-07	1.13	19.09	0.870502
Fidelity Cdn Disciplined Equity-B	1,021,928	29-Dec-06	2.24	18.98	1.019771
Fidelity Cdn Disciplined Equity-A	802,546	29-Dec-06	2.45	18.85	1.021164
Meritas Jantzi Social Index	74,262	31-Aug-07	1.94	18.81	0.872850
PH&N Community Values Cdn Equ-A	29,207	28-Sep-07	1.39	18.65	0.815829
Fidelity Cdn Disciplined Equ Cl-B	27,667	31-May-07	2.30	18.65	1.019219
Fidelity Cdn Disciplined Equ Class	38,425	31-May-07	2.50	18.52	1.020240
Manulife Canadian Equity Fund - A	369,908	29-Dec-06	2.23	18.38	1.046150
OTG Growth		29-Sep-06	1.30	18.37	0.933543

Source: Globefund

Source: Carrick, Rob, "How Canadian Equities Stack up against an ETF," *The Globe and Mail*, October 13, 2007, p. B17.

Buy-and-Hold Strategy

A buy-and-hold strategy means exactly that—an investor buys stocks and basically holds them until some future time in order to meet a particular objective. The emphasis is on avoiding transaction costs, additional search costs, and so forth. The investor believes that such a strategy will produce results that are as good as alternatives requiring more active management. Active management will invariably result in greater transaction costs and increase the likelihood of making errors in the stock selection process.

Notice that a buy-and-hold strategy is applicable to the investor's portfolio, whatever its composition. It may be large or small, and it may emphasize various types of stocks. Also note the critical importance of the initial selection decisions that must be made to implement the strategy. The investor must decide to buy stocks A, B, and C and not X, Y, and Z. Once the initial selections have been made, the investor will have to perform certain functions while the buy-and-hold strategy is in existence. For example, any income generated by the portfolio may be reinvested in the same or in other securities. Alternatively, a few stocks may do so well that they dominate the total market value of the portfolio and reduce its diversification. If the portfolio changes in such a way that it is no longer compatible with the investor's risk tolerance, adjustments may be required. The point is simply that even under such a strategy investors must still be ready to take certain actions.

Index Funds and Exchange-Traded Funds

As discussed in Chapter 10, an increasing number of mutual fund and pension fund assets can be described as passive equity investments. Using **index funds**, these asset pools are designed to duplicate as precisely as possible the performance of some market index, similar to bond index funds discussed in Chapter 12.

A stock index fund may consist of all the stocks in a well-known market average such as the S&P/TSX Index. No attempt is made to forecast market movements and act accordingly or to select under- or overvalued securities. Expenses are kept to a minimum, including research costs (security analysis), portfolio managers' fees, and brokerage commissions. Index funds can be run efficiently by a small staff.

While it is relatively straightforward for professional money managers to construct index portfolios, this may pose a problem to the average individual investor who may lack the necessary financial resources and/or investment knowledge. Fortunately, investors currently have a wide selection of index funds to choose from. In addition, as discussed in Chapter 3, the emergence of exchange-traded funds (ETFs) has provided investors with an alternative way of following an indexing strategy.

Recall that an ETF is an index fund holding a diversified portfolio of securities, priced and traded on public exchanges. Most ETFs are passively managed funds that own a basket of stocks (or bonds) designed to mimic the performance of a market index such as the S&P/TSX 60 Index, the S&P 500, or the DJIA. However, unlike mutual funds, investors are not buying shares from an investment company directly, but rather from another investor. Therefore, ETFs involve regular brokerage transactions and brokerage fees. Canadian ETFs trade on the TSX while US-based ETFs trade on US exchanges. Most ETFs are priced continuously during the day, can be sold short, and can be purchased on margin—unlike mutual funds. In addition, they usually have much lower management expense ratios (MERs) than the average index fund.

The most widely traded Canadian ETFs are the **i60s**, which represent units in the S&P/TSX 60 Index. I60s trade on the TSX (ticker: XIU) and currently have an MER of 0.17 percent. In addition, a growing number of Canadian-based small-cap, mid-cap, industry-based, style-based, and bond ETFs are available on the TSX.

Probably the best-known US-based ETF is the "Spider," Standard & Poor's Depository Receipts (SPDR), which was introduced in 1993 to reflect the S&P 500 Index. Other US ETFs include "Diamonds"® (the DJIA), "Cubes" (Nasdaq-100 Index Tracking Stock), "iShares" (S&P 500 as well as other S&P indexes for small-cap, mid-cap, and growth and value indexes, various Russell indexes, various Dow Jones sector funds, and various country funds), and "HOLDRS" (various sector funds). There are currently more than 75 different types of iShares. Most of the global-focused iShares MSCI (formerly WEBS) track Morgan Stanley Capital International indexes of various countries, providing investors with an opportunity to hold well-diversified country portfolios.

Index Funds

Mutual funds holding a bond or stock portfolio designed to mimic the performance of a particular market index.

INVESTING *tip*

Index funds and ETFs have become increasingly popular in response to the large body of evidence concerning the efficiency of the market that has demonstrated the inability of mutual funds to consistently outperform the market on a risk-adjusted basis. If the market is efficient, many of the activities normally engaged in by funds are suspect; that is, the benefits are not likely to exceed the costs. The available evidence indicates that many investment companies have failed to match the performance of broad market indexes. For example, over the 10-year period ending March 31, 2008, the average return for all Canadian equity funds was 6.9 percent, well below the S&P/TSX Total Return Index annual performance of 7.8 percent.

> **CHECK YOUR UNDERSTANDING**
>
> **14-3.** Your financial adviser urges you to adopt a passive investing strategy under which you will hold a broadly diversified portfolio of stocks. Your adviser argues that this will completely protect your portfolio from the collateral damage that occurs when an overvalued sector of the market declines. Do you agree with this argument? Explain your reasoning.

THE ACTIVE STRATEGY

Most of the techniques discussed in this text involve an active approach to investing. In the area of common stocks, the use of valuation models to value and select stocks indicates that investors are analyzing and valuing stocks in an attempt to improve their performance relative to some benchmark such as a market index. They assume or expect the benefits to be greater than the costs.

Pursuit of an active strategy suggests that investors believe they possess some advantage relative to other market participants. Such advantages could include superior analytical or judgement skills, superior information, or the ability or willingness to do what other investors, particularly institutions, are unable to do. For example, many large institutional investors cannot take positions in very small companies, leaving this field for individual investors. Furthermore, individuals are not required to own diversified portfolios and are not prohibited from short sales or margin trading, as are some institutions.

Many investors still favour an active approach to common stock selection and management, despite the evidence from efficient market studies and the published performance results of institutional investors. The reason for this is obvious—the potential rewards are very large, and many investors feel confident that they can achieve such rewards even if other investors cannot.

There are numerous active strategies involving common stocks. We consider the most prominent ones below. Because of its importance, we then consider the implications of market efficiency for these strategies.

Security Selection

The most traditional and popular form of active stock strategies is the selection of individual stocks identified as offering superior return–risk characteristics. Such stocks are selected using fundamental security analysis or technical analysis, or some combination of the two. Many investors have always believed, and continue to believe despite evidence to the contrary from the EMH, that they possess the requisite skill, patience, and ability to identify undervalued stocks.

We know from Chapter 1 that a key feature of the investments environment is the uncertainty that always surrounds investing decisions. Most stock pickers recognize the pervasiveness of this uncertainty and protect themselves accordingly by diversifying. Therefore, the standard assumption of rational, intelligent investors who select stocks to buy and sell is that such selections will be part of a diversified portfolio.

The Importance of Stock Selection

Evidence suggests that 80 to 90 percent of the total return on a portfolio is attributable to asset allocation decisions among various financial asset classes. If this is the case, then how important is stock selection in the overall investment process? Most active investors, individuals or institutions, are, to various degrees, stock selectors. The majority of investment advice and investment advisory services is geared to the selection of stocks thought to be attractive candidates at the time. *The Value Line*

Investment Survey, the world's largest investment advisory service in terms of number of subscribers, is a good example of stock selection advice offered to the investing public.

To gain some appreciation of the importance of stock selection, consider the wide variation observed in the returns across common stocks, referred to as cross-sectional variation in returns. Latané, Tuttle, and Jones were the first to point out the widely differing performances of stocks in a given year using the interquartile range.[3] Examining data through 1972, they found a remarkable constancy from year to year in the spread between the performance of stocks in the upper quartile and the performance of stocks in the lower quartile.[4]

A subsequent study by McEnally and Todd for the period 1946 to 1989 found that investors who successfully confined stock selection to the stocks in the highest quartile would have largely avoided losing years, and even the bad years showed only modest losses.[5] Conversely, for the bottom quarter, results were negative about 55 percent of the time, and about 25 percent of the time even the best stocks would have lost money despite generally favourable market conditions. The implication of these results is that "For those who do attempt to pick stocks, the rewards can be very high, but the risk and negative consequences of poor selection are substantial."[6] An additional finding of this study is that cross-sectional variation of returns has been increasing steadily over the decades, making stock selection even more important.

Although we outline an approach to security analysis below that logically places company analysis last, its importance is obvious. As Peter Lynch, one of the most celebrated portfolio managers and former head of **Fidelity's Magellan Fund**, states: "If it's a choice between investing in a good company in a great industry, or a great company in a lousy industry, I'll take the great company in the lousy industry any day." Lynch goes on to discuss what we can learn from the top 100 winners over the past decade. The basic lesson is that small stocks make big moves—the trick is identifying them. But as Lynch notes, "What do the great successes of the past 20 years tell us? It's the company, stupid."[7]

The Role of the Security Analyst

Two types of investors buy stocks: individuals and institutions. Institutional investors generally have their own analysts (often referred to as "buy-side" analysts), and individual investors may choose to rely on the recommendations of professional analysts ("sell-side" analysts) rather than attempt their own security analysis. An important part of the institutional side of stock selection and recommendation is the role of the security analyst (also called investment analyst or simply analyst) in the investment process.

The security analyst typically works for an institution concerned with stocks and other financial assets, but the analysts' product is often available to the individual investor in the form of brokerage reports and newsletters, reports from investment advisory services, and so forth. Therefore, when considering stock selection it is important to analyze the role of the analyst.

The central focus of the analysts' job is to attempt to forecast stock returns. This task usually involves a direct forecast of a specific company's return. Alternatively, it can involve the inputs to a valuation model such as those we considered in the previous chapter. Investors interested in stock selection use valuation models, and for inputs they can utilize their own estimates or use those provided by analysts.[8]

---

[3] In an ordered set of numbers, the interquartile range is the difference between the value that cuts off the top quarter and the bottom quarter of these numbers. The interquartile range is an alternative measure of dispersion.

[4] H. Latané, D. Tuttle, and C. Jones, *Security Analysis and Portfolio Management*, Second Edition (New York: Ronald Press, 1975), pp. 192–193.

[5] R. McEnally and R. Todd, "Cross-Sectional Variation in Common Stock Returns," *Financial Analysts Journal* 48 (May/June 1992), pp. 59–63.

[6] McEnally and Todd, p. 61.

[7] Peter Lynch, "The Stock Market Hit Parade," *Worth* (July/August 1994), p. 32.

[8] In Chapter 17, we will consider company analysis in detail, and this discussion will be organized around the two valuation models we studied in the previous chapter—the dividend discount model and the P/E ratio model.

What sources of information do analysts use in evaluating common stocks for possible selection or selling?[9] The major sources are presentations from the top management of the companies being considered, annual reports, as well as annual information reports that must be filed by companies with the appropriate regulatory body [such as the Ontario Securities Commission (OSC) for companies listed on the TSX]. According to surveys of analysts, they consistently emphasize the long term over the short term. Variables of major importance in their analysis include expected changes in earnings per share, expected return on equity (ROE), and industry outlook. The important point to note here is that the security analysis process used by financial analysts is the same one that we will examine in Part V.

One of the most important responsibilities of an analyst is to forecast earnings per share for particular companies because of the widely perceived linkage between expected earnings and stock returns. Earnings are critical in determining stock prices, and what matters is expected earnings (what is referred to on Bay Street or Wall Street as earnings estimates). Therefore, the primary emphasis in fundamental security analysis is on expected earnings, and analysts spend much of their time forecasting earnings. Security analyst earnings forecasts are publicly available through a variety of sources including securities firms' research reports, *The Value Line Investment Survey*, Institutional Brokers Estimate System (IBES) International, and Zack's Investment Research.

The information value of analyst reports depends upon a variety of factors and is generally enhanced by

- the amount of recent company information that is used
- the number of analysts following the stock
- the degree of consensus among analysts
- the quality of analysts following the stock

Empirical studies indicate that current expectations of earnings, as represented by the average of the analysts' forecasts, are incorporated into current stock prices. Perhaps more importantly, revisions in the average forecast for year-ahead earnings have predictive ability concerning future stock returns.

Investors should carefully study a company's earnings and estimates of earnings before investing. Estimates are available at many major investing websites. In other words, for better or worse, these estimates are quite widely reported and investors (and hence stock prices) reflect these estimates. For example, in 2002, *Business Week* concluded in an article that analysts still have a major impact on the market, and therefore investors need to pay attention.[10]

In connection with the *Business Week* article mentioned above, StarMine conducted an analysis that measured the impact of analyst changes in recommendations on stock prices. The results are reported in Figure 14-3 and show that on the day following an upgrade by analysts, stocks rise an average of 2.1 percent, while they fall an average of 5.4 percent following a downgrade. Downgrades tend to be more prominent because investors tend to focus more on bad news. StarMine also reports that there is a continued drift in prices for several months following the change in recommendation. This suggests that investors could still benefit from these changes in recommendation after the fact—contrary to the notion of market efficiency.

Intuitively, one would expect analyst earnings predictions to be superior to those obtained using historical data and trends in earnings, since they use more information. However, there is a great deal of evidence that analysts tend to be overly optimistic on average. Supporting US studies include O'Brien, and DeBondt and Thaler, while Canadian evidence is documented by Hennessey, and Ackert and Athanassakos.[11]

---

[9]This discussion is based on T. D. Coggin, "The Analyst and the Investment Process: An Overview," reprinted in *The CFA Candidate Readings*, Level I, Institute of Chartered Financial Analysts, Charlottesville, VA, 1992. The Candidate Readings and other publications issued by the institute are a valuable source of information for any serious investor as well as investment professionals.

[10]"Don't Sell Street Analysts Short," *Business Week*, October 21, 2002.

[11]P. O'Brien, "Analysts' Forecasts as Earnings Expectation," *Journal of Accounting and Economics* 10 (January 1988), pp. 53–83; W. DeBondt and R. Thaler, "Do Security Analysts Overreact?" *American Economic Review* 80 (May 1990), pp. 52–57; S. Hennessey, "Can Active Managers Profit from Earnings Forecast Revisions?" *Canadian Investment Review* 6 (Spring 1993), pp. 39–45; L. Ackert and G. Athanassakos, "Expectations of the Herd," *Canadian Investment Review* 9 (Winter 1996/97), pp.7–11.

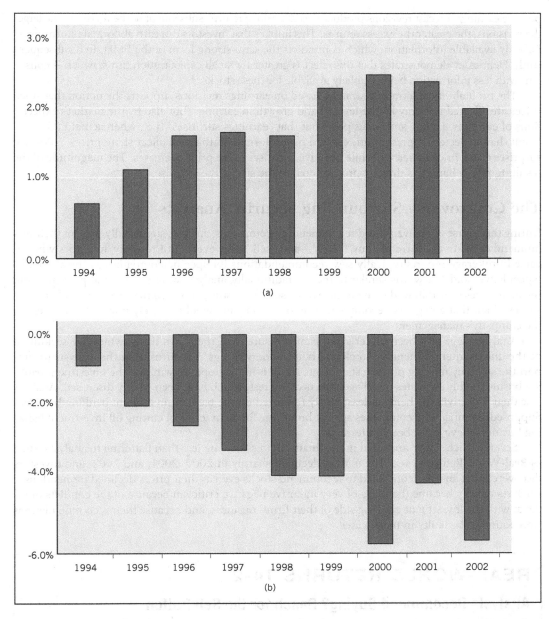

Figure 14-3
Average Percentage Amount a
Stock Moved in a Single Day
Following a Change in Analysts' Recommendations,
1994–2002 (a) Following an
upgrade; (b) Following a
downgrade

Source: StarMine Newsletter.
StarMine website, October
15, 2002. Reprinted with
permission.

The optimism of analysts is not surprising since they have greater incentive to issue buy rather than sell recommendations. They are under pressure by the companies they follow to avoid issuing sell recommendations. In fact, sell recommendations have traditionally been extremely rare, although changes to this practice are evolving, as discussed in the section below. This pressure will be greater if the brokerage firm they work for is trying to sell shares of the company being analyzed, or if there exists an investment banking relationship with the company. In addition, analysts may prefer to make estimates that do not stand out from the crowd. These notions are supported by the results of Ackert and Athanassakos, who find that analysts are "more optimistic when there is greater dispersion in earnings forecasts."[12]

Several empirical studies, including the 1993 Canadian study by Hennessey, suggest that investors can benefit from earnings estimate revisions. In particular, portfolios of stocks that have experienced

[12]L. Ackert and G. Athanassakos, "Expectations of the Herd," *Canadian Investment Review* 9 (Winter 1996/97), pp. 7–11.

positive earnings forecast revisions produce excess positive returns subsequent to the revision. The larger the revisions, the greater the excess returns. This implies that investors can earn abnormal returns using publicly available information, which contradicts the semi-strong form of the EMH. In a subsequent study, Hennessey demonstrates that this effect is greater for small capitalization firms, which is consistent with less information being publicly available for these stocks.[13]

The profitability of a trading strategy based on earnings revisions supports the notion that stock prices are affected not only by the level of and growth in earnings, but also by the market's expectations of earnings. Latané and Jones point out that "earnings surprises" (i.e., when actual EPS is different than expected) represent unexpected new information that will affect share prices.[14] Positive surprises cause price increases, while negative surprises cause price decreases. The magnitude of the resulting price changes is directly proportional to the size of the surprise.

The Controversy Surrounding Security Analysts

During the course of analyzing and recommending companies, analysts supposedly present their recommendations in the form of "buy," "hold," and "sell." However, until recently, investors who received brokerage reports typically saw recommendations for specific companies as "buy," "hold," "speculative hold," or words similar to these. Traditionally, analysts were under great pressure from the companies they followed to avoid the word "sell." One study reported that two-thirds of analysts surveyed felt that a negative recommendation on a company would severely impact their access to the company's management.

Analysts have also been under significant pressure from their own firms, which are seeking to be the underwriter on lucrative stock and bond underwritings. The firms want the analysts to support the stock by making positive statements about it in the hopes of winning the investment banking business. This generates massive conflicts of interest, which have been widely discussed. Analysts lose their objectivity by being at least partly rewarded on the basis of investment banking business. Supposedly, reprisals by companies against brokerage firms, in terms of cutting off investment banking business, have often been widespread.

Several articles have appeared in the financial press that are less than flattering to analysts, such as Real-World Returns 14-2. The market declined sharply in 2000, 2001, and 2002, and investors discovered that analysts continued to recommend stocks even as their prices declined tremendously. Analysts rapidly became the focus of very intensive negative criticism because of the conflicts of interest with the investment banking side of their firms' business, and because their recommendations were found to be faulty in many cases.

REAL-WORLD RETURNS 14-2

Analysts Recommend Buying? Reach for the Sell Button

These are turbulent times in financial markets. So now, more than ever, we should be putting our faith in analyst recommendations instead of trying to pick stocks ourselves, right?

After all, analysts are paid generously to spend all day scanning company financial statements, so of course they're in a better position to know which stocks will rise and which will sink.

Wrong. As it turns out, doing the opposite of what analysts recommend is often a better strategy than following their advice—a fact that should make investors think twice before blindly following the stock picks of brokerage firms in the hope of striking it rich.

---

[13]S. Hennessey, "Get the Drift," *Canadian Investment Review* 8 (Winter 1995/96), pp. 23–28.
[14]H. Latané and C. Jones, "Standardized Unexpected Earnings—A Progress Report," *Journal of Finance* 32 (December 1977), pp.1457–1465.

In a recent study, Thomson Reuters examined the performance of stocks in the S&P 400 MidCap index, dividing them into groups based on analyst recommendations. Care to guess which group fared the worst? That's right, stocks with the highest analyst ratings.

We're not talking about a short-term aberration, either. The study examined the period from March 31, 1994, to Dec. 31, 2007. Over that time, a group of the 80 lowest-rated stocks—rebalanced quarterly to reflect any changes in recommendations—posted an average annual return of 14.35 percent. The top 80 stocks returned just 10.96 percent—more than three percentage points less.

Thomson Reuters examined other indexes, with similar results. On the Dow Jones industrial average, the 10 stocks with the lowest analyst ratings posted an average annual gain of 13.87 percent. Over the same period, the Dow returned 12.17 percent and the S&P 500 11.04 percent.

The effect was even more dramatic for the S&P 100. "Poorly recommended stocks tend to do much better than highly recommended stocks," Thomson Reuters concluded. "Highly recommended stocks … underperform substantially."

There may be a simple explanation for this: Stocks that are hated on Wall Street are often pushed to unreasonably low levels, setting them up for a rebound. It's the same principle that underlies the "Dogs of the Dow" strategy, which calls for buying the Dow stocks with the highest dividend yields.

Jack Hough, author of Your Next Great Stock, has studied the relationship between analysts' recommendations and stock performance. Much of the academic research is contradictory, he says, but a few themes emerge.

One is that stocks with positive analyst recommendations do sometimes outperform lower-rated stocks, but only during bull markets. In bearish phases, like the one we've been in, highly rated stocks tend to lag the market. That may be because, during bull markets, analysts and investors favour growth stocks that do well in precisely that sort of environment.

Analyst recommendations are useful, but it's all in the way investors use them, he says. Rather than look at the absolute number of "buys," "holds" and "sells" on a stock, it's more important to examine changes in ratings. For example, if a stock has numerous "sells" and "holds" but one or two analysts have recently upgraded the company to "buy," that can be a positive signal.

For his part, when Mr. Hough is looking for value stocks, he deliberately avoids those with a lot of favourable ratings. "I'm looking for companies that have popularity left to gain, and if a company has an average recommendation of 'buy' or 'strong buy,' there's obviously not much more favour to gain on Wall Street," he says.

That's something to remember the next time you read a gushing "buy" report on a stock that's already shot up in price.

Source: Heinzl, John, "Analysts recommend buying? Reach for the sell button," *The Globe and Mail*, April 29, 2008, p. B16.

In mid-2002, the Attorney General of New York went to court to force Merrill Lynch, at the time the United States' largest retail brokerage, to change the procedures followed by its analysts in rating stocks (some Merrill Lynch analysts reportedly sent email among themselves castigating some stocks that the firm was recommending to its clients). Merrill Lynch agreed to a $100 million fine to settle charges that its analysts were overly optimistic in their research recommendations in order to win investment banking business. Some other large firms followed suit in changing their practices, primarily because of this action.

Merrill Lynch announced a new system of stock recommendations in mid-2002, with all stocks being rated "buy," "neutral," or "sell." Its stock recommendations would be tied to projections of total return and risk. The firm also provided investors with more disclosure on when it changes the ratings on a company. Many other firms have since followed suit.

Merrill Lynch's changes were in line with new rules adopted by the New York Stock Exchange (NYSE) and Nasdaq in May 2002, which were approved by the Securities and Exchange Commission (SEC). These changes—forcing analysts to limit and disclose contacts with the investment banking side—were a direct result of the enormously negative criticism the brokerage industry has received as a result of the above-mentioned problems.

In 2002, the SEC adopted new rules that should allow investors to understand more thoroughly what analysts are saying and what conflicts of interest may exist. The new rules include the following:

- Analysts must be clear about their recommendations, and use words such as "buy" or "sell."
- Reports must indicate the percentage of recommendations that are buy, hold, or sell.
- Reports must show the author's track record.
- Analysts must indicate for a stock when they initiated coverage and when they changed opinions.
- Price targets for a stock are to be shown, including if and when they change.
- Research must disclose any recent investment banking ties.

Sector Rotation

An active strategy that is similar to stock selection is group or sector rotation. This strategy involves shifting sector weights in the portfolio in order to take advantage of those sectors that are expected to do better, and avoiding or reducing emphasis on those that are expected to do worse. Investors employing this strategy are betting that particular sectors will repeat their price performance relative to the current phase of the business and credit cycle.

INVESTING *tip*

Perhaps because of their rarity, sell recommendations have a pronounced effect. According to one study, sell recommendations result in an average two-day decline of almost 5 percent and an additional 9 percent decline in the next six months. Another study confirmed the six-month decline but found that such stocks had a turnaround and subsequently beat the market.

An investor could think of larger groups as the relevant sectors, shifting between cyclicals, growth stocks, and value stocks. It is quite standard in sector analysis to divide common stocks into four broad sectors: interest-sensitive stocks, consumer durable stocks, capital goods stocks, and defensive stocks. Each of these sectors is expected to perform differently during the various phases of the business and credit cycles. For example, interest-sensitive stocks would be expected to be hurt during periods of high interest rates, and such periods tend to occur at the latter stages of the business cycle. As interest rates decline, the earnings of the companies in this sector—banks and other financial institutions, utilities, and residential construction firms—should improve.

The term "defensive stocks" needs some explanation. Included here are companies in such businesses as food production, soft drinks, beer, pharmaceuticals, and so forth, that often are not hurt as badly as other companies during the downside of the business cycle because people will still purchase bread, milk, soft drinks, and the like. As the economy worsens and more problems are foreseen, investors may move into these stocks for investment protection. These stocks often do well during the late phases of a business cycle.

Investors may view industries as they do sectors and act accordingly. For example, if interest rates are expected to drop significantly, increased emphasis could be placed on the interest-sensitive industries such as housing, banking, and utilities. Effective strategies involving sector rotation depend heavily on an accurate assessment of current economic conditions. A knowledge and understanding of the phases of the business cycle are important, as is an understanding of political environments, international linkages among economies, and domestic and international credit conditions.

Peter Gibson shows that while industry moves are generally in the same direction, relative differences in changes are often dramatic.[15] He suggests the key to industry timing is to identify the best

---

[15] P. Gibson, "Strategy," in Joe Kan, Editor, *Handbook of Canadian Security Analysis: A Guide to Evaluating the Industry Sectors of the Market from Bay Street's Top Analysts* (Toronto: John Wiley & Sons Canada, 1997), pp. 537–644.

industry leadership at each stage of the market cycle. In this regard, for purposes of industry analysis, industry groups should be formed on the basis of factors such as type of business, degree of economic sensitivity, and exposure to international markets.

Chapter 16 provides a detailed discussion of industry analysis; however, at this point we provide some general principles that must be kept in mind. First, prices for industries with similar economic sensitivity tend to move together (and hence display positive correlations among returns), which reduces the potential benefits of rotation gains. Second, it is important to focus on industry activity and not size. Third, be aware that diversification within and across industries is not a straightforward task in Canada. In particular, a few industries within the S&P/TSX Composite Index make up the majority of its total market capitalization. In addition, many S&P/TSX Composite Index industries are dominated by one or two companies, with the notable exceptions of the banks, the paper and forest producers, and the oil and gas producers.

The success of sector rotation strategies depends heavily on forecasting overall market activity, as well as activity within several industry categories. There are great potential benefits to this approach. However, as always, it is easy to say what should have been done after the fact, but it is a very difficult thing to predict which sectors will excel, ahead of time. The bottom line is that forecasting economic and market activity is a daunting task, and there is little evidence that it can produce superior results on a consistent basis.

Indirect Investing in Sectors

Investors can invest in sectors using mutual funds and ETFs. This indirect sector investing offers the potential of large returns, but the risks are also large. For example, for the year ending March 31, 2008, the Altamira Health Sciences fund produced a loss of 13.42 percent, while the Altamira Resource fund produced a 15.05 percent gain.

Market Timing

Market timers attempt to earn excess returns by varying the percentage of portfolio assets in equity securities. When equities are expected to do well, timers shift from cash equivalents, such as money market funds, to common stocks. When equities are expected to do poorly, the opposite occurs. Alternatively, market timers could increase the betas of their portfolios when the market is expected to rise and carry most stock prices up, or decrease them when the market is expected to go down. One important factor affecting the success of a market timing strategy is the amount of brokerage commissions and taxes paid with such a strategy as opposed to a buy-and-hold strategy. Some of the more common asset allocation strategies, based on the ability to time changes in the market, are discussed at the end of this section.

Market timing means that managers invest more aggressively in anticipation of strong markets and more conservatively in anticipation of slow markets. Robert Merton illustrated the astonishing profit potential associated with perfect market timing ability.[16] He showed that an investor with $1,000 to invest in 1927 could have accumulated $5.36 billion after 52 years (at the end of 1978), by correctly investing in either T-bills or the NYSE index (whichever produced a higher return during a given month). This amount dwarfs the $3,600 that would have been accumulated had the investor remained in T-bills the entire period, as well as the $67,500 that would have accumulated, had the investor held the market index the entire period.

Canadian evidence provided in Table 14-1 shows the results from following the monthly rebalancing strategy used by Merton in his study over the 1956–2003 period. An investor with perfect market timing would have experienced an average annual return of 32.99 percent, and would have seen $1,000 grow to over $581 million over that period, versus an annual return of 10.34 percent and accumulated wealth of only $57,793 had the investor remained fully invested in the stock market.

---

[16] R. Merton, "On Market Timing and Investment Performance: An Equilibrium Theory of Market Forecasts," *Journal of Business* 54 (July 1981), pp. 363–406.

Table 14-1

Canadian Market Timing Evidence
(February 1956 to March 2003)

	Average Annual Return	Ending Wealth of $1,000 Invested Initially
TSX	10.34%	$57,793
T-Bills	6.71%	$21,316
Perfect Market Timing (monthly)	32.99%	$581,642,466
Always Wrong	−11.78%	$2.12
TSX minus the best 5 months	8.91%	$32,359
TSX minus the best 10 months	7.80%	$20,423
TSX minus the best 15 months	6.82%	$13,545
TSX minus the best 20 months	5.90%	$9,137
TSX minus the best 40 months	2.81%	$2,375

The example above illustrates the importance of market timing ability for investors. However, like many issues in the investing arena, the subject of market timing is controversial. Can some investors regularly time the market effectively enough to provide excess returns on a risk-adjusted basis? The available evidence on the subject is mixed, and it is important to keep in mind that market timing is a broad topic and that it is difficult to summarize all viewpoints.

Much of the empirical evidence on market timing comes from studies of mutual funds. A basic issue is whether fund managers increase the beta of their portfolios when they anticipate a rising market and reduce it when they anticipate a declining market. Several studies found no evidence that funds were able to time market changes and change their risk levels in response. Veit and Cheney, for example, found in a study of 74 mutual funds that they were not able to successfully change their risk levels based on their timing strategies.[17]

Chang and Lewellen examined the performance of mutual funds and found little evidence of any market timing ability; furthermore, the average estimated downmarket beta turned out to be slightly higher than the average estimated up-market beta.[18] Overall, this study supported the conclusion that mutual funds do not outperform a passive investment strategy. This conclusion was also supported by Henriksson in a study of 116 mutual funds using monthly data.[19] He found that mutual fund managers are not able to successfully employ strategies involving market timing, and they were not even successful with market timing involving large changes in the market.

On the other hand, Weigel examined the market timing performance of 17 US managers who used a tactical asset allocation approach and found they had reliable market timing skills.[20] Studies by both Foerster and Turnbull, and Beveridge and Bauer have demonstrated the potential benefits of using market timing approaches in Canada.[21] There is also a great deal of evidence that international portfolio managers using dynamic asset allocation strategies can add considerable value to international portfolios.[22]

Mark Hulbert, publisher of a service that monitors the performance of investment advisory letters called the *Hulbert Financial Digest*, believes that the popularity of market timing follows a cycle

---

[17]E. T. Veit and J. M. Cheney, "Are Mutual Funds Market Timers?" *Journal of Portfolio Management* 8 (Winter 1982), pp. 35–42.

[18]E. Chang and W. Lewellen, "Market Timing and Mutual Fund Investment Performance," *Journal of Business* 57, Part 1 (January 1984), pp. 57–72.

[19]R. D. Henriksson, "Market Timing and Mutual Fund Performance: An Empirical Investigation," *Journal of Business* 57, Part 1 (January 1984), pp. 73–96.

[20]E. Weigel, "The Performance of Tactical Asset Allocation," *Financial Analysts Journal* 47 (Sept/Oct 1991), pp. 63–70.

[21]S. Foerster and A. Turnbull, "The Key to Effective Tactical Asset Allocation," *Canadian Investment Review* 6 (Spring 1993), pp. 13–19; S. Beveridge and L. Bauer, "How to Market Time Using Interest Rate Signals," *Canadian Investment Review* 7 (Summer 1994), pp. 13–16.

[22]For example, refer to R. Arnott and R. Henriksson, "A Disciplined Approach to Global Asset Allocation," *Financial Analysts Journal* 45 (Mar/Apr 1989), pp.17–28; M. Keppler, "The Importance of Dividend Yield in Country Selection," *Journal of Portfolio Management* 17 (Winter 1991), pp. 24–29; and, W. Fouse, "Allocating Assets Across Country Markets," *Journal of Portfolio Management* 18 (Winter 1992), pp. 20–27.

of its own.[23] If the market is strongly up, market timing falls into disrepute, and buying and holding is the popular strategy. Following a market decline, however, market timing comes into vogue and the buy-and-hold strategy is not popular. According to Hulbert, on a pure timing basis only 3 percent of the stock timing strategies tracked over the most recent five- and eight-year periods outperformed a buy-and-hold approach.[24]

Many successful portfolio managers such as Warren Buffet and Peter Lynch suggest that market timing is one of the most difficult things for an investor to accomplish. Based on this belief, they establish their investment policies with long-term objectives in mind in order to avoid having to continually make market timing decisions. On the other hand, there are several studies that indicate the potential benefits of market timing strategies. In fact, most funds employ market timing strategies to a certain degree, which is reflected in the varying cash ratios exhibited by their portfolios.

Considerable research suggests that the biggest risk of market timing is that investors will not be in the market at critical times, thereby significantly reducing their overall returns. Investors who miss only a few key months may suffer significantly. For example, over a recent 40-year period, investors who missed the 34 best months for stocks would have seen an initial $1,000 investment grow to only $4,492 instead of $86,650. Even T-bills would have been a better alternative in this situation.[25]

If you are still considering market timing as a strategy suitable for the average individual investor, consider the following US evidence. For the 10-year period 1986 to 1995, inclusive, returns on the S&P 500 Composite Index were as follows:

Fully invested annualized rate of return = 14.8 percent
Take out the 10 best days = 10.2 percent
Take out the 20 best days = 7.3 percent
Take out the 30 best days = 4.8 percent
Take out the 40 best days = 2.5 percent

Table 14-1 also provides Canadian evidence regarding the costs of missing out on some of the best months in the market. For example, we can see that $1,000 left invested in the market from 1956 to 2003 would have grown to $57,793 (an average annual return of 10.34 percent). However, if an investor was attempting to time the market and missed the best 20 months, the investor's ending wealth would have been only $9,137 (average annual return of 5.90 percent).

Asset Allocation Strategies

Asset allocation strategies are based on the ability to time the performance of the major financial asset categories, which include short-term money market instruments (such as T-bills and commercial paper), long-term bonds, and equity securities. The most commonly referred to strategy is tactical asset allocation (TAA), a moderately active asset allocation approach that allows managers short-term deviations from longer-term asset mixes to take advantage of market timing skills. Evidence was presented above regarding the relative success of such strategies.

Several other asset allocation techniques may be employed. Strategic asset allocation involves adhering to a long-term mix by monitoring and rebalancing the portfolio as necessary. In order to achieve a desired asset mix of, say, 60 percent equity and 40 percent bonds, rebalancing is necessary as equity and bond prices change through time, which alters the portfolio asset mix. The asset mix can be returned to the strategic long-term position by buying bonds (or stocks) when they become cheap and selling them when they increase in value. For example, suppose stock prices fell and bond prices rose, so that the actual asset mix changed to 55 percent equity and 45 percent bonds. This would require the manager to sell bonds, which had risen in price, and buy equities, whose prices had fallen. This buy low and sell high strategy is consistent with the notion underlying contrarian or value investment strategies.

---

[23]M. Hulbert, "New Tool for Contrarians," *Forbes*, November 18, 1996, p. 298.
[24]*Ibid*
[25]J. D. Pond, "The Harsh Reality of Market Timing," *Worth* (May 1994), pp. 117–118.

Insured asset allocation allows managers discretion in deciding asset amounts only if they exceed a base portfolio value that must be guaranteed by formula. This involves maintaining a predetermined amount in riskless securities or by using put options or futures contracts to "immunize" the portfolio value (i.e., portfolio insurance). Dynamic asset allocation is an active management technique that adjusts the mix between risk-free and risky assets as market conditions change by selling equities when markets fall and buying them when they rise. This strategy is consistent with the rationale underlying growth investment strategies.

Finally, integrated asset allocation represents an all-encompassing strategy including several of the approaches above. It examines market conditions and investor objectives and constraints separately, and based on this analysis, the optimal asset mix is determined. That asset mix is adjusted at regular intervals to reflect the fact that both market conditions and investor needs change through time.

Efficient Markets and Active Strategies

One of the most significant developments is the proposition that securities markets are efficient. This idea has generated considerable controversy concerning the analysis and valuation of securities because of its significant implications for investors. Regardless of how much (or how little) an investor learns about investments, and regardless of whether an investor ends up being convinced by the efficient markets literature, it is essential to be aware of the implications of market efficiency early in one's study of investments.

Much evidence exists to support the basic concepts of the Efficient Market Hypothesis (EMH), and it cannot be ignored simply because one is uncomfortable with the idea or because it sounds too improbable. It is appropriate to consider this concept with any discussion of active strategies designed to produce excess returns—that is, returns in excess of those commensurate with the risk being taken. After all, if the evidence suggests that active strategies are unlikely to be successful over time after all costs have been assessed, the case for a passive strategy becomes much more persuasive.

As we learned in Chapter 10, the EMH is concerned with the assessment of information by investors. Security prices are determined by expectations about the future. Investors use the information available to them in forming their expectations. If security prices fully reflect all the relevant information that is available and usable, a securities market is said to be efficient.

If the stock market is efficient, prices reflect their fair economic value as estimated by investors. Even if this is not strictly true, prices may reflect their approximate fair value after transaction costs are taken into account, a condition known as economic efficiency. In such a market, where prices of stocks depart only slightly from their fair economic value, investors should not try to employ trading strategies designed to beat the market by identifying undervalued stocks. Nor should they attempt to time the market in the belief that an advantage can be gained. Sector rotation also will be unsuccessful in a highly efficient market.

The implications of an efficient market are extremely important for investors. They include one's beliefs about how to value securities in terms of the two approaches to selecting common stocks discussed below—the fundamental and the technical—which, in turn, encompasses questions about the time and effort to be devoted. Other implications include the management of a portfolio of securities. Again, in terms of the above discussion, should management be active or passive? Efficient market proponents often argue that less time should be spent on deciding which securities to include in a portfolio and more on considerations such as reducing taxes and transaction costs and maintaining the chosen risk level of a portfolio over time.

Suffice it to say that an intelligent investor must be aware of this issue and form some judgement about its implications if he or she is to formulate a reasonable investment strategy. An investor's beliefs about market efficiency will have a significant impact on the type of stock strategy implemented. The efficiency of the market, and how investors should act in selecting portfolios of stocks, remains controversial.

Investors are constantly being bombarded with reports of techniques and procedures that appear to offer above-average returns, thereby contradicting the idea that the market is so efficient that they should not attempt to outperform it. Intelligent investors examine such claims and strategies carefully before using them.

CHECK YOUR UNDERSTANDING

14-4. Security analysts have often been accused of having a serious conflict of interest. What is the cause of this conflict?

14-5. Given the evidence supporting market efficiency, can investors have any confidence that really good security analysis will prove to be profitable year after year?

14-6. State two reasons why market timing strategies are unlikely to be successful for investors.

WAYS OF ANALYZING AND SELECTING STOCK

learning objective 4
Differentiate between technical and fundamental analysis.

The two traditional and well-known ways of analyzing and selecting common stocks are fundamental analysis and technical analysis. Both of these are given careful consideration in Part V, but greater emphasis is placed on fundamental analysis.

These two basic approaches are described briefly here, followed by a consideration of the concept of efficient market and its implications. The fundamental approach is then developed in some detail in the remainder of this chapter, setting the stage for the next three chapters, which analyze the fundamental approach in a specific, recommended order.

Technical Analysis

One of the two traditional strategies long available to investors is technical analysis, which is examined in detail in Chapter 18. In fact, technical analysis is the oldest strategy and can be traced back to at least the late nineteenth century.

The term **technical analysis** refers to the methodology of forecasting fluctuations in securities prices. This methodology can be applied either to individual securities or to the market as a whole (i.e., forecasting a market index such as the S&P/TSX Composite Index).

The rationale behind technical analysis is that the value of a stock is primarily a function of supply and demand conditions. These conditions, in turn, are determined by a range of factors, from scientific analyses to opinions and guesses, all of which play a part in determining the changes in prices. The price trends persist, or they may change with supply and demand conditions. Technicians seek to detect, and act upon, changes in the direction of stock prices.

In its purest sense, technical analysis is not concerned with the underlying economic variables that affect a company or the market; therefore, the causes of supply and demand shifts are not important. The basic question to be asked is: Does excess supply or demand exist for a stock, and can such a condition be detected by studying either the patterns of past price fluctuations or the movements of certain technical indicators or rules? Technicians study the market using graphical charting of price changes, volume of trading over time, and a number of technical indicators.

Technical Analysis
The use of specific market data for the analysis of both individual and aggregate stock prices for the purpose of identifying recurring price patterns.

Momentum Strategies

One of the most popular technical analysis techniques is that of **momentum investing**, which is basically a relative strength approach (relative strength is examined in Chapter 18). The basic premise of momentum investing is that if a stock has outperformed the market over some recent period, it is likely to continue to do so. In other words, this approach is one of following the trend.

Momentum Investing
Investing on the basis of recent movements in the price of a stock, which generally means buying stocks that have outperformed the market recently. In other words, it is following the trend.

Momentum investing is a short-run approach. For example, stocks that are strong for the prior six months tend to outperform the market only over the next six to 12 months. Evidence of the success of momentum investment strategies was discussed in Chapter 10.

Fundamental Analysis

Fundamental Analysis

The estimation of a stock's value using basic data such as its earnings, sales, risk, and so forth.

Intrinsic Value

The estimated or true value of a security as determined by an investor after examining a firm's underlying variables.

Fundamental analysis is based on the premise that any security (and the market as a whole) has an **intrinsic value**, which is the true value as estimated by an investor. This value is a function of the firm's underlying variables, which combine to produce an expected return and an accompanying risk. By assessing these fundamental determinants of the value of a security, an estimate of its intrinsic value can be determined. This estimated intrinsic value can then be compared to the current market price of the security, as discussed in Chapter 11 with regard to bonds, and in Chapter 13 with regard to common stocks.

In equilibrium, the current market price of a security reflects the average of the intrinsic value estimates made by investors. An investor whose intrinsic value estimate differs from the market price is, in effect, disagreeing with the market consensus of the estimate of either expected return or risk or both. Investors who can perform good fundamental analysis and spot discrepancies should be able to profit by acting before the market consensus reflects the correct information.

Efficient Markets and Behavioural Finance

The rise, and increasing acceptance, of the efficient market concept has had an impact on traditional investing practices. Hardest hit has been technical analysis. If prices fluctuate in accordance with the efficient markets model, there is little chance that pure technical analysis is valid.

The EMH also has implications for fundamental analysis. If the market is efficient, prices will react quickly to new information, and with many active investors buying and selling, prices should be close to their fair economic values. However, fundamental analysis is still needed in an efficient market, because without it, the market would be less efficient. One can argue that what makes the market efficient is the very fact that investors do fundamental analysis, based on the belief that the market is not efficient.

Given the widespread discussion of market efficiency, investors sometimes overlook the issue of psychology in financial markets—that is, the role that emotions play. Particularly in the short run, investors' emotions affect stock prices and markets, and those making investment decisions need to be aware of this.

As discussed in Chapter 10, behavioural finance is a hot topic in investing. Although traditional economics is built on the proposition that investors act rationally on the basis of utility theory, behavioural finance recognizes that investors can, and do, behave irrationally. Markets overreact, in both the up and down directions. Investors are motivated by numerous "irrational" forces, such as overconfidence, regrets about decisions, aversion to losses, and so forth. Unfortunately, despite several promising research findings, behavioural finance currently does not have a unifying theory that ties everything together.

CHECK YOUR UNDERSTANDING

14-7. In technical analysis, how useful is a stock's intrinsic value?

14-8. What are the implications of the efficient market hypothesis for technical analysts who make predictions based on charts of stock prices?

A FRAMEWORK FOR FUNDAMENTAL ANALYSIS

With any fundamental analysis, an investor will obviously have to work with individual company data. Does this mean that the investor should plunge into a study of company data first and then consider other factors, such as the industry within which a particular company operates or the state of the economy, or should the reverse procedure be followed? In fact, when doing fundamental analysis investors and security analysts may use each of these approaches, which are referred to as the "bottom-up" and the "top-down" approaches.

learning objective 5
Describe the bottom-up and top-down approaches in fundamental analysis.

Bottom-Up Fundamental Analysis

With the bottom-up approach, investors focus directly on a company's basics or fundamentals. Analysis of such information as the company's products, its competitive position, and its financial status, leads to an estimate of the company's earnings potential and, ultimately, its value in the market.

Considerable time and effort are required to produce the type of detailed financial analysis needed to understand even relatively small companies. The emphasis in this approach is on finding companies with good long-term growth prospects and on making accurate earnings estimates. To organize this effort, bottom-up fundamental research is often broken into two areas, growth investing and value investing.

Value Versus Growth

Growth stocks carry investor expectations of above-average future growth in earnings and valuations as a result of high price/earnings ratios. Investors expect these stocks to perform well in the future, and they are willing to pay high multiples for this. Examples include Microsoft and Intel, as well as the stocks of many Internet-related companies.

Value stocks, on the other hand, feature cheap assets and strong balance sheets. Value investing can be traced back to the value-investing principles laid out by the well-known Benjamin Graham, who wrote a classic book on security analysis that has been the foundation for many subsequent security analysts.[26]

Table 14-2

Annual Returns for Value and Growth Indexes, 1979–2002

Year	Russell 3000 Growth	Russell 3000 Value	Russell Top 200 Growth	Russell Top 200 Value	Russell Mid-Cap Growth	Russell Mid-Cap Value	Russell 1000 Growth	Russell 1000 Value	Russell 2000 Growth	Russell 2000 Value	S&P Index
1979	26.20%	21.85%	NA	NA	NA	NA	23.91%	20.55%	50.83%	35.38%	18.44%
1980	40.74	24.52	NA	NA	NA	NA	39.57	24.41	52.26	25.39	32.42
1981	-11.09	2.49	NA	NA	NA	NA	-11.31	1.26	-9.24	14.85	-4.91
1982	20.51	20.83	NA	NA	NA	NA	20.46	20.04	20.98	28.52	21.41
1983	16.29	29.24	NA	NA	NA	NA	15.98	28.29	20.13	38.64	22.51
1984	-2.75	9.28	NA	NA	NA	NA	-0.95	10.10	-15.83	2.27	6.27
1985	32.69	31.48	NA	NA	NA	NA	32.85	31.51	30.97	31.01	32.16
1986	14.25	18.78	13.99%	21.44%	17.55%	17.87%	15.36	19.98	3.58	7.41	18.47
1987	3.92	-0.13	6.45	2.20	2.76	-2.19	5.31	0.50	-10.48	-7.11	5.23
1988	12.00	23.63	10.88	22.02	12.92	24.61	11.27	23.16	20.37	29.47	16.81
1989	34.68	24.22	37.68	26.66	31.48	22.70	35.92	25.19	20.17	12.43	31.49
1990	-1.31	-8.85	1.37	-3.67	-5.13	-16.09	-0.26	-8.08	-17.41	-21.77	-3.17
1991	41.66	25.41	39.41	18.16	47.03	37.92	41.16	24.61	51.19	41.70	30.55
1992	5.22	14.90	3.89	9.07	8.71	21.68	5.00	13.81	7.77	29.14	7.67

(continued)

---

[26]Benjamin Graham and David Dodd, *Security Analysis: Principles and Technique* (New York: McGraw-Hill, 1934). This topic is discussed at some length in Chapter 10.

(Table 14-2 continued)

Year	Russell 3000 Growth	Russell 3000 Value	Russell Top 200 Growth	Russell Top 200 Value	Russell Mid-Cap Growth	Russell Mid-Cap Value	Russell 1000 Growth	Russell 1000 Value	Russell 2000 Growth	Russell 2000 Value	S&P Index
1993	3.69	18.65	-0.07	19.76	11.19	15.62	2.90	18.12	13.36	23.84	9.99
1994	2.20	-1.95	4.85	-1.90	-2.17	-2.13	2.66	-1.99	-2.43	-1.55	1.31
1995	36.57	37.03	38.65	40.03	33.98	34.93	37.19	38.35	31.04	25.75	37.43
1996	21.88	21.60	25.57	22.31	17.48	20.26	23.12	21.63	11.26	21.37	23.07
1997	28.74	34.83	33.73	35.47	22.54	34.37	30.49	35.18	12.95	31.78	33.36
1998	35.02	13.50	45.09	21.24	17.86	5.08	38.71	15.62	1.23	-6.45	28.58
1999	33.82	6.64	29.68	10.94	51.29	-0.11	33.16	7.35	43.10	-1.49	21.04
2000	-22.42	8.02	-24.51	2.31	-11.75	19.19	-22.43	7.02	-22.44	22.82	-9.11
2001	-19.63	-4.33	-20.50	-8.80	-20.16	2.33	-20.42	-5.59	-9.24	14.02	-11.88
2002	-28.04	-15.18	-27.98	-18.02	-27.41	-9.65	-27.89	-15.52	-30.26	-11.43	-22.10
Geometric Mean 1996–99	29.76	18.69	33.32	22.18	26.58	14.12	31.25	19.52	16.16	10.18	26.42
Geometric Mean 1979–2002	11.57	13.99					11.84	13.93	8.94	14.74	13.25
Standard Deviation 1979–2002	20.71	14.05					20.84	14.16	23.83	17.40	16.42
Geometric Mean 1986–2002	9.73	11.78	10.42	11.82	10.19	12.21	10.18	11.90	5.12	10.92	11.50
Standard Deviation 1986–2002	21.83	15.04	23.15	15.79	21.77	16.10	22.27	15.27	22.13	18.01	17.59
Percentage of years value exceeded glamour		54		53		65		50		67	

NA = not available.

Note: Returns for the Russell Top 200 and Russell Mid-Cap Growth and Value Indexes begin in 1986.

Source: "Value and Growth Investing: Review and Update," L.K.C. Chan and J. Lakonishok, *Financial Analysts Journal*, Jan./Feb. 2004, pp. 71–86.

As discussed in Chapter 10, value stocks have tended to outperform growth stocks over time. Evidence of this is provided in Table 14-2, which shows the performance for various US value and growth Russell indexes over the 1979–2002 period. For example, over the entire period, the mean geometric return on the Russell 3000 Value Index was 13.99 percent, with a standard deviation of 14.05 percent. Over the same period, the Russell 3000 Growth Index produced a geometric mean return of only 11.57 percent, with a standard deviation of 20.71 percent. However, growth stocks and value stocks tend to be in vogue over different periods, and advocates of each tend to prosper and suffer accordingly. For example, in Table 14-2, we can see that despite the long-term superior performance of the Russell 3000 Value Index, it only "beat" the performance of the Russell 3000 Growth Index in 13 out of 24 years (or 54 percent of the time).

In many cases, bottom-up investing does not attempt to make a clear distinction between growth and value. Many companies feature strong earning prospects and a strong financial base or asset value and therefore have characteristics associated with both categories. Real-World Returns 14-3 discusses a particular variation of a value strategy.

REAL-WORLD RETURNS 14-3

Picking Winners, Byte by Byte

Wall Street Journal columnist Jack Hough has devised some novel computer screening programs.

When Jack Hough was in junior high school, he was constantly skipping classes. But unlike most kids, you wouldn't find him slacking off at the video arcade.

He'd be in the library reading *The Wall Street Journal*.

"From a very young age I've always studied the stock market," says the author of *Your Next Great Stock: How to Screen the Market for Tomorrow's Top Performers.*

Mr. Hough's book is a useful guide for investors who want to make the most of the stock-screening tools proliferating on the Internet. It's the culmination of everything he's learned about investing, first as a curious kid scouring the stock tables for promising companies and later as a broker with firms such as Merrill Lynch—an experience that only reinforced his belief that people must learn to invest on their own rather than rely on a professional.

"I couldn't wait to work for a brokerage company. I envisioned it as being a place where everyone learned how to find great stocks. And it turns out it has nothing to do with that. It has entirely to do with staying on the phone all day asking people to buy a lot of [funds] that have a lot of high fees," he says.

At 35, he's returned to his first love: Hunting for great stocks. As a columnist for *Smart-Money* magazine and *The Wall Street Journal*, he's carved out a niche as an expert in stock screening—using computer software to sift through thousands of stocks to find the ones with the best attributes, whether they're young companies with great growth prospects or mature cash machines that return gobs of money to shareholders through dividends and share buybacks.

As if reading *The Wall Street Journal* as a kid wasn't peculiar enough, one of Mr. Hough's other passions is combing through academic papers on investing. As such, the screening methods in *Your Next Great Stock* are based, not on gut feelings or hunches, but on empirical research.

Consider his "New Dogs Screen." Back in 1991, Michael O'Higgins' book, *Beating the Dow*, popularized the strategy of buying the 10 Dow stocks with the highest dividend yields —the so-called "dogs of the Dow." But Mr. Hough takes the strategy a step further by adding share buybacks to the equation.

Why? Because a 2004 paper published in the *Journal of Finance* showed that companies with a combination of high dividend yields and large net share repurchases—in other words, those that return a lot of cash to shareholders—outperformed the market by an even wider margin than those with high dividend yields alone. (You can see results of The New Dogs Screen in the accompanying table; the "net payout yield" represents cash spent on dividends and buybacks over the past year, divided by the company's market value.)

The book covers some fairly challenging concepts, but it doesn't read like a dry academic study. That's a testament not just to Mr. Hough's knack for explaining arcane financial concepts in everyday language, but also to his sense of humour; it's not often that you find an investing author who spent year doing standup comedy in New York.

Take his explanation of herd behaviour:

"People will do some remarkable things simply because everyone else is doing them. They'll speed, yawn, kill, jump nude into icy water, grow mullets, and pretend to like cigars (usually not all at once). Herd behaviour is easy to see in the stock market. Crashes and bubbles happen when investors follow each other and not the facts," he writes.

That last point is central to understanding why stock screening is a useful tool. Contrary to what the efficient-market hypothesis holds—that it's impossible to consistently pick winning stocks because everyone is privy to the same information—Mr. Hough argues that human beings are prone to all sorts of foibles that create opportunities for smart investors.

For example, many investors shy away from stocks that have already doubled or tripled in price. This is because of a process called anchoring: They're looking at the stock in the context of where it used to trade—the anchor—which makes them feel like they've missed the boat and the stock is now too expensive. Instead, they should be judging the stock on its current merits, such as expected sales and profit growth, valuation and so on.

In fact, contrary to what many investors may think, studies have shown that stocks that have already risen sharply in the past six months to a year, and which are trading near their 52-week highs, are "overwhelmingly more likely to beat the market, and for a longer time," Mr. Hough writes.

(continued)

REAL-WORLD RETURNS 14-3 *continued*

That's not to say price momentum alone is enough to put a stock on your "buy" list. It isn't. But screening for high-fliers is a great way to spot companies with good growth prospects, as long as you do further research to determine whether the shares are still fairly priced. How many stocks like Research In Motion Ltd. or Potash Corp. of Saskatchewan have investors passed on because they thought they were too expensive, only to watch them soar even more?

Mr. Hough's "Buy High Sell Higher Screen" is one of his favourite ways to discover such breakout stocks, but it works best during bull markets. In today's volatile markets, his favourite is the "Impatient Value Screen," which looks for stocks that are showing price momentum but which are still trading at bargain levels. To make the cut, the stock must have a PEG ratio—price-to-earnings ratio divided by projected earnings growth—of less than 1.5 and be trading within 5 percent of its 52-week high, among other criteria. (You can run the screen yourself at www.smartmoney.com/jackhough.)

The book contains about 15 screens in all, including some that attempt to mimic the stock-picking prowess of legendary investors such as Warren Buffett and Peter Lynch. Using stock screeners alone won't turn you into to the next Oracle of Omaha; as Mr. Hough stresses, a screen is merely a starting point for further research on individual companies.

But in an age of ever-expanding information, screens are a great way to cut through the clutter—and they're a lot more efficient than scanning the stock tables.

The New Dogs of the Dow

Dow stocks with high dividend yields and large share buybacks—as measured by the net payout yield—have historically outperformed.

Company name	Stock ticker	Industry	Market cap. ($million)	Recent price	Price change yr.-to-date	Forward P/E (Current Yr.)	Return on equity	Yield	Net payout yield
Home Depot	HD	Home Improvement Stores	$46,426	$27.51	+$2.12	11.71	26.6%	3.27%	33.16%
Int'l Business Machines	IBM	Diversified Computer Sys.	$146,242	$106.13	−$1.82	12.96	48.7%	1.51%	11.96%
Pfizer	PFE	Drug Manufacturers /Major	$153,329	$22.45	−$1.23	9.51	11.5%	5.70%	11.11%
Walt Disney	DIS	Entertainment-Diversified	$60,859	$32.32	+$0.12	14.69	13.9%	1.08%	11.05%
Honeywell Int'l	HON	Aerospace/Defence Prd/Svc	$42,947	$57.51	−$6.59	15.34	29.6%	1.91%	9.66%
Citigroup	C	Money Center Banks	$128,214	$25.74	−$12.57	8.25	14.6%	4.97%	8.86%
JPMorgan Chase & Co.	JPM	Money Center Banks	$143,129	$42.61	−$2.38	10.42	12.8%	3.57%	8.37%
Exxon Mobil	XOM	Major Integrated Oil/Gas	$467,413	$85.55	−$8.69	10.86	33.1%	1.64%	8.25%
Hewlett-Packard	HPQ	Diversified Computer Sys.	$110,522	$43.26	−$14.30	12.88	18.9%	0.74%	7.81%
Microsoft	MSFT	Application Software	$265,249	$28.50	−$19.94	15.32	49.2%	1.54%	7.56%

Douglas Coull/*The Globe and Mail,* source: Smartmoney.com

Source: Heinzl, John, "Picking Winners, Byte by Byte," *The Globe and Mail,* February 19, 2008, p. B15.

Top-Down Fundamental Analysis

The top-down approach is the opposite of the bottom-up one. Investors begin with the economy and the overall market, considering such important factors as interest rates and inflation. They next consider industries or sectors of the economy that are likely to do particularly well. Finally, having assessed the effect of macro factors on equity investing, and having determined which parts of the overall economy are likely to perform well, individual companies are analyzed.

There is no "right" answer to which of these two approaches to follow. However, fundamental analysis can be overwhelming in its detail, and a structure is needed. This text takes the position that the better way to proceed is top-down in fundamental analysis:

1. First, analyze the overall economy and securities markets to determine if now is a good time to commit additional funds to equities.

2. Second, analyze industries and sectors to determine which have the best prospects for the future.

3. Finally, analyze individual companies.

This is consistent with the observation that between 80 and 90 percent of the return on a portfolio is determined by the asset allocation decision. Using this structure, the valuation models presented in Chapter 13 can be applied successively at each of the three levels.

Thus, we use the top-down version of fundamental security analysis here for our discussion. Part V explains fundamental security analysis in detail and we consider here only the justification for this approach.

Economy/Market Analysis

It is very important to assess the state of the economy and the outlook for primary variables such as corporate profits and interest rates. Investors are heavily influenced by these variables in making their everyday investment decisions. If a recession is likely or under way, stock prices will be heavily affected at certain times during the contraction. Conversely, if a strong economic expansion is under way, stock prices will be heavily affected, again at particular times during the expansion. Thus, the status of economic activity has a major impact on overall stock prices. It is, therefore, very important for investors to assess the state of the economy and its implications for the stock market.

In turn, the stock market impacts each individual investor. Investors cannot compete very well against market trends. If the market goes up (or down) strongly, most stocks are carried along. Company analysis is unlikely to produce high returns in a year such as 2002, when the stock market lost approximately 12 percent. On the other hand, most equity investors did well in 2003 to 2007 regardless of their specific company analysis, because the market provided approximate returns of 26, 14, 24, 17, and 10 percent respectively during those years, as measured by the S&P/TSX Total Return Index.

Another indication of the importance of the economy/market on common stocks is the impact on the earnings for a particular company. Available evidence suggests that from a quarter to a half of the variability in a company's annual earnings is attributable to the overall economy (plus some industry effect).[27]

The economy also significantly affects what happens to various industries. One has only to think of the effects of import quotas, record high interest rates, and so forth, to see why this is so. Therefore, economy analysis must precede industry analysis.

Industry Analysis

After completing an analysis of the economy and the overall market, an investor can decide if it is a favourable time to increase or decrease the amount invested in common stocks. The next step should

---

[27]E. J. Elton, M. J. Gruber, S. J. Brown, and W. N. Goetzmann, *Modern Portfolio Theory and Investment Analysis*, Sixth Edition (New York: John Wiley, 2003).

be industry analysis, since industry factors are the second most important component (after overall market movements) affecting the variability in stock returns.

Individual companies and industries tend to respond to general market movements, but the degree of response can vary significantly. Industries undergo significant movements over both relatively short and relatively long periods. Industries will be affected to various degrees by recessions and expansions. For example, the durable goods industries will be severely affected in a recession. Consumer goods will probably be much less affected during such a contractionary period. During a severe inflationary period such as the late 1970s and early 1980s, regulated industries such as utilities were severely hurt by their inability to pass along all price increases. Finally, new "hot" industries emerge from time to time and enjoy spectacular (if short-lived) growth (such as the Internet company "boom" and "bust" periods). Refer to Chapter 16 for related examples as well as a more detailed discussion of various industry categories.

Company Analysis

Although the first two steps are important, great attention and emphasis should also be placed on company analysis. Security analysts are generally organized along industry lines, but the reports that they issue usually deal with one specific company (sometimes more).

The bottom line for companies, as far as most investors are concerned, is earnings per share. There is a very close relationship between earnings and stock prices, and for this reason most attention is paid to earnings. After all, dividends are closely tied to past, present, and future earnings.

A number of factors are important in analyzing a company, but because investors tend to focus on earnings and dividends, we need to understand the relationship between these two variables and between them and other variables. We also need to consider the possibilities of forecasting earnings and dividends.

Because dividends are paid out of earnings, we will concentrate on the latter in our discussion of company analysis in Chapter 17. Earnings and interest rates are the real key to the fundamental analysis of a common stock. A good understanding of these concepts is vital if an investor is to understand, and perform, fundamental analysis.

The Framework for Fundamental Analysis in Perspective

It is useful to summarize the framework for fundamental analysis we are using because the following three chapters are based on it. Figure 14-4 depicts the fundamental valuation process. We should examine the economy and market first, then industries, and finally individual companies. Fundamental valuation is usually done within the context of a present value model (such as the dividend discount model) or a relative valuation model (such as the P/E ratio model). In either case, the two components of the value of any security being examined are (1) the expected stream of benefits, either earnings or dividends, and (2) the required rate of return or discount rate and/or the multiplier or P/E ratio. Investors should concentrate on these two factors as they systematically proceed through the three levels of analysis: economy/market, industry, and company.

CHECK YOUR UNDERSTANDING

14-9. As part of your analysis of the economy and market situation, you notice that interest rates have been increasing lately, and the indications are that they will to continue to rise. What impact is this likely to have on stock prices, in general?

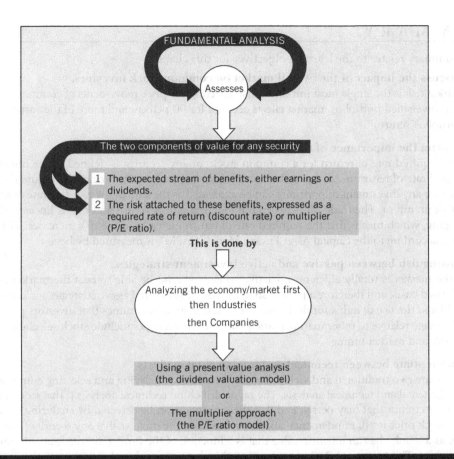

Figure 14-4
A Framework for
Fundamental Security
Analysis

SHOULD BROKERS AND ANALYSTS BE FINED FOR RUMOURS?

In early 2005, the former National Association of Securities Dealers (NASD) in the US announced it had fined a stock analyst $75,000 for spreading a rumour about a small semiconductor manufacturer. It was said to be a "sensational negative rumour" and the stock fell that day, although the company publicly denied the rumour the same day. The company complained to the NASD, which after investigation levied the fine.

The NASD alleged that the broker/analyst in this situation did not adequately investigate to determine if there was a reasonable basis for the rumour. Obviously, the question arises as to

what is "adequate." If the rumour had simply been fabricated, or the analyst spread it knowing it was false, there would be clear grounds for a fine. In this case, however, the charge was that the analyst simply circulated it.

Analysts and brokers are not fined for passing on rumours thought to come from a reliable source, or if the rumour is qualified by saying that the accuracy of the rumour could be in serious doubt. Furthermore, rumours are a daily part of trading stocks, happening regularly. Many investors sometimes invest on the basis of rumours or limited information, only later obtaining the actual facts.

DISCUSSION QUESTIONS

1. Should investors hold brokers accountable if rumours the brokers spread (whether or not they know they are false) result in investor losses, or should it simply be a case of 'buyer beware' where investors are concerned?

2. Who determines when an analyst has crossed the line?

3. Many websites offer what they claim to be 'hot stock tips'. Can these be considered a reliable source?

SUMMARY

This summary relates to the learning objectives for this chapter.

1. **Discuss the impact of the overall market on common stock investors.**

   Market risk is the single most important risk affecting the price movements of common stocks. For well-diversified portfolios, market effects account for 90 percent and more of the variability in the portfolio's return.

2. **Explain the importance of the required rate of return.**

   The required rate of return for a common stock, or any security, is defined as the minimum expected rate of return needed to induce an investor to purchase the stock. The required rate of return for any investment opportunity can be expressed as the sum of the risk-free rate of return and a risk premium. The trade-off between the required rate of return and risk is linear and upward sloping, which means that the required rate of return increases as the risk increases. The relevant risk, according to the Capital Asset Pricing Model (CAPM), is measured by beta.

3. **Distinguish between passive and active investment strategies.**

   If the market is totally efficient, no active strategy should be able to beat the market on a risk-adjusted basis, and therefore a passive strategy may be superior. Passive strategies include buy-and-hold and the use of index funds. Pursuit of an active strategy assumes that investors possess some advantage relative to other market participants. Active strategies include stock selection, sector rotation, and market timing.

4. **Differentiate between technical and fundamental analysis.**

   There are two traditional and well-known approaches to analyzing and selecting common stocks: fundamental and technical analysis. The rationale behind technical analysis is that stock prices will move in trends that may persist and that these changes can be detected by analyzing the action of the stock price itself. Fundamental analysis is based on the premise that any security (and the market as a whole) has an intrinsic value that is a function of the firm's (and the market's) underlying variables. This estimated intrinsic value may then be compared to the current market price of the security (and the market).

5. **Describe the bottom-up and top-down approaches in fundamental analysis.**

   Fundamental security analysis can be done following a bottom-up or a top-down approach. With the bottom-up approach, investors focus on information about a company such as products, competitive position, and financial status. The top-down approach used in Part V of this textbook considers, in order: (1) the economy/market, (2) the industry, and (3) the company.

KEY TERMS

Fundamental analysis, p.466	Momentum investing, p.465	Technical analysis, p.465
Index funds, p.453	Required rate of return, p.448	
Intrinsic value, p.466	Risk premium, p.448	

REVIEW QUESTIONS

14-1. What impact does the market have on well-diversified portfolios? What does this suggest about the performance of mutual funds?

14-2. What is meant by the required rate of return? Explain your answer in the context of an investor considering the purchase of Bombardier's common shares.

14-3. What are the two components of the required rate of return?

14-4. What is the shape of the trade-off between the required rate of return for a stock and its risk? Must this shape always prevail?

14-5. What is the rationale for passive investment strategies?

14-6. What does the evidence cited on market timing suggest about the likelihood of success in this area?

14-7. Identify and differentiate the two traditional approaches to analyzing and selecting common stocks.

14-8. What is the recommended framework for fundamental analysis? Is this a top-down or bottom-up approach? Explain the difference.

14-9. How does this recommended framework relate to the discussion about the impact of the market on investors?

14-10. What is the relationship between fundamental analysis and intrinsic value?

14-11. Explain how technical analysis is primarily based on supply and demand conditions.

14-12. Why is technical analysis inconsistent with the Efficient Market Hypothesis?

14-13. How does an investor in common stocks reconcile the large variability in stock returns, and the big drops that have occurred, with taking a prudent position in owning a portfolio of financial assets?

14-14. Given the drastic—some would say unprecedented—drop in the prices of Japanese stocks, how can Canadian investors justify owning foreign stocks?

14-15. Is there one required rate of return? If not, how many are there?

14-16. What is the required rate of return on the overall market?

14-17. Describe three active strategies that involve the use of common stocks.

14-18. What are the major sources of information used by security analysts in evaluating common stocks?

14-19. How does the cross-sectional variation in common stock returns relate to the issue of stock selection?

14-20. What is meant by sector rotation? What is the key input in implementing effective strategies in sector rotation?

14-21. What is the basic idea behind the Efficient Market Hypothesis?

14-22. What are the implications of the Efficient Market Hypothesis to both stock selectors and market timers?

14-23. What are the advantages and disadvantages to the top-down approach?

14-24. What are the advantages and disadvantages to the bottom-up approach?

14-25. Briefly explain why strategic asset allocation could be classified as a "buy-low, sell-high" strategy. Illustrate with the use of an example.

14-26. List and briefly describe three passive strategies for investing in common stocks.

14-27. For adequately diversified common stock portfolios, market effects often account for __ percent and more of the variability of the portfolio's return.

    a. 60

    b. 70

    c. 80

    d. 90

14-28. If security markets are totally efficient, the best common stock strategy to take is:

    a. an asset allocation approach.

    b. the modern portfolio theory.

     c. an active strategy.

     d. a passive strategy.

14-29. The equity risk premium for the market is 6 percent. What is the real risk-free rate if the expected return on the market is 11 percent, and expected inflation is 3 percent?

14-30. If more investors became passive investors, how would that affect investment companies?

14-31. How should active investors determine if their efforts are worth the cost relative to passive investing?

14-32. Vanguard's Health Care Fund (VGHCX) outperformed Vanguard's S&P 500 Index fund during the period 2000–2005, although it had a higher operating expense ratio. What is the reason for this outperformance?

PROBLEM

14-1. In Real World Returns 14-1, the five-year return figures for Canadian equity mutual funds and ETFs are presented. Although betas are also given for each fund, these figures are not taken into account when determining how the funds performed relative to the overall market. Let's do that for a selection of the funds; we'll work with the first 15 entries in the table (down to the "National Bank Canadian Index" fund). In a spreadsheet enter the fund name, 5-year return figures, and 5-year beta figures into columns A, B, and C respectively.

    a. Assume that the appropriate risk-free rate for this exercise is 4 percent per year. The return figure for the "iShares CDN Composite Index" ETF roughly reflects the overall market (its beta is very close to 1.0). However, this figure is net of the MER. Therefore, let's add the 0.25 percent MER onto that fund's annual return to calculate a more accurate value for the average market return.

    b. Using the figures from part (a) and the 5-year beta values along with the CAPM equation, calculate a risk-adjusted return for each fund. These figures will tell us what return was necessary to compensate for the level of risk (the beta) given the return in the overall market. Add a fourth column to your spreadsheet for these figures.

    c. Compare the figures in columns B and D. If the actual return (column B) is greater than the risk-adjusted value, then the fund has performed better than the market index, on a risk-adjusted basis. Did any of the funds that were ranked higher than the Composite Index actually have a worse performance (risk-adjusted), or did any of the lower ranked funds actually beat the Index?

PREPARING FOR YOUR PROFESSIONAL EXAMS

CFA PRACTICE QUESTION

14-1. All of the following indicate that the three-step (i.e., top-down) valuation process works *except*:

    a. Most changes in a firm's earnings can be attributed to general economic and market factors.

    b. There is a relationship between aggregate stock prices and various economic series such as employment.

    c. Empirical results show that it is possible to pick underpriced securities regardless of the direction of the economy.

    d. Changes in an individual stock's rate of return are best explained by changes in rates of return for the aggregate stock market.

CHAPTER 19

OPTIONS

Having heard about options from several sources, you decide this is one of those topics that you at least have to be able to talk about. If you are going to manage your inheritance without interference, you don't want to be left standing there looking foolish when someone asks you about writing calls or buying a put to protect against market declines. Even the popular press talks about calls and puts on a regular basis. Therefore, you see no alternative but to plow ahead and learn enough about derivatives in general, and options in particular, to let you hold your own. And, besides, this may turn out to be very valuable information you can use in the future when investing.

Learning Objectives

After reading this chapter, you should be able to

1. Define options and discuss why they are used.
2. Describe how options work and give some basic strategies.
3. Explain the valuation of options.
4. Identify types of options other than puts and calls.

CHAPTER PREVIEW

Derivatives are contracts between two parties (a buyer and a seller) that have a price and that trade in specific markets. The importance of derivative securities lies in the flexibility they provide investors in managing investment risk. Derivative instruments can also be used to speculate in various markets. Chapter 19 analyzes one of these derivative contracts—options—while Chapter 20 analyzes another: futures. Real-World Returns 19-1 alludes to the risks associated with derivatives when misused, pointing to the recent multi-billion-dollar losses generated by a rogue trader at the French bank, Société Générale. The article goes on to point out that derivatives per se are not bad, but the danger lies in the reckless action of their users.

REAL-WORLD RETURNS 19-1

Derivatives

How's this for timing: The January edition of *Risk* magazine named a certain French bank the Equity Derivatives House of the Year. A week later, that bank—Société Générale—was suddenly short $7.2-billion because of some unfortunate futures bets.

To be fair, not even *Risk* magazine's deep-thinking editors can predict a rogue trader. But still, that amusing little story does highlight an important point about derivatives. They're not dangerous in and of themselves. But in the hands of people who don't understand them or who have the wrong incentives, they're a powder keg. And since greed makes us all blind and stupid, investors should be extremely wary of any company that dabbles in derivatives.

There are too many kinds of derivatives to count, and more are invented all the time. A derivative is a financial position based on an underlying asset. Compared with a stock or a bond or real estate—traditional assets—derivatives are fleeting, with short life spans generally. They're also powerful because they bulge with leverage—a small change in the underlying asset's price usually means a much bigger change in the derivatives' value, up or down.

The Chicago Board Options Exchange has a price calculator for index options that will show you how a one-year option on an index can go up by 33 percent in value if the index moves from $90 to $91. If the index value moves from $90 to $89, the loss is 29 percent. Now you can see why SocGen's junior trader could do so much damage. But we can also start to see how misleading derivatives talk can be.

Lots of people who want to scare investors with talk of financial Armageddon will talk about the value of derivative positions and how they've mushroomed over the years. Measured in notional terms, that's true: JPMorgan's derivatives book has grown to $92-trillion in 2007 from $22-trillion in 1999. The total amount of US commercial bank derivatives was $172-trillion in the third quarter, $20-trillion more than in the second quarter.

Trillion is the best headline word after sex, drugs and Britney Spears, but is it accurate? In our example above, the notional value of a call option would be $90. It's not how much you can lose (or make). Entire indexes don't generally go to zero. They can drop a lot—say 20 percent, which in our example would cause the theoretical price of the option to go to zero. But the loss isn't $90, it's $1.70, the cost of the option.

So don't concentrate on that raw $172-trillion number. Most of that, in fact, is hedged—that is, the banks take a long position, a neutralizing short position and earn a small fee up the middle. SocGen's rogue trader pretended to be doing this but he was in fact making one-sided bets on future index values. If he thought an index would go up, he'd find someone who thought it would go down (or someone trying to lock in portfolio gains) and make a bet.

Back to the notion of notional: By far the most common derivatives that big US banks are involved in are swaps, whereby two investors agree to trade the return on different assets. Banks often use interest rate swaps to protect themselves (or their clients do it). For example, they may agree to pay a floating interest rate on a notional amount of principal in exchange for receiving a fixed rate from the counterparty. The bank isn't betting on the direction of interest rates; rather it's protecting itself because, in our example, it has to pay interest on debt and wants to make sure it has the cash to make the payments.

What we're saying is: Don't panic when you see big headline numbers. That said, don't be naive. While the absolute number of notional exposure isn't really that telling, the growth is a little more so, and so is that growth relative to bank assets. But even that doesn't hint at the real problem with derivatives, which is the computer programs that tell traders how to cobble together supposedly "safe" portfolios of derivatives. SocGen's problem, if you believe management, is straightforward: Thousands of little bets on the direction of stock indexes that went into the red (and that management liquidated in a panic, more than doubling the loss).

Most derivative explosions happen when a trader thinks he understands the co-relationships between a basket of related derivatives and learns, painfully, that his computer models were wrong. When a Calgary trader blew up hedge fund Amaranth in 2006, he wasn't just long or short a futures contract. He was long some and short others, hoping to earn a spread that flawed statistics told him would materialize. In short, he simply didn't know what he was doing.

The same holds true, in part for CIBC which, we note, has hired 40 consultants to help it work through its derivatives mess. Why didn't it employ these experts before plunging headlong into the derivatives world?

And as for greed, last year Wall Street bonuses were $33-billion. Credit-crunch-related losses, a lot of them caused by derivatives, are more than $100-billion. Shareholders lost that money; rest assured the bonuses won't be repaid to them.

To paraphrase the gun lobby, derivatives don't maul investors. People maul investors.

Source: Taylor, Fabrice, "The minefield of derivatives," *The Globe and Mail Report on Business*, January 30, 2008, p. B13.

This chapter briefly introduces the nature of derivatives in general, and then analyzes options, which are important derivative securities that provide flexibility for investors in managing investment risk and the opportunity to speculate in security markets. We explain the advantages of options and provide some basic strategies. We also discuss how options are valued using the Black-Scholes model. Although our focus is on put and call options, we take a look at interest rate, currency, and stock-index options at the end of the chapter.

INTRODUCTION TO OPTIONS

Rather than trade directly in common stocks, investors can purchase securities representing a claim—an option—on a particular stock or group of stocks. This option gives the holder the right to receive or deliver shares of stock under specified conditions. The option need not be exercised (and often will not be worth exercising). Instead, an investor can simply buy and sell these **equity-derivative securities** that derive their value from the equity prices of the same corporation. Gains or losses will depend on the difference between the purchase price and the sales price.

This chapter looks at put and call options. Appendix 11A discussed convertible securities, and Appendix 19B at the end of this chapter examines warrants and rights. All are equity-derivative securities.[1] We concentrate primarily on options on individual stocks and stock indexes, and to a much lesser extent on interest rate options. In Chapter 20, we consider futures contracts, which together with

Equity-Derivative Securities

Securities that derive their value in whole or in part by having a claim on the underlying common stock.

---

[1]Interest rate derivative securities, such as bond options and futures contracts on bankers' acceptances, are also commonly used derivatives, as discussed in Chapters 2 and 4. Interest rate swaps (which are discussed in Chapter 12) are used primarily by financial institutions and large corporations.

options constitute the most commonplace equity-derivative securities used by the average investor. Since we are focusing on investing instruments, we limit our discussion to financial derivatives.

Our emphasis is on how puts and calls work and on their importance to portfolio managers. As derivative securities, options are innovations in risk management, not in risk itself, and as such they should be both welcomed and used by investors and portfolio managers. Since our emphasis is on equity securities, our examples revolve around common stocks.

Options Basics

learning objective 1
Define options and discuss why they are used.

Options, which typically represent claims on an underlying common stock, are created by investors and sold to other investors. The corporation whose common stock underlies these claims has no direct interest in the transaction, being in no way responsible for creating, terminating, or executing put and call contracts.

Options

Claims that give the holder the right, but not the obligation, to buy or sell a stated number of shares of stock within a specified period at a specified price.

A **call** option contract gives the holder the right but not the obligation to buy (or "call away") a specified number of shares of a particular common stock at a specified price any time prior to a specified expiration date.[2] Investors purchase calls if they expect the stock price to rise because the price of the call and the common stock will move together. Therefore, calls permit investors to speculate on a rise in the price of the underlying common stock without buying the stock itself. For example, a Canadian Pacific Railway (CP) two-month call option at $74 per share gives the buyer the right (an option) to purchase 100 shares of CP at $74 per share from a writer (seller) of the option anytime during the two months before the specified expiration date.

Call

An option that gives the holder the right, but not the obligation, to buy a specified number of shares of stock at a stated price within a specified period.

A **put** option contract gives the buyer the right but not the obligation to sell (or "put away") a specified number of shares of a particular common stock at a specified price prior to a specified expiration date. If exercised, the shares are sold by the owner (buyer) of the put contract to a writer (seller) of the contract, who has been designated to take delivery of the shares and pay the specified price. Investors purchase puts if they expect the stock price to fall, because the value of the put will rise as the stock price declines. Therefore, puts allow investors to speculate on a decline in the stock price without selling the common stock short. For example, the writer (seller) of a CP two-month put at $74 per share is obligated, under certain circumstances, to receive from the holder of this put 100 shares of CP, for which the writer will pay $74 per share.

Put

An option that gives the holder the right, but not the obligation, to sell a specified number of shares of stock at a stated price within a specified period.

Why Options Markets?

An investor can always purchase shares of common stock if he or she is bullish about the company's prospects rather than buy a call (or sell a put). Similarly, one can sell a company's shares short if bearish about the stock rather than buy a put (or sell a call). Why, then, should we create these indirect claims on a stock as an alternative way to invest? Several reasons have been advanced, including the following:

1. Puts and calls expand the opportunity set available to investors, making available risk–return combinations that otherwise would be impossible or that improve the risk–return characteristics of a portfolio. For example, an investor can sell a stock short and buy a call. This decreases the risk on the short sale for the life of the call since the investor has a guaranteed maximum purchase price until the call option expires.[3]

2. In the case of calls, an investor can control (for a short period) a claim on the underlying common stock for a much smaller investment than required to buy the stock itself. In the case of puts, an investor can duplicate a short sale without a margin account and at a modest cost in relation to the value of the stock. In addition, the option buyer's maximum loss is known in advance. If an option expires worthless, the most the buyer can lose is the cost (price) of the option.

---

[2]It is important to remember throughout this discussion that the standard option contract on the organized exchanges is for 100 shares of the underlying common stock.

[3]Many stocks do not have puts and calls available in the organized options market exchanges. For example, the active options trading on the Montreal Exchange consists of less than a hundred stocks, while a few hundred stocks dominate the listings and trading activity on large US options markets such as the Chicago Board Options Exchange (CBOE). There are also a large number of stock options that trade in the over-the-counter market through brokers.

3. Options provide leverage by magnifying the percentage gains in relation to buying or short selling the underlying stock. In fact, options can provide greater leverage potential than fully margined stock transactions.

4. Using options on a market index such as the S&P/TSX 60 Index, an investor can participate in market movements with a single trading decision.

UNDERSTANDING OPTIONS

Options Terminology

To understand puts and calls, one must understand the terminology used in connection with them. Our discussion here applies specifically to options on the organized exchanges as reported daily in the financial media.[4] Important options terms include the following:

1. The **exercise (strike) price** is the per-share price at which the common stock may be purchased (in the case of a call) or sold (in the case of a put). Most options are available at several different exercise prices, thereby giving investors a choice. As the stock price changes, options with new exercise prices are added.[5]

2. The **expiration date** is the last date on which an option can be exercised. All puts and calls are designated by the month of expiration, with equity options expiring on the Saturday following the third Friday of the month. This forces clients to make their exercise decisions on the Friday. The expiration dates for options contracts vary from stock to stock.

3. The **option premium** is the price paid by the option buyer to the writer (seller) of the option, whether put or call. The premium is stated on a per-share basis for options on organized exchanges, and since the standard contract is for 100 shares, a $3 premium represents a cost per contract of $300, a $15 premium represents a cost of $1,500, and so forth.

Options exchanges have introduced combinations of standardized expiration dates (known as trading cycles) and standardized exercise prices. For example, Real-World Returns 19-2 describes Equity Option Cycles on the Montreal Exchange.

Exercise (Strike) Price
The per-share price at which the common stock may be purchased from (in the case of a call) or sold to (in the case of a put) a writer.

Expiration Date
The date on which an option expires.

Option Premium
The price paid by the option buyer to the seller (writer) of the option.

REAL-WORLD RETURNS 19-2

Equity Option Cycles

All equity options issued by the Canadian Derivatives Clearing Corporation (CDCC) and listed on the Montréal Exchange have expiry cycles. Expiry cycles are used to establish the length of time that an option will be listed and quoted by the equity option market makers.

Cycles vary in relation to the dividend that is being paid out by the listed underlying company and are comprised of four maturities: two near months and two quarterly months. Exceptions to this rule are the iShares and index options, which fall under cycle 4 having five maturities, as shown hereunder.

Montréal Exchange also has long-term equity options expiring in one-, two- and three-year intervals. These long-term equity options only have one expiry month, i.e. January (or March for long-term index options). Long-term options eventually get included as regular expiries when their cycle approaches nine months to its expiry.

(continued)

---

[4]Puts and calls existed for many years before the existence of organized exchanges. They could be bought or sold in the over-the-counter (OTC) market. The terms of each individual contract (price, exercise date, etc.) had to be negotiated between buyer and seller. This was clearly a cumbersome, inefficient process. The OTC market for options is unregulated, and transactions are not reported. Although specific information is not available, a very large OTC market for options does exist and is widely used by corporations and portfolio managers for hedging purposes.

[5]Options sold on these exchanges are protected against stock dividends and stock splits; both the exercise price and the number of shares in the contract are adjusted for dividends or splits, as necessary.

REAL-WORLD RETURNS 19-2 *continued*

Cycle 1 Four maturities — two near months and the next two months from the January, April, July, October cycle.

Cycle 2 Four maturities — two near months and the next two months from the February, May, August, November cycle.

Cycle 3 Four maturities — two near months and the next two months from the March, June, September, December cycle.

Cycle 4 Five maturities — three near months and the next two months from cycle 3.

Source: Retrieved from Montreal Exchange Equity Option Cycles Publication www.m-x.ca, May 26, 2008.

Figure 19-1 is an excerpt from Globeinvestor.com that shows the most actively traded call options on the Montreal Exchange on May 26, 2008. It reports the symbol for the underlying stock and for the call option, the option expiry date, the strike price, the underlying stock price, the last price for the option, the change in the option price in dollar figures and as a percentage, and the volume and open interest for the call option. The volume shows the number of options contracts that were traded the previous day, while the open interest represents the number of options of a particular series that are presently outstanding. It is usually used as a measure of liquidity, along with the volume of trading.

Figure 19-1
Equity Options

MOST ACTIVE - PRICE INCREASE (CALLS)

Stock	Symbol Option	Expiry Date	Strike Price	Underlying Price	Put/ Call	Last	Change $	Change %	Vol	Open Interest
TLM-T	TLMF2600	2008-06	26.00	24.70	CALL	0.75	0.45	150.00	125	5741
TLM-T	TLMF2800	2008-06	28.00	24.70	CALL	0.35	0.20	133.33	142	105
TLM-T	TLMF2400	2008-06	24.00	24.70	CALL	1.75	0.95	118.75	583	5957
TLM-T	TLMG2600	2008-07	26.00	24.70	CALL	1.10	0.50	83.33	45	1050
TLM-T	TLMG2800	2008-07	28.00	24.70	CALL	0.55	0.25	83.33	50	60
TLM-T	TLMG2400	2008-07	24.00	24.70	CALL	2.05	0.85	70.83	82	156
TLM-T	TLMI2600	2008-09	26.00	24.70	CALL	1.95	0.80	69.57	120	3522
TLM-T	TLMF2200	2008-06	22.00	24.70	CALL	3.10	1.25	67.57	90	3358
TLM-T	TLMG2200	2008-07	22.00	24.70	CALL	3.30	1.10	50.00	20	6
BCB-T	BCBA700	2009-01	7.00	3.61	CALL	0.15	0.05	50.00	40	0
PWF-T	PWFG4200	2008-07	42.00	35.60	CALL	0.15	0.05	50.00	10	526
BCB-T	BCBG500	2008-07	5.00	3.61	CALL	0.15	0.05	50.00	60	357
TLM-T	TLMI2400	2008-09	24.00	24.70	CALL	2.80	0.90	47.37	102	562
TLM-T	TLMF2000	2008-06	20.00	24.70	CALL	4.65	1.30	38.81	52	2447
TLM-T	TLMI2800	2008-09	28.00	24.70	CALL	1.10	0.30	37.50	20	973
TLM-T	TLMG2000	2008-07	20.00	24.70	CALL	4.90	1.30	36.11	14	0
TLM-T	TLMF1900	2008-06	19.00	24.70	CALL	5.75	1.45	33.72	10	1277
TLM-T	ZLMA2600	2009-01	26.00	24.70	CALL	2.45	0.60	32.43	40	861
TLM-T	ZLMA2400	2009-01	24.00	24.70	CALL	3.35	0.80	31.37	63	1185
TLM-T	ZLMA2800	2009-01	28.00	24.70	CALL	1.70	0.40	30.77	98	186
FNX-T	FNXF2600	2008-06	26.00	23.95	CALL	0.45	0.10	28.57	3	125
TLM-T	ZLMA2200	2009-01	22.00	24.70	CALL	4.45	0.95	27.14	86	887
TLM-T	TLMI2200	2008-09	22.00	24.70	CALL	3.55	0.75	26.79	31	1562
MBT-T	MBTF4000	2008-06	40.00	42.20	CALL	2.45	0.50	25.64	13	28

Stock	Symbol Option	Expiry Date	Strike Price	Underlying Price	Put/ Call	Last	Change $	Change %	Vol	Open Interest
TLM-T	TLML2800	2008-12	28.00	24.70	CALL	1.50	0.30	25.00	309	779
FTS-T	FTSG3000	2008-07	30.00	27.67	CALL	0.25	0.05	25.00	6	658
TLM-T	ZLMA2000	2009-01	20.00	24.70	CALL	5.80	1.10	23.40	193	1061
TLM-T	TLML2600	2008-12	26.00	24.70	CALL	2.15	0.40	22.86	110	388
TLM-T	TLML2400	2008-12	24.00	24.70	CALL	3.00	0.55	22.45	145	494
TLM-T	TLMI2000	2008-09	20.00	24.70	CALL	5.00	0.90	21.95	25	1206
BNS-T	BNSG5200	2008-07	52.00	48.20	CALL	0.30	0.05	20.00	8	1607
NG-T	NGA900	2009-01	9.00	8.58	CALL	1.85	0.30	19.35	15	0
HXD-T	HXDG1600	2008-07	16.00	16.38	CALL	2.50	0.40	19.05	3	0
FM-T	FMF8000	2008-06	80.00	77.15	CALL	4.15	0.65	18.57	10	21
BNS-T	BNSF4800	2008-06	48.00	48.20	CALL	1.30	0.20	18.18	60	3660
TLM-T	ZLMA1800	2009-01	18.00	24.70	CALL	7.25	1.10	17.89	31	552
CP-T	CPF7400	2008-06	74.00	71.95	CALL	1.00	0.15	17.65	12	346
NCX-T	NCXF2800	2008-06	28.00	27.84	CALL	1.00	0.15	17.65	20	96
TLM-T	ZLMA1600	2009-01	16.00	24.70	CALL	9.00	1.25	16.13	94	328
TLM-T	WLMA2600	2010-01	26.00	24.70	CALL	4.00	0.55	15.94	10	119
PDN-T	PDNF500	2008-06	5.00	5.71	CALL	0.75	0.10	15.38	101	442
TLM-T	TLMI1800	2008-09	18.00	24.70	CALL	6.50	0.85	15.04	5	452
BNS-T	BNSF5000	2008-06	50.00	48.20	CALL	0.40	0.05	14.29	47	1923
MFC-T	MFCG4400	2008-07	44.00	38.14	CALL	0.08	0.01	14.29	10	673
CP-T	CPG7400	2008-07	74.00	71.95	CALL	1.65	0.20	13.79	5	244
TLM-T	WLMA2000	2010-01	20.00	24.70	CALL	7.10	0.85	13.60	3	498
NCX-T	NCXF2600	2008-06	26.00	27.84	CALL	2.25	0.25	12.50	10	65
RY-T	RYF5000	2008-06	50.00	50.15	CALL	1.40	0.15	12.00	14	3993
CCO-T	CCOF4200	2008-06	42.00	40.94	CALL	1.40	0.15	12.00	25	568
TLM-T	WLMA1200	2010-01	12.00	24.70	CALL	13.35	1.40	11.72	5	125

Source: Retrieved from www.globeinvestor.com, May 26, 2008.

Consider the third last row referring to the **Royal Bank of Canada (RBC)** June 2008, $50 call options, reported as:

Stock	Symbol Option	Expiry Date	Strike Price	Underlying Price	Put/ Call	Last	Change $	Change %	Vol	Open Interest
RY-T	RYF5000	2008-06	50.00	50.15	CALL	1.40	0.15	12.00	14	3993

We can see that these options expire in June 2008, and they have an exercise price of $50, while the common shares of RBC closed trading on May 26, 2008, at $50.15 per share. The last trade price for these options was $1.40 per option (or $1.40 × 100 = $140 per option contract), the traded volume in this option series that day was 14 contracts, and the open interest was 3993 contracts.

Long-term options or **LEAPs** (short for Long-Term Equity AnticiPation Securities)[6] are options with maturities greater than one year and ranging to two years and beyond. They are available on several stocks, with more being traded all the time. For example, in May 2008, an investor could purchase long-term call options on **RBC** with maturity dates of January 2010 or January 2011.

Long-Term Options (LEAPs)

Options on individual stocks with maturities greater than one year.

---

[6]LEAPs is a registered trademark of the Chicago Board Options Exchange.

How Options Work

As noted, a standard call (put) contract gives the buyer the right to purchase (sell) 100 shares of a particular stock at a specified exercise price before the expiration date. Both puts and calls are created by sellers who write a particular contract. Sellers (writers) are investors, either individuals or institutions, who seek to profit from their beliefs about the underlying stock's likely price performance, just as the buyer does.

The buyer and the seller have opposite expectations about the likely performance of the underlying stock and therefore the performance of the option.

- The call writer expects the price of the stock to remain roughly steady or perhaps move down.
- The call buyer expects the price of the stock to move upward and relatively soon.
- The put writer expects the price of the stock to remain roughly steady or perhaps move up.
- The put buyer expects the price of the stock to move down and relatively soon.

EXAMPLE 19-1: BUYING A CALL OPTION ON RBC

Consider an individual named Carl who is optimistic about RBC's prospects. Carl instructs his broker to buy a June 2008 call option on RBC at a strike price of $50. Assume that the negotiated premium is $1.40 (i.e., the Last value reported in Figure 19-1). This implies the cost of one option contract is $140 plus brokerage commissions.

Three courses of action are possible with any option:

1. *The option may expire worthless.* Assume the price of RBC fluctuates up and down but is at $45 on the expiration date. The call gives the buyer (owner) the right to purchase RBC at $50, but this would make no sense when RBC can be purchased on the open market at $45. Therefore, the option will expire worthless.

2. *The option may be exercised.* If RBC appreciates above $50, Carl could exercise the option by paying $5,000 (the $50 exercise price multiplied by 100 shares) and receiving 100 shares of RBC. For example, if the shares appreciated to $60 before expiration, Carl could purchase 100 shares for $5,000 plus commission fees, and resell them in the market for $6,000 less commission fees. His resulting profit would be $6,000 – $5,000 – $140 (the original cost of the option contract) – total commission fees.

3. *The option can be sold in the secondary market.* If RBC appreciates, the value (price) of the call will also. Carl can easily sell the call in the secondary market to another investor who wishes to speculate on RBC because listed options are traded continuously. Most investors trading puts and calls do not exercise those that are valuable; instead, they simply sell them on the open market, exactly as they would the common stock.[7]

Puts work the same way as calls, except in reverse. A writer creates a particular put contract and sells it for the premium that the buyer pays. The writer believes that the underlying common stock is likely to remain flat or appreciate, while the buyer believes that the stock price is likely to decline. Unlike a buyer, a writer may have to take action in the form of taking delivery of the stock.

EXAMPLE 19-2: SELLING A PUT OPTION ON RBC

Assume a writer sells a June 2008 RBC put option contract with an exercise price of $52.00 when the stock price is $50.15. A premium of $2.35 (the Last price as of May 26, 2008) means a total

---

[7]One of the implications of the option pricing model to be considered later is that American calls on stocks that do not pay a cash dividend should never be exercised before the expiration date, but those with dividends might be exercised.

of $235 per option contract, which the buyer of the put pays and the writer receives (brokerage costs would be involved in both cases).

Suppose the price of RBC declines to $45 near the expiration date. The put owner (buyer), who did not own RBC previously, could instruct the broker to purchase 100 shares of RBC in the open market for $4,500. The buyer could then exercise the put, which means that a chosen writer must accept the 100 shares of RBC and pay the put owner $52.00 per share, or $5,200 total (although the current market price has fallen to only $45). The put buyer earns $465 before commission fees ($5,200 received less $4,500 cost of 100 shares less the $235 paid for the put contract). The put writer suffers an immediate paper loss because the 100 shares of RBC are worth $45 per share but have a cost of $52.00 per share, although the premium received by the writer reduces this loss by $235. (Brokerage costs have once again been omitted in the example.)

As in the case of a call, two other courses of action are possible in addition to the exercise of the put. If the market price of the shares was below $52.00 (the exercise price), it is far more likely that the put owner would sell the put in the secondary market for a profit (or a loss), rather than exercising the option. As in the case of calls, most put investors simply buy and sell their options in the open market. Alternatively, if the price of RBC is at or above $52.00, the put would expire worthless because the price of the common stock did not decline enough to justify exercising the put.

The Mechanics of Trading
The Options Exchanges

Most exchange listed equity options are American style, which can be exercised at any time up to and including the expiration date. Index options and over-the-counter (OTC) options are typically European, which means they can only be exercised on the expiration date. Options can be bought or sold through an exchange facility or privately arranged (OTC options).

As mentioned in Chapter 4, all exchange-traded options in Canada trade on the Montreal Exchange (ME), which officially merged with the TSX on May 2, 2008, to form the TMX Group. Five option exchanges constitute the secondary market in the US: the Chicago Board Options Exchange (CBOE), the American, the Philadelphia, the Pacific, and the newer International Securities Exchange (ISE) in New York. Traditionally, the first four exchanges controlled the trading of US options, each handling different options and competing very little. The ISE began trading in May 2000, and now has a substantial share of US trading volume in options. This all-electronic market is extremely efficient, and this competition has led to lower costs and narrower spreads for customers and quicker access to the market.

The options markets provide liquidity to investors, which is a very important requirement for successful trading. Investors know that they can instruct their broker to buy or sell whenever they desire at a price set by the forces of supply and demand. Liquidity problems, which often plague the OTC options markets, are overcome by

1. Offering standardized option contracts
2. Having all transactions guaranteed by a clearing corporation, which effectively becomes the buyer and seller for each option contract.

The same types of orders discussed in Chapter 5, in particular, market, limit, and stop orders, are used in trading puts and calls.[8] Certificates representing ownership are not used for puts and calls; instead, transactions are handled as bookkeeping entries. Option trades settle on the next business day after the trade. The exercise of an equity option settles in three business days, the same as

---

[8]While these orders are available, the manner in which some types of orders are executed on some of the options exchanges varies from that used on the stock exchanges.

with a stock transaction. An investor must receive a risk disclosure statement issued by the clearing corporation (discussed in the following section) before the initial order is executed.

Table 19-1 shows the option volume on the Montreal Exchange for 2006 and 2007.

Table 19-1

Option Product Group

Option Product Group	2006 Volume		2007 Volume	
Interest Rate Derivatives				
Future Options	605,806	4.7%	748,991	5.3%
Bond Options	2,275	0.02%	13,782	0.01%
Index Derivative				
Options on Index Derivatives	906,677	7.0%	814,880	5.7%
Equity Derivatives				
Equity Options	10,629,749	82.0%	11,903,402	83.6%
Leaps	787,009	6.1%	730,658	5.1%
Totals	**12,962,778**	**100.0%**	**14,246,602**	**100.0%**

Source: Retrieved from www.m-x.ca

While Table 19-1 indicates the volume of options traded in Canada has been increasing, a significant problem with the Canadian options markets has traditionally been thin trading. As a result, many investors have often taken their option trades to US markets, which deal with much larger trading volumes. For example, the largest options exchange in the world is the Chicago Board Options Exchange (CBOE). The volume of trading in all options on this exchange in 2007 was 944.5 million contracts—more than 66 times the volume of all ME option trades that year.

In addition to the equity options that are available on the ME and the OTC markets in Canada and through the US markets, there are a variety of alternative option products available to Canadian investors. Stock-index options on the S&P/TSX Index are available in Canada and options also trade on many of the Canadian-based ETFs discussed in Chapter 3, such as the i60 units, whose values are determined by the levels of the S&P/TSX 60 Index.

Index options on the Standard & Poor's 100 Index plus others in US are also available. Stock-index options are "cash-settled" based on 100 times the value of the index at expiration date. Bond options trade on the ME on Government of Canada bonds, while US dollar options are available on the ME and other currency options are available in US markets.

The Clearing Corporation

In Canada, all equity, bond, and stock index positions are issued and guaranteed by a single clearing corporation, the **Canadian Derivatives Clearing Corporation (CDCC)**, which is owned by the ME.

In the US, all listed options are cleared through the Options Clearing Corporation (OCC). Exercise on options trading on exchanges is accomplished by submitting an exercise notice to the clearing corporation. The clearing corporation then assigns the exercise notice to a member firm, which then assigns it to one of its accounts.

These clearing corporations perform a number of important functions that contribute to the success of the secondary market for options. They function as intermediaries between the brokers representing the buyers and the writers. That is, once the brokers representing the buyer and the seller negotiate the price on the floor of the exchange, they no longer deal with each other but with the

Canadian Derivatives Clearing Corporation (CDCC)

The clearing corporation that issues and guarantees all equity, bond, and stock index positions on options exchanges in Canada.

CDCC (or the OCC in the US). Through their brokers, call writers contract with the CDCC itself to deliver shares of the particular stock, and buyers of calls actually receive the right to purchase the shares from the CDCC. Thus, the CDCC becomes the buyer for every seller and the seller for every buyer, guaranteeing that all contract obligations will be met. This prevents the risk and problems that could occur as buyers attempted to force writers to honour their obligations. The net position of the CDCC is zero, because the number of contracts purchased must equal the number sold.

Investors wishing to exercise their options inform their brokers, who in turn inform the CDCC of the exercise notice. Once the option holder submits the exercise note, the process is irrevocable. The CDCC randomly selects a broker on whom it holds the same written contract, and the broker randomly selects a customer who has written these options to honour the contract. Writers chosen in this manner are said to be assigned an obligation or to have received an assignment notice.[9] Once assigned, the writer cannot execute an offsetting transaction to eliminate the obligation; that is, a call writer who receives an assignment must sell the underlying securities, and a put writer must purchase them.

One of the great advantages of a clearing house is that transactors in this market can easily cancel their positions prior to assignment. Since the CDCC maintains all the positions for both buyers and sellers, it can cancel out the obligations of both call and put writers wishing to terminate their position. For example, a call writer can terminate the obligation to deliver the stock any time before the expiration date (or assignment) by making a "closing purchase transaction" at the current market price of the option. The CDCC offsets the outstanding call written with the call purchased in the closing transaction. A put writer can also close out a position at any time by making an offsetting transaction.

Options cannot be purchased on margin, and buyers must pay 100 percent of the purchase price. With regard to puts and calls, *margin* refers to the collateral that option writers provide their brokers to ensure fulfillment of the contract in case of exercise. This collateral is required by the CDCC of its member firms whose clients have written options, in order to protect the CDCC against default by option writers. The member firms, in turn, require its customers who have written options to provide collateral for their written positions. This collateral can be in the form of cash or marketable securities (including shares in the underlying security).

CHECK YOUR UNDERSTANDING

19-1. Why might an investor prefer to buy a put on a particular stock rather than sell it short?

19-2. What does it mean to say a call buyer has a right but not an obligation? What about the call seller?

19-3. Assume that an investor buys a put on a stock. Describe three different outcomes that could occur for the investor holding this option.

19-4. How does the clearing house (or clearing corporation) help to ensure the fulfillment of put and call contracts?

SOME BASIC OPTIONS CHARACTERISTICS

In the Money, At the Money, and Out of the Money

Special terminology is used to describe the relationship between the exercise price of the option and the current stock price. If the price of the common stock, S, exceeds the exercise price of a call, E, the call is said to be *in the money* and has an immediate exercisable value. On the other hand, if the price of the common is less than the exercise price of a call, it is said to be *out of the money*. Finally,

---

[9]Assignment is virtually certain when an option expires in the money.

calls that are near the money are those with exercise prices slightly greater than current market price, whereas calls that are *at the money* are those with exercise prices equal to the stock price.

These same definitions also apply to puts, but in reverse.

In summary,

> If S > E, a call is in the money and a put is out of the money.
>
> If S < E, a call is out of the money and a put is in the money.
>
> If S = E, an option is at the money.

Intrinsic Values

Intrinsic Value (Option)

The value of an option if today was the expiration date.

If a call is in the money (the market price of the stock exceeds the exercise price for the call option), it has an *immediate* value equal to the difference in the two prices. This value will be designated as the **intrinsic value** of the call; it could also be referred to as the option's minimum value, which in this case is positive. If the call is at or out of the money, the intrinsic value is zero and the price of the option is based entirely on its speculative appeal. The intrinsic value can never fall below $0, since exercise is optional. Summarizing, where S_0 = current stock price:

(19-1)

$$\text{Intrinsic value of a call} = \text{Maximum } \{(S_0 - E), 0\}$$

EXAMPLE 19-3: CALCULATING INTRINSIC VALUE OF CP

We observe a closing price of $71.95 for the common shares of CP on May 26, 2008 (as shown in Figure 19-1). An October 2008 call option on CP with a $70 strike price is available at a premium of $6.40 (the last trade price). This option is in the money because the stock price is greater than the exercise price. The intrinsic value of the October 2008 call is

Intrinsic value of CP October 70 call

= Maximum [($71.95 − $70.00), 0] = $1.95

Puts work in reverse. If the market price of the stock is less than the exercise price of the put, the put is in the money and has an intrinsic value. Otherwise, it is at or out of the money and has a zero intrinsic value. Thus,

(19-2)

$$\text{Intrinsic value of a put} = \text{Maximum } \{(E - S_0), 0\}$$

EXAMPLE 19-4: CALCULATING INTRINSIC VALUE OF CP

There was an October 2008 put on CP stock available on May 26, 2008, with an exercise price of $74.00 (with a last trade price of $6.00). Given the market price for CP shares of $71.95 at that time, the intrinsic value for this put can be determined in the following manner:

Intrinsic value of CP October 74 put

= Maximum [($74.00 − $71.95), 0] = $2.05

PAYOFFS AND PROFITS FROM BASIC OPTION POSITIONS

We can better understand the characteristics of options by examining their potential payoffs and profits. The simplest way to do this is to examine their value at expiration. At the expiration date, an option has an investment value, or payoff, which equals the option's intrinsic value at that time. In addition, we can also examine the net profit, which takes into account the price of the stock, the exercise price of the option, and the cost of the option. We consider both variables because option traders are interested in their net profits, but option valuation is perhaps better understood by focusing on payoffs.

As part of this analysis, we use letters to designate the key variables:

$$S_T = \text{the value of the stock at expiration date T}$$
$$E = \text{the exercise price of the option}$$

Calls
Buying a Call

Consider first the buyer of a call option. At expiration, the investment value or payoff to the call holder is

Payoff to call buyer at expiration:
$$= S_T - E \text{ if } S_T > E$$
$$= 0 \text{ if } S_T < E$$

Notice that this payoff is the intrinsic value for a call option at time T, as presented in Equation 19-1. This payoff to a call buyer is illustrated in Figure 19-2(a). The payoff is \$0 until the exercise price is reached, at which point the payoff rises as the stock price rises.

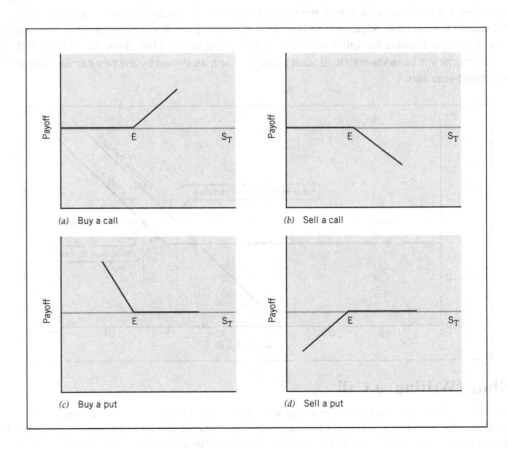

Figure 19-2
Payoff Profiles for Call and Put Options at Expiration

EXAMPLE 19-5: DETERMINING PAYOFF ON AN RBC CALL

Assume an investor buys an RBC July call option with an exercise price of $50. The payoff for the call at expiration is a function of the stock price at that time. For example, at expiration the value of the call relative to various possible stock prices would be calculated as in the following partial set of prices:

RBC stock price at expiration	$40	45	50	55	60
RBC call value (payoff) at expiration	$ 0	0	0	5	10

Notice that the payoff is not the same as the net profit to the option holder or writer. For example, if RBC is at $55 per share, the payoff to the option buyer is $5, but the net profit must reflect the cost of the call. In general, the profit to an option holder is the value of the option less the price paid for it. For the example above, if the cost of the RBC July 50 call option was originally $1.85, the net profit to the option holder (ignoring transactions costs) would be

$$\text{Net profit (option holder)} = \text{Option payoff} - \text{Option cost}$$

$$\text{Net profit (option holder)} = \$5 - \$1.85 = \$3.15$$

EXAMPLE 19-6: DETERMINING NET PROFIT ON CALL AND PUT OPTIONS

Figure 19-3 illustrates the profit situation for a call buyer. The price of the stock is assumed to be $48, and a six-month call is available with an exercise price of $50 for a premium of $4 per option, or $400 per option contract. If this call expires worthless, the maximum loss is the $400 premium. Up to the exercise price of $50, the loss is $4 per option. The break-even point for the investor is the sum of the exercise price and the premium, or $50 + $4 = $54. Therefore, the profit-loss line for the call buyer crosses the break-even line at $54. If the price of the stock rises above $54, the value of the call will increase with it, at least point for point, as shown by the two parallel lines above the $0 profit-loss line.

Figure 19-3
Profit and Losses to the
Buyer of a Call Option

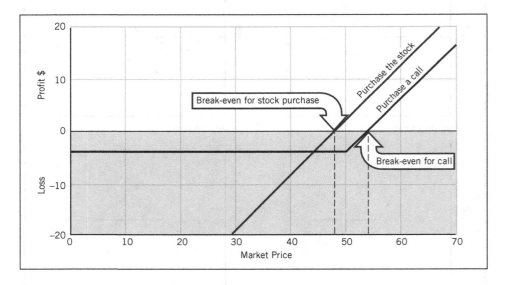

Selling (Writing) a Call

A "naked" or uncovered option writer is one who does not have their position "covered" in the underlying stock—in other words, does not own shares in the underlying stock to make available if the call option is exercised. Naked call option writers (or sellers) incur losses if the stock's price increases, as shown by the payoff profile in part (b) of Figure 19-2. The payoff is flat at the amount of the premium until the exercise price is reached, at which point it declines as the stock price rises. The call writer loses and the call buyer gains if the stock price rises.

Payoff to naked call writer at expiration:
$$= -(S_T - E) \text{ if } S_T > E$$
$$= 0 \qquad\qquad \text{if } S_T < E$$

The net profit line in Figure 19-4 is the mirror image of that for the call buyer, with positive profit levels up to the exercise price because the call writer is receiving the premium. The horizontal axis intercept in Figure 19-4 occurs at the break-even point for the option writer—the sum of the exercise price and the option premium received (note that the break-even point is identical to that of the call buyer). As the stock price exceeds the break-even point, the call writer loses. In fact, there is no conceptual limit to the call option writer's losses, since there is no upward limit on the price of the underlying share.

The mirror images of the payoff and net profit profiles for the call buyer [Figure 19-2(a) and Figure 19-3] and the call writer [Figure 19-2(b) and Figure 19-4] illustrate an important point. Option trading is often referred to as a zero-sum game, because whatever the option buyer gains, the option writer loses and vice versa. With commissions, options trading could be unprofitable for both buyers and sellers and must be unprofitable for both taken together since it is a zero-sum game. However, even though no actual wealth is created, both parties may achieve their investment objectives.

To illustrate this zero-sum game notion, consider the RBC July 50 call option discussed above that had a payoff of $5 to the option holder, when the ending share price was $55. Under the same circumstances, the payoff to the option writer would be −$5. Assuming this option writer had received $1.85 per option (the price paid by the option holder), the option writer's net profit would be the exact opposite of the net profit to the option holder, or

$$\text{Net profit (option writer)} = \text{Option premium} - \text{Option payoff}$$

$$\text{Net profit (option writer)} = \$1.85 - \$5.00 = -\$3.15$$

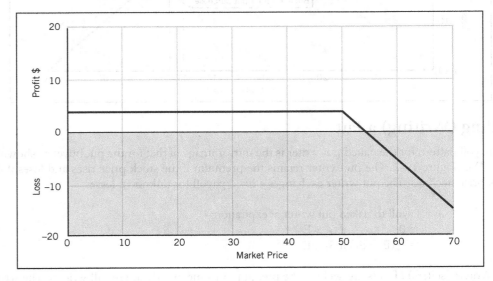

Figure 19-4
Profit and Losses to the Writer of a Call Option

Puts

Buying a Put

A put buyer makes money if the price of the stock declines. Therefore, as part (c) of Figure 19-2 illustrates, the payoff pattern is flat at the $0 axis to the right of the exercise price; that is, stock prices greater than the exercise price result in a \$0 payoff for the put buyer. As the stock declines below the exercise price, the payoff for the put option increases. The larger the decline in the stock price, the larger the payoff.

Payoff to put buyer at expiration:
$= 0$ if $S_T > E$
$= E - S_T$ if $S_T < E$

Notice, as with call options, that this payoff corresponds to the intrinsic value of the option at the expiration date.

Once again, the profit line parallels the payoff pattern for the put option at expiration. As Figure 19-5 illustrates, the investor breaks even (no net profit) at the point where the stock price is equal to the exercise price minus the premium paid for the put. Beyond that point, the net profit line parallels the payoff line representing the investment value of the put.

Figure 19-5
Profit and Losses to the Buyer of a Put Option

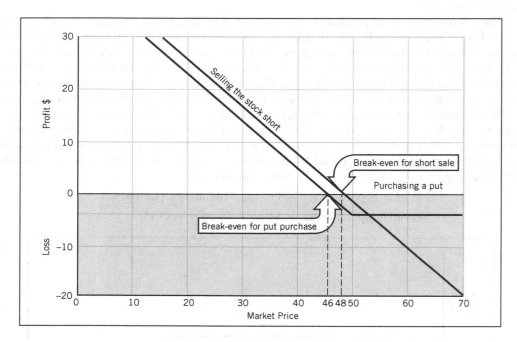

Selling (Writing) a Put

The payoff pattern for the naked put writer is the mirror image of that for the put buyer as shown in part (d) of Figure 19-2. The put writer retains the premium if the stock price rises and loses if the stock price declines. The put writer exchanges a fixed payoff for unknown losses.

Payoff to naked put writer at expiration:
$= 0$ if $S_T > E$
$= -(E - S_T)$ if $S_T < E$

Writers (sellers) of puts are seeking the premium income exactly as are call writers. The writer obligates himself or herself to purchase a stock at the specified exercise price during the life of the put contract. If stock prices decline, the put buyer may purchase the stock and exercise the put by delivering the stock to the writer, who must pay the specified price.

Note that the put writer may be obligated to purchase a stock for, say, \$50 a share when it is selling in the market for \$40 a share. This represents an immediate paper loss (less the premium received for selling the put). Also note that the put writer can cancel the obligation by purchasing an identical contract in the market.[10]

EXAMPLE 19-7: DETERMINING PROFITS AND LOSSES

Figure 19-6 illustrates the profit-loss position for the seller of a put. Using the previous figures, we see that a six-month put is sold at an exercise price of $50 for a premium of $4. The seller of a naked put receives the premium and hopes that the stock price remains at or above the exercise price. As the price of the stock falls, the seller's position declines. The seller begins to lose money below the break-even point, which in this case is $50 − $4 = $46. Losses could be substantial if the price of the stock declined sharply. The price of the put will increase point for point as the stock price declines. The maximum loss for the put writer is bounded, unlike that for the call writer, since the price for the underlying share cannot fall below zero. In this example, the most the put writer could lose is $4 − $50 = −$46 (where −$50 is the payoff if the shares became worthless).

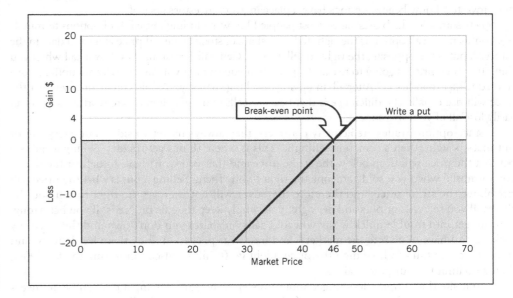

Figure 19-6
Profit and Losses to the Writer of a Put Option

Some Observations on Buying and Selling Options

Options are attractive because of the small investment required and the potentially large payoff. According to the studies that have been done, the odds favour the sellers. Writing calls produces steady, although not extraordinary, returns. Call writing is often profitable, and call buying is often unprofitable. When buying options investors should generally avoid options that expire in a few weeks—about 75 percent of the option premium disappears in the last three weeks of the option's life. Selling uncovered options is very risky. In effect, the reward (premium) does not justify the risk for most investors. Real-World Returns 19-3 discusses one investor's strategy for buying and selling call options.

---

[10]Of course, if the price of the stock has declined since the put was written, the price of the put will have increased and the writer will have to repurchase at a price higher than the premium received when the put was written.

REAL-WORLD RETURNS 19-3

Options

Why buying and selling calls has a place in even a conservative investor's playbook.

    I am not much of a gambler. Years ago I was at the Desert Inn in Las Vegas and tried using a "system" for winning big at roulette. I don't recall the fine points, but it involved doubling my bet every time I lost. I was down so far, so fast, it left my head spinning. I spent the rest of the night playing blackjack, determinedly eking out small gains until, many tedious hours later, I was even.

    For a long time I shunned options in the stock market as just another form of gambling. But a few years back, I bought some long-term call options, or "Leaps" (for Long-term Equity Anticipation Securities), which worked out quite nicely. Then a broker suggested I sell some calls on stocks I already own. In the process, I learned that selling these "covered calls" is deemed sufficiently conservative to be permitted in tax advantaged retirement accounts. Though I consider myself a cautious investor, I now believe options have a place in every investor's arsenal.

    Let's start with the basics, since most people I know, including myself, find options terminology confusing. A call option is the right to buy a share of stock at a fixed price at a fixed date in the future. A put is the opposite, the right to sell a share. Generally speaking, you buy a call when you think the stock price is going to rise and a put when you think it will fall. So why are options considered riskier than stocks? After all, in buying or selling shares, you're also predicting whether the price will rise or fall. The difference is that because calls and puts often expire worthless, you can easily lose all of your investment.

    Since options trades are actually contracts, they always have two sides: For every call or put that's bought, there's someone selling it. This is where things get trickier. Selling a call is a bet that the price will drop below the strike price and that you won't have to deliver the shares you promised when you sold someone the right to buy them. Selling a put is a bet the price will rise above the strike price, and therefore the buyer will not exercise the right to sell you the shares. If you sell calls or puts and bet right, you simply keep the sale proceeds. If you bet wrong, you can get into trouble quickly. Say you sold calls on shares you don't own and the price sky rockets. You have to go into the market—and into your pocket—to buy them for delivery, and since there's no limit to how high the price might go (think Qual-comm during the late '90s), there's no limit to your potential loss.

    To make this simpler, let's forget about puts entirely. Sure, buying a put can be an insurance policy against a declining market, but it's an expensive one, and selling a put is simply too risky for me.

    Calls are another matter. First of all, consider the actual risk. Yes, you can lose 100 percent of your investment. But stocks, too, can go to zero or close to it, as we've learned the hard way the past few years. And because an option price is always a fraction of the share price, you may be putting very little money at risk. If you sell covered calls, your potential losses are also capped by the fact that you already own the shares. Sure, you may have to deliver them at a price far below what they would then fetch in the market, but you're not out any additional money.

    I first bought some calls several years ago on shares of Tyco International. The stock had been hammered by short sellers, and then had been really clobbered when the Securities and Exchange Commission announced an investigation. Tyco denied any wrongdoing, and if the company was exonerated, there was potential for big gains. But if it wasn't, the share could go even lower.

    I had no idea what the SEC would conclude, but this is a situation where I like to buy calls. The negative sentiment meant that sellers were plentiful, driving down prices on the call options. But I needed an option lasting long enough for the SEC to reach a decision, which is when I discovered Leaps. I was able to buy options expiring more than a year in the future at a strike price barely above where the battered stock was already trading, for about $1 a share. (Finding real time option prices isn't easy. Unless you have something like a Bloomberg terminal, you have to ask a broker, which is a good way to make him actually earn his commission.) I bought 10 contracts, covering 100 shares each, for a total of $1,000. When the SEC exonerated Tyco eight months later, the stock—and option—prices soared, and I scored a big gain—all with just $1,000 at risk.

I had a similar experience buying calls on beleaguered Monsanto after it was attacked by anti-bioengineering activists. I figured the depressed stock would rebound once the benefits of such products as vitamin-enhanced "golden rice" became manifest. Little did I anticipate that Monsanto would be acquired by Pharmacia, which in turn was bought by Pfizer. My stake soared at each juncture. I exercised the options, and when the Pfizer deal closes, I'll own a nice position in the company for an extremely modest investment.

Yes, I've had losses, especially over the past three years in a steeply declining market. My $45 strike price Nortel Networks call options, needless to say, expired worthless this January. Still, with Nortel having plunged to less than $2, my loss was far smaller than if I had bought the shares outright. And as readers of my weekly online column already know, I recently hit a home run with AOL options at a strike price of $7.50. It doesn't take many of these to offset the losses.

So my rules of thumb are quite simple: I reserve buying call options for special situations that have driven a stock price down and soured investor opinion. And I buy only options with a long enough term—so far, at least a year—for the special situation to work itself out.

When I *sell* calls, I put the strategy into reverse. I have found this an excellent way to respond when the market hits one of my selling thresholds, as it did in November's rally. With the market feeling pretty euphoric, I sold covered calls on AIG and Microsoft for a lofty price of about $3.50 per share. Selling options on 500 shares of each stock generated $3,500 in cash right away.

At the time, AIG was trading at about $63, and the strike price was $70, with the contract expiring in January. That meant if AIG shares managed to reach that threshold—and that would require a 10 percent rise in just three months—I would have to deliver the 500 shares. Even if that happened and I wound up having to sell them for less than they were trading for, I figured I would still be happy to realize the $35,000 in proceeds.

After selling call options, you don't have to sit by passively and wait for the contracts to expire. By early December, with the market slumping again, those AIG options I sold for $3.50 were fetching just 20 cents, and the Microsoft options were at 90 cents. I could have stepped in and bought them back, keeping most of my profit and avoiding having to worry about what happened over the next month. But I decided to stand pat and let the hand play out. Odds are these options will expire worthless, and if not—if a sudden rally drives the stocks above the strike prices—I will still benefit from the discipline of selling into a rally, which is in line with my overall investing strategy. As this column went to press, I was still waiting to see whether my bet would pay off.

So here are my rules for selling calls: Sell only covered calls, look for big premiums suggesting a euphoric market sentiment about a stock's prospects, and sell short-term contracts. I have now sold calls on more than a dozen occasions, and every one of them has resulted in a net profit. In other words, I take a cautious, common-sense approach to options trading. Long-term, patient stock ownership remains the backbone of my investment approach, and options are a very small percentage of my portfolio. So far, my options trading has been very profitable. Yet curiously, my approach seems to be very unusual. Most options traders are technophiles and big institutions with sophisticated computerized strategies that seize on minor arbitrage possibilities and volatility aberrations. While I may just be experiencing beginner's luck, I'm beginning to suspect that the professionals have left some big opportunities for the rest of us.

SOME BASIC OPTIONS STRATEGIES

In the previous section, we examined the payoffs, and profit/losses, for basic uncovered (or naked) positions involving options. These four basic uncovered option positions are buy call, write call, buy put, and write put. In this section we analyze covered positions involving hedges. Spreads and combinations, which are also covered positions, are discussed in Appendix 19A.

Hedge

A strategy using derivatives to offset or reduce the risk resulting from exposure to an underlying asset.

A **hedge** is a combination of an option and its underlying stock designed such that the option protects the stock against loss or the stock protects the option against loss. In the next section, we consider some of the more popular hedges.

Covered Calls

Covered Call

A strategy involving the sale of a call option to supplement a long position in an underlying asset.

A **covered call** involves the purchase of stock and the simultaneous sale (or writing) of a call on that stock; that is, it is a long position in the stock and a short position in a call. The position is covered because the writer owns the stock and could deliver it if called to do so as a result of the exercise of the call option by the holder. In effect, the investor is willing to sell the stock at a fixed price (the exercise price), limiting the gains if the stock price rises, in exchange for cushioning the loss by the amount of the call premium, if the stock price declines.

Using our previous notation, the payoff profile at expiration is:

	$S_T \leq E$	$S_T > E$
Payoff of stock	S_T	S_T
− Payoff of call	-0	$-(S_T - E)$
Total payoff	S_T	E

Figure 19-7 illustrates the payoffs on the covered call hedge by showing all three situations: purchase of the stock, writing a call, and the combined position. Notice that the combined position is identical in shape to the payoff diagram from writing a put option as shown in Figure 19-2(d). The sale of the call truncates the combined position if the stock price rises above the exercise price. In effect, the writer has sold the claim to this gain for the call premium. At expiration, the position is worth, at most, the exercise price and the profit is the call premium received by selling the call.

As Figure 19-7 shows, if the stock price declines, the position is protected by the amount of the call premium received. Therefore, the break-even point is lower compared to simply owning the stock, and the loss incurred as the stock price drops will be less with the covered call position by the amount of the call premium.

EXAMPLE 19-8: CALL PREMIUM ON RBC

Assume that an investor had previously purchased 100 shares of RBC for $40 per share and when the stock price hits $48, writes a (covered) six-month call with an exercise price of $50. The writer receives a premium of $4. This situation is illustrated in Figure 19-8.

If called on to deliver his or her 100 shares, the investor will receive $50 per share, plus the $4 premium, for a gross profit of $14 per share (since the stock was originally purchased at $40 per share). However, the investor gives up the additional potential gain if the price of this stock rises above $50, as illustrated by the flat line to the right of $50 for the covered call position in Figure 19-8. If the price rises to $60 after the call is sold, for example, the investor will gross $14 per share but could have grossed $20 per share if no call had been written. However, should the price fall to $30, the investor would offset the loss of $10 per share held by the amount of the option premium ($4 per option) that was originally received, resulting in a net loss of only $6 per share.

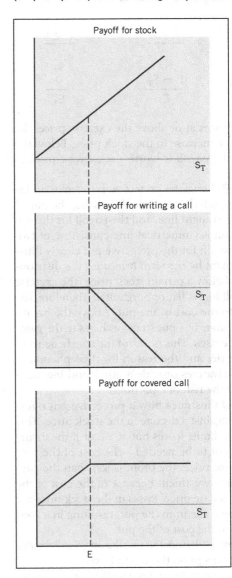

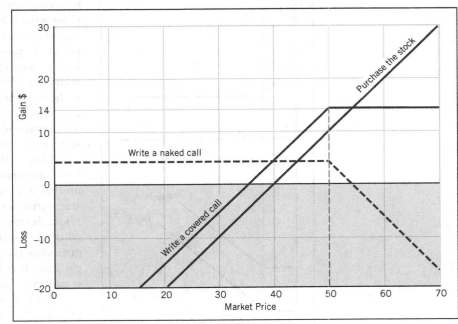

Figure 19-7
Payoff Profiles for a
Covered Call Position

Figure 19-8
Profit and Losses for a
Covered Call Position

Writing a naked call is also illustrated (by the broken line) in Figure 19-8. If the call is not exercised, the writer profits by the amount of the premium, $4. The naked writer's break-even point is $54. This position will be profitable if the price of the stock does not rise above the break-even point. Notice that the potential gain for the naked writer is limited to $4. The potential loss, however, is unlimited. If the price of the stock were to rise sharply, the writer could easily lose an amount in excess of what was received in premium income.

Protective Puts

Protective Put

A strategy involving the purchase of a put option as a supplement to a long position in an underlying asset.

A **protective put** involves buying a stock (or owning it already) and buying a put for the same stock; that is, it is a long position in both the stock and a put. The put acts as insurance against a decline in the underlying stock price, guaranteeing an investor a minimum price at which the stock can be sold. In effect, the insurance acts to limit losses or unfavourable outcomes. The largest profit possible is infinite (although the profit is reduced by the cost of the put option, as discussed below).

The payoff profile is:

Figure 19-9
Payoff Profile and
Profit/Losses for a
Protective Put Position

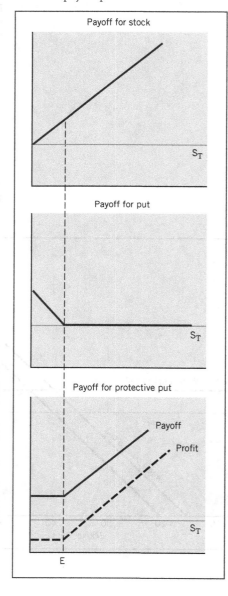

	$S_T < E$	$S_T \geq E$
Payoff of stock	S_T	S_T
+ Payoff of put	$E - S_T$	0
Total payoff	E	S_T

For stock prices at or above the exercise price, the payoff reflects the increase in the stock price. Below the exercise price, the payoff is worth the exercise price at expiration.

Figure 19-9 shows the protective put versus an investment in the underlying stock. As always, the payoff for the stock is a straight line, and the payoff for the option strategy is an asymmetrical line consisting of two segments. The payoff for the protective put clearly illustrates what is meant by the term *truncating* the distribution of returns. Below a certain stock price (the exercise price), the payoff line is flat or horizontal. Therefore, the loss is limited to the cost of the put. Above the break-even point, the protective put strategy shares in the gains as the stock price rises. This is one of the true benefits of derivative securities and the reason for their phenomenal growth—derivatives provide a quick and inexpensive way to alter the risk of a portfolio.

Figure 19-9 illustrates how a protective put offers some insurance against a decline in the stock price. This insurance feature limits losses but at a cost if the insurance turns out not to be needed—the cost of the put. Above the exercise price, the profit is less than the payoff profile for the investment because of the cost of the put. Below the exercise price, losses in the stock price are partially offset by gains from the put, resulting in a constant loss equal to the cost of the put.

This position is identical to purchasing a call except for a different intercept on the vertical axis.

The protective put illustrates a well-known concept called portfolio insurance, which is explained below.

Portfolio Insurance

The potential return–risk modification properties of options, and particularly the insurance aspects discussed above, are well illustrated by the technique known as **portfolio insurance**. This term refers to investment strategies designed to hedge portfolio positions by providing a minimum return on the portfolio while simultaneously providing an opportunity for the portfolio to participate in rising security prices. This asset management technique became very popular in the 1980s, with many billions of dollars of assets insured.

Portfolio Insurance

An asset management technique designed to provide a portfolio with a lower limit on value while permitting it to benefit from rising security prices.

There are several methods of insuring a portfolio, including the use of options, futures, and the creation of synthetic options (which refer to the creation of option-like payoffs by taking positions in other securities such as T-bills and market indexes). In practice, it is common to use futures contracts on market indexes (as discussed in Chapter 20). However, in principal options can be used in portfolio insurance strategies, and their use illustrates the basic nature of a hedge.

The idea behind portfolio insurance with regard to options is simple. A protective put can be purchased that allows the portfolio to be sold for an amount sufficient to provide the minimum return. The remaining portfolio funds are invested in the usual manner. The protective put provides insurance for the portfolio by limiting losses in the event stock prices decline. The portfolio's value at the end of the period must equal or exceed the exercise price of the put.

EXAMPLE 19-9: USING PORTFOLIO INSURANCE TO ENSURE MINIMUM RETURN

For simplicity, we assume an investor starts with $1.00 and purchases one unit of a stock market index that sells for $0.9097.[11] During a subsequent period, the value of the index has increased and the investor wants to lock in a guaranteed selling price of $1.05 for the index. To this end, the investor purchases a European put on this index for $0.0903. Notice the net investment equals $0.9097 + $0.0903 = $1.0000, and the put has a strike price of $1.05.

The investor has used portfolio insurance to ensure a 5 percent minimum return. If the value of the stock index exceeds $1.05 by the end of the investing period, the investor is ahead that much and allows the put to expire worthless. If the value of the index is less than $1.05 by the end of the period, the investor can exercise the option and sell the stock index for $1.05, thereby earning the required 5 percent minimum return on the initial investment of $1.00. Portfolio insurance has provided protection against the downside while allowing the investor to participate in stock price advances.

This example illustrates the conceptual use of puts in portfolio insurance strategies. In practice, however, puts and calls are not used to insure portfolios because those typically available to investors are American and not European. The exercise-at-any-time feature of American options makes them not only more valuable than corresponding European options but also much more costly for portfolio insurance purposes. Furthermore, it generally is not possible to find puts and calls with the exact time to expiration, exercise price, and so on that matches a particular portfolio.

It should also be noted that portfolio insurance is not without cost. The costs include

- The *cost of the option itself*—in our example, the put cost $0.0903. Obviously, if stocks advance and the put expires worthless, the cost of the put has been lost relative to an uninsured strategy. This can be thought of as the insurance premium.

- An *opportunity cost*. An investor who places 100 percent of investment funds in the stock index would participate fully in any market rise. In our example, the insured investor would participate in only 90.97 percent of any market rise.

---

[11]This example is based on R.J. Rendleman and R. W. McEnally, "Assessing the Costs of Portfolio Insurance," *Financial Analysts Journal* (May–June 1987), pp. 27–37.

CHECK YOUR UNDERSTANDING

19-7. Why is covered call writing considered a conservative strategy?

19-8. Explain why buying a put option on a stock you own can be thought of as a form of insurance.

OPTION VALUATION

learning objective 3
Explain the valuation of options.

A General Framework

In this section, we examine the determinants of the value of a put or call. An option's premium almost never declines below its intrinsic value. The reason is that market arbitrageurs, who constantly monitor option prices for discrepancies, would purchase the options and exercise them, thus earning riskless returns. **Arbitrageurs** are speculators who seek to earn a return without assuming risk by constructing riskless hedges. Short-lived deviations are possible, but they will quickly be exploited.

Arbitrageurs
Investors who seek discrepancies in security prices in an attempt to earn riskless returns.

Suppose a call option with an exercise price of $20 is selling for $2, when the price of the underlying share is $23. Notice that the intrinsic value of this option is $3, since the call enables you to purchase a share that is worth $23 for only $20. An arbitrageur (or anyone else recognizing that the option price is below its intrinsic value) could purchase an option contract for $200 ($2 × 100). The investor could then immediately exercise the option, purchasing 100 shares at a cost of $2,000 ($20 × 100). These shares could be sold in the market at a price of $23 per share, for a total of $2,300. The net result (ignoring transactions costs) would be a profit of $100: $2,300 − $2,000 (cost of exercising the options) − $200 (cost of the options). This profit is earned without assuming any risks and is referred to as arbitrage profit, hence the name arbitrageurs. Clearly, these opportunities should not exist in efficient markets, since rational investors will recognize them, exploit them, and hence eliminate them.

Time Values

Option prices almost always exceed intrinsic values, with the difference reflecting the option's potential appreciation, referred to as the **time value**. This is somewhat of a misnomer because the actual source of value is volatility in price. However, price volatility decreases with a shortening of the time to expiration, hence the term time value.

Time Value
The difference between the intrinsic value of an option and its market price.

Because buyers are willing to pay a price for potential future stock-price movements, time has a positive value—the longer the time to expiration for the option, the more chance it has to appreciate in value. However, when the stock price is held constant, options are seen as a wasting asset whose value approaches intrinsic value as expiration approaches. In other words, as expiration approaches, the time value of the option declines to zero.

The time value can be calculated as the difference between the option price and the intrinsic value:

(19-3)
$$\text{Time value} = \text{Option price} - \text{Intrinsic value}$$

EXAMPLE 19-10: CALCULATING TIME VALUE ON CP OPTIONS

For the CP options referred to in the examples of intrinsic value in the previous section:

Time value of October 70 call = $6.40 − $1.95 = $4.45
Time value of October 74 put = $6.00 − $2.05 = $3.95

We can now understand the premium for an option as the sum of its intrinsic value and its time value, or

$$\text{Premium or option price} = \text{Intrinsic value} + \text{Time value}$$ **(19-4)**

EXAMPLE 19-11: CALCULATING PREMIUM FOR CP OPTIONS

For the CP options:

Premium for October 70 call = \$1.95 + \$4.45 = \$6.40
Premium for January 30 put = \$2.05 + \$3.95 = \$6.00

Notice an important point about options based on the preceding discussion. An investor who owns a call option and wishes to acquire the underlying common stock will always find it preferable to sell the option and purchase the stock in the open market rather than exercise the option (at least if the stock pays no dividends). Why? Because otherwise, he or she will lose the speculative premium on the option.

Consider the CP October 70 call option, with a market price of the common share of \$71.95. An investor who owned the call and wanted to own the common share would be better off to sell the option at \$6.40 and purchase the common stock for \$71.95, for a net investment of \$65.55 per share. Exercising the call option, the investor would have to pay \$70.00 per share for shares of stock worth \$71.95 in the market, for a net investment of \$70.00 per share. Thus selling the options reduces the required investment to own a share of CP by \$4.45—the amount of the time value. (Brokerage commissions are ignored in this example.)

On the other hand, under some circumstances it may be optimal to exercise an American put early (on a non-dividend-paying stock). A put sufficiently deep in the money should be exercised early because the payment received at exercise can be invested to earn a return. Under certain circumstances it may also be desirable to exercise an American call option on a dividend-paying stock before the expiration date. (This is because dividends reduce the stock price on the ex dividend date, which in turn reduces the value of the call option).

Boundaries on Option Prices

In the previous section we learned what the premium, or price, of a put or call consists of, but we have not considered why options trade at the prices they do and the range of values they can assume. In this section, we learn about the boundaries for option prices, and in the next section we discuss the exact determinants of options prices.

The value of an option must be related to the value of the underlying security. The basic relationship is most easy to understand by considering an option immediately prior to expiration, when there is no time premium. If the option is not exercised, it will expire immediately, leaving the option with no value. Obviously, investors will exercise it only if it is worth exercising (if it is in the money).

Figure 19-10(a) shows the values of call options at expiration, assuming a strike price of \$50. At expiration, a call must have a value equal to its intrinsic value. Therefore, the line representing the value of a call option must be horizontal at \$0 up to the exercise price and then rise as the stock price exceeds the exercise price. Above \$50 the call price must equal the difference between the stock price and the exercise price.

For puts the situation is reversed. At expiration, a put must have a value equal to its intrinsic value. Therefore, the line in Figure 19-10(b) representing the value of a put option must be horizontal at \$0 beyond the exercise price. Below \$50, the put price must equal the difference between the exercise price and the stock price. Note that a put option has a strict upper limit on intrinsic value, whereas the call has no upper limit. A put's strike price is its maximum intrinsic value.

Figure 19-10
Determining the Boundaries
on Option Prices

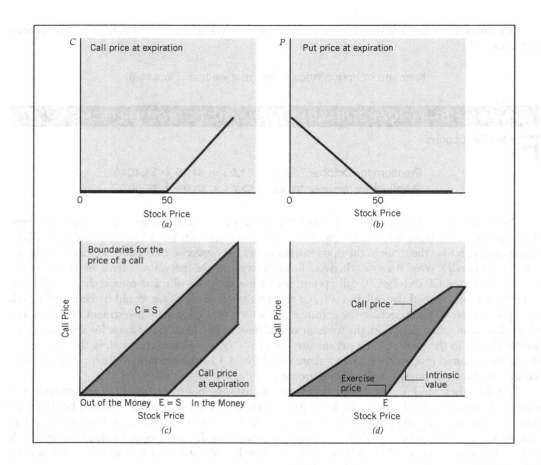

What is the maximum price an option can assume? To see this, think of a call. Since the call's value is derived from its ability to be converted into the underlying stock, it can never sell for more than the stock itself. It would not make sense to pay more for a call on one share of stock than the price of the stock itself. Therefore, the maximum price for a call is the price of the underlying stock.

Based on the preceding, we can establish the absolute upper and lower boundaries for the price of a call option, as shown in Figure 19-10(c). The upper boundary is a 45 degree line from the origin representing a call price equal to the stock price.[12] The lower boundary is the price of the option at expiration, which must be either zero or its in-the-money value. This is represented by the 45 degree line starting at the exercise price. Once again, the lower boundary can be interpreted as the value of the call at the moment the call is exercised, or its intrinsic value.

Finally, Figure 19-10(d) illustrates more precisely and realistically the variation in price for a call option by illustrating how the price of a call varies with the stock price and the exercise price. The call price is always above intrinsic value and rises as the stock price increases beyond the exercise price. The time value, represented by the shaded area in Figure 19-10(d), decreases beyond the exercise price.

To understand fully the price of a call option, we will examine the most common formal model used to estimate call prices, the Black-Scholes model. The price of a put can also be found from this model because of a parity relationship between put and call prices.

---

[12]Think of this as a call with a zero exercise price and an infinite maturity.

The Black-Scholes Model

Fischer Black and Myron Scholes developed a model for the valuation of European call options that is widely accepted and used in the investment community.[13] While the equation estimates the price of European call options on non-dividend-paying stocks, it is also used to evaluate American call options on non-dividend-paying stocks. This is a reasonable application, since we have seen that it is never optimal to exercise such American options before expiration date, so they should be worth approximately the same as the equivalent European option.

The formula itself is mathematical and appears to be very complex; however, it is widely available on calculators and computers. Numerous investors estimate the value of calls using the **Black-Scholes model**. The model is considered to be of such importance that Canadian-born Myron Scholes shared the 1997 Nobel Prize in economics, largely for this work. Black would almost certainly have shared in the award had he not died in 1995.

Black-Scholes model
A widely used model for the valuation of call options.

The Black-Scholes model uses five variables to value the call option of a non-dividend-paying stock.[14] These five variables, all but the last of which are directly observable in the market, are as follows:

1. The price of the underlying stock
2. The exercise price of the option
3. The time remaining to the expiration of the option
4. The interest rate
5. The volatility of the continuously compounded rate of return on the underlying stock

The first two variables are of obvious importance in valuing an option, because, as noted before, they determine the option's intrinsic value, whether it is in the money or not. If it is out of the money, it has only a time value based on the speculative interest in the stock.

Time to expiration (measured as a fraction of a year) is also an important factor in the value of an option because value generally increases with maturity. This is logical, because the longer to the expiration date, the more time is available to profit from price changes. The relationship between time and value is not proportional, however. The time value of an option is greatest when the market price and the exercise price are equal.

The interest rate affects option values because of the opportunity cost involved. Buying an option is a substitute to some degree for buying on margin, on which interest must be paid. The higher interest rates are, therefore, the more interest cost is saved by the use of options. This adds to the value of the option and results in a direct relationship between the value of a call option and interest rates in the market.

The last factor, and the only one not directly observable in the marketplace, is the stock's volatility. The greater the volatility, the higher the price of a call option because of the increased potential for the stock to move up. Therefore, a positive relation exists between the volatility of the stock and the value of the call option.[15]

The Black-Scholes option pricing formula can be expressed as[16]

$$C = S[N(d_1)] - E[N(d_2)] \times \frac{1}{e^{rt}}$$

(19-5)

[13]F. Black and M. Scholes, "The Pricing of Options and Corporate Liabilities," *Journal of Political Economy* 81 (May–June 1973), pp. 637–654.

[14]Options traded on organized exchanges are not protected against cash dividends, and this can have significant effects on option values. When a cash dividend is paid, the stock price should decline to reflect this payment. Any event that reduces the stock price reduces the value of a call and increases the value of a put.

[15]Volatility as used in the options model is not the same concept as a stock's beta as used in Chapter 9. Volatility is used here as a measure of the variability in the stock return (as measured by standard deviation) as opposed to sensitivity to market movements.

[16]This version of the model applies to non-dividend-paying stocks. Adjustments can be made for stocks that pay dividends.

where

C   = the price of the call option
S   = current market price of the underlying common stock
$N(d_1)$ = the cumulative density function of d_1 (assuming this variable is normally distributed)
E   = the exercise price of the option
e   = the base of natural logarithms (approximately 2.71828)
r   = the continuously compounded riskless rate of interest quoted on an annual basis
t   = the time remaining before the expiration date of the option, expressed as a fraction of a year
$N(d_2)$ = the cumulative density function of d_2 (assuming this variable is normally distributed)[17]

To find d_1 and d_2, it is necessary to solve these equations:

(19-6)
$$d_1 = \frac{\ln (S/E) + (r + 0.5\sigma^2)t}{(\sigma[(t)^{1/2}])}$$

(19-7)
$$d_2 = d_1 - (\sigma[(t)^{1/2}])$$

where

$\ln (S/E)$ = the natural logarithm of (S/E)
σ = the standard deviation of the annual rate of return on the underlying common stock

The five variables previously listed are needed as inputs. Variables 1 to 4 are immediately available. Variable 5 is not, however, because what is needed is the variability expected to occur in the stock's rate of return. Although historical data on stock returns are generally used to estimate this standard deviation, variability does change over time. A formula user should try to incorporate expected changes in the variability when using historical data. To do so, the user should examine any likely changes in either the market's or the individual stock's variability.

Variables 1 to 3 should be identical for a given stock for everyone using the Black-Scholes model. Variable 4 should be identical or very close among formula users, depending on the exact proxy used for the riskless rate of interest. Variable 5 will vary among users, providing different option values. Empirical studies have shown that estimates of the variance obtained from other than historical data are more valuable than the estimates based on historical data. Because the price of an option can be observed at any time, it is possible to solve the Black-Scholes formula for the implied standard deviation of the stock's return. This is an important application of the Black-Scholes equation that is frequently used by practitioners. Henry Latané and Richard Rendleman found that better forecasts of the actual standard deviation could be obtained by preparing forecasts from the model itself.[18]

EXAMPLE 19-12: USING BLACK-SCHOLES TO CALCULATE OPTION PRICE

The following is an example of the use of the Black-Scholes option pricing formula:

Assume

S = $40
E = $45
r = 0.10
t = 0.5 (6 months)
σ = 0.45

---

[17]This assumption does not mean that stock returns themselves are normally distributed, but that the variables d_1 and d_2 are normally distributed. In fact, one of the technical assumptions of the model is that stock prices are lognormally distributed.
[18]H. Latané and R. Rendleman, Jr., "Standard Deviations of Stock Price Ratios Implied in Option Prices," *Journal of Finance* 31 (May 1976), pp. 369–382.

Step 1: Solve for d_1.

$$d_1 = \frac{\ln(40/45) + [0.10 + 0.5(0.45)^2]\,0.5}{0.45\,[(0.5)^{1/2}]}$$

$$= \frac{-0.1178 + 0.1006}{0.3182}$$

$$= -0.054$$

Step 2: Use a cumulative probability distribution table (such as the one provided on the textbook's companion website) to find the value of $N(d_1)$.

$$N(d_1) \approx 0.4801$$

where $d_1 = -0.054$

Step 3: Find d_2.

$$d_2 = -0.054 - 0.45[(0.5)^{1/2}]$$

$$= -0.372$$

Step 4: Find $N(d_2)$.

$$N(d_2) \approx 0.3557$$

Step 5: Solve for C.

$$C = S[0.4801] - E[0.3557] \times \frac{1}{e^{(.10)(0.5)}}$$

$$= (40)(0.4801) - (45)(0.3557)(0.9512)$$

$$= 19.20 - 15.23$$

$$= \$3.97$$

The theoretical (fair) value of the option, according to the Black-Scholes formula, is $3.97. If the current market price of the option is greater than the theoretical value, it is overpriced; if less, it is underpriced—according to the Black-Scholes model.

Put Option Valuation

To establish put prices, we can take advantage of the principle of put-call parity.

The **put-call parity** principle expresses the relationship between the prices of European puts and calls on the same stock with the same exercise price that must hold if arbitrage is to be ruled out. In other words, unless the price of the put and the call bear a certain relationship to each other, there will be opportunities for earning riskless profits (arbitrage). The put-call parity can be expressed as

$$\text{Price of put} = E/(e^{rt}) - S + C$$

where all terms are as defined before.[19]

Put-Call Parity
The formal relationship between a European call and put on the same item that must hold if no arbitrage is to occur.

(19-8)

---

[19]Refer to Appendix 19C for a more detailed discussion of the no-arbitrage argument.

EXAMPLE 19-13: CALCULATING PUT-CALL PARITY

Use the information for the call given in the previous example. Since the Black-Scholes model uses continuous interest, the discount factor is expressed in continuous form.[20] It is equal to e^{rt} or $e^{10(0.5)}$. Using a calculator, this value is 1.051.

Therefore,

$$\text{Price of put} = 45/1.051 - 40 + 3.97 = \$6.79$$

Summarizing the Factors Affecting Options Prices

If we allow for stocks that pay dividends, we can summarize the factors affecting options prices into a table with six elements, as shown in Table 19-2. The plus sign indicates a direct relation, and a negative sign a negative relation. The assumption behind Table 19-2 is that all other variables remain fixed as we consider any of the six variables.

Table 19-2

Effects of Various Variables on Options Prices

Variable	Calls	Puts
Stock price	+	−
Exercise price	−	+
Time to expiration	+	+
Stock volatility	+	+
Interest rates	+	−
Cash dividends	−	+

The following discussion provides a basis for the intuition regarding how these six factors affect option prices (holding all other factors unchanged). Recall that the Option price = Intrinsic value + Time value (or speculative premium). Based on this framework, we note the following:

1. As share prices increase, the intrinsic value (IV) of calls increase and the IV of puts decrease.

2. As exercise prices increase, the IV of calls decrease and the IV of puts increase.

3. The greater the time to expiration, the greater the chance the option will be in the money, hence the greater the time value (or speculative premium).

4. As share price volatility increases, there is a greater chance that shares will end up in the money, so the time value, or speculative premium, increases.

5. As the riskless rate increases, the advantage of delayed ownership increases for call options. Conversely, the delay of exercising put options, which involves selling assets for cash today, becomes more costly.

6. Share prices fall by roughly the amount of a dividend that is paid. Hence, dividend increases tend to reduce share prices, which reduces the IV of calls and increases the IV of puts.

Hedge Ratios

A key concept with options is their use as a hedging device. Although risky assets themselves, options can be used to control risk. In particular, options can be used to control the riskiness inherent in common stocks.

---

[20]The value e^k is the equivalent of $(1 + r)$ in continuous compounding. If r is 5 percent, the value of e^k is $e^{0.05}$, or 1.051.

To hedge a long stock position with options, an investor would write one call option while simultaneously buying a certain number of common shares. The required number of shares is given by the **hedge ratio**, which is $N(d_1)$ from the Black-Scholes model for call options.[21] The hedge ratio for an option, commonly referred to as the option's delta, indicates the change in the price of the option for a $1 change in the price of the underlying common share. Since the hedge ratio with a call option is $N(d_1)$, for a put option it is $N(d_1) - 1$.

Hedge Ratio
The ratio of options written to shares of stock held long in a riskless portfolio.

EXAMPLE 19-14: DETERMINING THE HEDGE RATIO FOR OPTIONS

In Example 19-12, $N(d_1)$ was 0.48; therefore, for every call option written, 0.48 share of the common stock would be required to hedge the position. For a standard 100-share option contract, 48 shares of stock would be required. A $1 increase in the price of the stock should produce a $0.48 change in the price of the option. The loss on the call options written is 100 × $0.48, or $48, which is offset by the gain on the 48 shares of stock of $48. A perfectly hedged position leaves total wealth unchanged.

Since the maximum value for $N(d_1)$ is 1.0, hedge ratios are usually less than 1.0, except for the case of deep in the money options where the ratio tends to one. This indicates that option values change with stock prices on less than a one-for-one basis. That is, dollar movements in options prices are smaller than dollar movements in the underlying stock. However, percentage price changes on the option generally will be greater than percentage price changes on the stock; this is referred to as the leverage effect.

Using the Black-Scholes Model

What does it mean if we calculate an intrinsic value for an option that is significantly different from the market price? Although this may represent an investment opportunity, we must remember that the original Black-Scholes model is based on some simplifying assumptions, such as the non-payment of dividends, constant volatility, and continuous lognormally distributed stock prices. The standard deviation cannot be observed and must be estimated. Therefore, any observed discrepancies could reflect errors in the estimation of the stock's volatility.

Development of the Black-Scholes model was a significant event and has had a major impact on all options investors, both directly and indirectly. This model has been the basis of extensive empirical investigations into how options are priced. How well does this model work?

The numerous studies that have been conducted offer general support for the Black-Scholes model and the proposition that options are efficiently priced by the market. Some deficiencies have been noted.[22] The deviations and biases that appear to remain in option pricing models may derive from several sources. For example, the true stock-price volatility is unobservable. Despite any statistically significant biases that may exist in the prices generated by the option pricing models, however, the validity of these models remains intact.

CHECK YOUR UNDERSTANDING

19-9. Why does an option's price almost always exceed its intrinsic value?

19-10. What are the boundaries for the price of a call?

---

[21]Technically, the hedge ratio is the slope of the functional relationship between the value of the option (vertical axis) and the value of the stock (horizontal axis), evaluated at the current stock price. It is determined by taking the partial first derivative of the option price with respect to the underlying stock price.

[22]D. Galai, "A Survey of Empirical Tests of Option-Pricing Models," in M. Brenner, Ed., *Option Pricing: Theory and Applications* (Lexington, MA: Lexington Books, 1983), pp. 45–80.

AN INVESTOR'S PERSPECTIVE ON PUTS AND CALLS

What Puts and Calls Mean to Investors

Earlier we examined some simple strategies using puts and calls and briefly considered some more sophisticated strategies. It is important for investors to have an overall perspective on puts and calls and consider what they really add to the investment process.

Option contracts are important to investors in terms of the two dimensions of every investment decision that we have emphasized throughout this book—the return and risk from an asset or portfolio. Options can be used for various types of hedging, which involves the management of risk. Options also offer speculators a way to leverage their investment with a strict limit on downside risk.

The return–risk modification properties of puts and calls vary significantly from other derivative instruments such as futures contracts, which we consider in Chapter 20. The important point about options and portfolio return and risk is that the impact of options is not symmetrical. As discussed earlier, the distribution of payoffs is truncated, because in the case of buying a call the most the investor can lose is the premium, regardless of what happens to the stock price. The same is true when purchasing a put—relative to the profit-loss line when selling short, the distribution of possible profits and losses from purchasing a put is truncated. If the stock price continues to rise, adversely affecting the investor, the most that can be lost from the put purchase is the premium.

The Evolutionary Use of Options

Puts and calls on organized options exchanges have been available to investors since 1973, although financial derivatives were being used long before then. Puts and calls have been popular with individual investors since the beginning of CBOE trading, although the manner in which they are viewed has changed somewhat. At first, options were viewed more or less as speculative instruments and were often purchased for their leverage possibilities. Covered option writing was used to enhance portfolio yields. During the 1980s, many investors were selling puts in order to capitalize on the rising trend in stock prices. This strategy worked well until the famous market crash in October 1987. As a result of the losses, many investors once again viewed options as speculative instruments and options volume did not return to the level reached in 1987 for several years.

The current emphasis by the brokerage industry is on educating investors as to how options can be used efficiently as part of their portfolio. Investors' desire to hedge their portfolios against a market decline as well as the introduction of new products such as options on new indexes, country funds, and LEAPs, has drawn the public back into the market.

Today, options are increasingly valued for their use in strategic portfolio management. Options allow investors to create strategies that expand the set of outcomes beyond what could be achieved in the absence of options. In other words, investors and investment managers sometimes need the non-symmetric distributions of returns that options can provide. Options strategies increase the set of contingencies that can be provided for.[23]

OTHER TYPES OF OPTIONS

Newer innovations in the options market include **stock-index options**, **interest rate options**, and **currency options**. We briefly discuss interest rate and currency options, before confining our discussion to stock-index options, in keeping with the general theme of the chapter, which is to focus on equity options.

Primary US interest rate options traded on the CBOE include Treasury yield options. Interest rate options trade in Canada in the form of options on Government of Canada bonds, which have traded

learning objective 4
Identify types of options other than puts and calls.

Stock-Index Options
Option contracts on a stock market index such as the S&P/TSX 60 Index.

Interest Rate Options
Option contracts on fixed-income securities such as Government of Canada bonds.

Currency Options
Option contracts whose value is based on the value of an underlying currency, such as the Canadian dollar.

[23]This discussion is based on Richard Bookstaber, "The Use of Options in Performance Structuring," *Journal of Portfolio Management* 11 (Summer 1985), pp. 35–50.

on the ME since 1982. The volume of bond contracts outstanding represents a small proportion of the total options contracts that are traded in Canada. For example, Table 19-1 shows that these bond options accounted for a mere 0.01 percent of ME option trading in 2007. Index options, on the other hand, accounted for 5.7 percent of the 2007 ME option trading, while standard equity options on common shares accounted for approximately 84 percent of ME trading.

The only currency option that trades on the ME is on the US dollar; however, these and other currency options trade actively in the US.

The Basics of Stock-Index Options

Stock-index options presently trade in Canada on the ME and are available on the S&P/TSX 60 Index, and on various ETFs (such as the i60s), which derive their value from the appropriate stock indexes. There are also a variety of US stock-index options on market indexes, including (but not limited to) the S&P 100 Index (OEX), the S&P 500 Index, the NYSE Index, the Russell 2000 Index, the Major Market Index, the Value Line Index, the S&P Midcap Index, the Japan Index, and the OTC Index. Index options are also available on some US industry subindexes, including Pharmaceuticals, Computer Technology, and Semiconductors. In addition, long-term index options (LEAPs) are available for the S&P 100 and 500 indexes and for the DJIA.

Stock-index options enable investors to trade on general stock market movements or industries in the same way that they can trade on individual stocks. Thus, an investor who is bullish on the market can buy a call on a market index, and an investor who is bearish on the overall market can buy a put. The investor need only make a decision about the market as a whole, not on an industry or an individual stock.

Most index options are European style, including the S&P/TSX 60 Index options. Overall, stock-index options are similar to the options listed on the options exchanges. As usual, the exercise price and the expiration date are uniformly established. Investors buy and sell them through their broker in the normal manner. Index option information is read in the same manner as that for stock options. Unlike stock options that require the actual delivery of the stock upon exercise, buyers of index options receive cash from the seller upon exercise of the contract. The amount of cash settlement is equal to the difference between the closing price of the index and the strike price of the option multiplied by a specified dollar amount.

EXAMPLE 19-15: S&P/TSX 60 INDEX OPTION

Assume an investor holds an S&P/TSX Index call option with a strike price of 840 and decides to exercise the option on a day that the S&P/TSX Index closes at 880.75. The investor will receive a cash payment from the assigned writer equal to $100 multiplied by the difference between the option's strike price and the closing value of the index, or

| S&P/TSX 60 Index close | = 880.75 |
| S&P/TSX 60 Index option strike price | = 840.00 |

$$40.75 \times \$100 = \$4,075$$

Note the use of the $100 multiplier for the S&P/TSX Index option. The multiplier performs a function similar to the unit of trading (100 shares) for a stock option contract in that it determines the total dollar value of the cash settlement. Since options on different indexes may have different multipliers, it is important to know the multiplier for the stock index being used.

Strategies with Stock-Index Options

The strategies available for use with index options are similar to those for individual stock options. Investors expecting a market rise buy calls, and investors expecting a market decline buy puts. The maximum losses from these two strategies—the option premiums—are known at the outset of the transaction. The potential gains can be large because of the leverage involved with options.

EXAMPLE 19-16: LEVERAGE AND S&P/TSX 60 INDEX OPTIONS

In May, an investor expects the stock market to rise strongly over the next two months. This investor decides to purchase an S&P/TSX 60 Index July 920 call that was selling for $9.40 on a day when the S&P/TSX 60 Index closed at 880.75. The total cost to the investor would be $940 (i.e., $9.40 × 100).

Assume that the market rises, as the investor expected, to a level of 951.21 (an 8 percent increase) on the expiration date. The investor could exercise the option and receive a cash settlement equal to the difference between the index close (951.21) and the exercise price of 920, multiplied by $100, or

S&P/TSX 60 Index close	= 951.21
Call exercise price	= −920.00
	31.21 × $100 = $3,121

The investor's profit for this transaction (excluding commission fees) is:

$$\text{Profit} = \text{Payoff} - \text{Cost of option}$$
$$= \$3,121 - \$940 = \$2,181$$

The leverage offered by index options is illustrated in this example by the fact that an 8 percent rise in the index leads to a 132.0 percent profit on the option position (i.e., ($2,181−$940)/$940 = 232.0 percent). In this example, the investor would have benefited from the use of leverage. However, leverage can, and often does, work against an investor. If the market declined or remained flat, the entire option premium of $940 could be lost, for a 100 percent loss on the investment. As with any option, however, the investor has a limited loss of a known amount—the premium paid.

Investors can use stock-index options to hedge their positions. For example, an investor who owns a diversified portfolio of stocks may be unwilling to liquidate his or her portfolio but is concerned about a near-term market decline. Buying a put on a market index will provide some protection to the investor in the event of a market decline. In effect, the investor is purchasing a form of market insurance. The losses on the portfolio holdings will be partially offset by the gains on the put. If the market rises, the investor loses the premium paid but gains with the portfolio holdings. A problem arises, however, in that the portfolio holdings and the market index are unlikely to be a perfect match. The effectiveness of this hedge will depend on the similarity between the two.

EXAMPLE 19-17: HEDGING WITH S&P/TSX 60 INDEX OPTIONS

Assume an investor has a portfolio of TSX common stocks currently worth $264,000. It is June, and this investor is concerned about a market decline over the next couple of months. The S&P/TSX 60 Index is currently at 880.75 and an S&P/TSX Index July 880 put is available for $26.40. In an attempt to protect the portfolio's profits against a market decline, the investor purchases three of these puts (total cost = 3 × 100 × $26.40 = $7,920), which represents an aggregate exercise price of $264,000 (880 × 100 × 3 = $264,000).[24]

Assume that the market declines 10 percent by the July expiration date, so that the S&P/TSX 60 Index is 792.67 at that point.

Put exercise price	= 880.00
S&P/TSX 60 Index price	= 792.67
	87.33 × $100 × 3 (puts) = $26,199

---

[24] The exercise value of an index option, like any stock option, is equal to 100 (shares) multiplied by the exercise price.

If the value of the investor's portfolio declines exactly 10 percent, the loss on the portfolio of $26,400 will be almost exactly offset by the total gain on the three put contracts of $26,199. It is important to note, however, that a particular portfolio's value may decline more or less than the overall market as represented by one of the market indexes such as the S&P/TSX 60 Index.

As before, if the option is held to expiration and a market decline (of a significant amount) does not occur, the investor will lose the entire premium paid for the put(s). In our example, the investor could lose the entire $7,920 paid for the three puts. This could be viewed as the cost of obtaining "market insurance."

Stock-index options can also be useful to institutional investors (or individuals) who do not have funds available immediately for investment but anticipate a market rise. Buying calls will allow such investors to take advantage of the rise in prices if it does occur. Of course, the premium could be lost if the anticipations are incorrect.

Investors can sell (write) index options, either to speculate or to hedge their positions. As we saw in the case of individual options, however, the risk can be large. If the seller is correct in his or her beliefs, the profit is limited to the amount of the premium; if incorrect, the seller faces potential losses far in excess of the premiums received from selling the options. Although the writer of an individual stock call option can deliver the stock if the option is exercised, the writer of a stock-index call option that is exercised must settle in cash and cannot be certain that gains in the stock portfolio will *fully* offset losses on the index option.[25] It would be impractical (or impossible) to write a completely covered stock-index option if one had to buy the appropriate amounts of the individual shares comprising the stock index at all points in time. However, Canadian investors do have this luxury available to them due to the availability of ETFs such as the i60 units. As discussed in Chapter 3, these units can be purchased through a broker, and their value is determined by the value of the S&P/TSX 60 Index.

The Popularity of Stock-Index Options

Stock-index options appeal to speculators because of the leverage they offer. A change in the underlying index of less than 1 percent can result in a change in the value of the contract of 15 percent or more. Given the increased volatility in financial markets in recent years, investors can experience rapid changes in the value of their positions. Since introduced in 1983, stock-index options have grown in popularity and now account for close to 6 percent of options traded through the ME, and approximately 27 percent of CBOE trading. Much of the initial volume was accounted for by professional speculators and trading firms. However, as familiarity with index options has increased, individual investors are assuming a larger role in this market.

CHECK YOUR UNDERSTANDING

19-11. An investor has built a portfolio of Canadian stocks that is well diversified across many industries. She would like to hedge her portfolio against a decline in the price of these stocks, but finds that there are no options traded on most of them. What advice can you offer this investor?

---

[25]Writers of index options are notified of their obligation to make a cash settlement on the business day following the day of exercise.

SUMMARY

This summary relates to the learning objectives for this chapter.

1. **Define options and discuss why they are used.**

   Equity-derivative securities derive their value from the equity price of a corporation. They consist of puts and calls, created by investors, and warrants, rights, and convertible securities, created by corporations. A call is an option to buy a share of a particular stock at a stated price any time before a specified expiration date. Similarly, a put is an option to sell the stock. The seller receives a premium for selling either of these options, and the buyer pays the premium. Advantages of options include a smaller investment than transacting in the stock itself, knowing the maximum loss in advance, leverage, and an expansion of the opportunity set available to investors.

2. **Describe how options work and give some basic strategies.**

   Buyers of calls expect the underlying stock to perform in the opposite direction from the expectations of put buyers. Writers of each instrument have opposite expectations from the buyers. The basic strategies for options involve a call writer and a put buyer expecting the underlying stock price to decline, whereas the call buyer and the put writer expect it to rise. Options may also be used to hedge against a portfolio position by establishing an opposite position in options on that stock. More sophisticated options strategies include combinations of options, such as strips, straps, straddles, and spreads (which include money spreads and time spreads). These strategies are discussed in Appendix 19A.

3. **Explain the valuation of options.**

   Options have an intrinsic value ranging from $0 to the "in-the-money" value. Most sell for more than this, representing a speculative premium, referred to as the time value. According to the Black-Scholes option valuation model, value is a function of the price of the stock, the exercise price of the option, time to maturity, the interest rate, and the volatility of the underlying stock. The available empirical evidence seems to suggest that the options market is efficient, with trading rules unable to exploit any biases that exist in the Black-Scholes or other options pricing models.

4. **Identify types of options other than puts and calls.**

   Interest rate, currency, and stock-index options are also available to investors. Stock-index options are a popular innovation in the options area that allow investors to buy puts and calls on broad stock market indexes. A distinguishing feature of these option contracts is that settlement is in cash. In effect, stock-index options allow investors to make only a market decision and to purchase a form of market insurance. The strategies with index options are similar to those for individual stock options. Investors can both hedge and speculate.

KEY TERMS

Arbitrageurs, p.642
Black-Scholes model, p.645
Call, p.622
Canadian Derivatives Clearing Corporation (CDCC), p.628
Covered call, p.638
Currency options, p.650
Equity-derivative securities, p.621
Exercise (strike) price, p.623
Expiration date, p.623

Hedge, p.638
Hedge ratio, p.649
Interest rate options, p.650
Intrinsic value (option), p.630
Long-term options (LEAPs), p.625
Option premium, p.623
Options, p.622
Portfolio insurance, p.641
Protective put, p.640
Put, p.622

Put-call parity, p.647
Right (Appendix 19B), p.662
Spread (Appendix 19A), p.661
Stock-index options, p.650
Straddle (Appendix 19A), p.660
Time value, p.642
Warrant (Appendix 19B), p.663

REVIEW QUESTIONS

19-1. State three justifications given for the existence of options.

19-2. What does it mean to say an option buyer has a right but not an obligation?

19-3. How can the writer of a call option cancel his or her obligation?

19-4. Why is the call or put writer's position considerably different from the buyer's position?

19-5. Distinguish between call options, warrants, and rights. (Refer to Appendix 19B for this question.)

19-6. Explain the following terms used with puts and calls:
   a. Strike price
   b. Naked option
   c. Premium
   d. Out-of-the-money option

19-7. Who writes puts and calls? Why?

19-8. What role do clearing corporations play in options markets?

19-9. What is the relationship between option prices and their intrinsic values? Why?

19-10. What is meant by the time value of an option?

19-11. Why do investors write calls? What are their obligations?

19-12. What is an index option? What index options are available in Canada?

19-13. What are the major differences between a stock option and an index option?

19-14. How does writing a covered call differ from writing a naked call?

19-15. What does it mean to say that an option is worth more alive than dead?

19-16. What are the potential advantages of puts and calls?

19-17. Explain the factors used in the Black-Scholes option valuation model. What is the relationship between each factor and the value of the option?

19-18. Give three reasons why an investor might purchase a call.

19-19. What is a straddle? When would an investor buy one? Write one? (Refer to Appendix 19A for this question.)

19-20. What is a spread? What is its purpose? (Refer to Appendix 19A for this question.)

19-21. Explain two types of spreads. (Refer to Appendix 19A for this question.)

19-22. How can a put be used to protect a particular position? A call?

19-23. Which is greater for an option relative to the underlying common share, dollar movements or return volatility? Why?

19-24. Assume that you own a diversified portfolio of 50 stocks and fear a market decline over the next six months.
   a. How could you protect your portfolio during this period using stock-index options?
   b. How effective would this hedge be?
   c. Other things being equal, if your portfolio consisted of 150 stocks, would the protection be more effective?

19-25. Assume that you expect interest rates to rise and that you wish to speculate on this expectation. How could interest rate options be used to do this?

PROBLEMS

Assume the common stock of ABC Company trades on the TSX. ABC has never paid a cash dividend. The stock is relatively risky. Assume that the beta for ABC is 1.3 and that ABC closed at a price of $162. Hypothetical option quotes on ABC are as follows:

Strike Price	Call Apr	Call Jul	Call Oct	Put Apr	Put Jul	Put Oct
140	23.50	s	s	s	s	s
150	16	21	25	1	3.75	r
160	8.88	14	20	3	7	9
170	3	9	13.25	9	10	11
180	1.25	5.25	9	r	20	r

r = not traded; s = no option offered

19-1. Based on the ABC data, answer the following questions:

    a. Which calls are in the money?

    b. Which puts are in the money?

    c. Why are investors willing to pay 1.25 for the 180 April call but only 1.00 for the 150 April put, which has an exercise price that is closer to the current market price?

19-2. Based on the ABC data answer the following:

    a. Calculate the intrinsic value of the April 150 and the October 170 calls.

    b. Calculate the intrinsic value of the April 150 and the October 170 puts.

    c. Explain the reasons for the differences in intrinsic values in parts (a) and (b).

19-3. Using the ABC data, answer the following:

    a. What is the cost of 10 October 150 call contracts in total dollars (excluding commission fees)?

    b. What is the cost of 20 October 160 put contracts in total dollars (excluding commission fees)?

    c. On the following day, assume ABC closed at $164. Which of the options would you have expected to increase? Decrease?

    d. If the new quote on the October 150 call was 26, what would have been your one-day profit on the 10 contracts? What would have been your percentage return?

    e. If the new quote on the October 160 put was 7.50, what would have been your one-day profit on the 20 contracts? What would have been your percentage return?

    f. What is the most you could lose on these 20 contracts?

19-4. You are considering some put and call options and have available the following data (assume no dividends are paid by ABC or DEF):

	Call ABC	Call DEF	Put ABC
Time to expiration (months)	3	6	3
Annual risk-free rate	8%	8%	8%
Exercise price	$50	$50	$50
Option price	$3		$4
Stock price	$45	$45	$45

    a. Comparing the two calls, should DEF sell for more or less than ABC if their shares have the same volatility? Why?

    b. What is the call option time value for call option ABC?

    c. Based on the information for the call and the put for ABC, determine if put-call parity is working.

19-5. Assume that the value of a call option using the Black-Scholes model is $8.94. The interest rate is 8 percent, and the time to maturity is 90 days. The price of the underlying stock is $47.38, and the exercise price is $45. Calculate the price of a put using the put-call parity relationship.

19-6. Using the Black-Scholes formula, calculate the value of a call option given the following information:

Stock price = $50
Exercise price = $45
Interest rate = 7%
Time to expiration = 90 days
Standard deviation = 0.4
What is the price of the put using the same information?

19-7. Using the information in Problem 19-6, determine the sensitivity of the call value to a change in inputs by recalculating the call value if

a. the interest rate doubles to 14 percent but all other values remain the same.
b. the standard deviation doubles to 0.8 but all other values remain the same.
c. Which change causes the greatest fluctuation in the value of the call? What can you infer from this?

19-8. Given the following information, determine the number of shares of stock that must be purchased to form a hedged position if one option contract (covering 100 shares of stock) is to be written.

Stock price = $100
Exercise price = $95
Interest rate = 8%
Time to expiration = 180 days
Standard deviation = 0.6

19-9. Given the information in Problem 8, determine how the value of the call would change if

a. the exercise price is $100
b. the time to expiration is 80 days (use the original exercise price of $95)
c. the time to expiration is 8 days

19-10. Determine the value of Ribex call options if the exercise price is $40, and the option is currently $2 out of the money, the time to expiration is 90 days, the interest rate is 0.10, and the variance of return on the stock for the past few months has been 0.81.

19-11. Using the information in Problem 10, decide intuitively whether the put or the call will sell at a higher price and verify your answer.

19-12. An investor who purchased 100 shares of Stock G for $1,800 sells a six-month call with a strike price of $25 and a $5 call premium.

a. What is the investor's gross profit/loss if the price of the stock rises to $28 and the investor is called to deliver the 100 shares?
b. What is the investor's gross profit/loss if the price drops to $21?
c. What is the investor's gross profit/loss if the price drops to $16?
d. What is the investor's gross profit/loss if the price drops to $11?

19-13. Stock R closes at $16.25 on August 30, 2004. A May 2005 put option on Stock R has an exercise price of $18.05. This put was last traded at a premium of $3.10.

a. What is the intrinsic value of the put?
b. What is the intrinsic value of the put if the exercise price was $16.25?
c. What is the intrinsic value of the put if the exercise price was $14.44?
d. What is the intrinsic value of a March 2005 call option on Stock R, with an exercise price of $18.05?

e. What is the intrinsic value of the call if the exercise price was $16.25?

f. What is the intrinsic value of the call if the exercise price was $14.44?

19-14. Assume an investor buys a put option on Stock C for $4.90, with a strike price of $25. What is the payoff and the net profit for the put option if the price at expiration is $10, $15, $20, $25, or $30?

19-15. Assume an investor purchases a February 2005 call option of Stock B. It has an exercise price of $35 when the stock price is valued at $31.40 in the market, and it carries a premium of $2.15 for this standard contract. What is the investor's total wealth if:

a. The stock price went up to $36.50 and the call was exercised?

b. The stock price went up to $35?

c. The stock price went up to $33.20?

d. The stock price went up to $38.40?

e. What must the stock price be in order for this investor to break even?

f. In each of these cases above, is the call in the money, out of the money, or at the money?

 19-16. There are various ways to calculate the price of a call option using the Black-Scholes model. The spreadsheet breaks the required formulas into pieces to make it easy to work with. Column (1) shows the various inputs. The first five cells are the required inputs for a non-dividend-paying stock. The remainder of the cells are the formula parts. Column (2) shows a solved problem for a stock selling for $50, with an exercise price of $45, an interest rate of 6 percent, 90 days (one-quarter of a year), and a standard deviation of .235. Column (3) shows how the cell values in Column (2) were calculated. Once you have this set up in the spreadsheet, you can calculate the price of any call option by substituting the correct values in the first five cells of column (1).

Calculating a Call Price Using the Black-Scholes Model

S	50	
E	45	
r	0.06	
t	0.25	
s	0.235	
$\ln(S/E)$	0.105361	LN(B2/B3)
$r + 0.5\sigma$	0.087613	B4 + (.5)*(B6)^2
$\sigma(t)^{1/2}$	0.1175	B6*((B5) 0.5)
d_1	1.083095	(B7+(B8*B5))/B9
d_2	0.965595	B10−B9
$N(d_1)$	0.860617	NORMSDIST(B10)
$N(d_2)$	0.832877	NORMSDIST(B11)
$S*N(d_1)$	43.03084	B2*B12
E	2.7183	
$e-r^t$	0.985112	B15^−(B4*B5)
Call Price	6.109398	B14−(B3*B16*B13)

PREPARING FOR YOUR PROFESSIONAL EXAMS

CFA CURRICULUM AND SAMPLE EXAM QUESTIONS (©CFA INSTITUTE)

19-1. Assume the probability of bankruptcy for the underlying asset is high. Compared to the price of a US put option on the same underlying asset, the price of an equivalent European put option will most likely be:

a. lower.

b. higher.

   c. the same because the probability of bankruptcy does not affect pricing.

   d. the same because the possibility of early exercise only affects the pricing of call options.

19-2. With respect to put-call parity, a proactive put consists of a European

   a. put option and the underlying asset.

   b. call option and the underlying asset.

   c. put option and a risk-free bond with a face value equal to the exercise price of a European call option on the underlying asset.

   d. call option and a risk-free bond with a face value equal to the exercise price of a European put option on the underlying asset.

19-3. Unless far out-of-the money or far in-the-money, for otherwise identical call options, the longer the term to expiration, the lower the price for:

   a. European call options, but not US call options.

   b. US call options, but not European call options.

   c. both European call options and US call options.

   d. neither European call options nor US call options.

19-4. A call option with an exercise price of 65 will expire in 73 days. No cash payments will be made by the underlying asset over the life of the option. If the underlying asset price is at 70 and the risk-free rate of return is 5.0 percent, the lower bounds for a US call option and a European call option, respectively, are closest to:

Lower bound for US call option	Lower bound for European call option
a. 5.00	5.00
b. 5.00	5.63
c. 5.63	5.00
d. 5.63	5.63

19-5. A call option with an exercise price of 75 will expire in 73 days. No cash payments will be made by the underlying asset over the life of the option. If the underlying asset price is at 70 and the risk-free rate of return is 5.0 percent, the lower bounds for a US put option and a European put option, respectively, are closest to:

Lower bound for US put option	Lower bound for European put option
a. 4.27	4.27
b. 4.27	5.00
c. 5.00	4.27
d. 5.00	5.00

19-6. Compare a US call with a strike of 50 that expires in 90 days to a US call on the same underlying asset that has a strike of 60 and expires in 120 days. The underlying asset is selling at 55. Are the following statements true?

Statement 1: The 50 strike call is in-the-money and the 60 strike call is out-of-the-money.

Statement 2: The time value of the 60 strike call, as a proportion of the 60 strike call's premium, exceeds the time value of the 50 strike call as a proportion of the 50 strike call's premium.

Statement 1	Statement 2
a. No	No
b. No	Yes
c. Yes	No
d. Yes	Yes

19-7. Marla Johnson priced both a put and a call on Alpha Numero using standard option pricing software. To use the program, Johnson entered the strike price of the options, the price of the underlying stock, an estimate of the risk-free rate, the time to expiration of the option, and an estimate of the volatility of the returns of the underlying stock into her computer. Both prices calculated by the software program were substantially above the actual market values observed in that day's exchange trading. Which of the following is a plausible explanation?

    a. She put the wrong strike price into the program; most likely, she used too low a strike price.
    b. She put too low a value into the program for time to expiration of the options.
    c. She put too high a value into the program for the estimate of volatility.
    d. She put too low a value into the program for the estimate of volatility.

19-8. A call with a strike price of $40 is available on a stock currently trading for $35. The call expires in one year and the risk free rate of return is 10 percent. The lower bound on this call's value is:

    a. zero.
    b. $5 if the call is US-style.
    c. $1.36 if the call is European-style.
    d. $3.18 if the call is European-style.

19-9. A silver futures contract requires the seller to deliver 5,000 Troy ounces of silver. An investor sells one July silver futures contract at a price of $8 per ounce, posting a $2,025 initial margin. If the required maintenance margin is $1,500, the price per ounce at which the investor would first receive a maintenance margin call is closest to:

    a. $5.92.
    b. $7.89.
    c. $8.11.
    d. $10.80.

APPENDIX 19A

SPREADS AND COMBINATIONS

Puts and calls offer investors a number of opportunities beyond the simple strategies discussed in Chapter 19. We briefly describe here some combinations of options that can be written or purchased. We also consider the use of spreads.

Combinations of Options

Straddle

A combination of a put and a call on the same stock with the same exercise date and exercise price.

Options can be mixed together in numerous ways. Some typical combinations include a straddle, a strip, and a strap. A **straddle** is a combination of a put and a call on the same stock with the same exercise date and exercise price. A purchaser of a straddle believes that the underlying stock price is highly volatile and may go either up or down. Buying the straddle eliminates the need to predict the direction of the market correctly. The buyer of the straddle can exercise each part separately, and therefore can profit from a large enough move either way. However, the price of the stock must rise or fall enough to equal the premium on both a put and a call; therefore, the straddle buyer must be confident that the underlying stock has a good chance of moving sharply in at least one direction.

    Straddles can also be sold (written). The seller believes that the underlying stock price will exhibit small volatility but could go up or down. Unlike the buyer, the writer does not forecast that a substantial movement in one direction or the other is likely.

    Consider a stock selling at $75 with a six-month straddle available with an exercise price of $75 and, for simplicity, call and put prices of $5 each. The seller of such a straddle is protected (i.e., makes

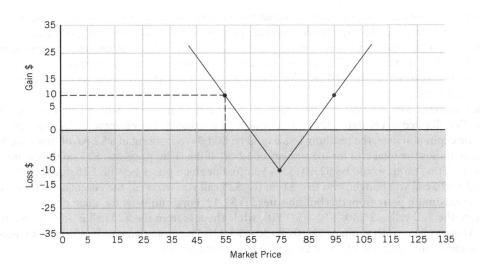

Figure 19-11
Straddle Profit Diagram

a profit) in the range of $65–85 (ignoring commissions). They earn the maximum return of $10, if the price remains at $75, since neither option would be exercised at this price. The buyers hope that the price exceeds one of these boundaries (i.e., $65 or $85) before expiration. In any event, if the price is above or below $75, one of the options would be in the money, and hence be exercised. However, in order for the buyer to achieve a positive profit by exercising the option, the price would have to move up or down by more than $10 (i.e., in order to cover the original cost of $10).[26] The profit diagram for this straddle is shown in Figure 19-11.

A *strip* is a combination of two puts and a call on the same security, again with the same expiration date and exercise price. In this case, the purchaser believes that the price will probably decline rather than rise and therefore wants two puts (but also wants some protection in the opposite direction). The seller obviously believes the opposite.

A *strap* is similar to a strip but combines two calls with a put. Here, of course, the purchaser believes the probability of a price increase exceeds that for a price decrease, and again, the writer expects the opposite.

Spreads

Rather than being only the buyer or the seller of various combinations of puts and calls, an investor can be both simultaneously by means of a spread. A **spread** is defined as the purchase and sale of an equivalent option varying in only one respect. Its purpose is to reduce risk in an option position, and it is a popular practice.

The two basic spreads are the *money spread* and the *time spread*. A money spread involves the purchase of a call option at one exercise price and the sale of the same-maturity option, but with a different exercise price. For example, an investor could buy an October 20 call and sell an October 25 call on the same underlying stock.

A time spread involves the purchase and sale of options that are identical except for expiration dates. For example, an investor could buy an October 25 call and sell a January 25 call on the same underlying stock.

Investors use particular spread strategies, depending on whether they are bullish or bearish. Assume you are bullish about a stock but wish to reduce the risk involved in options. The stock is selling for $22.83, with four-month call options available at exercise prices of $20 and $25 for $3.70 and $1.10, respectively. A bullish money spread consists of buying the $20 call and selling the $25 call.

Spread
The purchase and sale of an equivalent option varying in only one respect.

---

[26]Of course, we know that early exercise is generally less profitable than selling the option in the market, since the seller would receive a time value premium in addition to the intrinsic value (which is the value obtained if the option is exercised).

Your net cost is now $2.60, which is the maximum you could lose if the calls expire worthless because the stock's price dropped sharply. Should the share price rise above $20, however, your $20 call will be worth at least the price of the stock minus the exercise price of $20. This amount is netted against your profit or loss on the $25 call that you wrote. In effect, you give up some potential profit (what could have been earned on the $20 call alone) to reduce your risk (by reducing your net cost) if the stock price declines.

The maximum loss is $2.60, which would occur if the share price was $20 or below on the closing date. For all price levels above $20, this loss would be reduced. For example, if the share price is $22 on the expiration date, the resulting loss would be $0.60—consisting of a $2 payoff from the $20 call option, minus the total cost for the strategy of $2.60. If the share price was $25 on the expiration date, the resulting profit would be $2.40 ($5 – $2.60). For share prices beyond $25, for each $1 you gain on the $20 call you bought, you lose $1 on the $25 call you wrote, so the effects cancel out. As a result, the maximum profit from this bullish spread is $2.40. For example, if the share price is $30, the profit from the $20 call is $6.30 ($10 – $ 3.70), while the loss from the $25 call is –$3.90 ($1.10 – $5.00). This results in a net profit of $2.40 ($6.30 – $3.90). The profit diagram for this bullish money spread is shown in Figure 19-12. (This example ignores commission fees).

Figure 19-12
Bullish Money Spread
Profit Diagram

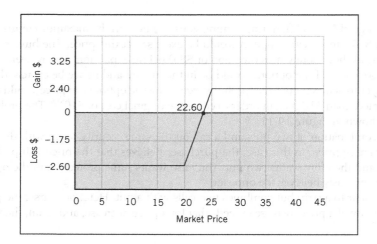

APPENDIX 19B

RIGHTS AND WARRANTS

Rights and warrants are similar to call options because they both give the holder the right to purchase shares at specified prices until the expiration date. Rights are generally short-term in nature, while warrants tend to be issued with maturities of three to five years. Unlike options, they are issued by the corporation itself, and result in dilution of the common equity capital base.

Right

A corporate-created option to purchase a stated number of common shares at a specified price within a specified time (typically a few months).

Rights

A **right** is the term applied to a privilege granted to a shareholder to acquire additional shares at a predetermined (subscription) price that is generally lower than the current market price. This creates value for the shareholder and induces them to exercise this option. Rights generally have short maturities consisting of a few weeks to three months. They are usually transferable, and certificates are mailed to shareholders on the record date. Shares trade ex rights two business days prior to a record date, which means they trade without the right privilege attached. Prior to the ex rights date, the stock is said to trade cum rights, since it trades with the right privilege attached. Typically the share price will drop by the theoretical intrinsic value of the right on the ex rights date.

Rights may be offered because

1. Current market conditions are not conducive to traditional common share issues.

2. Management wants to give existing shareholders the opportunity to acquire shares, possibly at a discount to present market price.

3. It enables new funds to be raised while providing existing shareholders the right to maintain their proportionate ownership of the company.

No commission is levied on the exercise of rights, and a ready secondary market can develop permitting the sale of rights by holders who do not wish to exercise. If the shares trade on an exchange, the rights are listed on the exchange automatically and trading takes place until they expire. Regular delivery requires settlement within three business days, prior to the expiration date of the rights, after which time the rights will trade only on a cash basis. The Exchange will cease trading of rights on the Exchange at 12:00 noon (Toronto time) on the expiration date. Because of their short lifetime, they are often bought and sold on a "when issued" basis, which implies that sellers agree to deliver the rights when they are received.

A rights holder may take four courses of action:

1. Exercise some or all of the rights

2. Sell some or all of the rights

3. Buy additional rights for trading or exercise purposes

4. Do nothing and let the rights expire (which would represent sub-optimal behaviour since the investor would gain nothing through this action)

Usually each shareholder receives one right, and a certain number of rights (N) is required to purchase one share (purchase of fractional shares may or may not be permitted, depending on the details of the issue). The theoretical intrinsic value (IV) of a right, by necessity, is calculated using two methods described below.

During the cum rights period:

$$IV = \frac{(\text{Market price of the stock} - \text{Subscription price})}{N + 1} \qquad \textbf{(19-9)}$$

The addition of 1 to N reflects the fact that the market price of the share includes the value of one right.

During the ex rights period:

$$IV = \frac{(\text{Market price of stock} - \text{Subscription price})}{N} \qquad \textbf{(19-10)}$$

EXAMPLE 19B-1: CALCULATING INTRINSIC VALUE CUM AND EX RIGHTS

A share is trading for $40 cum rights. Four rights are required to purchase a share at the subscription price of $35.

IV = (40 − 35) / (4 + 1) = $1.00

Two days after the ex rights date the share price above has fallen to $39.20.

IV = (39.20 − 35) / 4 = $1.05

Warrants

Warrants are corporate-issued securities with an option to buy shares from the issuer at a set price for a set period of time. Warrants are generally long-term in nature and tend to be issued with three to five

Warrant
An option created by a corporation to purchase a stated number of common shares at a specified price within a specified time (often several years).

years to maturity, although some have longer lives. They are often attached to debt or preferred share issues as a sweetener (to make the issue more attractive to investors). They are usually detachable either immediately or after a certain holding period, and then trade separately.

Investors may be attracted to warrants because they provide "leverage," which is attractive to speculators. In other words, the market price of a warrant is generally much lower than the price of the underlying security, yet its price moves together with the underlying asset price. The result is greater percentage swings in warrant prices than for the underlying asset, which magnifies gains (or losses) in percentage terms. A ratio that may be used to measure this leverage potential is

(19-11)
$$\text{Leverage potential} = \frac{\text{Market price of the underlying share}}{\text{Market price of the warrant}}$$

Generally speaking, the larger this ratio, the greater the leverage effect; however, other factors such as the amount of overvaluation must also be considered. Other factors to be considered by investors when selecting warrants include marketability and protection against stock splits and/or stock dividends (which is usually provided).

Warrants have an intrinsic value and a time value. The intrinsic value refers to the amount by which the market price of the underlying stock exceeds the exercise price of the warrant. It can never go below zero, since exercise is at the option of the warrant holder. Time value refers to the amount by which the market price exceeds the intrinsic value.

There is also usually an overvaluation associated with warrants, which is calculated as follows:

(19-12)
$$\text{Overvaluation} = \text{Market price of warrant} + \text{Exercise price of warrant} - \text{Market value of underlying asset}$$

This will equal the time value whenever there is a positive intrinsic value but may exceed the time value when the intrinsic value is nil.

EXAMPLE 19B-2: DETERMINING INTRINSIC VALUE, TIME VALUE, OVERVALUATION, AND LEVERAGE

Determine the intrinsic value, time value, percentage overvaluation, and leverage potential of the following warrants:

a. Share price is $50, warrant price is $8, and exercise price of warrants is $52.

b. Share price is $40, warrant price is $15, and exercise price of warrants is $30.

Solution:

a.   IV = Max (50 − 52, 0) = 0

     Time Value = 8 − 0 = $8

     Overvaluation = 8 + 52 − 50 = 10

     Percentage overvaluation = 10/50 = 0.20 or 20%

     Leverage potential = 50/8 = 6.25

b.   IV = Max (40 − 30, 0) = 10

     Time Value = 15 − 10 = $5

     Overvaluation = 15 + 30 − 40 = 5

     Percentage overvaluation = 5/40 = 0.125 or 12.5%

     Leverage potential = 40/15 = 2.67

Factors to be examined by investors in order to determine the appropriateness of warrant over-valuation include

1. The prospects for the underlying assets
2. Time to expiration
3. Volatility of underlying asset price
4. Higher premiums may be associated with higher price-earnings ratios of underlying shares
5. Lower over-valuations should result for warrants on assets paying higher dividends to compensate the warrant holder for not receiving the dividend

Some special types of warrants include

1. Piggyback warrants—may be received as part of the exercise of original warrants (and typically have higher exercise prices)
2. Put warrants—on stock indices, etc., which result in cash settlement if the price of the underlying is below a specified price
3. Commodity-indexed warrants—where the exercise price is linked to market prices of a specified commodity

APPENDIX 19C

PUT-CALL PARITY: THE NO-ARBITRAGE ARGUMENT

Unless the price of a European put and call on the same non-dividend-paying stock with the same exercise price bear a certain relationship to each other, there will be opportunities for earning riskless profits (arbitrage). We can prove this by using the following no-arbitrage argument, which ignores transactions costs. Consider the following investment portfolios: Portfolio A involves the purchase of a European call option for an underlying share that does not pay dividends (at a cost of C), and investing the present value of the exercise price on this option [PV(E) dollars] in a riskless investment (government T-bills) that will pay off E dollars at the maturity date; portfolio B involves the purchase of one share of the underlying stock (at a cost of S), and also buying one European put on the underlying share (at a cost of P). These actions and their payoffs at expiration date T are depicted below.

Portfolio	Action	Payoff at T	
		$S(T) < E$	$S(T) > E$
A	Buy 1 call	0	$S(T) - E$
	Invest PV(E) in T-bills	E	E
	Total Payoff	**E**	**S(T)**
B	Buy 1 share	S(T)	S(T)
	Buy 1 put	$E - S(T)$	0
	Total Payoff	**E**	**S(T)**

Notice that portfolios A and B always have the same payoff at T because they will both pay off S(T) at T when S(T) > E, and will both pay off E at T when S(T) < E. Since both the call and the put are European options, we also know that early exercise of either option is impossible. Therefore, since the two strategies must have identical payoffs at the expiration date, and since the options cannot be exercised early, they must have identical costs for constructing the portfolios. If they did not, investors could make riskless (or arbitrage) profits by taking a long position in the undervalued portfolio and taking a short position in the overvalued portfolio. For example, if the cost of constructing A was $10, while the cost of constructing B was $8, one could take a long position in B and a short position in A, and receive $2 today. Since both portfolios have the same payoff at T, the returns from B can always be used to pay off the short position in A, so there is no risk associated with this strategy, yet the payoff is positive. This condition could never exist in efficient markets and would quickly disappear as traders recognized the discrepancy and exploited it. So,

$$\text{Total cost to construct portfolio A} = \text{Total cost to construct portfolio B, or}$$
$$C + PV(E) = P + S$$

This can be rearranged to solve for the price of the put as follows:

$$P = PV(E) - S + C$$

Finally, we note that the present value of E using a continuous discount rate r, and with a time to maturity (in years) equal to t, can be expressed as $PV(E) = E/e^{rt}$, so we are left with Equation 19-8: $P = E/e^{rt} - S + C$.

CHAPTER 20

FUTURES

Quick—there is a freeze in Florida, so buy orange juice futures! You have heard this one before, but you never thought about doing it because you know nothing about futures contracts. Given all that you have had to learn lately as part of your investments education, you are not enthused about learning too much about futures contracts at this time. However, it would be nice to be able to understand what people are talking about when they discuss futures, and even to mull them over in your mind in case one day you want to use futures as part of your portfolio strategy. Therefore, you realize some effort in this area is worthwhile.

Learning Objectives

After reading this chapter, you should be able to

1. Describe the structure of futures markets.
2. Outline how futures work and what types of investors participate in futures markets.
3. Explain how financial futures are used.

CHAPTER PREVIEW

This chapter discusses financial futures, the other derivative security of primary importance to investors. As with options, futures allow investors to manage investment risk and to speculate in the equity, fixed-income, and currency markets. Here we discuss the structure of futures markets, explain the procedures of using futures, and give some basic strategies. We also consider interest rate and stock-index futures.

INTRODUCTION

Futures markets play an important role in today's investments world. New instruments in this area have proliferated, and techniques involving the use of futures, such as program trading, have captured wide media attention. Of particular importance to many investors is the array of financial futures now available. Anyone studying investments should understand what futures contracts are, the wide variety of choices now available, and how financial futures can be used both to hedge portfolio positions and to speculate in fixed-income and equity areas. Futures contracts are an important component of derivative securities and, like options, they represent a major innovation in risk management.

UNDERSTANDING FUTURES MARKETS

Why Futures Markets?

Physical commodities and financial instruments typically are traded in cash markets. A *cash contract* calls for immediate delivery and is used by those who need a commodity now (e.g., food processors). Cash contracts cannot be cancelled unless both parties agree. The current cash prices of commodities and financial instruments can be found daily in the financial media.

There are two types of cash markets: spot markets and forward markets. Spot markets are for immediate delivery.[1] The spot price refers to the current market price of an item available for immediate delivery. Forward markets are for deferred delivery. The forward price is the price of an item that is to be delivered at some specified time in the future.

Suppose that a manufacturer of high school and college class rings is gathering orders to fill for this school year and wishes to ensure an established price today for gold to be delivered six months from now, when the rings will actually be manufactured. The spot price of gold is not the manufacturer's primary concern, because the gold will not be purchased until it is needed for the manufacturing process. However, to reduce its risk, the manufacturer is interested in contracting for gold to be delivered in six months at a price established today. This will allow the manufacturer to price its rings more accurately.

Our manufacturer could find a gold supplier who was willing to enter into a *forward contract*, which is simply a commitment today to transact in the future. The other party to the contract, such as a mining company, agrees to deliver the gold six months from now at a price negotiated today. Both parties have agreed to a deferred delivery at a sales price that is currently determined. No funds have been exchanged. Both parties have reduced their risk in the sense that the mining company knows what it will receive for the gold when it is sold six months from now and the ring manufacturer knows what it will pay for the gold when it actually needs to take delivery six months from now.

Obviously, one of the parties may be disappointed six months later when the price of gold has changed, but that is the advantage of hindsight. If investors could foresee the future, they would know what to do to start with and would not have to worry about risk. The forward and futures markets were developed to allow individuals to deal with the risks they face.

---

[1]"Immediate" means in the normal course of business. For example, it may normally take two days for an item to be delivered after being ordered.

Forward contracts are centuries old, traceable to at least the ancient Romans and Greeks. Organized futures markets, on the other hand, only go back to the mid-nineteenth century in Chicago. Futures markets are, in effect, organized and standardized forward markets. An organized futures exchange standardizes the non-standard forward contracts, establishing such features as contract size, delivery dates, and condition of the items that can be delivered. Only the price and number of contracts are left for futures traders to negotiate. Individuals can trade without personal contact with each other because of the centralized marketplace. Performance is guaranteed by a clearing house, relieving one party to the transaction from worry that the other party will fail to honour its commitment.

The futures markets serve a valuable economic purpose by allowing hedgers to shift price risk to speculators. The risk of price fluctuations is shifted from participants unwilling to assume such risk to those who are. Another economic function performed by futures markets is price discovery. Because the price of a futures contract reflects current expectations about values at some future date, transactors can establish current prices against later transactions.

Current Futures Markets

To most people, futures trading traditionally has meant trading in commodities such as gold, wheat, and oil. However, money can be thought of simply as another commodity, and *financial futures* have become a particularly viable investment alternative for numerous investors. Therefore, futures contracts currently traded on futures exchanges can be divided into two broad categories:

1. Commodities—agricultural, metals, and energy-related
2. Financials—foreign currencies as well as debt and equity instruments.

Each category can be further subdivided as shown in Table 20-1, which shows the futures contracts traded in the United States. As we can see, the futures markets involve trading in a variety of both commodities and financials.

Table 20-1

Futures Contracts Traded in the United States, by Category

The major commodities traded in the United States can be classified into the following categories:

I. Commodities	
Grains and oilseeds	Wheat, corn, oats, soybeans, soybean oils, soybean meal, flaxseed, rapeseed, rye, and canola
Livestock and meats	Cattle (both live and feeders), pork bellies, and hogs
Foods	Cocoa, coffee, orange juice, and sugar
Fibres	Cotton
Metals	Copper, gold, platinum, silver, and palladium
Oil	Gasoline, heating oil, crude oil, gas oil, propane, and ethanol
Wood	Lumber
II. Financials	
Interest rates	Canadian government bond, Treasury bills, Treasury notes, Treasury bonds, municipal bond index, 30-day federal funds, Eurodollar, 1-month LIBOR, Sterling Long Gilt, Euromark, EuroSwiss, EuroLira, German government bond, Italian government bond, French government bond, 10-year swap, 5-year swap
Stock indexes	S&P/TSX 60 Index, S&P 500 Index, S&P MidCap 400, NYSE Composite Index, Major Market Index, KR-CRB Index, KC Value Line Index, Russell 2000, CAC 40, Nikkei 225 Index, GSCL, FT-SE 100 Index
Foreign currencies	Euro, Japanese yen, Canadian dollar, German mark, British pounds, Swiss franc, Australian dollar, and US dollar index

For each type of contract, such as corn or silver, different delivery dates are available. Each contract will specify the trading unit involved and, where applicable, the deliverable grade necessary to satisfy the contract. Investors can also purchase options on futures contracts (see Appendix 20A).

One of the striking features of Table 20-1 is the proliferation of foreign-based futures contracts on US futures exchanges. This is true for interest rate futures and stock-index futures and is good evidence of the move toward globalization that is occurring throughout the investing world. For example, Real-World Returns 20-1 discusses talks designed to initiate a new futures contract on Canadian crude oil on some US exchanges.

Real-World Returns 20-1

Futures Contract Sought For Canadian Crude

The growing importance of Canadian oil sands production could soon be rewarded with the ultimate status symbol, at least in oil market terms: a heavy crude futures contract.

Canadian oil producers say they're in negotiations with investment banks and commodities exchanges over the development of a futures contract for their heavy crude output. A contract on the New York Mercantile Exchange or the Intercontinental Exchange (ICE) for Western Canadian Select, a blend of heavy Canadian crudes, could be created in the next year if sufficient liquidity can be attained, these people say.

"We've spoken to the ICE and Nymex many times to see how we can set up a contract," said Walt Madro, senior vice-president of crude oil marketing at EnCana Corp., Canada's largest energy company.

"They're chasing this very aggressively. We wouldn't be surprised if they started providing quotes within the next 12 months." At present, Canadian firms trade their crude through private, over-the-counter deals with buyers such as refineries. The lack of transparency inherent in such a system means companies don't know what price their future supplies will achieve, creating uncertainty over revenue projections.

That's a problem producers would like to solve, considering crude output from Alberta's oil sands is expected to triple to three million barrels a day in 2015 and US refiners are showing greater interest in taking Canadian heavy output. ConocoPhillips Co. recently agreed to a huge supply deal with EnCana, while BP PLC and Marathon Oil Corp, have also said they're keen to source supply of more Canadian crude.

"Having a contract provides a great deal more liquidity with respect to moving volumes while providing improved price disclosure," said Rod Wilson, manager of domestic crude supply and natural gas liquids at Petro-Canada. "It's an uncertainty over revenue projections instrument for companies to lay off risk."

Both Nymex and the ICE refused to comment on the possibility of setting up a heavy crude contract. However, Nymex said earlier this month it had obtained authorization to offer the use of its electronic clearing and trading systems in Alberta. Meanwhile, the Toronto Stock Exchange owner, TSX Group Inc., is also mulling the introduction of a Canadian crude oil contract.

To be sure, the strong support in Canada for a heavy crude contract doesn't mean it will happen or be successful. New contracts frequently struggle to take away trading volumes from the traditional West Texas intermediate (WTI) and Brent benchmarks, resulting in an illiquid contract that's unable to attract traders. This month, a heavy crude contract for Russian Export Blend Crude Oil was launched on Nymex, but trading volumes haven't yet taken off.

However, the Canadian producers see a futures contract as a natural progression for their attempts to position Western Canadian Select as a North American benchmark for heavy crude. The blend, which consists of Canadian heavy conventional and bitumen crude oils, blended with sweet synthetic and condensate diluents, was launched by four producers—EnCana, Petrocan, Canadian Natural Resources Ltd. and Talisman Energy Inc—in late 2004. Production runs are at around 250,000 barrels a day, compared with the WTI and Brent benchmarks, both of which are near 350,000 barrels a day.

The level needed to maintain a contract is open to debate. Both EnCana and Canadian Natural, the largest producers of Western Canadian Select, think production of 300,000 barrels a day could sustain a contract, and could be reached within the next 12 months. However, both Petrocan's Mr. Wilson and Craig James, manager of crude and natural gas liquids marketing at Talisman, said a more realistic target is 400,000 barrels a day, which is unlikely to be reached in 2007.

Source: Scott, Norval, "Futures Contract Sought for Canadian Crude," *The Globe and Mail*, November 23, 2006, p. B18.

The only commodity exchange in Canada is ICE Futures Canada, formerly the Winnipeg Commodity Exchange, where trading has taken place in wheat, canola, flaxseed, oats, barley, and rye for several years. Futures on canola are by far the most active commodity futures that are traded in Canada, as shown in Table 20-2.

Table 20-2

Listed Futures Products on ICE Futures Canada for 2006 (formerly Winnipeg Commodity Exchange)

Commodity Futures	Trading Volume
Canola	2,427,697
Feed Wheat	65,802
Western Barley	193,324
Total	2,686,823

Options	Trading Volume
Canola	26,523
Feed Wheat	1,460
Western Barley	1,080
Total	27,603

Source: www.theice.com

Financial futures contracts presently trade in Canada on the ME. The ME trades contracts on three-month bankers' acceptances (which call for cash delivery), as well as on two-year and 10-year Government of Canada bonds. They also offer futures on 30-day overnight Repo Rates. Table 20-3 shows the 2007 volume for Canadian bankers' acceptances was 15.24 million contracts, while the volume for Government of Canada bonds was 9.3 million contracts. The ME trades several equity-based futures contracts, including those based on 200 times the S&P/TSX 60 Index and based on Sectoral Indexes, which all call for cash settlement. The 2007 volumes for the S&P/TSX 60 Index futures was 3.9 million contracts traded.

The centre of commodity futures trading in North America is the Chicago Board of Trade (CBT) and the Chicago Mercantile Exchange (CME); however, there are several other important exchanges in New York, including the Commodity Exchange, the New York Mercantile Exchange, the New York Coffee, Sugar and Cocoa Exchange, the New York Cotton Exchange, and the New York Futures Exchange. Futures markets in Canada are very small and much less developed than those in the US, both in terms of the variety of available products and trading volume. Real-World Returns 20-2 discusses the CME's takeover bid for Nymex Holdings Inc., which is the parent company for the New York Mercantile Exchange.

Table 20-3

Financial Futures Volumes on the ME (2006 and 2007)

Future Product Group	2006 Volume		2007 Volume	
Three-month Canadian Bankers' Acceptance Futures (BAX)	16,702,302	(60.6%)	15,237,958	(53.5%)
Ten-year Government of Canada Bond Futures (CGB)	7,691,797	(27.9%)	9,337,754	(32.8%)
Two-year Government of Canada Bond Futures (CGZ)	85,301	0.3%	6,363	0.0%
S&P Canada 60 Index Futures (SXF)	3,064,695	11.1%	3,885,872	13.6%
Sectoral Index Futures (SXA, SXB, SXH, SXY)	33,964	0.1%	25,507	0.1%
Total	27,578,059	100.00%	28,493,454	100.00%

Source: Montreal Exchange: www.m-x.ca

REAL-WORLD RETURNS 20-2

CME Takeover of Nymex

Chicago Mercantile Exchange parent CME Group Inc. said it had reached, as expected, a definitive agreement to buy New York Mercantile Exchange parent Nymex Holdings Inc. for around $9-billion (US), extending its position as the world's largest derivatives exchange.

CME's next challenge will be to expand its business in over-the-counter derivatives trading. In recent months, regulators have been increasingly worried about opaque trading in the over-the counter markets, where Wall Street firms have endured billions of dollars in mortgage-related losses.

While trading methods haven't caused these losses, some regulators have explored whether increasing the role of exchanges could boost transparency and reduce volatility in mortgage-debt and credit default swaps markets.

Nymex gives CME an added boost in that area. In the years after Enron and other energy players imploded, the resulting fears about counterparty risk provided opportunity for Nymex to extend its business into over-the-counter energy trading. With the recent credit market meltdown, CME is likely to accelerate this push into financial derivatives that usually trade over-the-counter between large Wall Street firms.

CME and Nymex shares were both hit amid the broader selloff in financial services shares. But because exchanges don't take trading and investment risks like big brokerage firms do, they've held up much better than the worst-hit investment banks. A combined CME-Nymex, for instance, would have a market value of about $32-billion.

CME requires approval from antitrust officials and Nymex members, some of whom have been agitating for richer terms.

The latest exchange deal retains the terms disclosed when the companies revealed they were in exclusive talks in late January, though the value has fallen with CME stock since then, reflecting uncertainty over the regulatory climate for the fast-growing futures and options industry.

Credit Suisse analyst Howard Chen said in a research note that the financial terms are reasonable. He also said the deal makes sense strategically, and that—through CME's acquisition of the Chicago Board of Trade last July—"CME management has proven to be strong integrators."

Nymex holders will receive 0.1323 of CME shares and $36 in cash for each Nymex share, or about $95 each.

CME will also pay up to $500-million to buy the trading rights from 816 Nymex members.

CME officials said they were confident of securing regulatory approval in six to nine months.

Source: Cameron, Doug, and Lucchetti, Aaron, "Derivatives drive CME's takeover of Nymex," *The Globe and Mail*, March 18, 2008, p. B13.

International Futures Markets

European futures exchanges are quite competitive. Most of these systems are now fully automated order-matching systems. Euronext was the first pan-European exchange, created in 2000 by the merger of the Amsterdam, Brussels, and Paris markets. On June 1, 2006, the NYSE and Euronext agreed to combine in a merger of equals. The new NYSE Euronext provides a marketplace for trading cash and derivative securities.

Japan, which banned financial futures until 1985, has been very active in developing futures exchanges. Commodity futures markets account for most of the futures trading. Japan has seven commodity futures exchanges, each of which trades specific contracts. Most foreign brokers concentrate on a small number of financial futures, such as the Nikkei 225 stock index and 10-year government bonds.

Futures Contracts

A **futures contract** is a standardized, transferable agreement providing for the deferred delivery of either a specified grade and quantity of a designated commodity within a specified geographical area or of a financial instrument (or its cash value). The futures price at which this exchange will occur at contract maturity is determined today. The trading of futures contracts means only that commitments have been made by buyers and sellers; therefore, "buying" and "selling" does not have the same meaning in futures transactions as it does in stock and bond transactions. Although these commitments are binding because futures contracts are legal contracts, a buyer or seller can eliminate the commitment simply by taking an opposite position in the same commodity or financial instrument for the same futures month.

Futures Contract
Agreement providing for the future exchange of a particular asset between buyer and seller at a specified date for a specified amount.

Futures contracts trading on the ME is regulated by provincial securities administrators. Futures trading on the ICE Futures Canada is regulated by the Canadian Grain Commission, which oversees trading on this market under provisions in the Federal Grain Futures Act. Futures trading in the US is regulated by the Commodity Futures Trading Commission (CFTC), a federal regulatory agency that is responsible for regulating trading in all domestic futures markets. In practice, much of the supervisory functions are performed by the self-regulatory organizations, which include the Investment Industry Regulatory Organization of Canada (IIROC) and the exchanges in Canada, and the National Futures Association in the US. In addition, each futures exchange has a supervisory body to oversee its members. In Canada, investment advisors must pass the Derivatives Fundamental Course and the Futures Licensing Course before dealing in futures or options on futures.

CHECK YOUR UNDERSTANDING

20-1. What are the main categories of futures contracts available for trading?

20-2. Forward contracts and futures contracts are conceptually very similar. Distinguish between these two instruments and state one advantage of each.

THE STRUCTURE OF FUTURES MARKETS

learning objective 1
Describe the structure of futures markets.

Futures Exchanges

As noted, futures contracts are traded on designated futures exchanges, which are voluntary, non-profit associations, typically unincorporated. The exchange provides an organized marketplace where established rules govern the conduct of the members. It is financed by both membership dues and fees charged for services rendered.

There are a limited number of memberships for futures exchanges, which, like stock exchange seats, can be traded at market-determined prices. Members can trade for their own accounts or as agents for others. For example, floor traders trade for their own accounts, whereas floor brokers (or commission brokers) often act as agents for others. Futures commission merchants (FCMs) act as agents for the general public, for which they receive commissions. Thus, a customer can establish an account with an FCM, who, in turn may work through a floor broker at the exchange.

The Clearing Corporation

Similar to options markets, futures markets use a clearing corporation to reduce default risk and to arrange deliveries as required. The clearing corporations also ensure that participants maintain margin deposits or earnest money, to ensure fulfillment of the contract. The Canadian Derivatives Clearing Corporation (CDCC) currently issues and clears futures and futures options contracts traded on the ME, in addition to options contracts (discussed in Chapter 19), while ICE Clear Canada is the designated clearing house for ICE Futures Canada. Futures contracts presently include those on 30-day overnight Repo Rates, the US dollar, two-year and 10-year Government of Canada bonds, 3-month bankers' acceptances, the S&P/TSX 60 Index, the S&P/TSX Sectoral Indexes, and single stock prices. Futures options contracts include options on the 3-month bankers' acceptance futures.

Essentially, the clearing house for futures markets operates in the same way as the one for options, which was discussed in some detail in Chapter 19. Buyers and sellers settle with the clearing house, not each other, and it is actually on the other side of every transaction and ensures that all payments are made as specified. It stands ready to fulfill a contract if either buyer or seller defaults, thereby helping to facilitate an orderly market in futures. The clearing house makes the futures market impersonal, which is the key to its success because any buyer or seller can always close out a position and be assured of payment. The first failure of a clearing member in modern times occurred in the 1980s, and the system worked perfectly in preventing any customer from losing money. Finally, as explained below, the clearing house allows participants to easily reverse a position before maturity because it keeps track of each participant's obligations.

THE MECHANICS OF TRADING

Basic Procedures

Short Position

An agreement to sell an asset at a specified future date at a specified price.

Long Position

An agreement to purchase an asset at a specified future date at a specified price.

Offset

Liquidation of a futures position by an offsetting transaction—buyers sell their positions and sellers buy their positions prior to the settlement of the contract (delivery).

Because the futures contract is a commitment to buy or sell at a specified future settlement date, a contract is not really being sold or bought, as in the case of T-bills, bonds, or stocks, because no money is exchanged at the time the contract is negotiated. Instead, the seller and the buyer simply are agreeing to make and take delivery, respectively, at some future time for a price agreed upon today. As noted above, the terms buy and sell do not have the same meanings here. It is more accurate to think in terms of a

- **Short position** (seller), which commits a trader to deliver an item at contract maturity.
- **Long position** (buyer), which commits a trader to purchase an item at contract maturity.

Selling short in futures trading means only that a contract not previously purchased is sold. For every futures contract, someone sells it short and someone else holds it long. Like options, futures trading is a zero-sum game, because the amount that is gained by one party is lost by the one on the other side of the contract.

Unlike an options contract, which involves the *right* to make or take delivery, a futures contract involves an *obligation* to take or make delivery. However, futures contracts can be settled by delivery or by offset. Delivery, or settlement of the contract, occurs in months that are designated by the various exchanges for each of the items traded. Delivery occurs in less than 1 percent of all transactions.[2]

Offset is the typical method of settling a contract. Holders liquidate a position by arranging an offsetting transaction. This means that buyers sell their positions and sellers buy their positions some-

---

[2]Instruments that can be used in a delivery are explicitly identified in delivery manuals issued by the appropriate exchange.

time prior to delivery. Thus, to eliminate a futures market position, the investor simply does the reverse of what was done originally. As explained above, the clearing house makes this easy to accomplish. It is essential to remember that if a futures contract is not offset, it must be closed out by delivery.

Each exchange establishes price fluctuation limits on the various types of contracts. Typically, a minimum price change is specified. In the case of S&P/TSX 60 Index Futures, for example, it is 0.1 of an index point or $20 per contract. Maximum daily price limits are also in effect for futures contracts. For the S&P/TSX 60 Index futures contracts, a trading halt will be invoked in conjunction with the triggering of "circuit breakers" in the underlying stocks.

With stocks, short-selling can be done only on an uptick, but futures have no such restriction. Stock positions, short or long, can literally be held forever. However, futures positions must be closed out within a specified time, either by offsetting the position or by making or taking delivery.

There are no specialists on futures exchanges and each futures contract is traded in a specific pit, which is a ring with steps descending to the centre. Trading follows an auction market process in which every bid and offer competes without priority as to time or size. A system of open outcry is used, whereby any offer to buy or sell is communicated verbally and/or through the use of hand signals, and must be made to all traders in the pit.

Brokerage commissions on commodities contracts are paid on the basis of a completed contract (both a purchase and sale), rather than being charged for each purchase and each sale, as in the case of stocks. As with options, no certificates exist for futures contracts.

The open interest indicates contracts that are not offset by opposite transactions or delivery. That is, it measures the number of unliquidated contracts at any time, on a cumulative basis.[3] The open interest increases when an investor goes long on a contract and is reduced when the contract is liquidated.

Margin

Recall that in the case of stock transactions the term *margin* refers to the down payment in a transaction in which money is borrowed from the broker to finance the total cost. A **futures margin**, on the other hand, is not a down payment because ownership of the underlying item is not being transferred at the time of the transaction. Instead, it refers to the "good faith" (or earnest money) deposit made by both buyer and seller to ensure the completion of the contract. In effect, margin is a performance bond. In futures trading, unlike stock trading, margin is the norm.[4]

Each clearing house sets its own minimum initial margin requirements (in dollars), which are identical for both buyers and sellers of futures contracts. Furthermore, brokerage firms can require a higher margin and typically do so. The margin required for futures contracts, which is small in relation to the value of the contract itself, represents the equity of the transactor (either buyer or seller). It is not unusual for the initial margin to be in the range of $1,500 to $2,500 per contract, representing some 2 to 10 percent of the value of the contract. Since the equity is small, the risk is magnified.

Assume the initial margin is equal to 5 percent of the total value and an investor holds one contract in an account. If the price of the contract changes by 5 percent because the price of the underlying commodity changes by 5 percent, this is equivalent to a 100 percent change in the investor's equity. This example shows why futures trading can be so risky!

In addition to the initial margin requirement, each contract requires a maintenance margin below which the investor's net equity cannot drop.[5] The net equity is defined as the value of deposited funds (or the marginable value of marketable securities) plus the open profit or minus the open loss. If the market price of a futures contract moves adversely to the owner's position, the equity declines. Margin calls occur when the price goes against the investor causing the investor's equity to fall below the

Futures Margin
The good faith (earnest money) deposit made by the buyer or seller to ensure the completion of a contract.

---

[3] The open interest can be measured using either the open long positions or the open short positions but not both.
[4] Because no credit is being extended, no interest expense is incurred on that part of the contract not covered by the margin, as is the case when stocks are purchased on margin. With futures, customers often receive interest on margin money deposited. A customer with a large enough requirement (roughly, $10,000 and over) can use T-bills as part of the margin.
[5] Maintenance margins are usually set at 75 percent of the initial margin requirements.

maintenance margin level, requiring the transactor to deposit additional cash or to close out the account. Conversely, withdrawal of funds from a futures account can only occur if net equity rises above the initial margin requirement. To understand precisely how this works, we must first understand how profits and losses from futures contracts are debited and credited daily to an investor's account.

Marked to the Market

All profits and losses on a contract are credited and debited to each investor's account every trading day.

All futures contracts are **marked to the market** daily, which means that all profits and losses on a contract are credited and debited to each investor's account every trading day.[6] Those contract holders with a profit can withdraw the gains, whereas those with a loss will receive a margin call when the equity falls below the specified variation margin. This process is referred to as daily resettlement, and the price used is the contract's settlement price.[7]

Table 20-4 illustrates how accounts are marked to the market daily and how a margin call can occur. Consider an investor who buys a stock-index futures contract for 870 and a second investor who sells (shorts) the same contract at the same price. Assume these contracts are on the S&P/TSX 60 Index, where the contract is for $200 times the index value. For example, a price advance from 870 to 871, or one point, represents an advance of $200 on the contract value. Each investor puts up an initial margin of $3,480, representing 2 percent of the contract value of $174,000 ($200 × 870). For purposes of this example, we will assume the maintenance margin is $2,784, or 80 percent of the initial margin requirement.

Table 20-4 traces each investor's account as it is marked to the market daily. At the end of Day 1, the price of the contract has dropped to a settlement price of 869.5, a decrease of one half an index point, causing a change in the futures contracts values of $100. This amount is credited to the seller's account because the seller is short and the price has dropped. Conversely, $100 is debited to the buyer's account because the buyer is long, and the price moved adversely to this position. Table 20-4 shows that the current equity at the end of Day 1 is $3,380 for the buyer and $3,580 for the seller.

Table 20-4

An Example of Investor Accounts, Using Stock-Index Futures, Marked to the Market

	Buyer (Long)	Seller (Short)
Account after one day		
Original equity (initial margin)	$3,480	$3,480
Day 1 mark to the market	(100)	100
Current equity	$3,380	$3,580
Account after two weeks		
Original equity (initial margin)	$3,480	$3,480
Cumulative mark to the market	1,000	(1,000)
Current equity	4,480	2,480
Withdrawable excess equity	$1,000	
Margin call		$1,000

Two weeks have passed, during which time each account has been marked to the market daily. The settlement price on this contract has reached 875.00. The aggregate change in market value for each investor is the difference between the current price and the initial price multiplied by $200, the value of one point in price, which in this example is 875 − 870 = 5.00 × $200 = $1,000.

---

[6]This is not true of forward contracts, where no funds are transferred until the maturity date.
[7]The settlement price does not always reflect the final trade of the day. The clearing house establishes the settlement price at the close of trading.

As shown in Table 20-4, this amount is currently credited to the buyer because the price moved in the direction the buyer expected. Conversely, this same amount is currently debited to the seller, who is now on the wrong side of the price movement. Therefore, starting with an initial equity of $3,480, after two weeks the cumulative mark to the market is $1,000. This results in a current equity of $4,480 for the buyer and $2,480 for the seller. The buyer has a withdrawable excess equity of $1,000 because of the favourable price movement, whereas the seller has a margin call of $1,000, assuming a $2,784 maintenance margin. In other words, the investor would have received a margin call since his or her equity value fell below the required margin of $2,784. The seller would be required to add $1,000 ($3,480 − $2,480) to restore the account to the initial margin level of $3,480.

This example illustrates what is meant by the expression that futures trading, like options trading, is a zero-sum game. The aggregate gains and losses net to zero. The aggregate profits enjoyed by the winners must be equal to the aggregate losses suffered by the losers. This also means that the net exposure to changes in the commodity's price must be zero.

CHECK YOUR UNDERSTANDING

20-3. Suppose you purchased several futures contracts. At the expiration date, the contracts are worth considerably more than when purchased, so that you have a large gain. How can you be assured that the party who sold you these contracts will make good on their obligations?

20-4. The short position's loss is equal to the long position's gain. Explain.

USING FUTURES CONTRACTS

learning objective 2
Outline how futures work and what types of investors participate in futures markets.

Who uses futures and for what purpose? Traditionally, participants in the futures market have been classified as either hedgers or speculators. Because both groups are important in understanding the role and functioning of futures markets, we will consider each in turn. The distinctions between these two groups apply to financial futures as well as to the more traditional commodity futures.

Hedgers

Hedgers are parties at risk with a commodity or an asset, which means they are exposed to price changes. They buy or sell futures contracts in order to offset their risk. In other words, hedgers actually deal in the commodity or financial instrument specified in the futures contract. By taking a position opposite to that of one already held, at a price set today, hedgers plan to reduce the risk of adverse price fluctuations—that is, to hedge the risk of unexpected price changes. In effect, this is a form of insurance.

In a sense, the real motivation for all futures trading is to reduce price risk. With futures, risk is reduced by having the gain in the futures position offset the loss on the cash position and vice versa. A hedger is willing to forego some profit potential in exchange for having someone else assume part of the risk. Figure 20-1 illustrates the hedging process as it affects the return–risk distribution. Notice that the unhedged position not only has a greater chance of a larger loss, but also a greater chance of a larger gain.

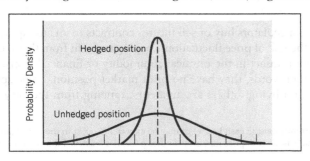

Figure 20-1
Return Distributions for Hedged and Unhedged Positions

The hedged position has a smaller chance of a low return, but also a smaller chance of a high return.

The use of hedging techniques illustrates the trade-off that underlies all investing decisions: Hedging reduces the risk of loss, but it also reduces the return possibilities relative to the unhedged position. Thus, hedging is used by investors who are uncertain of future price movements and who are willing to protect themselves against adverse price movements at the expense of possible gains. There is no free lunch!

How to Hedge with Futures

The key to any hedge is that a futures position is taken opposite to the position in the cash market. That is, the nature of the cash market position determines the hedge in the futures market.[8] A commodity or financial instrument held (in effect, in inventory) represents a long position because these items could be sold in the cash market. On the other hand, an investor who sells a futures contract has created a short position. Since investors can assume two basic positions with futures contracts, long and short, there are two basic hedge positions.

1. *The short (sell) hedge.* A cash market inventory holder must sell (short) the futures. Investors should think of short hedges as a means of protecting the value of their portfolios. Since they are holding securities, they are long in the cash position and need to protect themselves against a decline in prices. A **short hedge** reduces, or possibly eliminates, the risk taken in a long position.

2. *The long (buy) hedge.* An investor who currently holds no cash inventory (holds no commodities or financial instruments) is, in effect, short in the cash market; therefore, to hedge with futures requires a long position. Someone who is not currently in the cash market but who plans to be in the future and wants to lock in current prices and yields until cash is available to make the investment can use a **long hedge**, which reduces the risk of a short position.

Hedging is not an automatic process. It requires more than simply taking a position. Hedgers must make timing decisions as to when to initiate and end the process. As conditions change, hedgers must adjust their hedge strategy.

One aspect of hedging that must be considered is "basis" risk. The basis for financial futures often is defined as the difference between the cash price and the futures price of the item being hedged:[9]

$$\text{Basis} = \text{Cash price} - \text{Futures price}$$

The basis must be zero on the maturity date of the contract. In the interim, the basis fluctuates in an unpredictable manner and is not constant during a hedge period. Basis risk, therefore, is the risk that hedgers face as a result of unexpected changes in basis. Although changes in the basis will affect the hedge position during its life, a hedge will reduce risk as long as the variability in the basis is less than the variability in the price of the asset being hedged. At maturity, the futures price and the cash price must be equal, resulting in a zero basis. (Transaction costs can cause discrepancies.)

The significance of basis risk to investors is that risk cannot be entirely eliminated. Hedging a cash position will involve basis risk.

Speculators

In contrast to hedgers, speculators buy or sell futures contracts in an attempt to earn a return. They are willing to assume the risk of price fluctuations, hoping to profit from them. Unlike hedgers, speculators typically do not transact in the physical commodity or financial instrument underlying the futures contract. In other words, they have no prior market position. Some speculators are professionals who do this for a living; others are amateurs, ranging from the very sophisticated to the

Short Hedge

A transaction involving the sale of futures (a short position) while holding the asset (a long position).

Long Hedge

A transaction where the asset is currently not held but futures are purchased to lock in current prices.

---

[8]The cash position may currently exist (a cash hedge) or may be expected to exist in the future (an anticipatory hedge).
[9]The typical definition for basis is the cash price minus the futures price. For financial futures, the definition is often reversed.

novice. Although most speculators are not actually present at the futures markets, floor traders (or locals) trade for their own accounts as well as others and often take very short-term (minutes or hours) positions in an attempt to exploit any short-lived market anomalies.

Speculators are essential to the proper functioning of the futures market, absorbing the excess demand or supply generated by hedgers and assuming the risk of price fluctuations that hedgers wish to avoid. Speculators contribute to the liquidity of the market and reduce the variability in prices over time.

Why speculate in futures markets? After all, one could speculate in the underlying instruments. For example, an investor who believed interest rates were going to decline could buy Government of Canada bonds directly and avoid the bond futures market. The potential advantages of speculating in futures markets include

1. *Leverage*. The magnification of gains (and losses) can easily be 10 to 1.

2. *Ease of transacting*. An investor who thinks interest rates will rise will have difficulty selling bonds short, but it is very easy to take a short position in a bond futures contract.

3. *Transaction costs*. These are often significantly smaller in futures markets.

By all accounts, an investor's likelihood of success when speculating in futures is not very good and the small investor is up against stiff odds. Real-World Returns 20-3 discusses the benefits of using commodity futures to speculate on commodity prices.

REAL-WORLD RETURNS 20-3

Commodity Futures

One of the most effective ways to play the seemingly inexorable rise in commodity prices is also one of the scariest-sounding to the uninitiated.

Futures contracts present a higher level of complexity than stocks and funds, not to mention the risk of ruinous losses. But they also offer several advantages over traditional investments in energy, gold, metals and agricultural products. If you invest directly in a commodity producer, you're assuming the risk that the firm's management will make decisions that negatively affect returns. And unlike futures contracts, the performance of resource stocks and funds are influenced by the general mood on the stock markets.

You'll be relieved to know that you don't have to trade actual futures contracts to invest in commodity futures. An easier way is to buy an investment fund that tracks an index based on the performance of a diversified basket of commodity futures.

The idea of funds investing in the futures market recalls AGF Managed Futures, which was closed in 2007 after losing half its value in a year. But don't let that turn you off the idea of futures. Today, there is a small but growing collection of other choices in futures-based commodity fund vehicles.

One example is the Criterion Diversified Commodities Currency Hedged Fund, a tiny $20-million mutual fund offered by the mutual fund family Criterion Investments. Several other choices are available in the form of US-listed exchange-traded funds and exchange-traded notes, which are a cousin of the better-known ETF.

Two examples of exchange-traded notes are the iPath Dow Jones–AIG Commodity Index Total Return ETN, which trades on the New York Stock Exchange, and the awkwardly named Elements Linked to the Rogers International Commodity Index–Total Return, listed on the American Stock Exchange. Both of these ETNs track broad commodity indexes, but there are more specialized niche products available.

Commodity-based investments of all types have risen sharply in the past several years, so you're hardly buying low. But with oil and gold both hitting record highs this week, it's clear that

(continued)

REAL-WORLD RETURNS 20-3 *continued*

there's still a lot of momentum in the sector. If you see this continuing, and there are commodity bulls who do, then it's worth looking at funds and ETNs that expose you to commodity futures.

The Criterion diversified commodities fund is noteworthy in that it offers currency hedging, so your returns won't be affected by changes in the Canada–US exchange rate. Returns are linked to the Dow Jones-AIG Commodity Total Return index, which tracks 19 separate commodities. As of the end of January, the index was weighted 31 percent in energy, 21 percent in grains, 20 percent in base metals, 11 percent in gold and silver and the rest in so-called "softs"—sugar, cotton and coffee.

The Dow Jones-AIG Commodity Index is based on futures contracts, which set out a price and delivery date for a commodity at a future date. These contracts are continuously "rolled" or, in other words, sold before they reach their delivery date and replaced with new ones.

A benefit of using commodity futures is that they offer the prized attribute of negative correlation to the stock markets or, in other words, zigging when stocks zag. A study done a few years ago by finance professors at Yale University and the University of Pennsylvania's Wharton School found this to be true over the period stretching from mid-1959 through the end of 2004.

Here's a more recent example: In January, the Criterion diversified commodities fund made 3.3 percent while the S&P/TSX composite total return index fell 4.7 percent. "In the quest for non-correlated assets, commodity futures seem to have a great track record," said Ian McPherson, president of Criterion Investments.

Another benefit of commodity futures is that they insulate you from issues that can prevent the returns provided by resource stocks from mirroring the price of the commodity they produce. Mr. McPherson said an example would be the use of hedging, where a company presells some of its production at a set price and thus doesn't benefit if commodity prices soar. Resource stocks can also be held back by unexpected cost overruns and unforeseen events like Alberta's recent decision to raise the royalties paid by energy producers in the province.

The Yale/Wharton study found other benefits to investing in commodity futures. Returns came in at 5 percentage points higher than risk-free Treasury Bills on an average annual basis, and the risk profile was slightly lower than stocks. Also, commodity futures outperformed spot prices, which apply to immediate payment and delivery. The study's conclusion: Commodity futures are an attractive way to diversify traditional portfolios of stocks and bonds.

Exchange-traded notes are one way to get this diversification. Whereas an exchange-traded fund is a direct investment in a stock index, ETNs are bond-like securities that promise the returns of a particular index. ETNs fluctuate in value according to the value of their underlying index, just like ETFs. One way that they differ is in the fact that an ETN will mature at some point (the range is 15 to 30 years from now) at a value determined by the underlying index. There are no interest payments with ETNs, and no guarantee that you'll get your upfront investment back.

Sonia Morris, an analyst with the investment research firm Morningstar Inc. in Chicago, said there's another key difference between exchange-traded funds and notes. Because the notes are essentially debt, the creditworthiness of the backing financial institution is an important consideration. The iPath ETNs are backed by the giant global bank Barclays, while the Elements products are backed by the Swedish Export Credit Corp.

Ms. Morris said her favourite of the commodity futures ETNs is the broadly diversified iPath Dow Jones-AIG Commodity Index Total Return ETN. "I like it because it's not as energy-heavy as the competition. It caps the energy commodities, or any group, to one-third of assets, whereas some of the other supposedly diversified commodity ETNs have as much as 70 to 75 percent in energy."

If you're more interested in commodity sub-sectors, one to look at is the PowerShares DB Agriculture Fund. This ETF tracks an index called the Deutsche Bank Liquid Commodity

Index–Optimum Yield Agriculture index, which is equally weighted to corn, wheat, soybeans and sugar. Agricultural commodities have been hot lately and this fund has soared by about 25 percent this year, a contrast to the small losses posted by major stock indexes.

This is a classic example of the negative correlation that makes investing in commodities futures so attractive. Tempted to get it working in your portfolio? If so, be wary of commodities overload. Remember, your conventional mutual funds, ETFs and individual stock picks may have lots of exposure to the resource sector already. Also, let's not forget that commodities have come a long way in the past few years. They could go higher, but it's a long way down.

The Futures of Commodities

Here's a selection of investment funds that allow investors to get exposure to commodities through the futures market rather than through the shares of individual companies that produce oil, metals and agricultural products.

Fund	Category	MER	Ticker*	Info
Criterion Diversified Commodities Currency Hedged Fund	Mutual fund	2.65%	n/a	vengrowth.com
iPath Dow Jones-AIG Commodity Index Total Return ETN	Exchange-traded note	0.75%	DJP-N	ipathetn.com
iPath S&P GSCI Total Return Index ETN	ETN	0.75%	GSP-N	ipathetn.com
Elements Linked to the Rogers International Commodity Index - Total Return	ETN	0.75%	RJI-A	elementsetn.com
PowerShares DB Commodity Index Tracking Fund	Exchange-traded fund	0.83%	DBC-A	powershares.com
PowerShares DB Agriculture Fund	ETF	0.91%	DBA-A	powershares.com

*N=New York Stock Exchange; A = American Stock Exchange. Note: the iPath, Elements and PowerShares families also offer products for sector commodity investing. Source: AIG Financial Products Corp.

Source: Carrick, Rob, "Commodity futures can spice up your holdings," *The Globe and Mail*, March 8, 2008, p. B13.

CHECK YOUR UNDERSTANDING

20-5. The maturity date of a futures contract does not dictate realization of an investor's gains and losses. Explain.

20-6. What is the essential difference between a hedger and a speculator when it comes to owning the underlying asset involved in a futures contract?

FINANCIAL FUTURES

learning objective 3
Explain how financial futures are used.

Financial Futures
Futures contracts on financial assets such as equity indexes, fixed-income securities, and currencies.

Financial futures are futures contracts on equity indexes, fixed-income securities, and currencies. They give investors a greater opportunity to fine-tune the risk–return characteristics of their portfolios. This flexibility has become increasingly important as interest rates have become much more volatile and as investors have sought new techniques to reduce the risk of equity positions. The drastic changes that have occurred in the financial markets in the last 15 to 20 years could be said to have generated a genuine need for new financial instruments that allow market participants to deal with these changes.

The procedures for trading financial futures are the same as those for any other commodity, with a few exceptions. At maturity, stock-index futures settle in cash because it would be impossible or impractical to deliver all the stocks in a particular index.[10] As mentioned previously, the price fluctuations for the S&P/TSX 60 Index contracts are in increments of 0.1 index points. Price fluctuations are limited since a trading halt is invoked in conjunction with the triggering of "circuit breakers" in the underlying stocks. US stock-index futures typically have no daily price limits (although they can be imposed).

We will divide the subsequent discussion of financial futures into the two major categories of contracts: interest rate futures and stock-index futures. Hedging and speculative activities within each category are discussed separately.

Interest Rate Futures

Bond prices are highly volatile, and investors are exposed to adverse price movements. Financial futures allow bondholders and others who are affected by volatile interest rates to transfer the risk. One of the primary reasons for the growth in financial futures is that portfolio managers and investors are trying to protect themselves against adverse movements in interest rates. An investor concerned with protecting the value of fixed-income securities must consider the possible impact of interest rates on the value of these securities.

Today's investors have the opportunity to consider several different interest rate futures contracts that are traded on various exchanges.[11] Available short-term interest rate futures contracts include Three-Month Canadian Bankers' Acceptance (BA) Futures (BAX), which have traded on the ME since April 1988, and 30-day Overnight Repo Rate Futures (ONX). The price fluctuation for BAX is 0.5 basis point (i.e., 0.005) or $12.5 per contract for the nearest three listed contract months, and 1 basis point (i.e., 0.01) or $25 per contract for all other contract months, while the price fluctuation for ONX is 0.5 basis point (i.e., 0.005) or $20.55 (one-half of 1/100 of one percent of $5,000,000 on a 30-day basis) per contract. There is no maximum daily price fluctuation for either contract during regular trading sessions.

Available long-term interest rate futures contracts include 10-year Government of Canada bond futures (CGB), which have traded on the ME since September of 1989, and two-year Government of Canada bond futures (CGZ). The contract unit for the CGBs is $100,000 nominal value of Government of Canada bonds, with a 6 percent coupon rate, while for the CGZs, the unit is $200,000 nominal value of Government of Canada bonds with a 4 percent coupon rate. Prices for 10-year bond futures are quoted per $100 nominal value (e.g., 97.58), just like bonds, while they are quoted per $1,000 par value for the two-year bond futures. The minimum price fluctuation is one basis point for CGB and .005 for CGZ (or $10 per contract for both), and the maximum daily price fluctuation is three points (or $3,000 per contract for CGB and $6,000 per contract for CGZ) above or below the previous day's settlement price.

In the United States, the Chicago Mercantile Exchange trades contracts on US Treasury bills and the one-month London Interbank Offered Rate (LIBOR), as well as Eurodollars. The Chicago Board of Trade (CBT) specializes in longer-maturity instruments, including Treasury notes (of various maturities, such as two-year and five-year) and Treasury bonds (of different contract sizes). Contracts are available on various maturities of US Treasury notes in trading units of $100,000, on Treasury bonds in units of $100,000, and on Treasury bills in trading units of $1 million. The contracts for US Treasury bonds are by far the most important.[12]

Hedging with Interest Rate Futures

We now consider an example of using interest rate futures to hedge an investment position. Our objective here is to illustrate the basic concepts involved in such a hedge. In this example, we concentrate on

---

[10]Gains and losses on the last day of trading are credited and debited to the long and short positions in the same way—marked to the market—as was done for every other trading day of the contract. Therefore, not only is there no physical delivery of securities, but also the buyer does not pay the full value of the contract at settlement.

[11]The Chicago Board of Trade launched financial futures trading in 1975 by opening trading in Government National Mortgage Association (GNMA or Ginnie Mae) bonds. The concept accelerated in 1976, when the International Monetary Market started trading in Treasury bills. Treasury bond futures appeared in 1977.

[12]Futures prices on Treasury bonds are quoted with reference to an 8 percent, 20-year bond. Settlement prices are translated into a settlement yield to provide a reference point for interest rates.

the short hedge since it is by far the more common and discuss the concept of the long hedge later in the chapter.

Short Hedge

Suppose an investor has a bond portfolio and wishes to protect the value of his or her position. This type of hedge is sometimes referred to as the inventory hedge.

EXAMPLE 20-1: SHORT HEDGING ON GOVERNMENT OF CANADA BONDS

On November 1, 2008, a pension fund manager holds $1 million principal (or face) value of 7 percent Government of Canada bonds due June 1, 2018. The manager plans to sell the bonds four months in the future but wishes to protect their value against a rise in interest rates. Since assets are owned (a long position), a short hedge is used.

To protect the position, the manager hedges by going short (selling) in the futures market. As illustrated in Table 20-5, the manager sells 10 March 2009 10-year Government of Canada bond contracts (since each contract is worth $100,000) at a current price of $106.58. In this example, we assume interest rates have risen by March 1, 2009. This produces a loss on the cash side (i.e., in the prices of the bonds held in the cash market) and a gain on the futures side (i.e., the manager can cover the short position at a lower price, which produces a profit). The futures position in this example more than offsets the cash market loss resulting in a net profit.[13]

The manager in this example was able to offset more than 100 percent of the cash market loss because the Government of Canada bond contract is based on 6 percent coupon bonds, whereas the manager was holding 7 percent bonds. In this example, the dollar value of lower coupon bonds changes by a larger amount than the dollar value of higher coupon bonds for the given change in yields. However, if interest rates had fallen, the loss on the futures contract would have exceeded the profit on the long bond position, resulting in a loss. One way to overcome this difference is to execute a "weighted" short hedge, adjusting the number of futures contracts used to hedge the cash position. For example, using the data in Table 20-5, selling 9.5 March contracts would result in a profit on the futures position of $62,510, which is very close to the $63,300 cash market loss.

Table 20-5

Illustration of Hedges Using Interest Rate Futures: A Short Hedge

Cash Market	Futures Market
	Short Hedge
November 1, 2008	**November 1, 2018**
Hold $1 million principal value of 7% Government of Canada bonds maturing June 1, 2018	Sells 10, 10-year Government of Canada bond futures contracts at a price of $106.58
Current market price: $112.61 (yielding 5.15%)	
March 1, 2009	**March 1, 2009**
Sells $1 million principal value of 7% bonds at $106.28	Buys 10 bond futures contracts at $100.00 (to close out position)
Loss: $63,300 (i.e., $1,062,800 − $1,126,100)	Gain: $65,800 (i.e., $1,065,800 − $1,000,000)

[13]The $65,800 gain on the futures contract in Table 20-5 is calculated as follows: The gain per contract is $6,580 = [(106.58 − 100) × 1,000]. Since each contract is based on par value of $100,000, the gain is: $65,800 = ($6,580 × 10 contracts).

Other Hedges

An alternative hedge is the anticipatory hedge, whereby an investor purchases a futures contract as an alternative to buying the underlying security. At some designated time in the future, the investor will purchase the security and sell the futures contract. This results in a net price for the security position at the future point in time that is equal to the price paid for the security minus the gain or loss on the futures position.

Consider an investor who would like to purchase an interest rate asset now but will not have the cash for three months. If rates drop, the asset will cost more at that point in time. By purchasing a futures contract on the asset now, as a hedge, the investor can lock in the interest rate implied by the interest rate futures contract. This may be a good substitute for not being able to lock in the current interest rate because of the lack of funds now to do so. At the conclusion of this transaction, the investor will pay a net price that reflects the ending cash price minus the gain on the futures contract. In effect, the gain on the futures increases the rate of return earned on the interest rate asset.

Speculating with Interest Rate Futures

Investors may wish to speculate with interest rate futures as well as to hedge with them. To do so, investors make assessments of likely movements in interest rates and assume a futures position that corresponds with this assessment. If the investor anticipates a rise in interest rates, he or she will sell one (or more) interest rate futures, because a rise in interest rates will drive down the prices of bonds and therefore the price of the futures contract. The investor sells a contract with the expectation of buying it back later at a lower price. Of course, a decline in interest rates will result in a loss for this investor, since the price will rise.

EXAMPLE 20-2: SPECULATING ON GOVERNMENT OF CANADA BONDS

Assume that in November, a speculator thinks interest rates will rise over the next month and wishes to profit from this expectation. The investor can sell one December 10-year Government of Canada bond futures contract at a price of 106.58. One month later, the price of this contract has declined to 100.03 because of rising interest rates. This investor would have a gain of 6.55, or $6,550, and could close out this position by buying an identical contract.

The usefulness of interest rate futures for pursuing such a strategy is significant. A speculator who wishes to assume a short position in bonds cannot do so readily in the cash market (either financially or mechanically). Interest rate futures provide the means to short bonds easily.

In a similar manner, investors can speculate on a decline in interest rates by purchasing interest rate futures. If the decline materializes, bond prices and the value of the futures contract will rise. Because of the leverage involved, the gains can be large; however, the losses can also be large if interest rates move in the wrong direction.

Stock-Index Futures

Until recently, futures on individual stocks were not available. Today, they are available in the US, but they only exist on a few stocks and they are traded very thinly, which is the reason they only lasted on the ME for a few years. Stock-index futures trading was initiated in 1982 with several contracts quickly being created. Investors can trade futures contracts on major market indexes such as the S&P/TSX 60 and the S&P/TSX Sectoral Indexes. The contract size of each of these indexes is $200 times the index level. Several other futures contracts are available on other stock indexes around the world

Delivery is not permitted in stock-index futures because of its impracticality. Instead, each remaining contract is settled by cash on the settlement day by taking an offsetting position using the price of the underlying index. For example, the cash settlement price for the S&P/TSX 60 Index is $200 times the official opening index value to the nearest two decimal places, on the final settlement day.

Stock-index futures offer investors the opportunity to act on their investment opinions concerning the future direction of the market. They need not select individual stocks, and it is easy to short the market. Furthermore, investors who are concerned about unfavourable short-term market prospects but remain bullish for the longer run can protect themselves in the interim by selling stock-index futures.

The contract size for each of these indexes is $200 times the index level. Several other futures contracts are available on other stock indexes around the world.

Hedging with Stock-Index Futures

Common stock investors hedge with financial futures for the same reasons that fixed-income investors use them. Investors, whether individuals or institutions, may hold a substantial stock portfolio that is subject to the risk of the overall market; that is, systematic risk. A futures contract enables the investor to transfer part or all of the risk to those willing to assume it. Stock-index futures have opened up new, and relatively inexpensive, opportunities for investors to manage market risk through hedging.

Chapter 8 pointed out the two types of risk inherent in common stocks: systematic risk and non-systematic risk. Diversification will eliminate most or all of the non-systematic risk in a portfolio, but not the systematic risk. Although an investor could adjust the beta of the portfolio in anticipation of a market rise or fall, this is not an ideal solution because of the changes in portfolio composition that might be required.

Investors can use financial futures on stock market indexes to hedge against an overall market decline. That is, investors can hedge against systematic or market risk by selling the appropriate number of contracts against a stock portfolio. In effect, stock-index futures contracts give an investor the opportunity to protect his or her portfolio against market fluctuations.

To hedge market risk, investors must be able to take a position in the hedging asset (in this case, stock-index futures) such that profits or losses on the hedging asset offset changes in the value of the stock portfolio. Stock-index futures permit this action because changes in the futures prices themselves generally are highly correlated with changes in the value of the stock portfolios that are caused by marketwide events. The more diversified the portfolio, and therefore the lower the non-systematic risk, the greater the correlation between the futures contract and the stock positions.

Figure 20-2 shows the price of the S&P 500 Index futures plotted against the value of a portfolio that is 99 percent diversified. That is, market risk accounts for 99 percent of its total risk.[14] The two track each other very closely, which demonstrates that stock-index futures can be very effective in hedging the market risk of a portfolio.

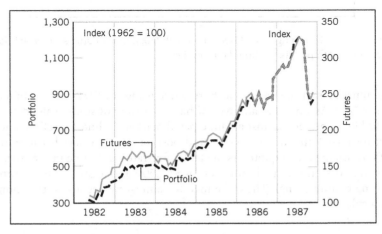

Figure 20-2
The Value of a Well-Diversified Stock Portfolio Versus the Price of the S&P 500 Index Futures

Source: Charles S. Morris, "Managing Stock Market Risk with Stock Index Futures," *Economic Review* 74 (June 1989), p. 9. Reprinted with permission from *Economic Review*.

[14]This example is taken from C. S. Morris, "Managing Stock Market Risk with Stock Index Futures," *Economic Review* 74 (June 1989), pp. 3–16.

Short Hedges

Since so much common stock is held by investors, the short hedge represents a natural type of contract for most investors. Investors who hold stock portfolios hedge market risk by selling stock-index futures, which means they assume a short position.

A short hedge can be implemented by selling a forward maturity of the contract. The purpose of this hedge is to offset (in total or in part) any losses on the stock portfolio with gains on the futures position. To implement this defensive strategy, an investor would sell one or more index futures contracts. Ideally, the value of these contracts would equal the value of the stock portfolio. If the market falls, leading to a loss on the cash (the stock portfolio) position, stock-index futures prices will also fall, leading to a profit for sellers of futures.

The reduction in price volatility that can be accomplished by hedging is shown in Figure 20-3, which compares the performance of a well-diversified portfolio (the unhedged one) with the same portfolio hedged by sales of the S&P 500 Index futures. Clearly, there is much less variability in the value of the hedged portfolio as compared to the value of the unhedged one. In fact, the volatility of the returns is 91 percent lower.[15] Notice in particular what happened in the great market crash of October 1987. The value of the unhedged portfolio fell some 19 percent, whereas the value of the hedged one fell only 6 percent.

Figure 20-3
The Value of a Well-Diversified Portfolio Versus the Value of the Same Portfolio Hedged by Sales of S&P 500 Index Futures

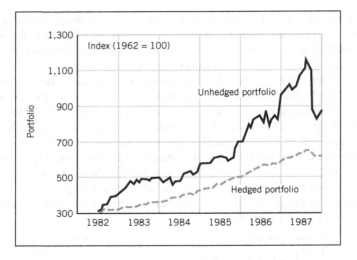

Source: Charles S. Morris, "Managing Stock Market Risk with Stock Index Futures," *Economic Review* 74 (June 1989), p. 10. Reprinted with permission from *Economic Review*.

Table 20-6 illustrates the concept of a short hedge using the S&P/TSX 60 Index futures contract when it is at 870. Assume that an investor has a portfolio of stocks valued at $175,000 that he or she would like to protect against an anticipated market decline. By selling one S&P/TSX 60 stock index future at 870, the investor has a short position of $174,000, because the value of the contract is $200 times the index quote. As the table illustrates, a decline in the stock market of 10 percent results in a loss on the stock portfolio of $17,500 and a gain on the futures position of $17,400 (ignoring commissions). Thus, the investor almost makes up on the short side what is lost on the long side.

---

[15]*Ibid*

Table 20-6

Examples of Short and Long Hedges Using Stock-Index Futures

	Short Hedge		
	Current Position	Position after a 10% Market Drop	Change in Position
(Long position) dollar value of portfolio	$175,000	$157,500	($17,500)
(Short position) sell one S&P/TSX 60 Index futures contract at 870.00	$174,000	$156,600	$17,400
Net gain or loss after hedging			($100)

	Long Hedge		
	Current Position	Position after a 10% Market Increase	Change in Position
(Long position) buy one S&P/TSX 60 Index futures contract at 870.00	$174,000	$191,400	$17,400
Amount of money to be invested in stocks (i.e., cost of stock position)	$175,000	$192,500	($17,500)
Net gain or loss after hedging			($100)

Long Hedges

The long hedger, while awaiting funds to invest, generally wishes to reduce the risk of having to pay more for an equity position when prices rise. Potential users of a long hedge include

- Institutions with a regular cash flow that use long hedges to improve the timing of their positions
- Institutions switching large positions who wish to hedge during the time it takes to complete the process (This could also be a short hedge.)

Assume an investor with $175,000 to invest believes that the stock market will advance but has been unable to select the stocks he or she wishes to hold. By purchasing one S&P/TSX 60 Index future, the investor will gain if the market advances. As shown in Table 20-6, a 10 percent market advance will increase the value of the futures contract $17,400. Although in this example, the investor has to pay 10 percent more (on average) for stocks purchased after the advance, he or she only pays $100 more than $175,000 because of the gain on the futures position.

Limitations of Hedging with Stock-Index Futures

Although hedging with stock-index futures can reduce an investor's risk, generally risk cannot be eliminated completely. As with interest rate futures, basis risk is present with stock-index futures. It represents the difference between the price of the stock-index futures contract and the value of the underlying stock index. A daily examination of Futures prices reported in the financial media will show that each of the indexes quoted under the respective futures contracts differs from the closing price of the contracts.[16]

---

[16]Futures prices are generally more volatile than the underlying indexes and therefore diverge from them. The index futures tend to lead the actual market indexes. If investors are bullish, the futures are priced at a premium, with greater maturities usually associated with greater premiums. If investors are bearish, the futures are normally priced at a discount, which may widen as maturity increases.

Basis risk, as it applies to common stock portfolios, can be defined as the risk that remains after a stock portfolio has been hedged.[17] Note here that stock-index futures hedge only systematic (market) risk. That is, when we consider a stock portfolio hedged with stock-index futures, the basis risk is attributable to nonsystematic (nonmarket or firm-specific) risk.

Figure 20-4a illustrates the effects of basis risk by comparing the value of a relatively undiversified portfolio with the price of the S&P 500 futures contract. In contrast to the 99 percent diversified portfolio in Figure 20-2, this one is only 66 percent diversified. Although the two series are related, the relationship is in no way as close as that illustrated in Figure 20-2. Therefore, stock-index futures will be less effective at hedging the total risk of the portfolio, as shown in Figure 20-4b. In this situation, the variance of returns on the hedged portfolio is only 27 percent lower than the unhedged position. Note that in the crash of October 1987, both portfolios fell sharply, demonstrating that the hedge was relatively ineffective. (It did better than the unhedged position, but not by much.)

From this analysis we can see that stock-index futures generally do not provide a good hedge for relatively undiversified portfolios.

Figure 20-4
(*a*) The Value of a Relatively Undiversified Stock Portfolio and the Price of the S&P 500 Index Futures Contracts (*b*) The Value of the Unhedged Portfolio and the Same Portfolio Hedged by Sales of S&P 500 Futures Contracts

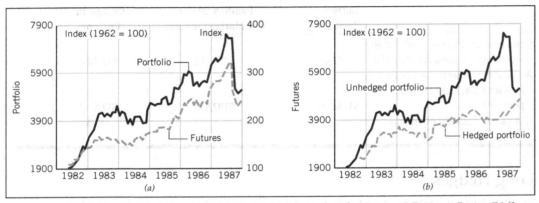

Source: Charles S. Morris, "Managing Stock Market Risk with Stock Index Futures," *Economic Review* 74 (June 1989), pp. 12–13. Reprinted with permission from *Economic Review*.

Index Arbitrage and Program Trading

Program trading (see Chapter 4) hit Bay and Wall Streets in the 1980s, and it has captured much attention and generated considerable controversy. It leads to headlines attributing market plunges at least in part to program trading, as happened on October 19, 1987, when North American and world stock markets plummeted. Because program trading typically involves positions in both stocks and stock-index futures contracts, the topic is within the general discussion of hedging.

Program trading is commonly used for portfolio insurance applications, which were discussed in Chapter 19. It is also used for **index arbitrage**, which refers to attempts to exploit the differences between the prices of the stock-index futures and the prices of the index of stocks underlying the futures contract. For example, if the S&P/TSX 60 Index futures price is too high relative to the S&P/TSX 60 Index, investors could short the futures contract and buy the stocks in the index. In theory, arbitrageurs should be able to build a hedged portfolio that earns arbitrage profits equaling the difference between the two positions. If the price of the S&P/TSX 60 Index futures is deemed too low, investors could purchase the futures and short the stocks, again exploiting the differences between the two prices.

If investors are to be able to take advantage of discrepancies between the futures price and the underlying stock-index price, they must be able to act quickly. Program trading involves the use of

Index Arbitrage

Exploitation of price differences between stock-index futures and the index of stocks underlying the futures contract.

---

[17]This discussion is based heavily on C. S. Morris, "Managing Stock Market Risk with Stock Index Futures," *Economic Review* 74 (June 1989), pp. 11–13.

computer-generated orders to coordinate buy and sell orders for entire portfolios based on arbitrage opportunities. The arbitrage occurs between portfolios of common stocks, on the one hand, and index futures and options, on the other. Large institutional investors seek to exploit differences between the two sides. Specifically, when stock-index futures prices rise substantially above the current value of the stock-index itself (e.g., the S&P/TSX 60 Index), they sell the futures and buy the underlying stocks, in "baskets" of several million dollars. Because the futures price and the stock-index value must be equal when the futures contract expires, these investors are seeking to "capture the premium" between the two, thereby earning an arbitrage profit. That is, they seek high risk-free returns by arbitraging the difference between the cash value of the underlying securities and the prices of the futures contracts on these securities. In effect, they have a hedged position and should profit regardless of what happens to stock prices.

Normally, program traders and other speculators "unwind" their positions during the last trading hour of the day the futures expire. At this time, the futures premium goes to zero, because, as noted, the futures price at expiration must equal the stock-index value.

The headlines about program trading often reflect the results of rapid selling by the program traders. For whatever reason, traders decide to sell the futures. As the price falls, stock prices also fall. When the futures price drops below the price of the stock index, enormous volumes of sell orders can be unleashed, which drive the futures prices even lower.

Speculating with Stock-Index Futures

In addition to the previous hedging strategies (and others not described), investors can speculate with stock-index futures if they wish to profit from stock market volatility by judging and acting on the likely market trends. Stock-index futures are effective instruments for speculating on movements in the stock market because minimal costs are involved in establishing a futures position, and stock-index futures mirror the market, offering just as much risk.

We can refer to one group of speculators as "active traders." These individuals are willing to risk their capital on price changes they expect to occur in the futures contracts. Such individuals are often sophisticated investors who are seeking the opportunity for large gains and who understand the risk they are assuming.

The strategies of active traders basically include long and short positions. Traders who expect the market to rise buy index futures. Because of the high leverage, the profit opportunities are great; however, the loss opportunities are equally great. The same is true for traders expecting a market decline who assume a short position by selling a stock-index futures contract. Selling a contract is a convenient way to go short on the entire market. It can be done at any time. (No wait for an uptick is required, as with stock short sales.)

Another form of speculation involves spreaders, who establish both long and short positions at the same time. Their objective is to profit from changes in price relationships between two futures contracts. There are two major types of spreads:

1. The intra-market spread, also known as a calendar or time spread. This spread involves contracts for two different settlement months, such as buying a March contract and selling a June contract.

2. The inter-market spread, also known as a quality spread. This spread involves two different markets, such as buying an S&P 500 Index contract and selling an S&P/TSX 60 Index contract (both for the same month).

Spreaders are interested in relative price as opposed to absolute price changes. If two different contracts appear to be out of line, the spreader hopes to profit by buying one and selling the other and waiting for the price difference to adjust. This adjustment may require the spread between the two contracts to widen in some cases and narrow in others.

Conclusion

We have focused our discussion of derivatives on options and futures in the last two chapters; however, many other derivatives are used frequently by investors, including swaps, which are discussed in Appendix 20B. The primary roles of most derivatives are hedging, speculation, and in some cases, price discovery.

CHECK YOUR UNDERSTANDING

20-7. Why are stock-index futures "cash settled" contracts?

20-8. If the cash price and the price of a futures contract must be the same at maturity of the contract, why do investors face basis risk? Would this type of risk be considered systematic or non-systematic?

SUMMARY

This summary relates to the learning objectives for this chapter.

1. **Describe the structure of futures markets.**
   Futures markets play an important role in risk management. Spot markets are for immediate delivery, while forward markets are markets for deferred delivery. An organized futures exchange standardizes the non-standard forward contracts, with only the price and number of contracts left for futures traders to negotiate.

2. **Outline how futures work and what types of investors participate in futures markets.**
   A futures contract designates a specific amount of a particular item to be delivered at a specified date in the future at a currently determined market price. Buyers assume long positions and sellers assume short ones. A short position indicates only that a contract not previously purchased is sold. Most contracts are settled by offset, whereby a position is liquidated by an offsetting transaction. The clearing house is on the other side of every transaction and ensures that all payments are made as specified. Contracts are traded on designated futures exchanges, which set minimum price changes and may establish daily price limits. Futures positions must be closed out within a specified time. There are no certificates and no specialists to handle the trading, so that each futures contract is traded in an auction market process by a system of open outcry. Margin, the norm in futures trading, is the good faith deposit made to ensure completion of the contract. All futures contracts are marked to the market daily; that is, all profits and losses are credited and debited to each investor's account daily. Hedgers buy or sell futures contracts to offset the risk in some other position. Speculators buy or sell futures contracts in an attempt to earn a return, and their role is valuable to the proper functioning of the market.

3. **Explain how financial futures are used.**
   Interest rate futures, one of the two principal types of financial futures, allow investors to hedge against, and speculate on, interest rate movements. Numerous contracts are available on both domestic and foreign instruments. Investors can, among other transactions, execute short hedges to protect their long positions in bonds. Stock-index futures are presently available on the S&P/TSX 60 and S&P/TSX Sectoral Indexes in Canada and on numerous international indexes. Investors can use stock-index futures to hedge the systematic risk of common stocks- that is, the risk of broad market movements. Short hedges protect a stock position against a market decline, and long hedges protect against having to pay more for an equity position because prices rise before the investment can be made. Index arbitrage refers to attempts to exploit the differences between the prices of the stock-index futures and the prices of the index of stocks underlying the futures contract.

KEY TERMS

Financial futures, p.681
Futures contract, p.673
Futures margin, p.675
Index arbitrage, p.688

Long hedge, p.678
Long position, p.674
Marked to the market, p.676
Offset, p.674

Short hedge, p.678
Short position, p.674
Swap (Appendix 20B), p.697

REVIEW QUESTIONS

20-1. What is a futures contract?

20-2. How do forward contracts differ from futures contracts?

20-3. Explain how futures contracts are valued daily and how most contracts are settled.

20-4. Describe the role of the clearing house in futures trading.

20-5. What determines whether an investor receives a margin call?

20-6. Explain the differences between a hedger and a speculator.

20-7. Given a futures contract on Government of Canada bonds, determine the dollar price of a contract quoted at 98.50.

20-8. Describe the differences between trading in stocks and trading in futures contracts.

20-9. How do financial futures differ from other futures contracts?

20-10. What is meant by basis? When is the basis positive?

20-11. Which side benefits from a strengthening basis? A weakening basis?

20-12. When might a portfolio manager with a bond position use a short hedge involving interest rate futures?

20-13. Is it possible to construct a perfect hedge? Why or why not?

20-14. What is the difference between a short hedge and a weighted short hedge using interest rate futures?

20-15. Why would an investor have preferences among the different stock-index futures?

20-16. What type of risk does stock-index futures allow investors to hedge? Why would this be desirable?

20-17. Explain how a pension fund might use a long hedge with stock-index futures.

20-18. When would an investor likely do the following?

    a. Buy a call on a stock index future.
    b. Buy a put on interest rate futures.

20-19. What is program trading? How does it work?

20-20. (Refer to Appendix 20A for this question.) With regard to futures options, fill in the following blanks with either "less than" or "greater than." The current futures price is 75.

    a. Put options with strike prices _____ 75 are in the money.
    b. Call options with strike prices _____ 75 are out of the money.
    c. Put options with strike prices _____ 75 are out of the money.
    d. Call options with strike prices _____ 75 are in the money.

20-21. How do futures markets serve a valuable economic purpose?

20-22. What are the two broad categories of futures contracts currently traded on futures exchanges?

20-23. How can buyers or sellers eliminate their commitments on a binding futures contract? How often are commitments carried out in the futures market?

20-24. What is meant by marked to market? Why is this done?

20-25. What is meant by the phrase, "futures trading is a zero-sum game"?

20-26. In what way are futures standardized?

PROBLEMS

20-1. An investor buys one March S&P/TSX 60 Index futures contract on February 1 at 870.00. The position is closed out after five days. The prices on the four days after purchase were 868.60, 869.80, 872.20, and 875.00. The initial margin is $7,000.

 a. Calculate the current equity on each of the next four days.
 b. Calculate the excess equity for these four days.
 c. Calculate the final gain or loss for the week.
 d. Recalculate (a), (b), and (c) assuming that the investor had been short over this same period.

20-2. Given the information in Problem 20-1, assume that the investor holds until the contract expires. Ignore the four days after purchase and assume that on the next to last day of trading in March the investor was long and the final settlement price on that date was 876. Calculate the cumulative profit.

20-3. Calculate the dollar gain or loss on Government of Canada bond futures contracts for the following transactions. In each case the position is held six months before closing it out.

 a. Sell 10 bond contracts at a price of 102.80 and buy 10 at 101.50.
 b. Sell 10 bond contracts at a price of 98.60 and buy 10 at 100.
 c. Buy 15 bond contracts at 110.20 and sell 15 at 112.30.
 d. Sell one bond contract at 98.50 and buy one at 105.

20-4. Assume a portfolio manager holds $1 million of 7.5 percent Government of Canada bonds due in two years. The current market price is 104.94, for a yield of 4.88 percent. The manager fears a rise in interest rates in the next three months and wishes to protect this position against such a rise by hedging in futures.

 a. Ignoring weighted hedges, what should the manager do?
 b. Assume two-year Government of Canada bond futures contracts are available at 102.11, and the price six months later is 99.20. If the manager constructs the correct hedge, what is the gain or loss on this position?
 c. The price of the Government of Canada bonds three months later is 101.31. What is the gain or loss on this cash position?
 d. What is the net effect of this hedge?

20-5. An investor buys a stock-index futures contract for $200 and the contract is for 400 times the index value. This contract requires an initial margin of 4 percent of the initial contract value. Assume the maintenance margin requirement is 75 percent of the initial margin. Assume that at the end of day one, the contract drops to a settlement price of $199.25. The price fluctuations for the next five days are as follows: $198.50, $199.75, $200.40, $201.05, $200.50.

 a. What is the initial margin required?
 b. Show how the account would look as it was marked to market daily.
 c. Did the buyer receive any margin calls? At what equity value would the buyer receive a margin call?
 d. What would the contract's settlement price have to drop to on the end of the seventh day for the buyer to receive a margin call?
 e. All other variables the same, show what the marked to market account would look like if the investor had been a seller rather than a buyer of this contract. Show how this contract is a zero-sum game.

20-6. On December 1, 2008, a portfolio manager holds $2 million face value of 10 percent Government of Canada bonds that mature on June 1, 2015. The manager is expecting an increase in interest rates, but he plans to sell the bonds in nine months.

The following is available in the market on December 1, 2008:
September 2009 10-year Government of Canada bond futures, with a contract size of $100,000 at a price of $131.49.
Current market price of 10-year, 10 percent Government of Canada bonds: $146.22

The following is available in the market on September 1, 2009:
March 1, 2010 10-year Government of Canada bond futures, with a contract size of $100,000 at a price of $119.21.
Current market price of 10-year, 10 percent Government of Canada bonds: $134.89

    a. In order to protect the value of the manager's position, show how the manager can hedge against the expected increase in interest rates by investing in 20 bond futures contracts. Did the hedge result in an overall gain or loss?

    b. In order to execute a weighted short hedge, how many futures contracts should have been used to hedge the cash position?

    c. What would you have expected the manager to do if he or she had strongly expected interest rates to decline rather than increase over the period?

20-7. Use a spreadsheet to find the price for the following interest rate swap. Swaps are discussed in Appendix 20B.

XYZ Corp. has a $5 million loan on which it pays a floating interest rate. At the beginning of each year the rate is set equal to the 1-year spot rate for corporate bonds of a similar quality. The company's CFO believes that interest rates will rise over the next few years, and has decided to enter into a 5- year swap agreement which will provide a fixed interest rate of 5.8838 percent per year on the amount of the loan. The spot rates on corporate debt are shown in the following table.

Maturity (Years)	Spot Rate
1	4.0000%
2	4.5000%
3	5.0000%
4	5.5000%
5	6.0000%

    a. Calculate the implied forward interest rate for each year (see Chapter 12).

    b. While the fixed-rate interest payments are known, the future floating rate interest payments cannot be known with certainty. However, their expected value is determined by the implied forward rates computed above. Under the swap contract, the company will pay (or receive) an interest payment at the end of each year based on the difference between the fixed rate and the floating rate set at the start of the year. Calculate the expected amount of each of these payments.

    c. Use the spot rates provided to discount the five expected payments to the present.

    d. Determine the actual cost of the swap by adding the present values of all five expected interest payments.

    e. Your figure in part d should be very small (close to zero). Does this make sense given that the loan amount was $5 million?

PREPARING FOR YOUR PROFESSIONAL EXAMS

CFA PRACTICE QUESTIONS

20-1. Futures contracts differ from forward contracts in the following ways:

    i. Futures contracts are standardized.

    ii. For futures, performance of each party is guaranteed by a clearing house.

    iii. Futures contracts require a daily settling of any gains or losses.

       a. i and iii only

       b. i, ii, and iii

       c. i and ii only

       d. ii and iii only

20-2. Trader A buys 50 contracts of wheat from Trader B. Later, Trader A sells 30 of these contracts to Trader C. Trader B also sells 40 wheat contracts to Trader D. After all of these trades what is the open interest in wheat?

    a. 50

    b. 70

    c. 90

    d. 120

20-3. A silver futures contract requires the seller to deliver 5,000 Troy ounces of silver. An investor sells one July silver futures contract at a price of $8 per ounce, posting a $2,025 initial margin. If the required maintenance margin is $1,500, what is the first price per ounce at which the investor would receive a maintenance margin call?

    a. $5.92

    b. $7.89

    c. $8.11

    d. $10.80

20-4. In futures trading, the minimum level to which an equity position may fall before requiring additional margin is the:

    a. initial margin.

    b. variation margin.

    c. cash flow margin.

    d. maintenance margin.

20-5. Which of the following statements about future contracts is false?

    a. Offsetting trades rather than exchanges for physicals are used to close most futures contracts.

    b. The major difference between forwards and futures is that futures contracts have standardized contract terms.

    c. To safeguard the clearing house, the exchange requires traders to post margin and settle their accounts on a weekly basis.

    d. The futures clearing house allows traders to reverse their positions without having to contract the other side of the initial trade.

CFA CURRICULUM AND SAMPLE EXAM QUESTIONS (©CFA INSTITUTE)

20-1. A private transaction in which one party agrees to make a single fixed payment in the future and another party agrees to make a single floating payment in the future is best characterized as a(n):

    a. futures contract.
    b. forward contract.
    c. exchange-traded contingent claim.
    d. over-the-counter contingent claim.

20-2. A public standardized transaction that constitutes a commitment between two parties to transfer the underlying asset at a future date at a price agreed upon now is best characterized as a(n):

    a. swap.
    b. futures contract.
    c. exchange-traded contingent claim.
    d. over-the-counter contingent claim.

20-3. The party agreeing to make the fixed-rate payment might also be required to make the variable payment in:

    a. an equity swap, but not an interest rate swap.
    b. an interest rate swap, but not an equity swap.
    c. both an equity swap and an interest rate swap.
    d. neither an equity swap nor an interest rate swap.

20-4. Agrawal Telecom is considering issuing $10,000,000 of 6.75 percent fixed coupon bonds to finance an expansion. Alternatively, Agrawal could borrow the funds in the Eurodollar market using a series of 6-month LIBOR contracts. A swap contract matching the maturity of the 6.75 percent coupon bonds is available. The swap uses 6-month LIBOR as the floating rate component. Identify the interest rate swap that Agrawal should use to evaluate the two alternatives.

    a. Agrawal would use a pay fixed, receive floating interest rate swap.
    b. Agrawal would use a pay floating, receive fixed interest rate swap.
    c. Agrawal would use a total return equity payer swaption to evaluate the two borrowing options.
    d. Given that Agrawal is a US corporation and is considering borrowing in the Eurodollar market, Agrawal would need to use a currency swap to evaluate the transaction.

20-5. The current price of an asset is 100. An out-of-the-money American put option with an exercise price of 90 is purchased along with the asset. If the break-even point for this hedge is at an asset price of 114 at expiration, then the value of the American put at the time of purchase must have been:

    a. 0.
    b. 4.
    c. 10.
    d. 14.

APPENDIX 20A

FUTURES OPTIONS

In Chapter 19 we discussed options (puts and calls) on common stocks. In this chapter, we discussed interest rate futures and stock-index futures. Futures options is a combination of the two. The development of this financial instrument is a good example of the ever-changing nature of financial markets, where new instruments are developed to provide investors with opportunities that did not previously exist.

Put and call options are offered on both interest rate futures and stock-index futures. In Canada in 2007, 748,991 option contracts on futures were traded, accounting for 5.3 percent of the total ME exchange-traded options. Available financial futures options in Canada include options on three-month BA futures, which trade on the ME. In addition, options trade on the ICE Futures Canada on canola futures, domestic feed wheat futures, and western domestic feed barley futures.

There are several options on futures contracts available in the United States, including (but not limited to)

- Options on foreign exchange: Pound, mark, Swiss franc, yen, Canadian dollar, and a US dollar index
- Options on interest rate futures: US Treasury bills, notes, and bonds and municipal bonds
- Options on stock-index futures: The S&P 500 Index (traded on the Chicago Mercantile Exchange (CME)), the NYSE Composite Index (traded on the New York Futures Exchange), and the Nikkei 225 Stock Average (CME)
- Options on commodities: Agricultural, oil, livestock, metals, and lumber.

Recall from Chapter 19 that an option provides the purchaser with the right, but not the obligation, to exercise the claim provided by the contract. An option on a futures contract gives its owner the right to assume a long or short position in the respective futures contract. If this right is exercised, the holder's position will be at the exercise (strike) price of the option that was purchased. For example, the exerciser of a call option buys the futures contract at the exercise price stated in the call option.

The key elements of an option contract on a particular futures contract are the exercise price and the premium. As in the case of stock options, premiums are determined in competitive markets. Each put and call option is either in the money or out of the money. With an in-the-money call option, the exercise price is less than the current price of the underlying futures contract. (If the exercise price is greater than the current price, it is out of the money.) For put options, the reverse is true.

Options on futures contracts can serve some of the same purposes as the futures contracts themselves. Specifically, both futures contracts and options can be used to transfer the risk of adverse price movements from hedgers to speculators. For example, a portfolio manager with bond holdings (a long position) who expects a rise in interest rates can hedge against the risk of the capital losses resulting from such a rise by selling futures contracts on government bonds. Alternatively, futures options on government bonds can be used to hedge against this risk because the option's price will change in response to a change in the price of the underlying commodity.

A rise in interest rates is bearish (bond prices will fall), therefore, the portfolio manager would either buy a put or sell a call. The value of these options would rise as the price of the futures contract declined. On the other hand, an investor bullish on bond prices (i.e., one who expects interest rates to decline) would either buy a call or sell a put. In addition to these simple strategies, a number of spreading techniques can be used with options on bond futures.

The general appeal of options on futures contracts is the limited liability assumed by the purchaser. Unlike a futures contract, which has to be settled by some means (say, by offset), once the contract is bought the purchaser has no additional obligation. Moreover, unlike futures, the purchaser is not subject to margin calls. Even if a speculator in futures is ultimately correct in his or her expectations, margin calls in the interim can wipe out all the equity. A writer (seller) of an option on a futures contract, however, does have an obligation to assume a position (long or short) in the futures market at the strike price if the option is exercised. Sellers must deposit margin when opening a position.

APPENDIX 20B

OTHER DERIVATIVE SECURITIES

Swaps

A **swap** is a type of cash settled forward agreement; however, unlike traditional forward agreements, there is a series of predetermined payments. In other words, one could view swaps as a series of forward agreements. The swap market is used extensively by banks for short-term (and to a much lesser extent for long-term) financing. Three types are discussed below: (1) interest rate swaps, (2) foreign exchange or currency swaps, and (3) swaptions.

1. *Interest rate swaps* represent agreements to exchange cash flows on an agreed upon formula. It is important to note that the notional or principal amount is not exchanged, either at initiation or maturity of the contract. The most common formula involves the exchange of payments based on a fixed interest rate, for floating rate payments of interest, based on some notional amount of principal. This is often referred to as a "plain vanilla" interest rate swap. Margins are required by both parties (unless one counter-party is a large chartered bank), and the floating rates are reviewed periodically. Floating rates are typically tied to Canadian bankers' acceptance rates or the six-month LIBOR (London Interbank Offered Rate).

Swap

A cash settled forward agreement with a series of predetermined payments.

EXAMPLE 20B-1: "PLAIN VANILLA" INTEREST RATE SWAP

The notional value for a swap is $10 million and the term is three years. Party A agrees to make fixed annual payments to Party B, based on a fixed interest rate of 4 percent (i.e., A agrees to pay B $400,000 per year). Party B agrees to make payments to Party A based on the prevailing bankers' acceptance rate plus 50 basis points (or 0.50 percent).

On the day the swap was arranged, the BA rate was 3.75 percent, so the floating rate to be paid by Party B would be 4.25 percent (or $10 million $\times$ 0.0425 = $425,000). As a result, the net payment would have B pay A $25,000 ($425,000 − $400,000). However, this is subject to change because the BA rate is a floating rate and its level changes on a daily basis. For example, the floating rate paid by Party B could fall to 3 percent (if the BA rate fell to 2.5 percent), or rise to 5 percent (if the BA rate rose to 4.5 percent). Obviously, B feels the floating rate will fall, while A feels it will rise, unless one of the parties has entered into the agreement for hedging purposes.

2. *Foreign exchange swaps or currency swaps* are similar to interest rate swaps; however, there are two important differences:

   i. The cash flows are denominated in two different currencies, and hence the notional amount is actually exchanged at the beginning and end of the contract.
   ii. These swaps do not necessarily have to be fixed for floating, but can be fixed for fixed.

   Currency swaps involve two market transactions—for example, the sale of US dollars to buy Canadian dollars today (the near date), and the sale of Canadian dollars and purchase of US dollars at a specified future date (the far date) and price. The difference between the spot price and forward price is referred to as a premium if the forward is greater than the spot. If it is less, it is called a discount. The size of the premium or discount depends on the interest rate differential between the two currencies.

EXAMPLE 20B-2: CURRENCY SWAP

Spot rate is $1.0006 Canadian per US$, term is 30 days, discount is 0.0004, so the forward price is (spot − discount) $1.0002 per US$. Suppose the US funds can be borrowed at a 3.50 percent interest rate.

This implies the equivalent cost of borrowing funds in Canada is: 3.50% − [(discount/spot) × (365/30) × 100] = 3.50% − 0.49% = 3.01%.

3. *Swaptions* are options that give the holder the right, but not the obligation, to enter into a swap agreement. The advantage of swaptions over straight swaps is the limited risk characteristics, as well as the non-obligation by the buyer of the swaption contract. In other words, a swap obligates a party to a future transaction, while a swaption provides the right, but not the obligation, to enter into such future transactions.

Embedded Options

Embedded options include features such as convertible, callable, retractable, and extendible features associated with some debt or preferred share issues. Convertibles enable the holder to convert the bond (or preferred shares) into common shares at a predetermined conversion price—hence they have an embedded call option. The price of this option can be inferred by the difference between the price of a convertible bond, and the price of a similar non-convertible bond (which should sell for less since it has no conversion feature attached).

Callable bonds enable the corporation to buy back the bonds at a predetermined call price, which implies the buyer of a callable bond is selling the bond issuer a call option. The cost of this option would be the difference between the price of a callable and a similar non-callable bond. The non-callable bonds would sell for a greater price because they do not provide the bond issuers with the call privilege (the risk of which is borne by the bondholder).

Retractable bonds enable the bondholder to sell the bond back to the corporation at a predetermined price. This is analogous to the bond issuer writing a put option on the bond, which is held by the bond owner. Once again, the option price can be viewed as the difference in the prices of similar retractable versus non-retractable bonds (which will sell for less because they do not contain the retraction privilege).

An extendible bond allows the bondholder to extend the maturity date of the bonds beyond some more recent maturity date. This can be thought of as a short-term bond, with an option to purchase an additional bond at a predetermined price. Hence they include an embedded call option that is held by the bond owner, and was written by the bond issuer. As a result of this privilege, extendible bonds sell for a greater price than similar non-extendible bonds, the difference representing the cost of the embedded call option.